SPIRITUAL GUIDANCE

Fundamentals of Ascetical Theology

Based on the Franciscan Ideal

Spiritual Guidance

FUNDAMENTALS OF ASCETICAL THEOLOGY

BASED ON THE FRANCISCAN IDEAL

by

ADOLPH KESTENS, O.F.M. Cap.

Adapted from the Latin by

ELMER STOFFEL, O.F.M. Cap.

VOLUME I

St. Anthony Guild Press, Paterson, New Jersey

FOREWORD
to the English Edition

Ascetical theology is the queen and mistress of all sciences, for it directs the soul to the highest possible perfection in this life. A detailed treatment of this science along Franciscan lines will therefore be a valuable aid to holiness among the sons and daughters of St. Francis of Assisi. Frankly, the English version of the *Compendium Theologiae Asceticae* by the Very Reverend Adolph Kestens, O. F. M. Cap., has been adapted to meet the need of all the followers of St. Francis as well as that of candidates for various other religious Orders and diocesan seminarians. The inspiration for undertaking this translation was given by a Friar Minor during the Franciscan Educational Conference when it met at Santa Barbara in 1947. His words of praise for Father Adolph Kestens' exposition as one of the best works on Franciscan asceticism and his pointed question why the Capuchins had not as yet produced an English version led to the present translation.

The original Latin *Compendium* first appeared in print in Hong Kong in 1921, being published by a missionary as a private enterprise. This first edition has been exhausted. We understand that the Capuchins of the Belgian Province, of which Father Adolph was a member, are considering the possibility of adapting and republishing the work in Latin. To our knowledge, however, little has been done in the matter.

A word may be said about the author's history. Father Adolph was eminently fitted to compile a treatise on Franciscan asceticism by reason of his excellent talents, his background, his studies and experience as well as the offices he held with distinction. He was born at Denderwindeke, Belgium, on May 1, 1863. His baptismal name was Audomar Kestens and his parents were truly devout Christians. He pursued his preparatory studies in the episcopal school until he felt certain of his Franciscan vocation. He was invested with the Capuchin habit on January 21, 1882. During the course of his philosophical and theological studies his instructors as well as his classmates noted his keen perception. He was ordained a priest on May 26, 1888. Shortly thereafter he was given an assignment as professor at the Seraphic College at Bruges, Belgium. From 1894 to 1925 he successively held the offices of preacher, local superior, custos general and novice master. During all these years he proved likewise a prolific writer, producing in all ten published works.

His *Compendium Theologiae Asceticae* is without doubt the most valuable and enduring. He compiled it and made use of it during his eighteen years as novice master. This becomes apparent in his Introduction; in the text, where he frequently used the term "Frater"; and in the direct address which he commonly employed throughout the work. The translator, however, has retained the use of the second person only in direct quotations from other writers.

Cardinal Mercier, who knew him for his extensive knowledge and experience in ascetical and mystical theology, employed Father Adolph in later life as investigator and examiner of the stigmatist Sister Rumolde. It was on his way to the convent at Herenthals, Belgium, on December 7, 1925, that Father Adolph was stricken. He died shortly afterward, having received Extreme Unction at the hands of the chaplain.

While the voice of Father Adolph is stilled in the pulpit and in the instructor's chair, he still teaches through the written word. May the vast army of Franciscan and kindred souls in English-speaking countries acquire a renewed eagerness for perfection as they study prayerfully his *Compendium Theologiae Asceticae* in its English version.

FR. CYPRIAN ABLER, O. F. M. CAP.,
Minister Provincial.

CONTENTS

VOLUME I

PART I

The Reformation of What Is Deformed, through the Purgation of Vices

BOOK I

The First Reformation:

Reformation of the Soul by Penance

BOOK II

The Second Reformation:

The Reformation of the External Senses and the Tongue through Accurate Custody

BOOK III

The Third Reformation:

The Reformation of the Bodily Members through Religious Discipline

BOOK IV

The Fourth Reformation:

Reformation of the Interior of "the Old Man" through Internal Custody

PART II

Strengthening What Has Been Reformed and Conforming to Christ through the Practice of Virtue

BOOK I

*Paragraphs preceded by an asterisk refer specifically to Franciscan religious.

SPIRITUAL GUIDANCE

Fundamentals of Ascetical Theology

Based on the Franciscan Ideal

ACKNOWLEDGMENTS

The translator wishes to acknowledge his indebtedness, first of all, to Very Reverend Father Mathias of Gandavo, O. F. M. Cap., formerly Minister Provincial of the Belgian Province of the Order of Friars Minor Capuchin, for permission to translate and adapt this work, originally entitled *Compendium Theologiae Asceticae* and written by Very Reverend Father Adolph Kestens, O. F. M. Cap.;

To Doubleday and Co., New York, N. Y., for permission to quote from *Amy Vanderbilt's Complete Book of Etiquette*, and to draw correct notions on etiquette from this same book, in chapter II, pp. 161-177, inclusive, of *Spiritual Guidance;*

To the Pustet Co., New York, N. Y., for permission to quote from the translation of *An Introduction to a Devout Life* by St. Francis de Sales;

To Benziger Brothers, New York, N. Y., for permission to adapt several quotations from the *Summa Theologica* of St. Thomas Aquinas, translated by the Fathers of the English Dominican Province.

The New Testament and the Pentateuch, Prophetical Books and Sapiential Books of the Old Testament have been quoted in the Confraternity of Christian Doctrine version, except where otherwise noted.

INTRODUCTION

1. A threefold Introduction to this work seems opportune, covering:

I. The purpose of this work and certain general notions regarding the science of ascetics;

II. The state in which man is placed by the decree of Divine Providence;

III. The universal principles by which man is directed to the purpose of his creation.

I. The Purpose of This Work and Certain General Notions concerning the Science of Ascetics

We wish to explain:

(1) That this work constitutes *A Summary of Ascetical Theology for the Use of Franciscans and Other Seminarians, as a Solid Foundation for Their Priestly and Religious Life;*

(2) The meaning of ascetical theology;

(3) The sources from which ascetical theology draws its doctrine;

(4) The development of this doctrine;

(5) The sources from which we ourselves derive the doctrine;

3

(6) The usefulness and necessity of applying ourselves to this study;

(7) The manner of proceeding.

1 — *Explanation of the Purpose of This Work*

2. A. This work is a summary, that is, a **Compendium.** One would therefore search it in vain for lengthy explanations. We propose to set forth clear, solid, and practical principles leading to religious and seraphic perfection. Those who desire further explanations will do well to consult other spiritual books, especially the works of St. Bonaventure.

3. B. A summary of **ascetical theology.**

Since the subject is theology, the work is subtitled: *Fundamentals of Ascetical Theology, Based on the Franciscan Ideal.* A further explanation of the meaning of ascetical theology will follow.

4. C. **A solid foundation for the priestly and religious life.** All the faithful without exception are called to perfection; for perfection consists essentially and principally in the love of God. When Jesus Christ said, "Thou shalt love the Lord thy God with thy whole heart, with thy whole soul, and with thy whole strength,"[1] He admitted no exceptions. Christ's Church does not have one kind of perfection for people living in the world and another for persons called to the priestly or religious life. Perfection is one, and only one. And it consists in loving God with one's whole soul.

Yet this perfection in itself has different degrees. Priests, because of their sublime dignity and the ministry incumbent upon them, have a more imperative duty to be perfect than the ordinary faithful, more so even than simple religious. Per-

---

1. Luke 10:27.

fection, indeed, is essentially one; yet there are various ways leading to it: namely, the way of the commandments and the way of the evangelical counsels. Religious bind themselves by vow to walk the way of the counsels. Although the diocesan priest does not by means of vows assume the obligation to walk the way of the counsels, he ought nevertheless to know in what it consists. For he is constituted by God as the light of the world and the salt of the earth. Many religious repeatedly consult him in the sacred tribunal of penance, seeking guidance from him in order to advance in perfection. In fact, it often happens that the spiritual direction of religious communities is entrusted to him. Since no one can teach what he has not learned, it is the duty of the diocesan priest to be versed in whatever pertains to the ways of perfection. But how much greater is this obligation in the religious priest, who has bound himself by solemn vow to the pursuit of perfection in the way of the counsels! Thus there are reasons for calling this Compendium a solid foundation for the priestly and religious life.

5. D. For the use of **Franciscans and other seminarians.** All religious approved as such by the Church tend to the highest perfection of divine love through the public observance of the three evangelical counsels. At least, they should. They bind themselves to the fulfillment of these counsels by a vow in the sight of Christ's visible Church. There are no essential differences between distinct communities, but there can be accidental variations. For in the Church there are many approved religious Orders. They differ from one another in their particular, specific, but accessory purpose. Some have the service of God as their special object; others, charity toward their neighbor. Each Order tends in its own way to its own end, some by means of a contemplative life, others by an active life, still others by a mixed life. Some bind themselves to a strict rule, others to a more lenient one.

Our Seraphic Father St. Francis, when founding his own Order, also proposed for it a particular end, over and above the general purpose of the religious state. This particular purpose is the imitation of the mixed life of our Lord Jesus Christ. To achieve this goal, he gave us a Rule in which he set down eminently suitable means, which the Most High Himself revealed to him. This end and these means distinguish the Order of St. Francis from all other Orders, and those who observe Francis' Rule faithfully should by the very fact be accidentally different in mind and spirit from the religious of any other Order. The methods of perfection cannot be the same in every Order, for the particular practices commendable in one institute may not apply in another. With this in mind, we have tried to direct all seminarians but particularly the children of St. Francis in the ways of perfection according to the method of the seraphic saint.

6. E. For **beginners** especially. This work was composed expressly for the novices and young religious of the Seraphic Order. In its entirety it comprises three volumes, of which this is the first. References, therefore, to "this manual" or "this work" pertain to the three volumes as a whole. Some parts of this work may be studied during the novitiate, others after simple profession; however, the entire three-volume work should be covered only during the course of theology. The use of this manual will depend upon the prudent judgment of the directors in charge of the young religious; it is their task to explain and clarify the chapters and sections which might seem difficult to beginners. This work is intended especially, but not exclusively, for young religious and seminarians. All religious and diocesan priests could use it to great advantage. Parts I and II, included in this volume, chiefly concern all souls aspiring to perfection. The few passages which pertain exclusively to Franciscans *are preceded by an asterisk.* The Franciscan

practices treated in this book have been duly approved by the Church and are esteemed by the whole Christian people.

NOTE. Some might have preferred a division of the work into two volumes: one for novices and one for the professed. There are reasons in favor of the division as it stands. Some of the novices might be gifted with an exceptional erudition; others may have already been raised to the dignity of the priesthood. Nothing would be more useful for the former during the time of their novitiate than to apply themselves most earnestly to the study of the spiritual life. However, the deciding factor in the choice of the present arrangement was the thought of the advantage to be gained by young religious if, at the very outset of their religious life, they were provided with a summary knowledge of religious perfection. If novices do not clearly and thoroughly understand the basic principles of the spiritual life, they may come to regard the object of their study as differing from the practice of these same principles. The foundation of the spiritual life is and always will be the reformation of the fallen man. If the foundation be removed, the building itself will collapse.

2 — Concept of Ascetical Theology

7. **Theology** is the science of God and of those things which refer to God. It is considered under different names according to its matter or its methods.

Theoretical treatises which have God for their object are called *natural theology* (theodicy) when they are explained by the light of reason alone. They are called *revealed* or *supernatural theology* when explained by the light of divine revelation. Supernatural theology is termed *dogmatic* when it simply explains revealed principles; *apologetic,* when its aim is to vindicate these principles against the enemies of the faith;

moral, when it directs and classifies moral conduct; *ascetical,* when it considers the regulation of life according to the norm of the Gospel; *mystical,* when it seeks to fathom the extraordinary ways by which souls are united to God, and to investigate the phenomena which often accompany this union. This definition of mystical theology is taken from a rather recent concept.

The present work is restricted to ascetical theology.

Meaning of the word. The word "ascetics" comes from the Latin "ascesis"; and "ascesis" is derived from the Greek term ἄσκησις, which signifies exercise, wrestling, struggle. Probably it has its origin in Sacred Scripture. The Apostle St. Paul compares the Christian to an athlete contending for an eternal crown.[2] Jesus Christ, by saying to all: "If anyone wishes to come after Me, let him deny himself, and take up his cross daily, and follow Me,"[3] clearly insisted upon self-sacrifice. The word "ascetics" was often used by the early Christians to designate the science of Christian perfection.

8. Nature of ascetical theology. The first step is to understand the nature of ascetical theology, to have a clear grasp of its characteristics.

A. Definition. Ascetical theology is the science of the perfection which any Christian can reach with the help of grace. It is a true science, both deductive and inductive, because it proceeds from certain, universal principles, and eventually reaches particular applications; and also because it proceeds from an accumulation of experimental facts which lead to probable principles and eventually again to particular applications. In its subject matter it also advances with greater certainty than other sciences, since it rests on principles made manifest through revelation and the wisdom of the saints.

---

2. 1 Cor. 9:24-25.
3. Luke 9:23; cf. Matt. 16:24.

B. **The difference between ascetical and dogmatic theology.** Dogmatic theology is speculative, while ascetical theology is practical; for ascetical theology points out the obstacles to be avoided and the means to be used to reach the supreme goal of perfection.

C. **The difference between ascetical and moral theology.** Moral theology deals only with practical duties strictly binding under pain of mortal or venial sin and directly or indirectly resting on all the faithful in general or particularly on a definite group. Ascetical theology presupposes that our actions are directed toward our final end, and investigates the rules of perfection, the approach to the union of perfect charity in God.

D. **The difference between ascetical and mystical theology.** The differences between ascetical, moral and dogmatic theology are easily understood, but greater difficulties arise when we have to decide whether a distinction should be made between ascetical and mystical theology. We shall investigate this point more thoroughly.

"Mystical," like the word "mystery," traces its origin to the Greek word Μύειν, which means "to close the mouth," "to lack a voice." It points to something secret or hidden which only the initiated can understand. The adjective "mystical" has had many meanings that are not based on its terminology. In common usage the words "mystic" and "mystical" have come to have the same signification as "occult" or "magic." They have been associated with the initiation rites of secret societies and with many dangerous pseudo-religious practices. The common connotation of these words implies something negative, secret, dark. There are "mystic signs" and "mystic occurrences" which have very little to do with love of God. Therefore it is most important to have a clear understanding of the traditional meaning.

In the favorable sense. Among Catholic authors the word "mystical" may be understood in a broad or in a strict sense.

(a) *In the broad sense* mystical theology does not differ from ascetical theology. "The mystical state," says St. Francis de Sales, "is union with God through love."[4] Father Weiss writes in the same strain: "What is the mystical state but the Christian life, the worthy life of a man drawn logically to perfection?" And again: "The mystical concept and action is a human alacrity for doing those things which lead us to our last end, God, a naturally mystical state."[5] And he adds: "Christian mysticism is merely that which the priest initiates at baptism, and that which a man promises at that time": to renounce evil and to unite himself with God. The mystical theology of the Middle Ages summarizes the ways of perfection in two words: departure and return; a departure from all that corrupts and fetters our nature, and a return to God in our inmost being. Our nature, after it has been freed from the obstructions that hinder it, joins itself to God. The use of the word "mystical" in the broad sense is not new: it originated in the fifth century. The Pseudo-Areopagite already gives it this meaning. In fact, nearly all the ancient authors made no distinction between ascetical and mystical theology. Under the term "mystical theology" they covered both the ordinary and the extraordinary way of perfection, while knowing full well that they were widely different.

(b) *In the strict sense.* Most contemporary authors admit a distinction between mystical and ascetical theology. The better to distinguish between the ordinary and the extraordinary ways of perfection, it has been agreed to designate as "ascetical

---

4. *Treatise on the Love of God,* Book VII, Chap. I.
5. *Apologie du Christianisme,* t. IX, First Conference, n. 4, and Nineteenth Conference.

theology" the science which treats of the ordinary ways and to reserve the term "mystical theology" for the study of the extraordinary. Remember that the object of our study is *ascetical theology.*

3 — Sources of Ascetical Theology

9. Since ascetics is a theological science, it must be based on the same sources as dogmatic and moral theology: namely, Sacred Scripture and Tradition. Ascetics is subordinate also to dogma and morals; as a distinct science it has its own principles, but it also relies on the subsidiary sources it finds in theology and the natural sciences.

(a) **Scripture, the chief source of ascetical theology.** The main principles of ascetics are found in the Gospels and in the writings of the Apostles, particularly St. Paul. The early Fathers of the Church, who left us their ascetical doctrines, always relied on the authority of Sacred Scripture. For the early monks continually studied and labored to interpret and examine the words of the Divine Master and the teachings of the Apostles, so as to draw from them the best methods of perfection. All important works on ascetics — as, for example, the *Imitation of Christ,* customarily attributed to Thomas a Kempis — are full of direct quotations from or expressions inspired by the sacred books.

(b) **Tradition is second in importance.** The Catholic Church is the only instrument by which God speaks to mankind. Ascetics, like any branch of theology, must consult the Church to learn the will of God concerning man. Any ascetical doctrine which does not rest upon the infallible teaching of the Church or which in fundamental form has not been continuously and unanimously accepted by theologians, must be emphatically rejected.

(c) **Ascetics, a branch of dogmatic theology.** Ascetical theology is evidently a branch of dogmatic theology. To explain its own doctrine, it must make clear the natural and the supernatural element in man. Revelation alone will help it to explain these with certainty. The supernatural, as we shall see later, absolutely transcends the power of human intelligence. As a result, reason alone cannot adequately direct us. Reason is merely a helper, a necessary helper which leads us to the very threshold of the supernatural. But its power stops at the door.

(d) **Ascetics, a branch of moral theology.** Ascetical theology must also rest upon the principles of moral theology. Before approaching the means to the final end, the nature of this end, according to the plan of Divine Providence as shown by revelation, must be clearly and well known. The available means must also be evident. This is the function of moral theology.

(e) **The special sources of ascetical theology.** Since the principles of dogmatic and moral theology are distinct, ascetics, in order to establish its own principles, has recourse to its proper sources: the teachings of the saints on Christian perfection.

Principles of ascetical theology established by the experience of the saints. All human knowledge is deepened by experience. Every art, every practical science, is submitted to the prudent application of theoretical rules. The testimony of others does not suffice; for, as Cassian says, a man cannot explain the sweetness of honey to one who has never tasted anything sweet. If a friar tells worldly people about the happiness derived from the penances of the Seraphic Order, they may indeed believe him, but they cannot fully appreciate such happiness unless they themselves have first experienced it. Gerson maintains that mystical theology, which is the summit of ascetical theology, is hidden "from many among the clergy, the learned, the wise, among philosophers and theologians. Such men, puffed up with philosophy, their vision clouded, go crushing under their sordid feet whatever they do not perceive, and tear to pieces with their snarling teeth whatever they do not understand."[6] And St. Paul says, "Now they who are according to the flesh mind the things of the flesh, but they who are according to the spirit mind the things of the spirit."[7]

As for the saints, it is through experience that they learned Christ's teaching on perfection. They sought the most powerful aids and obtained the happiest results. The experimental knowledge of the saints, and their instructions concerning the most suitable means of perfection, constitute the foundation of ascetical theology.

Due subjection of experimental knowledge to theology. In order that this experience of the saints may be genuine, it must be subject in its principal tenets to the science of theology. For if it is separated from doctrinal theology, ascetics easily falls into error. Even a holy man on the highest level of perfection will be helpless when he tries to direct others, unless he has a clear understanding of the theory of the spiritual life. At times, through ignorance, he will disapprove the most commendable practices. At other times he will encourage unsuitable habits because of their superficial appearance of goodness. Gerson advises that while those who are led along extraordinary ways of the spirit should not at once be spurned or rejected, they should not easily be given credence; they should be carefully tested according to the norms of ecclesiastical tradition, so that the worthy may be sifted from the impostor. In matters of doctrine, greater trust should be placed in a learned

---

6. *Mystic. Theol.*, in *Opera omnia*, Consid. 31.
7. Rom. 8:5.

man, eminent in virtue, than in a saint who is unlearned.[8] An author both learned and holy merits our greatest confidence. We can derive great benefit, then, from spiritual writers who have both qualities, as did St. Bonaventure, St. John of the Cross, St. Francis de Sales, and others. Many of the saints possessed a knowledge far more sublime than that of even the most learned man in the world.

(f) **Philosophy and the natural sciences are aids to ascetical theology.** Ascetical theology, although entirely supernatural, finds a useful ally in sound reason. For God, while redeeming us and elevating us to the supernatural life, does not deprive us of natural life. The duties He places upon us as men are not suspended by the obligations He imposes upon us as Christians.

A knowledge of metaphysics and psychology is beneficial to the spiritual life, for these lead to a practical knowledge of ascetical doctrine. Ascetical theology is a science, for it derives its premises from revealed principles, and from these it draws logical conclusions. As a science it will therefore fare the same as any other science. By their very nature dogmatic truths, which constitute the basis of ascetical theology, admit of no change.

---

8. NOTE. The learned man as such, even an eminently virtuous one, who has to rely solely on the power of his intellect, has a much more shallow insight than an inspired saint in those matters which are beyond the reach of human reason. Many uneducated saints have been the authors of brilliant treatises which far surpass the limits of human learning — for instance, St. Catherine of Siena, Blessed Angela of Foligno, etc. All the erudition in the world could never give us anything so deep and satisfying.

The opinion of a saint should be preferred to that of a virtuous learned man any time a saint speaks under the inspiration of the Holy Spirit.

A virtuous, learned man should be trusted more than a saint whenever the saint is merely expressing a personal opinion based on his human experience.

The general principle here should be: *the closer to God, the closer to truth.* And the problem is to determine *who is really speaking in the name of God's truth.*

Yet, inasmuch as these truths concern the living, both their interpretation and their application must be adapted. The times in which one lives, the person to whom the matter is addressed, even the teachers engaged in explaining these truths, call for such developments. Every human problem is properly unique and requires the unique application of immutable truths. This does not imply any change in principle, in morality or even in application, but merely the bringing forth, for the benefit of an individual case, the properly individual answer which was implied in the principles.

Spiritual matters are not always and in all things uniformly disposed. There are many divergent schools of the spiritual life, and none should be disparaged. The diverse ways they teach lead to the same final goal, union with God. Although these various methods in themselves may be useful and praiseworthy, yet they are not suited to all men considered individually. "Where the Spirit of the Lord is, there is freedom."[9] Without doubt, all men are destined for salvation, but all are not endowed with the same disposition. In fact, they are often subject to inconstancy of mind. Things which are stimulating at times, at other times cause aversion. What pleases us today arouses repugnance tomorrow. Considerations such as these are too often forgotten and underestimated. That is why some men once of good will abandon the spiritual life. Had they been guided according to their natural propensities, they would have attained true sanctity.

OTHER BENEFITS. Philosophy can also prove the importance of ascetics to the unlearned, and respond to the objections raised by reason. It can show the harmony between ascetical theology and sound reason. It can also explain spiritual doctrine in a clear manner. Many mistaken notions will crop up

---

9. 2 Cor. 3:17; cf. John 4:24.

even in a well-disposed mind if a doctrine is not correctly and clearly set forth.

Finally, spiritual life may involve something extraordinary. Such cases require the care not only of a learned theologian and of a spiritual master but also of someone endowed with a fund of pertinent scientific knowledge. The theologian will form his judgments according to revealed principles; the scientist draws his conclusions from externally observed facts; the spiritual director judges by the fruits.

The harmony between ascetical theology and philosophy. Philosophy, instead of opposing ascetics, helps by permitting a fuller investigation and a better understanding of it. We learn from experience that sound ascetics and true philosophy are not at variance with one another, but that the greatest concord and a permanent harmony necessarily exist between the two. If difficulties arise, they must be attributed either to a false ascetical doctrine or to a false philosophy.

Many ascetical principles seem contrary to philosophy. Some of the requisites of the ascetical way of life might at first sight seem contrary to sound philosophy — for instance, the advice of St. Francis that the eyes be made "blind," that the intellect and the will be immolated, and that we ourselves become like a corpse, the mere instrument of another's will.

But if we give these expressions their true meaning, we shall see that they represent effectual means for curbing our vices, our defects, and the perverse inclinations of our will; and this seems reasonable enough. A superior who imposes commands is held in the eyes of faith to take the place of God Himself. To him belong the right and the obligation of leading his subjects to the goal of their vocation. Yet his power is limited, for the various means he uses do not depend on the mere caprice of the superior. For wherever the specific purpose ceases or where his power does not serve the perfecting of his subjects, there also his power must cease. And if he exceeds his rights, he will be judged before God. The man hungering for perfection knows this. He places confidence in his superiors. If he receives a command from them, he carries it out faithfully, for he knows that this command constitutes the express will of God. Self-love, always dangerous, finds here ample material for mortification.

For man is really man only when he can restrain his inordinate desires, when he can impose sacrifices upon himself. A lover of Christian faith and holiness is at the same time something of a philosopher. For a saint using his reason in the most sagacious manner is the nearest approach to the perfection of human wisdom.

The science of ascetics will never lead anyone to unreasonable practices. If nature seems to be frustrated when someone tries to obey ascetical principles, if striving for humility seems to result in hiding one's light under the bushel, such defects do not originate from the science of ascetics itself, but from some misunderstanding or a lack of prudent application of the counsels given.

Exceptional cases. In some cases spiritual doctrine seems opposed to lawful natural inclinations. Many saints by their example seem to teach some very immoderate things. Some renounced their good name or afflicted their body with penances great enough to break even the hardiest constitution; others, such as our Seraphic Father, had no concern for the future. The teachings of ascetics and philosophy seem to contradict each other here. In fact, we must distinguish between the *ordinary* and the *extraordinary* way. The *ordinary* way, proposed to all Christians and to religious alike, as a rule does not demand such great hardships. On the contrary it is entirely opposed to them, since it calls for a reasonable caution in the practice of virtue. But the *extraordinary* way, in which God, by a special calling, inspires certain souls to follow seemingly useless and absurd practices, pertains to a higher state or order.

To understand this correctly, we are told to consider Jesus Christ. The manner in which He planned the redemption of man through sacrificing Himself on the Cross, brought some new elements into the spiritual life. Philosophy has no right to judge the actions of the saints, but it can assume a higher course than its own, the value of which it does not have the power to estimate. Reason should acknowledge and recognize a wisdom and prudence higher than its own, a wisdom and prudence whose laws are proclaimed by God Himself.

4 — Development of Ascetics

10. It is our purpose to show the development of ascetical theology, in the light of the aforementioned principles. The science of the saints, whereby we may arrive at our goal in the best possible way, begins with the words of the Divine Master to the young man: "Come, follow Me."[10] Jesus Christ has shown us by His words and His deeds how to arrive at the perfection of divine love. The work of the Apostles was to keep alive in the memory of the faithful the golden words which Jesus had engraved in their hearts.

(a) **From the apostolic age to the fourth century.** During this period the teaching of the saints on perfection, directed both to the man in the world and to the monk, remained very practical. It was not developed in a systematic way, but, when the occasion arose, it was explained concisely in letters, homilies, commentaries or tracts. In the writings of the early Church Fathers we often find exhortations on the practice of works of mercy, on virginity and other means of perfection. From the Holy Scriptures these teachers drew the thoughts

---

10. Matt. 19:21.

which they handed down to their followers as an inspiration for struggling against evil desires and thereby becoming better able to contemplate heavenly things.

In the Greek Church the learned Clement of Alexandria (prominent in 192 A. D.) explained the rules of the Christian life in his works *The Instructor* (*Paedagogus*) and the *Stromata*. Origen (fl. a. 230)[11] wrote much on the Christian life and perfection in his homilies, commentaries and various tracts, but only incidentally and without fixed order. Later he fell into error.

In the Latin Church the chief writers of this time are Tertullian and Cyprian.

Tertullian (fl. a. 199) treats of Christian doctrine and training. To teach the faithful, he composed many books dealing with asceticism — for example, treatises on Penance, on Patience, and on Virgins. But he too fell away from the Catholic Faith.

St. Cyprian (fl. a. 248) wrote admirably on the Lord's Prayer, on the value of patience, and on the conduct proper to virgins.

(b) **From the fourth to the sixth century.** This period is called the golden age of the Church Fathers. It was especially fruitful for the science of ascetics.

From the beginning of the Christian era many souls desired to imitate the perfect life of Christ our Saviour and of His Apostles. They renounced the riches and allurements of the world in order to lead an ascetical and solitary life. So great was the fame of holiness of these solitaries that it attracted many Christians to a similar mode of life. Inspired by God, they left the world and sought solitude. Under the guidance of some holy monk they sought to learn and to put into practice the lessons of saintly living.

---

11. *fl. a.: floruit anno:* he flourished or was at his prime in the year ——.

About the year 305 many hastened to St. Anthony, who was living in the Egyptian desert. He convinced them of the blessedness of the solitary life, and induced them to build monasteries in the desert and in the mountains. What St. Anthony did in Egypt, St. Hilarion achieved in Palestine about the year 307. A few years before, St. Pachomius had done the same on the island of Tabennisi, and St. Ammon in the desert of Nitria.

While monastic life progressed, ascetical and mystical theology came to be more perfectly expounded. The Doctors of the Church, celebrated both for their sanctity and for their learning, extolled the monastic life with the highest praises as the apex of Christian perfection, and urged others to adopt it. They themselves, whether hidden in the desert or raised to the episcopacy in the cities, lived a very austere life similar to that of the monks. All questions pertaining to ascetical theology and the more perfect life are treated in their writings, not only in letters, homilies, sermons and commentaries on Sacred Scripture, but also in their many tracts on the more important virtues or on the monastic state itself.

Eminent among the Greek writers were: St. Cyril of Jerusalem (fl. a. 347); St. Basil the Great (fl. a. 365), who wrote copiously on ascetics, and also composed a rule for an excellent system of monastic life; St. Gregory Nazianzen (fl. a. 375); St. Gregory of Nyssa (fl. a. 371); St. Ephrem, the Syrian (fl. a. 362); St. John Chrysostom (fl. a. 398); St. Nilus (d. circa 430) and St. John Climacus (fl. a. 590). This last author admirably described the perfection of monks in his work *Ladder to Paradise.*

At the same time in the Latin Church we find many Doctors of no less fame treating of perfection. St. Ambrose (d. 397), so highly renowned for learning and holiness of life, frequently treated ascetical matters. St. Jerome (fl. a. 385) in his commentaries on the Scriptures, and especially in his Letters, wrote much on contempt of the world and on Christian perfection. St. Augustine (fl. a. 430), the greatest of the Latin Doctors, explained almost all ascetical doctrines. Cassian (fl. a. 416) in his *Instructions for Cenobites* and *Conferences* gathered together the essence of the spiritual doctrine taught by the monks of Egypt. The author fell into the errors of Semi-Pelagianism. St. Caesar of Arles (d. 543) in his sermons and letters, and St. Gregory the Great (d. 604), especially in his work *Moralia in Job,* wrote brilliantly of perfection.

To the fifth century must also be attributed the works published under the name of Dionysius the Areopagite. These were written, not by a disciple of St. Paul who bore that name, but by an unknown monk, the Pseudo-Dionysius.

(c) **From the seventh to the twelfth century.** From the time of St. Gregory to that of St. Bernard the development of ascetics was greatly curtailed. Only a few names occur that are worthy of note. St. John Damascene (fl. a. 740) was eminent among the Greeks. Among the Latins there were St. Isidore of Spain (fl. a. 601), Venerable Bede (fl. a. 691), Alcuin (fl. a. 755), Rabanus Maurus (fl. a. 847), and St. Peter Damian (fl. a. 1057 A. D.). Of St. Bernard (fl. a. 1120) Mabillon says, "He was the last of the Fathers, but equal to the the best." He wrote so elegantly on the ascetical and mystical life that he merited the title "Doctor Mellifluus."

(d) **From the twelfth century on,** the science of theology received a more systematic, didactic and philosophical treatment. In their works, the Doctors of the Church not only set forth what a man must believe and do for his salvation, but also what he must do to attain to the perfection of the Christian life. They discoursed on ascetical questions in a scientific manner, hardly ever separating them from theology and at the same time laying down the solid, bedrock principles of this science.

From this point on, the many schools teaching theology were a great aid to the study of perfection.

One such institute was the school of Bec founded by Lanfranc and made famous by St. Anselm (d. 1109). This school, drawing conclusions by deduction from revealed principles, happily inaugurated the Scholastic method. The school of St. Victor (at Paris) is still of great importance in the study of ascetical and mystical theology. Among the doctors of this school, Hugh and Richard of St. Victor are outstanding. The most celebrated doctor of this time was Peter Lombard, who in the *Four Books of Sentences* collected a Summa of Theology from the Church Fathers and arranged it according to the Scholastic method.

(e) **Thirteenth century.** The Gospel life was wonderfully renewed by the founding of the mendicant Orders. These religious strove most intensely after the ideal perfection of Christ the Saviour, and practiced with new fervor the asceticism of the first centuries. The science of ascetics kept equal pace with this vital renewal. It rose to its highest perfection through the works of such illustrious masters as Alexander of Hales (d. 1245), St. Albert the Great (d. 1280), St. Thomas, and especially St. Bonaventure.

St. Thomas Aquinas (d. 1274), the Angelic Doctor, who developed a wonderful synthesis of all theology, also treated ascetical questions with extraordinary clearness.

St. Bonaventure (1221-1274), the Seraphic Doctor, who is truly a living image of the Fathers and of the ancient tradition of the Church, "must be numbered among the greatest in mystical theology, if not absolutely the greatest."[12]

"After Hugh and Richard of St. Victor," says Sanseverino in his *History of Mysticism,* "St. Bonaventure, by the best of standards, holds first place; even though St. Albert the Great,

---

12. Waffelaert, *Collationes Brugenses* (Bruges), t. XVIII, p. 128, nota.

St. Thomas and others might have here and there explained the more important of the fundamentals of mysticism, yet none of them engaged in this work of set purpose."[13] Nor should other great Franciscan authors be overlooked, namely: David of Augsburg (d. 1272); Bartholomew of Pisa (d. 1380); Bernard of Besse (d. 1272); John Peckham (d. 1292); Conrad of Saxony (d. 1279). All these men penned works of great importance to ascetical theology and to the spiritual life of the Order.

(f) **Fourteenth century.** While the science of ascetics was at a standstill in other regions, it received a new impetus in Belgium through the leadership of John Ruysbroeck (d. 1381). A great school of mystics sprang up about him and many distinguished writers borrowed their mystical doctrine from him: for instance, John Tauler, O. P. (d. 1361); Gerard Groote [Geert Groote] (d. 1384), founder of the Brothers of the Common Life; Gerard of Zutphen (d. 1398); and later St. Ignatius of Loyola. The principal authors of this period are: Master Eckhart (d. 1327) who, however, unwittingly fell into error; Blessed Henry Suso (d. 1366), whose mystical works are very pleasant and full of piety; Angelo Clareno (d. 1346); and Nicholas of Lyra of the Friars Minor (d. circa 1340).

(g) **Fifteenth century.** As in the previous century ascetical theology made little progress. However, the following men are among the most noteworthy: Gerson (d. 1428); Denis the Carthusian (d. 1471); St. Lawrence Justinian (d. 1453); Jean Mombaer; Jerome Savonarola (d. 1498); Thomas a Kempis (d. 1471), to whom the priceless little work *The Imitation of Christ* has long been attributed; and St. Vincent Ferrer (d. 1419). St. Bernardine of Siena (d. 1444), St. John

---

13. *Dynam.* V, iii, in *Coll. Brug.,* t. XVIII, p. 128, nota.

Capistran (d. 1456) and Harphius (d. 1477) are the most prominent Franciscan ascetical writers of this century.

(h) **Sixteenth century.** The science of ascetics, somewhat dormant during the fourteenth and fifteenth centuries, took on renewed vigor, and for nearly two centuries thereafter made great progress. The chief causes of this progress were: (1) a true renewal of the Christian and religious life brought about by the Council of Trent; (2) the founding or reforming of various Orders, for example, the establishing of the Capuchins, in 1525 by Matthew of Bascio; the founding of the Society of Jesus, in 1534 by St. Ignatius; and the reforming of the Carmelites, in 1562 by St. Teresa of Avila; (3) the invention of printing, whereby the ancient works of the Fathers and many works of theologians and pious writers on the spiritual life became more easily available to all.

The *Spiritual Exercises* of St. Ignatius, among ascetical works, and the works of St. Teresa, among the mystical, are of special importance. Leo XIII sums up the universal esteem in which St. Ignatius' exceptional book, the *Exercises,* is held: "It has been proved by the experience of three centuries and by the testimony of all men who during this period abounded in ascetical discipline and holiness of life, that the meditations of Ignatius can be of immense value to the eternal welfare of souls."[14]

St. John of the Cross (d. 1591), Doctor of mystical theology, author of *Spiritual Canticle, The Ascent of Mount Carmel,* and *The Dark Night of the Soul,* is, after St. John the Evangelist, probably the most profound writer who treated of the mysterious ways of divine love. Most of his works, instead of being pious and learned compilations of the Scriptures and the Church Fathers, are original outpourings of his

---

14. Letter of Leo XIII to Very Reverend Father Martin, General of the Society of Jesus, February 8, 1900.

own tremendous experiences. They beautifully develop the most authentic traditions while never conflicting with them. They are a refreshing and living expression of the eternal truths in their highest form, with the additional interest of unity of authorship which is a delight to the mind. St. John of the Cross is the eloquent father of a most austere doctrine which is also most sublime.

Other ascetical writers were: Blosius (d. 1563); Lansperg (d. 1539). Franciscan authors include: Marcus Vigerius (d. 1576); Anthony of Moneglia (d. circa 1527); Matthaeus Sylvaticus; Alphonsus of Madrid; John of Bonilla; John Baptist de Viñones; Francis Ortiz; Juan de los Angeles; Franciscus de Heira; Alphonsus de Ilha; Didacus Stella; John of Fano (d. 1539) and Francis Titelmans (d. 1537).

(i) **Seventeenth century.** By this time works treating of ascetical or mystical theology or of the spiritual life were appearing everywhere. Since the principles of the Christian life and the means of practicing virtue pertain to ascetical theology, ascetical doctrine was taught henceforth as an independent science.

Among the writers of this century, St. Francis de Sales (d. 1622) is the most eminent. A man filled with heavenly wisdom and the apostolic spirit, he taught a simple and agreeable way of perfection, even for persons living in the world. Other expounders of ascetical doctrine are: Louis of Granada (1505-1588); Alvarez de Paz (d. 1620); Venerable Louis de Ponte (d. 1624); Alonso Rodriguez (d. 1616); Cardinal Bona (d. 1674); John of Jesus and Mary (d. 1615); Thomas of Jesus (fl. 1609 A. D.). Among the Franciscans there are: Vincent Cardinal Laureo (d. 1693); Alexis de Salo (d. 1628); Constantine de Barbanson (d. 1631); Joseph of Paris [Francis Le Clerc du Tremblay] (d. 1638); Matthias Bellintani de Salo (d. 1611); Sanctes Sala of Palermo; Philip Gesualdi de Castrovillari; John Verri of Curianova; Benedict of Canfield

(d. 1610); Venerable Bartolomeo de Salutio (d. 1617); Santoro de Messina; John Evangelist of Bois-le-Duc; Clement Pelandi; Bernardine of Paris; François Soyer; Yves of Paris (d. 1678).

We shall not mention theologians of this and the preceding century, although some are worthy of high merit for their ascetical doctrine — for example, Suárez, Benedict XIV, and so forth.

(j) **Eighteenth and nineteenth centuries.** The development of ascetical doctrine again suffered a decline. This is not too surprising. For the principles of the spiritual life must be solidly proved, both by the light of natural reason and by the authority of the Scriptures and of the Fathers, so that practical rules for the perfect regulation of life can be drawn from them. During this period, scientific method was almost entirely lacking in ascetical writings. Ascetical theology was looked down upon by theologians and scientists. They cared but little for the motives and the means set down for eradicating vices, practicing virtue, and attaining the ideal of perfection which Christ Himself manifested by word and example.

Yet there were several noteworthy authors in this era: namely, St. Alphonsus Liguori (1696-1787); St. Leonard of Port Maurice (1676-1751); Ambrose of Lombez (d. 1778); Casimir of Marsala (d. 1762); Casimir Liborio Tempesti; Cajetan of Bergamo; Felix Alamin; Didacus of the Mother of God; Juvenal of Nousberg; Martin of Cochem (d. 1712); Ubald Stroiber; and Boniface Maes (d. 1706).

5 — Doctrinal Sources of This Work

11. The doctrines of Sacred Scripture, Tradition, and of the saints concerning Christian and religious perfection presented in these pages, are taken from excellent and approved authors. As our Constitutions recommend, the Seraphic Doctor St. Bonaventure and the Angelic Doctor St. Thomas find frequent expression in this work. In ascetical theology itself, sound teachings and wholesome practices warranted by reliable authorities have been chosen. It seems superfluous, however, to compile a list of the authors consulted; they will be met more than once in the course of this work.

The reader must not imagine that a different or new system of perfection is being proposed. For Franciscans, the way of St. Francis is always the best approach to perfection. These pages have been written to explain Franciscan asceticism — in other words, perfection according to the mind and spirit of St. Francis.

All doctrines contained in this book have been checked against the teachings of the most approved authors. Often their very words are cited; at times their statements are summarized and put into simple words so that the meaning may be readily understood. It is impossible, however, to recall the source of every annotation, because this work was not originally intended for publication; yet an attempt has been made, whenever possible, accurately to indicate the author.

6 — Necessity and Usefulness of Ascetical Studies

12. **The science of ascetics is a most excellent one.** The science of ascetics by its very nature is most commendable to all the faithful, especially to religious. Ascetical studies and ascetical teachings elevate human nature, for grace presupposes nature, grace elevates and perfects nature. Ascetics is queen and mistress of all sciences. It pertains not only to a choice group of religious persons but to all men who are called to salvation. We may give to its discipline, as did the holy Fathers, the name and beautiful title of "true philosophy," or

"philosophy of Jesus Christ." For while it is fed in different ways by other sciences, yet it retains for itself the glory of being the ultimate end toward which every natural and supernatural science must lead.

When a man claims that he is able to practice virtue while satisfying his craving for pleasure instead of restraining it, he is merely fooling himself and deceiving others; indeed, such blind self-indulgence is the very reason why so many are unfaithful to their duties as Christians and as men.

Our status as Christians obliges us to learn this science. On the day on which we were baptized we renounced the world and adhered to Christ by vows; indeed, through baptism a Christian is made to be another Christ: for this reason we are bound to come to resemble Jesus Christ more closely, and to put Him on, so that it is not we who live, but Jesus Christ who lives in us. This is the teaching of the holy Gospel.

Convinced of this truth, Christians will also understand the necessity and usefulness of ascetical studies, since these studies make known the means of reaching our great goal in the most perfect manner.

God Himself exhorts us to perfection. Indeed, the Lord said: "You therefore are to be perfect, even as your heavenly Father is perfect."[15] This is in accord with the precept to love our enemies, and to bear misfortunes with a tranquil spirit. From these words it is easy to see that all of us are really called upon to practice perfection. The same admonition is contained in the precept the Saviour gave us to love God with all our heart, with all our soul, and with all our strength.[16] But even though there is a general law to practice perfection, we do not commit a sin against the command if we fail to fulfill it perfectly, but only if we neglect and despise it.

---

15. Matt. 5:48.
16. Cf. Luke 10:27.

*Our status as Franciscans holds us to this in a special manner. As for us religious, on the day of our profession we as sons of St. Francis promised by solemn agreement to tend to the perfection of divine love by observing the evangelical counsels and the Rule of the Seraphic Order. Moreover, the Franciscans, called and dedicated to the labor of the Lord's vineyard and burdened with the duty of leading souls to greater heights of goodness, have a much greater obligation to master this divine science.

St. Teresa of Avila often said that it was very difficult to find a director who knew how to lead souls to perfection. She spoke from personal experience. Perhaps most directors will not be called upon to guide extraordinary souls to such holiness; yet all directors must be competent and capable of leading themselves and others to the summits of Christian and religious life. They will do well, therefore, to give themselves to the study of ascetical theology and to learn to know God, the final end of man. They should study the most powerful means of drawing souls to God, so as to reap a greater reward and become in truth holy men. Many spiritual dangers oppose the ascetical life. On the other hand there are certain great ascetical truths which, when properly proposed, lead the soul to knowledge of unsuspected heights of sanctity, and exemplify for it the perfect ideal of the good and the beautiful. A clear understanding of the supernatural protects against false mystical doctrines. Ascetical knowledge does not necessarily unite the soul with God; but this does not prove that it hinders perfection. For in order that a certain doctrine may be perfect, it must bear fruit: the truth according to which life is directed must be known. For the psalmist says: "I have more discernment than the elders, because I observe Your precepts."[17]

---

*TRANSLATOR'S NOTE. Paragraphs preceded by an asterisk refer specifically to Franciscan religious.

17. Ps. 118:100.

7 — *Manner of Proceeding*

13. The purpose of this work is to teach the necessary means and to show the best way of arriving at religious perfection, particularly in the Seraphic Order. To reach this high goal, we must, while trusting in the grace of God, begin to reform that which sin has deformed in us. This being done, at least in essentials, we must strengthen our progress by conforming our life to that of Christ. Finally, we must ascend to the height of virtue, which is the perfect observance of the Gospel.

In accordance with this threefold task and intention, this work is divided into three parts:

Part I treats of the reformation of the sinner and the restoration of everything distorted by sin.

Part II deals with the strengthening of the restored soul and its conformation to Christ.

Parts III and IV, not included in Volume I, take up the subject of perfection, or the perfect observance of the Gospel.

Although each part differs from the others, all are united by a methodical arrangement. The subdivisions, as well as the logical connection between the various matters, will be indicated in the book itself. Even a cursory glance through this treatise discloses the unity flowing through the many means of perfection, and shows that all are correlated with the noble Franciscan ideal and Franciscan goal.

The exposition of ascetical doctrine properly speaking could have started here. Yet it seems preferable to begin with an explanation of the true status of man, and of the universal principles underlying our spiritual doctrine. We must know the sublime destiny of man, for in this way we become acquainted at least in a general manner with the method of ascetical teaching.

II. The Actual State of Man's Existence
as Decreed by Divine Providence

14. This Summary treats of ascetical theology, a supernatural science which directs the soul to the highest possible perfection in this life. We shall do well to keep this vocation in mind and to consider the goal which God Himself has in view.

God's primary purpose is the manifestation of His glory. Next to this, He has no other purpose than that we should raise ourselves above all created things, attain holiness and purity of soul and, even while still on earth, begin to lead a heavenly life like that of the angels. In a word, that we be perfect as our heavenly Father is perfect. We shall approach this perfection more readily if we have a clear understanding of the state of man.

(1) **State.** State may here be defined as the fixed and lasting position of a thing in some setting proper to itself. When there is a question of the state of man or the state of a rational nature, it means a condition in regard to God or a relation to God as the final end, according to the arrangement of Divine Providence.

(2) **Various states.** There are many conditions in which a rational nature may exist. Therefore theologians discern various states of human nature, and the following are among the more important.

(a) *State of pure nature.* In this state nature possesses only what it is destined to have. It has its due, and nothing more.

(b) *State of integral nature.* In this state nature is whole and entire, without any defects which might spontaneously flow from it. It would therefore be free of rebellious concupiscence, death and other natural ailments. Yet it would not be destined for a supernatural end.

(c) *Supernatural state.* In this state man is destined for a supernatural end which exceeds the needs of every created nature. The necessary means to the end are provided in the state itself.

(d) *State of original justice and holiness.* This is the state of Adam before the fall.

(e) *State of fallen nature.* This is the state to which man was reduced immediately after Adam's fall. It was of short duration, since the Redeemer was soon promised.

(f) *State of restored nature.* This is the state in which we now exist.

It pertains to theology to treat dogmatically of these states. Here we shall give brief explanations in order to clarify knowledge of the spiritual life. We need to clarify the following: (1) the idea of nature, both in regard to the natural and the supernatural; (2) the state of original justice and holiness; (3) the gratuitousness of this state; (4) the fall and sin of Adam; (5) the effects of original sin; (6) the state of restored nature.

1 — The Notion of Nature, of the Natural and of the Supernatural

15. (a) **Nature.** Etymologically the word "nature" is taken from the Latin "natus" and means origin or birth. In a strict sense, however, it means the sum of qualities by which the substance of a thing is revealed. By means of these qualities the substance becomes known to us and is differentiated from everything else.

(b) **Natural.** In a strict sense "natural" means whatever constitutes the nature or essence of a thing or so pertains to the thing that it flows from its intrinsic nature; or whatever a nature is able to cause and effect by its powers; or what a nature must possess in order to pursue its proper end. Thus body and soul are natural to man because they constitute his essence. The intellect, the will, and other faculties are natural to man because they flow from his essence. The handiwork of man is natural to him because he is able to effect it by his powers. Reason and many other gifts are natural to man because of his position as a human being.

(c) **Supernatural.** In general "supernatural" signifies something above nature. The supernatural in no way pertains to the natural, but rather is added to a constituted nature. By being added to the natural, the supernatural perfects nature. Then it elevates what it has perfected and, by elevating, transfers the natural to a higher order. Since something can be above nature in various ways, the supernatural requires a division into:

(1) *Relative and absolute.* Something may be beyond the requirements of one being's nature, and yet not above that of another. Thus the ability to fly is supernatural to man but not to the bird. Such is the meaning of the term "relatively supernatural" or "preternatural." But something may transcend the powers and requirements of any nature and all natures and thus simply and absolutely exceed every created and creatable nature. This is the meaning of "supernatural" in the strict or absolute sense. For example, the beatific vision is supernatural in the strict sense. For no being is capable by reason of its own endowments, of beholding God face to face. The absolutely supernatural surpasses by its very act the essence, needs, and endowments of every created and creatable nature, and participates in the special good which is proper and natural to God

alone. In other words, the absolutely supernatural can exist in the divine order only, for it surpasses every created and every possible nature, and the most perfect creature is naturally entitled to those perfections only that fall short of the divine.

(2) *Supernatural as to effect and manner.* The vision of God is an example of supernatural effect. The raising of a dead man to life is an example of supernatural action. Since no creature of itself can attain to the vision of God, the enjoyment of this effect is supernatural. In the second case the attention is fixed instead upon the manner in which the effect is produced. Thus the life of Lazarus after his resurrection was perfectly natural, but the manner in which life was restored to him — by virtue of the words of Christ — was supernatural.

(3) *Supernatural in substance and accident.* The angels are in substance relatively supernatural compared to men. God Himself is absolutely supernatural in substance compared to all created or possible beings. There are various kinds of accidental supernaturality. We must distinguish between instances of the accidentally supernatural within us, such as sanctifying grace, infused virtues and the gifts of the Holy Spirit, and the accidentally supernatural actualities outside us, such as miracles and prophecies.

Having explained nature, the natural and the supernatural, we can proceed to the state of original justice and holiness, the state of our first parents.

2 — *The State of Original Justice and Holiness*

16. (A) The state of Adam was a **supernatural state.** God did not will to establish man in the state of pure nature, in which he could strive only for a natural end. He destined human nature, rather, for an end wholly supernatural. From the first instant of his creation, Adam was elevated by grace

to a state and condition above that of nature. Our first parent was endowed with sanctifying grace, and by this gift was made especially pleasing to God. This grace also justified him, and made him an adopted son of God, an heir to celestial glory, capable of meriting this glory.

(B) State of integral nature. Besides the absolutely supernatural gifts, God also conferred preternatural gifts upon our first parents.

(a) *The gift of integrity, or freedom from concupiscence.* The gift of integrity consists in the perfect supremacy of reason. In virtue of this gift Adam had such control over his lower nature that it never disturbed or prevailed over the deliberations of his mind, but depended upon rational commands. Reason could incite or restrain lower nature as it willed. This faculty is well named the gift of integrity, for it establishes a reign of perfect harmony and concord between lower and higher nature in man, and banishes the conflict aroused by concupiscence.

The other preternatural gifts are: **(b)** *immortality of the body;* **(c)** *impassibility;* and **(d)** *immunity from ignorance.*

3 — The Gratuitousness of Adam's State

17. The gifts bestowed on Adam before the fall were not in any way due to human nature, even in its innocence. They were not natural but supernatural and preternatural gifts.

A. **Sanctifying grace was a supernatural gift.** This can be proved from the effects of sanctifying grace. It was this grace which made Adam an adopted son of God. But adoption is a privilege due to no creature. Therefore sanctifying grace, which raised man so far above his nature and made him a son of God by adoption, must be a supernatural grace. Moreover, sanctifying grace enabled Adam to acquire the happiness of the beatific vision; and since this consists in an intuitive knowledge of God, it transcends all the natural faculties of man.

B. The gifts of integral nature were preternatural.

(1) *Freedom from concupiscence was not due to the nature of man.* The concupiscence of which we speak is an inclination of the appetite toward a sensible good contrary to the judgment of reason.

Thus understood, concupiscence includes: The attractions and aversions to the good and evil respectively in sensible things, which spontaneously flow from sensible perception, hinder the deliberations of reason, and by their allurements endeavor to entice the will to consent. When the will does not consent, a battle ensues between man's higher and lower nature, between reason and animal impulses. The appetites of the lower nature are linked with and give rise to corresponding bodily modifications. These in turn prepare the body to follow or reject the objects desired or disliked by concupiscence. And reason cannot repress these movements as it wills.

This concupiscence naturally emanates from the very constitution of man; for a sensible appetite naturally tends toward a sensible good, while the spiritual appetite, the will, naturally tends toward a spiritual good. Out of these contrary propensities, a battle necessarily ensues. But man is gifted with a free will, which presides over this battle so that the superior nature can subject the inferior, and thus preserve right order.

(2) *Immortality of body and freedom from pain and error are not due to the nature of man.* Man is composed of a body and a rational soul. Because of his body, he must naturally be subject to the conditions of every living being: that is, birth, growth, suffering, and dissolution or death. The death of the body is a sequel to its origin, and can occur by reason of an extrinsic cause, such as fire; or an intrinsic

cause, such as natural deterioration. God is not bound to hinder the effects of these causes. If immortality of body is not natural to man, neither is freedom from pain, since they are intimately associated. For human nature, in so far as it is sentient, is subject to agreeable and disagreeable sensations caused by natural agents.

CONCLUSION. — *The state of pure nature is possible.* If the gifts of sanctifying grace, the supernaturally infused gifts and the preternatural gifts were not Adam's right before the Fall, then man could have been created without them. In other words, the state of pure nature was possible.

St. Thomas teaches that "in the beginning when God created man, He could have formed another man out of the slime of the earth whom He might have left in the condition of nature. This man would have been mortal, subject to suffering and the struggle between concupiscence and reason. Nothing would have been wanting to the human nature in him because all these things follow from the principles of nature. Yet this defect of existing in the condition of pure nature would not have been a fault or a punishment because there would have been nothing voluntary about it."[18]

It would be unfair to judge the state of pure nature by the defects discovered in the states of fallen and restored nature; for many such defects depend very much on particular causes: for example, parents, education and other circumstances that make up our environment. In the state of pure nature, man would have possessed natural foresight and all the requirements necessary to live a wholesome physical and moral life.

4 — *The Fall and Sin of Adam*

18. "When the first man, Adam, had transgressed the law of God in paradise," says the Council of Trent, "he immedi-

18. *In. II Sent.,* d. 31, q. 1. a. 2.

ately lost the sanctity and justice in which he had been created, and through this offense of disobedience incurred the indignation of God. He also became liable to death, . . . and along with death he became captive under the power of him who has 'the empire of death'; that is, he was subject to the power of the devil. Through this sin of disobedience the whole Adam was changed for the worse in body and soul."[19] Therefore, an explanation of what we mean by original sin or the sin of Adam, and the manner in which it is a voluntary sin of the whole human race, is called for.

(1) **Meaning of original sin.** "Original sin is the privation of original justice resulting from the voluntary act of our first parent, not because he was an individual person, but because he was the fount, the beginning of our nature, and hence was to transmit either the supernatural excellence of sanctity if he remained faithful, or the deprivation of it if he acted otherwise."[20] The state of justice, or the state in which Adam and the human race were, by divine dispensation, rightly ordered toward God, their last end, was supernatural sanctity. God destined this grace for the entire human race because it formed one family with Adam. Thus God formally conferred grace on Adam as the principle for propagating human nature, and it consequently followed as a law that Adam, unless he himself lost this grace, would transmit it to posterity along with his human nature. By voluntary transgression of God's command, Adam suffered the loss of this right relationship toward God, his last end. Consequently Adam voluntarily deprived not only himself of this right order toward God, but also deprived the whole human race. Notice, therefore, that original

---

19. Sess. V, Decret. *De peccat. orig.*

20. De Baets, *De ratione et natura peccati originalis,* in *Coll. Brug.,* t. IX, p. 372.

sin is not actual but habitual, not personal but a fault of our nature.

(a) *Original sin is not an actual sin or an evil human act;* for infants, inasmuch as they are incapable of the use of reason, are unable to perform a morally bad deed. Original sin is a habitual sin, the permanent guilt of a sinful act.

(b) *Original sin is not a personal fault but rather one of our nature.* Human nature, concentrated in Adam, incurred the disfavor of God. We are made sharers in this nature by our generation. We spring forth from the fruitful but tainted root of our first parent.

(2) **How original sin is voluntary for the whole human race.** Adam sinned and all posterity sinned in Adam. But how is it possible that an act of Adam's will is voluntary for us? Because under one aspect the will of Adam was our will. How was the will of Adam our will? Not as that of an individual man, but because Adam, as we have seen, was the origin or principle of the propagation of human nature. Since he had voluntarily turned from God, the entire human family was deprived, in him, the father of our human nature, of its rightful adherence to God through the loss of sanctifying grace. Therefore, this privation is "voluntary" in all in so far as they partake of this nature. We must realize, however, that difficulties as well as mysteries lie hidden in this dogma of original sin, which will never be fully explained. St. Thomas teaches that original sin is most serious by reason of the loss incurred; for we are bereft of a supreme good, one which was, however, not due to us. In truth, original sin is least serious in respect to sin as such, because it is the least voluntary; for it is not voluntary through one's own will but by the will of Adam, the father of the human race.

5 — Effects of Original Sin

19. From what has been said about the nature of original sin, we should be able to distinguish its effects. They are as follows:

(1) *Privation of sanctifying grace,* which for Adam and his posterity is a moral sanction, since it is the result of a sin most freely committed.

(2) *The loss of all supernatural gifts.* By losing sanctifying grace man also lost all its formal effects: divine adoption, etc.

(3) *The loss of the preternatural gifts.* Adam lost all the preternatural gifts and man was made subject to concupiscence, mortality, sorrow, and ignorance.

(4) *Captivity under the power of the devil.* After original sin man suffered captivity by the devil.

(5) *Other evils.* If the center of the universe was thoroughly disturbed, no wonder that the whole cosmic order was troubled and all visible things made subject to vanity. The Council of Trent asserted that Adam was changed for the worse in body and soul by his disobedience. The change of nature is not, however, to be taken in a philosophical sense, but in comparison to that state, enriched with so many gratuitous gifts, in which Adam was established before his sin. This same Council also declared that free will was weakened and inclined to evil because of the loss of graces, and the loss of the gift of integrity and the increased rebellion of man's members.

6 — The State of Restored Nature

20. Fallen man could in no way *extricate* himself from his unhappy state, and therefore he lay under necessity of perishing in such misery. But (1) God repaired this damage through Christ; (2) this reparation was brought about by spiritual regeneration in Christ; (3) through baptism, by which (4) the supernatural gifts were restored to man (5) but none of the preternatural gifts.

(1) **Fallen nature was redeemed by Christ.** Moved by mercy, God the Father sent His Son to save the human race. Assuming our nature and emptying Himself, Jesus Christ was made like to man, and appeared in the form of man. He solicitously took care of us, healed our wounds, restored our lost goods, and in this way repaired the ruin of Adam. This reparation, therefore, was not particular or personal to Adam alone, but universal, and for all nature.

(2) **Spiritual regeneration in Christ.** "Although Christ died for all," states the Decree on Justification of the Council of Trent, "not all receive the benefits of His death but only those to whom the merit of His passion is communicated. For just as man is born defiled only through propagation of the seed of Adam, so also man will be justified only by rebirth in Christ."[21]

(3) **Spiritual regeneration in Christ is accomplished through baptism.** This justification the Council of Trent calls "transference from that state in which man is born a son of the first Adam, into the state of grace and adoption as a son of God through the second Adam, Jesus Christ our Saviour. Since the promulgation of the Gospel, however, this transference cannot be accomplished without the cleansing water of regeneration or at least a desire for it; for, as it is written, 'Unless a man be born again of water and the Holy Ghost, he cannot enter into the Kingdom of God' (John 3:5)."[22]

---

21. Council of Trent, Sess. VI, Decret. *De justif.*, cap. III.
22. *Ibid.*, cap. IV.

(4) **The supernatural gifts are restored to the regenerated soul.** "Through the grace of our Lord Jesus Christ,
conferred in baptism, the guilt of original sin is remitted and
all that has the true character of sin is also taken away. In
the regenerated soul there is nothing that God detests, for
nothing deserving damnation remains in those who are truly
buried with Christ in death through baptism. They no longer
walk according to the flesh but, having put off the old man
and put on the new, who is created according to God, they
are made innocent, unstained, pure, and blameless. They are
loved by God, they are heirs of God and co-heirs with Christ,
so that nothing further should keep them from reaching
heaven."[23]

(5) **The preternatural gifts are not restored to the regenerated soul.** Although sanctifying grace and the supernatural gifts are restored, the preternatural gifts are not. Baptized
persons are still subject to concupiscence, sorrow, ignorance
and death.

Since these imperfections are not in themselves sinful, they
can most powerfully serve to promote the glory of God and
secure our salvation. God allowed holy men, His well-beloved
Son, and even the spotless Mother of His only-begotten Son
to be subject to misery, and even death itself. From this it is
clear that the absence of the preternatural gifts is not opposed
to divine wisdom and goodness, for the present life is a
diminished one, even though it has been restored. It is not
a peaceful and happy contest but one of agony and struggle,
in which eternal reward will not be received without strenuous
combat. Therefore concupiscence, sorrow and hardship can
be occasions of multiple good, merit and the exercises of virtue.

CONCLUSION. The state in which we now exist is the state
of fallen though restored nature. Man continues to be destined

---

23. Council of Trent, Sess. V, Decret. *De peccat. orig.*, n. 5.

for a supernatural end, as God has ordained. Although he is incapable of reaching this end of himself, since he is born in original sin, yet through Christ he is able to regain grace and all the means to attain the end for which he was destined. Hence we must briefly explain the general principles which guide man to this end in his state of fallen but restored nature.

III. The General Principles by Which Man Is Directed to His End

21. Since no edifice can sustain itself without a foundation, how could the edifice of the science of the spiritual life stand up without one? This foundation consists in general principles from which the entire doctrine of the spiritual life is drawn; these principles can be reduced to the following three points:

(1) Man comes from God: God is his Author;

(2) Man journeys to God: God is his end;

(3) Man has the means of reaching his end.

1 — *Man Comes from God: God Is His Author*

22. Man was created by God: He Himself, and not our parents, made us; because that which is born of the flesh is flesh, but the soul is spiritual. God Himself, in order to bring forth the flesh, makes use of parents as one would of hired help in building a house. He is the Architect, the Author, the Father not only of the soul but also of the body; thus He wills to be, and to be called, the Father of the entire man. Thus the Spirit of the Lord says through Moses: "Is He not your Father who created you? Has He not made you and established you?"[24] and through Job: "With skin and flesh You clothed me, with

---

24. Deut. 32:6.

bones and sinews knit me together";[25] also through that truly wise woman, the mother of the Machabees: "I know not how you were formed in my womb: for I neither gave you breath, nor soul, nor life; neither did I frame the limbs of every one of you — but the Creator of the world that formed the nativity of man and that found out the origin of all."[26]

Hence the Wisdom of God, Christ the Lord, said, "Call no one on earth your father; for one is your Father, who is in heaven."[27] Now if God is the Author of your body and soul, whatever you have or hope for, you hope for from Him. With what great confidence and affection must David have said: "I am Yours; save me."[28]

2 — Man Journeys to God: God Is His End

23. (1) **Man's destiny.** Man is destined to share in the divine life for all eternity by participating in the knowledge and love by means of which God knows and loves Himself.

(a) THE BEATIFIC VISION. St. John speaks of the beatific vision, saying: "Beloved, now we are the children of God, and it has not yet appeared what we shall be. We know that when He appears, we shall be like to Him, for we shall see Him just as He is."[29] And St. Paul writes, "For we know in part and we prophesy in part; but when that which is perfect has come, that which is imperfect will be done away with. . . . We see now through a mirror in an obscure manner, but then face to face. Now I know in part, but then I shall know even as I have been known."[30]

25. Job 10:11.
26. 2 Mach. 7:22-23.
27. Matt. 23:9.
28. Ps. 118:94.
29. 1 John 3:2.
30. 1 Cor. 13:9-10, 12.

(b) BEATIFIC LOVE. As a result of the beatific vision, love for the highest good must arise in the will, as by a natural necessity. And this highest good will be immediately recognized as such. This beatific love is signified by the Apostle when he says, "So there abide faith, hope, and charity, these three; but the greatest of these is charity"[31] — because it continues for all eternity.

(2) **The end of man consists in the knowledge and love of God** to which he is destined; and through this knowledge and love he promotes the *glory of God and his own beatitude.*

(a) THE GLORY OF GOD. In creating, God acts most wisely; for He creates everything with a purpose. Since He is completely happy in Himself, He cannot intend His own advantage or joy. He wills rather to manifest His glory externally, and to obtain formal external glory from man. This formal external glory is a clear knowledge and praise of the excellence of God.

Man was created by God, therefore, to know His Creator, to praise Him and to venerate Him as his kind and most high Lord. Even while on earth man can and must accomplish this, yet he will be able to do it perfectly and fully only when he has attained at last to the vision of God and its consequent love. The Holy Spirit rightly gives this command: "The Lord thy God shalt thou worship and Him only shalt thou serve."[32] What can be easier, sweeter, more agreeable than to love Goodness, Beauty and Love — our Lord and our God? How well David expresses this in the psalm: "The ordinances of the Lord [all the more so, the Lord Himself] . . . are more precious than gold, than a heap of purest gold; sweeter also than syrup or honey from the comb."[33] Certainly if we strive through

---

31. 1 Cor. 13:13.
32. Matt. 4:10.
33. Ps. 18:10, 11.

knowledge and hope to realize this high purpose of our existence, we should blush with shame when we contend for possessions of this earth, when we are downcast because of the loss of temporal things or overjoyed over temporal gain. We who are companions of the angels, sharers in the friendship of God and in His inestimable good should blush when we discover ourselves desiring the same gratifications as animals. By knowing and loving God, by doing precisely that for which he is made, man prepares his own happiness, and contributes to God's external glory.

(b) THE HAPPINESS OF MAN. Perfect human happiness consists in the possession and perfect enjoyment of the highest good. But man most perfectly possesses and enjoys this highest good in the intuitive vision of God and in the love which necessarily follows upon it. "For You, O Lord, are good and forgiving."[34] Who would not serve God with his whole heart, especially since God has promised such a splendid reward through His Apostle St. James: "He will receive the crown of life which God has promised to those who love Him."[35] And what is the crown of life except an even greater good than we can imagine or desire? St. Paul speaks of it when he says, "Eye has not seen nor ear heard, nor has it entered into the heart of man, what things God has prepared for those who love Him."[36] Man therefore is destined for eternal happiness; he is to glorify God for all eternity. The glory of God is the primary ultimate purpose of man, and eternal happiness his secondary purpose. If we reach this end we will be happy. If we fall short of this end, we will be wretched. With this in mind, we must consider as truly good for ourselves whatever leads to our goal, and as harmful whatever causes us to fall away from it. Prosperity and adversity, abundance and neces-

---

34. Ps. 85:5.
35. James 1:12.
36. 1 Cor. 2:9, from Isaia, 64:4.

sity, health and sickness, honors and dishonors, life and death, in themselves must neither be sought nor avoided. If, however, they lead to the glory of God and our everlasting happiness, they are good and desirable; if they are a hindrance, they are bad and to be avoided.

3 — Man Has the Means of Reaching His End

24. Since God has destined man for the beatific vision, it follows that within this very destiny is contained the means necessary to achieve this ultimate goal. Here we do not wish to consider the external means which our Lord has established for this end, but only the interior means which enable the soul to strive for its goal. These means are: (a) sanctifying grace; (b) the theological virtues; (c) the moral virtues; (d) the gifts of the Holy Spirit; and (e) actual grace.

(a) **Sanctifying grace.** Sanctifying grace is a certain beautiful and exquisite quality inherent in the soul. By this grace man is made just and acceptable to God, His friend and adopted son, and a sharer in His divine nature. Grace may well be compared to oil because it does for the soul what oil does for the body. Indeed, sanctifying grace is the oil of salvation which heals our internal wounds: an invigorating oil which strengthens our weakness, anointing us as athletes for the fight against the devil. It is the oil of peace which, after victory has been obtained, reconciles the soul with God. It is the oil of light that dispels the darkness of sin and ignorance, and shines forth with the truths of faith. It is the oil of splendor, causing us to appear beautiful and fair before God; the oil of joy which gladdens the inner man. It is a nourishing oil, enriching the spirit with devotion. And just as oil floats above other liquids, so sanctifying grace supersedes all the other gifts God grants us during our pilgrimage on earth.

The infused virtues are also required. Just as ointment is compounded of many sweet-smelling fluids mixed with oil, so sanctifying grace, the spiritual ointment, is completed by what it brings along with it: namely, the supernatural virtues and the seven gifts of the Holy Spirit. For after the manner of oil, grace penetrates our innermost being, strengthening all the powers of the soul and anointing them for the pursuit of their ultimate end.

In the first place, sanctifying grace requires the theological virtues.

(b) **The theological virtues.** The theological virtues are habits infused by God enabling man to practice supernatural acts whose motive or formal object is God or some absolute divine perfection. They are three in number: faith, hope, and charity. St. Paul writes of them in his Epistle to the Corinthians: "So there abide faith, hope, and charity, these three; but the greatest of these is charity."[37] The theological virtues direct man toward eternal happiness; faith sees God as the highest and ineffable Truth; hope as the Omnipotent Being, faithful to His promises; but charity looks to Him as the highest Good. Those who seek perfection should persevere in faith, hope, and charity, for these are the powers which cause us to lead a life befitting the sons of God; these are defensive and offensive weapons: the shield of faith, the helmet of hope, and the sword of charity. He who loves God seeks Him through faith, strives toward Him through hope, and possesses Him in charity.

(c) **Moral virtues.** Man is directed toward his last end by means of the theological virtues. But this is not sufficient. He should also be duly disposed and instructed in the means to this end. This is accomplished by the moral virtues, the habits infused by God whose formal object or motive is a

---

37. 1 Cor. 13:13.

right conduct. Four of the moral virtues are called cardinal virtues: prudence, justice, fortitude, and temperance. All the others are connected with and can be reduced to these four.

After Adam's sin, human nature remained in a weakened state, pierced as it were with as many wounds as there are senses, appetites, concupiscences, and passions. For this reason man did not retain his heavenly riches, nor did he preserve the merits of his good works nor guard the waters of divine grace. But the moral virtues serve to heal these wounds. Their office is to watch over the doors of the senses, to bridle the appetites and concupiscences, and in the best possible way to repair human nature so that all its faculties — the intellect, the will, the appetites, both irascible and concupiscible — may be ordered to the pursuit of man's ultimate goal. Temperance restrains the concupiscible appetite; fortitude and justice conform the irascible appetite to the will; and prudence instructs reason and the practical intellect.

(d) **The gifts of the Holy Spirit.** Inasmuch as sanctifying grace and the theological virtues elevate the soul and unite it with the Holy Spirit, they require the infusion into the soul of His gifts. These gifts are certain qualities through which man naturally and immediately obeys the promptings of the Holy Spirit who dwells within him. Three of these gifts, namely, wisdom, understanding, and knowledge, enlighten the eye of faith and make it see revealed truth more clearly and more deeply. Counsel foresees what must be done, while piety, fortitude and fear of the Lord help one to do it.

Words are inadequate to express the sublime truths available to the mind, the deep affections offered to the soul, the powerful appeal to heroic virtue which flow from the action of the Holy Spirit. Although remaining unseen, the Holy Spirit is active, sharpening the eyes of faithful souls and directing their interior vision. Invisible also is the union of the

Holy Spirit with souls; yet souls who are docile to Him are led to ever higher levels of spirituality, to ever greater perfection.

(e) **Actual grace.** We need the natural help of God to perform natural deeds; we absolutely need supernatural help called actual grace, to elicit supernatural acts. Through this grace God supernaturally concurs with every supernatural action, so that His help anticipates, accompanies, and perfects it. St. Paul had this in mind when he wrote: "Not that we are sufficient of ourselves to think anything, as from ourselves, but our sufficiency is from God."[38] And writing to the Philippians he says, "For it is God who of His good pleasure works in you both the will and the performance."[39] St. Augustine also plainly states: "Even though the eye is very healthy, unless it is aided by the luster of light it cannot discern; so also man, even one who is completely justified, unless he is assisted by the eternal light of justice, cannot live correctly."[40]

But do not fear, for we have a Helper who assists us along the way of salvation, the same who in Egypt was not wanting as a Liberator. Say, therefore, with the Psalmist: My help is not from riches, nor from power and strength, nor from men, but "my help is from the Lord."[41]

RECAPITULATION. These are the general principles by which man tends to the purpose of his vocation.

Man was *created by God.* If I come from God, then I do not come from myself, nor from society, nor from anything else. Therefore, I must obey God. All other necessities are vain in comparison. It is right, honorable, pleasing, and praise-

---

38. 2 Cor. 3:5.
39. Phil. 2:13.
40. *De natura et gratia,* cap. XXVI in fine, in Migne, *P. L.,* t. XLIV, col. 261.
41. Ps. 120:2.

worthy to protect one's own good and the common good, but it is not necessary if it cannot be accomplished without disobedience to God.

Man is *created for God*. If I exist for God, the hope for any other happiness is vain. All I have comes from God. I hope to obtain the object of my desire from Him and not from riches, nor from my own will, nor from the pleasures of the body. The only profitable service is the service of God.

Think of all the favors bestowed on us by God: sanctifying grace, the infused virtues, the gifts of the Holy Spirit, the natural gifts. Nature externally and grace internally offer us their treasures, so that we are inexcusable if we do not serve God.

Yet it is not enough simply to serve God: God has destined us to the state of perfection. It is not enough to love God above all things as He has prescribed. We must strive for the perfection of love. If we do not possess perfect love, then by reason of our state we are bound to keep on striving for it.

In the light of these general principles, we can more easily find the way to our eternal home, the kingdom of heaven. The object of the following pages is to point out the safest way to this heavenly home.

Divisions

25. We must rise to perfection in an orderly way. For, even though the charity in which Christian perfection consists always tends in its desires and its ambition toward the highest and best, yet in actual practice it only reaches such summits gradually and by degrees. It would be indiscreet and dangerous for anyone immediately to engage in the practices of perfect souls without first learning the beginner's lesson. By rashly trying to jump from one bank of a river to the other, we will not only lose the place where we stood and fail to reach the

other shore, but we will also fall into the stream and perish. The religious life according to St. Paul consists in the following:

I.   *In the reformation of what is deformed, through the purgation of vices;*

II. *In the strengthening of what has been reformed, by spiritual means;*

III. *In conforming to Christ, by the practice of virtue;*

IV. *In the consummation of what has been strengthened and conformed to Christ, through the perfect observance of the holy Gospels.*

I.   *The reformation of what is deformed* is accomplished through the purgation of vices, for, as the Apostle wrote, "As regards your former manner of life, you are to put off the old man, which is being corrupted through its deceptive lusts. But be renewed in the spirit of your mind."[42]

II. and III. *The strengthening of what has been reformed, and conforming to Christ,* are achieved through the exercise of virtue, for St. Paul continues, "Put on the new man which has been created according to God in justice and holiness of truth."[43]

IV. *Finally, the consummation of what has been strengthened* is effected by perfect observance of the holy Gospels, as the Apostle concludes: "Be you, therefore, imitators of God, as very dear children and walk in love, as Christ also loved us and delivered Himself up for us an offering and a sacrifice to God to ascend in fragrant odor."[44]

---

42. Eph. 4:22-23.
43. *Ibid.* 4:24.
44. *Ibid.* 5:1-2.

PART I

THE REFORMATION OF WHAT IS DEFORMED, THROUGH THE PURGATION OF VICES

PART I

THE REFORMATION OF WHAT IS DEFORMED, THROUGH THE PURGATION OF VICES

26. **Divisions.** The corruption of human nature necessarily flowed from the defection of our first parents from the end which God had ordained for them. It came in the form of original sin. Having lost their original sanctity and justice, and consequently having been deprived of supernatural and preternatural gifts, our first parents fell into so many evils that the multitude of their imperfections exceeds description.

From original sin comes blind concupiscence which oppresses the soul and binds it to earth. From original sin result love of transitory things and even aversion from God, giving rise to uncontrolled passions. From original sin comes ignorance which involves our mind in a dark mist. From this source comes an impious rebellion against the Divine Will. In a word, man, after sinning, is powerfully drawn toward self by the weight of self-love; he loses sight of his last end and relies solely on himself, so that at last his ego becomes the center of all his activities.

The man of sin, or "the old man," must heal in his nature the wounds of sin; that is to say, the soul itself must undergo a reformation together with the external and internal senses and the various members of the body.

There are, therefore, four books in Part I:

Book I — The reformation of the soul of "the old man" by penance.

Book II — The reformation of the exterior of "the old man," or the reformation of the external senses and tongue through accurate custody.

Book III — The reformation of the bodily members of "the old man" through religious discipline.

Book IV — The reformation of the internal senses of "the old man" through internal custody.

BOOK I

The First Reformation:
Reformation of the Soul by Penance

27. Divisions. Since the soul is corrupted by sin, in this discussion we must study the following:

    I.   The nature, the kinds, and the causes of sin;

    II. The eradication of mortal sin;

    III. The eradication of venial sin and the final reformation of the soul.

CHAPTER I

SIN AND ITS CAUSES

Article I — The Nature of Sin

28. What is sin? Man, under the guidance of his conscience, tends toward his ultimate end through human acts conformable to law. But because of his human weakness, or rather his malice, he sometimes wanders from the straight path through transgression of the laws of God. When the sin is grave, man is turned away from his last end; but if the sin is venial, he does achieve his end but only after some delay.

Difference between mortal and venial sin. St. Bonaventure makes this distinction between mortal and venial sin: "Actual sin is an actual disordering of the will. This disordering of the will may be such that it destroys the order of justice and is called mortal sin, because it takes away life by separating the soul from God, through whom a just soul derives life; or the disordering may be so mild that it does not destroy that order but disturbs it in some way — and this is called venial sin, as we are able immediately to obtain forgiveness: 'venia' — for grace is not removed nor is divine enmity incurred."[1]

Article II — The Causes of Sin

29. The *efficient cause* of sin is the free will of man. Man's will is attracted toward sin either through: (1) *intrinsic* or (2) *extrinsic* causes.

§ I. The Intrinsic Cause

30. The intrinsic cause of sin is *concupiscence.*

What is concupiscence? Concupiscence means the perverse tendency of the appetites, both the lower and the higher. This

---

1. *Breviloquium*, Pars III, cap. VIII.

perverse tendency is born of original sin, by which man is moved toward things which are contrary to right reason. For though by nature flesh and spirit are brothers, they became enemies after the fall of Adam. For just as Rebecca bore two sons who struggled with each other, so each one of us bears within himself appetites of the body and of the soul which bitterly conflict with each other; but according to the law and plan of God, the flesh must serve the soul and be subject to it. But, in actual fact, the flesh rebels against the spirit to the extent that it nurtures inclinations in opposition to the soul, just as Esau opposed Jacob. Our carnal man, like Esau, is so inclined toward pursuit of pleasures that he employs his five senses to seize for himself the alluring goods and useful possessions of this world and solicitously seeks and even idolizes them. But our spiritual man, like Jacob, is by nature simple and serene, a lover of peace and given to the contemplation of the supernatural, lest his flesh should disturb him.

Concupiscence is the cause of sin. St. James teaches us that this is the cause of sin: "But everyone is tempted by being drawn away and enticed by his own passion. Then when passion has conceived, it brings forth sin. But when sin has matured, it begets death."[2] Consequently, concupiscence is not in itself a sin, but is the principal tinder of sin, a continual inducement to sin.

Material for concupiscence. St. John sets up a threefold matter upon which concupiscence hinges: "Because all that is in the world is the lust of the flesh, and the lust of the eyes, and the pride of life."[3] Therefore, when sin occurs, it exists through an unruly affection for pleasures, riches and honors. Not that it is a sin per se to live amid pleasures, riches and

---

2. James 1:14-15.
3. 1 John 2:16.

honors; but to seek after such objects inordinately constitutes a grave danger; thus a bridle must be thrown on the appetite, and if any deformity is already present, it must be reformed.

The severe struggle against concupiscence. Concerning this struggle the Apostle says, "But I see another law in my members, warring against the law of my mind."[4] "Moreover," states Thomas a Kempis, "this internal struggle is most painful and difficult for us all, begotten as we are in corruptible and sinful flesh. For what is more painful, more difficult, to every man desiring peace than daily to fight against himself, to struggle against nature, to restrain lust, to overcome concupiscence itching within? ... An exceedingly heavy burden and an intricate war: to nurse the flesh, to nourish an enemy, to clothe, warm, wash, dry, caress it so that it does not complain; and yet to chastise it so that it does not rebel. To encourage it so that it does not lose hope; yet to rebuke it so that it does not grow slothful. To subdue it so that it is not puffed up, and to strengthen it so that it does not faint; to instruct it so that it does not err, to repress it so that it does not become insolent; to love it as a companion, but to hate its lust as the snare of death itself. But in this warfare no man is overcome unless he is corrupted by an evil will and has, of his own accord, turned away from God. Beware, then, of the dangers in the daily conflict of the flesh; for as long as we live in the world eating and drinking we are tempted in many ways."[5]

§ II. The Extrinsic Causes

31. There are two principal extrinsic causes which entice us to sin: the world and the devil.

---

4. Rom. 7:23.
5. Thomas a Kempis, *Serm. ad Novit.,* Serm. 19, n. 8, 9.

I. **The world.** What is the world? The world with which we are concerned is not the whole of living mankind but the empire of the evil spirit. In other words, it is that portion of humanity that is in revolt against God's will; it comprises those who seek the satisfaction of their own appetites, with no regard for the moral law. It includes all those who live for the sake of pride, honor, power, or wealth; who despise the humble and the poor, and have regard only for created and temporal values.

In this world there are many dangers. This world is full of snares and traps. For this reason David says, "In the way along which I walk, they have hid a trap for me."[6] And Sirach warns us to step between these snares. There are as many vices as there are traps; there are as many sins as there are stumblings into these traps. These pitfalls consist of temptations, trials and occasions of sin; the traps are the plots, deceits, and subterfuges of the enemies of our salvation. "Everything in the world," says St. Leo, "is full of dangers, full of snares. Things of the world arouse the passions; their enticements ambush us; worldly gains allure us, temporal losses dishearten us."[7] Such snares are found both in the abundance of riches and in the squalor of poverty — in fact, in the excess or defect of any human activity and as regards any object.

Yet these dangers do not arise directly from created things but from their abuse through the concupiscence mentioned by St. James: "Whence do wars and quarrels come among you? Is it not from this, from your passions, which wage war in your members?"[8] For this reason St. John calls the concupiscence of the flesh and of the eyes enemies in our wicked world. For the images of sensible objects enter through the eyes and ears, and these images arouse our concupiscence. And

6. Ps. 141: 4.
7. *Serm. 5 de Quadrages.*, in Migne, *P. L.*, t. LIV, col. 282.
8. James 4:1.

concupiscence so ravages the soul through the use of the eyes and indeed is so blind that as a result it will open further the windows of the senses so that death may enter.

II. **The devil.** The devil assails us. St. Peter warns us about this battle: "Be sober, be watchful! For your adversary the devil, as a roaring lion, goes about seeking someone to devour."[9] And St. Paul writing to the Ephesians says, "Put on the armor of God, that you may be able to stand against the wiles of the devil. For our wrestling is not against flesh and blood, but against the Principalities and the Powers, against the world-rulers of this darkness, against the spiritual forces of wickedness on high."[10]

This battle between the devil and man began in paradise, after the creation of the first man. And "it will last as long as the human race walks upon the earth. . . . And he [Satan] deceives not only the simple but the learned also and famed masters and religious, suggesting to them diverse vanities. He is busy day by day tempting man by the five senses of the body: now enticing by the flesh, now by levity, now by arousing anger.

"As is frequently experienced, the devil in his malice never ceases doing harm, nor does he allow others to rest; and where he himself does not come, he sends his accomplices to vex the sheep of Christ. And if he cannot carry them off, if he is forbidden to slay them, he at least strives to injure them by his terrors. And if he sees one of them wandering, one of them idle, remiss in good work, study or prayer, he approaches the more freely to tempt him because such a one has incautiously laid down the arms that resist the foe."[11]

Now we must consider how the soul, deceived and deformed by concupiscence, the world, or the devil, can be reformed.

---

9. 1 Peter 5:8.
10. Eph. 6:11-12.
11. Thomas a Kempis, *loc. cit.*, n. 6, 7.

CHAPTER II

REFORMATION OF THE SOUL DEVASTATED BY MORTAL SIN

32. (1) The souls even of religious can be disfigured by mortal sin. Although the faithful are regenerated in Baptism, strengthened in Confirmation, and nourished by the Holy Eucharist, they can and should not only safeguard their own spiritual life, but also perfect it. Since they enjoy free will and are exposed to the alluring baits of the world, the snares of the devil, and the enticements of concupiscence, they will readily fall into temptation and sink not only into venial but even mortal sins, unless they are ever alert and prayerful. Knowing this full well, our holy Father St. Francis, in the seventh chapter of his Rule, speaks about "The penance to be imposed on friars who sin." And he is not concerned therein with friars who sin secretly but with those who commit mortal sins openly, for he says: "Let him have recourse as quickly as possible and without delay to (the Ministers)." "This action," says St. Bonaventure, "is taken only for notorious sins, since secret crimes should not be publicized."[1]

Our holy Father also points out the reason for such falls in the words: "at the instigation of the enemy." For, as the Seraphic Doctor remarks, "The higher the perfection one strives for, so much more insidious are the snares the devil plots for him."[2]

(2) The Sacrament of Penance is necessary. Left only to their own resources, men cannot merit the forgiveness of the infinite God for the sins they have committed. But the Son of Man made ample reparation for the offenses of man against God, and instituted the Sacrament of Penance for the purpose of applying His merits to us. Whence it follows that

---

1. *Expos. super Reg.*, cap. VII, 2.
2. *Ibid.*

this Sacrament, at least "in desire, by the necessity of means," is necessary for the salvation of all who, after Baptism, have fallen into mortal sin. For the remission of a mortal sin committed after Baptism is certainly essential for our salvation. Christ has given us the means whereby we may obtain this remission: the Sacrament of Penance, which must be received, if possible, in reality; and if this is impossible, at least in desire.

Although contrition with perfect love may reconcile us to God before reception of the Sacrament, it does not restore us to God's favor without desire for the Sacrament, a desire which is implicitly contained in true contrition. This doctrine is based on the fact that in the New Testament there is no forgiveness of mortal sins independent of the power of the keys. We are able to receive the forgiveness of our sins through the merits of Christ applied to us only by the means which He has prescribed: "For there is one God, and one Mediator between God and men, Himself man, Christ Jesus."[3] "In whom we have our redemption, the remission of our sins."[4]

CONDITIONS NECESSARY FOR THE SACRAMENT OF PENANCE. According to St. Bonaventure, the reformation of the sinner takes place (1) "through the repentance of sorrow conceived in the heart by compunction [that is, contrition] (2) expressed orally through confession, and (3) consummated in deed by satisfaction."[5]

Article I — Contrition

33. Contrition, as the term is generally applied, means the sorrow of the soul and the detestation of the sin committed, with the resolution of avoiding sin in the future; in other words, it is an act whereby the sinner is diverted from evil and

---

3. 1 Tim. 2:5.
4. Col. 1:14.
5. *Brevil.*, Pars VI, cap. X.

directed toward good, i. e., toward God. Contrition can be divided into two kinds: one, *perfect*, which is simply called contrition; the other, *imperfect*, which is properly known by the term "attrition."

To understand the nature of this conversion of the soul to God through contrition, we must note:

(1) The difference between contrition and attrition;
(2) The necessity of the realization and acknowledgment of our own guilt, which results in the death of the soul;
(3) The nature and necessity of sorrow;
(4) The essential requisites of sorrow; and, lastly,
(5) The firm resolution of avoiding sin in the future.

§ I. The Difference between Contrition and Attrition

34. Contrition and attrition are distinct in their motive and in their effect. The former has its origin in love and justifies the sinner even outside the Sacrament; the latter springs from a less worthy cause and does not justify the transgressor, unless accompanied by the actual Sacrament of Baptism or of Penance.

To understand this distinction we must give our attention to the following points: (1) the distinction between the detestation of sin springing from love and an abhorrence effected by some other motive; and (2) the effects of contrition and of attrition.

I. THE MOTIVES FOR CONTRITION AND ATTRITION

35. The motive for contrition, or the reason for sorrow and detestation of sin, consists in this: that sin offends God, who is to be loved above all things. God may be loved not only because of His infinite goodness, or because of the totality of all His perfections, but also because of His individual perfections, as, for example, His power, goodness, mercy, etc. If we hate sin because it is directed against God's infinite goodness, which is to be our primary object of love, or because of some other divine attribute, we make an act of perfect contrition.

The motive for attrition is not indeed a motive of love, but an inferior motive. Yet it is related to God. The Council of Trent reduced the motives of attrition to these three:

1. *The vileness of sin.* For sin contains in itself a manifold baseness or malice: disobedience, ingratitude, contempt, etc.; in addition, mortal sin always produces most fatal effects in the sinner: it deprives his soul of sanctifying grace; it debases it before God; it makes it Satan's possession and renders it odious in the eyes of God.

2. *The fear of hell,* or the fear of supernatural and eternal punishment which God inflicts because of mortal sin. This punishment consists in the loss of merit, the deprivation of beatitude, and the pains of the body.

3. *The fear of punishment,* or the fear of temporal punishment either in this life or the next. These punishments do not follow sin naturally but accordingly as God, who is offended by sin and avenges transgressions, wills to inflict them.

II. THE EFFECTS OF CONTRITION AND ATTRITION

36. We cannot determine a priori (deductively) the effects of abhorring sin through a motive of love and the effects of detesting it because of some other inferior motives. From revelation, however, we learn the conditions established by an offended God through which He wills to forgive insults. One thing certainly evident in revelation is that wherever perfect love flourishes, there exists at the same time the friendship of God. Friendship and enmity are incompatible in the same subject. Therefore, when love is present, it banishes sin. "If anyone love Me," says Jesus, "he will keep My word, and My

Father will love him, and We will come to him and make Our abode with him."[6]

Through perfect contrition the sinner loves God and so fulfills the last disposition required by Him for the infusion of sanctifying grace.

Nevertheless, in the New Law this contrition does not justify us without a desire for the Sacrament; for after the institution of the Sacrament, it is the design of the divine will to forgive sin only when sin is brought into relation with the keys of the Church. Therefore the obligation remains for the sinner to submit his sin to the power of the keys through sacramental confession whenever possible.

Privileges, especially supernatural ones, must not be presupposed, but are to be proved. Perfect charity confers the privilege of reconciliation before actual confession when desire for confession is all that is immediately possible — not the reception of the actual Sacrament. Since by attrition the sinner returns to God's friendship not from a motive of love but from some other inferior motive, the same privilege must not be ascribed to attrition. Therefore we cannot say that attrition outside the Sacrament justifies the sinner.

Yet, since a detestation of sin through attrition more or less resembles love, such detestation is real and sufficiently disposes the sinner toward recovering justification through the Sacrament, as the Council of Trent clearly points out.

Through attrition the sinner begins to love God. Still that incipient love is not the motive for sorrow, but is an act concomitant with sorrow and is always contained in the requisite dispositions for justification, whether in the hope of forgiveness, or in the resolution, or in the sorrow itself.

------

6. John 14:23.

§ II. The Necessity of the Realization and Acknowledgment of
Our Plight, i. e., The Death of the Soul

37. In order that he may return to God's friendship, the
sinner should realize and acknowledge that his soul is dead.
Let him exclaim with Ezechia: "I will recount to Thee all my
years in the bitterness of my soul."[7] Or he can confess with
David: "I acknowledge my offense, and my sin is before me
always."[8] In this regard St. Cyprian offers this advice: "O
most beloved brethren, in your penitent and sorrowful condition, be aware of your sins, acknowledge the grave crime of
your conscience, open the eyes of your heart in order to understand your sin; do not despair of God's mercy, yet do not
demand forgiveness as though you had a right to it."[9]

Malice of the sinner. The malice of the sinner appears
terrible because he has so soon squandered the great gifts bestowed on him at Baptism in favor of some vile creature, in-
flicting almost infinite injury on the Giver.

"Be amazed at this, O heavens, and shudder with sheer
horror, says the Lord. Two evils have My people done: they
have forsaken Me, the source of living waters; They have dug
themselves cisterns, broken cisterns, that hold no water."[10]

For what citizen of heaven would not be amazed, were it
possible for him, or what heavenly power would not be desolate and moved with grief when observing the sinner abandon
the God of all grace, the fountain of living water? What indeed is sin except, as we have seen, a turning away from
immutable goodness, an abandoning of God, the Source of
all good? And what is the reason for this aversion, except
that the sinner is turned toward changeable and transitory

---

7. Isa. 38:15, Challoner-Douay version.
8. Ps. 50:5.
9. *De lapsis*, XXXV, in Migne, *P. L.*, t. IV, col. 507.
10. Jer. 2:12-13.

good, a situation like that of the man who digs for himself cisterns which hold no water to quench his thirst and cannot serve as secure storage tanks?

Wretched condition of the sinner. The sinner should attentively consider his own wretchedness. He is a counterpart of the prodigal son who received his inheritance from his father, left his parents' home, and set out for a distant region. There he dissipated his fortune by riotous living, then sought the favor of one of the citizens of that region, who commanded him to feed his swine. Tortured with hunger, he desired to fill his stomach with the husks the pigs ate, but no one gave him any. Deep calls upon deep, and the sinner, commencing with slight faults, slips into worse, ever more serious falls. On this score St. Paul relates: "But the wicked and impostors will go from bad to worse."[11] The sinner in a certain sense plunges himself into a fathomless abyss of misery in seven stages of wickedness.

(1) *He rebels against his Father.* For, in the first place, he wishes to be his own law, the judge in his own case, and not to submit to the rule and protection of his Father. "Long ago you broke your yoke, you tore off your bonds. 'I will not serve,' you said."[12]

(2) *He leaves his Father's house.* In forsaking God, he commits an additional evil, and this not by means of the body but rather of the intellect. He abandons his paternal home and the companionship of his brothers and intimates, and he ignores the example and admonition of the saints, who wish to restrain him from evil.

(3) *He travels to a distant region.* He journeys on foot to a distant land which must be a frigid, dark and dismal region akin to the shadow of death, since it is a great distance

---

11. 2 Tim. 3:13.
12. Jer. 2:20.

from God, the Sun of Justice. It is a long distance away because it is alienated from the just. As long as he abides in this
region, his only companions are sinners; with these he freely
associates, and their code of morality — wrongdoing — he
willingly observes.

(4) *He squanders his inheritance.* Freely following in
the footsteps of the wicked, this wretched youth spends all
his inheritance. For one who dissipates grace and charity and
the gifts of the Holy Spirit by living luxuriously, yielding to
his own concupiscence and gratifying every desire of the senses,
dissipates all his strength, all his resources. He even glories in
such disgraceful conduct, saying: This is my lot, my portion,
my good fortune, my life.

(5) *He clings to the devil.* He clings to a citizen of that
land; that is, the devil; and this is the same as making a
covenant with death and a union with the inhabitants of hell.
See how he has been taken captive! For he attaches himself to
one of his vices involving grave matter. As every sinner clings
more tenaciously to one predominant vice, this vice — a king,
or rather a tyrant — orders him about like a lowly possession.
This vicious habit compels him as if by violence to obey and to
serve it in all matters. For this reason the Evangelist remarks,
"he sent him to his farm to feed swine."[13] And the prodigal
immediately obeyed this order.

(6) *He feeds swine.* This is the sixth and most horrible
evil: to feed swine, not only his own, but those of others; that
is to say, he "feeds" not only his own senses and appetites,
which have degenerated into the filthiness of swine, but he
"feeds" even those of other evil-doers, whose keeper, leader
and teacher he has become. This was commanded by the
wicked citizen to whom he adhered, who stands for pride, the

---

13. Luke 15:15.

principal and chief of all vices: "erring and leading into error."[14]

(7) *He perishes with hunger.* Now he reaches the worst stage of his sin, when his desire for sinning is so insatiable that it cannot be satisfied. "And he longs to fill himself with the pods that the swine were eating, but no one offers to give them to him."[15] Earthly goods are called pods, because they are empty on the inside, soft on the outside, and man is not invigorated by them, but only stuffed, so that they are a burden rather than a benefit. It might be objected that since he was a swineherd no one could stop him from taking the husks for which he hungered. The actual meaning is that oftentimes a sinner falls into such depths that he would rather sin in order to obtain an object than acquire it through honest labor. And while he sees others given to revelries and drunkenness and debaucheries, contrary to the dictates of divine law, and longs for forbidden pleasures, he languishes in his envy, is troubled in heart, and continually desires to satisfy his hunger with these empty husks. But often either ability or opportunity to indulge in such base delights is lacking. God in His mercy has so arranged circumstances that such occasions are removed from the sinner, preparing his return to the Master he has abandoned.

EFFECT OF THIS KNOWLEDGE. Knowing the condition of his own wretchedness, the sinner climbs out of the depths into which he has fallen and, following the example of the prodigal son, desires to repent. He says to himself: "How many hired men in my Father's house have bread in abundance, while I am perishing here with hunger?"[16]

We sinful creatures should look into our heart and consider the evils which we have committed; think of the count-

---

14. 2 Tim. 3:13.
15. Luke 15:16.
16. *Ibid.* 15:17.

less miseries that have befallen us because of these very evils. May at least the horror of these miseries be the occasion of our resolution to return to our Father's house, where not only sons but even servants have plentiful bread. For the Lord feeds and consoles the perfect and the imperfect. Let us take the right road and determine in our heart: I will say to my Father, "Father, I have sinned against heaven and before Thee."[17] I do not seek bread as one of Your children; I desire to be allowed to labor in Your house as a servant, and to earn my bread in the sweat of my brow.

§ III. The Nature and Necessity of Sorrow

38. (1) **The nature of sorrow.** The sorrow of the sinner must be an anguish of soul which resides in the will and not in the senses. Yet sensible sorrow is sometimes aroused by the soul's contrition. This is desirable but not necessary, since it is not within man's power to evoke this sensible sorrow at will. This sorrow should also contain the resolution to avoid sin in the future; otherwise the contrition is false and insincere. God, speaking through His prophet Jeremia on the merits of such contrition, says, "And . . . the traitor sister . . . did not return to Me wholeheartedly, but insincerely."[18] And for this reason Isaia exclaims, "Wash yourselves clean! Put away your misdeeds from before My eyes; cease doing evil. Learn to do good."[19] And St. Gregory the Great remarks, "Penance consists in bewailing the evil we have done, and in not repeating the deeds that cause us to weep."[20]

(2) **The necessity of sorrow.** This contrition, this sorrow, is definitely needed to convert the sinner from evil and to direct him toward good, as Sacred Scripture rightly teaches:

---

17. *Ibid.* 15:21.
18. Jer. 3:10.
19. Isa. 1:16-17.
20. *Homil. XXXIV in Evang.,* n. 15, in Migne, *P. L.,* t. LXXVI, col. 1256.

"Yet there too you shall seek the Lord your God; and you shall indeed find Him when you search after Him with your whole heart and your whole soul."[21] "Return to Me with your whole heart, with fasting and weeping and mourning, and rend your hearts, not your garments."[22] The Wisdom of God, our Lord and Master Jesus Christ, reminds us that "Unless you repent, you will all perish in the same manner."[23] And the Apostle taught the Jews this doctrine: "Repent therefore and be converted, that your sins may be blotted out."[24]

The Church Fathers are in agreement that nothing is more important for the sinner than contrition: "Nor can anyone," says St. Augustine, "proceed from error to truth, nor can he pass over to true amendment of sin, whether great or small sins, without penance."[25]

§ IV. The Necessary Qualities of Sorrow

39. For this sorrow or contrition, whether perfect or imperfect, to be sufficient for the valid reception of the Sacrament, the sorrow should be: (A) internal; (B) supernatural; (C) supreme; (D) universal.

A. **Internal sorrow.** Sorrow must be real, sincere, interior; not merely on the fringe of the mind or on the surface of the imagination, nor with bare sound of empty words or forced tears. It must arise from the innermost recesses of the will. Nothing demonstrates this sincerity more completely, more satisfactorily, and more certainly than the avoidance of sin and the performance of good works. "For man seeth those things that appear, but the Lord beholdeth the heart."[26]

---

21. Deut. 4:29.
22. Joel 2:12-13.
23. Luke 13:3.
24. Acts 3:19.
25. *Epist. 93,* n. 53, in Migne, *P. L.,* t. XXXIII, col. 347.
26. 1 Kings 16:7.

B. **Supernatural sorrow.** Sorrow must be supernatural both in respect to its principle, i. e., divine grace, and in regard to its motive.

(a) SORROW MUST BE SUPERNATURAL IN RESPECT TO ITS PRINCIPLE. For there can be no salutary cleansing of the soul without the aid of grace and the influx of the Holy Spirit. The reason for this is that the means must be proportioned to the end, and accordingly must be of the same order. Since contrition was given to us by God as the means of our justification and of our obtaining sanctifying grace, it must be in the supernatural order, as are sanctifying grace and justification themselves.

(1) **Necessity of this grace.** We are always in need of God's grace, not only while in the state of grace, but even more so while in the state of mortal sin, for grace is a necessary condition of our return to God. Jesus Christ said, "No one can come to Me unless the Father who sent Me draw him. . . . No one can come to Me unless he is enabled to do so by My Father."[27] The sinner left to his own resources can do nothing. He may be compared to a saw lying on the ground. It is unable to raise itself from the earth, nor can it do any kind of work, unless it is lifted and operated by the carpenter. Therefore, even though the sinner freely returns to God through contrition, he has no reason to glorify himself rather than God. He may not attribute his conversion to himself, but must acknowledge that it is due to God's mercy, since it would not have been effected unless God had first drawn and assisted him. Recognizing his poverty, his insufficiency, let him pray as a mendicant, let him ask God for what he needs, saying, "Draw me! Draw me out of the abyss of my sins." For the mercy of God inspires us to pray and to seek to do whatever pleases God, since according to St. Paul we are not sufficient of our-

---

27. John 6:44, 66.

selves, but our sufficiency is from God. And no one can cry out, "Lord Jesus," except by the Holy Spirit, who inspires and guides every man to invoke Him, to praise Him, or to ask something in His name.

(2) **Various ways in which God calls us to conversion.** God's grace arouses the sinner to conversion principally in three ways:

The first way occurs through a superabundant and extraordinary mental enlightenment and a strong impulse of the will which so transform the sinner's heart that, by a divine and heavenly strength, he repels every carnal and worldly desire of which his vices, his passions and his temporal possessions were the occasion. He then willingly begins to seek Christ by contrition and perfect conversion. In this extraordinary way, our Lord gained such eminent sinners as Mary Magdalene, Matthew, and Saul.

The second way whereby God attracts sinners with His grace occurs through the manifold benefits and gifts He bestows on them, such as He lavished on David after he committed adultery. For Nathan the Prophet addressed David in this manner: "Thus saith the Lord the God of Israel: I anointed thee King over Israel; and I delivered thee from the hand of Saul. . . . If these things be little, I shall add far greater things unto thee. Why therefore hast thou despised the word of the Lord to do evil in My sight?"[28] Nathan recalled to David such an abundance of divine benefits that David, moved by this display and interiorly drawn and compelled by God, cried out: "I have sinned against the Lord."[29] And so it came about that he soon broke the fetters of iniquity and was completely reconciled with God.

In this manner God converts certain sinners, attracting them with His benefits, drawing them with the chains of His

---

28. 2 Kings 12:7, 8-9.
29. *Ibid.* 12:13.

love, granting them innumerable favors in the natural order or in the order of grace.

The third and usually the ordinary way in which God converts sinners, is through consideration of the punishment deserved for sin. By this means God instills fear into the hearts of the sinners. Likewise the consideration of the possible loss of temporal goods induces some to repent; for, as St. Gregory remarks, some hear the voice of God much more readily when deprived of the things which delight them in this life. For this reason David prays for sinners: "Darken their faces with disgrace, that men may seek Your name, O Lord."[30]

(b) SORROW MUST BE SUPERNATURAL IN RESPECT TO ITS MOTIVE. Though the sinner may be reconciled to God outside the Sacrament, the call of grace is not sufficient in itself. The sinner must convert himself to God from a supernatural motive proportionate to justification and sanctifying grace, toward which contrition is ordained.

Contrition with a merely natural motive is insufficient for salvation. Such was the contrition of Antiochus who wept, not because his sin was an offense against God, but because of the very great disease that afflicted him. Such is the contrition of all those who abandon their sinful ways through fear, or through the hope of some temporal good.

The motive for even imperfect contrition must in some way spring from love, at least from initial, imperfect love, such as is contained in the hope of forgiveness, in the fear of eternal punishment and the loss of eternal bliss, in shame before the baseness of sin considered as an offense against God, and in other sentiments of a similar nature which pertain to the supernatural order. Yet we should not entirely spurn natural motives, for the soul is often deeply stirred by them, the flames of passion extinguished, and access provided for loftier ends.

---

30. Ps. 82:17.

C. Sorrow must be supreme *appreciatively,* not necessarily *intensively.* We elicit intensively supreme sorrow when we feel in our hearts a deeper sorrow for the sins committed than any sorrow we might experience for some temporal loss. Even though it is not indispensable, this sorrow should be earnestly desired. It is not indispensable, because arising usually in the sensible part of our soul, it is not always dependent upon our will, and therefore cannot be included among our obligations. David wept more passionately and for a greater length of time over the death of his son than for his sins. Nevertheless, his repentance was sincere and satisfactory, since he merited hearing these words from the mouth of the prophet: "The Lord . . . hath taken away thy sin."[31]

But it is absolutely essential that contrition be appreciatively supreme. We have appreciatively supreme sorrow when our mind considers sin the greatest evil, and our will turns from that greatest evil in such a way that we prefer to suffer the loss of all things rather than commit another sin.

Necessity of such contrition: The necessity of such contrition is evident from the nature of sin which, since it is offensive to God and deprives us of the greatest good, is the greatest evil and hence must be hated and avoided above every other evil. Christ said: "He who loves father or mother more than Me is not worthy of Me; and he who loves son or daughter more than Me is not worthy of Me."[32]

D. Universal sorrow. Finally, contrition must be universal, extending to every sin committed, or at least to all mortal sins. The Bible makes this eloquent plea: "But if the wicked man turns away from all the sins he committed, . . . he shall surely live."[33] St. Gregory the Great asks, "What benefit is there for one to lament his sins of impurity and yet burn with

31. 2 Kings 12:13.
32. Matt. 10:37.
33. Ezech. 18:21.

the passion of avarice? Of what avail is it to be sorry for faults
of anger and at the same time to waste away with the fires
of jealousy?"[34] The point to be learned is that contrition is
sorrow for sin inasmuch as sin offends God; therefore, if our
contrition is real and sincere, we must detest all our sins, for
every sin offends God. Anyone who retains an attachment to
even a single sin is not really sorry for transgressing God's law.

St. Bonaventure brilliantly explains why this condition is
necessary for true contrition: "Because all mortal sins turn
men away from the one God, and are opposed to the one grace,
and pervert the one principle of righteousness in man, in order
that the remedy of penance be sufficiently effective and integral
in every way, man must have repentance for all sins: for the
past, through remorse for the perpetrated acts; for the present,
by abstaining from sinful acts; and for the future, by the resolve never to fall again into the same or into any other sin."[35]

§ V. The Firm Purpose of Amendment

40. This firm purpose of amendment consists in the resolution, the determination of the will to sin no more. This is
essential for a sincere conversion. The sinner cannot really
detest a sin he has committed if at the same time he wishes
to commit it again. Both the actually committed sin and the
intended sin offend God, and are an obstacle to the attainment
of our final end.

I. **The requisites of a firm purpose of amendment.** A
good purpose of amendment, as far as mortal sin is concerned,
must be (A) firm; (B) universal; (C) efficacious.

A. FIRM. For the purpose of amendment to be firm, the
penitent must be so disposed that he really wills to fulfill his
resolutions, and prefers to endure any evil, and to be deprived

---

34. *Homil. XXXIV in Evang.*, n. 15, in Migne, *P. L.*, t. LXXVI, col. 1256.
35. *Brevil.*, Pars VI, cap. X.

of every good, rather than offend God seriously. This firmness is not destroyed by the thought or the fear that we actually might sin again. For such a thought is an act of the intellect which foresees a possible relapse on account of the frailty of human nature, and the thought can coexist with an act of the will sincerely resolving not to sin again.

B. UNIVERSAL. The purpose of amendment is universal when it extends to the avoidance of all mortal sins in the future. Here we must distinguish between universal contrition and universal purpose of amendment. Universal contrition extends to all sins that have been committed and not yet forgiven. But the purpose of amendment is not universal unless it includes the intention of avoiding absolutely all mortal sins in the future. Our purpose of amendment must always proceed from a universal motive. However, the purpose of avoiding all mortal sin may be general. We do not have to review each sin in particular.

C. EFFICACIOUS. A purpose of amendment is efficacious when the will is moved to use those means which are necessary for the avoidance of future sins — such as fleeing proximate occasions, making reparation for harm done, forgiving injuries, etc. For one who sincerely desires to attain the end, must be determined to use the necessary means to that end. As long as we have no desire to avoid the occasions of sin, to return stolen goods, or to pardon an offense, we remain attached to our sin.

II. **The necessity of persevering in the purpose of amendment.** A firm purpose of amendment includes the obligation of the penitent to persevere. Heed the words of Paul of St. Magdalen, a very holy man of our Seraphic Order, who received the martyr's crown in London in 1643: "It is not enough for you to reveal in confession the wounds of your conscience and to receive the grace of Christ through the compunction of your heart; mindful that you have returned to

Christ, as to your true Master, you must be aware of your obligation to be His faithful servant in the future, to give your whole life to Him with a complete devotion to His will. You should endeavor as far as possible to conform your conduct to His own.

"Therefore, for the future, plan to lead a life different from that of the past: a life characterized by the formation of new habits, by interest in other activities; even choose new companions, provided such friendships will please God in the end. Just as the basest condition of man consists in yearning to commit sin, so, on the other hand, receding from the corruption of a carnal life constitutes the greatest nobility of soul.

"It must be remembered that a small degree of sorrow or an ordinary devotion does not suffice for us if we are to destroy the old man and completely put on the new man. As a matter of fact, the more we have yielded to the old man in the past, the more deeply ingrained our bad habits have become, the longer and more fiercely we will have to struggle to gain the upper hand.

"Arise, then, with a good heart, act courageously, continue to proceed with simplicity. Consider what a long journey still stretches before you, what fierce battle you must wage before you can gain complete victory over self.

"Do not let discouragement, or profitless idleness, hinder your progress; by your reconciliation you have now proclaimed yourself an enemy of sin, a servant of Christ, a soldier of penance, an adversary of the devil, a pilgrim bent on heaven, a spouse of the Redeemer, a temple consecrated to the Holy Spirit. You have received grace, you have regained your liberty, you have confessed your iniquity — how then can you ever return to your vomit without bringing deep sorrow to your Eternal Father?

"Listen to the words of your Lord and Judge as He earnestly admonishes: 'Behold, thou art cured. Sin no more, lest something worse befall thee!' (John 5:14)."[36]

Article II — Confession

41. **Meaning of confession.** As we have seen, the sinner turns from evil by means of contrition. But the sinner's conversion is completed only through the confession of his sins. This manifestation of all his sins is preceded by a diligent examination of conscience in order to remove the veil of ignorance, by a heartfelt contrition in order to discard the cloak of malice, and lastly, by a manly fortitude in order to destroy the mantle of false shame. Therefore, we will treat of: (1) the examination of conscience; (2) the characteristics of a good confession; (3) the effects of a good confession; (4) the reasons why confession should not be delayed.

§ I. Examination of Conscience

42. **Examination of one's whole life.** We are considering here the case of novices converting to a life of perfection. According to the decree of Clement VIII entitled *De Reformatione Regularium:* "Immediately upon the reception of the habit novices shall cleanse their consciences by means of a general confession of all the sins of their past life."

Therefore we shall consider: (1) the advantages of a general confession; and (2) the manner of making it.

I. **Advantages of a general confession.** St. Ignatius enumerates the advantages of a general confession in his *Spiritual Exercises.*

---

36. Paul of St. Magdalen, *Soliloquia seu documenta Christianae perfectionis* (Quaracchi, 1892, 3rd edition), p. 128.

(1) We receive much profit and merit on account of the greater sorrow for sins.

(2) The nature and wickedness of sin is considered and seen in a much clearer light.

(3) We are better disposed to receive Holy Communion, we more joyfully flee from sin and are more eager to preserve and increase the graces received.

Another advantage of a general confession is that the penitent need never again, even at the hour of death, confess the sins committed while living in the world.

II. **Manner of making a general confession.** A good life is one in which man conforms himself to the will of God by observing His commandments. For these commandments proximately and directly determine the acts by which we must strive toward our ultimate end according to the will of God. There are three kinds of commandments: (A) the precepts of the theological virtues; (B) the commandments of God; (C) the commandments of the Church.

To make easier a general examination of conscience, the penitent should examine his life according to the commandments, and discover what sins he has committed. Let him recall the outstanding periods in his life — as, for instance, the period before and shortly after his first Holy Communion, the sins committed during that time, in thought, desire, word, deed, or omission. Let him remember how he acted at home, in church, in school, and toward his neighbor.

But before engaging in the general examination of his whole life, the penitent should consider whether or not a general confession is necessary on account of some mortal sins he deliberately failed to confess. If he voluntarily omitted mortal sins, then all the sins of his sacrilegious confessions must be repeated, and as far as he is able, the number of these sins, their nature and the circumstances which change their gravity.

Since the penitent is not required to confess venial sins, he may omit their number and circumstances. However, authorities on the spiritual life recommend the confessing of venial sins committed with malice, the mentioning of their number and their aggravating circumstances.

Examination of Conscience Preparatory to General Confession

43. I. *Have you made any sacrilegious confessions?* Did you ever fail to mention mortal sins because you were ashamed of them? How often? Did you receive Holy Communion in such a state? Did you receive your Easter Communion in that state? How often? Did you culpably omit to perform your penance?

II. *Theological virtues.* Have you sufficiently often made acts of faith, hope and charity? Have you the necessary knowledge of the principal mysteries of faith — namely, that there is a God and that He is the remunerator of good and evil; the mysteries of the Holy Trinity, the Incarnation, and the death of Jesus Christ? Or have you perhaps denied your faith? Have you doubted any religious truth or denied it? Have you spoken against religion? Have you read forbidden books? Sold them? Did you lend them to others?

Have you perhaps despaired of God's mercy? Why? Have you presumed upon God's goodness?

Or have you been negligent regarding the commandments of God and Church through human respect?

Have you given scandal to your neighbor? Or evil advice, or bad example? Have you lingered in, or sought out, occasions of sin?

III. *Commandments of God.* Did you violate any of God's commandments? 1st: Superstition? Divination? Vain worship? Idolatry? The habit of never or rarely praying?

2nd: Oaths? Vows? Or blasphemy?

3rd: Work on Sunday or feast days? Missing Mass or attending indevoutly?

4th: Disobedience to parents, employers or pastor? Murmurings? Insults? Blows? Wishing the death of another person?

In regard to children, servants or other subjects: Have you cared for their education, instruction, and health? Have you removed proximate occasions of sin? Have you been watchful in regard to their religious duties? Given bad example, or become angry?

5th: Have you injured your neighbor in body or soul? Hated anyone or desired revenge? Quarreled with others? Wished others evil, fought with them or struck them?

6th or 9th: Have you given in to any unchaste thoughts or desires? Morose delectations? Were you guilty of any indecent words, jokes, or songs? Or did you willingly listen to them? Have you read obscene books? Have you been guilty of any unchaste deeds? With yourself? By touch? Through pollution? By sight? With others? Was the other person single, married, related or bound by vow? Of the same sex? Are there any proximate occasions of sin at present?

7th and 10th: Have you been guilty of unjust damage, theft or fraud? Have you retained or defrauded the laborer of his just wages? Neglected to make restitution? Committed small thefts?

8th: Did you tell any pernicious lies? Are you guilty of rash judgments? Detraction? Calumny? (Remember the obligation of making reparation when another's name has been injured, or when other serious damage has been inflicted.)

IV. *Commandments of the Church.* Have you broken the laws of fast and abstinence? Omitted confession or neglected your Easter duty?

V. *Capital sins.* Did you commit any sins of drunkenness, pride, sloth, envy, anger, or avarice?

All these points should be diligently examined, so that nothing will remain lurking in the hidden recesses of our soul when the Judge comes and says: "I will explore Jerusalem with lamps"[37] — that is, we must thoroughly illuminate all the streets and byways of our soul in order that we may find whatever filth there is in them, for nothing may remain unpunished. "Like the mud in the streets I trampled them down."[38] Having completed the examination, we should consider whether there is anything else on our conscience: perhaps this will be our last confession.

We must beware lest the devil, the enemy of our salvation, should deceive us. Since he knows that a good confession is a fountain of God's grace out of which sinners draw salvation, he makes every effort to turn it into a fountain of death, often by inducing us to be silent about certain shameful and grievous sins because of a perverse fear. How many thousands may now suffer in the flames of hell for having fallen victim to such a pernicious temptation! When this battle has to be fought, we should hasten to the refuge of sinners, the Blessed Virgin Mary, and also ardently implore our patron saints.

What spiritual joy, what an abundance of grace, what happiness in the pursuit of virtue, if once and for all we have wiped out all our sins by a truly sincere confession! In all purity of heart we can truly begin a seraphic life! How easy and agreeable the monastic life will be if we begin it and follow it through with a pure and tranquil conscience! Listen to Jesus saying: "Come to Me confidently in the person of your confessor, to Me your Redeemer, the most loving and fond Father of your salvation. Behold My extended arms on the Cross by which I powerfully protect you, My penitent!

---

37. Soph. 1:12.
38. Ps. 17:43.

Or, if you will, enter confidently into My heart which is wholly prepared to receive you. Come, My son! Come quickly!"[39]

§ II. Characteristics of a Good Confession

44. The absolution of the priest, coming after the required self-accusation of the contrite penitent, acts like a sharp sword and separates the soul from all sin, even the most enormous, as soon as this sin has been made to appear in the rite of confession. There are, however, certain characteristics which must be found in every good confession. Our sins must be told with (1) humility; (2) simplicity; (3) completeness; (4) sorrow; (5) faithfulness; (6) truthfulness.

IN THE FIRST PLACE a confession must be *humble;* that is, we must truly recognize ourselves as sinners, and so confess. St. Gregory says: "These are the evidence of humility: that one both recognize his iniquity and voice this knowledge in his confession."[40]

The old and well-tried manner of confessing in our Order attended to this condition in a special way. It prescribed that the penitent, putting aside his mantle and sandals, with hands joined and eyes downcast, kneel at the side of the confessor, and bowing low, say: "Bless me, Father, for I have sinned," and kiss the floor.

THE SECOND CONDITION for a good confession is *simplicity.* St. Bernard says: "The confession must be simple. Then the penitent will not try to excuse his sin, if he is guilty, nor minimize the guilt when it is grievous, nor throw the blame on another, since no one can be forced to act against his will. Excusing one's sin is not a confession but a defense, which aggravates rather than lessens the guilt. Minimizing guilt is a

---

39. Cf. Gaudentius Guggenbichler, *Introductio ad vitam Seraphicam,* Pars I, Tract IV, pp. 338 et seq.

40. *Homil. XXXVI in Evang.,* Lib. II, n. 6, in Migne, *P. L.,* t. LXXVI, col. 1269.

subterfuge that is indicative of ingratitude; for the more the guilt is minimized, the less glory there is to the one who pardons. . . . Hence whoever believes that he is already forgiven depreciates the office of the forgiver . . . , and that is exactly what anyone does who tries to lessen his guilt. . . . Another ruse consists in the clever attempt to blame someone else for one's sins. Wishing to excuse oneself when one is rebuked is in no way beneficial; on the contrary, it is harmful. David in the psalms calls making excuses for sins 'evil words' [Ps. 140:4, Challoner-Douay version]. Therefore he prayed and begged the Lord not to let his heart revert to excuses."[41]

IN THE THIRD PLACE the confession must be complete. This means that each and every mortal sin must be *confessed*. If a wounded man refuses to reveal to the physician every mortal injury he has received, his body cannot be healed; so also the sinner cannot be cured who fails to show to the priest every deadly wound of his soul.

THE FOURTH CONDITION of a good confession is that it must be accompanied by grief and *contrition* of soul. St. Ambrose says: "Judas could not find a remedy when he said: 'I have sinned in betraying innocent blood' (Matt. 27:4), for he entertained an evil fire in his heart which inflamed him to go toward the noose. He was not worthy of a remedy, for his conversion did not cause him to mourn from the depths of his soul nor did he seriously do penance. And so he acted, even though the Lord Jesus in His goodness would have remitted even such a crime if Judas had desired His mercy."[42]

THE FIFTH CONDITION is *faithfulness*. To be faithful, the confession must in the first place be free from all misrepresentation; i. e., the penitent must tell what is certain as certain

---

41. *In Cant.*, Serm. 16, n. 11, in Migne, *P. L.*, t. CLXXXIII, col. 853.
42. *Ad simpliciam*, Epist. 67, no. 10, in Migne, *P. L.*, t. XVI, col. 1283.

and what is doubtful as doubtful. For, as Sirach says: "Never gainsay the truth."[43]

Secondly, the confession must be free from all deceit. The priest cannot remit this deceit nor the sin of him who presents himself in a fraudulent manner. And so the sinner is left in his sin.

Thirdly, the penitent must be confident of forgiveness. St. Bernard comments on this condition as follows: "Your confession will be faithful when you confess with hope, entirely confident of forgiveness; otherwise you will not justify, but condemn yourself by your words. Judas, the betrayer of our Lord, and Cain, the murderer of his brother, confessed and despaired; the one said: 'I have sinned in betraying innocent blood' (Matt. 27:4); the other: 'My punishment is too great to bear' (Gen. 4:13). And though they admitted the truth, such an unfaithful confession did not profit them."[44]

THE SIXTH CONDITION is *modesty*. Wisdom testifies to the fact that modesty is twofold: For "there is a sense of shame laden with guilt, and a shame that merits honor and respect."[45] St. Ambrose speaks of the latter, saying: "We must blush and condemn sin, not defend it; for a fault is minimized by shame, but increased by defense. For the Lord Himself says: 'Tell your iniquities and you will be justified' (cf. Isa. 43:25-26). The grace of feeling salutary shame is so great that it obtains justification and takes away the guilt of sin."[46]

We shall treat of reprehensible shame when discussing belated confession.

§ III. The Effects of a Good Confession

45. FIRST EFFECT: **The remission of sin.** After the penitent has correctly confessed his sins, the priest grants absolu-

---

43. Sirach 4:25.
44. *In Cant.*, Serm. 16, n. 12, in Migne, *P. L.*, t. CLXXXIII, col. 854.
45. Sirach 4:21.
46. *Loc. cit.*, n. 5, col. 1282.

tion; that is, he grants the remission of all sins. How boundless is the mercy of God!

SECOND EFFECT: **Sweetness or consolation.** What is sweeter and more consoling than that phrase, "Ego te absolvo a peccatis tuis — I absolve thee of thy sins"?

(a) *For God.* These words are sweet to the ears of God; for nothing is sweeter to Him than hearing the sighs and laments of the penitents, so that He may forgive them: "Because this my son was dead and has come to life again; he was lost, and is found."[47]

(b) *For the priest.* These words are sweet to the ears of the priest; for after the example of Christ, the true Father and Shepherd, he receives the penitent in the same manner in which the kind father received his prodigal son; and like Christ, he joyfully carries the sheep back to the evangelical fold.

(c) *For the penitent.* But these words are sweetest to the ears of the penitent, for they fill him with joy and gladness and lift up his humiliated heart. His soul revives at the words of absolution.

THIRD EFFECT: **Bestowal of gifts from God.** (a) *Union with God.* Although God uses the ministry of the priest to justify the sinner through the Sacrament of Penance, He Himself hastens to him through grace, and is intimately united with him; while He as it were embraces him through the absolution, and at the same time confers on him the finest garment — sanctifying grace — and clothes him with the wedding garment of charity, which covers a multitude of sins. And this robe does not merely cover the sins as a precious garment draped over a leprous body; it entirely washes away the leprosy of sin and adorns the soul with an unspeakable internal beauty.

---

47. Luke 15:24.

(b) *Infusion of the virtues and gifts.* God Himself places the ring of a living faith on the hand of the penitent, for He takes his soul to Himself as a bride, and desires that it be faithful to Him. And since He gives strength to the penitent to fulfill those things which are proper to a child and friend of God, He also furnishes the sandals of the infused virtues whereby the steps of affection are directed toward God so that he may advance without harm in the way of the Commandments.

(c) *Application of the merits of Christ.* God Himself brings forth and kills the fattened calf, since He applies to the penitent the fruits of the Passion of Christ, who was slain for sinners on the altar of the Cross. From the purest flesh and the most precious blood of this divine Victim, God prepares a banquet for the penitent and manifests His great joy to the soul.

§ IV. Reasons for Not Delaying Confession

46. Why is confession delayed? A sinner whose conscience is burdened with the most grievous sins often puts off confession from day to day. A great number of people delay their conversion so as to enjoy at more length the pleasures of this world, and thereby fully satisfy their appetites. Another cause is shame, concerning which St. Bernard writes: "The soul afflicted with shame might be asked: Why are you ashamed to confess the sin you were not ashamed to commit? Or why are you ashamed to confess sins to God, from whose eyes you cannot hide anything? If you fear exposing your sins to one man, who is also a sinner, what will you do on the day of judgment, when your conscience will be exposed, entirely laid bare to all? To overcome this shame, have recourse to these three means: namely, use of reasonable judgment, respect for the knowledge of God, and comparison with a greater disorder."[48]

---

48. *Serm. 104, De diversis* n. 2, in Migne, *P. L.,* t. CLXXXIII, col. 731.

The danger in deferring confession. Why does the sinner put off his confession from day to day? God surely is ready to hear his confession and grant him pardon. He should beware lest God close His ears and become inattentive: for He has promised pardon to those who confess their sins, not to those who procrastinate. Although the procrastinator may sometimes obtain pardon, yet he may just as easily perish in his dawdling, as Sirach warns: "Delay not your conversion to the Lord, put it not off from day to day; for suddenly His wrath flames forth; at the time of vengeance, you will be destroyed."[49] The Holy Spirit, who directed the pen of Sirach, inspired this saying on the importance of not deferring repentance.

Today the voice of the penitent will be sweet to God, because now He desires to hear it; perhaps tomorrow He will answer as He did to the foolish virgins: "I do not know you."[50] "Confess, my brothers," says St. Augustine, "and do not put it off; hasten to reap the sacred fruits of confession. For it is the salvation of souls, the disperser of crimes, the restorer of virtues, the assailant of demons, the terror of hell, an obstacle to the devil, the garment of angels, the confidence of the churches, the leader, the staff, the light, and the hope of all the faithful. O holy and admirable confession, you obstruct the mouth of hell, and you open the gate of paradise. Without you the sinner is reckoned as dead," but through you he rises to glory.

Article III — Satisfaction

47. The necessity of satisfaction. By means of contrition, confession, and absolution, God, like the father of the prodigal son, forgives the offense of which the penitent accuses himself. Yet, as a wise legislator, He imposes a temporal punish-

---

49. Sirach 5:8-9.
50. Matt. 25:12.

ment to ensure future observance of His laws, to deter us from evil, and to preserve the balance between mercy and justice.

Triple satisfaction. There are three kinds of satisfaction for sins committed. First, there is sacramental satisfaction, which is imposed upon the penitent in the tribunal of confession. Then there is the satisfaction of supererogation. Man, knowing that he cannot be saved unless he carries the cross and suffers with Christ and completes in his flesh that which in a certain sense is lacking in the Passion of Christ, mortifies himself in different ways, such as fasting and the like. Finally, there is a satisfaction communicated to us by the Church from the treasury of the saints. Christ gave the Church the power to impose satisfactions on penitents for sins committed. He also bestowed upon it the faculty of granting indulgences from the infinite treasury of His merits. By means of these indulgences the remaining temporal punishment can be remitted after the valid reception of the Sacrament of Penance.

The three kinds of satisfaction are, therefore: (1) sacramental satisfaction; (2) satisfaction of supererogation; (3) satisfaction through indulgences.

§ I. Sacramental Satisfaction

48. **(1) Definition.** Sacramental satisfaction is the voluntary performance of the penance imposed by the confessor to compensate for the injury done to God and to obtain remittance of the temporal punishment which is ordinarily due, even after sin and the eternal punishment have been remitted.

The punishment due to sin is not always entirely remitted by God; the temporal punishment remains to be expiated after sin has been forgiven, though the eternal punishment is remitted through absolution.

(2) Office of the priest. (a) *The priest offers God a sacrifice of justice through the penitent.* The priest offers God both the Eucharistic sacrifice and the sacrifice of justice. The penitent also offers the sacrifice of justice. Through the priest, salvation comes to us from God. The priest certainly does not perform his office with a vindictive spirit, but with compassion, and like a kindhearted physician comforts the heart and heals the wounds. The penalties of satisfaction recall us from sin, check our evil tendencies, and make us more careful, more watchful in the future.

(b) *The priest acts with mercy.* Speaking in the Rule in the section concerning Ministers Provincial and priests, our holy Father St. Francis says: "They shall with mercy impose upon them a penance. . . . And they shall take care not to get angry or disturbed by the sins of another, for anger and vexation are hindrances to charity both to themselves (the confessors) and to others" (the penitents).[51] Therefore according to the Rule, the Ministers and priests shall mercifully impose the penance upon the penitent, and in imposing it they shall remember that if God would judge us with strict justice, few or none would be saved; therefore they shall attend to the salvation and not to the loss of the souls of the afflicted brethren.

(3) **Obligation of the penitent.** Let the penitents take care to fulfill the obligation of satisfaction with diligence and devotion, not only as regards the strictly sacramental satisfaction, but also any other works imposed upon them as preventive means by their confessor or director; for the works selected by the confessor are better suited to heal our sickness and our wounds, and are also more conducive to salvation. They should be appreciated not so much because of the greatness of their function but because of their being chosen by God. Nor should they be despised if they are slight, for their healing power proceeds more from obedience to God than from their magni-

---

51. Chap. VII.

tude. Thus Naaman was cleansed from leprosy, not because he washed in the Jordan; for many lepers washed there and were not cleansed; but because he washed there out of obedience to Eliseus.

§ II Supererogatory Satisfaction

49. (1) **Suitableness.** The true penitent desires to satisfy divine justice and holiness not only through the works imposed upon him by the confessor, but also through other works of supererogation, as St. Gregory teaches: "Whoever has done nothing unlawful may by right use the things which are lawful. If, however, one has fallen into a grave fault, inasmuch as he remembers that he has perpetrated something illicit, by so much should he also abstain from what is licit. Therefore it is just that he occasionally give up many desirable things which are allowed, such as food, drink, sleep, riches and other goods of this kind, in order to satisfy God more fully."[52]

(2) **Examples of the saints.** Mary Magdalene is a wonderful model for the converted sinner in that she loved much and washed the feet of our Lord with her tears, in order to obtain forgiveness of her many sins. St. Peter wept bitterly because of his triple denial. And because he greatly loved the Master, even though he had denied Him, he was moved to labor and suffer for Christ by a real sentiment of compunction, which proceeded from the fire of love and produced such copious tears that it washed away the stains of his sins.

(3) **Three works of penance.** The three foremost works of penance are fasting, prayer, and almsgiving. All others can be reduced to these three. They remove the sources of sin, which sources St. John calls the concupiscence of the flesh, the concupiscence of the eyes and the pride of life.[53]

---

52. *Homil. XXXIV, in Evang.*, n. 16, in Migne, *P. L.*, t. LXXVI, col. 1256 et seq.
53. 1 John 2:16.

(a) *Fasting.* The concupiscence of the flesh is diminished by fasting and mortification of the flesh; concupiscence of the eyes by almsgiving, for it indicates a disregard for worldly possessions; and the pride of life through prayer. When speaking to Tobias, the Angel united all three: "Prayer is good with fasting and alms: more than to lay up treasures of gold."[54] The term "fasting" includes every act by which the flesh is weakened and emaciated.

(b) *Prayer.* By prayer we not only mean prayers of petition but also strong affections of the heart directed to God by means of which the sinner offers to God the merits, sufferings, works and wounds of Christ in satisfaction for his own sins. These offerings are undoubtedly sufficient to fully satisfy God's justice in regard to all sins.

(c) *Almsgiving.* By the term "almsgiving" we mean works of mercy and of virtue which tend to the reformation of life. These are always accompanied by mortification and prayer; for whoever prays worthily and denies himself soon abounds in all good works.

(4) **Other works of satisfaction.** To these penances, undertaken of our own accord, we must add those inflicted by God and patiently endured. For God often permits us to be tried by various adversities, by sufferings of body and soul. When these are patiently endured, particularly when they are united to the sufferings and death of Christ, they offer ample opportunities for satisfaction. The greater the joy and love with which it is embraced, the more efficacious is this kind of patience.

§ III. Satisfaction through Indulgences

50. Indulgences form another very effective means of satisfying for sin.

---

54. Tob. 12:8.

(1) **Concept.** An indulgence is a remission before God of the temporal punishment due to sin, granted outside the Sacrament of Penance by a legitimate superior from the treasury of the Church.

(2) **The spiritual treasury of the Church and its dispenser.** The spiritual treasury of the Church is composed of the superabundant satisfaction of Christ, the Blessed Virgin Mary, and the saints. The supreme dispenser of this treasury is the Holy Father, who for a just reason can use it to remit the debts of the faithful. By granting an indulgence, he does not simply remit the temporal punishment, but offers the penitent something with which to pay: the superabundant satisfactions of Christ, His Mother and the saints.

(3) **The various kinds of indulgences.** By reason of their effect, indulgences are divided into plenary and partial. A plenary indulgence remits all the unrequited punishment; a partial indulgence remits only a part of the punishment, in the sense that as much of the indebtedness is forgiven as might have been remitted, for example, through forty or one hundred days of canonical penance in the early days of the Church.

*(4) **The treasury of indulgences of the Seraphic Order.**[55] Since this united treasury of the merits of Christ and the saints is opened to us by the Church, let us hasten with trust and love to make the best use of it. We will be eager to use especially the benefits which have so abundantly been granted to the Seraphic Order by the Roman Pontiffs as to be compared to a great sea. We will gladly acquit ourselves of the debt of punishment which might impede and retard our entrance into heaven. Moreover, by gaining indulgences we will not be compelled to suffer a long time in Purgatory after death. After the Holy Sacrifice of the Mass, indulgences are

---

55. Passages such as this, preceded by an asterisk, are specifically intended for the use of Franciscans.

also our best means of helping other souls detained in Purgatory.

§ IV. The Necessity and Utility of Satisfaction

51. (1) **Necessity.** We were set free from sin and the servitude of the devil by baptism and have received the gift of the Holy Spirit; yet we have again willfully profaned the temple of God. It becomes Divine Justice not to remit our sins without some satisfaction.

(2) **Practice in the early Church.** Early Christians had a much better understanding of the necessity of penance. They considered how much easier the satisfaction for sins was on this earth than in Purgatory, and gladly undertook and completed long and difficult penances lasting as long as seven years, twenty years, or even a whole lifetime. During the entire time of their penance they fasted frequently, prayed frequently, and stayed away from occasions of enjoyment; their entire life was nothing but contrition, humility, and atonement.

(3) **Practice today.** But today nothing is more common than sin and nothing more rare than true and perfect repentance. With Jeremia we can say: "I listen closely: they speak what is not true; no one repents of his wickedness, saying 'What have I done!' "[56]

(4) **Glory of repentance.** How glorious to weep over our sins. The penitence and the confession of Job were so wonderful that St. Gregory was carried away in admiration and said: "That man might seem great in his virtues to anyone, but to me he appears truly exalted, even in the admission of his sins. Others admire his continence, integrity of justice, and interior piety; I admire no less his humble confession of sins, which is so high a sign of virtue."[57]

---

56. Jer. 8:6.
57. *Moralia,* Lib. XX, cap. XV, in Migne, *P. L.,* t. LXXVI, col. 273.

CONCLUSION. Behold, O religious soul, the penance by which a sinner is turned from evil and converted to good. Behold the law which man must follow to reform his disfigured soul and to arrive at his last end. The Lord said: "Bring forth therefore fruits befitting repentance"; and "Return to Me with your whole heart." [58]

---

58. Luke 3:8; Joel 2:12.

CHAPTER III

THE REFORMATION OF THE SOUL WEAKENED BY VENIAL SIN

52. (1) *The just more easily perceive how much the soul is deformed by venial sin.* At the approach of daylight, says St. Francis de Sales, we perceive more clearly in a mirror the spots and stains that disfigure our faces; so, as the inward light of the Holy Spirit more and more enlightens our consciences, we see in a more distinct and clear manner the sins, inclinations, and imperfections which prevent us from attaining to our perfection. The same light which enables us to perceive these spots and blemishes inflames us with a desire to cleanse and purify ourselves of them.

(2) *The requirements for reforming a soul weakened by venial sin.* We should first know: (1) the nature and kinds of venial sin; (2) its effects; (3) the importance of avoiding venial sin; (4) the nature of imperfections.

Article I — Nature and Kinds of Venial Sin

53. Concept. Venial sin, as we have already seen, is an act in which the moral order and the divine law are not entirely rejected but only slightly violated. It does not interrupt our habitual abiding in God. But since it does violate His law, it is and must be considered a real offense against God. It displeases Him and is a just cause for His indignation.

Various kinds. Some venial sins are slight by reason of their object, because the law transgressed imposes only a slight obligation, or the slightness of the transgression results in no serious disturbance of the moral order. Others are slight for a subjective reason: they arise suddenly and do not proceed from a fully deliberate will; however, if they become habitual, they will lead to mortal sins and cause the death of the soul.

Various ways of committing venial sin. Men commit venial sins in various ways, but we shall give special attention to those committed: (1) deliberately; (2) through habit; (3) through the impulse of concupiscence.

§ I. Deliberate Venial Sins

A soul sins deliberately when it knowingly and willfully despises some command of God.

54. Formal contempt. Man can sin even mortally when he belittles the will of God in small matters; that is, when he violates a law through formal contempt. This contempt is the transgression of a law from the motive of revolting against an ordinance of God. Actions of this type seriously oppose the reverence due to the commands of the Divine Majesty. "Venial offenses," says St. Bernard, "should not be considered criminal except when they are altered through contempt, and then it is not the objective nature of the sin that is considered but the intention of the sinner."[1] St. Bernard is speaking here of religious; for, in the case of religious, contempt of little things contradicts their very profession. Religious are bound to tend toward perfection by following the Rule, which under penalty of grave sin they are not allowed to condemn.

Anxiety. Although a soul does not ordinarily transgress the divine law out of formal contempt, yet if it knowingly and willingly resists a command of God, it will often be in doubt as to whether the transgressions are grievous or light; e. g., when there is doubt as to the gravity of the matter. It is easy to define mortal and venial sins but often very difficult to distinguish them in practice.

Disposition leading to mortal sin. Any sin, as soon as it is minimized, has power to ruin the soul. It disposes the

---

1. *Lib. de Praecep.*, cap. XI, in Migne, *P. L.*, t. CLXXXII, col. 876.

heart for an easy fall into mortal sin. As bodily infirmity prepares for the death of the body, so venial sin inclines the soul to mortal sin. As the disposition to adhere to created things grows, so the desire to sin increases in proportion, so much so that even in matters of greater moment the human will may incline toward a creature contrary to the will of God. Anyone who at first yields only slightly to resentment may easily consent to temptations of fierce anger. Therefore, even a little excessive affection for creatures should not be considered trivial; for the devil, clever as he is, makes of such little things the handles by which he seizes and destroys the soul. St. Dorotheus says that an eagle, free to use its head, its wings, and its body, can easily be killed if it is caught by a single claw.

"No matter how much a city may be fortified with high walls and firmly locked gates," says Cassian, "it may be laid waste by the discovery of one unguarded rear gate, no matter how small. What difference does it make whether the pernicious enemy enters the city over high walls, through the wide-open gates, or through a small, concealed hole?"[2]

Since the devil is more insidious with the more advanced, one who is of greater holiness must set up a better guard lest he knowingly and willingly consent to venial sin.

§ II. Venial Sins of Habit

55. Concept. By venial sins of habit we mean those committed through carelessness and levity.

Danger of falling into mortal sin. (a) *The enemies of the soul become stronger.* The soul remains exposed to many enemies who try to rob it of sanctifying grace. Such enemies are, for instance, evil inclinations of the soul and vices which

---

2. Lib. V, cap. XI, in Migne, *P. L.,* t. XLIX, col. 226.

simulate virtue. The apostate angels are also our enemies, for they use venial sins to incite us to evil thoughts, which gradually undermine the soul and lead to its destruction.

(b) *Horror of mortal sin diminishes.* The man accustomed to overlook little sins soon reaches a state where serious sins are no longer abhorrent to him. And the less he fears sin in little things, the more disdainful, the more fearless he becomes in graver matters.

Hence Sirach warns: "He that contemneth small things shall fall by little and little."[3] Scripture does not say "he who commits little sins," for even the perfect fall through surprise — "for in many things we all offend."[4] But if we repeatedly commit small sins, without being concerned about them, we shall gradually fall into more serious offenses. The Fathers of the Church explain this danger through various comparisons: for example, in time, dripping water will carve out a rock as deeply as a chisel can.

(c) *The soul is weakened.* By frequently and willingly committing venial sins, we abuse grace, resist the inspirations of the Holy Ghost and thus deprive ourselves of more abundant help; finally, we find ourselves too weak to overcome serious temptation.

§ III. Venial Sins Committed through the Impulses of Concupiscence

56. Concept. By sins committed through impulse we mean those proceeding from passion which have surreptitiously gained our consent. We can quickly cleanse ourselves from these sins of impulse, as Solomon testifies: "The just man falls seven times [a day] and rises again."[5]

---

3. Ecclus. 19:1, Challoner-Douay version.
4. James 3:2.
5. Prov. 24:16.

It is impossible to avoid all these over an entire lifetime. Without a singular privilege of grace, no one can avoid every venial sin; for this implies victory over every temptation, the repression of every unexpected impulse of concupiscence, continual diligence in prayer and other duties. But no man, however holy, can accomplish this unless his faculties are particularly aided by a very special grace; in the present state our will is incapable of such fortitude and constancy.

Faintheartedness must be avoided in regard to venial sins. The just man does not lose heart because of these almost indeliberate defects, but consigning them to the divine clemency and resigning himself to God, he remains humble, tranquil and peaceful; even if out of human frailty he falls a hundred or a thousand times a day, each time he rises with a holy hope of forgiveness; for where the love of Christ burns fervently, such venial sins are consumed like straw.

Distrust of self and confidence in God. We must always propose to ourselves an ideal of greater purity and tend to it with greater caution. We should not be too self-confident but should commit ourselves entirely to the goodness of God and to the help of His grace, which will never be wanting to those who humbly ask for it. We know that the passions and certain smaller vices will, by the permission of God, remain unconquered so that our soul will always struggle with a certain anxiety. One of the reasons why God allows these faults is that as long as we perceive the enemies within us, we shall be afraid of them and shall not unduly rejoice over past victories.

These venial sins can be turned to personal advantage. A vice as yet unconquered may humbly be turned to our advantage; a very strong and disturbing passion tamed by virtue may become a powerful help, and very often assist reason in its arduous work.

Let us humbly pray to our Lord: Behold, him whom Thou lovest is sick; I have sinned, O Lord, not indeed out of malice, but through the stress of concupiscence, which I try to resist; alas, what I desire I am not able to accomplish; but as often as I sin, I am anxious to rise again promptly, admitting my injustice, and Thou, O Lord, immediately forgivest my iniquity, because "for this shall every faithful man pray to You."[6] The time to pray in such instances is when we first realize the fall, lest the enemy of our soul more seriously undermine our holiness and beauty of soul by making us rejoice in our venial sin.

Difference between venial sin and an affection for it. There is a great difference, says St. Francis de Sales, between venial sins and an affection for venial sins; for although we can never be entirely free from such sins, so as to live without them for a long time, we should live at least without affection for them. For it is one thing to lie once or twice in a spirit of hilarity and lightheartedness in things of small moment; but it is quite another to be satisfied in one's lie and to have an affection for this kind of sin.

Beginners should be aware of this difference. We must call attention to this difference; otherwise beginners, and those who are hidden in the cloister and occupied with the contemplation of God alone, will be scandalized by the minor defects which they observe in prelates and others who are charged with the salvation of their neighbor.

We do not mean that those who are engaged in directing others will be confronted with more dust of venial sins than those who live in solitude, but that, as St. Gregory maintains, whatever their faults they will be consumed by the fire of love which burns in the heart of those who seek the salvation of others. These faults and venial sins are compensated for by the greatness of the work performed.

---

6. Ps. 31:6.

Article II — The Effects of Venial Sin

57. Concept. Venial sin does not extinguish or decrease sanctifying grace, nor does it affect the soul with the fullness of the stain of sin. Yet such sins produce pernicious effects, especially when frequently and deliberately committed, and committed with pleasure.

They diminish the fervor of charity. Besides the danger of leading to mortal sin, venial sins diminish the fervor of charity. For if we commit venial sins deliberately and with pleasure, we shall lose our inclination to do everything for love of God, and in many instances we shall deliberately choose to please ourselves instead of God. Venial sins destroy devotion and entangle the powers of the soul with bad habits so that active charity, which is true perfection, can no longer be exercised.

Guilt of venial sin. Venial sin brings on what theologians call: (a) the guilt of fault; (b) the guilt of punishment.

(a) *The guilt of fault.* Venial sin makes us guilty of displeasing God, and although we do not lose the divine friendship, our love for God grows cold.

A certain devout virgin once desired to know the state of her soul in order to perfect it. In a vision she beheld her soul in the image of an emaciated infant, whose face was covered with flies. The flies signified small defects and unsuitable thoughts. Such faults must zealously be driven away and exterminated before the soul can become beautiful and pleasing to God.

(b) *The guilt of punishment.* Every venial sin must be punished either in this life or in Purgatory, with a temporal punishment proportionate to the crime, as our Lord teaches: "But I tell you, that of every idle word men speak, they shall give account on the day of judgment."[7] And St. Bernard gives

7. Matt. 12:36.

an interpretation of Christ's words to St. Peter: "If I do not wash thee, thou shalt have no part with Me."[8] That is: "Peter, do not resist My washing your feet, for every sin, even the smallest, must be purged by My blood, and unless it is first dispelled in this life or in Purgatory, you cannot be admitted to the kingdom of heaven, for nothing defiled can enter there."

Article III — The Importance of Avoiding Venial Sin

58. No precept should be considered slight. The aim of all religious is the most perfect union with God through the observance of the Rule, the Constitutions and the counsels of superiors. Religious must very carefully avoid even small sins and take adequate precautions not to destroy the splendor of virtue in their soul. The *Mirror of Discipline* says: "To disregard small sins is by no means a small offense, for their moral stain is all the greater — these small sins were committed through neglect, while they could so easily have been noted and avoided."[9] If we wish to be great before God we should not look down upon any precept; for he who breaks one of the least commandments shall be called the least in the kingdom of heaven.

Avoidance of venial sin is the best protection against mortal sin. By means of mortal sin the devil inflicts two evils upon man: he destroys sanctifying grace and some of the virtues and gifts of the Holy Spirit; he subjects our powers and appetites to his will. We who are regenerated must make every effort to overcome this formidable enemy by suppressing vice, by recovering virtue and by restoring our powers to their original freedom under the light of reason.

---

8. John 13:8.
9. Prologue to the *Mirror of Discipline*, ii.

Principles. The best rule is to break up small inordinate inclinations, immediately capturing and exterminating them as we would a little fox the first time it comes out of its den. If we see a slight fire in a house, we are immediately disturbed, for if we do not attend to the initial blaze, we may later be forced to run and fight a total conflagration. Any vice in the soul is worse than a burning flame, and therefore must be extinguished at once.

We must continually be on guard against improper thoughts and affections which proceed from the higher cognitive and affective faculties of the soul. But if we do not quickly resist a temptation which springs from the heart, it will become stronger by reason of the delay which allowed it to grow. Once it exists in the mind it easily triumphs in external deeds.

Let us also cleanse our soul of the guilt of punishment. For venial faults are dispelled in many ways, e. g., by contrition, by saying the Lord's Prayer, by enduring physical inconvenience for the love of God, by using holy water, by genuflections, and by other acts of humility piously and religiously performed. The confession of even the smaller offenses is advantageous to man and pleasing to God.

The soul must guard against venial sin. We ourselves are placed as guards around the vineyard of our soul so that at the hour of death we will not be forced to cry out like the spouse of old: "My own vineyard I have not cared for."[10] Let us therefore continually watch, for sins must be avoided as offenses against God. He Himself will help us conquer; and to those who conquer He will give a crown of glory.

CONCLUSION. Since a pure conscience is the sign of man's salvation, we should, laying everything else aside, strive with every effort to obtain it. We should dedicate all our powers to the purpose of keeping our conscience pure and clean. "For

---

10. Cant. 1:6.

what does it profit a man, if he gain the whole world but ruin or lose himself?"[11]

Article IV — Imperfections

59. We must carefully distinguish venial sins from imperfections. Venial sin is always a transgression of a law and therefore a moral evil in itself. An imperfection is a lack of some suitable good, which is, however, not prescribed by a divine law.

This lack occurs: (1) in actions; (2) through omissions; (3) through inclination.

§ I. A Less Perfect Action

60. **All actions performed according to the dictates of reason are good.** All actions regulated by right reason, recognized as such and actually performed, are morally good. No one can judge himself guilty of sin when he uses the pleasant and delectable things of nature moderately and according to the dictates of reason. When we converse, eat, drink, play and recreate we should not believe that, because these things are pleasant, we are doing something wrong; on the contrary, we are doing something positively good, for if the Author of nature made so agreeable and delightful these actions which contribute to the conservation and perfection of nature, it is precisely for the sake of inducing us to perform them.

These actions, however, are on the lowest scale of perfection. The value of such actions, in terms of merit, is very slight; and, in relation to other actions explicitly ordered to our final end, they can even be considered as imperfections. For the value of an action increases in proportion to the higher and nobler intention of the agent, and also in proportion to the clarity and the effectiveness of the intention.

---

11. Luke 9:25.

They are dangerous for religious. Pleasurable actions, although not evil in themselves, are always dangerous, and much more so for religious. Games, recreation, and eating are certainly licit and permitted by the Rule and Constitutions. Yet it is true that too great an inclination and disposition toward them is contrary to the spirit of devotion.

They are to be enjoyed in the right manner. These actions are well regulated by our superiors. It is harmful to a religious, however perfect, to put his heart in the things of earth, for these then supplant spiritual inspirations, sap the strength of the soul, and obstruct worthy inclinations. We do not mean to say that we should abstain entirely from these dangerous things, but that we must use them correctly. Nor can we ever become attached to them without great loss of grace.

They are an obstacle to prayer and meditation. The human heart which burdens itself with useless, superfluous and dangerous affections while striving for religious perfection, cannot promptly, easily and painlessly turn to God in prayer and meditation, which are the goals of a true religious. Those advanced in years and experienced in the religious life, who are vehemently and excessively drawn to these superfluous and dangerous things, who desire them even beyond the prescribed limits, appear ridiculous to seculars as well as to their fellow religious.

§ II. The Omission of Good Works

61. **In themselves these omissions are not sinful.** The doctrine concerning less perfect actions also holds for the omission of counseled or unprescribed good works. If good works are omitted for a reasonable motive, such omissions are good. But when considered as unaccomplished good works, the omissions may be called imperfections — especially since the omission of good works ordinarily proceeds from sensuality or sloth or some other vice.

§ III. Evil Inclinations

62. Evil inclinations in themselves are not sinful. Other unintended actions or omissions arise which are certainly not sinful, such as involuntary distractions at prayer. Yet in relation to the laws of morality, they are considered imperfections.

These inclinations must be corrected. Some people are light-minded by nature, others harsh or unyielding, still others impatient, so that very few are entirely without defect. Even if these imperfections are personal and natural in each individual, they must be corrected and moderated with care.

Manner of correcting evil inclinations. (a) *Discover them.* First of all we should be aware of these evil inclinations, for they are camouflaged enemies. Pusillanimity is often mistaken for humility, anger for zeal, indolence for mildness, haste for fervor; some men even expect a reward for things of which they should be ashamed. Hence these imperfections are hard to correct. This is especially true when vice is mistaken for virtue, for as long as we are not ashamed of what we do, it will be hard to get rid of the evil inclinations from which such deeds arise.

Since we are not ashamed of evil nor in fear of punishment, we more easily do what we consider justifiable, without thinking about correcting what we mistakenly approve.

(b) *Seek light from God and from superiors.* How shall we capture these hidden enemies? By seeking enlightenment from those who know how to capture them. For He who commands us to overcome them will not fail to give us the power to do so. Holy Mother Church provides masters and teachers who know where the enemy lurks. Evil inclinations, posing as virtues, can be detected by them for they have the spirit of God.

(c) *Examine your conscience.* The examination of conscience is another means of discovering evil inclinations. These internal affections are always accompanied by disorders and restlessness. Although those who suffer from them seem to prefer what is good, yet when their intentions are placed under close surveillance, a hidden tendency toward what is irreligious and worldly can be discovered. Thus these inclinations may be distinguished from real, pious affections which are from God, and which are sweet, tranquil, disdainful of earth and of whatever is mundane and carnal, and intent only on what is spiritual and heavenly.

(d) *Change the apparently good inclinations into true virtues.* Once these enemies are detected, they must be captured immediately. In other words, the propensities which have only the appearance of virtue must be apprehended and changed into such true and solid virtue as will please God and edify the Church and the Order. For whatever is of value in a natural inclination should be preserved and converted into virtue. For example, pusillanimity should be transformed into true humility, anger into true zeal, carnal love into that which is spiritual. St. Gregory says: "In our striving to overcome inclinations to vice, we may put the vice itself at the service of virtue. One who is troubled with anger can subjugate his irascibility and place it at the service of holy zeal. Another is easily inflated with pride; training his soul to the fear of God, he may change this pride into a defense of justice."[12]

(e) *Practice the virtue opposed to the particular vice.* Just as good qualities and natural inclinations can be turned to evil by bad habits, so also by the grace of God, with the assistance of a spiritual director and of personal diligence, bad qualities and inclinations can be transformed into good ones.

---

12. *Moralia,* Lib. III, cap. XXXVII, in Migne, *P. L.,* t. LXXV, col. 632.

CONCLUSION. We must, therefore, attentively consider and energetically apply the admonitions and exercises provided in the Seraphic Order for putting off "the old man." For, by the aid and application of these expedients we can purify our souls not only of mortal sin but also of dangerous affections and imperfections, and fortify our conscience more and more against all sin.

BOOK II

The Second Reformation:
The Reformation of the External Senses and the Tongue through Accurate Custody

63. After sin has been conquered, the senses must be purified. Once we have expelled sin from our soul, there still remains for us a lengthier and more irksome battle against the passions, against evil propensities and vices and vicious habits. These usually remain imbedded in us as a result of our former misdeeds. "Although all the Israelites," says St. Francis de Sales, "departed in reality out of the land of Egypt, yet they did not leave that country willingly: wherefore many of them regretted in the wilderness their lack of the onions and flesh pots of Egypt. In like manner, there are penitents who depart from sin, but do not leave it willingly. They propose to sin no more but it is with a certain reluctance of heart that they deprive themselves of, or abstain from, an unfortunate delectation in sin. They would rejoice if they could sin and not be damned."[1]

Requisites for purifying the exterior man. If we have determined to make progress in the religious life, we must not only avoid sin, but in addition completely root out all affection for sin from our heart. Such affection arises in the first place from the use of the external senses and of the tongue. To control these external senses and the tongue, we shall now direct our attention to their custody.

There are two principal points in our discussion: (I) the custody of the external senses; (II) the custody of the tongue.

---

1. *Introduction to a Devout Life* (New York, N. Y., Pustet, 1917), translated by Alan Ross, Part I, Chap. VII.

CHAPTER I

CUSTODY OF THE EXTERNAL SENSES

Article I — Introduction

64. **The morality of the external senses.** "God endowed man with external senses," says St. Bonaventure, "because the First Principle created a sensible world to make Himself known, so that, as through a vestige and mirror, man should be led to loving and praising God the artificer."[1] "Whoever is not enlightened by the all-pervading splendor of created things, and fails to behold them, is blind; he who is not awakened by such thunders is deaf; he who, looking on such effects, is not inspired to praise, is dumb; and he who in the presence of such clear footprints of God cannot trace the First Principle of Creation, must be a fool. Open therefore thine eyes, draw near with ears of spiritual hearing; unseal thy lips and apply thy heart, that in all created things thou mayest see, praise, love, hear, worship, magnify and honor God, lest perchance the universal frame of things rise up against thee."[2]

Guarding the external senses. The external senses of man allow him to know and praise God. Yet man must be aware that from his youth these faculties are prone to evil, and that they possess an ill-bent propensity for perceiving and desiring the things of this world. But in guarding the senses, custody should not be so rigid and controlled in every operation as to hamper contact with external reality.

We have a frequent need of external things. We should not say, "Destroy the external senses," but rather, "Control them discreetly and allow them a wholesome exercise in their

---

1. *Brevil.*, Pars II, cap. XI.
2. *Itinerarium mentis in Deum*, cap. I, n. 15.

114

proper operations." Rule out whatever is injurious, and do not permit the faculties of the senses to wander at large from one object to another, particularly when they are inflamed with the fires of disorderly passions.

The five external senses. There are five external senses: (1) sight; (2) hearing; (3) smell; (4) taste; (5) touch. Let us examine them so as to be able to reform them through earnest mortification.

Article II — The Five External Senses

§ I. Custody of the Sense of Sight

65. Sight is the noblest of the senses. Sight is the noblest of the external senses with which God has endowed the human body. It furnishes our imagination with more images of external reality than any of the other senses; by means of such images the mind forms ideas, then fashions judgments, regulates our speech, and produces other beneficent effects.

Its great danger. Owing to the importance of its operation, this sense is probably more dangerous than the others. We can say with St. Augustine: "I resist the enticements of the eye, lest the feet with which I walk Your road should be entangled in the snare; and I raise the eyes of my soul to You, that You may pluck my feet from that snare. Repeatedly You pluck them out, for indeed they are ensnared. But You do not cease to pluck them out however often I fall into the snares that are spread all about us. For Thou shalt neither slumber nor sleep, Thou that keepest Israel. How innumerable are the things — made by various kinds of art and through manufacture, in clothing, shoes, vessels, and all kinds of contrivances, going far beyond what is necessary for our use and what is reasonable and of pious significance — that men have added for the delight of their eyes, externally engrossed in what they make, interiorly abandoning Him by whom they were made, and destroying what He made them."[3]

Custody of the eyes. Since the sight is exposed to such perilous and diverse dangers, it certainly must be mortified; the eyes must be carefully guarded.

The nature of this custody. Now the nature of this custody lies in: (1) the avoidance of an evil or curious gaze upon any indecent object, any object enticing to sin: this is a very necessary and mandatory custody; (2) for love of God, a restraint, as far as humanly possible, from curious, valueless and often even indifferent glances at material objects: such a restriction of the sense pleases God; (3) occasionally viewing things which create natural revulsion, and yet bring on no moral danger: such a mortification is very meritorious before God.

Havoc caused by lack of custody. The importance of guarding one's sight will be clearly apparent if we reflect for a moment on the havoc created when such custody is lacking. (1) Nearly all the passions which war against the soul have their root in unguarded sight, since the greater part of our images is introduced to the intellect through the eyes. (2) Moreover, an impure passion, or at least immoral temptations frequently result from these images. Aroused by the consideration of such imagery, animal instincts are stirred and set in motion. As a consequence, the will is gradually drawn to yield its consent to such carnal delights. For this reason St. James remarks, "Then, when passion has conceived, it brings forth sin."[4] Jeremia says, "Death has come up through our windows."[5] (3) Lastly, innumerable distractions are created in the intellect, causing it frequently and readily to wander off its course. This is what prevents us from true devotion. This is what hinders

---

3. St. Augustine, *Confessions,* Book X, Chap. XXXIV, n. 52, in Migne, *P. L.,* t. XXXII, col. 801.
4. James 1:15.
5. Jer. 9:20.

and even destroys the spirit of prayer. And because of this, David ardently besought the Lord: "Turn away my eyes from seeing what is vain."[6]

Manner of mortifying the eyes. It is of the greatest importance to one's spiritual life to learn to put into practice the means of mortifying the eyes. There are seven general rules.

(1) Never look at the unseemly parts of your own or another's body, even though such persons might be of tender and innocent years. "It is shameful for a religious to gaze upon any nude body. Any decent man has a dread of appearing nude, unless manifest necessity should compel him to it."[7]

(2) The eyes must be restrained when they glance at drawings, paintings, statues; also at pictures in anatomical books. For the Lord says, "So if thy right eye is an occasion of sin to thee, pluck it out."[8] And St. Gregory remarks that: "Our eyes, which resemble human vultures, ought to be shut tight against sin. For whoever rashly views the things of the exterior world through the windows of the body, generally succumbs, though perhaps unwillingly, to the delights of sin, and compelled by the yearnings of concupiscence, begins to wish for things which he did not desire before he beheld them."[9]

(3) Maintain a prudent custody of the eyes in the presence of women, without being either too free or too reserved. For he who desires to avoid sin should be on his guard against every occasion of sin. If David had not imprudently looked at Bethsabee, his soul would not have been mortally wounded. Scripture says, "Through woman's beauty many perish."[10]

---

6. Ps. 118:37.
7. *Mirror of Discipline,* Part I, Chap. XXV, n. 6.
8. Matt. 5:29.
9. St. Gregory, *Moralia,* Lib. XXI, cap. II, in Migne, *P. L.,* t. LXXVI, col. 189.
10. Sirach 9:8.

When Frater Roger's spiritual director asked him on one occasion why he, who was especially favored by God with an extraordinary love of purity, so assiduously avoided women, he replied: "Father, when a man does what lies in his power to avoid the occasion of sin, God in turn will do all in His power to guard and protect him. But when man rashly casts himself into the occasion of sin, he is justly forsaken by God. And so, because of nature's corruption, it frequently happens that one falls into grievous sin."[11] Precious words of wisdom, which should be printed in letters of gold!

(4) Guard the eyes while walking in public. This practice both edifies people and provides them with a good example for their imitation. Moreover, such modest conduct lessens the danger of sin.[12]

(5) Restrain your eyes in church and in choir, and outside choir or church when prayers are being recited.[13] "The eyes of a fool are on the ends of the earth."[14]

(6) It is most praiseworthy to abstain from looking at things out of mere curiosity, when there would be no advantage, reason or necessity in looking at them. The greater our inclination and desire to see such objects, the greater the merit of abstaining. Gaudentius Guggenbichler writes: "Occasionally it may be permissible and suitable to grant a respite to our sense of sight or to any other, for some good reason — for example, to relieve our bodily forces to some extent after study, labor, etc.; to restore them and to conserve our energies for devotion to God. If we exclude such situations, there are still many other instances when we have the opportunity to mortify our sight, and when it will neither harm us nor injure our

---

11. *Analecta Franciscana* (Quaracchi), t. III, p. 384.
12. Cf. St. Prosper, *De vita contemplativa,* Lib. III, cap. VIII, n. 1, in Migne, *P. L.,* t. LIX, col. 484. (Attributed erroneously to St. Prosper; the true author is Pomerius.)
13. Cf. *Mirror of Discipline,* Part I, Chap. XXIV, n. 1.
14. Prov. 17:24.

health to do so. When no one else is aware of this self-denial, and there is consequently no danger of vainglory, such an act is motivated by the purest intention and is pleasing to God."[15]

(7) Finally, it is very commendable for us to fix our gaze upon objects which in themselves are licit and afford us no moral danger, but which are adverse to our passions and against our nature. For example, we may have such a natural aversion for some person that we cannot think about him without displeasure, nor even look at him; yet for love of God and for the sake of peace and Christian charity we look at him with kindness. This can sometimes even be a heroic act of virtue.

CONCLUSION. Since our path is strewn with moral dangers for the eyes, it behooves us to guard them well. We must turn away from every suggestive scene, not permitting the eyes even momentarily to dwell on any object whose nature could entice us to commit sin or impede our efforts toward self-perfection. In such cases, look elsewhere as fast and as carefully as if you were fleeing from a plague-ridden city. The religious considers all things from a Christian viewpoint; observing the visible phenomena of this world, he rises to the contemplation of the invisible God. For God alone is true beauty, from whom the rivulets of created beauty flow in all directions as from a spring.

Let us imitate our Seraphic Father: "As the three youths in the flames of the fiery furnace calmly besought all creation to praise and glorify the Creator, so did he, filled with the Spirit of God, ceaselessly glorify, praise and bless in every element, in every being, the Author and Ruler of all. When he saw flowers brightening the land, he began to preach to these beautiful creatures in his usual way, urging them to praise their Maker as if they had the use of reason. He also addressed the waving fields of grain, the purple vineyards, the stones and

---

15. Gaudentius Guggenbichler, *Introductio ad Vitam Seraphicam*, Pars I, Tract. IV, cap. II, § 2.

the forest, the splendors of the plains, the running streams and the verdant flowers, the earth and the fire, the air and the wind; and his message to each and to all was an exhortation to love, serve, and glorify God with the purest intention. Finally, he called all his fellow creatures his brothers. In this singular manner, in a way unfamiliar to others, he often reached into the inmost depths of creatures with such perspicacity that it was apparent that he had already attained the noble liberty of the sons of God."[16]

When we use the sense of sight properly and with internal purity, we discover the handiwork of God in all things, we perceive the traces of God in all His works. As soon as we are in the habit of venerating God as manifested in His creatures, we shall be able to elevate our soul through them to the delightful contemplation of the Divine Majesty.

§ II. Custody of the Ears

66. **Morality of the sense of hearing.** "Hearing is one of the senses used in acquiring knowledge. Through this faculty the mind obtains many ideas of truth and wisdom. The ears are often referred to as gateways or portals. Consequently, man must guard his ears with prudent alertness lest falsehood instead of truth, folly instead of wisdom, penetrate the inmost recesses of the heart."[17]

Custody of the ears. As in the case of the sense of sight or any other external sense, custody of the ears is pleasing to God, useful, meritorious, and at times even a necessity, and this for the same reasons as explained above. In general it is easier to avoid every approach of evil pleasure than to control

---

16. Celano, *Legenda Prima* (Edward of Alençon edition, Rome, 1906), cap. XXIV, n. 80-81.
17. Cf. Cardinal Bona, *Manuductio ad coelum,* cap. X, n. 3.

our senses when occasions for such pleasures actually arise. Since we have learned from infancy to pamper our external senses, even though we may have realized the fragility and emptiness of such gratifications, preconceived notions of these "pleasures" remain in our mind and are strongly imbedded in our imagination. It is only through meditation and the practice of contrary acts of virtue that such notions gradually vanish and the solid principles of Christian living are impressed on the intellect.

Nature of this custody. This custody consists in restraining the ears from listening to what is illicit, harmful, or useless. It also demands control in hearing conversations that might be lawful in themselves, but that are replete with idle, curious, or pointless talk. Furthermore, such custody also enjoins us, when charity demands, to listen to conversations that are proper and harmless enough, but boring and perhaps even disagreeable to us. In many instances custody of the ears is advantageous, meritorious and to some extent required. It is sometimes a strict necessity.

Particular occasions for custody of the ears

(1) *In no instance should we pay attention to detractors or murmurers.* One should never listen to people who speak ill of their neighbor, of secular priests, or of priests of one's own or another Order. We should particularly avoid giving ear to adverse remarks about our own superiors. For it is a sin against charity not only to speak in this manner but also to listen to such talk without good reason. Whenever we hear such talk, we will do well to interpret the words or the facts in their best possible light. We shall try to excuse such words or deeds, or at least attribute a good intention to the persons apparently guilty of detraction. We shall put the best possible construction on their actions. Finally, we shall try, with a proper religious spirit, to change the topic of conversation.

(2) *We should be an enemy of indecent speech.* Indecent speech defiles the soul and, like glue, leaves a sticky, slimy trail. Listening to immodest language deceives, entices and eventually induces us to speak likewise. Obscenity often inflicts a mortal wound on a soul, especially that of an innocent person, and thus destroys the spiritual life of this soul. St. Bonaventure advises: "Be careful to avoid all idle words and immodest speech, so that you neither listen to it nor repeat it, because, according to St. Paul, 'Evil companionships corrupt good manners'" (1 Cor. 15:33, Challoner-Douay version).[18] For this reason Holy Scripture teaches us: "As you hedge round your vineyard with thorns, set barred doors over your mouth."[19] Father Gaudentius remarks: "When conversing with seculars, if the discussion shifts to a worldly topic, either get up and leave the place if you can do so prudently, or with pious dexterity change the subject. If you are unable to use either of these methods, manifest your displeasure by keeping your eyes modestly downcast.

"We should likewise be imbued with the same strong convictions about obscene conversations presented in a jocose, humorous, and insidious manner; for the Fathers call such speech the 'poison of the soul.'"[20]

(3) *Disregard current and strange rumors about the world.* Invariably such news produces distractions in our spiritual life. Let our holy Father St. Francis be our model in this respect, for according to Celano, "the glorious saint lived within himself and, traversing the breadth of his own heart, he was wont to prepare a dwelling place suitable for his God. Consequently, the din of the world did not reach his ears, nor could the sound of another's voice disturb his contemplation. He did

---

18. St. Bonaventure, *Regul. Novit.*, cap. X, n. 1.
19. Sirach 28:24.
20. Gaudentius Guggenbichler, *loc. cit.*, § 3.

not allow the magnitude of some of his missions to interfere with his spiritual reflections."[21]

(4) *Do not be attentive to praise and adulation.* The imperfect man, the man of weak or mediocre virtue, is consumed with the fire of adulation. The fumes of this fire pour forth blinding clouds of vanity. But the man who has acquired some degree of perfection is made humbler by such attentions, since he finds nothing inside or outside himself to justify such praise. Whatever perfection he possesses he attributes to God, to whom alone he gives all the credit. "Hence," says St. Gregory, "it often happens that the unjust man is poisoned by his own self-esteem, while the just man is purified by the praise of others. For the God-fearing man hearkens to the voice of his conscience and reforms what is reprehensible in his nature; whereas the good he possesses he refers to God."[22] "For they who praise me, scourge me,"[23] remarks St. Ignatius of Antioch.

Be careful not to imitate men of the world who respond to flattery by showing the satisfaction they derive from it. As they themselves are flatterers, you should severely reprimand them, if you have authority over them. However, when someone praises you in good faith, discourage such action by humbly and truthfully presenting reasons against his doing so, lest such a person should persist in his adulation.

(5) *Heed the admonitions of your superiors and teachers* with an obliging, humble and obedient spirit of submission. Also accept their commands, corrections and instructions, for the Lord has shown His way to your superiors and through them you become subject to Him. There are some, especially among younger religious who, when they are rebuked, try to find excuses. Some even go so far as to defend their actions,

---

21. Celano, *Legenda Prima,* cap. XVI, n. 45.

22. *Moralia* Lib. XXII, cap. VII, in Migne, *P. L.,* t. LXXVI, col. 222.

23. St. Ignatius of Antioch, *Epist. ad Trallianos,* cap. IV, in Migne, *P. G.,* t. V, col. 678.

or try to blame others, following in this the example of our first parents. Others are even worse in this regard. For when reprimanded by superiors, their faces redden, not from a decent sense of shame but because of undue ire, provocation, and rage. They are inflamed with anger when corrected, like a madman who in his fury bites the hand of the physician who tries to heal him. They wish to abound in virtue, yet with insults they harangue those who correct them and expose their faults, though this has been done only to improve their spiritual condition. True it is that they are sorry; yet their regrets are not motivated by an awareness of their shortcomings but rather by the detrimental effect their faults may have on their reputation. The novice in religion who earnestly desires to reach the state of perfection does not act in this manner. Even when innocent, he is happy when criticism is directed against him; in fact, he rejoices in his humiliations. If he is justly rebuked, he should remain silent, and show his sorrow by silence and a holy shame-facedness. He will, by so doing, show his respect for his superior or the confrere who has reproved him.

(6) *With patience and in a spirit of tranquillity, listen to the praises* lavished on your rivals or your enemies. "You will never be happy as long as you are envious of another's good fortune. Do you think you can snatch away his prosperity, which is cause of your envy, and use it yourself? Your neighbor has wealth, he abounds in knowledge, he has a high social standing. Yet all these are yours if you love him. For he who loves his neighbor has a superabundance of wealth."[24]

CONCLUSION. "Avoid," says St. Bonaventure, "those little gatherings of idle and giddy persons. Detest the blandishments of flatterers and despise their gifts. Always abhor the talk of whisperers, murmurers, hypocrites, and detractors, for these, according to Sacred Scripture, are 'hateful to God' (cf. Rom.

---

24. Cardinal Bona, *Manuductio ad coelum,* cap. VIII, n. 2.

1:30)."[25] Do not be deceitful like the serpent. Heed not outpourings of venom. Close your ears to idle chatter and rumors, shut them to idle gossip, so that your conversation may be heavenly, for the less frequently you listen to men, the more frequently will you hear God speaking within your soul.

§ III. Custody of the Sense of Smell

67. Morality of the sense of smell. The sense of smell, or the olfactory sense, was given us by God in order that we might distinguish the various foods and other gifts of nature that are beneficial or harmful to our constitution. It is the most innocent of the five senses and probably affords the least occasion for sin. St. Augustine remarks, "As for the allurement of sweet scents, I am not much troubled: when they are absent, I do not seek them; when they are present, I do not refuse them."[26]

Custody of the sense of smell. The olfactory sense must be guarded in order to prevent transgressing the limits of right reason, decency, and fraternal charity. Therefore we must try to learn how the pruning knife of mortification can help.

Principles concerning custody of the sense of smell

(1) It is a matter of ordinary courtesy to disregard unpleasant odors: polite people simply do not let on that they have noticed them.

(2) This disinterestedness and self-control is all the more properly expected of religious and priests. Naturally, our self-control in this as in all things should be supernaturally motivated; but, certainly, what others can do as a matter of courtesy, we can do for the love of God.

---

25. St. Bonaventure, *Regul. Novit.*, cap. X, n. 1.
26. St. Augustine, *Confessions*, Lib. X, cap. XXXII, in Migne, *P. L.*, t. XXXII, col. 799.

(3) From a motive of saving souls or doing a good work, valiantly, unflinchingly endure unpleasant odors. No stench should hinder us from performing acts of charity. Follow the example of St. Francis. "The sight of lepers was repugnant to him. When he was living a somewhat superficial life in the world, he would look at a colony of lepers from a point almost a mile away and would hold his nose so as not to perceive the putrid emanations of their rotting, festered flesh. But after his conversion the saintly lover of total humility used to go to meet the lepers and to live with them. He would take tender care of their ravaged bodies for love of God. He would gently bathe these living corpses and would even cut away their corrupted ulcers."[27] In his *Testament* he sets the basis for Celano's statements: "Whilst I was in sin, it seemed to me too bitter a thing to see lepers, but the Lord Himself led me among them and I showed compassion to them."

CONCLUSION. "Be intent on the pursuit of virtue, and your life will be a fragrant odor unto God."[28] In this, we should also follow the example of St. Francis and learn from him to glorify God in all the elements of nature. "What exhilaration the beauty of flowers brought to his mind as he perceived their beautiful shapes and sensed their sweet fragrance. He immediately bent his consideration to the beauty of that heavenly Flower who in the Springtime came forth brightly from the root of Jesse and raised with its fragrance countless thousands of the spiritually dead."[29]

§ IV. Custody of the Sense of Taste

68. Morality of the sense of taste. The main function of the sense of taste is to distinguish foods and liquids. The

---

27. Celano, *Legenda Prima,* cap. VII, n. 17.
28. *Manuductio,* cap. X, n. 3.
29. Celano, *Legenda Prima,* cap. XXIX, n. 81.

principle of determination is the flavor of the thing to be consumed. The sense of taste distinguishes wholesome foods from harmful. It directs the appetite away from unpleasant and unsuitable foods and guides it to those which are tasty and satisfying to the particular consumer. "This appetite for food has been given to us that we might keep our nature in a fit condition and be able to persevere in God's service and gain much merit. A well-ordered, sparing and regular use of food conserves our strength longer, while it never retards but rather revives our faculties."[30]

Custody of the sense of taste. Moderation of the sense of taste consists not only in refraining from an intemperate and illicit use of food and drink; in addition, it also implies frequently abstaining from even a licit use. The Apostle says, "The kingdom of God does not consist in food and drink, but in justice and peace and joy in the Holy Spirit."[31]

There are many ways of abusing food and drink. St. Gregory reduces them to five.

Abuses of the sense of taste. (a) "Eating at improper times; (b) desiring more sumptuous repasts; (c) desiring to have food better seasoned; (d) eating an inordinate quantity of food; (e) eating greedily."[32]

Gluttony, properly so called, consists in deriving inordinate pleasure from food and drink. Vices which originate from an immoderate use of food and drink merely for the sake of satisfying the taste are considered the offspring of gluttony.

Consequences of gluttony. St. Thomas enumerates five evil consequences of gluttony: (1) undue levity; (2) scurrility; (3) immorality; (4) loquacity; (5) dullness of the faculty of understanding.

---

30. David of Augsburg, *De exterioris et interioris hominis compositione,* Lib. II, cap. XXIII.

31. Rom. 14:17.

32. St. Gregory, *Moralia,* Lib. XXX, cap. XVIII, in Migne, *P. L.,* t. LXXVI, col. 556.

Moderation of the appetite

(1) The Lord remarks in the holy Gospel: "Take heed to yourselves lest your hearts be overburdened with self-indulgence and drunkenness."[33] St. Bonaventure urges us continually to strive to avoid such excesses and to espouse sobriety. St. Bernard says that we should eat to satisfy our hunger and not for the gratification of our sense of taste. Eat only for necessity. Never desire to eat more than you need, merely for the pleasure it may afford you. Heed the wisdom of St. Augustine: The mind surfeited by food loses the power of prayer.

(2) Purely secular banquets and celebrations should be avoided by religious; and conduct at the banquets they do attend — religious jubilees, wedding anniversaries, etc., for instance — should be modest and decorous.

(3) Be content with any dish that is set before you. "If a favorite course is served, partake of it with moderation, as becomes a servant of God and a follower of most holy poverty."[34] Be careful not to accuse of gluttony those who eat sumptuous or carefully prepared foods. Their state of health or some festive event may warrant such exceptions. Be mindful of the words of our holy Father St. Francis: "I admonish and exhort them [the brethren] not to despise or judge those whom they see ... use choice food and drink: but rather let everyone judge and despise himself."[35] Never eat outside the refectory unless compelled by necessity or infirmity.

(4) A true son of St. Francis should approach the dinner table with the thought that as a poor mendicant he deserves only bread and water. If delicacies or more pleasing items are on the menu, let him select those which are somewhat more unpalatable and distasteful to him as more suitable for a follower of holy poverty. "Remember that God is sufficient

---

33. Luke 21:34.
34. St. Bonaventure, *loc. cit.*, n. 2 et 3.
35. *Rule*, Chap. II.

for the poor man, and that we can be happy and content with very little in this life."[36]

(5) On certain days let us abstain from some particular food which our nature or appetite particularly craves. This practice will become easy if we recall the fasts and almost incredible penances of the saints, and remember that we should follow the example of Christ, who drank gall and vinegar.

(6) Never complain about the quality of the food or about its faulty preparation. Patiently endure these hardships in the spirit of poverty. Be mindful of the example of St. Francis: "He never or seldom ate cooked food. But he often ate food which was seasoned with ashes and he would destroy the flavor of the repast with cold water. . . . What should I say about his drinking wine when he would not allow himself even sufficient water though he might be burning with thirst?"[37]

(7) Love of God, the example of our holy Father St. Francis, and the desire of virtue will readily suggest various other methods of mortifying the sense of taste. Yet we must always proceed with caution.

Standard to be observed in the moderation of the appetite. As Blosius observes: "A novice should not pursue an extraordinarily austere life, even though he knows that many saints led an extremely rigorous life. The saints were more fully enlightened by the Holy Spirit, and knew that their austerities pleased God. Many beginners experience this fervor during their initial conversion. But since such austerities usually impose too heavy a load on the weakness of human nature, life under this load often proves a great burden to them. Such imprudence might even draw some novices away from the service of God. Practices such as wearing a hairshirt, sleeping on a hard bed, dining on bread and water, taking the

---

36. Blessed John Ruysbroeck, *Commentaria in tabernaculum foederis,* cap. LXXIX.
37. Celano, *Legenda Prima,* cap. XIX, n. 33.

discipline, and so forth, if performed purely for the honor of God, are certainly pleasing to Him and are aids in destroying the carnality of robust youth. However, true love for God binds man much closer to God than any of these practices."[38]

St. Francis was endowed with a high degree of Christian prudence. "In his opinion indiscreetly depriving the body of its due was as much a sin as yielding to gluttony. 'My Brothers,' he repeated, 'this I wish to say, that each one should consider his own nature, for one can subsist on less food than another and the one who needs more food should not imitate the one who can do with less in this matter, but considering his own nature should provide it with what is necessary. For, just as we should refrain from overeating, which is detrimental both to body and soul, so also should we avoid a too extreme abstinence; yes, even more so, for God is more concerned with a merciful heart than with material sacrifice."[39]

Beginners in religious life should not by their own will burden themselves with excessive abstinence; on the other hand, they should not be too worried about the care of the body. Discretion and moderation should be their guides. The prudent counsels of superiors will protect them against excesses or deficiencies.

CONCLUSION. "Having food and sufficient clothing, with these let us be content."[40] Whoever is satisfied with these essentials is so much the more happy and perfect. In this way natural strength is conserved and the body is offered to God as a living sacrifice, for such subjection is within the limits of reason.

Our basic food should be spiritual. When the Apostles asked our Lord to eat, He replied: "I have food to eat of

---

38. Cf. Blosius, *Institutio spiritualis,* cap. II, § 2.
39. *Mirror of Perfection,* n. 24.
40. 1 Tim. 6:8.

which you do not know. . . . My food is to do the will of Him who sent Me, to accomplish His work."[41]

The food of the spirit affords much more satisfaction than the food of the body. "The precepts of the Lord are right, rejoicing the heart; . . . the ordinances of the Lord are true . . . , sweeter . . . than . . . honey from the comb."[42] St. Gregory writes that the greater the amount of food taken, the greater the satiety and loathing; for this is the way with corporal things: when pleasure is indulged in to excess, it turns into pain. On the contrary, when spiritual food is taken, it stimulates spiritual desire and appetite. Carnal delights quickly pass, spiritual joys endure, extending into eternity.

§ V. Custody of the Sense of Touch

69. Morality of this sense. The sense of touch was given by God chiefly for the conservation of the human species. Unlike the other senses, which are localized in a particular part of the body, this sense extends throughout the entire human organism. Therefore its custody is of the greatest importance.

Caution in the use of the sense of touch. St. Basil writes: "The sense of touch is the most pernicious and seductive of all the corporal powers, dragging the other senses along with it into its foul disorders. For this reason the chaste soul will watch as attentively as possible to preserve itself immaculate; all the more so because one is seldom forewarned against such attacks of sensuality."[43] The sense of touch is not evil as such, for nothing created by God can be evil as such — that would be contradictory. The sense of touch can be vile in its abuse only. Of course, it is particularly important to discipline this sense in the religious life, but the right way to do so is not to

---

41. John 4:32, 34.
42. Ps. 18:9, 10, 11.
43. St. Basil, *De vera virgin.*, in Migne, *P. G.,* t. XXX, col. 679, n. 5B.

condemn it as evil, but to recognize its worth, to limit its use, and to seek the immense spiritual value of such a sacrifice. No human faculty is useless. The sense of touch, properly controlled and often mortified, can be the origin of great good.

Nature of custody of this sense. Mortification of the sense of touch implies the following precautions:

(1) Care in touching the private parts of the body: We recall, first of all, that cleanliness is an aid to virtue, and that all parts of the body are good in themselves. Hence, whatever is necessary for cleanliness and proper care of the body is not only permitted but good and holy, a part of our observance of the fifth commandment. At the same time, however, we must remember that unnecessary touches of the private parts of one's body are dangerous and can be seriously sinful. This is all the more true when the private parts of another's body are touched: only in case of real necessity can this be permitted.[44]

(2) A prudent reserve must be upheld in touching even the modest parts of another's body, even those of a person of the same sex. Salutations are to accord with the customs of the place. Religious and devout persons are looked up to as models in this matter, and people expect them to be more dignified in their way of life.

(3) Great care is demanded in our association with women. Without being stiff and formal, the religious will avoid unnecessary and familiar physical contact with the opposite sex. In this as in all things, the good religious strives for the perfect balance between excessive familiarity and a cold reserve; yet, if one must fall short of that perfect balance, it is better to do so by being too reserved. In this spirit we can understand the detailed, if somewhat extreme, examples given in the following sentences of the *Mirror of Discipline:* "The religious . . . should

---

44. Obviously, this very brief treatment presupposes more detailed reference to some work of moral theology.

decline all feminine attentions, all tactile proximity or contact. They should never touch the hand of a woman, nor her head, nor her body, without an evident reason or manifest necessity. . . . "[45]

Above all in this matter, beware lest excessive self-confidence deceive you. He who does not fear has already fallen. "This confidence causes a religious to pretend that his familiarity is motivated by necessity, custom or pure intention," says Cardinal Bona, "but under the guise of good, enormous evils are hiding. For dangerous liberties, harmful conversations, thoughtless levity, neglect of modesty, hilarity, and other abuses gradually break down and finally destroy all modesty."[46]

(4) Do not engage in familiarities such as pressing the hand, especially of the opposite sex, under the pretext of friendship, affection, etc.; and do not allow others to hold your own hand in this manner. Such signs of affection, while not evil in themselves, easily become the first small loopholes by which sin may enter. For by degrees, almost without realizing it, the mind will be affected by these sensual impulses unless they are immediately checked. Beware of holding the hand of another even in jest. "I cannot regard that person as chaste or modest," says Bernard of Besse, "who does not shrink from touching or being touched by a woman. For how can it be permissible to touch that on which one is not even allowed to gaze?"[47]

(5) Do not seek softness or luxury in clothing or bedding; desire to provide yourself only with what is necessary.

CONCLUSION FOR THE CUSTODY OF THE FIVE SENSES. From what has been said, it is evident that we should keep a careful watch over all our senses. And in order to fully appreciate

---

45. *Mirror of Discipline,* Part I, Chap. XXX, n. 4.
46. *Manuductio ad coelum,* cap. V, n. 4.
47. *Mirror of Discipline, loc. cit.,* n. 4.

this truth, we should remember the words which God spoke when He created man: "Let us make mankind in Our image and likeness."[48]

God wished to sign man with the seal of His own image, that man might know that he is not independent, but dependent upon God; and that man, who is truly something of God, may conduct himself as befits a being of such high dignity, raising himself up to divine standards, shrinking from what is bestial. When Christ was shown the coin of the empire, He asked, "Whose are this image and the inscription?" When told it was Caesar's, He said, "Render, therefore, to Caesar the things that are Caesar's, and to God the things that are God's."[49] Let us in this way recall the facts of our creation. When we behold a man and ask: "Whose are this image and inscription?" what is the answer? "It is the image of God." Clearly, then, we should render to God the things that are God's. God has impressed His image upon us that we may know that we belong wholly to Him and therefore should give ourselves entirely to Him. Although this image is primarily in the soul, it extends to the body, reminding us that the body also is subject to Him and that it also has a celestial destiny. The human body stands upright, and is directed toward heaven, while the bodies of other animals are inclined toward the earth, as St. Bernard says, and this is the sign of the destiny of man: heaven and God Himself, who is in heaven.

Let us be on our guard lest secular and mundane things ensnare us, lest the things of earth impede our heavenly journey. What is so precious as the image of God? Let us see to it that we do not lose this gift. For the Lord will punish those who, made to His likeness, do not preserve the great treasure. In the grip of sin we begin to be another person, and that which we were we cease to be. But we will guard this

48. Gen. 1:26.
49. Matt. 22: 20, 21.

image which God has imprinted upon our body if we make
sure that we practice purity of sight, chastity of hearing,
temperance of taste, and that we are modest with regard to
the sense of smell, and untainted in the use of touch.

CHAPTER II

CUSTODY OF THE TONGUE

Article I — Custody of the Tongue in General

70. Morality and importance of custody of the tongue.
The tongue is the instrument of the mind. With regard to God
it should give praise and thanksgiving; with regard to our
brethren, it should speak truth and charity. It would be foolish
to debase so noble an instrument with unworthy speech. "Of
such importance is custody of the tongue," says Cardinal Bona,
"that greater care should be exercised in guarding it than in
guarding the pupil of the eye, for 'death and life are in the
power of the tongue' (Prov. 18:21). He who cannot hold his
tongue is comparable to an open city without walls."[1] The
tongue cannot be controlled without the special help of God.
"Man can tame a ferocious beast," says St. Augustine, "but
not his tongue; he tames the lion but does not curb his speech;
it overcomes him, but he does not overcome it; he overcomes
his fears, but he does not fear what he should in order to
overcome himself."[2] Loquacity is innate in human nature. We
have a tendency to speak out at once whatever we think or
desire.

Necessity of the custody of the tongue. The spiritual
man should consider that he has accomplished nothing if, after
he has checked his external senses, he does not control his
tongue. The Holy Spirit is our authority for this. "Many have
fallen by the edge of the sword, but not as many as by the
tongue."[3] And we can add the memorable words of St. James:

---

1. *Manuductio,* cap. XI, n. 1.
2. *Serm. 55,* cap. I, n. 1, in Migne, *P. L.,* t. XXXVIII, col. 375.
3. Sirach 28:18.

"If anyone does not offend in word, he is a perfect man."[4] Heed also the advice of Giles: "Consider your words that you may know before they reach the tongue that they are suitable for the tongue's utterance. Beware also of superfluous speech, for he who talks much harms his soul."[5]

Faults of the tongue. According to St. Gregory, we may sin by means of the tongue in two ways: " . . . by speaking unjustly and by keeping silent when justice demands that we speak. For if it were never a sin to keep silent, the prophet would not have said, 'Woe is me because I have held my peace' (Isa. 6:5, Challoner-Douay version)."[6]

Article II — Custody of the Tongue in Particular

71. **Evils of the tongue.** The evils of the tongue treated in the following paragraphs are: (1) detraction; (2) lies; (3) revelation of secrets; (4) idle talk; (5) scurrility; (6) contention; (7) murmuring; (8) flattery; (9) boasting.

§ I. Detraction

72. The reputation of another can be injured either by detraction or by calumny. Detraction consists in injuring our neighbor's good name by the unjust revelation of a fault which, while true, is hidden. Calumny consists in doing so by imputing false defects.

Malice of detraction. Detraction is generally the first to be treated among the sins of the tongue, for, as Thomas a Kempis says, "It is generally the custom to speak about absent persons; first, about one, then about another. And in such conversation the speaker freely expresses what pleases or displeases him in

---

4. James 3:2.
5. Lemmens, *Documenta antiqua franc.*, Pars I, p. 63.
6. St. Gregory, *Moralia*, Lib. III, cap. X, in Migne, *P. L.*, t. LXXV, col. 608.

others; he forgets to be careful not to hurt anybody, for it is easy to offend even gravely by word. Often he says something for which he is immediately sorry, and if he could do so he would recall his words and repair the damage done; he regrets having spoken in such a manner. Would that by falling once a man could be taught the injury he inflicts upon himself and upon others, so that he might not fall a second time."[7]

Evil effects of detraction. The detractor, by one movement of his tongue, is able to commit a threefold "murder." Very often he spiritually slays his own soul and that of his listener, as well as the good name and character of the one from whom he detracts with his stinging, deadly words. St. Bernard said that both he who detracts and he who listens have a devil, the first on his tongue and the other in his ears. And according to St. Basil, "These two should be separated from the rest of society."[8] If we could only take a burning coal from the holy altar and touch the lips of men to remove their wickedness and cleanse them from sin! One who would eliminate detractors from the world would remove a huge amount of its sin and iniquity.

Ineffectual detraction is also sinful. There is harm done even if the one who is detracted from accepts the defamation with equanimity. The detractor sins in spite of the fact that his words fall on deaf ears, and do not succeed in harming anyone's reputation. Any man shooting a gun at another commits a grave sin, even though he may not succeed in hitting him. There is still the damage done to a man's honor, even when the detraction does not wound his soul.

Detractors must make reparation. Let the detractor remember that besides confessing the sin he has committed he must repair the damage done to the good name of the insulted

---

7. Thomas a Kempis, *De Silentio,* xx.
8. St. Basil, *Reg. 26 ex Brevior.* in Migne, *P. G.,* t. XXXI, col. 1102.

person. No one can go to heaven with stolen goods, even if these goods be imponderables, such as the honor due to others.

Perniciousness of detractors. St. Francis abhorred detractors above all sinners. They have a poisoned tongue and infect others with their venom, as he said. According to Celano, Francis would never listen to gossip or to biting remarks but would turn away lest his ears be corrupted by such conversations.

Punishment of detractors. Francis not only abhorred detraction but punished the detractors. "Such conduct is disgraceful. ... Detractors are a menace to religious and must be shunned, for the most sweet odor of many virtuous persons will be changed into a stench unless the poisonous mouths of detractors be closed." And Thomas of Celano writes: "For what indeed are the detractors if not the gall of mankind, the ferment of iniquity and the disgrace of the whole world? They praise only those whose good graces they desire to enjoy, and are silent when they see no earthly gain for their praise. By assuming the pallor of one who fasts, they try to sell their poisonous flatteries; taking on the appearance of spirituality, they presume to sit in judgment over all persons and things and will not bear to be judged by any. They take great delight in their imaginary sanctity but not in good works; they rejoice in the reputation of an angel, not in angelic virtue."[9]

CONCLUSION. Reflect often and seriously on your speech. Beware of detraction which is born of wicked parents. Perverse ambition is its father, envy is its mother. If you hear others being defamed and accused, challenge the detraction if possible. If you cannot do this, excuse the intention of the accused. If you are unable even to do this, show compassion in some way or change the topic of conversation. Remind those present that those who have not yet fallen should thank

---

9. Celano, *Legenda Secunda*, cap. CXXXVIII (Edward of Alençon edition, 1906), p. 306.

God for this grace. In a subtle way, lead the detractor to examine himself; and if possible counteract the evil done by narrating some praiseworthy act of the person defamed.

§ II. Lies

73. A lie is any speech that conveys a meaning contrary to what is in the mind, with the intention of deceiving. By the term "speech" we mean all exterior manifestations by which interior thoughts are signified, such as words, signs or acts.

Malice of lying. A person who tells a lie even in a small matter commits a sin, for no liar can be close to God; in fact, every lie is something foreign to God. It is written, "When he [the devil] tells a lie, he speaks from his very nature, for he is a liar and the father of lies."[10] Note that the Lord refers to the devil as the father of lies. God, on the contrary, is Truth. "I am the Way, and THE TRUTH, and the Life."[11] See, therefore, from whom you withdraw and to whom you adhere when you lie.

The sin of lying is very easily committed. Even religious fall into this sin. "A lie is told in conversation," says St. Dorotheus, "when, for instance, a lazy religious, while urging others to rise for the night office, spares himself and later says, 'I suffered from fever and debility and was not able to rise; my strength failed, I was weak,' when he should have said, 'Forgive me, Father! It was because of my slothfulness and negligence that I did not rise.' Such a religious will lie many times to appear honorable and to avoid humiliation."[12] He wanders far from the right path by trying to conceal his failings under the appearance of virtue.

Baseness of the lie. Lying was always hateful to our Seraphic Father. Thomas of Celano tells us of St. Francis' re-

---

10. John 8:44.
11. *Ibid.* 14:6.
12. Dorotheus, in Migne, *P. G.,* t. LXXXVIII, col. 1719.

action to a young man who knelt and asked admission to the Order. "Studying him, the man of God at once realized that the young man was not moved by the Holy Spirit, and he said to him: 'Miserable and carnal youth, how is it that you believe that you are able to lie to the Holy Spirit and to me? Your request is carnal, for your heart is not with God.' "[13]

Never resort to a lie. Our holy Father made no allowance for a lie, even when used with the intention of cultivating virtue. To a friar who asked forgiveness for a fault he had not committed, St. Francis said: "Beware, Brother, lest under the guise of humility you tell a lie."[14]

Exaggerations are to be avoided. "Not only lies — for they are criminal — but also exaggerations and all duplicity must be avoided. Conjectures regarding future and doubtful matters should never be related as truth, but all pertinent circumstances should be mentioned."[15]

CONCLUSION. Beware of duplicity. In ordinary conversation, when you are justly interrogated, it is a misrepresentation to twist words so that they convey a meaning contrary to their usual sense. Even if occasionally it is lawful to hide the truth by artful use of words, St. Francis de Sales says this should be resorted to but rarely, and only in matters of great moment, when the honor and glory of God manifestly demand it. And such practices are dangerous, for in Scripture we read that the Holy Spirit does not dwell in an insincere and hypocritical soul. Worldly prudence and carnal cunning may be part and parcel of the sons of this world; but the sons of God walk straightforward without any shifting or roundabout ways; neither is there any guile in their hearts. "He who walks honestly walks securely,"[16] says Proverbs. Untruth, duplicity

---

13. Celano, *Legenda Secunda,* cap. XI, p. 200.
14. *Ibid.*
15. *Mirror of Discipline,* Part I, Chap. XX, n. 3.
16. Prov. 10:9.

and simulation reveal a weak and worthless soul. "He that speaketh sophistically, is hateful."[17] Faults such as these and similar ones are indeed small sins, but they are indicative of one who has little care for purity of conscience. Therefore resolve never to tell any lie, never to resort to any duplicity. In all that you do, always adhere to the truth.

§ III. Revelation of Secrets

74. **The revelation of secrets is prohibited.** There is danger not only in telling a lie but also at times in revealing the truth — for instance, in the disclosure of what should not be publicized. Regarding this subject, the author of the Proverbs says, "Discuss your case with your neighbor, but another man's secret do not disclose; lest, hearing it, he reproach you, and your ill repute cease not."[18] For what is worse than to simulate friendship while harboring enmity?

Causes of unjust revelation of secrets. St. Ambrose enumerates the causes from which the betrayal of secrets proceeds. "This vice springs from four causes: adulation, avarice, glory and loquacity. While wishing to flatter one person, the revealer pours forth the secrets of another. Others in their desire for profit seek the wages of treachery, selling the secret of another for what they can get for it. Still others, wishing to seem important in the knowledge they hold, make known things that should be concealed. Finally, there are those who speak without thinking, giving out information they are later unable to recall."[19]

Revelation of one's own secrets. It is imprudent to reveal even our own secrets.

---

17. Ecclus. 37:23, Challoner-Douay version.
18. Prov. 25:9-10.
19. St. Ambrose, *In Ps. 108,* Serm. 2, n. 26, in Migne, *P. L.,* t. XV, col. 1284.

"Secrets of the heart," says Brother Giles, St. Francis' companion, "are not to be publicized, for this is foolish and the occupation of fools."[20] His heavenly secrets Francis revealed to no one; he says: "Blessed is the man who knows how to guard and conserve the secrets of God, for there is nothing hidden that will not be revealed, according to the wish of the Lord, and when He so desires. . . . I fear for myself," he said, "and therefore, if secrets are to be revealed, I would much rather that they be revealed by another."[21] Our Seraphic Father also left an example for our serious consideration, as recorded by Thomas of Celano. "It was his custom rarely if ever to reveal a secret. For from experience he knew that it is a great evil to communicate all things to all men. He knew that a man cannot be holy if his secret affairs are not more perfect and more numerous than that which appears outwardly, or if from his appearance everyone can know all about him."[22]

But how should we answer imprudent and rash questions? The Holy Spirit teaches us the proper response. "Answer not the fool according to his folly, lest you too become like him"[23] — that is, if out of curiosity he interrogates you regarding a secret or the hidden sin of your neighbor, you should not make these known to him; nor should you satisfy his curiosity if he inquires about inane or harmful things. But in all these matters, act according to the advice of Sacred Scripture: "Answer the fool according to his folly, lest he become wise in his own eyes."[24] That is, answer him as his foolishness demands, so that he may be convinced that the secret sins of his neighbor are not to be made known to him any more than he would like his sins to be broadcast by others.

20. Lemmens, *Documenta antiqua franc.*, Pars I, Scripta Fr. Leonis, p. 63.
21. *Ibid.*, p. 44.
22. Celano, *Legenda Prima*, cap. III, n. 88, pp. 99, 100.
23. Prov. 26:4.
24. *Ibid.* 26:5.

When a secret may be revealed. Superiors are as fathers to their subjects, and it is their duty to correct their sons in order to bring about amendment of the past and good resolutions for the future. For this reason hidden defects of subjects may be made known to superiors. Such manifestations cannot be considered as complaints or detraction, but as charity. Sometimes we are obliged to give such information, but ordinarily we should first resort to fraternal correction.

At times there is an obligation to reveal the secret of a neighbor. This is true especially in three cases: (1) when an innocent person would be deceived or corrupted; (2) when a spiritual, hidden "ulcer" might corrupt and destroy the whole man — for it is a slighter evil that a little honor be sacrificed than that the danger to the soul be allowed to continue; (3) when the common good, which must always be preferred to the particular good, would suffer.

Fraternal and private correction should precede if possible. Unless a private admonition is first administered, it is not fair to reveal defects. For Christ Himself taught as follows: "If thy brother sin against thee, go and show him his fault, between thee and him alone,"[25] inviting no man to witness his unknown fault. Otherwise you are not a corrector, but a betrayer; nor will he be cured in this way; rather will he more quickly sink to his ruin by this treatment, for detrimental shame will incite him to defend his fault and thus continue in his perversity for a longer time than otherwise.

Cases in which fraternal correction may be omitted. There are two cases in which one may reveal a fault to a superior as to a father without previous fraternal correction: when knowledge of the offense is spreading, or when we rightly think that our correction will be of little value on account of the haughtiness of the offender and the insignificant authority of the corrector.

---

25. Matt. 18:15.

§ IV. Idle Talk

75. Idle talk means that which is devoid of all utility, both spiritual and temporal. If one converses with an upright intention — for example, in order to correct a misunderstanding, with a view to reconciliation of friendship or cheering the sick — even if such conversation is somewhat lighthearted or jocose, as long as it remains within the bounds of propriety it is not idle but useful. For then it builds up, it edifies, it serves a good purpose.

Idle talk was hateful to our Seraphic Father. Empty, idle talk always displeased our holy Father St. Francis. According to Thomas of Celano, "The man of God considered that prayer devoid of profit which was followed by idle conversation; and to avoid falling into this fault, he proposed a remedy, saying: 'Whenever a brother is guilty of idle talk or useless conversation, he must confess his fault at once, and for each idle word say one Our Father. And it is my wish that, if he accuse himself of the fault, he say the Our Father for his own soul; but if he must first be reminded by another, that he offer the prayer for the friar who reminded him.' "[26] We shall appreciate the merit of this admonition of St. Francis when we consider the words of our future Judge: "But I tell you, that of every idle word men speak, they shall give account on the day of judgment."[27] Furthermore, idle talk easily degenerates into scurrilous, disgraceful conversation.

Idle talk disturbs the conscience. Although idle conversation may not always have dire results, it tends to disturb the conscience and diminishes the spirit of devotion. "Nothing," says St. Lawrence Justinian, "so weakens the mind, destroys compunction, leads to confusion, deprives of respectability, and inclines toward tepidity, as insolent, inane loquacity."[28]

---

26. Celano, *Legenda Secunda,* cap. XIX.
27. Matt. 12:36.
28. St. Lawrence Justinian, *De discipl. monast.,* cap. XV.

CONCLUSION. Following our Seraphic Father, let us flee from idle talk and vain conversation and listen to the counsel of Thomas a Kempis: "Have no time for idle conversation yourself; it would also be well to admonish those who engage in this practice. Christ desires to speak to you; therefore, you must free yourself from useless conversation, and influence your brother to seek peace and satisfaction in his cell."[29]

§ V. Scurrility

76. Scurrility, buffoonery, vulgarity, biting wit are opposed to religious austerity. For they promote indecency by provoking laughter through circuitous, covert, subtle and caustic speech. By the use of such language man plays the part of a clown. To put it mildly, he demonstrates his imprudence, if not his folly.

Scurrility is injurious. By reason of its sharpness, scurrilous speech penetrates deeply into the soul: the keener the blade, the more readily it pierces the body. Even though we do not intend any evil, yet the devil may instill much harm into such words; for he secretly uses scurrilous conversation as a weapon to wound sensitive hearts.

Scurrility is always dangerous. Many improper words are said without any bad intention, but the audience may attribute a bad meaning to them, far different from that which the speaker had in mind. If spoken before the imperfect, these words will linger in their hearts. Just as a single drop of oil which is spilled on a piece of cloth will spread and cover a large portion of the cloth, so also scurrility, by its effect on the mind and soul of the weak, will gradually extend and be the cause of the corruption of many.

Listen to the words of St. Bernard to religious: "You have consecrated your mouth to the Gospel, and so opening it to

---

29. Thomas a Kempis, *De fideli dispensatore,* § 14.

speak what is wrong is to accustom yourself to sacrilege."[30] Such a reprimand is well deserved, for even serious-minded lay-folk do not approve of such facetious speech. Refuse to make your mouth the sounding brass of vulgar jests, or the tinkling cymbal of cheap, worldly talk, for like a sacred harp it has been dedicated to the praise of divine things. Our Saviour, who reads the hearts of men, declares: "Out of the abundance of the heart the mouth speaks."[31] According to St. Francis de Sales, those who consider themselves cultured and refined yet engage in this type of conversation, are truly ignorant of the purpose of conversation. For those who converse should be as a swarm of bees collecting holy and sweet honey from their exchange of words; not as a horde of wasps or beetles gnawing and devouring a putrid corpse.[32]

CONCLUSION. If some foolish person speaks in an unbecoming manner in your presence, show that you are offended, or take leave of him as quickly as possible, or teach him a much-needed lesson in some other manner, as opportunity affords and prudence suggests.

§ VI. Contention

77. **Malice of contention.** Contention is an ill-regulated battle of words or a dispute in which the truth is defended or attacked with too much asperity. The tongue is at fault when it engages in contention; hence Paul wrote to Timothy: "Recall these things to their mind, . . . not to dispute with words, for that is useless, leading to the ruin of the listeners."[33] And St. John Chrysostom asks, "How does it conform to right

---

30. St. Bernard, *Lib. de consid.,* Lib. II, cap. XIII, in Migne, *P. L.,* t. CLXXXII, col. 756.

31. Matt. 12:34.

32. St. Francis de Sales, *Introduction to a Devout Life,* Part III, Chap. XXVII.

33. 2 Tim. 2:14.

reason when men who are brothers, who share the same nature, who are of the same family, who live in this world as pilgrims and strangers, and who ought to be teachers of gentleness, clemency, and all philosophy, contend and dispute among themselves?"[34] Our Father St. Francis charitably warned his brethren against this vice when he said in his Rule: "They shall not dispute . . . with others, but let them be meek, peaceful and modest, . . . speaking courteously to everyone, as is becoming."[35]

Effects of contention. Dreadful evils have resulted from contention. "Contention," says St. Lawrence Justinian, "is the fiery lance of the devil for accomplishing the death of souls. How many are the quarrels, how great the hatred, which spring from contentious words! Truly contention is very grave, for through it the ties of friendship are broken and the sweet bonds of affection severed."[36]

We should never contradict anyone without a good reason. Listen to the warning of St. Francis de Sales: "Never contradict the sayings and words of another, unless, because of your assent, some sin or great injury would follow."[37] For this reason he advises that the door to all disputes, strifes, and quarrels should be closed. When someone must be contradicted, or when we must oppose another's opinion, we should do it with great kindness and skill. Otherwise it may seem as if we were forcing the other's mind and inclinations to yield to our own. We gain nothing when we treat our fellow men rudely or harshly.

CONCLUSION. What procedure should we follow if, through human frailty, through the deceptive temptations of the devil, we have poured out the venom of contention? We should

---

34. *Homil. XXXIII in Gen.*, in Migne, *P. G.*, t. LIII, col. 308.
35. Chap. III.
36. *Lib. de discipl.*, cap. XIII.
37. St. Francis de Sales, *loc. cit.*, cap. XXX.

imitate the example of our holy Father's companions. If any of them spoke disturbing words to another, immediately prostrating himself on the ground, he acknowledged his fault. By humbling ourselves in such circumstances we will give joy to our beloved Seraphic Father. Concerning acts of reconciliation, Thomas of Celano says: "[Francis] rejoiced greatly when he learned that his sons gave evidence of such proofs of holiness among themselves."[38]

§ VII. Murmuring

78. The tongue errs by murmuring, that is, by engaging in complaints against superiors or others. A servant of God should consider in his heart what great harm he incurs by murmuring.

The evils of murmuring. If murmuring is tolerated in the cloister, where is the regular silence, where is the holiness of the religious state, where is the silence prescribed by the Order, where is the bond of charity? Murmuring produces strife, extinguishes peace, begets quarrels.   .

What a sad state of affairs if we find murmurers even in religious Orders — not only occasional murmurers but those who complain with great pleasure and gusto. Nothing pleases them more than to speak of and to interfere with the affairs of others, particularly if their attacks are spurred by hatred. We shall do well to examine the causes of murmuring.

The causes of murmuring. According to Louis de Ponte, there are four passions which particularly prompt the tongue to murmur.[39]

(1) *Hatred.* Murmuring can be caused by hatred; it was this sentiment which drove the Pharisees to murmur against Christ and His deeds.

---

38. Celano, *Legenda Secunda,* cap. CXV, p. 286.
39. L. de Ponte, *De christiani hominis perfectione,* t. II, Tract. III, cap. X.

(2) *Jealousy.* Murmuring can be caused by jealousy: when others seem to be more esteemed and honored than we are. Dathan and Abiron murmured in this way against Moses and Aaron.

(3) *Impatience.* Murmuring can be caused by impatience: when we complain against those through whom we suffer wrongs. Thus did the sons of Israel murmur on account of their misfortunes and hardships and lack of food and drink in the desert.

(4) *Covetousness.* Finally, murmuring can be caused by covetousness when the desire for things advantageous and convenient to us makes us speak against everyone who stands in the way. Judas murmured against Magdalene's waste of ointment, which might have been sold for thirty denarii, part of which he planned to keep for himself.

Occasions for murmuring will be present every time carnal desires must be subjected to restraint, particularly those regarding the use of temporal goods and the obedience due to superiors.

REGARDING THE USE OF TEMPORAL GOODS. Let us listen to the advice of St. Bernard: "You should not contend for food, drink, or clothing, but accept without murmuring what is provided for you by your superiors. Let it not concern you if your brother receives something better than you. For you have not come to the religious life for the sake of wealth but to practice poverty. You have not come to the monastery to possess earthly riches, but to acquire heavenly virtues. You did not enter a religious Order to do your own will, but to obey the will of another, and to despise all earthly goods for the love of God. It would have been better for you to have remained at your father's house than to create scandal, to quarrel, or to murmur about mundane and transitory things among servants of God."[40]

REGARDING OBEDIENCE DUE TO SUPERIORS

(1) *It does not pertain to an inferior to judge a superior.* We do not know the reasons which prompt superiors to do, command, or prohibit something. Therefore the duty of judging is God's concern, and the concern of superiors, to whom the Lord has given the power of governing. How then can an inferior presume to judge a superior, thus casting his sickle into the harvest of another and manifesting his unjust judgment to his confreres or to others?

A superior may rule well or badly. Superiors may exercise their office imperfectly or perfectly. If they fulfill their office imperfectly, remember that they still take the place of God Himself, who says: "Touch not My anointed, and to My prophets do no harm."[41] He meant by this: "It should be sufficient for you to know that they are Mine, and that they take My place." This thought should inspire such holy fear in our heart that we will never dare by our ill-advised speech to touch either their words or their actions; it should lead us to sincere veneration of their office and their dignity.

The superior is a man, not an angel. Therefore we should not proclaim it a wonder if we find one or the other defect in him. The superior is our father. If, therefore, we try to conceal the faults and defects of the father who begot us in the flesh, why do we not from a higher motive conceal the defects of our spiritual father? Let us listen, rather, to the advice received from God Himself: "In word and deed honor your father, that his blessing may come upon you."[42] And again,

40. Attributed to St. Bernard, but actually by an unknown author; in Migne, *P. L.,* t. CLIV, col. 1230.

41. Ps. 104:15.

42. Sirach 3:8.

"Glory not in your father's shame, for his shame is no glory to you! His father's honor is a man's glory."[43]

If superiors rule perfectly, and grumbling persists because of the very perfection of their direction, then with Moses they can answer the murmurers, "Your grumbling is not against us, but against the Lord."[44]

(2) *Tolerance with superiors.* A superior may happen to be unmerciful, harsh, unpleasant. He may not know how to have compassion for the weaknesses of his subjects. He may not show the heart of a father but that of a stern judge. We who claim to be men of God should bear patiently with such a superior, for we can gain a glorious victory: we can overcome his severity by our patience. We should try in all possible ways to love this superior. We should never permit ourselves to speak any evil of him. On the contrary, we should resolve to pray for him for the love of God.

CONCLUSION, TAKEN FROM THE WARNING OF ST. BERNARD AGAINST MURMURING. We must therefore guard our tongues against murmuring lest we tempt Christ, as some of the Israelites tempted God and perished by serpents. He tempts Christ who murmurs about food, drink, clothing or the like, just as it is written of that same people: "They tempted God in their hearts by demanding the food they craved" (Ps. 77: 18). He who asks for earthly and transitory things in the monastery sins against Christ and tempts his superiors to do wrong.[45]

§ VIII. Reticence and Flattery

79. **Two evils to be avoided.** Charity unites the faithful and establishes harmony through the use of agreeable and kind

---

43. *Ibid.* 3:10, 11.
44. Exod. 16:8.
45. Cf. St. Bernard, *De modo bene vivendi,* cap. XLVII passim, in Migne, *P. L.,* t. CLXXXIV, col. 1268 et seq.

words. And yet we must avoid two extremes; one of which is evil through excess, and the other by defect.

(a) *Through defect:* **Reticence.** We err when we are reticent about the merit of our neighbor at the place, time, and occasion in which it should be made manifest. This reticence is evil because it is usually born of rancor and envy.

How to bestow praise. The just man does not live for himself, but for Christ. Therefore, when he is praised, he should not be praised for himself, but for Christ's sake; for it is by Christ's grace that his gifts are what they are. Therefore a virtuous man, when he is present, should be praised in such a manner that he is led to call to mind Him who is the Author of all good and virtue. For then he will give all the credit to God and will suffer no harm from these commendations.

With all due caution we can sometimes and for special reasons offer a word of approbation — for instance, if someone is very sad and in need of consolation. St. Paul in his letters often lauded the virtues of those who were discouraged.

When to praise a good person in his absence. It may be necessary to praise a confrere in order to save him from evil and misfortune or when his honor and reputation are at stake. We should also acknowledge the good in our neighbor by agreeing with those who praise him, especially when they also ask our opinion. Finally, let us extend a word of approval whenever it is expedient that strangers and confreres should have a good opinion of their neighbor. We should particularly praise and commend worthy superiors in this way.

(b) *By excess:* **Flattery.** Those who praise others too much sin through excess, and are guilty of flattery.

The circumstances of flattery. Flattery is sinful in four instances:

(1) In the first instance, flattery is sinful when the EVIL ACTIONS of others are praised. Let us take care not to approve

any murmurings or any vengeful action committed by anyone against his enemy. This is mortally sinful if the matter is grave; venially sinful if the matter is only light. Sacred Scripture clearly testifies: "He who condones the wicked, he who condemns the just, are both an abomination to the Lord."[46]

(2) There is also flattery when someone is praised and extolled beyond reason and solely on account of his *external appearance.* Celano cites an instance in his *Legends:* "As far as could be externally observed, a certain brother was of exceptional sanctity. Absorbed in prayer at all times, he observed silence with such great strictness that he used to speak not in words but only with a nod of the head. He was considered thrice holy by all. It happened, however, that our blessed Father came to the place. And while everyone else was commending and praising the brother, our Father answered: 'Let him be, brethren, and do not praise his diabolical traits to me.' Not many days later, the so-called 'saint' of his own free will left the Order, fled to the world, and returned to the vomit."[47] The Holy Spirit therefore advises us in Sacred Scripture: "Praise not a man for his looks."[48]

(3) A third instance of flattery occurs when there is reason to believe that our praise will incite an otherwise upright man to *vainglory and pride.* Our holy Father abhorred those who praised him, and when they called him blessed he exclaimed: "Do not praise anyone but the secure. No one should be praised whose end is uncertain."[49] Confirming this, Scripture says, "Praise not any man before death,"[50] as though he were holy.

(4) A fourth instance of flattery occurs when we lavish our praises on others, either to make them PRAISE US, or to

---

46. Prov. 17:15.
47. Celano, *Legenda Secunda,* cap. II, p. 190.
48. Sirach 11:2.
49. Celano, *loc. cit.,* cap. XCVI, p. 270.
50. Ecclus. 11:30, Challoner-Douay version.

obtain some *temporal favor* from them. This way of acting was far removed from the saints of God, who could say with their leader St. Paul: "If I were still trying to please men, I should not be a servant of Christ."[51]

AVOID FLATTERY. A true man of God will have nothing to do with flattery. St. Gregory says: "Praise tortures the just, and makes the wicked exult. But while it tortures the just, it also purifies them; while it gladdens the wicked, it displays their empty pretentions. They are gratified by praise, because they do not seek the glory of their Creator. But those who seek the glory of their Creator are tortured by praise. For they fear that inwardly they are not what they are outwardly said to be. Even when the things commended are true, they fear that before the eyes of God they may lose their reward on account of having been praised. They fear lest human praise weaken the steadfastness of their mind, causing it to incline toward self-love. They fear that praise, which should be an aid to efficient work, may be the sole reward of their labor."[52]

§ IX. Boasting

80. Boasting means to extol ourselves above our true worth, or to promise more than we truthfully intend to fulfill. This can be done in a twofold manner.

Ways of boasting. He boasts, in the first place, who praises himself and his possessions, extols his lineage, and too highly esteems his natural gifts or those of his family.

The second instance of boasting occurs when we exaggerate our knowledge, virtue, and merits, and the work we have undertaken for God.

Evil consequences. Through such a desire for false glory, we lose the reward which we had merited from God. Our

---

51. Gal. 1:10.

52. *Moralia,* Lib. XXVI, cap. XXXIV, in Migne, *P. L.,* t. LXXVII, col. 386.

Seraphic Father says that it is "worse to abuse virtue than not to possess it."[53] The Pharisee who went to the temple to pray lost the merit of the good works which he so boastfully proclaimed.

CONCLUSION. A religious who has left the world, who praises and exalts the virtues which he once despised, should never boast. "Beware of boasting," says St. Bernard; "flee the desire for vainglory. Despise the praise of men, and do not inquire whether someone is praising or censuring you. Praise must not mislead you, censure must not break you."[54]

Indeed, religious should not boast even about the Order itself. The *Mirror of Discipline* says: "They should never commend our Order by descending to particulars; but if it is necessary, they should commend it in general only, without making comparisons or detracting from other Orders. The worst praise is that which glorifies self by bringing injury to others."[55]

General conclusion on the custody of the tongue. Let us remember before speaking that our words will be heard by the Lord, our future judge. In the presence of this Supreme Majesty, let us not engage in any conversation which we would be ashamed to hold before a prelate or a man of blameless life. Let us follow the example of spiritual-minded men: "Let every man be swift to hear, slow to speak."[56] We should first think and then talk. Blessed Giles says: "I do not believe that the virtue of silence is a lesser virtue; it seems to me that man should have a neck like a crane, so that his words would travel a long way before they come out of his mouth."[57]

---

53. Celano, *Legenda Secunda,* cap. I, p. 274.
54. *De modo bene vivendi,* cap. XXXVIII, in Migne, *P. L.,* t. CLXXXIV, col. 1259.
55. *Mirror of Discipline,* Part I, cap. XXXI, 3.
56. James 1:19.
57. *Dicta B. Aegidii,* cap. XVII.

BOOK III

The Third Reformation:
The Reformation of the Bodily Members
through Religious Discipline

81. The members of the body must be sanctified. The external senses are not the only ones in need of sanctification; the members of the body, by means of which men commit evil, must also be sanctified. They must be restored to their moral excellence. This restoration is obtained by the practice of religious discipline.

DIVISIONS

I. *Meaning of religious discipline and consequences of its observance and of its neglect;*

II. *Practical rules to be observed.*

RELIGIOUS DISCIPLINE IN GENERAL

82. Meaning of religious discipline. Discipline, which some call civility or even modesty, has been defined by Hugh of St. Victor in these words: "good and honorable conduct which is not content with avoiding evil, but even tries to perform faultlessly what it does well. Discipline is likewise the orderly movement of all the members of the body, and their proper disposition in every action and habit."[1]

83. Advantages and necessity of religious discipline. "Discipline is the prison of evil desires, the bridle of lust, the yoke of excessive elation. It controls intemperance, restrains levity, stifles all disordered activity of the mind. As inordinate motions of the body are the signs of an inconstant mind, modest restraint of the body manifests and develops strength and constancy of mind. The intellect within us will gradually become disposed to moderation, and improper movements will not proceed from it."[2]

Observance of discipline edifies, non-observance offends. External modesty is greatly admired by men. The religious who modestly composes his eyes, voice, and every gesture seems like an angel among men. He is readily followed; he easily persuades others, for he seems to have descended from heaven and to be speaking in the name of God. Even when his tongue is silent, he preaches more effectively by his example. Our holy Father St. Francis gave excellent sermons on this subject. On the other hand, a religious who lacks self-control and proper composure in his external movements will not only fail to

---

1. Hugh of St. Victor, *Instit. Novit.,* cap. X, in Migne, *P. L.,* t. CLXXVI, col. 935.
2. *Ibid.*

persuade, but will even seem ridiculous, and with just cause will be found blameworthy. For the dignity of the ministry does not go hand in hand with levity, nor the religious habit with disordered movements.

"A scoundrel, a villain is he who deals in crooked talk. He winks his eyes, shuffles his feet, makes signs with his fingers."[3] In other words, he is undisciplined in his external actions.

It is a mistake to reject the practice of religious propriety. Whoever belittles and spurns external discipline is at fault. Bernard of Besse remarks: "Those who are moved by the spirit of God devote themselves to exemplary morals. But proud and foolish persons despise such principles. At one time they call them superstitions and at another time mere ceremonies. They even assail them with specious accusations. 'The fool takes no delight in understanding, but rather in displaying what he thinks' (Prov. 18:2)."[4]

The obligation of superiors in regard to the observance of religious propriety. St. Bonaventure warns us concerning the observance of religious modesty: "The neglect thereof is to be guarded against, since it is established to preserve religious decorum and to make spiritual life easier. To disregard it is a sign of neglect of conscience and of interior levity."[5]

The example of our holy Father and his companions. When recommending propriety to his brethren, our holy Father St. Francis says in his Rule: "I counsel, admonish, and exhort my brethren in our Lord Jesus Christ, that when they go out into the world they shall not dispute, or contend in words, or judge others: but let them be meek, peaceful, and modest, well-mannered and humble, speaking courteously to everyone, as is

---

3. Prov. 6:12-13.
4. *Mirror of Discipline,* Prologue, ii.
5. St. Bonaventure, *De sex al. Seraph.,* cap. III.

becoming."[6] He not only enjoined this propriety, but also observed it with his companions as carefully as possible. According to Thomas of Celano, this holy companionship abounded with "sweet conversation, modest laughter, pleasing appearance, guileless eyes, soothing speech, gentle replies, pleasant subjects of discourse, ready deference to others, and untiring help. The actions of Francis' brethren were disciplined, in accordance with the example of their Founder. Their every approach was unassuming. Their senses were so mortified that they scarcely allowed themselves to hear or see anything unless it commanded their attention. With their eyes cast to the ground, they fixed their minds on heaven. Hatred, malice, rancor, contradiction, suspicion and harshness had no place among them. Instead, there was much peace, continual calm, thanksgiving, and words of praise. These were the lessons with which our holy Father instructed his new sons, not only in word and discourse, but mostly in deed and in truth."[7]

Religious propriety is the ornament of other virtues. Religious modesty is of great importance as a sign of humility and charity. It is not only a virtue in itself, but lends particular charm to all other virtues and makes them all more attractive.

Affectation must be avoided. Religious modesty demands that we diligently refrain from all affectation in our words and actions. Excessive politeness, insistence on ceremony, uncalled-for compliments are annoying. Flattery and other acts of so-called politeness performed with an air of elegance; a fashionable veneer assumed by men of the world and particularly by effeminate youth, are all a source of disgust, even to seculars. So it is with the greatest care that we should follow the rules of religious propriety.

------

6. *Rule,* Chap. III.
7. Celano, *Legenda Prima,* cap. XV, pp. 41, 44.

POLITENESS AND COURTESY

84. Politeness and courtesy are phases, and not unimportant ones, of the virtue of charity. It has been pointed out that the finest rules for behavior are to be found in chapter 13 of the First Epistle to the Corinthians — in St. Paul's beautiful dissertation on charity.[1] The rules of politeness and courtesy are merely extensions, practical applications, of the practices extolled by St. Paul in that chapter. Those practices are, moreover, part of our imitation of St. Francis, the most knightly of the saints, who brought the flowering of chivalry to the service of religion and who exhorted his friars in the third chapter of the Rule to speak "courteously to everyone, as is becoming."

The practices and observances of polite and well-mannered people are no more innate in fallen human nature than are the other virtues. They must, then, be learned and practiced if one is to possess them. And the time for religious and seminarians to review them and thus reinforce that learning and practice is at the beginning of their religious life or during the first days in the seminary.

It might be well to recall, first of all, that good manners are not merely a veneer cast over a man, which he can put off and on at will, like the medieval coat of mail. To be pleasing and effective, good manners must become part of a man's makeup; they are not merely things to be done on certain occasions, but they are part of a way of life. To be sure, a good many of these practices are merely conventional, agreed upon by human beings living in society — though even on that score alone they are part of our condition as social beings. Yet a conventional

---

1. Cf. *Amy Vanderbilt's Complete Book of Etiquette* (New York, N. Y.: Doubleday, 1958), p. 140. The material in this chapter has been adapted from the Vanderbilt work, with the permission of the Doubleday Company.

that always stays in place, if such there be; hence, together with frequent combing and daily brushing, some kind of hair dressing is certainly in place for religious. But it must not be used so freely as to show; it should appear to be quite natural, and hair dressings with heavy odors should be avoided. Whatever hair dressing is chosen should be shampooed out at least once a week, if for no other reason than to wash out the unpleasant odors which the hair of even the cleanest person will pick up.

In common with the rest of men, some priests and religious perspire more heavily than others, and that fact must be borne in mind when one is considering the frequency of bathing. A daily shower or bath is not at all extravagant, and for some men may not be sufficient.

Finally, it is not a part of religious indifference, but merely of carelessness and perhaps even of laziness, to neglect chapped hands or lips, pimples and blackheads, stained teeth or dandruff.

86.

II. Table Manners

Table manners are the touchstone of good breeding, being at one and the same time an essential thing, and the hardest to put on for a momentary show. They need, then, to be studied and practiced constantly until they become second nature. Naturally, some informalities are permitted at meals in religious houses and seminaries; moreover, those things which are approved as customary in the community take precedence over the general rules of etiquette. Yet it is certainly both poor taste and contrary to charity to feel that one need not observe the niceties at table when eating among one's own. For one thing, the closer nature or grace brings us to certain people, the more delicate should be our consideration for their feelings and sensitivities; and secondly, if the priest or religious is to practice good manners with an unstudied ease when a guest in the homes of others, he must prepare himself by observing good manners in his own home.

At the same time, it must be remembered that courteous observance at table varies considerably with the formality of the meal. Therefore no absolute standards can be given that would be applicable in every case. Moreover, since this is such a broad topic, nothing approaching completeness can be attempted here; rather, a few principles will be given, the rest being left to books on etiquette.

(1) Guests begin eating only after several people have been served, although it is not necessary to wait until all have been served, lest the food be cold.

(2) The napkin is placed entirely in the lap, completely open or half open, depending on its size (only children tuck the napkin in). Guests do not pick up their napkins until the hostess has picked up hers.

(3) It is more acceptable at present to reach for things than to ask another to pass them, provided one can do so gracefully, and always without rising from his seat.

(4) If some silverware is lacking, the proper thing to do is simply to pause, without saying anything, until the hostess notices it.

(5) It is quite permissible now to convey food to the mouth with the fork held in the left hand, when one has, for instance, just cut a piece of meat — that is, without putting down the knife, picking up the fork with the right hand, and thus conveying the food to the mouth. But when so used (in the left hand), the tines of the fork are kept down, whereas they are always kept up when used with the right hand.

(6) No matter what the beverage, nothing is taken until the mouth is empty and has been wiped with the napkin, so as not to leave any kind of mark on the rim of the cup or glass.

The only exception is that a sip of water may be taken immediately if one has inadvertently put into his mouth food that is too hot.

(7) Tumblers are held near their base, small-stemmed glasses by the stem, and tall-stemmed glasses at the base of the bowl.

(8) Gravy (except that in which there are larger pieces of meat or fish, etc.) and liquid sauces (Worcestershire, etc.) are ladled only onto the meat, never on potatoes, rice, etc.; but if one wishes, one may dip the potatoes, with one's fork, into the gravy that has escaped from the meat. Horseradish, applesauce, relish, etc., are put on the side of the plate, and then eaten as desired, a bit being put on the fork together with the food it is intended for.

(9) A bit of bread may be used, when necessary, to push food onto a fork; or, if no bread is available, the knife may be used.

(10) It should not be necessary to mention that a whole slice of bread, or a whole roll, is never buttered all at once; instead, bite-size pieces are broken off with the fingers and buttered as needed. Nor is a whole serving of meat cut up at once: again, a bite-size piece is cut off as needed.

(11) If one wishes to butter his potatoes or vegetables, he takes the butter from the individual butter plate with the dinner fork; only bread is buttered with the butter knife.

(12) Any foreign matter which has been put into the mouth beyond one's intention is removed from the mouth with thumb and forefinger and placed on the side of the plate. If foreign matter is found in a dish, it is removed in the same way; the food need not be eaten, if one prefers not, but nothing is ever said about it. Simply pass that dish by unless the hostess offers to serve you another.

(13) Soup or dessert dishes may be tipped, but only away from, not toward, the eater.

(14) It is permitted to rest one's elbows on the table only between courses.

(15) Conversation and laughter at table must always be kept low and quiet. Guests never become so involved in a conversation with each other as to completely avoid their near neighbors or the hostess. If the table is narrow, guests talk across it, and when a partner on either side seems unoccupied, they draw him or her into the conversation as naturally as possible. Highly controversial subjects (religion and politics) or squeamish ones (illnesses, operations, etc.) are not discussed at table.

(16) How to eat various foods: This list is by no means complete; it includes only the more common dishes which might cause some difficulty.

Apples and pears: At table, they must always be peeled; or, if one wishes, they may first be quartered and then peeled. After a section has been cored, it is eaten either with the fingers or with a fork. Apples and pears are not bitten into, whole, at table.

Asparagus: May be eaten with the fingers, but it is preferable to use a fork, especially if eating the asparagus with the fingers is likely to be messy.

Bacon: If very crisp, eaten with the fingers; otherwise, with the fork.

Bananas: Peel them completely, then break them into small pieces as needed and eat with the fingers. Only at picnics may they be peeled half way and the lower half of the peel used as a holder.

Berries: Eaten with a spoon, except for strawberries served whole with the stems on; then they are grasped by the stem and eaten in one or two bites, the stem then placed on the side of the plate.

Celery and Olives: Taken from the serving plate with the fingers, and eaten with the fingers. Small stuffed olives are popped whole into the mouth; large ones are eaten in bites, and the stone is not cleaned in the mouth.

Chicken: Eaten with the fingers only at picnics. Bones are never put into the mouth at table. Joints may be cut at table only if it can be done gracefully.

Corn on the cob: Silver spears for handling the ear may be used, but it is perfectly acceptable to hold the cob directly with the fingers, even when the spears are provided. If the ear is long, it may be broken in half. Only a row or two is eaten at a time, and so only that much is buttered or salted at any given time.

Fish: Small fish bones which have been taken into the mouth are thoroughly cleaned in the mouth, and then removed with the thumb and forefinger and laid on the edge of the plate.

Fresh apricots, cherries and plums: Eaten in one or two bites, the stone cleaned in the mouth and then dropped into the cupped hand and placed on the side of the plate.

Fresh peaches: Halve them, then quarter them, pull off the skin from each segment, and eat them with a fork.

Grapes: Eaten one at a time. If you prefer not to eat the skins, clean them in the mouth (but don't chew them), drop them into the cupped hand together with the pits, and place them on the side of the plate. Or, if preferred, the inside of the grape may be popped into the mouth, if it can be done gracefully.

Oranges and tangerines: Peeled with a knife in a continuous spiral, then broken into segments, and eaten with the fingers, unless the segments are too large: then they are cut in half and eaten with a fork.

Pickles and radishes: Whole pickles, like radishes, are eaten with the fingers.

Pineapple: Eaten with a spoon if served cut up; if served in slices on plates, eaten with a fork.

Potatoes: Baked potatoes, if served already buttered, are held with the left hand and eaten from the skin with the fork; if served whole and uncut, they are broken apart with the fingers for buttering and seasoning, and eaten as above. The skin may be eaten, if you wish, after it is cut into small pieces (never cut up the whole skin at once). Potato chips are eaten with the fingers, French fried potatoes with a fork; shoestring potatoes also are eaten with a fork, unless they are very crisp, in which case they may be eaten with the fingers.

Stewed or preserved fruit: The pits or cores are dropped into the spoon and placed on the side of the plate.

Sandwiches: If small, they may be eaten with the fingers; otherwise, with a fork.

87.
III. Conduct for Various Social Occasions

(1) As a guest in the home of others, a priest or religious should remember that cigars are not smoked at table unless the host or hostess offers them, or at least unless permission is first obtained. It is also a matter of courtesy to ask for an ash tray which will be sufficiently large if none appears immediately available.

If a cigar is smoked in the living room, the butt should be put into the garbage can, if you are that familiar in that particular home; otherwise, run it under water, wrap it in paper and drop it into a waste basket. Such precautions need not be taken, however, if the ash trays are being emptied frequently.

Pipes should not be cleaned in another's home, except when one is alone; the discarded contents of the bowl and the used pipe cleaner should not be left in the ash tray but disposed of. Any loud sucking noises on the pipe must be avoided.

No one may smoke in a sickroom, unless the patient is smoking and has given his visitors permission to smoke.

Smoking is not acceptable in elevators, even though a "No Smoking" sign is not visible there; nor should one smoke in taxis or cars unless permission is first obtained from all the other occupants of the car. Used matches and cigarette or cigar butts are never ground out on the floor of the car. Also, one should never throw lighted or used matches or cigarettes or cigars out the window. An ash tray is usually available somewhere in the car.

(2) Upon being introduced to each other, men shake hands standing (no one ever shakes hands while seated). Nothing need be said, although some phrase such as, "It is nice to meet you" (never "charmed" or "delighted") is proper. The proper answer to "How do you do?" is simply "How do you do?"; and to "How are you?" an adequate reply is "Fine, and how are you?" ("How's yourself?" is both ungrammatical and unacceptable.) One never indulges in an actual exposé of one's feelings or state of health at such moments.

A man does not take the initiative in shaking hands with a woman; and a man is always presented to a lady, not vice versa, unless one is introducing her to a priest or religious or a civil dignitary.

(3) It is much more correct to be slow in using people's first names — all the more should priests and religious be careful in this, since they never permit others (except perhaps members of their own family) to use their first names. A man never calls a woman by her first name unless he has been asked to do so. Priests and religious who have a secretary address her as "Miss" or "Mrs." during office hours.

(4) If you cannot recall a person's name, try to cover up that fact with some pleasant generalities until the other gives a clue to his or her identity. One never presumes that he is

remembered by another; but whenever there is any doubt about whether one is remembered or not, he offers his name at once: "How do you do? I'm Father So-and-so; I met you . . . ," etc. It is absolutely boorish to pin another down with some statement such as: "You don't remember me, do you?"

(5) No one need answer a question which he feels is too personal (unless it is asked by one's own superior, of course); but the refusal to do so should be tactfully evasive, if possible. If no such tactful evasion presents itself to you, it is quite proper to say something like: "I'm sorry, but I consider that a very personal question which I am unwilling to answer."

(6) A man always rises when a woman enters the room, unless she is his secretary who has come in to take dictation, or an applicant for some such position. He ought also to rise for any priest, religious, or layman who is much older than himself. A man who introduces a woman to another also rises.

(7) One's hat is kept on in crowded elevators and the corridors of public buildings, but is removed when one enters the office of any woman. When merely approaching an information desk presided over by a woman, a man may simply touch the crown of his hat (not merely the brim unless he is wearing a stiff-brimmed "Panama") as if to remove it; it is neither necessary nor quite in place to remove the hat on such occasions. But if a man is greeting a woman on the street or elsewhere, he actually removes the hat, and keeps it off during the conversation unless the weather is bad, in which case he puts it back on without offering an apology.

(8) If it can be done without awkwardness, an inferior allows his superior to precede him from a room. But a woman is always allowed to go first.

(9) A man lights a woman's cigarette for her, even if he doesn't smoke himself. If he does smoke in a woman's presence,

he must offer her a cigarette first — and that each time he takes one himself, unless she tells him that she doesn't smoke.

(10) In answering the phone for another, one does not ask who is calling, unless an explanation is made first: "I'm sorry; Father So-and-so is very busy right now, but I can call him for you if you wish. May I ask who is calling?"

On the other hand, the person who calls someone else always announces himself as soon as the other person says "Hello."

(11) If a man gives up his seat in a bus or train, etc., to a woman, he never engages in conversation with her afterwards; instead, he stands as far away from her as conveniently possible, and looks in another direction.

(12) A man does not enter a room before a woman, unless the room is dark and he wishes to snap on the light for her. Nor does he seat himself while ladies are standing.

88.
IV. Importance of letter writing

The practice of letter writing is perhaps the one social duty which is most often neglected by priests and religious. That this is unfortunate goes without saying, for letter writing is not only socially graceful and at times necessary, but is also important for priestly and pastoral work. The letters written by a priest or religious should naturally be dignified and reserved, but nonetheless interesting for all of that. A letter is nothing else than conversation put into writing, and the remembrance of that simple fact can make letters a joy to receive and at least much less of a chore to write. As we enjoy conversation with our friends, so we ought also to enjoy writing to them — and we will if we go about it in the right spirit.

It is not at all out of place to talk about oneself in a friendly letter; in fact, for the most part, it is this alone that will make our letters interesting to our friends. News about common friends, our joys and hopes and little disappointments, all have a place in our friendly letters.

Business letters, obviously, are a must for priests and religious, on various occasions, and should be rigidly correct as to form. They are expected to be brief and to the point, and it should not be necessary to insist that all business letters of any degree of importance should be typed in duplicate and kept on file until the business discussed is concluded, or even longer, if it is at all probable that future reference will be made to this same business matter. It is a serious mistake for priests and religious, as for anyone else, to trust to their memories to such an extent as to send off a business letter of which they have no copy.

89.
V. Formalities of letter writing

Any gift, however small, deserves an acknowledgment or thank-you note, and that all the more from a priest or religious. Unfortunately, it is only too true that priests and religious are notoriously remiss in this important duty. Remember, too, that any overnight stay as a guest in another's home requires a letter of acknowledgment, or "bread and butter" note. If one has been a guest for part of a day, or for a meal, an oral thank-you upon leaving one's host or hostess is sufficient, unless some extraordinary trouble or expense has been gone to for one's comfort or entertainment.

Letters of condolence and letters of congratulation must always be written in longhand; other letters, even friendly and social ones, may be typed if one prefers, and should be typed if one's handwriting is not very legible. In particular, if a person's signature is illegible, it is a matter both of courtesy and prudence for him to type out his name below the handwritten signature; this is all the more important when one is writing a business letter.

A priest or religious should use only the conservative blue or black inks.

Social usage prefers that the return address be written or printed on the flap of the envelope, but post-office authorities prefer to have it on the front upper left corner of the envelope. If the return address is written in longhand, it should, of course, be written small enough to make it plainly distinguishable from the address of the intended recipient.

No commas or abbreviations are used on the envelope; i. e., no comma is placed at the end of a line, and enough lines are used to contain all the necessary information. Thus:

MR. DONALD BROOKS
   19278 HILAND AVENUE
     CHICAGO
      ILLINOIS

The word "Personal" may be marked on the outside of the envelope only when a letter is sent to someone at his office, and the sender has reason to believe that it may be opened by a secretary. To mark this on an envelope sent to a person's home is an insult to the rest of the family.

If you don't know a person's address, it is permissible to send the letter to his former address and mark the envelope "Please Forward."

The abbreviation "Messrs." is correctly used as the plural of "Mister" only when one is addressing brothers, never for a father and son or men who are not related at all.

If your stationery has no printed letterhead, your address should appear at the top of the letter, toward the right corner, unless you are very well known to the recipient of the letter. The date may be put either directly below the letterhead or the handwritten address, or at the end of the last page, after your signature. If you are writing to a close friend it is sufficient to put down the month and day; in all other letters, the full date should appear.

90.

VI. Letters to ecclesiastics: Correct forms of address

Obviously, this list cannot be complete; only the more important persons and the more common occasions are considered here. Futhermore, only the name and title of an ecclesiastic appear here; his actual address will have to be added to the form of address given here.

The Pope
> HIS HOLINESS THE POPE *or*
> HIS HOLINESS POPE JOHN XXIII
> VATICAN CITY
> ROME
> ITALY

Cardinals
> HIS EMINENCE FRANCIS CARDINAL SPELLMAN

Bishops and Archbishops
> THE MOST REVEREND JAMES STEVENS, D. D.

Abbots
> THE RIGHT REVEREND ABBOT JOHN J. FOSTER (the proper letters, designating his religious Order, are added)

Domestic Prelates
> THE RIGHT REVEREND MONSIGNOR ARNOLD JONES

Papal Chamberlains
> THE VERY REVEREND MONSIGNOR EUGENE SMITH

Secular Priest
> THE REVEREND JOHN SHELDON

Priest of a Religious Order

THE REVEREND CHARLES MALONEY (with the proper letters designating his Order or Congregation)

The Superior General of a Religious Order or Congregation

THE MOST REVEREND JOSEPH WILLIAMS (with the proper letters to designate his Order or Congregation)

The Provincial Superior of a Religious Order or Congregation

THE VERY REVEREND JOHN WILKINS (with the proper letters to designate his Order or Congregation)

Religious Brothers

THE VENERABLE BROTHER JUDE, *or simply*
BROTHER JUDE (in either case, add the proper letters to designate his Order or Congregation)

Religious Sisters

THE VENERABLE SISTER THEOPHANE, *or simply*
SISTER THEOPHANE (again, with the proper letters to designate her Order or Congregation)

A Rabbi

RABBI JOSHUA KLEIN (if he has a scholastic degree, the proper letters should be added)

Protestant Bishop

THE RIGHT REVEREND ANDREW GRAVES, D. D.

Protestant Clergyman

THE REVEREND STEPHEN LORD (if he has a scholastic degree, the proper letters should be added)

91.

VII. Civil dignitaries: correct forms of address

The President of the United States
THE PRESIDENT
THE WHITE HOUSE
WASHINGTON, D. C.

The Vice-President
THE VICE-PRESIDENT
UNITED STATES SENATE
WASHINGTON, D. C.

Cabinet Officers
THE HONORABLE ELY WILLIAMSON
SECRETARY OF THE INTERIOR
WASHINGTON, D. C.

Assistant Secretaries
THE HONORABLE GEORGE SMITH
ASSISTANT SECRETARY OF LABOR
WASHINGTON, D. C.

Chief Justice of the Supreme Court
THE CHIEF JUSTICE
THE SUPREME COURT
WASHINGTON, D. C.

Associate Justice
MR. JUSTICE O'ROURKE
THE SUPREME COURT
WASHINGTON, D. C.

Judges
THE HONORABLE JUDGE ALBERS
JUDGE OF HURON COURT

American Ambassador
>THE HONORABLE MARK SIMMONS
>AMERICAN AMBASSADOR
>LONDON
>ENGLAND

American Minister
>THE HONORABLE STUART KING
>AMERICAN MINISTER TO SWITZERLAND
>BERN
>SWITZERLAND

Foreign Ambassador
>HIS EXCELLENCY THE AMBASSADOR OF BRAZIL
>WASHINGTON, D. C.

Senators
>THE HONORABLE BRUCE GREGORY
>UNITED STATES SENATE
>WASHINGTON, D. C.

Speaker of the House of Representatives
>THE HONORABLE PETER QUEENS
>SPEAKER OF THE HOUSE OF REPRESENTATIVES
>WASHINGTON, D. C.

Representatives
>THE HONORABLE EDMUND HOHILAN
>HOUSE OF REPRESENTATIVES
>WASHINGTON, D. C.

Governors
>THE HONORABLE NORBERT KANE
>GOVERNOR OF VERMONT
>MONTPELIER, VERMONT

Mayors
>THE HONORABLE DAVID WHITNEY
>MAYOR OF PORTLAND
>OREGON

BOOK IV

The Fourth Reformation:
Reformation of the Interior of "the Old Man" through Internal Custody

92. Up to this point we have explained the reformation of the exterior of "the old man" in us. But without an internal spirit of truth, the practice of external virtue is nothing but hypocrisy and sham. Many fail in the pursuit of Christian perfection because their works are not guided by a spirit of truth.

We live among men imbued with false doctrine. We must examine ourselves all the more repeatedly to learn whether or not we are doing what is right. This requires a certain knowledge and watchfulness of the internal faculties.

The internal senses are twofold: sensitive and spiritual, as they pertain to the lower or higher faculties of man.

DIVISIONS

The following discussion is divided into two sections:

I. *The sensitive powers;*

II. *The spiritual powers.*

Section I

Custody of the Internal Sensitive Powers

The internal senses or powers of the sensitive faculties of man are either "cognitive" or "appetitive."

CHAPTER I

THE COGNITIVE SENSES OF THE LOWER FACULTIES OF MAN

93. The sensible cognitive powers in the lower faculties of man are designated by a single term, "perception," which also covers "imaginations" and "phantasms." Although the objects of the external senses — the objects seen, smelled, heard, tasted, and touched — are perceived also through different internal senses,[1] we designate their perception as one operation, whether the objects are present or not.

Difficulties in guarding the internal senses. No matter how well a man succeeds in combating the unruly invasions of the external senses, it is only with great difficulty that

---

1. There are four internal senses, according to Scholastic tradition:

(1) *The common sense.* All the external senses refer every sensation they receive to the common sense as to a sort of common receptacle or treasury. This, according to many authors, is not actually a distinct faculty.

(2) *The imagination.* The imagination is the power to form images or phantasms of perceived objects, and to reproduce these in the absence of the object.

(3) *The estimative sense.* The estimative sense in man is called the cognitive power. It distinguishes the sensate from the insensate; it compares and sets in order the material received, and collects ideas from phantasms. For instance, sheep obtain their idea of enmity from the image of a wolf, the notion of friendship from the phantasm of a dog.

(4) *Memory.* Memory is the power to recall past objects and states of consciousness, etc., and to recognize them as a part of former experiences.

he can counteract their effects on the internal senses. David complained about the prevalence of evil thoughts, saying, "They are more numerous than the hairs of my head, and my heart fails me."[2] And St. Gregory declares, "Our mind is fittingly called a tent in which we are hid when we are not seen at work. We must first relax the grip of iniquity and then cast injustice from our tent. For whoever wishes to cut himself off from external sin, must enter into himself and examine what ideas hold sway in his mind, lest the fault which he does not commit in deed should persist in his thoughts. Solomon says: 'Complete your outdoor tasks, and arrange your work in the field; afterward you can establish your house' (Prov. 24: 27)."[3]

Therefore we shall cover: (1) the causes of perverse and harmful thoughts; (2) their danger; (3) the suitable means of mortification.

Article I — Causes of Perverse and Harmful Thoughts

94. *First cause:* **Objects perceived by the external senses.**

Depraved and harmful thoughts or imaginations arise from what has been heard, seen, or perceived by the external senses. Images are left in our mind, and whatever is pleasing to the passions stubbornly clings. We are scarcely able to eradicate such things from our memory.

Second cause: **Sense appetites.** "Do you wish to know where your treasure is?" asks St. Lawrence Justinian. "Then discover what you love. Do you wish to know what you love? Then pay attention to your thoughts. In this way you recognize your treasure from your love and your love from the direction

---

2. Ps. 39:13.
3. St. Gregory, *Moralia*, Lib, X, cap. XV, in Migne, *P. L.*, t. LXXV, col. 935.

of your thoughts."[4] And St. Gregory: "What do we desire, if not what we seize actually or by thought? 'I made a covenant with my eyes,' declared Job, 'that I would not so much as think upon a virgin' [Job 31:1, Challoner-Douay version]. In order that his heart might remain chaste he made an agreement with his eyes, lest he should rashly look upon something which he might later love against his will."[5]

Third cause: **The instability of the human heart.** The alert man thinks constantly, and unless he diligently seeks good thoughts he is bound to have illicit and idle ones. "In the present life," says Cassian, "the mind is surrounded on every side by a torrent of temptations. Since it can hardly be free of waves of thought, which it must accept or prepare itself to meet, it should zealously and diligently provide for this encounter."[6]

Fourth cause: **The cunning of the devil.** When the devil is not able to wound with depraved and lewd thoughts, he tries at least to smite with vain and useless daydreams. Job warns: "His breath sets coals afire,"[7] because his instigation excites perverse thoughts and drives to impure desires.

Article II — Dangers from Perverse and Harmful Thoughts

95. There are three kinds of thoughts. The first are impure thoughts which are centered on the vices of the flesh. These soil the soul with detestable filth, and unless speedily ejected they will cause spiritual death. Secondly, there are idle, curious, useless thoughts, of practically no value. Thirdly, there are thoughts about necessary things, such as food and drink and the like — things absolutely requisite to sustain life.

---

4. St. Lawrence Justinian, *In ligno vitae,* Tract. de caritate, cap. IV.
5. *Moralia,* Lib. XXI, cap. II, in Migne, *P. L.,* t. LXXVI, col. 190.
6. Cassian, *Coll. I,* cap. XVIII, in Migne, *P. L.,* t. XLIX, col. 508.
7. Job 41:13.

Yet while these things are essential, there is often no need to think about them.

Dangers. To maintain purity of life, we should not only banish improper thoughts, but also avoid foolish thoughts. "We strait-jacket the insane lest they injure someone; in the same way we must also put a halter on our imagination lest it overwhelm our minds with false notions."[8] Thoughts are the fountains of words, desires, and deeds. The man who harbors harmful fantasies easily indulges in harmful desires, improper words, and evil deeds.

Harmful desires. An idle thought is the beginning of an evil or unsuitable desire, for we desire only what we have first contemplated.

Improper words. The Jews said of Jeremia: "Come, . . . let us destroy him by his own tongue; let us carefully note his every word."[9]

Evil deeds. Our Lord teaches that "Out of the heart come evil thoughts, murders, adulteries."[10] This is as if He had said that murder is first deliberated, then perpetrated.

Improper thoughts dissipate the powers of man and corrupt his spiritual life. What good can abide in us when improper thoughts fill our minds? They hinder divine praise, they impede devout prayers, they induce forgetfulness of heavenly things, they drag us down to earthly, worldly concerns. Hence the necessity of mortifying our thoughts.

Article III — Mortification of Perverse and Harmful Thoughts

96. If we desire perfection, we will constantly labor to restrain all corrupt thoughts and fantasies — to cut them off, as it were, with the knife of mortification. Both general and spe-

---

8. Cardinal Bona, *Manuductio,* cap. XII, n. 1.
9. Jer. 18:18.
10. Matt. 15:19.

cial means are available for this purpose — various kinds of blades for this "pruning."

§ I. General Means for Mortifying
Depraved and Harmful Fantasies

Petition for divine assistance. David credits God with being our ally in this war. He says, "Blessed be the Lord . . . , my shield in whom I trust, who subdues peoples under me."[11] And St. Gregory declares, "Men are best trained to holy thoughts when a strict severity banishes foolish ideas. Then they will not run along the uneven paths of fantasies, but will humbly find rest in a heart subject to reason."[12]

Resistance to the first assaults. "He is blessed," says St. Dorotheus, "who will not permit himself to harbor depraved or evil thoughts, nor yield ground to them in the beginning, enabling them to coalesce and to increase and in the end to wreak havoc."[13] "As long as man does his part," declares Blessed Roger, "by avoiding with all his might sinful and evil occasions, God will do His share and preserve him from evil. If you expose yourself to the danger of sinning in matters toward which man is most inclined on account of the corruption of his fallen nature, God may rightly leave you to your own strength. Without Him, you cannot resist temptation even for a moment."[14]

Opening one's heart to the spiritual director. John Climacus tells us that this was the practice in ancient Christian times, and we know that it was also the habit of most of the saints.

Reflection upon God. "See to it that you do not ponder in the presence of God what you would blush to say in the

---

11. Ps. 143:1-2.
12. St. Gregory, *Moralia,* Lib. XXVI, cap. LXVI, n. 84, in Migne, *P. L.,* t. LXXVI, col. 398.
13. St. Dorotheus, *Doctr.,* XI, in Migne, *P. G.,* t. LXXXVIII, col. 1739.
14. *Analecta Franciscana,* t. III, p. 384.

presence of an upright man. Your thoughts should be peaceful, simple, pure, and devoid of all malice. They should be such that if you were questioned about your thoughts unexpectedly, you could without shame admit what abides within your heart. We should be ashamed to think of what we would be ashamed to say."[15]

If harboring useless thoughts in the presence of men causes us to be abashed, how much more should we flee such thoughts in the presence of God, who sees everything in our mind. How often He is displeased by what His eyes behold within us!

Contemplation of proper objects. "During the time of rest from external labor," says Thomas a Kempis, "a psalm, a praise of God should at once arise in the heart and from the lips. The heart is not able to remain quiet nor the tongue silent for a long time. The heart conjures up thoughts — good or evil. It considers sorrows and ponders joys as a cloud formation set in motion by the wind. As a precaution against the sudden attack of evil, and a protection against its blows, you should sow holy words like heavenly grain in your heart; and diligently ruminating on them, convert them into food. If only you spoke good words as often as you speak idle ones! If only you thought and pondered on the good and the noble as much as you are concerned with the evil and the harmful! Open your heart to Christ! Close it to Satan! In this way your soul will be in heaven and not in the world. Christ speaks to you in every word of God and in every book written under the inspiration of the Holy Spirit. Whatever you read, whatever you understand, whatever you draw out of the Scriptures is a consolation to the faithful soul in the time of tribulation, a remedy against the poison of the devil. It also recalls the wandering mind to its God in heaven."[16]

---

15. Cardinal Bona, *Manuductio*, cap. XII, n. 2.
16. Thomas a Kempis, *Manuale parvulorum*, cap. VI.

§ II. Special Means of Mortification against Perverse and Harmful Thoughts

97. Against impure thoughts: **Remembrance of profession.** St. Bernard says: "In order that a rushing multitude of thoughts, which should be put out like a common rabble from a hall, may not force God from our memory, we should place the remembrance of our profession like an attendant at the door. And when we feel our soul weighed down with base thoughts, we should chide ourselves, saying: 'O priest, cleric, monk — remember what you are! Should a servant of God, a lover of Christ, think such things?' Thus the remembrance of our profession shuts off the flow of illicit thoughts."[17] In his answer to Brother Giles, Brother Juniper furnishes us with another efficacious means. Brother Giles had asked: "What do you do against temptations of the flesh?" Juniper replied, "When I perceive such diabolical suggestions, clamoring, as it were, in the castle of the flesh, I firmly close the portals of my heart without delay, and occupy the entire fortification of my heart with holy thoughts and with devout prayers for its secure protection. When these suggestions beat upon the gate of my heart in order to agitate me, I answer from behind the portal, which I always keep locked, saying, 'Stay out, for the guest chamber is occupied and you cannot also be quartered there'; and so I never permit them to enter. Then they, victims of complete rejection, leave me."[18]

Against fickle and harmful thoughts: **Invocation of Christ.** Against such thoughts, take as your battle cry: "Get thee behind me, Satan!" "O soldier of Christ," says Thomas a Kempis, "use these words against every evil phantasm of the devil. Your weapons are the holy words and works of Christ.

---

17. St. Bernard, *Sermo de triplici judicio,* Serm. 32, n. 4, in Migne, *P. L.,* t. CLXXXIII, col. 626.
18. *Analecta Franciscana,* t. III, p. 60.

Therefore, against the fiery darts of the flesh, weigh the wounds of Christ. Against weariness of heart, the sweet name of Jesus be always on your lips. Against all suspicion and disdain of others, balance all your own faults committed from the time of your birth to the present, and you will cease to be indignant."[19] Finally, against idle, curious, useless thoughts learn to reflect on the stupidity of frittering away the precious time allotted to you for knowing and loving God. Such empty daydreams are not only without any fruit of merit for eternity, but also are greatly detrimental to your spiritual welfare.

Against excessive thoughts about necessary things: **Recollection of Divine Providence.** Since God cares for you, there is no reason for anxiety about necessary things. The Lord says, "Seek first the kingdom of God and His justice, and all these things shall be given you besides."[20] If you practice virtue, you will never suffer want in necessary things, except in the form of a trial, which you will always have the grace to overcome.

---

19. Thomas a Kempis, *Manuale parvulorum,* cap. VI.
20. Matt. 6:33.

The Appetitive Senses of the Lower Faculties of Man

98. The movements of the lower part of the soul are called "passions." These we wish to examine (1) in general; (2) and in particular.

Article I — Passions in General

The objective of our study is to know: (1) the number of passions; (2) their morality; (3) the obligation of mortifying them.

§ I. The Number of Passions

99. In man, as in animals, there are two kinds of inclinations which move him in relation to sensible objects inasmuch as these objects are *pleasant* or *unpleasant*. The concupiscible appetite tends toward an object that is pleasant. *Love* is a yearning for what is good without regard to its presence or absence. *Desire* is a quest for *absent* good. *Joy* is the satisfaction arising from a *present* good. On the other hand, *hatred* is complete dislike of some evil; *flight* (or *aversion*) shuns an *absent* evil. *Sadness* grieves over *present* evil. The irascible appetite opposes an *unpleasant* sensible object; tends toward a pleasant object which cannot be attained without effort. When a good is *possible* although difficult of attainment, *hope* arises; when it appears *impossible, despair* results. In the question of a future evil, when we see a chance of overcoming it, *courage* appears. When an evil difficult to avoid is encountered, *fear* sets in. When a *present evil* incites the desire for revenge, *anger* flares up.

All the passions are stimulated by love. St. Augustine says, "Love, desiring to have what is loved, is cupidity; possessing and delighting in it, is joy; fleeing from it, is fear; feeling the loss of it, is sorrow."[1]

§ II. Morality of the Passions

100. **The passions in themselves are good.** All the passions are good in themselves if subjected to right reason and ordered to our final end. "Reason is sufficiently the master," says Cardinal Bona, "when it has curbed and moderated them. The Stoics who labeled every affection as evil were wrong. Affections are not evil nor are they so much useless furniture provided by nature. The loss of all these inner forces would mean the loss of all virtue. Where there are no contests, there are no victories."[2]

"The others who followed the word — what sort of persons are they? They were mortal creatures like you; subject to suffering, like you; bearing in themselves like you the conflict between the flesh and the spirit. Such was Paul, My Herald, such were the multitude of My saints, every one of whom, in one way or another, was impassioned."[3]

They may be dangerous. Since the fall of Adam, man is prone to evil, and he often uses the passions for doing wrong. When vehemently aroused, the passions, like a fog, obscure the light of reason. Therefore nothing is more harmful for the soul than to arouse the sense appetites by exciting the passions. If not curbed by penance and by the power of grace, the passions inflict grievous wounds on man and often leave him half dead, crushed under the blows of sin. Sadness wounds the soul by lessening spiritual fervor. Many similar examples could

---

1. *De civitate Dei,* Lib. XIV, cap. XII, in Migne, *P. L.,* t. XLI, col. 410.
2. Cardinal Bona, *Manuductio,* cap. XII, n. 3.
3. St. Catherine of Siena, *Dialogue,* Chap. VI.

be drawn from the sensitive inclinations. Hence the necessity
of mortifying the passions.

§ III. The Obligation of Mortifying the Passions

101. **The passions must be regulated.** From the preceding it can be concluded that the passions are not to be destroyed.
Rather, they are to be kept under control. At the first sign of
excess, they must be checked.

Control must start early. A little boy can pull up a small
shrub, but even a strong man cannot uproot a tree. St. Dorotheus says, "The same holds true for our passions. While they
are shallow and weak, we can uproot them easily. But if we
neglect them, they become obdurate, and the more obdurate
they become, the more effort and labor are required to overcome
them."[4]

Article II — The Passions in Particular

A. THE PASSIONS OF THE CONCUPISCIBLE APPETITE

§ I. Love

102. **The nature of love.** Love is the complacency of an
appetitive power in an agreeable good. Strictly speaking, love
differs from dilection and charity.

Love (amor) means complacency in an object loved, and
in this sense is common both to men and animals.

Dilection (dilectio) goes beyond love and adds free choice;
it can be present both in the good and in the wicked.

Charity (caritas) adds a certain perfection or divine infusion to dilection.

Love is a natural impulse. This appetite is naturally inclined to good. The human soul cannot exist without love;

---

4. St. Dorotheus, *Doctr., loc. cit.,* XI, in Migne *P. G.,* t. LXXXVIII, col.
1738.

it must love itself or something outside itself. Hence love is good in itself.

The morality of love. St. Augustine states, "What you love is not evil, nor is the fact that you love, evil; but because you love evilly, that is evil, and it is the whole evil."[5]

Therefore we must consider what we love. "Two cities fostered two loves: Jerusalem fostered the love of God, Babylon toyed with the love of the world. Let each one ask himself therefore, what he loves and determine of which city he is a citizen."[6]

The causes of love. There are various incentives to love. Often goodness and beauty impel people to love; similarity in habits, compatibility of spirit, external modesty, natural acumen, industry, belief, and other embellishments of body and soul may do the same. Various interior dispositions may make certain human beings more apt to love. "Jovial, warmhearted, vital people, and people who are mild and affable by nature are predisposed toward love."[7]

The effects of love. (1) Love is primarily the force which *unites* the lover with the beloved person or thing. Hence (2) the lover is always *thinking* of that person or thing. Therefore, if one thinks more of the world than of God, he loves the world more than God. (3) The lover also *defends* the rights of the beloved, removes what is harmful, and (4) makes great *sacrifices*. Where love abides, no sacrifice is too great, for, says St. Augustine, "Regarding the object of love, either there is no labor, or if there is, we love the labor."[8]

"O how unhappy the lover who does not love God," exclaims Cardinal Bona. "He who loves God is in God; ceasing

---

5. St. Augustine, *De substantia dilect.*, cap. II, in Migne, *P. L.*, t. XL, col. 845.

6. St. Augustine, *Super Psalm. 64*, n. 2, in Migne, *P. L.*, t. XXXVI, col. 773.

7. Cardinal Bona, *Manuductio*, cap. XIII, n. 2.

8. St. Augustine, *De bono viduitatis*, cap. XXI, in Migne, *P. L.*, t. XL, col. 448.

to live in himself, he lives in Him in whom all things live. Human love is often violent and bitter. Divine love is always humble and tranquil. Jealousy crucifies in human love; in divine love there is no rivalry. Human love fears that another may love; divine love wishes that all should love."[9] Hence we should seek as earnestly as we can for ways and means of directing our love away from earthly or dangerous objects and channeling all our love toward God.

Means of moderating love

First remedy. The first remedy for inordinate love is the removal *of human causes.* For example, we should remove certain images and affections from our eyes and our mind. We should seek only representations which are consonant with piety and sanctity. The good and the beautiful expand human affections, while the base and the reprehensible enkindle a perverse, ardent fire in the heart. "The chaste and gentle love permitted man is not attached to sensuality, but rather contemplates the eternal in transitory things."[10]

Second remedy. Some souls will find a remedy for inordinate love if they will take their eyes away from the apparently good qualities of the object of their love, so that they may discover also *the bad points,* the numerous physical evils with which it abounds. There is something destructive of beauty and loveliness in every creature. For instance, we know that death will destroy the beauty of the human body.

Third remedy. We should occupy the mind with other matters which call for our attention and divert our thoughts from the beloved object.

Fourth remedy. The fourth remedy for inordinate love is *flight.* We should depart from the beloved object, and if it is

---

9. Cardinal Bona, *loc. cit.,* n. 3.

10. Richard of St. Victor, *De grad. caritat.,* cap. III, in Migne, *P. L.,* t. CXCVI, col. 1202.

a person, avoid his company if possible, avoid conversing with him. Conversation strengthens an unbecoming friendship; separation and forgetfulness dissolve it. St. Chrysostom warns, "Do not retain instigators to evil as friends, tempters, who care more for your table than for your friendship. If you deprive them of the delights of your table, they will soon withdraw their friendship."[11]

Fifth remedy. We should consider the consequences of inordinate love. How many suspicions, jealousies, quarrels, dissensions and perplexed consciences have not resulted from perverted love! Let us remember particularly that immoderate love provokes God to wrath and that He pursues it with unspeakable anger.

Sixth remedy. This consists in directing our love toward *good and proper objects.* If we wish to be absolutely freed from the vices of depraved love, we must as far as we are able enkindle in ourselves the fire of divine love. If we choose the sweetness of divine love unreservedly, we will not care for temporal sweetness.

§ II. Hatred

103. **The nature of hatred.** Hatred is displeasure for what is considered repugnant and injurious. Just as a good thing is the object of love, so an evil thing is the object of hatred.

The morality of hatred. It is good to hate objects that are opposed to right reason and to the welfare of the soul. As St. Augustine says, "Love is perverted by hatred and hatred is turned to good by love";[12] again, "To perish, let a man love his own life; to live, let him hate it. If you hate well, then

---

11. St. Chrysostom, *Homil. XLIX super Matt.,* in Migne, *P. G.,* t. LVIII, col. 496.

12. *Serm. 368,* in Migne, *P. L.,* t. XXXIX, col. 1653.

you love. Happy are they who have preserved their life by hating it, lest they lose it by loving it."[13]

The causes of evil hatred. Evil, or rather the absence of good, is the cause of hatred, for hatred is caused by love. Since the good is loved, whatever blocks the attainment of the good is hated. Likewise, hatred frequently arises from anger, envy and other passions.

The ignorant, the fainthearted and the suspicious, fearing injury from almost every direction, easily fall prey to this passion. "If a person of this type opposes you," says Cardinal Bona, "do not hate him but treat him with pity."[14]

The effects of vicious hatred:

(1) *Estranging of souls.* "All nature is united in a bond of love," says the same author. "Love gathers and unites the galaxy of stars in the heavens, flocks of birds in the sky, droves of cattle in the fields, herds of goats on the mountains, packs of beasts in the forests. This noble bond is disrupted by hate alone, for as love tends toward union, so hatred tends toward disunion."[15]

(2) *Personal unhappiness.* The man who hates inflicts graver injuries upon himself than upon anyone else. "What reward is there for hatred," asks St. Jerome, "except the terrifying darkness of soul and the horror of a confused mind? Ever displaying a bitter countenance — the counterpart of an embittered soul — the hater torments himself with the very fury with which he hopes to injure another."[16]

(3) *The anger of God.* Lastly, he incurs the anger of God, as Blosius explains: "Although you fast much, constantly

---

13. St. Augustine, *Tract. 51 super Evang. Joan.,* cap. XII, in Migne, *P. L.,* t. **XXXV**, col. 1767.
14. *Manuductio,* cap. XIII, n. 5.
15. *Ibid.*
16. *Epist. I ad Demetr.,* in Migne, *P. L.,* t. **XXX**, col. 19.

go to church, and pray continuously, if you hate your brother you are not numbered among the children of God."[17]

Remedies for perverse hatred:

First remedy. Hatred is restrained by LOVE, inasmuch as love is its opposite. "Hatred stirs up disputes, but love covers all offenses,"[18] says Solomon.

Second remedy. Hatred is overcome by the search for the good qualities hiding in the hated person or object. These good qualities will make the person appear lovable.

Third remedy. If hatred is directed toward a fellow man, we must bear in mind that as long as this ill humor is voluntarily nourished we may not approach the sacraments. Nor can we recite the Lord's Prayer without deceit; for Christ plainly orders us to say, "And forgive us our trespasses AS WE FORGIVE those who trespass against us." Moreover, Scripture says, "Everyone who hates his brother is a murderer";[19] and "If anyone says, 'I love God,' and hates his brother, he is a liar."[20] The brother whom we hate is loved by God and destined for eternal glory.

Fourth remedy. There will be no room for hatred if we *put a good interpretation upon everything.* The mind, therefore, must be trained to think well of anyone whom we are tempted to dislike. We must praise him before others and honor him by signs of deference. Such considerations soften the heart of the one who hates, and show that his enemy is worthy of his love in some way. Consider the example of the saints who excelled in loving their enemies, and accordingly were far removed from the fault of hatred.

Fifth remedy. We must be careful not to become offensive, spiteful or bitter about the petty failings of others, but always

---

17. Blosius, *Canon vitae spir.*, cap. XXXI.
18. Prov. 10:12.
19. 1 John 3:15.
20. *Ibid.* 4:20.

to have a kind word for them. Let us do nothing which would stir up hatred, but rather perform little services and deeds which will silently promote mutual friendship. Let us administer the twofold medicine prescribed by Christ, the great Physician of souls: "Love your enemies, *do good* to those who hate you, and *pray for* those who persecute and calumniate you."[21] For this is sublime virtue: to overcome hatred by kindness. This is the height of pure dilection: to repay hatred with love.

Sixth remedy. Finally, hatred must be directed toward the object which deserves to be hated: sin. "In order to excite and obtain a perfect hatred of sin, consider in detail *the sufferings of Christ,* as if He endured all these pains for no other reason than that through them He might stir up and produce in you a hatred for all your sins, and move you to eliminate your inordinate tendencies and affections."[22] We must realize, however, that only the wrong in evil deeds must be hated; the subject who committed them must be loved.

§ III. Desire

104. **The nature of desire.** Desire is a quest for some future good not yet attained, or a longing for things which are absent.

The morality of desire. There are good and evil desires. "We may be lifted up to God by a good desire, while an evil one may cast us headlong into hell,"[23] says St. Augustine. Holy desires spur us on toward a Christian life. Evil desires drag us down into the muck of sin.

Causes of evil desires. There are three outstanding causes of evil desires: wealth, pleasure and honors; uncontrolled de-

---

21. Matt. 5:44.
22. Scupoli, *Pugna spirit.,* cap. XXVII.
23. St. Augustine, *Super Psalm. 122,* in Migne, *P. L.,* t. XXXVII, col. 1629.

sires are kindled by wealth, immoral desires by pleasure, vain desires by honors. How many are the yearnings that torture the hearts of men! Some covet gold, others silver; some hanker for money, others set their hearts on the mirage of elusive honors. Everyone has his goal, his pet ambition. Some form of desire burns in every human heart.

Effects of evil desires. As a result of evil and useless desires, the mind becomes unstable and restless. In its attempt to grasp what it desires, the mind never rests and is literally driven around in circles. What a continual headache! What a perennial misery!

Moderation of desires. The remedies prescribed for moderating perverted love should also be used against evil desires.

First remedy. We should consider that the coveted object, even when attained, cannot satisfy us. We shall be as poor and as restless as before. Let us have the courage to check the multitude of desires within us. St. Francis de Sales says that a great variety of food, particularly when eaten in great quantity, always burdens the stomach; and if the stomach is weak, such excess causes sickness. We should not fill our soul with too many desires, whether worldly or spiritual. It is clear that worldly desires corrupt, and the greater the number of desires the greater the corruption. But what is not so apparent, yet nonetheless true, is that even too many spiritual desires may impede our progress and result in anxiety. Once our soul is cleansed, it ardently longs for what is divine and spiritual, and seeks to give itself to all kinds of pious exercises, such as prayer, fraternal charity, mortification, humiliations, etc. Such longing is an excellent sign of progress; but we must first ask ourselves whether we can digest everything we wish to "eat." Therefore let us seek the advice of our spiritual director and select with his help from among our desires those which can be prudently satisfied.

Second remedy. We should not desire anything dangerous to the soul, such as dignities, offices, human favors; for great peril, vanity and deception lie hidden under the surface of these things. Once we attain our goal, we shall soon despise such goods. For they will heap annoyances upon us and overwhelm us with a thousand difficulties. Before long we shall wish to be free and to turn to other desires, other activities. And yet soon we shall take the same view of these new "toys"; yearning until we attain them, then rejecting them and acquiring a longing for something else. Some form of imperfection will be found in all such objectives. It is better, therefore, to dismiss all desire for a harmful thing and to condemn it from the start than to throw it away after having obtained it. The wheel of desire allows no rest to those who are unable to stop it.

Third remedy. We should use moderation even in our desire for lawful things. A religious who does not seek more than nature requires will never suffer from a lack of necessities. But one who lives immoderately will be in want even when he has everything he needs. "For a few things suffice nature, while nothing can satiate cupidity."[24] Therefore let us not desire absent or future goods; too many people are wearied and tormented and finally lose heart unnecessarily because of their desire for impossible delights.

Fourth remedy. We should analyze our desires, lest perhaps the deceitful serpent is hiding himself under the mask of devotion. For this reason St. Francis de Sales says, "I can in no way counsel or approve of the man who, having devoted himself to some office or state, wishes to take up another kind of life over and above what is suitable to his condition and talents, or wishes to observe practices which are incompatible with his present state and duties. If I [already confirmed in my voca-

---

24. Cardinal Bona, *Manuductio,* cap. XIV, 3.

tion] desire the solitude of the Carthusians, I am wasting my time; if, while I am sick, I wish to undertake the exercises of the healthy, I foster useless desires which I allow to usurp the place of better ones, such as the desire to be as patient, resigned, mortified, gentle and obedient in pain and trouble as I can be."[25]

Let us not wish for heavier crosses until we have learned to bear patiently those we presently have to carry. It would also be rash to desire temptations. In our imagination we fight with monsters, but in reality, through our lack of attention, we are often felled by a little serpent on our path.

Fifth remedy. The most efficacious remedy is complete submission to the divine will. "My son, say this on every occasion: 'Lord, if it be pleasing to Thee, so let it be. Lord, if it be Thy honor, let this be done in Thy Name. Lord, if Thou dost see that this is expedient and dost approve it as profitable for me, then grant that I may use it to Thy honor. But if Thou knowest that it will be harmful to me and not profitable for the salvation of my soul, take away from me such a desire.' "[26] If we diligently examine each desire, we will be surprised at how quickly we will learn to cast out the worthless.

§ IV. Flight or Aversion

105. The nature of aversion. Aversion is the passion which makes us recoil from evil. The morality of aversion and its causes and effects are the same as those of hatred.

The curbing of aversion. The remedies for aversion consist in checking our repugnance, curbing our desires to avoid and abhor many things which must not be avoided or abhorred: for many things which we flee and detest are really useful for us.

---

25. St. Francis de Sales, *Introduction to a Devout Life*, Part III, Chap. XXXVII.

26. *Imitation of Christ*, Book III, Chap. XV.

(1) Whatever hurts us but teaches us a lesson is first among the remedies for aversion. Death, poverty, ignominy, sickness, and similar experiences beyond our control are not really evils but circumstances which can be turned to our advantage. If we drink bitter medicine which brings health to the body, why do we not also accept bitter occurrences which bring health to the soul?

(2) Oftentimes the patient bearing of something bitter results in its becoming sweet by the very acceptance of it. Things which at first were harsh and disagreeable to the body seem sweet once we have accustomed ourselves to them. Our Seraphic Father writes in his *Testament:* "For whilst I was in sin, it seemed to me too bitter a thing to see lepers, but the Lord Himself led me amongst them and I showed compassion to them. And when I left them, what before seemed bitter was changed into sweetness of soul and body."

(3) We cannot observe the precepts of the divine law unless we meet with some difficulty; for as gold is tried by fire, so the virtue of man is tested by the trials of life. Hence we should say with the royal Psalmist, "For the sake of the words of Thy lips, I have kept hard ways."[27]

(4) Those who endure adversities will reap a rich reward. For "we are . . . heirs indeed of God and joint heirs with Christ, provided, however, we suffer with Him, that we may also be glorified with Him."[28]

§ V. Delights and Joy

106. **Nature of delight and joy.** Delight or delectation is a complacency of the soul in the possession of some good which it loves. Strictly speaking, delight differs from joy in that joy has its origin in the rational appetite, while the origin

---

27. Ps. 16:4, Challoner-Douay version.
28. Rom. 8:17.

of delectation is in the carnal appetite. However, not much attention is paid to this distinction.

Morality of delight. We cannot live without love, delight, joy and pleasure. This is a postulate of our very nature. Therefore, delightful things are not evil in themselves, nor per se can they divert us from our final end. There is, however, a vast difference between spiritual and corporal delight, as we shall presently discover.

CAUSES AND EFFECTS OF DELIGHT. *Sensual men* (1) delight in sumptuous foods which, when taken too liberally, cause headaches and stomach-aches, bring on incurable diseases, and can lead to decay. (2) They enjoy wealth and fine clothing; yet in the end, death will strip them of all these things which even now give them nothing but care, worry, fear and anxiety. (3) They delight in the misty aura of renown, the smoke of ephemeral glory and human favor, which is nothing but empty vanity, a breath of wind, and pure hypocrisy!

Spiritual men, however, delight in the Lord. For He is their food which refreshes without satiety and satisfies without disgust. He is their strong, delectable, savory food. "Taste and see how good the Lord is."[29] This food cannot be purchased with money. It will not make us ill. It will not distend our spirit with self-esteem. On the contrary, it enriches the mind, cures the disease of sin, lifts the oppressed, and satisfies the needy.

Curbing of delight. Taking delight in harmful or useless things is as vain as feeding on empty husks, for it fails to glorify God. Such delectation should be completely avoided. For whether it results in mortal or venial sin, in every case it is an obstacle to the pursuit of virtue.

(1) We must, then, make a firm resolution to stay away from such things. For since Jesus Christ turned away from

---

29. Ps. 33:9.

Causes. Adversities and their attendant evils engender a natural sorrow and sadness in the soul, and unless these latter are checked they will overwhelm it or cause it to become indignant and to seek vengeance.

The well-founded causes of sorrow are our sins and vices in which we become so involved that we can seldom contemplate heavenly things or even obey any spiritual impulses.

Effects. In his *Introduction to the Devout Life* St. Francis de Sales teaches us the effects of sadness. Only two good effects are produced: pity, which is sorrow over the evil in another; and remorse, which is sorrow because of evil in ourselves. But, he says, there are six harmful effects: anxiety, hatred, indignation, jealousy, envy and impatience.

Sirach has written: "Drive away sadness far from thee. For sadness hath killed many and there is no profit in it."[39] Because of this harmful sadness, the soul becomes troubled and restless, suffers from inordinate fears, loses its taste for prayer, and the mind is benumbed and oppressed. Have we not all seen sad, harsh, melancholy men wearing sullen, gloomy looks as if they were enveloped in a fog? The affliction is even greater when the sorrow lies undisclosed in the human heart. "Sorrow," says St. Bernard, "deliberates very little, is unashamed, does not consult reason, fears not the loss of dignity, disobeys the law, refuses to accept judgment, and is ignorant of custom and order."[40]

Moderation of sadness. It is apparent from the foregoing that we must reject all harmful sadness. We can accomplish this in the following manner:

(1) Drive away all worldly sadness with spiritual joy, for a spirit of joy makes life flourish, whereas a spirit of sad-

---

39. Ecclus. 30:24-25, Challoner-Douay version.
40. St. Bernard, *Epist. I ad Robertum*, n. 1, in Migne, *P. L.*, t. CLXXXII, col. 169.

ness dries up the bones. Joy of heart is man's support. A sad person always offends and grieves the Holy Spirit within him. Of all evil dispositions, worldly sadness is certainly the worst and most harmful to the servants of God. "Sadness lies in the heart like a tortuous serpent in foul water."[41] Worldly sadness injures, bruises, wounds the servants of God. The Holy Spirit does not encourage such sadness. Listen to the words of our holy Father St. Francis: "The devil rejoices most when he can rob the servant of God of joy of spirit. Satan's game is won when the heart is opened ever so little to allow him to inject a speck of dust with which to tarnish candor of mind and purity of life. But as long as the heart is filled with spiritual joy, the infernal serpent endeavors in vain to instill his deadly poison. The devils cannot harm the servant of Christ when they behold him filled with holy joy. But when the soul is in ill-humor, if discouraged and desolate, it easily becomes a prey to complete unhappiness or turns to vain pleasures."[42] Therefore, at all times let us retain spiritual joy which finds grace before God. Spiritual joy of every kind is good, inspires wholesome thoughts, and banishes futile sadness. The Psalmist declares: "The just man is glad in the Lord, and takes refuge in Him; in Him glory all the upright of heart."[43]

(2) Sadness which is according to the will of God promotes salutary repentance. We should cultivate it but temper it with spiritual joy. They are wise indeed whose sadness is according to the will of God, since to them our Lord says in the Gospel: "Rejoice rather in this, that your names are written in heaven."[44] St. Paul also counsels us to be "sorrowful yet always rejoicing";[45] and again, "Rejoice in the Lord always;

---

41. *Mirror of Discipline,* Part I, Chap. II, 3.
42. Celano, *Legenda Secunda,* cap. LXXXVIII, p. 265.
43. Ps. 63:11.
44. Luke 10:20.
45. 2 Cor. 6:10.

again I say, rejoice."[46] And it is this beneficial spiritual sorrow of which the Beatitudes speak: "Blessed are they who mourn: for they shall be comforted."[47]

But, as a contemporary of St. Bernard advises, we must be guided by moderation. "Mourn at the thought of your sins and rejoice in the love of Jesus Christ, your Spouse. Weep at the memory of your past offenses and exult in the hope of heavenly bliss. Grieve over your faults and negligences and delight in the promise of the heavenly kingdom. Be saddened by your past misdeeds and be cheerful in the hope of the eternal reward."[48]

(3) Reason itself teaches us the advantages of avoiding baneful sadness. For the tribulations that afflict us are part and parcel of our human lot — the cup that others as well as we must drink. We should try to imitate those who patiently endure and earn a great reward for themselves, rather than those who, through their impatience, fail to reap any profit. Finally, let us keep in mind the fact that hugging sadness to our heart in no way removes or mitigates the cause of sorrow, but only increases it. Locking sorrow in our heart and throwing away the key is no remedy; a balm will be found in hope and equanimity.

(4) After mature deliberation, we should engage ourselves in external good works, particularly in those which have no relation to our sorrow and which divert our minds from it. We should perform these external labors with fervor, even when all taste for them is lacking.

(5) There is also the most excellent remedy so frequently recommended by the Holy Spirit — prayer. "Is any one of you sad?" He asks through St. James. Then, "Let him pray."[49]

---

46. Phil. 4:4.
47. Matt. 5:5.
48. *De modo bene vivendi,* cap. XI, in Migne, *P. L.,* t. CLXXXIV, col. 1220.
49. James 5:13.

Prayer is the most effective remedy for those burdened with anxieties; it lifts the soul to God, our only joy and consolation. But in our prayer we must be careful to form affections and words which inspire us with love and confidence in God. "Our holy Father St. Francis," says Thomas of Celano, "took the greatest care to avoid sadness and quickly turned to prayer when it threatened to becloud the joyous ardor of his soul. He was accustomed to say: 'If a servant of God, as may easily happen, is sad for any reason, he must turn to prayer immediately and tarry before the face of the most high Father until He restores His salutary joyfulness.' "[50]

(6) Lastly, we must place ourselves in God's hands and adapt ourselves with patience to any annoying and wearisome sorrow. We should also bear it as a just punishment for our vain pleasures. But we must never doubt that God, after He has tried us for a time, will deliver us from this evil.

We shall never be sad if we live well and piously. A good life is a joyful life. Let us often recall the words of our Seraphic Father to the sad brother: "It behooves not a servant of God to show himself sad and ill-humored before men; he should, on the contrary, always be of good cheer. If thou hast sinned, go, and examine thyself in thy cell and weep over thy sin before God. But when thou returnest to thy brothers, put aside thy sadness and be cheerful as are the others."[51]

B. THE PASSIONS OF THE IRASCIBLE APPETITE

108. The affections or passions residing in the irascible appetite expose us to equally grave dangers and require the same important means of control as the passions residing in the concupiscible appetite.

---

50. Celano, *Legenda Secunda,* cap. LXXXVIII, p. 265.
51. Celano, *loc. cit.,* cap. XCI.

§ I. Hope

Nature. Hope is the appetite which bears us toward a thing loved, whose acquisition seems possible though difficult.

Morality. If the object is good, although difficult to attain, and we strive to obtain it by lawful means, together with guidance and prudence, this hope is good. Righteous hope rests on God, evil hope on what is false.

Causes. We are aroused to hope by various causes, among which love and experience are outstanding.

Love. No one begins to hope for anything, no matter how beautiful or desirable it appears, as long as his love for it is weak or altogether lacking.

Experience. Experience builds up hope because it increases confidence. For instance, if we know by experience that a certain priest is a kindly confessor, we will go to him with greater confidence.

Effects. Anxiety and sadness are the usual consequences of worldly hope. For we cannot possibly have peace as long as we place our trust in men. We are easily made sad as long as we hope for the things of this world. Celestial hope, on the contrary, strengthens us and frees us from tribulation, elevates and refreshes our minds. The farmer living in the hope of the harvest scarcely minds his labors; so the soul rejoicing in hope thinks little of the sufferings of this life. Such hope overcomes vain fears, banishes worldly consolations, and raises our thoughts toward heavenly delights.

Moderation. Whoever sets his hope on perishable things is building on flowing water. Man often trusts that he can achieve harmful, vain and impious objectives and undertakes great labors in order to acquire pleasure and honor; but his hope is founded on a very weak and frail base — like the house resting on sand. He builds walls of mud instead of marble, so that the slightest wind can blow them down. If a thief should steal his riches, what will happen to the hope of the avaricious man? And if the ambitious man should ever lose the favor of another through some true or even false suspicion, how will his hope survive? We must not expect any of our desires to be fully realized, for death is ever ready to destroy the walls of clay. Other means of regulating this passion will be studied in the sections on the virtue of hope. For the present, we must learn to turn our hearts toward the things of heaven and strive to obtain them, expelling all inordinate hope.

§ II. Despair

109. Nature. Despair is a withdrawing of the irascible appetite from a good judged impossible of attainment.

Morality. "Despair is twofold," says Cardinal Hugo, "both good and evil. Through the former we lose faith in the friendship of this world; through the latter we lose faith in the mercy of God. The first separates us from the world, the second from God."[52]

Causes. Slothfulness, despondency, excessive fear of difficulties, depression over personal vices, and the lack of diligence and moral stamina are all causes of despair.

Effects. Nothing is more disastrous than despair, for one affected by it loses all constancy in fortitude, and abandons hope, the anchor of his soul. "For despair prevents the rising of those who have fallen and causes the fall of those who stand."[53]

Moderation. If we despair of the very things we should hope for, the door is opened to a multitude of evils. We must be confident of forgiveness of our sins, of perseverance in our chosen state of life, of victory over temptations, of alleviation

---

52. Cardinal Hugo, *Super Job,* cap. VII, in t. I, p. 407, col. 3.
53. St. John Chrysostom, *Homil. VI, De poenit.,* in Migne, *P. G.,* t. XLIX, col. 314.

from our trials and of help for attaining perfection. If we are infected with despair in any of these matters, we need to be healed. The following remedies are suggested:

(1) We should remember the divine liberality. When tried by overwhelming misfortune and calamity, let us consider that we are men formed by God's hands, endowed with reason and intelligence, with which we contemplate Him and all created things, and that without doubt our soul will be encouraged and consolation will return. God Himself has prepared for us a crown of glory, an everlasting kingdom and a paradise of delights. Even more! The Son of God valued us so highly that He preferred to lose His own life rather than our soul.

(2) We should consider the divine mercy. "I take no pleasure in the death of the wicked man, but rather in the wicked man's conversion, that he may live."[54] And again, "Though your sins be like scarlet, they may become as white as snow."[55] Consider the lesson taught by souls who might well have despaired of divine mercy because of very grievous sins, but who were finally cleansed by penance and attained eternal salvation. "Although we are of the earth," reads an ancient Christian work, "and although we walk upon the earth, yet our conversation is in heaven. Although you are a sinner, do not despair. Many worldly men have become heavenly and many heavenly men have become worldly. The unfortunate Judas was a heavenly man, and became worldly. St. Paul, when he persecuted the Church, was of the world; he confessed, and became heavenly. The man intent on heaven should not feel too secure; nor should the worldling despair of attaining eternal life."[56]

---

54. Ezech. 33:11.
55. Isa. 1:18.
56. *Super Psalm. 133*, in Migne, *P. L.*, t. XXVI, col. 1300 (erroneously attributed to St. Jerome).

(3) We should consider the divine power. This power, together with His boundless love, God lavishes on us in the form of countless, superabundant aids in all our undertakings, our trials, our necessities. A worried friar once asked Blessed Giles: "What shall I do if I commit sin and become sad and despair?" "You will do well," answered Giles, "if you are saddened by sin, but moderate your sorrow, remembering that God's power to forgive is greater than your ability to sin."[57]

(4) Devotion to the Blessed Virgin Mary is another remedy for despair, as Father James of Milan teaches. "Fly to His mother, the refuge of sinners, if it seems that Christ is angry with you because of your sins. If you honor her as the Mother of God, contritely and perseveringly asking her aid, never ceasing or doubting, you will receive the grace you ask through her."[58]

(5) The same author offers the best remedy to those who despair of being saved and feel that perhaps they are not predestined for heaven. "If any thought of predestination or of the foreknowledge of God troubles your mind, answer such promptings of the devil in the following manner: 'Whatever my lot, yours is certainly that of the damned. Even if I foresaw my loss of God in the next life, I would strive with all my strength to possess Him as much as I can in this life, lest I should be deprived of so great a good both here and hereafter. Even if my future life is to be one of eternal misery, I shall not lose a moment of time for the rest of my life; but, inasmuch as I can, I will enjoy Him totally and always rejoice in that supreme pleasure. . . . Regardless of my future lot, I will never desist from the service of God. Woe to you, because you cannot serve so great a Lord nor enjoy His sweet presence.' "[59]

---

57. Quoted in *Analecta Franciscana,* Chron. Gen., XXIV, p. 94.
58. Fr. James of Milan, *Stimulus amoris* (Quaracchi, 1905), p. 30.
59. *Ibid.,* pp. 15, 18.

(6) Finally, in despair, as in other temptations, we must consult a spiritual director. In his treatise on spiritual direction the Carthusian Guigo wrote: "There are three that a monk should have in his cell: God, his conscience, and his spiritual director."[60]

§ III. Fear

110. **Nature.** Fear is a movement of the irascible appetite which makes us shrink from a future evil difficult to avoid. Cardinal Hugo divides this passion into six types:

(1) Sluggishness, or fear of work, unwillingness to make strenuous efforts;

(2) Apprehension, or fear of disgrace in the performance of an act;

(3) Shame, or fear of disgrace for an act already perpetrated;

(4) Alarm, or fear of an imagined evil when the means of avoiding it is not seen;

(5) Anxiety, or fear aroused by habitually imagining ills;

(6) Agonizing fear, or fear aroused by the realization of a suddenly impending evil which is difficult to avoid.

Morality. Fear, good in itself, becomes vicious when we have so great a dread of worldly or other apparent temporal evils, that we omit some duty, forsake some worthy project, or commit some sin. Salutary fear can also deteriorate and become a vicious trepidation when we are too fearful of real evils or when we are frightened by things we should not fear.

Causes. All fear has its beginning in love, since no one is afraid to lose what he does not love. Thus love and fear have

---

60. *Epist. ad fratres de Monte Dei,* I, cap. IX, n. 27, in Migne, *P. L.,* t. CLXXXIV, col. 325.

a common origin. Lack of courage is another cause of fear, since weakness disposes us to fear.

Effects. By curbing our fear we become more courageous in resisting evil. Concerning the effects of fear of the Lord, St. John Chrysostom writes: "Where there is fear, there will be zeal for almsgiving and attentiveness to prayer, fervent and continuous tears and sighs of contrition. The fear of God corrects evil-doers, protects against sin, preserves innocence and gives continuous strength. No thief, robber, or evil-doer would dare to go near a house guarded at all times by an armed soldier; if our soul were equally well guarded by fear, no unwarranted disturbance could easily enter it, but would rather flee and be repelled and even banished by the command of fear."[61]

Moderation. Harmful fear must be restrained.

(1) The first and most universal remedy is a good conscience. Our Seraphic Father once said to his companion, who feared the opinion of men: "Unburden your conscience and fear God more than men."[62]

(2) We can more forcefully deal with fear when we think of those valiant souls who in similar circumstances remained undaunted, and did not surrender their virtue to a threatening evil. . . . Stephen prayed to God with a peaceful mind while he was being stoned; Lawrence rejoiced in the midst of the flames and scoffed at his persecutors; inspired by God, the virgin Apollonia threw herself without hesitation on the burning funeral pyre prepared for her.

(3) We should consider the objects we fear as devoid of real evil, or at least as not being as evil as we imagine. Car-

---

61. St. John Chrysostom, *Homil. XV ad Pop. Antioch.*, in Migne, *P. G.*, t. XLIX, col. 154.

62. Celano, *Legenda Secunda*, cap. IV, p. 192.

dinal Bona expresses this when he says: "Brush aside your own personal explanation for the evils which befall you and accept the common causes. Admit that you have a frail, mortal body, subject to many diseases and, at length, to death. Say to yourself: 'For a long time I have known that many adversities threaten me; why should I fear them now? Am I to be sick? Sickness of body will be good for the health of my soul. Shall I be reduced to poverty? Then greater security will be mine, and life will be more peaceful. Shall I lose my wealth? All its many cares and endless dangers will vanish with it. Shall I suffer disgrace? If it is deserved, I will deplore the cause; if undeserved, my conscience will be consoled. Will something I hoped for be denied me? Neither are all the wants of kings satisfied. Will exile be my lot? I shall go willingly and make it a journey, a pilgrimage. Shall I become blind? My path will be freed of many hurtful desires. Are men to speak evil of me? Then they will act as they always do and according to my deserts. Shall I die? I entered life upon the condition that I should leave it. But shall I die away from my monastery? No place on earth is foreign to one who has not here a lasting city. Shall I die before my time? No one, except an insane man, complains if he is unshackled and freed from prison before his time. Death, exile and sorrows must not be feared as punishments but should be looked upon as the lot of our mortality. It is foolish to fear things you cannot avoid."[63]

(4) It will be well to remember that what we fear will perhaps never occur. As Scripture says, "There have they trembled for fear, where there was no fear."[64] Even if some great harm is to befall us, there is no sense in torturing ourselves with the thought of it before it happens. "Sufficient for the day is its own trouble"[65]

---

63. *Manuductio,* cap. XVII, 3.
64. Ps. 13:5, Challoner-Douay version.
65. Matt. 6:34.

(5) We must by all means curb our fear in regard to sins committed in the past. The Chronicle records that after hearing the words of Scripture, "Be not without fear about sin forgiven,"[66] Brother Christopher became troubled about the sins he had committed in the world. But a holy friar, learned in the ways of heaven, reassured him: "Rather than fear because of what has been committed, we should persevere in the good we have undertaken."[67] For it is one thing to fear because we have sinned and another to fear lest we sin again. The former is dread of the penalty, the latter, fear of offending God.

(6) The most efficacious remedy for fear is true charity; for by charity we love God and are convinced that God loves us. The Psalmist says: "They who trust in the Lord are like Mount Sion, which is immovable; which forever stands."[68] "The Lord is my light and my salvation; whom should I fear?"[69]

§ IV. Courage

111. **Nature.** Courage is a movement of the irascible appetite which overcomes an imminent danger. There is a difference between courage and fear; fear shrinks from some future evil, while courage challenges it with hope of victory.

Morality. Courage is good in itself, but it is vitiated when we attempt something forbidden or contrary to the divine will; or when, of our own free will and without any just cause, we undertake what is seriously dangerous or what evidently is beyond our abilities.

Causes. Anything that increases and sustains hope supports courage. For instance, valor is augmented by the physical or

---

66. Ecclus. 5:5, Challoner-Douay version.
67. *Analecta Franciscana,* t. III, Life of Brother Christopher, p. 162.
68. Ps. 124:1.
69. *Ibid.* 26:1.

moral excellence of a person. Defects such as ignorance may incidentally or indirectly cause actions which appear to be courageous.

Effects. The effect of virtuous courage is perseverance in the service of God, in spite of great dangers or obstacles. Brash, uncontrolled courage, although it is quick and fierce in the beginning, frequently collapses and often leads to despair.

Moderation. (1) Audacity or boldness in evil-doing is checked by the justice of God. For almighty God severely punishes those who transgress His commandments and many a time forcibly resists all their attempts to work iniquity.

(2) In difficulties beyond our own power, courage should be tempered by humility and discretion. "When the Holy Spirit forms the dispositions of the upright," St. Gregory writes, "He makes them at certain times courageous, at other times fearful. He instills courage into them, to give them confidence. He inspires them with fear, so that they will not become proud. And so He urges them to beg for necessities and deters them from excessive presumption, lest they develop the vice of temerity."[70]

§ V. Anger

112. **Nature.** Anger is a movement of the irascible appetite toward revenge. Anger differs from hatred. For hatred wishes evil on another in so far as he is evil; but anger breathes forth enmity for reasons of vengeance. There is a distinction between anger and irascibility. Anger arises from some present provocation; irascibility, or a disposition to be easily incensed, is a natural defect, a deeply ingrained, abiding fault. There is also a difference between anger and fury: anger is prolonged indignation, fury is a sudden eruption of ire, like an explosion.

---

70. St. Gregory, *In I Reg.*, Lib. IV, cap. IV, n. 26, in Migne, *P. L.*, t. LXXIX, col. 253.

Morality. There is one kind of anger induced by impatience, and another prompted by zeal for justice; the former is born of vice, the latter of virtue. It is of this latter that the Psalmist speaks when he says: "Be ye angry and sin not."[71] "But when the soul is moved by zeal," says St. Gregory, "the greatest caution must be taken that the same anger used as an instrument of virtue does not become master of the mind and dominate it like a lord. For even just anger must always remain the handmaid of zeal; it should never leave the feet of reason. For, though anger may arise from zeal for what is right, once control over it is lost, it overcomes the mind, and disdains to serve reason any longer. And the more it regards impatience as no vice but rather as something good, even something virtuous, so much more imprudently it gives itself rein to plunge forward into a host of evils."[72] Our task, then, is to become angered not at ourselves but at our sins, not at our neighbors, but at their wrongdoings. "Pursue justice," says St. Augustine, "that you may hate only vices, and love all men."[73]

Causes. All the causes of anger can be reduced to contempt and insult. When these are inflicted on man or his friends and relatives, they incite anger.

Effects. The most pernicious effects flow from uncontrolled anger: "Under the stimulus of anger, the heart throbs rapidly, the body trembles, the face reddens, the eyes become wild, the tongue entangles itself, and friends are no more recognized. The mouth produces a bellowing outcry, but what the shouting means the wrathful person himself hardly knows."[74] St. Augustine writes: "From anger proceeds rancor; from rancor, hate, which is wrath long brewing in the mind; of this is born

---

71. Ps. 4:5, Challoner-Douay version.
72. St. Gregory, *Moralia,* Lib. V, cap. XLV, n. 83, in Migne, *P. L.,* t. LXXV, col. 727.
73. *Serm. 49,* cap. VII, in Migne, *P. L.,* t. XXXVIII, col. 324.
74. St. Gregory, *loc. cit.,* in Migne, *P. L.,* t. LXXIX, col. 724.

murder, if not in deed, at least in desire; then insult, detraction, suspicion and injury, all works of the flesh and of the devil. . . . Ire stifles reason, unbalances justice, darkens the sun of sanctity, loosens the bonds of friendship, drives away peace, tramples wisdom underfoot, makes fools of the wise, works ruin among monastics, dissolves chastity, tears to shreds the dignity of pastors,"[75] and does great harm to the body.

Moderation. Since anger can wreak such havoc, let us consider the words of St. Francis de Sales: "Simply and without exception: Never become angry if this is possible for you, nor open the gates of wrath under any pretext. . . . However, I do not deny that you must constantly and steadfastly resist all evil, and decisively reprove the vices of those entrusted to your care; but this should be done pleasantly and lovingly. . . . As long as reason gently reigns, its corrections and reproofs, though as firm as ever, are nevertheless applied with kindness. Everyone likes and approves such a procedure. But when anger, passion, bitterness, ill-humor . . . are mustered as its soldiers by reason, then it makes itself terrible — dreadful rather than appealing. 'It is more advantageous,' as St. Augustine affirms,' . . . to refuse access even to anger that is just and reasonable than to permit it entrance, no matter how small a dose of ire it may be.' "[76] Here are some suggestions:

(1) Whenever we begin to feel angry and are conscious of it, we must promptly gather together again all our inner strength, not violently and impetuously, but gently and earnestly.

(2) After applying this gentle violence, we should implore the aid of God as the Apostles did when they were tossed in the midst of the sea by the tempest and the winds, and cried out: "Lord, save us! We are perishing!"[77] And He

---

75. *Serm. 9 ad Fratres in Eremo,* in Migne, *P. L.,* t. LX., col. 1251.
76. *Introduction to a Devout Life,* Part III, Chap. VIII.
77. Matt. 8:25.

will order our passions to be still, and soon there shall settle over our soul a great calm.

(3) After we have stemmed our wrath for a time, we should strive to repair the damage by an act of meekness; the best remedy for anger is to erase it as quickly as possible by a contrary act of benignity. As the old saying goes, it is easier to heal a fresh wound than one long neglected.

(4) Once we are well calmed and have no further occasion to become angry, it would be advisable to keep watch over ourselves in regard to meekness and kindness.

(5) It will help us to know that it is only human to be disturbed and to become angry, and that wrath is common to both the good and the bad. For this reason we must never despair over our sins of anger. "To become angry is human," says St. Jerome; "to do no injury is Christian."[78] But to persist in anger is diabolical. We read of Blessed Giles: "When he tarried in a place (Setone), he built himself a cell in a garden where there grew many fine heads of cabbage. While he stood there with his staff in his hand, saying a Pater Noster, a certain Brother, perhaps to test him, approached with a large sword and began to slash the cabbage heads, chopping them to pieces. As soon as Brother Giles saw this, he ran to him shouting, seized him and threw him out of the garden. His confrere said to Giles, 'Brother Giles, where is your patience and your sanctity?' When he caught his breath, Giles answered, 'My Brother, forgive me, for you came upon me so suddenly. I was unarmed and could not defend myself on such short notice.'"[79]

(6) Perhaps the best remedy of all is to imagine, before we get into serious trouble, all the insults we could possibly

---

78. St. Jerome, *Epist. 12 ad Anton.*, in Migne, *P. L.*, t. XXII, col. 346.
79. *Analecta Franciscana*, Chron. Gen., t. III, pp. 108-109.

suffer and, united in thought to the infamy of the Saviour, be prepared to meet any adversity. This was the practice of our Seraphic Father. Let us remember what he said about the conditions for perfect joy.

(7) Here is one last remedy. When we see the excesses of others, let us remember the sins we have committed in like circumstances. Recognizing our own weakness, we will soon learn to excuse the faults of others.

Section II

Custody of the Internal Spiritual Senses

113. The training of the interior man consists not only in the correct and pious use of the sensitive powers, but especially in the correct use of our spiritual faculties. The senses or faculties implanted in man's higher nature are the intellect (Chapter I) and the will (Chapter II).

CHAPTER I

CUSTODY OF THE INTELLECT

Article I — General Nature of the Intellect

A. **Nature of the intellect.** The intellect is that power of the soul which apprehends and forms immaterial and intelligible ideas or notions. By the light of intelligence the human soul perceives not only colors, tastes and other sensations that affect the bodily senses, but also arrives at a knowledge of their underlying substance; and in general, it comes to the knowledge of beings in both their individual and their universal qualities. Through the intellect, the soul knows not only the present, but is also able to make conjectures about the future; it can transcend the heavens and penetrate the abysses; from causes it arrives at effects; from the effects it searches the causes. It has even the power to touch upon the nature and existence of God through the things He made, as the Doctor of the Gentiles testified in his letter to the Romans: " . . . what may be known about God is manifest to them. For God has manifested it to them. For since the creation of the world, His invisible attributes are clearly seen — His everlasting power also and divinity — being understood through the things that are made."[1]

B. **Excellence of the intellect.** Nothing can excel the intellect. It is the spouse of most exalted truth, and the union of truth with intellect begets the noble offspring of good thoughts. Led by this benign light, the soul understands what it must do and what it must avoid. By this power man is likened to God, and is set apart from every type of mere animal.

C. **Function of the intellect.** This faculty has a twofold function. In the first place it explores truth, which is the work of the speculative intellect. Secondly, it decides what should be done and what should be omitted, and this is the work of the practical intellect (or practical judgment).

D. **Morality of the intellect.** The sin of Adam weakened and decreased the power of our intellect while impairing the perfection of our will.

Ever since the loss of preternatural knowledge, ignorance or blindness has been the main defect of our intellect. As a result man errs in his notion of truth, and is often unable to discern what he or his neighbor should do or avoid. The intellect requires three kinds of knowledge.

THE THREEFOLD KNOWLEDGE NEEDED BY THE INTELLECT

(1) The first is a knowledge of God and of the wonderful works He uses to guide and govern us.

(2) The second is a knowledge of ourselves, of the evil tendencies and defects which man experiences in his nature, and the benefits he receives from His Creator or which are superadded by grace.

---

1. Rom. 1:19-20.

(3) The third is the mastering of such science of the spiritual life as leads us to a more perfect knowledge of God and ourselves. These three kinds of knowledge contain the perfection of the Christian and religious life and are the root of all good affections and deeds.

PROOF THAT CHRISTIAN PERFECTION RESTS ON THIS THREE-FOLD KNOWLEDGE OF THE INTELLECT. We can draw a comparison between this threefold knowledge and the ladder of Jacob. Its lowest part, near which the Patriarch rested on the ground, is knowledge of ourselves; this leads to humility, contempt and a holy hatred of self — the foundation of the spiritual edifice. The upper part of the ladder, reaching into the heavens to the throne of God, is knowledge of God through faith; this generates hope and charity, the peak of perfection. The intermediary rungs are the knowledge of other things which advance the knowledge of God and of self. First of all, we must strive to obtain the twofold knowledge of God and self. St. Augustine begs God for this: "Noverim te, noverim me — that I might know Thee, and know myself!" With these words he begins to build the heavenly Jerusalem, whose citizens are all the just. But what a shame! Often men learned in natural sciences are ignorant of these three important branches of knowledge. How different was our Seraphic Father! On one occasion, while St. Francis was explaining the words of a prophecy, a holy man and doctor of sacred theology of the Order of Preachers declared: "My brethren, the theology of this man, drawn from purity and contemplation, soars aloft like an eagle, while our science crawls upon the ground on its belly."[2] It will be good to examine the causes of this ignorance.

E. The causes of ignorance in the intellect. Negligence. We are often too lazy to advance in the knowledge proper to

---

2. Celano, *Legenda Secunda,* cap. LXIX, p. 248.

our state in life. We do not learn what we should, and hence we remain ignorant.

Curiosity. A common failing is to use our desire for knowledge in studies that are without utility. Such pursuits are useless if they are unprofitable for the service of God, of no avail to our fellow men, or fruitless in regard to our vocational state. To study superfluous matters is not harmful in itself, but it can be injurious if in doing so we waste some of the time allotted for necessary things.

F. **The effects of ignorance.** This ignorance brings heavy damage to the soul.

(1) Ignorance of self and of God gives rise to inordinate self-love, lack of confidence, and contempt of God. These are the "hands" that build the city of Babylon, wherein reign error and indecision, wavering doctrines and inability to reach the only Truth.

(2) These evils are the forerunners of even worse consequences: "Man lives in truth when reason governs the pursuits of the soul and the spirit of God influences him. But if man is subjected to the tyrannical rule of voluptuousness, his soul slips from truth to vanity; he is goaded by emotions which are as fickle and changeable as weather vanes: now by fear, now by intense longing; sometimes by anxiety, again by vain joy; at times by sorrow over some loss, at other times by the craving for some worldly good; now tormented by an injury suffered, now consumed with desire for revenge. Thus vanity and voluptuousness are the sources of all the evils which vex the tortured soul."[3]

(3) St. Bernard writes that those who follow their own judgment "are wreckers of unity, enemies of peace, destitute of charity, swelled with pride, pleasing to themselves, and

---

3. Cardinal Bona, *Princip. vitae christ.,* Part II, § 1.

great in their own eyes."[4] The author of *The Spiritual Combat* enlarges on this when he writes: "These men totter on the brink of grave danger and are rescued only with difficulty; for pride of intellect is far more dangerous than pride of the will. One who has become proud only as regards his will does not cease to obey at some time or other, because he prefers the judgment of others to his own, and considers them more mature. But if one is intellectually proud and insists that his opinions are better than those of anyone else, who will be able to convince him of his wrong?"[5]

Article II — Regulating the Speculative Intellect

114. (1) We should learn what is necessary and useful. A threefold knowledge is a definite necessity for everyone. We should therefore devote ourselves to it and cast aside all vain curiosity. We should reject all desire to please men, all ambition to shine in the spotlight of fleeting human glory. We must learn what is profitable to ourselves and how to become proficient in whatever pleases God. We are to study and to understand how to serve our neighbor, how to improve our own life.

We should, it is true, master the natural sciences required for the study of theology. But any religious spending much or almost all his free time in reading profane poets and authors deserves serious blame. The works of such writers are often useless, frivolous and dangerous, and make a man worldly rather than Christian. Some religious, neither truly spiritual nor wholeheartedly consecrated to God, will not heed this admonition and will perhaps even ridicule it. We ask them to judge, in the light of their conscience, in view of their lost taste for spiritual things, and with the wisdom of experience,

---

4. St. Bernard, *Serm. 3 Paschae*, n. 4, in Migne, *P. L.*, t. CLXXXIII, col. 290.

5. Scupoli, *Pugna spirit.*, cap. IV.

how much these frivolous pursuits have cooled their devotion, how often fruitless reflections have distracted them during times of prayer.

(2) **We should learn what is useful in a proper manner.** By a proper manner we mean by applying our intellect correctly, moderately, and in an orderly way to advantageous learning.

Correctly. We instruct our intellect correctly when we seek truth for some good purpose, such as the glory of God, the salvation of our fellow man, or the perfecting of our own soul. "We should cautiously guard against taking pleasure or esteeming any project without first examining our motives and praying to God for light to know truly whether these projects are good or bad. We should do this not only in regard to profane undertakings but even in regard to pious matters. Devout works, good in themselves, may prove unsuitable on account of circumstances of time or place, or because of their great number, or because of our vow of obedience. Thus it happens that otherwise good and praiseworthy labors are often the cause of shipwreck for many."[6]

Moderately. We seek knowledge moderately when we try to restrain our mind from undue curiosity. "Show yourself humble and discreet, even while investigating heavenly things: and desire to know nothing other than Christ crucified; let your chief book be His life and death."[7]

In an orderly way. We learn in an orderly way when we pursue knowledge as a means to an end, and not as the end in itself, not as the goal of virtue. Our scholarship is orderly when we divide our time with discretion between study and work, and do not infringe on the hours reserved for divine worship and prayer. St. Augustine writes: "Knowledge should be used like a machine, to erect the structure of charity, which

6. Scupoli, *loc. cit.*
7. *Ibid.*

will remain forever, even when knowledge is destroyed. With charity as its end, the use of knowledge is most practical; but knowledge in itself, without any such purpose, is not only superfluous, but even pernicious."[8]

(3) **We should restrain the deviations of the mind.** In the following paragraphs, intellectual deviations are considered from the moral aspect.

(a) *Teaching others without first acquiring the requisite doctrine.* St. Ambrose says: "We must learn before we speak. Train your ears to catch the counsels of the wise. The tongue must be held in check, the ears keen to hear."[9] This truth concerns all who are inexperienced in spiritual matters and who, for that reason, cannot know how to direct others toward higher things. If such ignorant persons would restrain themselves and listen to others before they speak, or would direct to wiser counselors those who consult them, they would not thrust so many stumbling-blocks into the way of their hearers.

(b) *Neglecting oneself and foolishly bothering about the affairs of others.* This detestable vice arises from a vicious forgetfulness of self. Pomerius says, "As long as a person is too inquisitive about the affairs of others, he will remain ignorant of his own sins which he should know and bewail. But let him turn his eyes on himself, let him earnestly examine his own conduct, and he will find much to regret and deplore, and he will not go about seeking what he may discover that is particularly blameworthy in others."[10] And St. Gregory writes: "A well-directed mind takes notice of what it owes to itself and to its neighbors; it does not neglect its own pursuits by becoming immoderately solicitous about others' affairs, nor

---

8. St. Augustine, *Epist. 55,* cap. XXII, n. 39, in Migne, *P. L.,* t. XXXIII, col. 223.
9. St. Ambrose, *Liber de Noe,* cap. XXXI, in Migne, *P. L.,* t. XIV, col. 434.
10. Pomerius, *De vita contemplativa,* cap. VI, in Migne, *P. L.,* t. LIX, col. 450.

does it give less consideration to others by becoming too vigilant about its own good."[11]

CONCLUSION: *We should search for knowledge by praying and meditating.* It remains for us to seek knowledge also by praying and meditating. For we can often solve problems or penetrate hidden truths more easily, more completely, by prayer than by lengthy investigation.

Article III — Moderation of the Practical Intellect or Judgment

115. As we have already seen, the intellect is called the practical intellect, or judgment, from its proper act of discerning and judging what is to be done in a given instance. This judgment can be either true or false. It is true if it is in accord with the nature of the thing it judges, or with what should take place in a certain action; and false if it perceives and judges some object or action other than it really is.

A judgment is called personal if it is not conformable to the judgment of God or of wise men; it is singularly our own inasmuch as it differs from the definition and opinion of others. This personal judgment must be mortified by the following remedies.

(1) **Elimination of false ideas.** "A wise man," according to Cardinal Bona, "is one who weighs matters for himself and evaluates things as they are, and not as they are spoken of or appraised by others. There seem to be two sides or faces to some things; one genuine, the other painted, simulated. The true face is conformed to the divine decrees and to the ideas that exist in the mind of God; the masked face is molded according to the notions and sentiments of men, fashioned by the depraved prescriptions of self-love."[12] Let us judge things as they really are and not as they rank in the opinion of men.[13]

---

11. St. Gregory, *Moralia,* Lib. II, cap. XLVIII, in Migne, *P. L.,* t. LXXV, col. 591.
12. Cardinal Bona, *Princip. vitae christ.* Pars I, § XXXV.
13. Cardinal Bona, *loc. cit.*

(2) **Avoidance of erroneous opinions.** As soon as we are able correctly to evaluate creatures, we will find it easy to reject erroneous judgments and false opinions. Judgment exercises its tyranny over men in various remarkable ways. Is it not this judicial power that makes man happy or miserable by his own choice? For no one is happy and secure unless he judges himself to be happy and secure. Aman, for example, held the first place in the kingdom of Assuerus. He possessed boundless wealth and innumerable honors, and yet in his own opinion — that is to say, in his own judgment — he was most unhappy. For he considered himself as having nothing if it should happen that even one of the captives failed to rise in his honor when he entered the palace. All treasures and dignities in the world, even if personally awarded us, will not be sufficient to content us unless in our own judgment we consider ourselves content. The saints of God and the adherents of the devil are sometimes subject to the same unhappy lot in the world; yet the saints glorify God, the minions of Satan blaspheme Him. Whence does such great divergence arise if not from their judgment? While the saints see human miseries as opportunities for acquiring merit, the followers of the devil see nothing in them but the black cloud of undeserved punishments. Man can never entirely avoid erroneous judgments, for he is prone to color things according to his own lights, to interpret things differently from what they actually are. It is certainly diabolical to love our own opinions too dearly, or to despise better ideas because they are presented by others. However, it only belongs to angelic perfection to interpret all things faultlessly. Let us acquire the habit of asking the Father of lights to flood our intellect with the true light of His grace. For judgment is correct only in the degree in which it is made clear by true light.

(3) **Renunciation of personal judgment.** If we really seek the truth, we will not refuse to mortify our own private

judgment. We must be careful not to rely on our own judgment and our own prudence, for they depend upon the sensible and outward appearances of things. We could easily be deceived and the death of our soul would probably be the result. We should renounce our personal judgment in the following instances:

(a) *In whatever pertains to doctrine.* The word of no man is certain, but only the word of Truth. However, if we put our trust in truly probable opinions or prefer one opinion to another, on the strength of the basic laws of reasoning, we do not commit the fault of clinging to our own personal judgment. But it is a vice to insist that an opinion is true without any solid reason, particularly when truly wise men teach that it is false.

(b) *In whatever is approved by the whole Order.* "What pride can be greater," asks St. Bernard, "than for one man to prefer his own judgment to that of an entire congregation, as if he alone had the spirit of God?"[14] Cassian writes: "The Fathers of the desert would say to a newcomer: 'If, as we believe, you are inclined to emulate our ideals for love of God, then, after you have decidedly renounced all the practices which hindered your initial efforts, in all humility imitate the actions and traditions of your elders. Be of firm purpose. Neither retreat nor deviate from that imitation, even if the reason for some works or practices is not clear. Full knowledge, acquired by experience and effort, will reward those who, instead of engaging in destructive criticism, faithfully strive with a well-directed and simple outlook, to imitate whatever traditions or conduct they see manifested in their elders.' "[15]

(c) *In our manner of acting in religious life.* The path followed by all good religious of the Order will be safe and

---

14. St. Bernard, *Serm. 3 Paschae, loc. cit.*
15. Cassian, *Collat. XVIII,* cap. III, in Migne, *P. L.,* t. LXIX, col. 1092.

pleasant for us; but dangerous and sad is the road if it is one selected by ourselves; the tendency to this latter is called singularity. We should take good care to lead our spiritual life according to the instructions of our superiors. He who disdains to be the disciple of another man will himself turn out to be a teacher of error. He who makes himself his own teacher becomes the disciple of a fool. Never listen to those who prick your ears with clever language, who seek novelties, who are avid destroyers of traditions, who speak only of what pleases the senses. They are serpents, transforming themselves into angels of light. Follow, instead, the teachings on which the saints of the Seraphic Order were fed: the doctrine of the Gospel, the Rule and the Constitutions handed down to us by our superiors, who were pious and learned men in the Order. Concerning such doctors of the law, the Lord, speaking through Jeremia, says, "I will appoint over you shepherds after My own heart, who will shepherd you wisely and prudently."[16] And when Paul asked Christ, "Lord, what wilt Thou have me do?" the Lord said, "Arise and go into the city, and it will be told thee what thou must do."[17] God feeds our superiors, our superiors feed the minds of the religious, and the religious rule their senses and appetites through the doctrine they receive from their legitimate instructors. If the fervent aspire to the most severe austerities, to immoderate labors and unbearable burdens, and on the other hand the lukewarm shrink from every hardship and cast away every burden, the spiritual director will advise against the indiscretion of the former and rouse the indolence of the latter; by docility toward their superiors, religious will escape all harm, even the great obstacles to spiritual progress. We should, therefore, not hand over the reins to our own judgment but submit to the counsels and opinions of our superiors.

16. Jer. 3:15.
17. Acts 9:6.

CHAPTER II

CUSTODY OF THE WILL

Article I — Nature of the Will in General

116. Nature of the will. The will is the rational appetite or free agent by which we strive for intellectually perceived good and shun intellectually perceived evil. This rational appetite enables the soul to pursue not only present, particular, corporal goods, such as brute animals also seek; it empowers man to aim at the attainment of unseen, spiritual goods, known through faith or reason, and, above all, to the highest, the infinite good — God Himself. Moreover, this faculty endows man with a capacity for great virtues, especially charity, queen of all virtues. The will, with its freedom of choice, is of eminent nobility and surpassing excellence: it is high above and worlds away from the rest of mere visible creation.

The will is prone to evil. But through the sin of our first parents, the freedom of the human will has been weakened and is easily inclined to choose what is evil or harmful. Our will is indeed free to will or not to will, free to be willing or unwilling. But in this simple determination, as well as in other matters, it is not always strong enough to carry out what it wills and to prevent what it does not will. Listen to the complaint of the Apostle in his Epistle to the Romans: "For it is not what I wish that I do, but what I hate that I do."[1] Is there any of us who at times does not feel the same way? We may wish to pray attentively, and we command our imagination not to wander about; but before long we find ourselves tricked by our imagination. Thoughts of other things insinuate themselves. The spirit, in truth, battles against the flesh, and the flesh against the spirit. A more bitter, more ruthless, more

---

1. Rom. 7:15.

interminable warfare can hardly be imagined. Here is a struggle in which will is so opposed to passion and passion to will
that the final victory of either is impossible until the end of
life; neither foe yields any ground; both wait for a chance
to strike.

The will governs the entire man. The will always holds
sway over all man's powers, and everything we learn about the
necessity and manner of purifying our external and internal
senses pertains in some way to the volitional faculty. The will
resembles a royal horseman giving orders to the other faculties
and directing them to their end, as St. Ambrose explains. The
horse is our body with its appetites; the horseman rules the
flesh and its impulses and curbs them with guiding reins.
But this royal equestrian stands in need of an adviser, since
he also must be governed by something higher: the divine
laws. His adviser, as we have seen, is the intellect. The understanding does not use for itself alone the intellectual treasures
it receives. It places these impressions before the will. Thus
the will and its lower faculties can reach a happy conclusion
in determining some project or course of action.

The cause of defects in the will. Although the will governs the senses, the causes of all defects of the will are re-
ducible to these same sensitive powers. For all our knowledge
begins with the senses, which are called the portals or windows
of the soul — by which all images and species of sensible
things enter. From these perceptions the mill of the intellect
grinds out its judgments and reasonings. If the senses are not
guarded and well-directed, the will goes astray.

A depraved will is the cause of all evils. A perverse will
changed good angels into devils. Later, many demons, who
once had been just and holy, became reprobates and were
damned solely by reason of their evil wills. St. Anthony of
Padua says: "An evil will is a bad tree: its root is cupidity;

its trunk, obstinacy; its branches, perverted works; its leaves, vain words; and its fruit, eternal death."[2]

Control of the will. The will must not be allowed too much liberty. In his Rule, our Seraphic Father mentions the obligation of controlling our will: "But the brethren, who are subjects, shall remember that for love of God they have renounced their own wills."[3]

Devout religious have always heeded this admonition of our holy Father. It is said of Friar William of Esseby that "When Friar Gregory, the Minister General in France, asked him if he wished to go to England, he answered that he did not know if he wished to go. When the Minister General wondered at such a response, Friar William replied that the reason he did not know what he wished was that his will was not his own, but the Minister's."[4] Do not overestimate the value of the days you have spent here in mere physical renouncement of the world; consider yourself as having lived well on that day only in which you denied yourself your own will, for you passed that day without any transgression of the Rule.

For the will to correct and to set itself in order, it must, with the help of God's grace, subject itself to the divine will, and then courageously resist all evil desires. More will be said concerning the subjection of our will to the will of God when we discuss the virtue and vow of obedience. But here we must consider the will in so far as it subjects sensuality to right reason.

---

2. St. Anthony of Padua, *Serm. 8 post Trinit.*
3. *Rule,* Chap. X.
4. *Analecta Franciscana,* t. I, p. 218.

Article II — Self-love

§ I. Self-love in General

117. **Concept.** Love in a rational creature is an affection of the soul by which a person wills what is good for himself or for others. But by self-love a person wishes good for himself and flees anything adverse to his own good; in other words, he looks to himself as the end of all his actions. This love of self is not the natural love with which we are commanded to love our neighbors as ourselves and of which the Apostle speaks: "For no one ever hated his own flesh."[5] It is a corrupt love, nurtured by our fallen nature: an egocentric love by which we strive for our own advantage only, without any consideration of the divine glory or other honorable purposes.

Perversity of this self-love. To love ourselves as our own end is, by its very nature, an inordinate, depraved, culpable thing. For man is created, not for himself but for God: "The Lord has made everything for His own ends."[6] The proper way to seek created goods, therefore, is to seek them not for ourselves but for God, who is their end and the end of all things. St. Augustine says that love of God builds a heavenly city in proportion to our contempt of self, and love of self builds, in proportion to our contempt for God, an earthly city over which the devil rules. For since God has commanded that all things be referred to Him, whoever looks only to himself or to his own advantage, certainly directs none of his works to the acquisition of eternal life. The Doctor of the Gentiles says, "We are debtors, not to the flesh, that we should live according to the flesh."[7]

---

5. Eph. 5:29.
6. Prov. 16:4.
7. Rom. 8:12.

Tragic effects of self-love. St. Paul pointed to self-love as the root of all evils: "Men will be lovers of self." Consider what a long list of evil consequences he enumerates as growing from self-love: "Covetous, haughty, proud, blasphemers, disobedient to parents, ungrateful, criminal, heartless, faithless, slanderers, incontinent, merciless, unkind, treacherous, stubborn, puffed up with pride, loving pleasure more than God; having a semblance indeed of piety, but disowning its power."[8] We should meditate on each of these words, and dwell on them for a long time.

Self-love in a religious stirs up the three concupiscences and produces evil consequences, among which four are predominant.

(1) STIMULATION OF THE THREE CONCUPISCENCES

(a) **Concupiscence of the eyes.** Religious who are deceived by self-love are not attentive to the duties of their state nor are they much concerned about things prohibited by their profession. They desire temporal good, not only out of necessity, but to the point of superfluity and worldliness. It is worldliness and vanity to devote ourselves to perishable, exterior things that must be left behind at death.

(b) **Concupiscence of the flesh.** Religious who are imbued with excessive self-love desire unnecessary pleasures of the body. These pleasures excite the external senses or captivate the interior faculties. In this state of mind, a religious will hanker for beautiful, empty and worthless things: for books, journeys, pleasures of the flesh and so forth. Such self-love is not good for the body, because it reaps corruption and death. Such self-love is damaging to the soul, for it serves iniquity and is the occasion of eternal death.

(c) **The pride of life.** Finally lovers of self desire honors, praise, high offices. Nothing is more powerful and

---

8. 2 Tim. 3:2-5.

dangerous than such desires. For the road to vanity is broad and short, and it is easier to fall down on the earth and to tumble into hell than to rise and to be lifted up to heaven.

(2) THE FOUR MOST HARMFUL CONSEQUENCES OF SELF-LOVE

(a) *Sadness.* The soul is never satisfied by the goods offered by carnal concupiscence; it is merely saddened, for these goods lack the requisites of happiness: perfection and eternity.

(b) *Envy.* Those who love themselves try to obscure the virtues and gifts of others, lest anyone be preferred to themselves. And that is envy.

(c) *Impatience.* Deceived by self-love, they are indignant, irked, irritated against all who stand in the way of their desires. This is impatience.

(d) *Scruples.* The religious who indulges in self-love will be troubled by an unsettled conscience and at times by a thirst for exalted virtue. This results in unrest and scrupulosity.

SELF-LOVE MUST BE MORTIFIED ESPECIALLY IN THE FOLLOWING INSTANCES:

(1) *Complacency in natural or supernatural gifts.* By regarding one's gifts, whether natural or supernatural, not as given by God but as due to his own merits, man deceives himself, thinks himself to be something great, is self-complacent in all he does. He excuses his own defects, and with a certain underlying motive and hidden desire eagerly seeks his own glory and honor.

(2) *Exaggerated self-esteem.* Honor and glory belong to God alone. But the man who is ignorant of this, desires to be loved, feared, esteemed, and praised, not for love of God but for his own sake. In his anger, this man will quarrel, murmur,

lash with unfair judgment his superiors and confreres who give little satisfaction to his improper craving.

(3) *Fear of humiliation.* Humiliation harms no one. Religious who do not know this are ashamed of the defects that spring from their very nature or flow from their innate weaknesses. But the man guided by supernatural light is ashamed of sin alone; he is aware of no other real cause for confusion. He does not strive to please men, but God. For he knows humble and devout acts of submission are always acceptable to his heavenly Father.

(4) *Hiding defects and making display of good works.* The Lord spoke to David through the mouth of Nathan: "For thou didst it secretly: but I will do this thing in the sight of all Israel, and in the sight of the sun."[9] The true religious shows himself outwardly just as he is inwardly. But the man who chooses self-love and not faith and reason as the light of his soul will act like a hypocrite. He will hide his vices, defects, and shortcomings, not for the edification of his neighbor but to acquire a reputation for holiness in the minds of others. He will perform with the greatest care all the works which will be seen by men, while neglecting those which God alone can see. A lofty speech and a lukewarm prayer are a discordant psalmody. Self-love, like a cruel sword, makes many spiritual men martyrs, not of God, but of the world and of vanity.

(5) *Avoidance of the things condemned by the world.* We should always pursue whatever is good, whatever pleases God. Reason itself teaches this, but man often forgets it. To avoid worldly shame he will omit good works. Pernicious love seals the lips of counselors who are afraid of freely speaking the truth. It fetters the hands of laborers, so that they will not engage in any tasks which might seem degrading, even

---

9. 2 Kings 12:12.

though these works are actually pleasing to God. It weakens the heart of the servants of God so that they do not dare to abandon the company of the tepid and to follow a more perfect way of life.

§ II. Control of Self-love

118. **Control of self-love is difficult.** The egocentric person is inclined to seek his own convenience in all things. This prevents his intellect from holding fast to Christian principles and to the Christian pattern of life, and makes the subjugating of self-love very difficult. "Is there anyone," inquires Cardinal Bona, "who can persuade a man who loves himself that everything the world holds dear is vain and of no moment, and that honors and dignities are nothing else but a most apparent slavery and affliction of the spirit? Or that it is the part of the strong and magnanimous man not to take notice of personal enemies and to do good to those who hate him? That it is more praiseworthy to conquer oneself and hold one's appetite in rein than to overcome the most fortified strongholds? These things seem hard and incredible to the man who loves himself. But the sons of God are governed by the spirit of God so that they live, not according to the flesh, but according to the spirit."[10]

How to control self-love. We must first realize how vicious the inclination to self-love can be, for then our will can more effectively control its lower appetites. As light disperses darkness, so the will, by the illumination of the intellect, is enabled to repel this perverse love. Let us consider the following points:

(1) FREQUENT SELF-EXAMINATION. "Is it not admirable that despite the diversity of men and human ways, all are agreed on this: that no one seems odious to himself, and none wishes

---

10. Cardinal Bona, *Princip. vitae christ.*, Pars I, § XXX.

to yield or submit to another? Each one wants to predominate."[11] Therefore "Know thyself!" Learn to know who and what you are. The sun rises for all other men as well as for you; God, who is the Lord of all, has given His gifts not only to you but to the rest of men also. If, then, in the final analysis you are only one of the crowd and not superior to it, you have no cause for demanding more love or praise, more exemptions or a preferential treatment.

(2) CAREFUL CONTROL OF ACTIONS. Our actions are either bad, theoretically indifferent, or good. We must study these distinctions. "Whoever neglects to take inventory of his life," says St. Gregory, "either despises or does not know how to examine what he does, what he says, and what he thinks, . . . and he who is not careful day by day to examine and know himself is really not acquainted with himself. He truly knows himself who pays as close attention to his own actions as if they were those of another. For the sins we commit are many, but they do not seem very serious to us because we love ourselves, close our eyes to our defects, and caress our very self-deceptions."[12]

(a) *Bad actions.* "All men are ignorant of themselves, but never of others," says Cardinal Bona. "They hold tenaciously to their opinions, admire their own possessions, approve only their own deeds and pleasures, and disapprove of the same in others. They make a display of their ignorance as if it were wisdom, and although they know nothing, they are of the opinion that there is nothing of which they are ignorant. They conceal their vices, and, conscience unheeded, feign a good life."[13] We should carefully examine these vices and strive to correct them.

---

11. *Ibid.,* cap. XXXII.
12. St. Gregory, *In Ezech.,* Lib. I, *Homil. IV,* n. 8-9, in Migne, *P. L.,* t. LXXVI, col. 819.
13. Cardinal Bona, *loc. cit.,* cap. XXXII.

(b) *Actions indifferent in the abstract.* "Whether you eat or drink, or do anything else, do all for the glory of God,"[14] says the Apostle. If anyone desires these gratifications for himself and not for love of God, he does not avoid the danger of sinning; for whatever he does is not done with the proper intention: for God. He is greedy for pleasure, solicits wealth, honors, dignities, all for self-gratification, self-glorification.

We should instead imitate the saints who, "when they were forced, out of human necessity, to perform something gratifying to the flesh, endeavored not to be attracted to it through self-love but restrained the depraved desires of the flesh from a supernatural motive. Lovers of self maintain that discretion is necessary in corporal matters; however, this discretion is really desirable and worth striving for when inspired by heaven — for the prudence of the flesh is death."[15]

(c) *Actions good in themselves.* Even actions good in themselves must be inspected with the lamp of reason and especially in the light of faith. There are spiritual men who trample underfoot the things of earth, who prudently love their friends and neighbors, but who are deceived by this unsuspected trap of self-love. The love of their own deeds, their private exercises, their spiritual consolations, seduces them; hence they fall into the vice of singularity, and gradually lose fraternal charity and sympathy toward the needy. "Since sham, deceit, hypocrisy are companions of our self-seeking nature, we should scrutinize the innermost recesses of our soul and beware lest any motive of self-advantage vitiate the beginning, the middle, or the end of any of our actions, even though they may seem holy and innocent. The philosophy of Christian life is this: not to seek or love anything except in reference to God, and to hate what is our own."[16]

---

14. 1 Cor. 10:31.
15. Cardinal Bona, *loc. cit.,* cap. XXX.
16. *Ibid.,* cap. XXXII.

(3) PRESENTATION OF ALL THINGS TO GOD WITH A GOOD INTENTION. If we wish to please God, we should always act out of love of God, both in the performance of good and in the avoidance of evil. Every work, even every attempt to virtue, every good desire, every action that proceeds from a faulty intention is corrupt. Therefore let us have a good intention in all things, not only a good intention that is habitual or virtual, but as far as possible actual. For if we frequently renew our good intention, then in whatever we think or desire, in whatever we say or do, we shall seek not ourselves but God and His good pleasure and glory.

Conclusion of the Entire Discussion on the Reformation of "the Old Man" in Us

119. We have examined everything that has been deformed by sin: the disorders of the internal and external senses and of the members of the body. We have also learned how to use the tools needed for the reformation of "the old man" in us. But let us be assured that this reformation is not accomplished suddenly, or by leaps and bounds. It is a gradual and continual process.

(1) THE REFORMATION OF "THE OLD MAN" IN US IS A GRADUAL PROCESS. "The soul that rises from sin to piety may be compared to the dawning of the day," says St. Francis de Sales, "which, as it approaches, dispels the darkness not suddenly, but gradually."[17] A gradual cure is indeed the safest. Diseases of the soul, like those of the body, are easily contracted but slow in being cured. Let us progress with fervor, and bear with patience the time-consuming slowness of our reformation.

(2) TWO EXCESSES TO BE AVOIDED. *The first excess.* Some souls who hold fast to the way of purgation for a period of

---

17. *Introduction to a Devout Life,* Part I, Chap. V.

time, and discipline themselves as long as they perceive their various imperfections, soon begin to be restless and disturbed and slacken their pace. Little by little they succumb to temptation, abandon what they have begun, and recede to their former position.

The second excess. By way of temptation on the other extreme, some souls imagine themselves already purged of all their imperfections: they are on dangerous ground. They believe that they are made pure by their first efforts; they wish to fly without wings. They are in great peril of falling back because of their hasty withdrawal from the care of the physician.

(3) PURGATION IS NEVER ENTIRELY COMPLETED. We must be convinced that this process of the soul's purgation should not cease until the end of our life. Let us not be perturbed by our imperfections, for our perfection consists in fulfilling our capacity to struggle against our imperfections. This state of war is really best for us; for if we desire, we can always be victorious by using the means ordained by God.

(4) WE SHOULD ALWAYS APPLY THE GENERAL MEANS. What are these means, we might ask. The prophet Job answers: "Behold, the fear of the Lord is wisdom; and avoiding evil is understanding."[18]

Fear of the Lord. The fear of the Lord is like medicine for the sick. Just as well-chosen medicine overcomes sickness and the effects of poison, so the fear of God repels all sin and all occasions of sin. Casting off sin and its occasions — this is the same as putting off "the old man."

Manner of growing in fear of the Lord. The manner of acquiring fear of the Lord and wisdom that will keep us far from sin is this: in everything to look to our last end, toward which all our actions tend.

---

18. Job 28:28.

Meditation on the last things. Consideration of and meditation on death, the particular and the general judgments, Purgatory and hell: These are the negative ways of growing in the fear of the Lord, and also of avoiding sin. "In whatever you do, remember your last days, and you will never sin."[19] Sin, as we have already mentioned, derives its origin from pleasure. When pleasure approaches dangerously close to the sinful, it must be repressed by the thought of the horrible and unending punishments of hell. Any man can resist a whole multitude of vices if only he will consider how God, with ever-watchful eye, beholds all his works; if only he will weigh carefully the brevity of voluptuousness, the filth of sin, the shortness of the present life, the uncertainty of death, the peace of a good conscience, the anxiety of a conscience infected with sin, and, finally, either eternal joy or eternal torture. What indeed is this thing called life if man, having hardly come forth from one sepulchre, constantly moves in the direction of another and in the end is buried in the everlasting flames of hell? St. Bernard writes: "First he would think of his sins, their nature and number. But this thought would not have profited him much if he did not fear to be punished for them in hell. Thus the consideration of hell was aptly joined to the reflection of sin. Again, if one meditated on the torments of hell and how great they are, and forgot all about his sins, perhaps the mind would feel safe against hell, since there would be no recollection of its sins to terrify it. For this reason, when one is meditating, both sin and hell should be linked together and thus a salutary fear will well up in the heart."[20] Preaching to his people, St. John Chrysostom said: "Nothing so eats away sin, gives such growth to virtue, as a holy, unceasing fear.

---

19. Sirach 7:36.
20. St. Bernard, *Parab. de Nupt. filii Reg.,* in *Opera S. Bern.* (Paris, 1640), col. 1723.

Wherefore he cannot live well who lives without fear; just as, contrariwise, it is impossible for one living in holy fear to sin."[21]

"Evil men at the same time both hate and love their vices," says Cardinal Bona, " and even while they indulge in them, detest them. What does it profit a man to reject evil by his words and to embrace it by his deeds? No one has such a hardened conscience that his vices do not at times nauseate him; and yet before long he begins to relish them again. A man really converted to God lays the ax to the root and eradicates the smallest fibers of vice. Always mindful of his weakness, he earnestly avoids every occasion of sin and, filled with holy fear, runs and leaps away as it were from any object of evil."[22]

Every morning, therefore, when we return to our cell after Divine Office, let us always make a short meditation on the last things. Once this practice becomes a custom, it will be a powerful means for exterminating "the old man" in us.

The way of love. Parallel to "the fear of the Lord" — which after all is only "the beginning of wisdom" — and far above it, is the way of love. Sin can be cast out by fear of reprisals, by visions of Purgatory and hell, by meditations on death, but this is the way of the weak and of the beginner. It does not sufficiently consider the infinite goodness of the offended God. It is too full of self-pity. The main reason for avoiding sin is not that it brings punishment to the sinner, but that it offends God and that it adds to the agony and sufferings of Christ.

The contrition of fear, even though sufficient for the Sacrament of Penance, is imperfect and incomplete. The protection given by fear is limited and founded upon egotistical motives. Not so the contrition and protection of love.

---

21. St. John Chrysostom, *Homil. XV ad pop. Antioch,* in Migne, *P. G.,* XLIX, col. 154.
22. Cardinal Bona, *Manuductio,* cap. III, 2.

When we consider that every sin is an insult to the Infinite Love; when we compare the love of God, giving us His only Son, and when we think of Christ dying for us on the cross, and of our shame and audacity in rejecting this love, we should burn with such a fire of remorse, such a flame of belated love, as to make even the fire of hell disappear. This is not the abjection of a trembling slave, but the tremendous rising of a fallen soul: the glorification of God in all things, even through our weaknesses. This is perfect contrition.

Contrition through fear is negative and lowly. It is based on our own imperfection. It tries to overcome imperfection through imperfection: the imperfection of sin through the imperfection of fear. It attempts to cast out sin through the effects of sin on the sinner. It never rises above the limited world of the ego. It draws no merit and no grace.

Not so the contrition of love. When God is properly loved, every sin, every fall is understood first of all as a failure of love. Often the idea of punishment in the loving soul is so remote that its deterrent power is almost nil compared to the sorrow for having offended God. When God is properly loved and contrition is perfected through this love, such an abundance of grace descends upon the sinner that, instead of being merely restored to his former integrity, he rises from the dead with an additional treasure, with a stronger purpose toward good and a more abundant love.

PART II

STRENGTHENING WHAT HAS BEEN REFORMED AND CONFORMING TO CHRIST THROUGH THE PRACTICE OF VIRTUE

PART II

STRENGTHENING WHAT HAS BEEN REFORMED AND CONFORMING TO CHRIST THROUGH THE PRACTICE OF VIRTUE

120. We have set forth an excellent method for reforming man's corrupt nature. We have shown the necessity of our quest for God. Now we shall prescribe ideal means for confirming this reformation of the soul that has discovered God through His love and His grace. Conformation to Christ will be effected by the practice of virtue, according to the example of St. Francis. The proposed confirmation of the reformed nature of man and his conformity to Christ are implied in the words of David: "Happy the men whose strength You are! Their hearts are set upon the pilgrimage: when they pass through the arid valley, they make a spring of it; the early rain clothes it with generous growth. They go from strength to strength; they shall see the God of gods in Sion."[1]

These words contain the necessary means for the fulfillment of this confirmation and conformity to Christ, and furthermore they reveal to us the manner of advancing in both. First of all, we must bear in mind that God, who is the beginning and end of all creation, influences our spiritual progress as the Primary Moving Cause. Both confirmation and conformation to Christ, which will enable us to reach our last end in a state of complete perfection, are a sublime operation. Yet progress is quite arduous and difficult since the powers of human nature usually are unstable and unequal to so weighty an affair. God Himself is our goal, and He promises His help.

---

1. Ps. 83:6-8.

And by His aid we are enabled to progress, to ascend, and ultimately to unite our whole selves with Him. Well does David exclaim: "Happy the men whose strength You are!" For without divine assistance we shall accomplish nothing. Without God we shall not be happy but wretched. We shall not ascend to lofty heights of prayer. We shall not strengthen our reformed nature. We shall not conform our life to Christ. Worse, we shall descend into the abyss. For "Destruction is thy own, O Israel: thy help is only in Me."[2]

God, who gratuitously bestows His aid on us, demands our consent and co-operation. He presents the means by which we prepare our hearts for making further progress in perfection. The various spiritual exercises constitute such means. They enkindle our love for God, manifest His will, increase and perfect the life of Christ in us. Relying on the divine assistance, we can climb the mountain of perfection. With the help of the Almighty "who made heaven and earth," we can advance from virtue to virtue, from strength to strength, from one degree of holiness to another, from one state of soul to another more sublime.

This section will treat of the strengthening and conforming of the new man to Christ under the following divisions:

1. Spiritual means;

2. Practice of virtue.

---

2. Osee 13:9, Challoner-Douay version.

BOOK I

Initial Strengthening and Conforming of "the New Man" to Christ through Spiritual Means

121. **We must conform our life to the life of Christ.** Perfection consists in the love of God, or in the conformity of our will to the divine will. In Christ we have a faultless model of this perfection; consequently, we must pattern our lives after His.

The life of Christ demands imitation. "Christ died for all, in order that they who are alive may live no longer for themselves, but for Him who died for them."[1] In these words St. Paul declares that the passion and death of Christ should in a special way stimulate in the faithful the desire to live for God alone and to pursue a virtuous, more perfect life.

We must meditate on the life and passion of Christ. If we are to live for God alone, it is sufficient for us to study diligently the book of the Crucified! "I do not need many things," says St. Francis; "I know the poor crucified Christ."[2] Jesus Himself, when He was about to enter upon the ocean of His sorrows, said to the Apostles, and through them to all the faithful: "I have given you an example, that as I have done to you, so you also should do."[3] He urges us to the conscientious practice of this imitation, saying: "Open to Me, My sister";[4] open your heart by consent and preparation for receiving My gifts. The more you open and enlarge your heart, the more

---

1. 2 Cor. 5:15.
2. Celano, *Legenda Secunda,* cap. LXXXI.
3. John 13:15.
4. Cant. 5:2.

intimately shall I come to you, that you may conform your life to Mine. I shall confer more ample gifts on you by which you will become more virtuous and holy.

Keys to this conformity. We must learn how to throw open the portals of our hearts. We must prepare the keys which will open our souls so that the life of Christ may enter. There are four of these keys, which as it were unlock our intellect, our will, our senses and passions, and finally our actions. These keys abundantly strengthen us in the grace of God and conform us more perfectly to the life and teaching of Christ. Our intellect is opened to Christ by instruction, our will by conformity to the divine; our passions by subjection to reason and Christian doctrine; and our actions by imitation of the divine model.

DIVISIONS

We shall examine more closely these spiritual keys:

I. *Instruction of the intellect;*

II. *Conformity of the human will to the divine;*

III. *Subjection of the senses and passions;*

IV. *Proper ordering of actions.*

FIRST KEY: INSTRUCTION OF THE INTELLECT

122. The faculties of man perform various functions within his soul. In relation to other faculties the intellect may be considered the gateway inasmuch as every act begins with a motion of the intelligence. We must condition this faculty, "unlock" it by learning what is needed for its conformation to Christ, and "lock" it in respect to transitory and worldly thoughts.

According to the Fathers, the following are the means of furnishing the intellect with Christian doctrine:

1. Sermons or spiritual exhortations;

2. Spiritual reading;

3. Examination of conscience;

4. Mental prayer, meditation;

5. Spiritual direction.

Article I — Spiritual Exhortation

§ I. Necessity

123. Christ, Uncreated Wisdom, descended to earth from the bosom of the Father to found His Church and to instruct it in His holy doctrines. On the day of His Ascension into heaven He most earnestly recommended to the Apostles the preaching of His divine word, saying, "Go into the whole world and preach the Gospel to every creature."[1]

St. Bernardine gives us an excellent reason for this command: "Since man consists of body and soul, he must have a

---

1. Mark 16:15.

twofold food. He obviously needs material bread for the nourishment of his body. Moreover, he requires spiritual bread — specifically, the word of God — as sustenance for his soul. Christ assigns the function for each sort of nourishment in man's life when He says: 'Not by bread alone does man live, but by every word that comes forth from the mouth of God' (Matt. 4:4). Now this word of God constitutes the sweet spiritual food of the soul.

"It refreshes the soul in the same manner in which food nourishes the body. For if we support only the flesh and do not nurture the soul with the word of God, we sate the servant and starve the lady of the house."[2] Holy Mother Church, recognizing this necessity, commands the superiors of all religious Orders zealously to provide spiritual food, the word of God, for their subjects.

"We admonish all superiors in the Lord," says Clement VIII, "to be mindful of the reckoning which on the last day they will have to give for the flock entrusted to them . . .; it will be very opportune if a sermon is delivered each week in every convent concerning religious discipline and regular observance."[3] St. Francis at all times met this obligation as carefully as possible. He always regarded religious conferences to the friars as an excellent tool for the construction of their spiritual dwellings.

§ II. God Demands the Preaching of the Word

124. Although the Holy Spirit can use the voice and talents of anyone for the ministry of the word, yet He placed "pastors and teachers" both in the Church and in every religious community "in order to perfect the saints for a work of ministry, for building up the body of Christ, until we all attain" not

2. St. Bernardine, *Serm. 5 in Dom. Quadrag.*
3. Clement VIII, *Nullus omnino* (1601).

only "to the unity of the faith and of the deep knowledge of the Son of God," but also "to perfect manhood, to the mature measure of the fullness of Christ." We are to "practice the truth in love, and so grow up in all things in Him who is the Head, Christ."[4]

Preachers must be heard. As the faithful devoutly listen to the word of God, the Holy Spirit gently enters into the soul, especially into religious souls. This most blessed Light is infused into the minds of those who proclaim God's word. For the Lord Jesus said to the Apostles, and through them to all pastors of souls: "I will ask the Father and He will give you another Advocate to dwell with you forever, the Spirit of truth, whom the world cannot receive, because it neither sees Him nor knows Him. But you shall know Him, because He will dwell with you, and be in you. . . . But the Advocate, the Holy Spirit, whom the Father will send in My name, He will teach you all things, and bring to your mind whatever I have said to you."[5] Therefore we must without question listen to those who preach the word.

Preachers should not be despised because of their imperfections. Concerning the obedience which should be shown the commands of superiors, Christ says: "The Scribes and the Pharisees have sat on the chair of Moses. All things, therefore, that they command you, observe and do: but do not act according to their works; for they talk but do nothing."[6] We too are bound to heed this admonition of our heavenly Master toward all ministers of the Gospel as long as they teach the orthodox faith and the pure truth, even if their conduct is sinful, and their life unchristian. Let us never despise their doctrine, but beware of following their example.

---

4. Eph. 4:11, 12-13, 15.
5. John 14:16-17, 26.
6. Matt. 23:2-3.

§ III. The Matter of Spiritual Exhortations

125. Briefly St. Paul indicates to Timothy the material for his exhortations: "Preach the word."[7] That is to say, "Preach the word of God." Or, as Christ proclaimed, "Preach the Gospel." St. Francis de Sales followed this precept by instructing his priests to preach continually on virtue and vice, heaven and hell. Sacred Scripture affords such ample material on these subjects that we need not search elsewhere. In his holy Rule St. Francis prescribes the same for friars who are preachers. He wishes them to discourse on "vices and virtues, punishment and glory."

No other source is needed. Of course, prelates may use the arguments of the Fathers of the Church in their exhortations. St. Francis de Sales teaches that there is no more difference between Sacred Scripture and the doctrines of the Fathers of the Church than between a whole loaf of bread and the same cut into many slices. Indeed, the holy Fathers are heralds through whom God makes known the true meaning of His word.

Our preachers are warned against profane and abstruse arguments which are above the ordinary mental grasp of their audiences. In sermons they should refrain from inept verbiage and be able to declare with the Apostle: "We, at least, are not, as many others, adulterating the word of God; but with sincerity, as coming from God, we preach in Christ in God's presence."[8] "And I, brethren, when I came to you, did not come with pretentious speech or wisdom, announcing unto you the witness to Christ."[9]

---

7. 2 Tim. 4:2.
8. 2 Cor. 2:17.
9. 1 Cor. 2:1.

§ IV. Results of Exhortations

126. The word of God expressed by our superiors always produces beneficial results. God speaks of this in the Book of Isaia: "So shall My word be that goes forth from My mouth. It shall not return to Me void, but shall do My will, achieving the end for which I sent it."[10] "The divine word," says St. Bonaventure, "has power to illumine our intellect, to purify our heart and to perfect our works."[11] What could be better, what could be sweeter, what more profitable for man than devoutly to listen to the word of God?

For the word of God is the mirror of truth which flatters no one, misleads no one, but reveals a man as he really is.

Results are slow to appear. The Lord Jesus said: "The seed is the word of God."[12] For we observe by experience that some seeds, even though they are very small, will grow little by little and develop into tall trees. The tiny seed of the word of God, which can scarcely be perceived, develops in the course of years into a tree which reaches to the very stars. Who can count how many souls have reached an eminent degree of sanctity by having heard merely one word of God? As the seed does not suddenly bloom and ripen, so the exhortation of God's word does not fructify all at once; it grows slowly, in its own good time bearing the luscious fruits of virtue. In periods of temptation and trial, in time of studies and active life we shall perhaps recall the word of God heard in our novitiate. At such times, with the help of God's grace, the word may cause our amendment, perhaps even our salvation. The devil vividly realizes that the word of God, addressed to us through exhortations, is a special instrument for the perfection of religious. For this reason he strives in all possible ways to impede us from hearing, cherishing, or obeying this word.

---

10. Isa. 55:11.
11. St. Bonaventure, *Serm. 2 de purificatione B. M. V.,* Prothema.
12. Luke 8:11.

§ V. How Exhortations Are To Be Received

127. Diligence is requisite before, during and after an exhortation.

(a) BEFORE EXHORTATION. We should always have a great desire for the word of God; for this yearning is a sign of our call to eternal glory. When our Saviour said: "My sheep hear My voice . . . ; and I give them everlasting life; and they shall never perish,"[13] He clearly expressed proof of our eternal calling. He promised heavenly beatitude to all who willingly hear the word of God. St. Anthony of Padua says, "It is a great sign of election to listen with pleasure to the word of God and to reports of our heavenly country, just as some willingly listen to reports of their earthly country."[14]

(b) DURING EXHORTATION. The word of God will be fruitful in our soul only if we listen to it with attention and meditate upon it with care. St. Ambrose writes: "You should desire to hear the word of God so as to be able to repeat it, and tell what you have heard to others, in your homes, in your gardens, wherever you may be. With persistent thought, ruminate on the spiritual food of God's word, as animals chew the cud. Then, with the help of God, you will accept it, you will make it as it were part of your flesh and blood, and you will also pass it on to others."[15]

St. Jerome, writing on the sermons of the Egyptian monks, describes what happens when the spiritual father begins to preach: "And while he talks there is total silence; no one dares to look about or cough. The applause of the speaker consists in the weeping of the hearers. Silent tears roll down their cheeks; their sorrow does not burst forth into loud sobbing. And when he begins to speak of the kingdom of Christ,

---

13. John 10:27-28.
14. St. Anthony of Padua, *Serm. in Domin. Pass.*
15. St. Ambrose, *Sermo 4 in die Cineris;* in App., *Opera S. Aug.,* Sermo dubius 141; cf. Migne, *P. L.,* t. XXXIX, col. 2022.

future happiness, eternal glory, you can hear their restrained sighs, and you can see their eyes lifted heavenward, as if saying among themselves, 'Had I but wings like a dove, I would fly away and be at rest' (Ps. 54:7)."[16]

(c) AFTER EXHORTATION. After the exhortation we must diligently guard the word of God in our heart and transfer it into action, if we wish to profit by it. We should not let the words of spiritual conferences go into one ear and out the other. St. James condemns such levity: "Be doers of the word, and not hearers only, deceiving yourselves. For if anyone is a hearer of the word, and not a doer, he is like a man looking at his natural face in a mirror: for he looks at himself and goes away, and presently he forgets what kind of man he is. But he who has looked carefully into the perfect law of liberty and has remained in it, not becoming a forgetful hearer but a doer of the work, shall be blessed in his deed."[17] Take heed that a sermon or spiritual talk always bears fruit. Praise is due to Mary, our sweet Mother, not only because she bore the Word of God in her womb, but also because she perfectly observed the precepts of God in her actions. What a great multitude would suddenly fill paradise if all who listened to sermons and spiritual conferences had practiced what they had heard!

CONCLUSION. "Since you already know that what you have heard is from God," says St. Gregory, "let each of you reflect whether or not the voice of God has gained ground in your heart. For there are some who disdain to learn the precepts of God by listening. Some listen to them but have no desire to embrace them. Again, some willingly accept the word of God, moved even to weeping; but after their tears, return to their former iniquities. They do not sincerely hear the word of

---

16. St. Jerome, *Epist.* 22, *ad Eustoch.*, n. 35, in Migne, *P. L.*, t. XXII, col. 420.

17. James 1:22-25.

God who disdain to put it into practice."[18] If we wish to lay
open our intellect to Christ, let us diligently listen to devout
exhortations. And to render the word efficacious, let us lend
not only our ears to hear, but also our heart to absorb the
doctrine of Christ. Then the same sentiment of love, the same
harmony of speech, will prevail among all.

Article II — Spiritual Reading

§ I. Excellence and Usefulness of Spiritual Reading

128. (1) **The excellence of spiritual reading.** Spiritual
reading offers another means of instructing the intellect. Sermons are very beneficial; yet the word of God is more deeply
impressed on the mind when we read it with our own eyes.
Father Roderick, S. J., gives an excellent explanation of spiritual
reading. "Although reading does not possess such inherent
force as listening to an animated voice, yet it has many advantages lacking in sermons. *First*, it is not always possible to
have a preacher on hand, while it is always possible to have a
spiritual book. *Second,* one quickly forgets what is said in a
sermon and therefore the words do not bear full fruit. But
the contents of a good book can be thought over, reread, and
pondered to produce a strong and lasting effect. *Third*, a
good, sincere, candid book is a better counselor. The philosopher Plutarch aptly states: 'What a friend or an adviser does
not dare tell me, a book says undauntedly, reminding me of
my vices and faults, sometimes reproaching me and at other
times exhorting me' (Demetrius Phalerius, *Plutarch in apoph.*).
Fourth, by reading a person converses with the authors. He
blends his words with those of a Bernard, a Gregory, a Basil,
and a Chrysostom; in a sense he becomes one of their disciples,

---

18. St. Gregory, *Homil. XVIII in Evang.*, in Migne, *P. L.*, t. LXXVI, col.
1150.

listening to what they say as if they were in his presence. The Fathers of the Church call good books a public, life-giving treasure, because of the immense stream of wealth they pour forth. *Finally,* spiritual reading contains so many and such great advantages that it is difficult to estimate them. St. Jerome, while speaking of the interior fire of the soul, asks on what this fire and flame subsists. He answers without the slightest hesitation that they subsist on the reading of sacred writings which inflame the soul with love for God and cleanse it of all vice (cf. St. Jerome, *Epist. 18, ad Damasum,* n. 6)."[19]

(2) **The usefulness of spiritual reading.** (a) *Our Lord recommends it.* Christ our Lord, whose actions are our instructions, clearly recommends spiritual reading by His own example. For St. Luke writes: "He entered the synagogue . . . ; and stood up to read. And the volume of Isaia the prophet was handed to Him. And . . . He opened the volume."[20]

(b) *Spiritual reading is endorsed by the Doctors of the Church.* By His example our Lord suggests that we read the Scriptures; for after the sin of Adam this reading became a necessity, as the Seraphic Doctor, St. Bonaventure, explains. "The book of creatures was destroyed through the sin of Adam, but Sacred Scripture restored the book of the world. As long as man remained good and upright, he realized the true value of created things and their presence moved him to praise, honor and love God. The purpose of created things is to lead men to God. Since man lost this knowledge through the fall, he could not return this praise to God. Therefore another book was needed to clarify this book of the world, which had been closed and destroyed. This second book is Scripture, which presents similitudes, properties and metaphors of the things which are written in the book of the world. The

---

19. *Perfectio christiana,* Pars I, Tract. V, cap. XXVIII, n. 13.
20. Luke 4:16-17.

book of Scriptures, therefore, is the restoration of the entire world to God, who must be known, praised and loved."[21]

St. Thomas of Villanova confirms this opinion of St. Bonaventure: "The art of arts is to serve God. The supreme wisdom is to have learned to live well. If you know this, although you know nothing else, you are most wise. He who does not know this, whatever else he may know, is most ignorant. All Christians profess this truth. For what else is Christianity but the art of teaching men to live piously and to please and serve God? We learn, moreover, the art of living according to the dictates of divine law by reading the sacred books. The Gospel and Sacred Scripture teach the rules and regulations of this art."[22]

(3) **Fruitfulness of spiritual books.** The fruits of Sacred Scripture and of spiritual books are proof of their usefulness.

(1) Without Scripture there is nothing but blindness.

(2) In Sacred Scripture we find a powerful aid toward salvation.

(1) *Blindness in the absence of Scripture and tradition.* Some truths have been bequeathed to us by the Apostles in writing; others in tradition. Scripture and tradition are the fountains of truth. If the Church of Christ did not have Sacred Scripture and tradition and many other spiritual books, the world would be in a state of blindness and ignorance. "Reading the Scriptures is a great defense against sin," says St. John Chrysostom. "Ignorance of the Scriptures is a steep precipice, a bottomless abyss. It is a great danger to salvation not to know the divine laws, for this ignorance produces heresies and results in corrupt living."[23]

---

21. St. Bonaventure, *In Hexaem.*, Coll. XIII, n. 12.
22. St. Thomas of Villanova, *Conc. 2 in Dom. 1, Quadr.*
23. St. John Chrysostom, *De Laz.*, Conc. III, n. 3, in Migne, *P. G.*, t. XLVIII, col. 995.

(2) *Sacred Scripture is a powerful aid toward salvation.*
The Apostle St. Paul highly esteemed the study of Sacred
Scripture and the application of our mind to it. A man of God
and one highly favored with spiritual gifts, he still devoted
much of his time to reading. He had been taught as in paradise by Uncreated Wisdom, and he possessed infused knowledge, yet he devoted the whole power of his intelligence to
spiritual reading. When writing to his disciple Timothy, he
earnestly advises wholesome reading, saying, "Be diligent in
reading."[24] "All Scripture is inspired by God and useful for
teaching, for reproving, for correcting."[25]

SACRED SCRIPTURE IS PROFITABLE FOR TEACHING. The
psalms indicate this heavenly profit: "The revelation of Your
words sheds light, giving understanding to the simple."[26]
Spiritual reading and the study of the Sacred Scriptures enlighten all who implore the divine aid. St. John Chrysostom
writes: "God will never neglect anyone who applies himself
to Scripture with great fervor and ardent desire. In the
absence of a teacher, the Lord Himself will enter our hearts
from above, enlighten our minds, penetrate our reason with
His radiance, reveal His secrets and teach us things of which
we are ignorant."[27] St. Augustine tells in his *Confessions* that
one day, while still a Manichaean, he heard a voice saying:
"Take and read." Impelled by these words, he read, and thus
arrived at a perfect knowledge of God as he himself testifies:
"I took it, opened it and read it . . . ; all the darkness of my
doubts was made to flee, as if dispelled by a light of certitude infused into my heart."[28] We may say with St. Bonaventure: "All

---

24. 1 Tim. 4:13.
25. 2 Tim. 3:16.
26. Ps. 118:130.
27. St. John Chrysostom, *Homil. 35 in Gen.*, n. 1, in Migne, *P. G.*, t. LIII,
col. 321.
28. St. Augustine, *Confessions*, Lib. VIII, cap. XII, in Migne, *P. L.*, t.
XXXII, col. 762.

Scripture is the heart of God, the mouth of God, the tongue of God, His book written within and without."[29]

In other words Sacred Scripture is a communication which the living God has sent to all His creatures to enlighten and stabilize their erring and wavering minds.

SACRED SCRIPTURE IS PROFITABLE FOR THE EXAMINATION OF CONSCIENCE. St. Gregory teaches that "Sacred Scripture is placed before the eyes of our mind like a mirror, so that we may behold in it the image of our inner self. This mirror shows us our good and bad qualities. In this way we learn how far we have advanced and how far we have yet to go before attaining perfection."[30] The mirror of spiritual reading will show us what we really are and the direction in which we tend.

SACRED SCRIPTURE IS PROFITABLE FOR CORRECTION. The Scriptures and spiritual books disclose our sins and imperfections. The ignorant will find therein an admonition to learn; the obstinate and the sinful will find reasons to fear the scourge of future judgment. The good laborer will find the promise of future glory and of life everlasting, so that he will be stimulated to greater effort. Spiritual reading inflames the will and moves it to work swiftly; it abolishes all tepidity and coldness. We can say with St. Paul: "Thou hast known the Sacred Writings, which are able to instruct thee unto salvation by the faith which is in Christ Jesus. All Scripture is inspired by God, and useful . . . for instructing in justice; that the man of God may be perfect, equipped for every good work."[31] The reading of sacred and devout books is most useful, except when we do not concentrate upon them. Let us choose our books wisely and read them well.

---

29. St. Bonaventure, *In Hexaem.*, Coll. XII, n. 17.
30. St. Gregory, *Moralia*, Lib. II, cap. I, in Migne, *P. L.*, t. LXXV, col. 553.
31. 2 Tim. 3:15-17.

§ II. Which Books To Read

129. The choice of spiritual books. Many books, such as the Sacred Scripture, spiritual writings, the lives of the saints, are food for the soul and the means of its most perfect development.

(1) **Sacred Scripture.** Each day, before all other reading, we should read from Sacred Scripture.[32]

(2) **Books on the spiritual life.** Next in importance to the Sacred Scriptures are books treating of the spiritual life. We must always eat some spiritual food to sustain our spiritual strength, lest we faint along the way of virtue. The human mind is unstable in its consideration of the supernatural; but in books on the spiritual life it discovers valuable aids to virtue.

*FRANCISCAN AUTHORS. When choosing books on the spiritual life we should always prefer Franciscan authors. "They err and speak contrary to the Seraphic spirit who, neglecting the prudent treatment of ascetics by excellent Franciscan doctors, occupy themselves wholly in reading the works of others. The works of Franciscan authors have a special value in educating and correctly directing Friars Minor. The words of non-Franciscan authors are not always suited to our calling. Moreover, their exclusive use could very easily obscure or adulterate our own traditions. The result would be a mixture of asceticism which has lost the Seraphic spirit."[33]

St. Bonaventure, foremost among Franciscan authors. We should always prefer the writings of St. Bonaventure, of whom it has been written: "Many authors teach doctrine; many preach devotion; but few offer both in their works. Bonaventure rose above these authors, since his doctrine taught devotion, and

---

32. Cf. Hugh of St. Victor, *Erud. didasc.* Lib. V, cap. VII, in Migne, *P. L.,* t. CLXXVI, col. 794.

33. *Analecta O. M. C.,* t. III, p. 45.

his devotion taught doctrine. If you wish to be devout and well instructed, read his works."[34]

(3) **The lives of the saints.** The masters of the supernatural life and the spiritual Fathers highly recommend the lives of the saints. As Franciscans we should frequently read the life and writings of St. Francis and of his blessed companions, and other books of the Order, such as the Chronicles, which portray for us the mind of our Seraphic Father. Concerning these Franciscan books, we can say what St. Basil wrote of Sacred Scripture: "In these books the heroic deeds of God's champions are portrayed, the lives of the blessed pass in review before the mind's eye — living examples of a heavenly life on earth. In a word, the most exalted models for imitation are proposed."[35]

(4) **Advice on the use of spiritual books.** Unswerving orthodoxy is a primary requisite in every book we are to read. If at any time, as occasionally happens in Sacred Scripture, there is mention of something carnal, follow the advice of Blosius. "Let such matters slip by the eyes of the mind casually and simply, as if mention were made of stones."[36] In all passages which seem in any way obscene or arouse the least spark of sensuality, let us flee as far as possible from the snare. If these things trouble us and grow to be actual temptations, let us use our intelligence against them; let us refuse our consent; let us make the sign of the cross and direct our whole attention to God. In this way we shall escape injury.

§ III. Conditions for Fruitful Reading

130. There are certain necessary conditions to be observed before, during, and after reading.

---

34. Joannes Trithhemius, O. S. B., *De script. eccles.*, c. 464; cf. *Analecta O. M. C., loc. cit.*, p. 46.

35. St. Basil, *De virtut. et vitio*, n. 5, in Migne, *P. G.*, t. XXXII, col. 1121.

36. Blosius, *Spec. monachorum*, Divisio III.

(1) BEFORE READING. We should: (a) determine what to read and when to read it; (b) seek spiritual fruit and not the satisfaction of curiosity or the enjoyment of style; (c) always implore the grace of the Holy Spirit.

(a) *When and what to read.* A certain time must be set aside for spiritual reading, and we must hold to it. "One may sometimes defer the hour designated for this reading if necessity arises, but should never omit it entirely. Some hour in the morning is usually more advantageous, more convenient and more free from other occupations."[37] "Keep definite periods of free time for specific reading," says St. Bernard. "Reading that is light, diversified, taken up haphazardly, does not build up, but tends to unsettle the soul. Things easily received easily vanish from the memory."[38] Light reading can be helpful — for instance, in sadness or temptation. Outside such occasions it is always best to avoid it.

(b) *Our purpose should be the spiritual fruit.* We should not read to satisfy our curiosity nor seek the pleasure of style. We should read books in the spirit in which they were written, and be prepared to read wisely to obtain abundant fruit. As Blosius explained, "In reading, seek profit for the soul, spiritual consolation, the love of God; not the allaying of curiosity, nor superfluous understanding and knowledge, nor ornateness and elegance of words. For the kingdom of God is not in elegance of speech but in holiness of life."[39]

We should not be disappointed when a book is not well written; but when it is adequate in this respect, we may rejoice, for perfection of style is a gift of God. Let us receive all things in a spirit of thanksgiving, and all things will turn to our salvation. As the wise bee collects honey from flowers,

---

37. Cardinal Bona, *Horol. ascet.,* cap. II, § 2, n. 3.
38. St. Bernard, *De vit. sol. ad fratres de Monte Dei,* I, cap. X, in Migne, *P. L.,* t. CLXXXIV, col. 327.
39. Blosius, *Spec. monachorum,* Divisio III.

so we must gather from our reading some choice food for our soul.

(c) *We should call upon the Holy Spirit.* Before reading, or before listening to a reader, we should always pray. The Holy Spirit is the key to the treasures of divine knowledge and wisdom; of Him Christ says: "He will teach you all things."[40] St. James expresses it clearly when he says: "If any of you is wanting in wisdom, let him ask it of God."[41] "O Lord Jesus Christ, open the ears of my soul, give sight to the eyes of my heart, that I may hear Your words, understand them, and do Your will."

(2) DURING READING. Different rules apply to public and private reading:

(a) *Public reading.* We should listen attentively, so that both body and spirit may be strengthened and encouraged to imitate Christ crucified. St. Bernard says: "Behold, already while you wash your hands He prepares a table in your sight, that you may live not on bread alone but on every word which proceeds from the mouth of God and that in the strength of that food you may run in the way of His commandment."[42]

(b) *Private reading.* In private, we should read carefully, prayerfully and practically.

CAREFUL READING. We should read with great peace of soul and not rush through the book. We should, when necessary, read the same sentence two or three times or even more. Our aim should not be to read much, but to get much out of our reading. (*Multum, non multa.*) Carelessness is no way to learning. Let us stop after every few lines. A cloudburst is not good for the crops: it drowns the seed and leaves barren fields.

---

40. John 14:26.
41. James 1:5.
42. St. Bernard, *Serm. 24 de Multipl. util. verb. Dei,* n. 3, in Migne, *P. L.,* t. CLXXXIII., col. 604.

Superficial and hasty skipping over many books does not enrich the soul with new life and devotion, but often confuses it and causes spiritual indigestion.

PRAYERFUL READING. We should seek God in all we read, and we shall find Him by means of a spirit of prayer. Through reading, the soul soars like a bird. As a bird drinks, it raises its head to the sky and, then lowering it, drinks again. A virtuous soul, while reading a book on spiritual topics, should lift the mind to God from time to time and then read some more.

PRACTICAL READING. Reading should be a source of knowledge to the intellect, but also and even more, a goad to stimulate the will. Reading points out our pathway and its dangers. We can always make much progress if we put into practice what we read. St. Gregory says, "You have sown much, but produced little. A man who receives heavenly inspiration from much reading and listening, and yet fulfills this inspiration negligently, will achieve meager results. Knowledge of spiritual things can make you a good spiritual director, but not a good religious. We do not have spiritual books merely to get knowledge out of them but to translate solid doctrine into deeds."[43]

Dislike for spiritual reading. Reading can become a bore and a burden in two ways. A book may be unintelligible, and therefore poor in quality; or it may be too long and therefore excessive in quantity. We should take care in both cases not to be suffocated by what was meant as refreshment.

(3) AFTER READING. "Always select noteworthy passages from what you have read and copy them into a notebook kept for this purpose. For then you can more easily commit them to memory, think on them more frequently, increase the flame of devotion and keep distracting thoughts from entering the

---

43. St. Gregory, *Homil. XV in Evang.*, in Migne, *P. L.*, t. LXXVI, col. 1132.

mind. Conclude the reading with a short thanksgiving. Implore God's help, that you may live what you have learned, and achieve what you have proposed."[44]

CONCLUSION. Spiritual reading fills the intellect with knowledge of God. To omit this reading is to neglect our soul. Let us enlighten our minds, so that, lacking nothing, we may become perfect. Celano wrote of St. Francis: "Whenever he read from a sacred book and had committed anything to his soul, it remained indelibly written in his heart. He had a memory for books. For, once he had heard something he turned it over in his mind with continuous devotion. He said that the way to teach and to read fruitfully was not to wander into innumerable subjects."[45]

Article III — Examination of Conscience

131. **Conscience: The monitor and instructor of the soul.** An academy or school is in the charge of a director. So too, in the school of the Christian life there is one assigned by Divine Providence to man's weak nature, a director who urges man on to better things and reproves his faults. This director is our conscience which, like a lighted candle, has been placed by God in the center of our heart to reveal what is hidden within. Besides instructing our intellect by exhortation and spiritual reading, we must diligently examine our conscience. Our Constitutions with good reason advise all the brethren to do so daily.

Twofold examination of conscience. There are a general and a particular examination of conscience. (1) The general examination, according to the sacred custom of our Order, is usually made before retiring. By this examination we daily scrutinize our faults and defects and repent with a firm purpose

---

44. Cardinal Bona, *Horol. ascet.,* cap. II, § 2, n. 9.
45. Celano, *Legenda Secunda,* cap. LXVIII, p. 247.

of amendment. (2) The particular examination is made early
in the morning or before dinner, and is directed against a
specific vice opposed to a certain virtue we wish to acquire.

§ I. General Examination

132. Necessity. The power inclining us toward evil is so
great, the enticement of demons to sin so numerous, the occasions of falling so frequent and so dangerous that it is impossible for the soul to overcome all these attacks without
suffering some injury. It is therefore most useful and salutary
to stand each evening before retiring as if arraigned before the
tribunal of a judge and to give an account of every one of
our thoughts, words and deeds. For if we fail to see our
progress clearly during the activities of the day, now at least,
at the close of the race, we shall have leisure to check our
advance.

The task of a lifetime. Even if we ascend to a sublime
degree of perfection, if we rise higher and higher and our soul
becomes as beautiful as the moon, as bright as the sun and we
dwell in high heaven with the angels, we must still continue to
examine and search ourselves for stains and say with the psalmist: "In the night I meditate in my heart: I ponder and my spirit
broods."[46]

Different examination for imperfect and perfect souls.
The imperfect frequently, deliberately, and at times maliciously
fall into the briers of smaller offenses. They cast their eyes
on the thorns, when they should set about eradicating and burning them. Perfect souls with resolute will try to decrease the
number of their faults and defects. They do not knowingly
and deliberately commit the slightest sin. They do fall into
some sins. But when they do it is only because they are taken
by surprise, or because their good works are mixed with im-

---

46. Ps. 76:7.

perfections, performed without sufficient care or in the wrong circumstances.

Method for general examination:

(1) BEFORE EXAMINATION. "When embarking on this examination, imagine that your guardian angel brings you before the tribunal of divine clemency to render an account. You have been assured of receiving pardon and mercy if you wash away your sins by contrition, atone for them by penance and compensate for them by fervor of spirit. Therefore, with a good intention and an unfaltering trust in God, your most loving Father, with great humility, reverence and confidence, cast yourself down before the throne of divine grace among the army of saints who by this practice once washed their robes in the blood of the Lamb."[47]

(2) DURING EXAMINATION. There are five points to consider:

FIRST POINT: REMEMBRANCE OF THE GOODNESS OF GOD, AND A FERVENT ACT OF THANKSGIVING. Our own depravity produces greater shame when contrasted with the divine liberality. We should briefly but fervently thank God for His general and particular benefits of the past, the present and even the future.

SECOND POINT: PETITION FOR THE GRACE TO KNOW OUR FAULTS. After an act of gratitude we should ask the Holy Spirit for grace to enlighten our mind. Since the heart of man is perverse and inscrutable, it can scarcely recognize its evil-doing unless the Father of all light sends down light from above.

THIRD POINT: INVESTIGATION INTO THE MATTER OF THE EXAMINATION:

(1) **Investigation into the matter of imperfect souls.** If up to now we have been guilty of many deliberate venial

---

47. Cf. Bona, *Horol. ascet.,* cap. IV, § 1, n. 1.

sins, we should conduct an examination of conscience in such a manner as to discover our true self. This examination is easy and fruitful if it is performed exactly, concisely and with order.

Exactly. An exact examination is one which weighs each thing as if the examiner were immediately to explain it in confession.

Concisely. He makes a concise examination who does not spend too long a time examining each defect.

With order. An orderly examination demands three steps:

(a) First, an examination of thoughts: "Have my thoughts been loving toward God, charitable toward my neighbor, humble concerning myself, and pure in regard to the flesh and the world?"

(b) Then, an examination of the senses: "Have my senses been disciplined, guarded, modest; or curious, and dissipated on a variety of vain objects? Have I been brief, measured, and circumspect in my speech?"

(c) Finally, an examination of acts and omissions. First, acts: "Have I done what I should have done? Were all my deeds permissible, fitting, expedient?" Then omissions: "How careless have I been in my prayers and good works? In correcting my defects, in resisting temptations, in advancing in virtue, in performing works of supererogation when occasions presented themselves?" We should ask ourselves, in a word, whether we have sinned against God, our neighbor or our own self by thought, word, deed or omission.

(2) **Matter of examination for perfect souls.** A threefold examination is required:

(a) Works and fruits of virtue;

(b) Internal affections and desires;

(c) Thoughts, which are the fountainhead of other operations.

(a) *Works and fruits.* This examination begins with the more noteworthy deeds. That is, how we have acted and spoken, what aroma and fragrance our deeds have had before God and our neighbor, and whether we have performed them with humility, so that they may deservedly be called perfect deeds.

(b) *Desires.* We should examine the internal desires and the intentions of our soul to see whether these are strong enough to produce abundant fruits.

(c) *Thoughts.* Finally, we must revert to the seeds or roots, the causes of the flowers and fruits—that is, the thoughts and intentions which permeate the soul, from which affections and actions proceed.

FOURTH POINT: THANKSGIVING, DETESTATION OF SIN, AND THE FIRM PURPOSE OF AMENDMENT. If upon completing our investigation we find that all has gone well, we must thank the generosity of God, the Author of all good. If, however, we find anything lacking, we should repent and ask for grace and exclaim with St. Bernard: "How dare I, such an evil son, raise my eyes to the face of my Father, who is so good? It is a disgrace to have done such things when I have the dignity of being a child of God. I should be ashamed of living as a degenerate son of such a Father. Bring forth streams of water, O my eyes: let confusion veil my face, shame cover my countenance and darkness fill my soul."[48]

FIFTH POINT: PENANCE FOR SINS. After the examination of conscience has been completed, we often realize that we were on the edge of the chasm, in imminent danger of falling. We often discover that we have already fallen into the dark water, and nearly drowned; that we not only have failed to rise or even to walk along the steep path, but that we have actually gone down. We must make a firm purpose of amend-

---

48. St. Bernard, *In Cant.,* Serm. 16, in Migne, *P. L.,* t. CLXXXIII, col. 580.

ment for the future, and humbly recommend it to Christ, the Blessed Virgin Mary and the saints. We must also impose upon ourselves a penance, such as the recitation of an Our Father or Hail Mary, or the performance of some other penitential work.

AFTER THE EXAMINATION: After the examination we should reflect on the examples and works of the servants of God, from whom we can learn the art of holiness and thereby make greater progress. Consider how roughly, how harshly some saints punished their bodies; how resolutely others chose the last place. We should admire their patience in adversity, their humility in prosperity. Great is our gain if, in studying the way of the saints, we perceive our own weakness and exclaim with Job: "I sinned and did wrong."[49] For by reflecting on men better than ourselves we realize that we are sinners. We try to improve, and in time advance with quicker strides. St. Gregory says, "We are strengthened with great yearning for personal advancement when we perceive in others the virtue we do not possess."[50]

§ II. Particular Examen

133. **Necessity.** Like the general examination, the daily particular examen is necessary for our spiritual perfection. We cannot, with a single blow, remove all inordinate desires, nor tear out once and for all every vice rooted in the soul. All the masters of the spiritual life agree that we must follow a certain orderly procedure in reforming our ways, and this procedure is the daily particular examen. The Church Fathers also have recommended this practice for its effectiveness. It is a serious mistake to neglect it.

---

49. Job 33:27.
50. St. Gregory, *Moralia*, Lib. XXIV, cap. VIII, in Migne, *P. L.*, t. LXXVI, col. 297.

Matter for the particular examen. As in the general examination, the needs of each individual determine the matter for the particular examen. Let the imperfect religious work at removing his most deeply rooted vice. He must prepare to battle first against his externally defective acts; then he should attack vicious internal affections. If we are burdened with many vices, let us begin by fighting a weaker fault. As soon as it is eradicated, we can proceed to the assault of other more difficult vices. If, however, our faults are of equal gravity, we should make a central attack. That is, we are to struggle against the vice which is the root and fountainhead of the others. The proficient should concentrate on a virtue most decidedly needed for his further progress.

Success depends upon careful choice. The efficacy of this examination depends largely upon the selection of the matter. If an imperfect soul discovers some ruling passion which is the wellspring of many other vices, he should attack it and thoroughly overcome it by means of the particular examen. What applies to imperfect souls applies also in due proportion to the proficient and the perfect. They must discover the virtue which will be the source of many other virtues for their soul in its present state. Their particular examen should above all concern itself with this virtue.

Method of particular examen

(1) Once we have selected the matter for the particular examen — either a virtue or a vice — we must each morning firmly resolve to cultivate the desirable virtue or conquer the detestable vice. It is distinctly helpful to renew this intention often throughout the day, particularly during meditation or Mass, etc. If we frequently forget to renew our intention, we must post a sign at some definite place to serve as a reminder.

(2) When we perceive that we have failed in this duty, we should regret the omission, and humbly strike our breast if

we can do so without attracting the attention of others. An act of the virtue which is the opposite of our fault should be performed, so that one and the same operation may root out the fault and strengthen the good habit.

(3) Before meals we should examine our conscience in detail. In the evening, this examen is made in connection with the general examination of conscience, in order to record the number of times we have failed during the day. The following method should be used during the time allotted for the examination.

(a) We should first thank God, ask light of the Holy Spirit, etc., observing the same preparations as for the general examination.

(b) We should consider every act; examine our progress, the number of falls; the places and occasions that have caused the greatest difficulty. For the purpose of conquering a vice or acquiring a virtue, it is strategically expedient to divide the topic of the examination — for instance, fraternal charity. First, external actions: "Did I fail in word, inclination or deed?" Then internal acts: "Did I foster a bitter disposition, show contempt," etc.?

(c) We must persevere until we have accomplished the purpose of the examen — that is, victory over the vice or acquisition of the determined virtue. Every gain brings us nearer to the general objective: integrity or true purity of heart.

"The suppression of certain vices, such as those against modesty," says Le Gaudier, "and the acquisition of certain minor virtues do not require a long time. In fifteen days, for instance, a diligent person can overcome the obstacles to external decency and silence, and learn to avoid scurrility and detraction. On the other hand, we might profitably strive after any of the greater virtues — as, for instance, perfect humility, patience, conformity to the will of God — not merely for a year, but two or more, or even throughout our lifetime. At the same time we may, with great profit, occasionally work at eradicating some other vice or establishing some virtue. We could, for instance, resolve that for fifteen days we shall specially keep watch over sins of speech."[51]

(d) Once or twice daily let us note the number of transgressions on a card which is boxed off by lines into weeks of the month and days of the week.

"Do not despise the practice of the particular examen or consider it trivial or puerile. St. Ignatius, St. Alphonsus Liguori, St. Alphonsus Rodriguez and other eminent teachers of the spiritual life taught and commended this practice. Innumerable saints have made use of the particular examen and our Fathers have handed it down to us, as their writings clearly demonstrate. Therefore, you too must use the particular examen with perseverance, that you may profit by its effects."[52]

(e) Day by day, week by week, we should inspect our notes on the particular examen to ascertain our progress. If we have advanced but little, we would do well to try a stronger remedy. The struggle should never become excessive, to the point of producing a feeling of forced bondage or slavery. Let us avoid all that overtaxes, all that destroys freedom of the spirit, or impedes the devout movements of the will. We should not tie ourselves down to such strict assignments that the breaking of them would seem sinful. We should each follow the method best suited to our individual needs.

(f) We should also consult our confessor and give him an exact account of our failures in respect to the particular examen, and having obtained the confessor's permission, impose on ourselves some mortification proportionate to the gravity of our sins.

---

51. *Loc. cit.,* cap. VIII.
52. Gaudentius Guggenbichler, *Introductio ad vitam Seraphicam,* Pars I, Tract. IV, cap. VI, n. 2 nota.

CONCLUSION. The general and the particular examination of conscience will teach the soul to proceed in the proper way along the road to perfection. By neglecting these exercises, we expose ourselves to serious danger; by observing them perfectly, we shall escape from this danger and rise to an exalted degree of holiness.

Neglect of the examination of conscience. This exposes one to the danger of falling. The Apostle St. John is convinced that it is impossible at the same time to know God and to offend His divine majesty: "He who says that he knows Him, and does not keep His commandments, is a liar and the truth is not in him."[53] Light is incompatible with darkness: "Let us therefore lay aside the works of darkness, and put on the armor of light."[54] Experience proves that even religious well instructed in the law of God and in the holy Rule may be a bad example to their confreres and even to seculars.[55] Some novices, too, cast off the yoke of religious life and return to their worldly desires. Why do they loosen the reins of religious observance and live as if neither God nor Rule nor Constitutions existed? The answer is: because of ignorance resulting from neglect of the examination of conscience.

The examination of conscience warns us of danger. The story is often told of a traveler who lost his way in the darkness and could not find a place to sleep. He finally discovered a cave, the hiding place of robbers and lay peacefully down to rest. What was the reason for such great boldness? The poor man did not know that the cave was the den of robbers. Had he known it, he would have been horrified and would not have been able to sleep, nor even to close his eyes. In the morning, he saw his great danger and, shaking with fright, he crept away. A soul in the darkness of sin often dwells with robbers

---

53. 1 John 2:4.
54. Rom. 13:12.
55. Cf. St. Jerome, *Letter 60* (alias 3), § 11, to Nepotianus.

who will set a trap and threaten the sinner with eternal death. These robbers are our vices and unbridled passions. By the light of grace and through the influence of the examination of conscience, both general and particular, the soul recognizes its plight and, by answering the call of grace, flees to the shelter of sanctity.

Article IV — Mental Prayer

134. Holy Scripture indicates an even more excellent method of acquiring wisdom, of illuminating the mind and of enlightening the intellect, when it says, "I pleaded, and the Spirit of Wisdom came to me."[56] Through the prophet Jeremia, God suggests the reason why the world approaches its ruin. The reason is evidently the lack of mental prayer. "With desolation is all the land made desolate, because there is none that considereth in the heart."[57] We must know exactly what is meant by mental prayer. For many do not understand it and do not explain it properly.

Prayer in general. Prayer is an act of the virtue of religion, or an act of supreme worship (*latria*) which is due to God alone. By virtue of the fact that we petition benefits from God we acknowledge His power and goodness and profess our dependence on Him, our need of Him who is the Author of all good. All this pertains to the virtue of religion.

Definition: St. John Damascene defines prayer as "the lifting up of the mind to God or the petition for suitable things from God."[58]

(a) *In the broadest meaning* prayer is every ascent or movement of the intellect and will toward God. According to St. John Damascene's general definition, mental prayer is that

---

56. Wisd. 7:7.
57. Jer. 12:11, Challoner-Douay version.
58. St. John Damascene, *De fide orthod.*, Lib. III, cap. XXIV, in Migne, *P. G.*, t. XCIV, col. 1090.

prayer which embraces the various internal acts of religion and the acts of the other virtues.

(b) *In a more restricted meaning* it is the ascent of the mind to God by which we praise Him, thank Him for His gifts, and seek His aid.

(c) *In the strict sense,* prayer is "a petition for suitable things from God."

PETITION is an act by which we appeal to the benevolence of another in order to receive something from him as a favor.

SUITABLE THINGS are goods which we can desire because of their quality and usefulness. Spiritual favors are eminently suitable; temporal favors are suitable if they lead to salvation.

FROM GOD. Not every petition is called a prayer. In order to be a prayer, it must be directed to God. For prayer, as we have said, is an act of religion. We can pray only to God as the principal Author and Giver of all good. Praying to the saints in this way would be actual idolatry. The saints should be invoked as patrons and intercessors before the throne of God.

Petition will honor God and be properly a prayer in the strict sense when it proceeds from the intention of worshiping God. For a prayer to lead to salvation, it must originate from actual grace and receive support from faith and hope.

Division of prayer. Prayer is divided into vocal and mental prayer. Vocal prayer proceeds proximately from spoken words and ultimately from thoughts. For the mere production of words with the lips and the raising of the voice to God cannot be called prayer. Mental prayer is performed by the mind without any words being said.

Mental prayer is called *simple thought* when we merely keep our mind devoutly on some pious topic for a time. This is something like an internal ejaculation.

Prayer is called *meditation* when we earnestly and lovingly think upon and penetrate the depths of a question. Prayer is known as *contemplation* when the soul does not consider its object in any formal discursive way. *Contemplation* consists in a certain simple gaze of the mind, replete with admiration of the divine truth and the perception of love. Contemplation is used in a strict and a broad sense; it will receive detailed treatment later.

EXPLANATION OF MENTAL PRAYER. Mental prayer is commonly called meditation when it occurs in the usual way through the free use of the faculties under the influence of grace; it is called contemplation when attained in an extraordinary way. Over and above this division some authors use the term "meditation" not only to include the act of "meditating" properly so called, but also to embrace in a general way all the acts performed in this pious exercise. St. Bernard — or more precisely, the author of *The Ladder of the Cloistered* (*Scala claustralium*) — reduces these acts to four: reading, meditation, prayer, and contemplation. These are the rungs of the ladder by which the religious engaged in mental prayer will rise from earth to heaven. The bottom of the ladder rests on the earth, while the top pierces the clouds. "These rungs are distinct in order and function as well as in name and number. . . . Reading seeks the sweetness of a blessed life, meditation finds it, prayer asks for it, contemplation tastes it. Our Lord Himself says: 'Seek, and you shall find; knock, and it shall be opened to you' (Matt. 7:7). We seek by reading and find by meditating: we knock by prayer and the door is opened to us by contemplation. Reading is like putting solid food into our mouth; meditation chews and masticates it; prayer develops the taste; contemplation is the sweetness which delights and refreshes. Reading is the shell, meditation the core, prayer the request for what is desired, and contemplation is delight in the acquired sweetness."[59]

---

59. *Scala claustralium*, cap. I et II, in Migne, *P. L.*, t. CLXXXIV, col. 475, 476.

At the time assigned for mental prayer we should always do these four things, for they form an inseparable whole. "Reading without meditation is dry; meditation without reading is rambling; prayer without meditation is tepid; meditation without prayer is fruitless; prayer without the sweetness of contemplation is burdensome; the attainment of contemplation without prayer is either rare or miraculous."[60]

Necessity of mental prayer. "Without zeal for internal devotion," says Father David of Augsburg, "the life of a religious is like a honeycomb without honey, a wall without mortar, food without seasoning. In these days a great many neither relish nor seek, desire, nor love the gift of devotion; they do not even believe in it; they make fun of it in others. These people should know that the life of every religious who does not seek the marrow of divine sweetness, who does not make special efforts to acquire the spirit of prayer and internal purity, is dry and imperfect and close to ruin. St. Paul clearly says: 'The Spirit Himself gives testimony to our spirit that we are sons of God' (Rom. 8:16)."[61]

And so the main purpose of mental prayer is to open the gates of our soul to the outpourings of the Spirit, to make ourselves receptive to its constant flow of love, and to reciprocate this love in our own small measure by expressing our gratitude in the most sincere, personal, and childlike movements of our heart. These movements may find their origin in a formal meditation on some event of the life of Christ or on some point of faith, but the important thing to remember is that the perfection of mental prayer does not consist in the quality of its logical development but in its depths and sincerity as an expression of love. It is no use trying to dazzle the Lord with our brilliant mind: He made it Himself, and knows all about

---

60. *Ibid.,* cap. XII, col. 482.
61. David of Augsburg, *De exterioris et interioris hominis compositione,* Lib. III, Proc. VII, cap. LIX, n. 4.

it; and He is not seeking a display of scholarly wit, but an act of gratitude, praise, and love.

Prayer is our spiritual teacher, the mother and nurse of all virtue. "He who neglects prayer," St. Thomas declares, "is like a soldier without weapons since he lacks both the light and the holy impulses which are so necessary to preserve his spirit."[62]

135. **Divisions of mental prayer.** Mental prayer is so important that the holy Fathers see in it the source of true wisdom, from which flows knowledge of God and of divine things. We shall now consider what must be done: (1) before mental prayer; (2) during mental prayer; (3) after mental prayer; (4) in various circumstances.

§ I. Preparation

136. **Preparation is necessary for prayer, especially for mental prayer.** He who prays without preparation tempts God by appearing improperly before the divine majesty. Sirach says: "Before prayer, prepare thy soul and be not as a man who tempteth God."[63]

KINDS OF PREPARATION. St. Ambrose explains the preparation to be made before prayer and the meaning of Sirach's words: "Before prayer," he says, "prepare your soul, that your manners may indicate, your faith support and your works commend that for which you pray."[64] St. Lawrence Justinian writes: "Those who wish to approach the throne of an earthly king dispose themselves so becomingly that nothing either in their appearance or speech may displease the sovereign. How much more should they prepare themselves who desire to stand

---

62. Quoted by Bernard of Andermatt, *Litterae de observ. Reg.* in *Analecta O. M. C.,* t. XVII, p. 274.

63. Ecclus. 18:23, Challoner-Douay version.

64. St. Ambrose, *Exhort. virginitatis,* cap. X, n. 70, in Migne, *P. L.,* t. XVI, col. 372.

before the King of men and angels!"[65] The same saint divides this preparation into two parts: (1) remote preparation; (2) proximate preparation.

I. REMOTE PREPARATION

137. **Definition.** "Remote preparation consists in the praiseworthy life of the one who prays. It will be a great aid to devout prayer, if at all times, in every place and deed, we refrain from illicit actions and obey the divine precepts."[66] Therefore:

Conscience must be cleansed before prayer. St. Paul writes truthfully that those who transgress the divine laws "crucify again for themselves the Son of God."[67] By what right can anyone whose hands are tinged with the blood of the crucified Son of God presume to appear in the presence of the eternal Father and demand gifts and favors from Him?

Even though God does not listen to the prayer of a confirmed sinner who is in the state of mortal sin, if the sinner has recourse to prayer for the purpose of hating his sin and of obtaining the grace to hate it, God will listen to this prayer, as clearly appears from the example of the publican. "But the publican, standing afar off, would not so much as lift up his eyes to heaven, but kept striking his breast, saying, 'O God, be merciful to me the sinner.' "[68] His words and behavior manifest the necessary and sufficient conditions to be met by every true and worthy penitent. First, a recognition of his own unworthiness; then, arising from this recognition, a change of heart and a salutary shame.

A sinless life, condition of an efficient prayer. Mental prayer is conversation with God, and should therefore proceed

---

65. St. Lawrence Justinian, *Lignum vitae*, De oratione, cap. III.
66. *Ibid.*
67. Heb. 6:6.
68. Luke 18:13.

familiarly, as among friends and acquaintances. Contemplative, prayerful souls are chiefly found in religious cloisters, where penitential and sinless lives are lived. Contemplative souls are seldom found amid the noise of the world.

The habit of recollection is also needed for the greater efficacy of prayer. This will be treated along with the conditions for acquiring and retaining the spirit of prayer.

II. PROXIMATE PREPARATION

138. Proximate preparation consists in the acts required to dispose us immediately for prayer. By this preparation we adapt all our faculties to the task before us and call upon God to aid us by His grace. We must first prepare the subject matter, set our memory in order for this exercise, stir our will to receive the fruits of prayer and in all earnestness invoke God's help.

The subject matter of prayer in general. St. Peter of Alcantara writes: "Since prayer has for its purpose to enkindle in our hearts the love and the fear of God and fidelity to His commandments, the best subject matter for prayer will be that which most nearly approaches this purpose. Certainly, all material things, all Sacred Scripture may serve this purpose. But generally speaking the mysteries of faith contained in the Apostles' Creed are the most efficacious, the most effective for achieving the desired end. The Creed treats of the divine beneficence, the last judgment, the pains of hell and the glory of heaven. Reflections on such matters powerfully arouse the hearts of men and move them to the love and fear of God. The Creed also embraces the life and Passion of our Lord and Saviour Jesus Christ, the fount and source of all our good. . . . In order to help novices and beginners walk along the path of mental prayer and to give them food for meditation, as it is given already prepared to small children, I shall

offer two sets of meditations — one for the morning and one
for the evening — taken almost entirely from the mysteries of
our faith. As we strengthen our bodies with two [*sic*] meals
a day, so we should also give two meals to our soul, which is
nourished by meditation on things celestial. Some of these
meditations are on the Passion and Resurrection of our Lord,
the remainder on the other mysteries of faith."[69]

The subject matter of prayer in detail. (a) *The mysteries of faith as subject matter.* Before all else we should
strive to acquire the virtues opposed to our predominant vices;
at the same time we should try to develop the virtues which
are considered more fitting for our state and our particular
needs. Some people are fainthearted; others are bold. In Scripture there are many words, deeds, examples and parables which
drive away fear and strengthen hope. Others are designed to
reprove the overconfidence and audacity of the proud. We
should be careful not to choose any subject or material too
advanced for our particular condition: Bread is good for a
man but harmful for an infant.

(b) *The life and Passion of Christ as subject matter.* Meditation on the life and Passion of our Lord is very useful for all
souls, but particularly for the Friars Minor. The specific precepts and counsels of our Order are founded on mortification
of the flesh, self-abnegation and the carrying of the Cross; this
is the true life of the Friars Minor. In the life and Passion
of Christ we can see the gentleness of our Lord, and learn how
to conform our actions to His. Jesus is the Light of the world
in whom and through whom all must be illumined. "As little
children," says St. Francis de Sales, "begin to learn by hearing
their mothers talk, and finally speak their language, so we also,
by earnestly meditating on our Saviour's life and observing
His words, actions and affections, shall, by the help of His

---

69. St. Peter of Alcantara, *Tractatus de orat. et med.,* cap. II.

divine grace, learn to speak, to act, and to make the right deci-
sions as He does. . . . There is no more excellent material for
meditation than the life of Christ."[70]

§ II. Acts during Prayer

139. FIVE PARTS. Mental prayer has four aspects: reading,
meditation, prayer, and contemplation. It is preceded by immediate preparation. We shall now treat each of these in turn.

PART I: The Immediate Preparation

140. **Posture at prayer.** "When you are about to meditate in the place assigned for prayer," says St. Peter of Alcantara, "assume a suitable posture, either on your knees or standing or even seated, should necessity or health demand it. Then
arm yourself with the sign of the Cross. Gather the scattered
powers of your soul. Above all, control your imagination,
withdrawing it from all sensible objects. Raise your intellect
to God by calling to mind the Divine Presence. Have the same
reverence and attention you would have if you were actually
in His presence, for this is really the case. Make a general act
of contrition, if it is the morning meditation. If it is the evening
meditation, examine your conscience on all your thoughts,
words, actions of the day, your forgetfulness of God and divine
things; and purge it of the sins of that day and of your entire
previous life. Then humble yourself profoundly before the
majesty of God, in whose presence you stand, saying with the
holy Patriarch, Abraham, 'I have ventured to speak to the Lord
though I am but dust and ashes' (Gen. 18:27)."[71]

Curbing the imagination. We should often meditate on
these words of St. Peter of Alcantara, since they show how
to begin correctly and fruitfully the holy exercise of prayer.

---

70. *Introduction to a Devout Life,* Part II, Chap. I.
71. St. Peter of Alcantara, *loc. cit.,* cap. VI.

Whoever is subject to any vice, passion, or irregular affection is exposed to many distractions, vain, useless and perverse thoughts, fantastic and strange desires related to the object of his evil attachment.

Even the more perfect involuntarily suffer from the delusions of useless thoughts insinuated by the devil. Often they cannot extricate themselves from these snares except through the assistance of God Himself. For God alone, when He visits and directs the soul by means of His illuminations and holy inspirations, can suppress and subdue these troublesome vagaries.

Petitioning God's grace

(1) *Grace to overcome mental vagaries.* Everyone must beseech God to dispel these delusions. We should all pray with the psalmist,

"My heart fails me. Deign, O Lord, to rescue me; O Lord, make haste to help me";[72] visit me in Your goodness, that I may meditate with tranquillity.

Often a person suffers imaginative wanderings and distractions at the beginning of prayer and spends much time checking the imagination and calming the affections of the heart. It is well, then, always to seek enlightenment from God. He will rout these wanderings from the start, lest what seemed a little speck in the beginning may turn out to be a huge beam in the end. For one who is tepid at the beginning of prayer grows steadily more negligent and cold.

(2) *Grace to pray well.* We generally know from faith, Scripture, and theology what we should ask for and in what way to ask for it. However, in each particular petition both the matter and the manner of prayer remain concealed from us unless the Holy Spirit directs, moves, and inflames us to pray as we should. "For we do not know what we should pray for

---

72. Ps. 39:13-14.

as we ought," says St. Paul; "but the Spirit Himself pleads for us with unutterable groanings."[73] A contemporary of St. Bonaventure comments: "Unless divine communication or inspiration rouses the mind to meditate, and inspires the soul as to the matter and manner of reflecting on divine truths, human meditation remains empty and useless because it does not burn with the fire of devotion, but rather with the flame of vanity and cupidity."[74] "When one meditates, therefore," says St. Peter of Alcantara, "he should beg our Lord to give him the grace to stand before so great a majesty with the proper attention, interior recollection, fear and reverence, and so to spend the time of holy prayer that he may come forth from it with renewed strength and fervor, ready to do or suffer all things in His service. Prayer which does not produce this fruit is tepid, imperfect and of little worth in God's eyes."[75]

PART II: Reading

141. **Kind of reading.** After the immediate preparation comes the reading, or the recollection, of the subject for meditation. "The subject matter must not be read hurriedly," says St. Peter of Alcantara, "but carefully, slowly, and devoutly, applying to it not only the intellect, so as to understand what is read, but, above all, the will, so as to perceive and relish it.

"And when one comes to some passage which especially absorbs his attention, he should pause a while that he may more deeply imprint it on his heart. The reading should not be too long. Thereby more time will be gained for meditation, which will be all the more profitable and fruitful to the extent that one intelligently penetrates the matter under consideration,

---

73. Rom. 8:26.
74. *De septem itiner. aetern.,* Itin. II, Dictinctio 5, in t. VII, p. 147, in *Opera S. Bonav.* (Mainz edition, 1609).
75. St. Peter of Alcantara, *loc. cit.,* cap. VI.

and elicits more affections.[1] If, however, the mind is too distracted to lend itself with ease to prayer or meditation, one should delay a little longer over the reading, or combine reading with meditation, repeating the process of reading a passage and then meditating on it."[2]

PART III: The Meditation Proper

142. **Elements of the meditation.** The reading is followed by the meditation proper. This meditation sets in action the imagination, the intellect, and the will.

I. THE WORK OF THE IMAGINATION

The imagination brings to mind the chosen scene. By showing it as if it were happening before our eyes, it brings it more vividly to our mind and awakens our senses to keener perceptions. Indeed, it can be very useful to imagine in our hearts that we are present, that the mystery we are thinking of is actually happening now. For instance, if we wish to meditate on our crucified Saviour, we imagine that He is on Mount Calvary and we see everything that happened and was said there on Good Friday. We may do the same when we meditate on death, or hell, or on mysteries in which there is something that is offered to the senses. But when it comes to mysteries such as the divine attributes, divine goodness or clemency, or any of God's other perfections, the mind cannot function except through analogy, for these perfections cannot properly be represented even by the intellect. Whatever we "imagine" of God is certainly wrong. "Therefore, until God

---

1. That is, acts of various virtues or sentiments such as sorrow, desire, love, shame, etc.

2. St. Peter of Alcantara, *loc. cit.*, cap. VII.

draws a person higher, let him contain himself in this low valley and not overstep his bounds."[3]

II. THE WORK OF THE INTELLECT

143. **The part of the intellect.** After the imagination, the intellect is set to work. It draws from the vision of the imagination one or more considerations which turn our affections to God and to the things of God. The function of the intellect in meditation is not study, nor consideration for the purpose of acquiring knowledge or writing or arguing. It is a function in which our mind, enlightened by faith and aided by God, evokes the divine mysteries for the purpose of increasing in truth and in virtue. In truth, for if we hope to attain a perfect knowledge of God we have to enlighten our intellect, purge it from error and strengthen it in faith. In virtue, for meditation should not only result in an increase of our knowledge of God, but also in a deeper glow of love. We should carry out, by the practice of virtue, what we have learned in the exercise of meditation. "We may contemplate divine things in two ways: either by means of some sublime views or contemplations, or through certain practical aspects or principles. The first way is speculative, the second, practical; the former is suitable for the more experienced, the latter for beginners; the one moves the will little or not at all, the other efficaciously stimulates the will to action."[4]

United effort of the intellect and the will. The work of the intellect and the work of the will are inseparable. The intellect proposes to the will the things it loves; and the will, in turn, moves the intellect to seek and to find the objects worthy of love, and to propose them clearly and forcibly. The intellect

---

3. Cf. St. Peter of Alcantara, *loc. cit.,* cap. VIII; cf. St. Francis de Sales, *Introduction to a Devout Life.*

4. Cardinal Bona, *Horol. ascet.,* cap. II, § 11, n. 11.

should continue in meditation and in discursive prayer until the will catches the spark of holy charity, and is set afire by it.

The examination of conscience and the intellect. Meditation will be more practical if during this exercise we examine our conscience. Often, during the day, we take care of our personal cleanliness: we should in the same way examine our conscience at the time of meditation to cleanse it from sin. "Carefully examine the old ledger of your past life, filled in your case as in that of other mortals, with vice and error. Look into your heart, scrutinize yourself, examine the book of your conscience which shall be opened at the last judgment to God and to the entire world. Search and judge yourself, lest on that tremendous day you be judged and damned. . . . Recall to mind how you have lived or how negligent you have been in thought, word, deed; in desire, in respect to inordinate and unjust fears; in listening to illicit talk, in unregulated love and insincere sorrow; in instability, in excesses, in duplicity, dissimulation, hypocrisy; in performing useless actions, or omitting profitable works, and finally in any other deeds committed outside or against the rules."[5]

Ignorance of self is misery; knowledge of self is great wisdom, for it is the wisdom of the saints who said with St. Bernard, "I will search my ways and my desires so that He who will search Jerusalem in the light may find in me nothing which has not been duly examined and discussed. For no one is to be judged twice on the same matter."[6]

III. THE WORK OF THE WILL

144. **The part of the will.** Once the intellect has been properly instructed, devout affections arise, or, at all events, should be aroused in the will. The affections are: love of God

---

5. Ruysbroeck, *De septem custodiis libellus,* cap. XXI.

6. St. Bernard, *In Cant.,* Serm. 55, n, 3 in Migne, *P. L.,* t. CLXXXIII, col. 1046.

and neighbor, desire for paradise and heavenly glory, zeal for the salvation of souls, and for imitation of the life of our Saviour, compassion, fear of offending God, dread of eternal judgment and of hell, hatred of sin, confidence in the goodness and mercy of God, shame for the sins of our past life. "The will," says St. Francis de Sales, "must exert all its powers on these affections."[7]

Devotion not to be forced. Let us follow the advice of St. Peter of Alcantara: "We will determine certain boundaries for the activity of the will, beyond which it may not pass without committing a fault. For, in its exercise the will should not act too vehemently or passionately. Forgetting this, many people only dry up their hearts and render them unfit for divine visitation. A forced way of meditation often injures the health of the body and sometimes leaves the soul so disgusted that it fears again to face this exercise in which it has experienced so much pain."[8]

Artificial methods of little avail. "Recent authors," says Cardinal Bona, "have proposed various ways of moving and increasing the affections; for example, by admiration, thanksgiving, etc. However, this exercise of the heart depends more on the unction of grace than on merely human devices. For 'The Spirit Himself pleads for us with unutterable groanings' (Rom. 8:26)."[9]

Necessity of resolutions. The will must not only be affective, but also effective. Good resolutions must be made. They must be practical, particular, suited to our present state, proportioned to present strength, founded on solid motives, and humbly dependent upon the help of grace. After prayer we should turn all the strength of our love toward Christ; we

---

7. *Introduction to a Devout Life,* Part II, Chap. VI.
8. St. Peter of Alcantara, *loc. cit.,* cap. XII, documentum III.
9. Cardinal Bona, *Horol. ascet.,* cap. II, § 11, 6.

should love only in relation to Him and because of Him. We should so love God as not to condemn our neighbor, and so love our neighbor as not to lessen our love for God. Prayer forms, nourishes and increases the life of Christ in the soul. Perfect love of Christ demands both internal affections of the heart and external acts, for the performance of external acts proves the worth of our love.

Part IV: Prayer

145. Prayers of thanksgiving and oblation logically follow meditation.

Thanksgiving. We should praise God and sincerely show our gratitude and remembrance of past and present benefits before we ask for any grace. It is bad to ignore a benefit, it is worse to make no return, but the blackest ingratitude consists in forgetting all about the favors granted us. At the time of prayer we must first remember the benefits God has conferred upon us, so that by giving thanks we may burn with a more intense love for God and become worthy to receive new gifts. To thank God and to glorify Him for His generosity in the past is the best way to be sure of His grace in the future.

Oblation. St. Peter of Alcantara recommends this method of making an oblation. "After we have rendered heartfelt thanks to God for all the benefits received, our hearts will naturally overflow with the affection felt by the royal prophet David when he exclaimed: 'How shall I make a return to the Lord for all the good He has done for me?' (Ps. 115:12) We may in some way satisfy this desire by offering God whatever we possess and can offer. Let us first offer ourselves to God as His servant forever, wholly surrendering ourselves and resigning our will, so that God may do with us whatever He

wishes. We should make an offering at the same time of all
our thoughts, words, deeds, and direct all that we do and
suffer to the greatest honor and glory of God's name. Then
we should present to God the Father the merits and obedience
of His only-begotten Son together with all His labors and
sorrows . . . , and the benefits derived from the most holy life
of Christ, . . . since this is the greatest and most excellent offering anyone can possibly make to God."[10]

Prayer or petition. After such an excellent offering we
may safely pray. In prayer we ask God for a share in the
graces and virtues of His Son. We beseech God to bless our
resolutions and enable us to fulfill them faithfully. "We should
also pray for certain important virtues which help us keep a
more careful guard over ourselves; for instance, temperance in
eating and drinking, restraint of the tongue, custody of the
senses, a modest and composed attitude, good example to our
neighbor, rigor and austerity toward ourselves and other
similar virtues."[11] Then let us pray for others, for the welfare
of the Church militant and for His Holiness the Pope, that
grace may be given him to see clearly, to will efficaciously, and
to carry out successfully all that may redound to the honor and
glory of the Divine Majesty, the salvation of the Christian
people, and the conversion of heretics and infidels. Let us pray
for the Cardinals, bishops, and other prelates of the Church,
and particularly for superiors, pastors of souls, parents, bene-
factors, friends; let us pray for both the living and deceased,
and implore the intercession of the Blessed Virgin Mary, of
the holy angels and of our patron saints.

This petition should not last too long and should conclude
with a fervent plea for divine love.

---

10. St. Peter of Alcantara, *loc. cit.*, cap. X.
11. *Ibid.*, cap. XI.

PART V: Contemplation

146. Relation between contemplation and meditation.

"In the exercise of prayer we must associate meditation and contemplation, for meditation is a ladder leading to contemplation."[12] The beginner may be almost totally ignorant regarding contemplation. A complete explanation is necessary. We shall explain: (1) the nature of contemplation; (2) the practice of active contemplation in general; (3) the degrees of active contemplation; (4) passive, or infused contemplation.

I. THE NATURE OF CONTEMPLATION

147. Explanation. The word "contemplation" has a broad and a strict sense. In the *broad sense* contemplation not only signifies intuition or cognition, but also a searching gaze, meditation, and any other consideration which tends to the acquisition of truth. Speculations of the philosophers may be called contemplation in this broad sense.

In the *strict sense,* according to its usage by theologians and the Fathers of the spiritual life, contemplation signifies the summit of spiritual searching, a simple gaze at truth which has been sought and found.

Difference between meditation and contemplation. "We must understand," says St. Peter of Alcantara, "that the work of meditation is to consider diligently and attentively divine and heavenly things and to ponder now one, now another, in order to stir up in our hearts pious affections, as one would strike a flint to get a spark. In contemplation, which follows meditation, the fire is already lighted; that is, the affection sought after so laboriously has been found and is enjoyed in silence and tranquillity of spirit; not amid much reasoning and

---

12. *Ibid.,* cap. XIII, documentum VIII.

speculation of the intellect, but with a pure and simple gaze at truth."[13]

In contemplation the soul rests in and enjoys the presence of God. If we unite ourselves spiritually with Christ through meditation, if we place Him in our hearts by means of a never-failing remembrance and love, so that the soul can say, "I am Yours and You are mine; I possess You and You me; for what I have is in heaven, and besides You, what do I desire on earth; if You are mine, what more do I seek?,"[14] our soul has acquired this rest and the taste of contemplation and therefore rightfully puts aside the burdens of discursive or disquisitive prayer. It is content with the simple vision and the remembrance of God, as if it saw Him present, and it enjoys the affections of pure love, admiration and joy which God bestows upon the soul.

THE PRESENCE OF GOD AS CONTEMPLATED BY PHILOSOPHERS AND BY PIOUS MEN. The wise of this world contemplate God differently than pious men. Philosophers see God through created things; they are led by the light of nature. Little knowledge is derived from this source and also little love and spiritual fervor. St. Paul said of the pre-Christian philosophers: "Although they knew God, they did not glorify Him as God or give thanks, but," lifted up by the cold wind of pride, "became vain in their reasonings."[15] Devout men ascend from creatures to the contemplation of the Creator, not as if He were afar off, but as He is, existing within them. The light of grace illumines them and they exult and rejoice in His presence. They speak with Him as being present, for "He is not far from any one of us. For in Him we live and move and have our being."[16]

---

13. *Ibid.*, cap. XII, documentum VIII.
14. *Ibid.*
15. Rom. 1:21.
16. Acts 17:27-28.

The will directs contemplation toward holiness. Contemplation is properly an act of the intellect. The will must direct it toward the love of God by means of antecedent and subsequent acts.

(a) *Antecedent act of the will.* Contemplation is an act of the virtue of religion. It should therefore proceed from affection toward God, from divine worship.

(b) *Subsequent act of the will.* Since contemplation originates from charity, charity itself increases after contemplation because the soul has a better knowledge of God.

True contemplation demands two acts: one of the intellect, intuition of a truth; the other, of the will, love of God. Intuition without affection is possible because affection follows freely, not necessarily. But such intuition would deserve the name of study or curiosity rather than prayer or contemplation.

Kinds of contemplation. There are two kinds of contemplation: natural and supernatural.

Natural contemplation is that which is practiced through mere natural powers.

Supernatural contemplation is that which is practiced through supernaturally elevated powers.

Two kinds of supernatural contemplation. On the part of the contemplative, supernatural contemplation may be twofold, either more active or more passive. We say *more* passive because the intellect, which is a vital power, can never be entirely passive.

ACTIVE CONTEMPLATION. Contemplation is more active when the soul makes more use of her own efforts, not only of her faculties in their natural condition but also of these faculties elevated by the infused virtues and by the gifts of the Holy Spirit, and influenced by habitual and actual grace.

PASSIVE CONTEMPLATION. Contemplation is more passive when the contemplative is more acted upon by God than active of himself.

Distinction between active supernatural contemplation and passive, or infused, contemplation. To understand the difference between the two kinds of contemplation, we need to know something of the gifts of the Holy Spirit. The intellectual gifts of knowledge, understanding and wisdom are the eliciting principles in both active and passive contemplation. For these gifts are habitual sources through which the just man quickly obeys the promptings of the Holy Spirit, which may be made in an ordinary or extraordinary way.

The ordinary way. In regard to divine contemplation, the Holy Spirit can move the mind by lights and inspirations according to the usual plan of Divine Providence, just as He can move to action by the principles underlying the practical reason, provided it has been instructed in the common articles of faith. This is the ordinary way. In this case contemplation is active, since it is effected by our own effort and industry. Yet it is supernatural in so far as it is prompted by the Holy Spirit and elicited by the gifts of the same Spirit, as from a formal and proximate source.

The extraordinary way. The Holy Spirit can move us to divine contemplation through charismata, or gratuitously given graces. Contemplation will then be passive, since the contemplative receives rather than actively practices it; he experiences divine things rather than meditates on them. The distinction between the two kinds of contemplation consists in the different ways in which the gifts are activated: either by the ordinary workings of the Holy Spirit, or by His extraordinary activity through charismata.[17]

---

17. Some authors give to active supernatural contemplation the name "acquired contemplation," to distinguish it from infused contemplation. Now "virtue" is correctly divided into acquired and infused. But this division should be avoided as regards contemplation, since contemplation is not so much acquired as practiced, and this in two ways: either by the strength of nature alone, or by the faculties when elevated by the Holy Spirit; on the other hand, infused

(*continued on p. 301*)

Hence, while active supernatural contemplation in a certain sense may be called acquired or infused, in the strict sense we classify as acquired contemplation only that which is purely natural; and as infused contemplation, that which comes by charismata.[18]

The habit of contemplation. Now the question may arise whether we can acquire the habit of contemplation, that is, a way of practicing contemplation freely, constantly and delightfully. The answer is yes. But we must remember that this habit *in itself* will always remain natural, whether acquired by natural or supernatural acts. Waffelaert teaches that, "Just as a person may acquire theological knowledge by constantly studying and applying his mind to the truths of faith, so he

---

virtue is not acquired by our own powers, however elevated. Active supernatural contemplation may result in union mainly because of our own effort, and in this sense can be said to be acquired; yet it is still supernatural and infused in so far as it is performed under the influence of supernatural habits and infused gifts. — Cf. Waffelaert, *De donis Spiritus Sancti in particulari*, in *Coll. Brug.*, t. XVIII, p. 121, nota, and p. 122.

18. Those who disclaim any supernatural contemplation outside the infused do not realize that logically they should also deny the supernatural character of every pious thought or meditation, although these latter nevertheless constitute true mental prayer. Many, moreover, speak with much confusion in this matter. They distinguish only two kinds of contemplation: the one, natural, which they also (less fittingly, as we have said) call acquired; the other, supernatural, which they term infused. In treating of this, they claim its eliciting principle to be sometimes a gift of the Holy Spirit — knowledge, wisdom, or understanding — sometimes a higher principle or gratuitously given grace, or a brief concession of the light of glory. But if the eliciting principle is a usual gift of the Holy Spirit which every just man enjoys, what hinders the movement of the Holy Spirit from being ordinary also; what hinders active contemplation from making use of the ordinary gifts of the Holy Spirit and being at the same time truly supernatural in character? If the Holy Spirit actually moves the contemplative soul by gratuitously given grace, with reason may this quasi-passive contemplation be called infused, and remain distinct from that which is generally called infused, and yet have for its eliciting principle the habitual gifts of the Holy Spirit. Besides, charismata, which do not per se sanctify, are not indispensable for salvation or perfection; much less infused contemplation as we have defined it, although it is well suited to the state of perfection. Therefore, we may safely conclude that there is another kind of supernatural contemplation besides the infused. — Cf. Waffelaert, *Coll. Brug.*, t. XIX, p. 10, nota 2.

may acquire the habit of contemplation by practicing active contemplation of God and divine things, whether natural or supernatural. This habit, like theological knowledge, will be only a natural habit even though the acts of contemplation are practiced supernaturally and are true mental prayer. Theology may be studied so devoutly that it amounts to a continuous consideration of and supernatural meditation on divine truths; yet the acquired habit of knowledge will be natural only."[19] We said *in itself* ("per se") because God can infuse the habit of contemplation or of theological knowledge incidentally ("per accidens") while the habit in itself remains natural.

II. THE PRACTICE OF CONTEMPLATION IN GENERAL

148. **Meditation tends toward contemplation.** St. Peter of Alcantara urges us to rise to contemplation after each meditation. "We can do this at the end of each exercise, after the petition for divine love, and for two reasons: First, we may presuppose that our labor in meditating will produce some devout affections toward God for, as the wise man says, 'Better is the end of speech than its beginning' (Eccles. 7:8); secondly, after the labor of meditation and prayer, it seems only right to let the intellect breathe freely for a little while and rest peacefully in the arms of contemplation.... Whenever the soul feels this operation of divine love, at any moment of prayer, let it by no means resist but rather spend the whole exercise in this state. For just as we should abandon vocal prayer if it retards devotion, so should we relinquish meditation if it hinders contemplation."[20]

BREVITY OF CONTEMPLATION. The act of contemplating, that is, the intuition of the thing contemplated, is brief. The

---

19. Cf. Waffelaert, *Coll. Brug.*, t. XIX, p. 9.
20. St. Peter of Alcantara, *loc. cit.*, cap. XII, documentum VIII.

contemplation we are considering here is not special or infused, but performed by ourself with the help of grace. "Blessed is the man whom God allows to abide even for a moment on this high plane," writes the author of the *Scala claustralium*, who could truly say, "Behold I feel the grace of the Lord, behold I contemplate His glory on the mountain!"[21]

POSSIBLE EXTENSION OF OUR MEDITATION ON THE CON-TEMPLATED OBJECT. Although the act of contemplating may be brief, by meditation we may dwell for a long time on that which was contemplated. "Since the weak vision of the human mind cannot behold the vivid representation of true light for a longer time," says St. Bernard, "it descends gently and in an orderly way to any one of the three steps by which it has ascended and stops on one after another of them according to its free choice and according to the time and the place, remaining as near to God as it is distant from the first step."[22]

We must set a limit for the intellect and the will in this meditation which aims at contemplation. For the enemies which try to deceive intellect and will are very subtle. They endeavor to make these faculties exceed their proper limits.

Deception of the intellect. The intellect is deceived when it curiously searches into the majesty of God with an over-avidity for knowledge; also when it busies itself in the effort to know more than it should. Again, it is tricked when it is so delighted by the truths it sees that it does not communicate them to the will nor draw the will to love and embrace what the intellect contemplates, as though knowledge were the only object of its search. The learned, who desire knowledge more than the disposition of charity, often fall into this error and search more deeply than is suitable into the mysteries of God. They should listen to Solomon: "As it is not good for a man to eat much honey, so he that is a searcher of majesty shall be

---

21. *Scala claustralium,* cap. XII, in Migne, *P. L.,* t. CLXXXIV, col. 483.
22. *Ibid.*

overwhelmed by glory."[23] Although in itself it is good and pleasant to taste the knowledge of the Divine Majesty, it is dangerous to investigate it beyond the power of our comprehension. St. Paul warns us "not to be more wise than it behoveth to be wise, but to be wise unto sobriety, and according as God hath divided to everyone the measure of faith."[24] The intellect should therefore impart to the will a love for the contemplated object, and make the will feed on it and thus enkindle a love for it.

Deception of the will. We must also be careful not to let our will adhere inconsiderately to the delight of contemplation lest it be so captivated by its sweetness as to be overwhelmed by it, or to have the greatest difficulty in tearing itself away from this spiritual relish, even when we are called upon to help our neighbor in need. God must be loved for His own sake and not for our pleasure.

THE GRACE OF CONTEMPLATION COMES AND GOES. Father Anthony of the Holy Spirit says: "The grace of contemplation is often withdrawn. God approaches and withdraws. He approaches and illumines us by His approach, He withdraws and allows us to suffer in darkness and grief."[25] God holds to this manner of acting both with beginners and with the advanced.

Active contemplation is bestowed on novices and also withdrawn: BESTOWED. For a brief time at the beginning of their conversion, God usually gives novices the grace of consolation and contemplation. He knows that after tasting the sweetness of the spirit they will more readily renounce carnal desires, condemn earthly things, and remain in the secure harbor of a religious Order.

WITHDRAWN. Later this sensible grace is withdrawn from them so that, grounded more thoroughly in self-abnegation,

---

23. Prov. 25:27, Challoner-Douay version.
24. Rom. 12:3, Challoner-Douay version.
25. Anthony of the Holy Spirit, *Direct. Mystic.*, Tract III, D. 3, s. 7.

they may dispose themselves to receive the same grace more abundantly and securely.

Contemplation is also accorded to and withdrawn from the advanced: BESTOWED. If religious advanced in the spiritual life abandon external concerns and affairs at the right times and meditate a while to replenish their spiritual forces, they will then apply themselves all the better to their duties. Let them beg for the help of God and for His inspirations, which are the source of the vital energy of their soul. Let them seek contemplation, which gives them strength to accomplish all difficult undertakings. For if they never find the consolations and lights of meditation, their heart will dry up, their mind become dark, their interior strength fail, their passions run wild, their senses prevail, and their faculties become listless and shy away from all good works.

WITHDRAWN. Sometimes the gift of active contemplation is denied even to the advanced. They lose that which for them had been a great joy. The contemplation of Christ's glory of Mount Thabor was undoubtedly delightful to St. Peter. For he exclaimed: "Lord, it is good for us to be here. . . . Let us set up three tents, one for Thee, and one for Moses, and one for Elias,"[26] but as the Evangelist observes, "not knowing what he said"[27]; that is, he was ignorant; he suggested what was neither proper for himself nor fitting for Christ. Whenever advanced souls are deprived of the grace of contemplation, they realize that it furthers their own spiritual gain, or promotes the glory of God, or that perhaps it is in expiation for their sins.

It is for their own spiritual gain. This privation will enable them to work more efficiently at the duties entrusted to them, to mortify earthly affections, correct defects, and dispose themselves for higher things.

---

26. Matt. 17:4.
27. Luke 9:33.

Likewise the privation may be *for the glory of God*, lest, forgetful of their duties, they rest in contemplation more than is right. Contemplation is withdrawn from these souls that they may go out into the fields of labor to work according to the divine will and exercise the duties imposed upon them. It is not right for them always to remain within their own privacy, for their vocation calls for works of both the contemplative and the active life.

For the expiation of sins. Contemplation is sometimes denied because of a proud and puffed-up spirit, because of vehement passions which are not sufficiently mortified, or because Christ is not sought with zeal and order.

Yet contemplation should always be sought. We know now the reasons why active contemplation is at times denied by God to beginners. Let us not lose courage if we happen to be deprived of it, but rather try earnestly to recover it: (a) by avoiding whatever might prove an impediment to it; (b) by making use of the means which promote it.

(a) **Avoiding impediments.** All obstacles to contemplation may be reduced to these four: (1) the concupiscence of the flesh, oppressing the devout soul; (2) laziness, by which man flees labor and seeks idleness; (3) excessive solicitude, anxiety, hankering for business affairs and external occupations; (4) the pride of life.

(1) THE CONCUPISCENCE OF THE FLESH. All men naturally desire the sweetness and rest of contemplation, all desire divine consolations, but many wish at the same time to retain carnal delights.

But this is impossible. No one can taste divine sweetness without overcoming the flesh and its concupiscences. It is impossible to find heavenly riches among earthly pleasures.

(2) LAZINESS. Some people, although they seem to love God, to desire contemplation, and seek it, do not find it, be-

cause they are self-indulgent. They avoid work and seek leisure. St. Bernard says: "Let us rise up, all of us who are in this condition. Let us renew our souls, regain our vigor by casting off pernicious tepidity, if not because it is dangerous, then at least because it is burdensome, full of misery and sorrow."[28]

(3) EXCESSIVE SOLICITUDE. Others are bent upon feverish pursuit of honors and dignities, under the pretext of necessity or piety. Those who are led by this spirit walk in darkness; their troubled and unstable heart darkens the eyes of the mind, forces them to roam about through many shifting activities, and renders them unfit for contemplation. For this reason St. Paul warned the good soldier of God not to entangle himself with secular affairs. Immoderate occupation, in so far as it is immoderate, does not proceed from good will but from ambition or self-love. St. Bonaventure makes the same observation: "Just as noxious fluids flow where there is an [infected] lesion in the body, and, unless they are carefully removed, turn the wound into a running sore or an ulcer, so the business affairs of one who allows himself to be occupied by them increase more and more until they extinguish the feeble flame of the spirit."[29]

(4) PRIDE OF LIFE. The evil spirit deceives others with subtle pride. This pride appears under the guise of some good — as, for instance, a more ardent love of God; or zeal, when it inclines the mind toward meditation at an improper time, when obedience to superiors or a neighbor's need calls for something else, when it impels one to devote too much time to contemplation, so that the body becomes weak and the spirit is overwhelmed.

Required dispositions. Four dispositions are especially favorable for contemplation: (1) the denial of self and of all

---

28. St. Bernard, *Serm. 3 de Ascens.*, n. 7, in Migne, *P. L.*, t. CLXXXIII, col. 308.

29. St. Bonaventure, *De sex al. Seraph.*, cap. VI, n. 14.

earthly things which impede the friendship of God; (2) the earnest desire to imitate Christ; (3) tranquillity of heart whereby all else is put out of mind during the time of meditation; (4) a profound reverence and submission before the Divine Majesty.

(1) SELF-ABNEGATION. Many obstacles to contemplation are removed through self-denial. By a mortified life the onslaughts of the flesh are curbed, the senses bridled, the appetites and the passions conquered; and by the practice of the moral virtues all actions are properly ordered.

(2) THE IMITATION OF CHRIST. The imitation of Christ is the most excellent practice of all for obtaining the gift of contemplation. A great likeness to Christ attunes us to the divine communications. Indeed, the Lord Jesus Himself calls the clean of heart blessed, "for they shall see God."[30] That purity of heart which makes them similar to God makes them also contemplators of God.

(3) PEACE OF HEART. "Look to Him that you may be radiant with joy and your faces may not blush with shame," says the psalmist.[31] If we approach God unworthily, we shall not be enlightened. Therefore, when we prepare ourselves for prayer, desiring to enter into familiar converse with God and to delight in His presence, let us bear in mind what God said to Moses: "Remove the sandals from your feet";[32] that is, put aside all earthly things, that your heart may remain free, not bound to any creature but dedicated to God alone.

(4) PROFOUND REVERENCE. When we are intent on praying, let our reverence not only be internal but also external. Let us observe the external marks of reverence instituted by the Church, by keeping our head uncovered, genuflecting, pros-

---

30. Matt. 5:8.
31. Ps. 33:6.
32. Exod. 3:5.

trating ourselves, or by some other observance. If while striving diligently to acquire virtue, we make this outward preparation for prayer, we will enjoy contemplation in peace. If
we do not obtain the desired peace, let us not be troubled, but
wait until we are told: "Friend, go up higher!"[33]

III. THE DEGREES OF ACTIVE CONTEMPLATION

149. Mental prayer, which is common to all, implies reading, meditation and prayer, and also contemplation, as has been
explained. There are less common ways of praying. These are
designated by various names according to their foremost acts:
(1) the prayer of recollection; (2) the prayer of silence;
(3) the prayer of quiet.

In these forms of prayer the activity of the soul is more perfect, so that it comes closer to passive or infused contemplation,
since the Holy Spirit directs and aids in this activity.

(1) **The prayer of recollection.** The active prayer of
recollection is also designated by other names: "the recollection of the faculties," "the prayer of simple intuition," "the
prayer of pure faith," "the prayer of the simple presence of
God," "the prayer of contemplation," "interior prayer," and
sometimes, but less correctly, "the prayer of silence," which
is the object of the next article.

The prayer of recollection is a withdrawal of the soul from
exterior things and a devotion of all its powers to interior
matters, so that the soul is occupied with God alone. It brings
about a simple, loving and affectionate gaze upon God or a
simple, affectionate attention to Him.

(2) **The prayer of silence.** In the prayer of silence the
intellect does not frame words, but the entire will rests in the

---

33. Luke 14:10.

Loved One, and perfects its acts in an even more intense way
than in the prayer of recollection.

(3) **The prayer of quiet.** The prayer of quiet consists in
the enjoyment of true peace and internal sweetness, which can
be felt only in the superior part of the soul, for by this prayer
we not only come close to God, but in some way we perceive
His presence.

The acts of this prayer. This prayer is called the prayer of
quiet, not because the internal faculties sleep and do nothing,
but because, tranquil now, they are free of impediments in
their action. The intellect is alert and gazes on the Object
with delight and love. The will is vigilant and elicits ardent
affections of love toward the Beloved. The rational appetites
are attentive, eliciting divine affections. In a word, soul, mind
and all their powers are alert. God is more ardently loved
with the whole soul, with the whole mind, and all its strength
and in an altogether more excellent and perfect way than in
common prayer. This kind of prayer is not yet infused by God,
but is attained by man with the help of grace.

The practice of this prayer. Exceptional prayer is surely
not expected of novices. Yet it can happen that after we have
applied ourselves earnestly and for a long time to ordinary
prayer, it is almost impossible not to attain the prayer of quiet.

We may experience great consolation and spiritual profit
while praying in a more simple way. We should in such a
case consult our spiritual director. He will teach us how to
act so as not to be deceived by the devil.

IV. INFUSED OR PASSIVE CONTEMPLATION

150. **Definition.** Infused contemplation is "a simple intellectual gaze, together with a pure delight in revealed truth,
proceeding from God in a special way through the application
of the intellect to knowing, and of the will to loving, the

things revealed, while the gifts of the Holy Spirit also concur, especially the gifts of understanding and wisdom, together with a great illumination of the intellect and an inflaming of the will."[34]

This contemplation entirely transcends common laws, and is infused directly by God into the soul. The soul itself remains passive, as if yielding to the divine action. In the twinkling of an eye God Himself may impress many mysteries or heavenly truths on the mind and stir up ardent affections which abide for a long time, while the soul, adhering to the supreme joy it has received, delights in the presence of her sweet Spouse.

We should strive for this kind of contemplation. Infused contemplation can rightfully be desired and asked of God, *if it is for His glory.* "Eternal union with God through contemplation or vision and blessed enjoyment is desirable and may be asked of God," says Cardinal Laureo; "there is on this earth no man in his right mind who, if he were acquainted with it, would not desire it and ask for it with all his strength."[35] Even while still on earth, we may desire and ask God for this perfect union, as well as for the proximate dispositions for it, for it is the pledge of the Beatific Vision. "Infused contemplation does not depend on our efforts, attention and human diligence," says the same author, "since it is a gift of God and a favor coming forth from His generosity. Yet nothing prevents man, with the divine assistance, from acquiring some dispositions for contemplation, in view of which, out of His generosity, God may deign to grant the gift of contemplation."[36] Along with St. Augustine, the Council of Trent teaches: "God wishes that the things which are His gifts be merited

34. Cardinal Laureo, O. M. Conv., *Opuscula octo de oratione christiana in tyronum orantium gratiam* (Rome, 1685), p. 413. Cf. Benedict XIV, *De sanct. Beatif. et Canon.,* Lib. III, cap. XXVI, n. 7.

35. *Op. cit.,* pp. 436, 437.

36. *Op. cit.,* p. 436.

by us.''[37] For no greater gift can be imagined than eternal beatitude, and God wills that through our merits, which He Himself deigns to grant, we should reach this beatitude as our reward and crown.

Required dispositions. Many necessary means and many dispositions are required to arrive at active contemplation. Infused contemplation, however, demands many more favorable dispositions. It requires above all that the subject lead a perfect life. This perfect life will be treated of in a later volume.

Infused contemplation is difficult. The dispositions by which God in His goodness can be moved to grant this supernatural contemplation are difficult and laborious. In fact, they seem arduous not only to worldly but also to spiritual persons. Perfect purgation is painful, and the practice of all the moral virtues, as opportunities present themselves, is quite difficult. The number of those who actually arrive at infused contemplation is very small.

A person of great charity must not lose courage if infused contemplation is denied him, for this happens to a great number of people, either for their spiritual progress or because of a special arrangement of Divine Providence.

(a) *For spiritual progress.* Just as infused contemplation is ordinarily granted to those who have deep foundations in humility, so it is generally refused to others who would turn it into an occasion of pride.

(b) *Through a special arrangement of Providence.* Theologians teach that infused contemplation is occasionally withdrawn from the perfect, and sometimes granted to imperfect souls such as beginners; and again it may be lacking in many holy and blessed souls who are not contemplatives.

---

37. Sess. VI, *De justif.*, cap. XVI.

In any case it is necessary unto salvation that all men follow Christ, walk in His footsteps, and apply well the means of grace He offers, but it is by no means necessary that they enjoy the gift of infused contemplation. Like the Apostles, we are chiefly concerned with the imitation and following of Christ. We need not be envious of others who enjoy special gifts. Jesus chose only three of the Apostles "and led them up a high mountain by themselves, and was transfigured before them."[38]

NOTE: The assertion that contemplation can rightfully be desired if it is for God's glory, says Waffelaert, "does not contradict the common doctrine of the mystics by which they claim that one is not allowed to desire gratuitously given graces for himself because it may be an omen of pride. They maintain this with regard to the charismata considered formally and in themselves. Our assertion must be understood with respect to the sanctifying effect of the charismata under the supposition that God will grant them. Besides, prophetical knowledge, by which we mean all the charismata pertaining to knowledge, has a certain unrestricted meaning, so that in the strict sense it is truly a gratuitously given grace, while in a broader sense it is something imperfect in relation to prophecy, and not a genuine charisma. From this viewpoint, however, it does include those special illuminations and inspirations of the Holy Spirit which make active, supernatural contemplation approach infused contemplation."[39]

CONCLUSION. After finishing our prayers, let us thank God and again implore the intercession of the Blessed Virgin Mary. "But," as St. Francis de Sales says, "conclude by collecting a little devotional bouquet."[40] At the end of the meditation let us select one, two, or at most three thoughts or points

---

38. Matt. 17:1-2.
39. *Op. cit.,* t. XIX, p. 11, nota.
40. *Introduction to a Devout Life,* Part II, Chap. VII.

abuse than even the lack of virtue."[43] This, of course, applies to private communications. It does not concern the gift of prophecy which by its very nature must be revealed, but always in conformity with the advice of a spiritual director; for few things are more detrimental to the Church than a false prophet acting under a personal delusion or the inspiration of the devil.

Frequent remembrance of the presence of God. After prayer we should often recall the Divine Presence. Let us not imagine that this delight in God and this remembrance of Him are proper only to the time of prayer. As there is no interruption in divine love, we should at no time be unmindful of the presence of God.

§ IV. Various Circumstances Which Present Themselves in Mental Prayer

152. Various circumstances. Here we wish to consider some of the moral aspects connected with mental prayer: (1) the necessity for all the religious of the Seraphic Order to apply themselves to this pious exercise; (2) the purpose of this exercise; (3) the proper circumstances of place and time; (4) the various difficulties encountered in mental prayer; (5) the most fruitful methods.

As to the material for meditation, this point has already been explained.

*I. MENTAL PRAYER IS INCUMBENT ON ALL FRANCISCANS

*153. **Natural dispositions vary with different persons.*** Divine Providence has so arranged natural traits as to grant to some souls an inherent peace by which they seem fitted for mental prayer, but unfit for action. Others, on the contrary, have such an inclination toward external activity that they seem to be unsuited for the quiet of prayer. St. Paul says:

---

43. *Ibid.,* cap. LXV, p. 244, and cap. CI, p. 274.

"Each one has his own gift from God, one in this way, and another in that."[44] For the mystical body of the Church, just like the natural body of man, requires that there be many members, allotted to different functions. For if the whole body were an eye or an ear, what would do the work of the hands and feet? Everyone should be content with his lot and remain in his vocation, and care for one thing only: to please God.

THESE DISPOSITIONS CAN BE PERFECTED BY GRACE. The grace of God enhances, perfects, and elevates nature. No one need consider himself absolutely unsuitable for the grace of prayer, nor deem himself entirely unfit for action. For the love of God often goads the listless to labor; the fear of God often binds the restless with the sacred ropes of prayer. Extroverts can make their active life serve as a remote preparation for mental prayer. Sluggish souls can promote prayer by external works. All this is truly applicable to members of the Seraphic Order, who lead a mixed life and are engaged sometimes in active ministration like Martha, sometimes in silent contemplation like Mary.

THE ACTIVE AND CONTEMPLATIVE LIFE ARE INSEPARABLE IN THE SERAPHIC ORDER. In this Order everyone can say with the royal Prophet: "The Lord is my shepherd; I shall not want. In verdant pastures He gives me repose."[45] For as Jeremia says, "He guards them as a shepherd his flock."[46] The shepherd at one time feeds his sheep and at another leads them to their resting place. The sheep, while browsing, do not remain in the same place but wander from one part of the meadow to the other, yet within the limits appointed by the shepherd. After they have eaten, they are led to shady places

44. 1 Cor. 7:7.
45. Ps. 22:1.
46. Jer. 31:10.

where they can rest, chew their cud, and be protected from the heat of the sun, and later be led again to new pastures.

CHRIST FEEDS FRANCISCANS IN THE ACTIVE LIFE WITH SPIRITUAL FOOD. Thus Christ, the most kind shepherd of the Friars Minor, guides the sons of St. Francis through the works of the active life, offering them food by which they may be nourished unto life eternal. He Himself used such food, as He said: "My food is to do the will of Him who sent Me, to accomplish His work."[47] All holy works undertaken by Franciscans in the active life are spiritual nourishment with which Christ the Shepherd deigns to feed them. Yet we must realize that it pertains to the Shepherd to lead the sheep, to assemble them in the place of pasture and to lead them forth from it. The sheep follow the shepherd, obey his voice and go wherever he wishes to lead them for pasture.

CHRIST PERMITS HIS SHEEP TO REST IN THE CONTEMPLATIVE LIFE, OFFERING THEM A SWEETER FOOD. Over and above the food of the active life, Christ our Lord grants other food to His Franciscan flock. For the royal Prophet continues, saying, "Beside restful waters He leads me; He refreshes my soul."[48] The sheep lie down to rest, chew their cud, or sleep; in the same way the exercises of the contemplative life follow those of the active life. They consist in listening to the word of God, reading spiritual books, and above all in mental prayer: that is, in the meditation on holy mysteries, in petition, praise and thanksgiving. This is without doubt sweet, delightful and very wholesome spiritual food. Our soul must rest now and then from labor and stop all external activities. We must attentively consider our work, and the manner in which it is accomplished, investigate the mysteries of faith and receive from them our spiritual nourishment and delight. Finally, our

---

47. John 4:34.
48. Ps. 22:3.

soul will enter the sweet repose of contemplation. While our senses and passions sleep in this heavenly bliss, our mind and heart watch for God, having leisure only to gaze on Him.

THIS IS CONFIRMED BY OUR HOLY RULE. Our Seraphic Father confirms this teaching in his Rule, for he says that he wishes the brethren to have above all things the spirit of prayer and devotion. But to these he joins work, saying: "They shall work faithfully and devotedly in such wise that avoiding idleness, the enemy of the soul, they yet do not extinguish the spirit of holy prayer and devotion."[49] And the brethren who occupy themselves with the work of the sacred ministry are warned that "they shall sometimes leave the multitude and return to solitude, by ascending with our loving Saviour the mountain of holy prayer and contemplation. There let them remain, till once again, full of God, the impulse of the Holy Spirit will move them to go forth to spread the divine grace over the world. Let them endeavor to become inflamed as the Seraphim with sacred love, so that, all on fire themselves, they may enkindle others."[50]

The Franciscan's need of prayer becomes evident when we investigate the purpose of this exercise.

II. THE ORIGIN AND PURPOSE OF MENTAL PRAYER

154. **Mental prayer arises from love and tends toward love.** All mental prayer originates in love directed by the intellect, and also tends to inflame the heart with love of God.

Origin of mental prayer. Mental prayer grows out of love, for the soul that ardently loves God desires nothing more intensely than to know the way and manner in which it can obtain a better knowledge of Him. The soul which loves and is loved aspires to greater and higher things until it arrives at the perfect day.

---

49. *Rule,* Chap. V.
50. *Capuchin Constitutions,* n. 209.

Purpose of mental prayer. Just as true mental prayer begins with supernatural charity and is directed by the intellect to a more profound knowledge of God, so it tends to inflame the heart with a more fervent love for the contemplated Perfection. The intellect first seeks the truth, finds it and feeds on it, then shares its fruit with the will, so that love of God may burn more ardently.

CONCLUSION. The life of the Friars Minor is a life of ardent love for Jesus Christ. The friars should practice mental prayer with the greatest zeal, and this in accordance with the rules of the Order concerning time and place.

III. THE TIME AND PLACE FOR MENTAL PRAYER

155. **In general.** Except when hindered by some appointed occupation, vocal prayer and even mental prayer are proper everywhere and at all times. St. John Chrysostom says: "You can set up your altar wherever you are, for the place does not matter, nor the time. . . . Pray wherever you happen to be. You yourself are a temple, and therefore need not seek out a place. When temptations arise, have recourse to God, for God is always near. If you have a clean heart, detached from vicious affections, whether you are standing at the marketplace, the highway, inn or workshop — wherever you are, you will certainly obtain your request when calling on God."[51]

*The place for mental prayer is determined by the Order.

For mental prayer of any length, we need a place suitable to this conversation with God, and removed from the gaze of men. In such a haven the religious can enjoy peace and quiet. For us, the court of God, the choir, is prescribed so as to remove the danger of the empty praise of men. When we pray

---

51. St. John Chrysostom, *Ecloga de oratione,* Homil. 2, in Migne, *P. G.,* t. LXIII, col. 585.

there, our mind is less tempted to wander and to follow the distractions of the senses. For private prayer we should also choose a becoming place, and remain there in an attitude of great reverence and devotion. Yet we should at all times take into account our physical constitution and any bodily infirmities we may have.

CONCLUSION

1. Throughout the course of our life we should highly esteem and most diligently engage in mental prayer at the appointed time and place, after the example of the Fathers of the Church, ascetical men and all the saints, especially those of our Order.

2. Those who shorten or avoid mental prayer for false or questionable reasons are in a bad way and deprive themselves of much fruit.

3. They err gravely and also inflict a serious injury on themselves who give themselves so entirely to external affairs— even good works — that they find no time for prayer or leave this important task unfinished. Such excessive activity has often been openly condemned, through word and example, by our Seraphic Father, by many saints and blessed, and by innumerable illustrious men of the Order. Of our Seraphic Father, Celano declares: "He began all his occupations with holy prayer."[52]

IV. DIFFICULTIES IN MENTAL PRAYER

156. **Prayer requires effort.** Man, as we know, is bound to seek God. But he cannot reach this goal except through his efforts and his intellectual labor. For man does not approach God by the movement of his feet, but through the exercise of

---

52. Thomas of Celano, *Legenda Prima,* cap. XIV, p. 38.

his reason and free will. Grace perfects nature. And just as man since creation is born to work, so through Baptism he is born again in order to work more gloriously and more perfectly according to the graces and virtues infused by God. The Holy Spirit also repeatedly spurs man on to make efforts, to perform suitable works. And the best of these works is mental prayer.

EFFORT IS REQUIRED. To pray in a fitting manner, we have to remove the impediments and acquire certain dispositions. Let us remember here what has been said about contemplation, and not spare any reasonable effort.

Yet effort should not be overemphasized. There is here a serious pitfall. Many exaggerate this endeavor and only produce dread where rest and joy were the goal. For some imagine that the way of mental prayer is strewn with a thousand difficulties, exposed to many illusions, and most painful to the body. The light of prayer will dispel this fear conceived in the darkness of ignorance.

SOME DIFFICULTIES REQUIRE PARTICULAR ATTENTION. These difficulties are: (a) aridity; (b) distracting thoughts; (c) drowsiness.

157. Aridity. *Our attitudes during culpable aridity.* We should not be disturbed if we experience no ardor or consolation during mental prayer. We should place ourselves in the presence of God and approach Him with a sense of guilt. We should examine our conscience with care to find out whether we have culpably rejected His grace. And if we have, we should humbly but confidently beg His forgiveness. We should beseech Him to show us the patience with which He bears with us, and the indulgence with which He treats us even when we have sinned. Then we should carefully review the subject matter of the meditation until our soul becomes peaceful and glows with the flame of love.

Our attitude during guiltless aridity. Whenever we are well prepared to converse with God, we can always purely and simply enter upon holy prayer. Then, if it pleases the Divine Majesty to speak and to converse with our souls, we shall be honored and supremely happy. But if God does not wish to speak to us, if He acts as if He did not see us and we feel no consolation, we must accept this as an occasion for deeper humility. We should be careful not to omit our usual exercises of prayer, even when they seem insipid and useless. For no great virtue is required to lengthen the time of our prayers when divine consolations abound. But it takes real virtue to continue in prayer when this sweetness is withheld.

Usefulness of aridity. Aridity can be rich in fruits of humility, patience and perseverance. St. Peter of Alcantara says that anyone in a period of dryness "should accept it calmly and endure it. He ought to consider it sufficient that he has offered himself and everything he possesses as a sacrifice and most pleasing oblation, that he has denied his own will and put himself into the hands of God and under His power, that he has crucified all his inordinate desires, entered into a struggle with his faults and passions, and has done whatever he could on his part. And although he has not honored the Lord with an adoration made real to his senses, it is sufficient that he has adored Him in spirit and in truth, for such is the adoration which He demands."[53]

CONCLUSION. If we receive consolation during mental prayer, we should thank God for this generous and gratuitous gift. For our Seraphic Father says: "If, while praying, a servant of God is visited by some new consolation from the Lord, he should, before departing from prayer, lift his eyes toward heaven and with joined hands say to God: 'O Lord, You have sent me this consolation and sweetness from heaven, though

---

53. St. Peter of Alcantara, *loc. cit.*, cap. XII, documentum V.

I am a sinner and unworthy of it. I will return it to You in order that You may preserve it for me, because I am a robber of Your treasures.' And again: 'O Lord, deprive me of Your good in this life in order to preserve it for me in the next.' "[54] But if God delays His coming for a long time, we must humble ourselves before Him and confess our unworthiness of this grace; and if He does not come at all, we should consider it a great honor to be close to Him and in His very sight.

158. (B) **Manner of dealing with distracting thoughts.** When distracting thoughts assail us, we should heed the advice of St. Peter of Alcantara: "The remedy against attacks of distracting, unprofitable thoughts that so often and in such number annoy you while at prayer is this: Struggle bravely against them, do not permit them to master you. Yet as far as possible do not allow this battle to be accompanied with great labor and distress of spirit; for the grace of God and humility of the heart bring more success than much display of strength. Therefore, whoever is assailed by this kind of temptation should turn himself toward God without scruple or anxiety of mind (since this is by no means his fault, or at least very little so) and with humble submission and devotion of heart say: 'Behold, O Lord, how little I avail! Will my ground ever bring forth any fruit besides thorns and thistles? What good can it bring forth, O Lord, unless You cleanse it from all its evil growths?' After this, he should proceed to gather the threads of his meditation, and patiently await the visit of the Lord who never fails the humble. But even if this tumult of thoughts has not ceased, he should still resist them firmly and perseveringly, and courageously repel their attack. For he receives greater profit and merit (I think) from this persevering effort than from the greatest consolations he has received at other times during meditation."[55]

---

54. Thomas of Celano, *Legenda Secunda,* cap. LXV, p. 244.
55. St. Peter of Alcantara, *De devotione,* cap. IV, documentum 2.

Remedies against drowsiness. If the cause of drowsiness is bodily fatigue, we should remember that the body must not be denied what it has a right to expect, lest in turn it become a burden to us. If drowsiness comes from sickness, then we must be careful not to disturb or afflict the body even more, since there is no guilt in this kind of drowsiness. In this case we should resist drowsiness moderately and as much as our strength permits, by a careful balance of effort and concern for our health, lest prayer be entirely lost; for without prayer we will acquire very little in this life. Often torpor proceeds from laziness. If this is the cause, bodily mortifications are the best cure.

As for other difficulties which may occur during mental prayer, such as blasphemous thoughts, despair, and so forth, the best remedy is to be without fear. Let us forget about these difficulties and consider them as nothing. For when we actually are afraid of them, this very fear generally makes them worse and unleashes greater terrors. A further remedy is to seek help from Him who is always prepared to give it, particularly to those who fervently and perseveringly ask.

V. VARIOUS METHODS OF PRAYER

159. For a better and more secure practice of mental prayer, and to conquer many of its difficulties, a definite method of prayer should be selected. Although the Holy Spirit is the teacher of *infused* prayer, and is likewise the principal director in both common and private prayer, experience proves that a definite method of prayer is necessary for all, especially for beginners.

There are various methods of prayer. Different methods of prayer have been established by holy and spiritual men. All of them vary in certain accidental points, but agree in the essentials.

Essentials. The essentials of every method are: remote and proximate preparation; exercise of the memory, intellect and will; pious affections, good resolutions, petitions. These are in fact all the things which necessarily serve to attain the end of mental prayer.

Accidentals. The accidentals are the means proper to each method. They help either the intellect or the will. Hence all methods can be reduced to the following:

Three general methods of prayer

(1) The method which pays special attention to the instruction of the intellect.

(2) The method (Franciscan) which especially spurs the will to union with God through sanctified love.

(3) The method which to a greater degree disposes the soul for contemplation.

THE REASON FOR THIS DIVERSITY IN METHODS OF PRAYER. "Where the spirit of the Lord is, there is freedom," says St. Paul.[56] Just as the Holy Spirit, who is the instructor, the leader and the director of all who pray, does not guide everyone in the same manner along the way of prayer, so the saints and spiritual directors who have left us countless methods of prayer, did not wish to compel everyone to follow the same way. The saints kept the end in view; they chose methods that would more perfectly aid them to reach this objective. All these methods of prayer are good and holy, and each person should select the one which is most suited to his temperament, abilities and needs.

CAUTION IN THE USE OF A METHOD. Mental prayer and our method of prayer should be adapted to the requirements of our vocation and profession. There is a certain danger for all

---

56. 2 Cor. 3:17.

religious, no matter how perfect, in abolishing all method, or in abandoning, for some trivial reason, a method once used. Some may even desire to pray with affections only. This rashness may expose them to serious mistakes.

No one is allowed to give up all method; yet the method is not the end of prayer. It is a means of attaining the end with less difficulty. Therefore we must not adhere to a method which in some way keeps us from greater devotion. But neither should we discard it for superficial reasons.

St. Peter of Alcantara and St. Francis de Sales approve this doctrine

(1) St. Peter of Alcantara says: "We may perhaps resolve to consider some truth in its various aspects. We may divide this subject into several distinct points to be considered at several distinct periods of prayer. This is a good system. But we should never restrict ourselves to it so completely as to think it is wrong to pass, at least occasionally, to some other method or matter in which we find more devotion and profit. Since the purpose of all our exercises of prayer is devotion, whatever most directly helps us to attain devotion should be regarded as the best method for us, our most fruitful mode of prayer."[57]

(2) St. Francis de Sales says: "Some people have an exaggerated notion about the necessity of a method of mental prayer. They anxiously seek out a number of ways or rules indispensable (so they think) to mental prayer. They are continually examining their manner of prayer to see how they perform it, or how, in their opinion, they should discharge this obligation. They think they dare neither cough nor move during mental prayer for fear the Spirit of God will depart. What foolishness! As if the Spirit of God were so fastidious as to

---

57. *Tractatus de orat.*, cap. V.

depend on their method and posture. I do not say that a definite method should not be used, but that we should not slavishly adhere to it as some do who think they have not prayed well unless their own rubrics and fancies precede the affections inspired by the Lord; whereas these pious sentiments are the true end and goal of all considerations. Such souls are like travelers who, finding themselves at the very place to which they intended to go, turn back because they have not reached it by the road which had been pointed out to them."[58] Let us always follow some method; but if at any time, whether in the beginning or in the middle of prayer, we are entirely drawn to God, let us give free rein to the affections, for there is then no more reason to follow any method.

With this doctrine clear in our minds, let us now turn our attention to the methods themselves. Since an explanation of all the methods is beyond the scope of this work, we will explain only two: the Franciscan and the Ignatian.

*A. **The Franciscan method.** Various Franciscan writers, among whom the most eminent is St. Peter of Alcantara, extracted the Franciscan method from the life and the words of our holy Father St. Francis and his companions, and particularly from the writings of St. Bonaventure. There is a definite simplicity in its whole arrangement. It recommends itself to those who find it difficult to persevere attentively and for a long time in intellectual considerations. In this method we converse with God in humble simplicity and filial love, as did our Seraphic Father.

The parts of the Franciscan method are:

1. Preparation: (a) remote; (b) proximate; (c) immediate.

2. Body of meditation: (a) the reading; (b) meditation; (c) thanksgiving, oblation and prayer; (d) contemplation.

---

58. *Colloq. spirit.,* colloq. 18.

And throughout these different parts we are free to evoke pious affections and petitions.

3. Conclusion: Thanksgiving, invoking the intercession of the Immaculate Virgin Mary. Since we have explained the individual parts above, it is unnecessary to repeat them here. From this brief explanation we can see that the Franciscan method allows great freedom, so that we can use it according to our natural dispositions and the influence of God's grace.

B. **The method of St. Ignatius.** St. Ignatius outlined his method very exactly, and clarified it with many examples in his famous book of *Exercises*.

REMOTE PREPARATION. Removal of the obstacles: The spirit of this world, dissipation of mind, etc. . . . Application of the opposite virtues: the spirit of humility, mortification, prayer, etc.

PROXIMATE PREPARATION. Rereading of the meditation of the day before; thinking since early morning about the meditation of the day; fostering thoughts and affections on the subject of the meditation.

BEGINNING. Recalling of the presence of God; adoration; offering of self for God's greater glory.

Preludes: (1) imagining the mystery to be contemplated just as if it were taking place before one's eyes; (2) petition for the expected fruit.

BODY OF MEDITATION

I. With the aid of *memory*, recalling of the subject matter of the meditation.

II. Weighing by the *intellect* of:

1. What truth should be considered;

2. What practical conclusions can be derived from this truth;

3. What motive should induce this practical conclusion; (Is it becoming, useful, easy or necessary?)

4. How has this point been observed so far?

5. What will be done from now on?

6. What obstacle must be removed?

7. What means should be chosen?

III. *Operations of the will.* 1. Arousing of devout affections throughout the whole meditation. These affections should come more from the heart than from the lips; for example, praise, gratitude, humility, sorrow, love, hope, etc.

2. Formation of resolutions that are particular, practical, adapted to some present necessity, and founded on solid motives.

END OF MEDITATION. Addressing our Lord, our heavenly Father, as sons would address their father, servants their master, friends a friend, the sick their physician, as little lambs might speak to their shepherd; and speaking to Our Lady as sons to their mother.

CONCLUSION. (1) Prayer is the principal work of the day. It is the guide of our journey, the companion of our life, our support in the performance of duty. What a happy hour, wherein the soul contemplates the divine! This short period of prayer is sweeter than any honey, more pleasant than any food or drink. The soul while still on earth is on fire with love of God and with heavenly sentiments. Even now the soul speaks with God, the soul melts as it hears God speak His ineffable words. The intellect and the affections are elevated above the earth, and the soul is lifted far above all creatures to the fatherly heart of God.

(2) If we wish to reap the desired fruit of prayer, we must adapt our life to prayer and to divine conversation. This adaptation means that we must, as far as possible, avoid all faults and defects, free our heart from worldly affections, and stay away from the snares of vain, worldly occupations.

(3) Mental prayer must be preferred to all other occupations. If we are not free to pray during the appointed time, let us seize the first opportunity to do so. The Psalmist says, "Blessed be God who refused me not my prayer or His kindness."[59] Many pray fervently in the beginning of their religious life, only to become cold and even negligent. Never, under any pretext, should we omit prayer. If we cannot come to meals at the proper time, we eat afterwards. If we cannot sleep at the proper time, we rest and sleep at the next convenient hour. And why? Because these things are so necessary that we could not live very long without them. It should be the same with prayer, for prayer is the food of the soul.

Article V — The Spiritual Director

160. **Importance of a spiritual director.** The guidance of a spiritual director is another means for the proper instruction of the intellect. A religious can understand the elaborate structure of all the virtues by means of instruction, spiritual reading, examination of conscience, and, above all, by means of mental prayer. Yet, by subtle snares, the devil often weakens the soul and suppresses its virtues while the religious is unaware of the damage. The chief ruse of the devil is to hide himself and to deceive souls under the appearance of good. God, who admonishes us to flee the devil, will grant, to those who seek it, the ability to penetrate this camouflage of Satan. God is the only one who can reveal the hidden form of the

---

59. Ps. 65:20.

evil beast and expose him in his true horror; He gives this light of discernment to some of His beloved, particularly to those in religious Orders. For it is here He has placed His teachers and doctors, men instructed by Him to recognize the wiles of Satan, men who are to see to it that we are not deceived by him.

We shall consider: (1) the necessity of having a spiritual director; (2) the obligations of the disciple toward his spiritual director; (3) the diligence required in the selection of a spiritual guide.

§ I. The Necessity of Having a Spiritual Director

161. The whole supernatural life is like a pilgrimage. During this pilgrimage all the religious are bound to hasten toward God in the most perfect manner. But in difficult travels, such as the one toward religious perfection, we need a guide to help us reach our destination more easily, securely and quickly. All the spiritual authorities agree that a guide is necessary for all religious, even for those who are far advanced along the way of perfection.

162. (a) **A spiritual director is necessary for novices.**

(1) The necessity of a spiritual director for novices is proved from the *practice of the Church.* The ways of youth are inconstant and unstable. Proverbs says: "Three things are hard to me, and the fourth I am utterly ignorant of. The way of an eagle in the air, the way of a serpent upon a rock, the way of a ship in the midst of the sea, and the way of a man in youth."[60] Because of this instability, Holy Mother Church wishes novices and newly professed to be trained in those houses only in which perfect common life and strict regular observance reign; in which are stationed only serious, faithful,

---

60. Prov. 30:18-19, Challoner-Douay version.

exemplary religious, followers of the pure observance of the Rule, and given to prayer and mortification. Without such examples, religious life cannot exist. Novices and young religious should walk in the footsteps of the perfect and learn their practices. Because of the inconstancy of youth, Holy Mother Church further prescribes that they be under the direction of a suitable master who is experienced in the ways of perfection.

(2) The necessity of a spiritual director for novices is also proved from the fact that it is a *common practice among all religious*. The Fathers of the desert already advocated a spiritual director as a means of perfection. Cassian recalls that Photius frequently recommended and inculcated this doctrine. St. Jerome earnestly admonished his monk Rusticus with these words: "It pleases me indeed that you enjoy the companionship of holy men, and that you do not instruct yourself; that you have not entered on a new way of life nor immediately turned away from another path without the counsel of a director; that you have revealed your doubts, and are making progress more or less as you should; that you are taking care neither to exhaust your strength through haste, nor to fall asleep through delay."[61] St. Bonaventure also gives us reasons for having a spiritual director: "Beginners need a director from whom to learn things of which they are ignorant — that is, the tools of their salvation and spiritual progress, the necessity and utility of these instruments. . . . They need a director so as to be protected from falling into sin, or from too little concern about the practice of virtue. . . . They need a guide so as to be corrected, for one offense always leads to another, and he who falls into error corrects himself with difficulty unless he is aided by someone who is more stable."[62]

---

61. St. Jerome, *Epist. 125*, n. 9, in Migne, *P. L.*, t. XXII, col. 1077.
62. St. Bonaventure, *De sex al. Seraph.*, cap. I, § 2.

163. (b) A spiritual director is also necessary for older religious. Young men are not all alike in their conduct and fervor, nor equally well established in religious discipline and customs. Older men also differ in their ways and perfection, and not all can be recommended as exemplary or as of the highest caliber. For a man should be judged by his virtue and not by his age. Yet virtue is rarely so perfect in any religious that he does not need the help of a spiritual director. The Seraphic Doctor says: "The man who needs no spiritual director must possess a knowledge so complete that he never errs in the doctrines which are necessary for all. . . . He must be so enlightened that he will never be deceived by men or by his own perceptions when something only appears to be good. In other words, he must be divinely endowed with the gift of discernment of spirits. . . . He must be so filled with the fervor of devotion that without the promptings of another he is conscious of striving faithfully, effectively for every virtue. . . . He must be so steadfast in his love of good that abhorrence of every evil is second nature to him. . . . He must be so humble in all things that he neither desires to be praised for his good habits, nor imagines himself entirely free from faults, and minutely judges his every excess in thought, word and omission, correcting such lapses by severe punishments. And in all things he must be so constant that nothing — neither fickleness, nor distraction, nor hardships, nor fear — will make him change his state in life."[63] And since it is difficult to find a man of such quality, we can conclude with St. Augustine: "As the blind can hardly walk on the right path without a guide, neither can man without a spiritual director."[64] "To live better and more securely," says St. Bonaventure, "it is necessary that everyone should submit himself to others, by whom he can be directed. This holds true even of the Supreme Pontiff, who,

---

63. St. Bonaventure, *loc. cit.,* § 3.
64. *Ibid.*

as the Vicar of Christ, is at the head of the whole Church Militant."[65]

Our Seraphic Father St. Francis also had a spiritual director in Brother Leo, to whom he had recourse in all his anxieties. When Brother Leo was absent, he asked some other Brother to show him the way of truth. For he knew of nothing more dangerous than to guide himself. He said: "I once saw a blind man who had a little dog as a guide on his journey."[66] And Celano says of him that "he most diligently inquired, and most earnestly desired to know, in what measure and in what way or in what circumstance he could be of use to the Lord God, and how he could perfectly adhere to the counsel and good purpose of His will. This was always his supreme philosophy of life, his most burning desire as long as he lived — to inquire of the simple, the wise, the perfect and the imperfect, how he might apprehend the way of truth, and attain to higher objectives."[67]

§ II. Obligations of the Disciple toward His Spiritual Director

164. What should be revealed? The spiritual director should always be as an angel in the disciple's esteem. We should not consider him simply as a man, nor trust in him only because of his human knowledge. We should confidently approach him without hesitation, as if approaching God Himself. Then God will speak to us through him as His organ and instrument. Through his mind and tongue God will inform us of what is necessary for our well-being, for our spiritual good, our progress, our salvation. Therefore, we should be open and candid with him, sincere and truthful. We should reveal all to him, the good and the bad, without reserve,

---

65. St. Augustine, *Serm. 202, in App.,* in Migne, *P. L.,* t. XXXIX, col. 2324.
66. Thomas of Celano, *Legenda Secunda,* cap. CV, p. 278.
67. Thomas of Celano, *Legenda Prima,* cap. II, p. 95.

duplicity or dissimulation. "Often beg him to point out any disorderly affections he may observe in you, lest they grow stronger. This he should do frequently, without fearing to hurt your feelings by pointing out your vices. But if he says that he can find nothing worthy of censure, you must not immediately conclude that you are faultless. For he may remain silent because he fears your ill will or because he despairs of your amendment. In such a case, urge him earnestly to lay bare your wounds. Show him by your deeds how much you desire to make progress. Begin of your own accord to disclose your faults to him, and reform your conduct according to his direction. Rejoice when he reproves your corrupt inclinations. Thus you will always depart from him a better man, or with the will to improve."[68]

Good deeds should be revealed. We should submit to our spiritual director the manner in which we perform the religious exercises, particularly our method of mental prayer and of examination of conscience; also our mortifications, whether internal or external; the virtues with which we are blessed; the remedies applied in opposing our chief fault. Richard of St. Victor says, "Sometimes the devils hide evil under the appearance of good — and in order to lead us into evil, even announce future events. . . . They beguile us with false devotion, conjuring up within the soul prayers, meditations and sweet affections, even tears. These empty exercises sap the body of its strength and lead the soul into error or self-exaltation. . . . Some persons the demon inspires with too much solicitude for the salvation of others, inciting them and urging them to convert and edify people living far away from them, so that they lose their own tranquillity and profit. Hence, when the thought of some works to be performed comes to our mind, we should consider well whether there is any indis-

---

68. Cardinal Bona, *Manuductio*, cap. II, n. 3.

cretion in the proposed deeds; whether the deceit of the enemy
lurks behind such actions."[69] As this is very difficult to determine by ourselves, we should have recourse to a spiritual
director who will tell us what should be done in each instance
of this kind.

Christ our Lord warned us to be careful lest the light that
is in us should become darkness. That is, we must beware lest
our minds, which have obedience and humility as their light,
be covered with the darkness of pride and of our own judgment. The Book of Proverbs also cautions us: "On your own
intelligence rely not."[70] Cassian, the distinguished master of
the spiritual life, said: "The devil cannot lure a monk into any
more dangerous fault than persuading him to neglect the
counsels of his elders, and to trust his own judgment, his own
knowledge, his own way of explaining things."[71]

Temptations should be revealed. The practice of consult-
ing our spiritual director not only enables us to advance prudently along the right path but, as Cassian asserts, preserves
us unharmed amid the hundred and one deceits and the snares
of the enemy. As soon as a wicked thought is revealed to the
spiritual guide, it vanishes. And even before the spiritual director can give his considered advice, the hideous serpent will
be brought forth from his dark and subterranean abode into
the light by virtue of your disclosure. And once he is exposed,
he flees in disgrace. For his noxious suggestions have dominion
over us only as long as they are kept secret in our hearts.
Therefore we should immediately and candidly inform our
spiritual director about the troubles of our conscience, that is,
our temptations, weariness, scruples, etc. There is no reason to
be ashamed of disclosing temptations to our director, for it is

69. Richardus, *In Cant.*, cap. XVII, in Migne, *P. L.*, t. CXCVI, col. 456.
70. Prov. 3:5.
71. Cassian, *Coll. II*, cap. XI, in Migne, *P. L.*, t. XLIX, col. 541.

not the wicked but the holy whom the devil attacks, to snatch away their heavenly treasures.

Sins should be revealed. In the Sacrament of Penance we are bound by precept to confess only our mortal sins to the priest. But in spiritual direction there is no law but only a counsel urging us to reveal both the good and the bad in our souls, as also our sins, whether grave or small. Then our souls will be clear as water in a crystal vase in the sight of our spiritual director. Father Alvarez says, "A person who thinks he is sick is easily induced to reveal his sickness in order to obtain medical aid. If a man wishes to have a doctor or some medicine for his sickness, he cannot have the blessings of either without revealing his disease. Likewise, how can anyone enjoy relief from the diseases of his soul without a spiritual doctor or without consenting to take the medicine prescribed by him? Never fear this manifestation, for it is easier to expose your deadly wound to a doctor than to hide it. For calling a doctor and exposing our diseased body to his eyes brings great consolation, banishes sickness, moves the beholder to pity, and restores our health to its former condition."[72] St. Gregory says: "Unopened wounds hurt more, but when the putrefaction which is fermenting within us is cast forth, the affliction gives way to sound health."[73]

We should place full confidence in our spiritual director, but we must approach him with a holy reverence. The two go hand in hand: Reverence should not lessen confidence; confidence should not decrease reverence.

§ III. Choosing a Spiritual Director

165. **In the novitiate.** Ordered by his parents to set out for Rages, young Tobias objected: " . . . Nor did I ever know

---

72. Alvarez de Paz, Lib. IV, Pars IV, cap. V.

73. St. Gregory, *Reg. Pastor,* Pars III, cap. XIV, in Migne, *P. L.,* t. LXXVII, col. 72.

the way which leadeth thither." His father answered, "Go now, and seek thee out some faithful man to go with thee."[74] The young religious who wishes to conform "the new man" in him to Christ must also look for a faithful man who will direct and lead him. According to St. Francis de Sales, this is the first and most important of all admonitions and counsels.

For the novice this searching is unnecessary. For just as God provided an angel from heaven for young Tobias, so through the lawful authorities He provides the novice with a master who is to him a real friend and a trustworthy leader.

When studies have been completed. Once studies are finished, it is good to choose a director who can extend a helping hand, point out dangers, detect snares, and lead us through struggle to victory. But whom should we choose? Cardinal Bona answers, "A faithful and wise man who has both the willingness and the ability to assist you on the road to holiness. A man whom you revere rather than fear; who does not punish the erring but rather leads them to amendment; and whose life is proved by his deeds rather than by his words. He is a poor director who gives good advice but does not practice it."[75]

We cannot overemphasize the importance of the spiritual director! St. John of the Cross lamented the fact that he found so few spiritual directors, and Father Godinez says, "Scarcely ten out of every thousand souls whom God calls to perfection, respond to His call. And from every hundred whom God calls to contemplation, ninety-nine fail to respond. I maintain, therefore, that many indeed are called but very few are chosen. Besides the great and insuperable difficulties of our human frailty with which this task is surrounded, one of the greatest causes of failure is the scarcity of spiritual directors, who are, after divine grace, the navigators that steer souls aright through

---

74. Tob. 5:2-4.
75. Cardinal Bona, *Manuductio,* cap. II.

this unknown sea of the spiritual life."[76] One of the greatest factors of success on the road to perfection consists in finding a qualified spiritual director.

Use the proper means. "A faithful friend," says Sirach, "is a sturdy shelter; he who finds one finds a treasure."[77] But who can discover this friend? "He who fears God"[78] — that is, the humble of heart, those who seek with all their might to make spiritual progress, who earnestly ask God to give them someone who is a man after His own heart.

CONCLUSION. Throughout his life the religious must continually fight, not against an enemy that can be seen, but against an invisible, inveterate antagonist. He must wage this ruthless war not against one or two, but against an innumerable, hostile horde. To be victorious in this fierce conflict the religious must report to his spiritual captain (the director) all that transpires in his heart, and then exactly follow the orders, counsels, directions of the spiritual guide.

---

76. N. Godinez, *Praxis Theol. Myst.*, Lib. VIII, cap. I, Opusc. select.
77. Sirach 6:14.
78. *Ibid.* 6:16.

CHAPTER II

SECOND KEY: MEANS OF CONFORMING THE HUMAN WILL
TO THE DIVINE

166. The various means for instructing the intellect constitute the "key" which opens the human mind to Christ and to His doctrine. The "key" which opens the human will to Christ is the conformity of the human will to the divine will. The will of man is drawn to this conformity by devotion.

Devotion is the desire to give ourselves readily to whatever pertains to the service of God. This is the devotion to which, as our Seraphic Father teaches, "all temporal things ought to be subservient."[1] And St. Peter of Alcantara says, "The highest recommendation this virtue can receive is that devotion is the one virtue which is an inducement to all the other virtues. Hence, whoever desires to walk along the path of virtue without difficulty, must adopt this virtue for his mainspring; otherwise he will not be able to control the rebellious, lustful beast which is his animal nature."[2]

The various means. There are many means for acquiring this disposition of soul, particularly: (1) the practice of the presence of God; (2) the Divine Office; (3) mental and vocal prayer; (4) special devotions and Franciscan devotions; (5) devotion to the Holy Eucharist; (6) certain occasional exercises.

Let us open our will, that most noble faculty; open wide this door of the soul to Christ our Lord. Let us willingly adopt the holy means suggested, for through them we shall obtain the important virtue of devotion. Through these means we not only acquire tenderness of heart and abundant consolations, but also promptitude and alacrity in moving our will. We can say with the royal Prophet: "I will run the way of Your

---

1. *Rule,* Chap. V.
2. *De devotione,* cap. I.

commands when You give me a docile heart."[3] Human life grows into a familiar friendship and conversation with God. Hearts burn with love for Him, and through this union of love they draw nearer to Christ, adhere to Him more closely, and conform to Him more perfectly.

Article I — The Practice of the Presence of God

167. Among the means assisting us in conforming our will to the divine will with promptitude and alacrity — in other words, with devotion — nothing is more excellent than the practice of the presence of God. We shall therefore treat of this means under the following three headings: (1) the doctrine of the Divine Presence; (2) the fruit of this practice; (3) practical methods of walking in the presence of God.

§ I. The Doctrine of the Divine Presence

168. In Sacred Scripture the Holy Spirit teaches us to be aware of the actual presence of God continuously in every place and at all times. For the psalmist says:

> "Where can I go from Your spirit?
>   from Your presence, where can I flee?
> If I go up to the heavens, You are there;
>   if I sink to the nether world, You are present there.
> If I take the wings of the dawn,
>   if I settle at the farthest limits of the sea,
> Even there Your hand shall guide me,
>   and Your right hand hold me fast.
> If I say, 'Surely the darkness shall hide me,
>   and night shall be my light' —
> For You darkness itself is not dark,
>   and night shines as the day."[1]

---

3. Ps. 118:32.

---

1. Ibid., 138:7-12.

For, as theologians assert, God is present everywhere through His *Knowledge,* His *Power,* and His *Essence.* God's presence everywhere through His knowledge is proved from St. Paul, who says: "And there is no creature hidden from His sight."[2]

Through His power He is present everywhere inasmuch as all things are subject to Him: for His wisdom "reaches from end to end mightily and governs all things well,"[3] "upholding all things by the word of His power."[4]

St. Paul teaches us that God is present in all things by means of His essence; as Paul says, "He is not far from any one of us. For in Him, we live and move and have our being."[5]

God, therefore, sees all things. "There is an eye," says St. Bernard, "to which all things are apparent, but the eye itself is not seen. I fear the gaze of that observer who stands behind a wall, whose keenness of vision Scripture compares to that of the roe. Yes, I fear this hidden observer."[6] Jeremia, speaking of the inscrutability of human hearts, wrote, "More tortuous than all else is the human heart, beyond remedy; who can understand it?"[7] He immediately adds, "I, the Lord, alone probe the mind and test the heart"; for the divine eye looks into the depth of our hearts and sees all our thoughts and imaginations. He sees them very distinctly, not only those in our minds at present, but also those of the future. He sees them all, in their smallest detail, for as St. Augustine teaches: "All things, no matter how deep, were known to God before He created them. Whatever I do, You are always equally present, a perpetual observer of all my thoughts, intentions, pleasures and works."[8]

---

2. Heb. 4:13.
3. Wisd. 8:1.
4. Heb. 1:3.
5. Acts 17:27-28.
6. *In Cant.,* Serm. 55, in Migne, *P. L.,* t. CLXXXIII, col. 1346.
7. Jer. 17:9.
8. *Soliloq.,* cap. XIV, in Migne, *P. L.,* t. XL, col. 875, inter apocrypha S. Aug.

The blindness of man. Among the other afflictions which befell the human race as a result of original sin, is this: that man ventures to persuade himself that he can hide from the eyes of God. The Scriptures say of Adam and Eve: "The man and his wife hid themselves from the Lord God."[9] But they were greatly deceived, as St. John Chrysostom remarks: "Notice how foolishly they now act, . . . for they are trying to hide themselves from God who is present everywhere."[10] And St. Augustine, commenting on this incident, says, "[God] must be feared in public and in private. When you go abroad, you are seen; when you light a lamp, He sees you; when the light is extinguished, He sees you; when you have a change of heart, He sees you. . . . If you wish to sin, find a place where He will not see you, and do what you please. But since God is everywhere, your will must guard you everywhere against sin."[11]

§ II. The Fruits of This Exercise

169. When God proposed Abraham to the whole world and to all future ages as the father of all believers and at the same time as the prototype and exemplar of all true virtue and perfection, He also recommended the manner by which Abraham could prepare himself for this great dignity: the practice of the presence of God. For He said, "Walk in My presence and be perfect."[12]

(1) **The practice of the presence of God preserves us from every sin, particularly from the sins of the flesh:** (a) *From every sin.* Why do atheists of our day fall into every kind of wickedness? Because, foolishly, they try to persuade themselves that there is no God. All the crimes they commit spring from this principle. "The fool says in his heart, 'There

---

9. Gen. 3:8.
10. *Homil.* XVII, *in Gen.,* n. 2, in Migne, *P. G.,* t. LIII, col. 136.
11. *Serm. 132,* cap. II, in Migne, *P. L.,* t. XXXVIII, 736.
12. Gen. 17:1.

is no God.' "[13] And the result: "Such are corrupt; they do abominable deeds; there is not one who does good."[14] Every pretext for transgressing the law of God will be abolished immediately if we consider that God is ever beside us, and is not only an unseen witness at the time of our transgression, but also our future inexorable judge. St. Basil could say: "A single recollection, if it is intense, can be the sufficient means of deterring any vice."[15] And Claude Arvisenet says: "Behold, a short but very useful counsel: Always remember the presence of your God, and you will not sin."[16]

(b) *It preserves us particularly from the sins of the flesh.* Where did Joseph find the heroic virtue to resist the solicitations of the wife of Putiphar? St. John Chrysostom offers the explanation: "Although she planned her solicitation out of the sight of her husband and all who dwelt in the house, Joseph said to her: 'How can I do this wicked thing and sin against my God? Do you imagine that although we could perform this evil deed without the knowledge of others, we could be free from the observance of Him who never sleeps? Him alone should we fear, hold in awe, and dread, lest we do anything evil in His sight.' "[17]

This presence of God also strengthened Susanna, and guarded her chastity amid the flatteries and threats of the incontinent old men. One of them assailed her with these words so full of guile: "Look, the garden doors are shut and no one can see us."[18] To these words "Susanna sighed and said, . . . 'It is better for me to fall into your hands without doing it than to sin in the sight of the Lord.' "[19]

---

13. Ps. 13:1.
14. *Ibid.* 13:1.
15. *Reg. fusius tract.*, Interrog. V, in Migne, *P. G.*, t. XXXI, col. 922.
16. *Memor. vitae sacerd.*, cap. XLV, 3.
17. *Homil. 62 in Gen.*, n. 4, in Migne, *P. G.*, t. LIV, col. 538.
18. Dan. 13:20.
19. *Ibid.*, 13:22, 23.

We shall never sin if we can persuade ourselves that God is an observer and witness of our every temptation, as He actually is. We shall not sin, either openly or secretly, for though no man will see what we do in secret, we shall be afraid to sin because of our conscience and because of God Himself, who sees the secret depths and recesses of our soul.

(2) **It goads us on to greater perfection.** When we think of God as the fountain of all holiness, we will more readily understand that we need to be adorned with all the virtues in order to please the Divine Majesty. "You therefore are to be perfect, even as your heavenly Father is perfect."[20] As a soldier fights more bravely under the eyes of his leader, so we also shall be spurred on to greater efforts when we bear in mind that our Leader is present with us in our battles. Praying, frequenting the Sacraments, hearing the word of God, bodily macerations, fasts, mortifications, and all other acts of penance are certainly effective means of acquiring and maintaining perfection. But to keep ourselves always in the presence of God surpasses them all. Corporal austerities restrain and check the body; but remembering the divine presence also curbs the soul, the primary agent upon which depends all our internal and external operations.

(3) **It gives joy.** Who will not become joyful in difficulties and in temptations when he remembers that God Himself is present in his heart? With a joyful heart Jeremia the Prophet could declare: "But the Lord is with me, like a mighty champion: my persecutors will stumble, they will not triumph. In their failure they will be put . . . to lasting, unforgettable confusion."[21]

(4) **It arouses confidence.** "If God not only dwells within us, thoroughly penetrating and sustaining us, but also externally surrounds and encompasses us, then who can harm

20. Matt. 5:48.
21. Jer. 20:11.

us unless by a special permission of God?" asks Lessius. "But if He permits it, we should certainly accept it patiently and willingly from His hand, for He does this so that all things may work together unto good for those who love Him."[22]

To those who are experienced in the practice of the presence of God, we can apply the words of the Queen of Saba to the servants of King Solomon: "Blessed are thy men ... who stand before thee always";[23] and we can add, "before Thee who art so much greater than Solomon."

Since this holy practice of the presence of God produces so many fruits of sanctity, we must discover the manner in which it can most perfectly be conducted.

§ III. Practical Methods of Walking in the Presence of God

170. We can suggest a threefold method of walking in the presence of God. In the first, the imagination is more active; in the second, the intellect; in the third, the affections.

This first method, through the services of the *imagination,* is somewhat imperfect. In this method Christ is pictured as lying in the crib, or crowned with thorns, crucified, rising from the dead, or ascending into heaven. "Imagine yourself prostrate at His feet, and with great reverence, fear and trembling, with keen understanding, most ardent love, and with a contrite heart ask forgiveness for your sins. Then, pierced with the sword of compassion, consider the sacred Passion of the Son of God and, mournful and weeping, place yourself before His Cross and be wounded with Him. And perceiving the innumerable and immense benefits of His Passion, make acts of thanksgiving."[24] We shall then behold Him walking before us, accompanying us, seeing us, observing all our thoughts, words, and actions.

---

22. *De perfec. divinis,* Lib. III, cap. III, n. 21.
23. 3 Kings 10:8.
24. St. Bonaventure, *Epist. de XXV memorialibus,* n. 22.

The second method is more perfect and is accomplished through the *intellect* by a realization that God is present everywhere through His essence, His knowledge, and His power. For the Lord fills heaven and earth with His immensity; all things are open and exposed to His eyes, and He searches our heart and our dispositions. It will be easy for us, in the course of our usual day, to venerate God present in all things and creatures; in our superiors and our inferiors; in plants, flowers, and trees; in the animals of the earth and the birds of the air. Our Seraphic Father St. Francis related everything he saw and heard to the Passion of Christ. If a noise occurred, or a tumult, or the stroke of a hammer; if he saw a ladder, or wood, a lance, or a nail, or anything else, he seized upon it as an occasion to recall the Passion of Christ to his grateful mind.

The third method is the most perfect, and is accomplished through *fervent acts of love and intimate union* with God. By reason of this love and union we behold God present within us with all His attributes and perfections, in all His glory, majesty, omnipotence, and so forth. Christ says, "The kingdom of God is within you";[25] and the Apostle of the Gentiles, "Do you not know that you are the temple of God and that the Spirit of God dwells in you?"[26] Whenever we consider the presence of God within us, we should yearn for Him as our last end, and aspire to union with Him by acts of faith, hope, and love. This exercise is more a matter of the affections than of speculation; more abundant fruit is obtained through ardent colloquy with God than through mere consideration of Him.

171. Means which facilitate the practice of walking in the presence of God. There are three powerful means:

(1) The frequent elevation of our heart to God by means of fervent *aspirations* and ejaculatory prayers; (2) the renewal

25. Luke 17:21.
26. 1 Cor. 3:16.

of our *good intention* at various times throughout the day; (3) *examining ourselves* in regard to this practice during our particular examen and during the examination of conscience in the evening, and occasionally during mental prayer.

Father Le Gaudier says that "many people approach this practice with too much confidence in their own efforts. They never or very seldom ask help from God, although this practice most certainly depends upon God and upon His special grace."[27] We should ask God for this grace, saying to Him with all the fervor of our souls: "Look upon me and have mercy on me, and show Thy face to me. Thy face, O Lord, do I seek. Do not turn it away from me but have compassion on Thy servant that he may always walk before Thee in this land of exile and may enjoy Thee in heaven for all eternity."

We should endeavor to attain to such stature of spirit "that, detached from all things, desiring nothing of earth, despising all creatures, we may tend toward our Creator with such force of mind and fervor of desire that we become as it were oblivious of all inferior things. Whatever you do, wherever you abide, during every occupation, day and night, at every moment and every hour, always be mindful of God, knowing for certain that you are in His presence, convinced that He sees you no matter where you are."[28]

Article II — The Divine Office

172. The Divine Office is a potent instrument for aligning our will with the divine will. Concerning the Office, the Most Reverend Minister General of the Capuchins, Pacificus a Sejano, wrote: " 'As oil poured out,' it puts its mark on our whole life, it sanctifies our whole life ... ; the mind is raised to the celestial, the heart is inflamed with pious affections, the spirit is enriched with supernatural charismata. Through it,

---

27. *De perf. vitae spirit.* t. II, Pars V, sect. VIII, cap. IX.
28. St. Bonaventure, *Epist. de XXV memorialibus,* n. 22.

religious souls adhere to God; through the Divine Office they quaff great draughts of the supernatural life, tasting the sweetness of divine truth. In short, this daily offering of ourselves, by means of the sacred and Divine Office, incites us to holiness."[1] We shall explain: (1) the excellence of the Divine Office; (2) the manner of saying it.

§ I. Excellence of the Divine Office

173. The excellence of the Divine Office becomes apparent when we discover: (A) the reasons why Holy Mother Church instituted this salutary exercise; (B) its antiquity; (C) its content; (D) the fruits which it so abundantly produces; (E) that the recitation of the Divine Office is a very distinguished function.

A. REASONS WHY THE DIVINE OFFICE WAS INSTITUTED

174. The Seraphic Doctor gives these reasons: "The Holy Spirit instituted the Divine Office in the Church for five reasons: First, *in imitation of the heavenly harmony* by which the saints and angels in heaven continually sing the praises of God in His presence. Second, to remind us of the divine favors, and of the fact that at fixed hours *we should give thanks to God for these favors by praising Him and praying to Him.... As* it is only just that we should never forget these benefits, so it is expedient that we always recall them at fixed times. Third, in order that we may continually *prompt ourselves to devotion* and enkindle the fire of divine love, lest it grow cold through our slothfulness or occupation with other affairs. *This is the perpetual fire which shall never go out, which the priest shall feed on the altar, putting wood on it every day in the morning* (cf. Lev. 6:12-13). This fire is the fervor of devotion, which should always burn on the altar of our hearts. The devout

---

1. Pacificus a Sejano, O. M. Cap., *Analecta O. M. Cap.,* t. XXVI, pp. 12, 13.

priest should always nourish it by placing on it the fuel of divine praises, so that it may never be extinguished. Fourth, that we may accustom the faithful to the practice of prayer by means of the Divine Office. Fifth, *it is becoming to the Christian religion.* For it is truly proper . . . that those who possess the holy Sacraments should often meet to celebrate and venerate these sacred mysteries, and chant a solemn praise to their Author. Through these devotions we shall obtain more graces from God, yes, life eternal; through this divine psalmody we shall lead the faithful to greater reverence and love for their holy religion."[2]

B. THE VENERABLE ANTIQUITY OF THE DIVINE OFFICE

175. Holy Mother Church instituted common prayer from her very origin, and always favored it with singular blessings. For the first followers "continued steadfastly in the teaching of the Apostles and in the communion of the breaking of the bread and in the prayers, . . . continuing daily with one accord in the temple."[3] And as to the psalms, the faithful were intent on their recitation from the beginning. "The psalms were composed by divine inspiration," says St. Pius X, "and as a collection placed among the sacred writings. From the very beginning of the Church, this collection not only powerfully influenced and nurtured the piety of the faithful . . . but also, out of a love already evident in the Old Law, found a conspicuous place in sacred liturgy itself and in the Divine Office."[4]

C. THE CONTENTS OF THE DIVINE OFFICE

176. We should frequently consider the contents of the Divine Office. For in this work of God (*opus Dei*) God Him-

---

2. St. Bonaventure, *De sex al. Seraph.,* cap. VII, n. 5 et seq.
3. Acts 2:42, 46.
4. St. Pius X, *Divino Afflatu,* Nov., 1911.

self places on our lips words, canticles, and hymns which are His own or those of His saints. What shall we say about the immortal, sweet psalms, which the Holy Spirit brings forth from the heart of a man according to the heart of God? Let us listen to St. Ambrose: To him a psalm means "the benediction of men, the praise of God, the applause of the people, the laud of all, the sermon of the universe, the voice of the Church, a harmonious acknowledgment of faith, complete devotion to authority, the happiness of liberty, a cry of delight, resounding joy."[5] For the singing of the psalms lifts up to heaven our pious desires, our deep sighs, our prayers and praises, and brings back celestial lights, consolations and aids of grace. We should consider the truth of the divine saying: "He that offers praise as a sacrifice glorifies Me; and to him that goes the right way I will show the salvation of God."[6]

D. THE FRUITS OF THE DIVINE OFFICE

177. **(1) For those reciting the Divine Office.** We can apply to the Divine Office what St. Bernard said of the most holy name of Jesus: "It enlightens, nourishes, anoints."[7] As a response to the psalmody, God in a way opens the heavens and rains down a sweet manna. It is like the Jordan, a sacred bathing place, into which we are immersed seven times a day and washed of our stains, so that the youthfulness of our soul is renewed. "It is good to give thanks to the Lord, to sing praise to Your name, Most High."[8]

The Lord will hear all the pious entreaties of the Divine Office; for it is endowed with the special blessing of all prayer in common: the promise of being heard. The Saviour Himself made this pledge: "For where two or three are gathered

---

5. *Enarrat. in Ps.,* I, n. 9, in Migne, *P. L.,* t. XIV, col. 968.
6. Ps. 49:23.
7. *Serm. XV super Cant.,* in Migne, *P. L.,* t. CLXXXIII, col. 846.
8. Ps. 91:2.

together for My sake, there am I in the midst of them."[9] Wherefore, "if two of you shall agree on earth about anything at all for which they ask, it shall be done for them by My Father in heaven."[10] In a choir of praying religious, Christ is the Head, the Leader and the Mediator, interceding for all; and "the Spirit Himself pleads for us with unutterable groanings."[11]

(2) For the faithful. Abundant graces will flow upon the faithful through the recitation of the Divine Office. For public worship induces the Divine Sower to scatter His seed. Hence comes the hope, the confidence which Holy Mother Church and the Christian people place in the canonical hours; so much so that they call everyone who recites the Divine Office another Moses raising his arms on the holy mount, obtaining victory for the people of Israel.

E. THE RECITATION OF THE DIVINE OFFICE IS A GLORIOUS DUTY

178. By chanting the Divine Office the religious resemble the beautiful Sion, chosen to fulfill the august and glorious ministry of worshiping on earth, for there are holy angels among the choirs of praising religious, says St. Nicetas, and these angels exult when the chanters sing the lauds distinctly, attentively, vigilantly, ardently, harmoniously, humbly. St. Augustine says: "My psalter is my joy."[12]

§ II. Manner of Reciting the Divine Office

179. "Of all exterior observances," says St. Bonaventure, "the recitation of the Divine Office is the one which requires the greatest care, for it has to be done with order, promptitude

---

9. Matt. 18:20.
10. *Ibid.* 18:19.
11. Rom. 8:26.
12. *In Ps. CXXXVII*, n. 3, in Migne, *P. L.*, t. XXXVII, col. 1775.

and devotion. For in the other practices we work for God; here we wait upon God and direct our whole being to Him, speak to Him and at the same time personally ask His help in our needs."[13] Hence we should (A) prepare our minds before reciting the Office; (B) recite the Office earnestly and devoutly.

180. (A) **Preparation before the Office.** Clerics and priests who are not prevented or legitimately excused from the choral recitation of the Office should promptly assemble in the choir at the first sound of the bell and prepare their minds for the Lord. With devotion, composure, mortification, recollection and silence, they shall remember that they are in the presence of God, and about to engage in the angelic function of singing the divine praises.

(1) **At the first sound of the bell.** As soon as the bell rings for the Divine Office, either during the day or at night, we must immediately be on our way. If it rings while we are at work, we must abandon the work. If while we are writing a letter, we should stop writing.

Anything we happen to be doing must be left unfinished. Let us imagine the angels themselves are announcing: "Behold the bridegroom is coming, go forth to meet Him."[14] And with the holy kings we reply: "This is the sign of a great King, let us go and seek Him, and offer Him gifts."[15] As we hasten to choir in gravity and silence, our minds should be concentrated on God.

This promptitude is particularly fitting at night, lest culpable delay cause the grace of God to recede from us and our spirit to be left dry and desolate.

---

13. *De sex al. Seraph.,* cap. VII, n. 9.
14. Matt. 25:6.
15. Magnificat antiphon, First Vespers, Office for the feast of Epiphany.

(2) **Legitimate excuses.** Let no one be deceived by frivolous excuses, or lightly dispense himself from attendance at
Divine Office. "The religious who is not detained by some
task and yet does not wish to attend choir unless he is forced,
should not be retained in the Order. He is not secure in
regard to his own salvation. For anyone wishing to live peacefully in the Order should accustom himself to attend choir.
Whosoever is an enemy to the choir will become intolerable
to religion or will finally become an apostate."[16]

(3) **Preparation of the mind for the Lord.** We must
leave all worldly thoughts behind when entering choir and
promptly dispose our souls, lest God reject us as He does the
hardened sinner: "Why do you recite My statutes, and profess
My covenant with your mouth?"[17] We should ask for divine
help, so that He who alone can do so will quiet the rabble of
our unruly thoughts and affections. Next, with a lively faith,
let us recite the *Aperi, Domine.* "Spiritual things," says St.
Bonaventure, "must always and everywhere have priority over
everything else. Therefore when you are in church or in some
other place for the purpose of reciting the Divine Office, you
should not appear with a wandering heart, nor attempt to mix
distracting or injurious thoughts with the holy sentiments
suggested. St. Bernard says that it is a great abuse for the body
to be present in choir while the heart is outside."[18]

(4) **Angelic function.** The Psalmist says: "In the presence of the angels, I will sing Your praise."[19] These words
can be explained in two ways. "In one sense, they mean that
we sing with the angels who are present, for God is not without His messengers and ministers. In another, they mean

---

16. Cf. Francis Alban of Rüdesheim, O. M. Cap., *Tyrocinium Seraphicum*
(Mainz, 1772), p. 270.
17. Ps. 49:16.
18. *Regul. Novit.,* cap. I, n. 1.
19. Ps. 137:1.

that since we contemplate in our hearts what our lips express, our purpose is the same as that of the angels."[20]

Before the recitation of the Office, it is well to remember that the Church Triumphant in heaven is united with the Church Militant on earth, which aspires to heaven. We should rejoice that God is glorified in this way by all His saints, and we should ardently desire to have the fervor and love of all the saints and angels for the performance of our divine work.

181. (B) **Requisites for an earnest and devout recitation of the Office.** Two rules will help us recite the Office properly. The first concerns external composure, the second, interior dispositions.

I. **External composure**

(a) *In general.* Pope Benedict XII gives these general rules about external comportment: "In the churches or chapels each and every monk must humbly and devoutly join the assembly at the time appointed for the recitation of the Divine Office, and chant it with sincere devotion, slowly, distinctly, agreeably and dutifully; not hurrying through it or omitting syllables or in any way impeding its proper recitation; observing silence so that his heart may be attentive to divine things. All who disobey these rules should be punished."[21] St. Bernard adds: "I admonish you, dearly beloved, always to offer the divine praises faultlessly and promptly. In a lively way, to be sure, so that as you assist at the divine praises reverently, you may also appear eager and willing in the 'work of God'; not reluctant, not sleepy or lazy, nor sparing the voice so that it quavers . . . ; but as is proper with manly voice and affection, sounding out the words of the Holy Spirit."[22]

---

20. Hildemarus, Commentary on the Rule of St. Benedict, in Migne, *P. L.*, t. LXVI, col. 478.

21. Constitution *Summi Magistri*, cap. XXVII, a. 1336.

22. *In Cant.*, Serm. 47, in Migne, *P. L.*, t. CLXXXIII, col. 1011.

(b) *In particular.* The following rules should always be observed with care.

(1) Whether standing, sitting, kneeling or bowing, let us always maintain a modest, dignified and reverent position in choir. A respectful posture of the body promotes interior devotion and is a sign of reverence during the recitation of Office.

(2) Unless the rubrics direct otherwise, let us always stand for the recitation, body erect, eyes down, hands properly joined.

(3) All frivolous movements, such as turning the head, allowing the eyes to wander, rubbing the hands, brisk turning of pages, or any other superfluous actions should be avoided.

Our Seraphic Father has set the example. "He prayed the canonical hours with as much reverence as devotion. Although he suffered from weakness of the eyes, the stomach, the spleen and the liver, yet while he said the Office he would never lean against the wall, but always stood erect and bareheaded, without any wandering of the eye or any other interruption."[23]

(4) For all these things to be the better observed, the acolytes and the hebdomadary should prepare themselves so that the Office proceeds with order, without disturbing breaks due to errors. Then all can say the Divine Office with gravity, the pauses being properly observed and the voice pitched neither too high nor too low, but moderately in a monotone. "The psalmody should be uniform, so that the Office continues and ends in the same tone as it was begun, without any lowering of voices, variation or dissonance. Moreover, the voice should not be too feeble or jerky, nor too loud or bellowing; but sufficiently high-pitched, clear, devout, humble and sweet. The voice should be raised enough so as to be readily heard and to be distinctly audible; it should be devout and humble so as to move the minds of the faithful to compunction; and

---

23. Thomas of Celano, *Legenda Secunda,* cap. LXIII, p. 242.

sweet so that it calms the hearts of the attentive and inspires them to praise God."[24]

II. **The interior dispositions of the soul.** This second rule considers the intention and the attention:

(1) *Intention.* With all fervor we should make a most simple and pure intention, offer all our thoughts, words and actions for the honor and glory of God, and resign ourselves perfectly to His good pleasure. Heeding the advice of the Seraphic Doctor, let us give thanks particularly to Christ Jesus at every hour of the Divine Office. "He was born of the Virgin Mary at night; in the morning, He appeared at the court for judgment; at daybreak, He arose from the dead; He was scourged at the third hour, and about that time He sent the Holy Spirit on the Apostles; and at the sixth hour He was crucified, and at the ninth He died on the Cross for us; in the evening while at table He gave us the Sacrament of His body and blood; and at Compline He was buried."[25]

(2) *Attention.* The Divine Office should be said with great devotion and due attention. Attention is an act of the intellect, the application of the mind. This attention is partly external and partly internal. External attention consists in avoiding every external action that is incompatible with internal attention. External attention, then, requires no more than this: that the Divine Office be performed in a human manner. That is, the religious, while reciting the Office, should intend to do what he is doing, and should pronounce the words well.

Attention is *internal* when the mind is centered on the Office itself. Internal attention is threefold:

(a) *Verbal* attention consists in pronouncing all the words entirely, perfectly and distinctly. As is evident, everyone is bound to this attention.

---

24. *Monita et Declarationes de divino cultu et disciplina regulari Definitorii Generalis,* 18 Junii 1912, in *Analecta O. M. Cap.,* t. XXVIII, p. 219 et seq.
25. *De sex al. Seraph.,* cap. VII, § 6.

(b) *Literal* attention has reference to the literal meaning of the words. The psalmist commends this attention, saying: "Sing ye wisely."[26] "When one directs his thoughts," says St. Basil, "to every word of the psalms, as in tasting to discern the different kinds of food, then he fulfills the admonition: Sing ye wisely."[27] Examining this attention, Cassian says: "As they begin to chant the psalms, all recognize in them their own sentiments, not so much as intended by the Prophet, but as composed by themselves, like a personal prayer, drawing compunction from the depths of their hearts. They consider the psalms to be directed to themselves personally; they regard the sentiments of the psalms not only as experienced by the Prophet and fulfilled in him, but as daily experienced and fulfilled in themselves. Perceiving the same affections of which the Prophet speaks, the same sentiments described by the psalm, they take the attitude of its composer and anticipate his thought rather than follow it."[28] Cardinal Bona says that this kind of attention is suitable only to the learned who grasp the literal and mystical sense of the psalms. Yet it is easier than any of the others, more profitable and less subject to mental wandering. It is more in conformity with the patristic doctrine and the spirit of the Church.

(c) Attention is *intellectual* when our thoughts are centered on God. This attention is common to the learned and unlearned. Spiritual authors have advanced various methods of being continually mindful of God while one prays, by the use of various signs as reminders. "But this exercise," declares Cardinal Bona, "can hardly be reduced to practice without distractions or serious vexations of the mind. For continuous at-

---

26. Ps. 46:8, Challoner-Douay version.
27. *In Regul. apud Rufin.*, cap. LVII, quoted in cap. XIX of the Commentary on the Rule of St. Benedict, in Migne, *P. L.*, t. LXVI, col. 477.
28. *Coll. X*, cap. XI, in Migne, *P. L.*, t. XLIX, col. 838; cf. Cardinal Bona, *Horol. ascet.*, cap. III, § 3, n. 2.

tention to these different signs over a long period of time tires the brain; and if the exercise is interrupted, distractions ensue."[29] We more easily conserve our strength when we make acts of love of God and acts of humility, or when we simply speak to God. Our Seraphic Father has given us an example, for according to St. Bonaventure, "He said the psalms with as much attention of mind and spirit as if God were actually present; and when the name of the Lord occurred in the psalms, it seemed to linger on his lips with charming sweetness."[30]

In private recitation. "Although outside the convent all the rules cannot be strictly observed, the religious should be marked in all circumstances by a certain religious atmosphere," says the *Mirror of Discipline*.[31] If you are not able to observe all the usual prescriptions, says Cardinal Bona, it is sufficient to perform your duty of prayer attentively, devoutly and reverently, pronouncing all the words completely and distinctly; observing the proper time, unless excused by necessity; and finding an appropriate place, one that is less conducive to distractions. Care should be taken when reciting the Office privately that it is not hastily or negligently discharged. Let us observe the above rules as well as possible, paying special attention to the preparation, intention and attention; otherwise our prayer will provoke the wrath of God.

As to distractions and weariness which occur during Office, consult the later section on prayer. "Before leaving the oratory after the canonical hours," says the *Mirror of Discipline*, "they offered some small voluntary gift of prayer or praise to God, whom they had frequently offended through negligence in the saying of the prescribed Office. They became accustomed to this holy habit through frequent and constant

---

29. *Ibid.*
30. *Legenda S. Franc.*, cap. X, n. 6.
31. Part II, Chap. I, n. 9.

practice, and learned to add a little act of reparation to God for the soul's distractions."[32] After this act, let us proceed in silence to our appointed work.

CONCLUSION. "It is of great importance to us," says Pacificus of Sejano, "that regular observance, which is a source of blessings and of holiness, be conspicuous and flourishing in our convents. We command you to maintain this regular observance, to attend choir at fixed hours in the day and similarly at night, to persist in prayer and devoutly to sing the divine praises like the saints, or rather, I should say, the angels. Woe to us if, through a lax spirit or by the collapse of piety, this observance declines and the Divine Office in the choir and church is neglected! This would surely be the ruin of the religious and the destruction of the Order, a sign of pride as it were, which St. Catherine of Siena very well explains: 'The pleasure of choir attendance seems like a venomous serpent or a poisonous food to the negligent friar, so much is he affected with aversion and disgust for the place. The *pride, disobedience* and *ingratitude* with which he is filled have stultified his interior taste. The obedient friar, on the other hand, thinks of the choir as a garden, regards his cell as heaven on earth. . . . He puts forth every effort to observe the rules, customs and ceremonies of his Order.' "[33]

Article III — Prayer

182. If we fully grasp the implications of the spiritual life, it will be plainly evident to us that we should practice our Seraphic Father's way of life in order to discern and fulfill the will of God. But what is St. Francis' way of life if not one of holy prayer and devotion? It was ever his intention that the friars should particularly devote themselves to prayer. He

---

32. Part I, Chap. XII, n. 6.
33. *Littera 80.*

urges all his friars in these words: "Let them endeavor to
have, what is to be above all things desired, the spirit of the
Lord and His holy operation: Let them endeavor to pray
always with a pure heart."[1] And although he obliged the
friars to work, he nevertheless willed that "they do not extinguish the spirit of holy prayer and devotion, to which all
temporal things should be subservient."[2] Rightly, then, do we
speak of the spirit of prayer as the mainstay of holiness, the
chief ornament of the true Friar Minor. "Prayer is like the
armor protecting the soldier, like a lamp lighting up the way,
like a dove carrying an olive branch," writes a contemporary of
St. Bonaventure.[3] And in a work attributed to St. John
Chrysostom we find the remark: "Just as when a queen enters
a city to reside there, all the wealth from far and near flows
into that city; so, too, once prayer enters the soul all the
virtues accompany it."[4] Against this background, we shall
treat of: (1) the necessity of prayer; (2) various kinds of
prayer; (3) precautions to be taken against the soul's instability; (4) requisites for acquiring and preserving the spirit
of prayer.

§ I. The Necessity of Prayer

183. (A) **In general.** St. Thomas Aquinas clearly indicates the necessity of prayer for all the faithful. "Now after
baptism man needs to pray continually in order to enter heaven:
for though sins are remitted through baptism, there still remain the tendencies to sin assailing us from within, and the
world and the devils assailing us from without, and therefore
it is said pointedly that 'Jesus also having been baptized and

---

1. *Rule,* Chap. X.
2. *Rule,* Chap. V.
3. *Diaetae salutis,* Lib. II, cap. V, found in the Mainz edition of the works
of St. Bonaventure and formerly attributed to him; cf. t. VI, p. 284.
4. *Serm. de precat.,* II, of doubtful authorship, in Migne, *P. G.,* t. L, col. 786.

being in prayer, . . . heaven was opened . . . ' (Luke 3:21); for after baptism the faithful stand in need of prayer."[5]

This need of prayer is a truth of faith revealed by God and transmitted to us by the Church. The need of prayer can be easily proved from the history of the Christians on earth, and confirmed by the glory of the blessed in heaven. Without continual prayer, neither the sanctity nor the eternal happiness of the blessed can exist or even be conceived as a possibility.

*184. (B) **In particular for the Friars Minor.** Our life is a mixed life, both contemplative and active. And what is "the contemplative life but an elevation of the mind to God, a continuous union with Him, an association with celestial beings in paradise, the bliss of eternal joys, a living with the mind fixed on heaven and raised to the consideration of the divine?"[6] Contemplation and the elevation of the mind to God are so necessary that if they are neglected we cannot lead a truly religious life, since prayer must always precede, accompany and follow all our work.

"In his incomparable wisdom, our Seraphic Father ordered that our first task, our chief duty, should be the apostolate of prayer. Thus the Friars Minor, like the Apostles, must first draw from prayer what is necessary for their own sanctification, and then pour out on their neighbors what they have absorbed during the peace of contemplation."[7]

"We firmly believe," says Cajetan Mary of Bergamo, "that holy prayer is of the greatest necessity for our state, and that, as far as in us lies, we should strive never to omit prayer. This all the more so, as it is the precise intention of our Seraphic Father St. Francis. He wished us never to omit prayer because

---

5. *Summa theol.*, III, q. 39, a. 5. (From the second revised edition of the *Summa* translated by the Fathers of the English Dominican Province; used with the permission of the publisher and copyright owner, Benziger Brothers, New York, N. Y. The quotations from the *Summa* on pp. 430, 439, 499, 529, 578, 589, 593, 595 and 597 are adapted from the Benziger publication.)

6. Pacificus a Sejano, in *Analecta O. M. Cap.*, t. XXVII, p. 142.

7. *Loc. cit.*, p. 140.

of any other task. The composition of sermons for the development and the conversion of souls is certainly a holy occupation. Yet we must not neglect prayer on account of preaching, for the law of charity obliges us to be more solicitous for the welfare of our own soul than for that of others.

"The preacher may reflect on eternal truths while preparing his sermon. But it is one matter to think of these truths with the intention of applying them to an audience, and another to consider their application to one's own person for the purpose of correcting his own defects. Medicine is beneficial to those who use it, not to those who produce it. And so it easily happens that one becomes vain and worldly while he actually preaches against vanity and worldliness. Now, if prayer should never be omitted because of the office of preaching — in which the virtue of seraphic zeal is actually exercised — how can prayer possibly be neglected for frivolous causes and useless occupations?"[8]

Considering this truth, St. Bonaventure said: "We should carefully avoid anything that disturbs our fervor or our devotion. Fervor and devotion are to sustain every good religious institute, to increase the exercise of virtue. Any Order which is not fed by this oil is unproductive. The structure of good works which is not connected with an abundance of devout prayer is unsteady, like a stone wall without cement. The religious Order in which the fervor of devotion has grown lukewarm also declines and grows feeble in the practice of the other virtues."[9] It is of the greatest importance that the maxim of our Seraphic Father should remain engraved on our minds: "A religious should ardently desire the grace of prayer, without which nothing will prosper in the service of God, nor any good come from the religious."[10]

---

8. *Capuccinus solitarius,* Dictamen practicum, II, Diei VII.
9. *De sex al. Seraph.,* cap. II, n. 10.
10. St. Bonaventure, *Legenda S. Franc.,* cap. X, n. 1.

"My dearly beloved brethren," says Father Pacificus of Sejano, "would that we, endowed with the spirit of grace and of prayer, and esteeming the apostolate of prayer most highly, might strive with all our strength to become great men of prayer, apostles of prayer! If religious grasp the vital importance of this, there will arise among us other men like Moses and Samuel whose prayers will appease the wrath of the Lord, and Israel will triumph over the enemy."[11]

§ II. Various Kinds of Prayer

185. Prayer, as we have seen, is the act of praising God or of giving thanks to Him, or the petition of becoming things from God. Prayer is either *public,* made in the name and by the authority of the Church, as for example, the Divine Office; or *private,* made only in the name of the person praying.

In respect to the persons praying, prayer is either *individual,* if it is solitary, performed by one person only; or it is *common,* if it is recited by many persons at the same time.

Public prayer, that is, the Divine Office and the manner in which it is said, has already been explained.

Mental prayer, which also has been treated (cf. n. 134 above), is from its very nature individual, although it is practiced by the religious in a common place. Besides mental prayer, there are other, shorter prayers prescribed in the Order and in the different Provinces, which should be recited in common and everyone should conscientiously join in them. Our Lord recommended common prayer in a special way when He said: "Where two or three are gathered together for My sake, there am I in the midst of them."[12]

In the following paragraphs, some particular prayers will be explained: (A) morning and evening prayers; (B) spiritual recollection; (C) ejaculatory prayers.

---

11. *Loc. cit.,* t. XXVII, p. 144.
12. Matt. 18:20.

A. MORNING AND EVENING PRAYERS

186. Morning and evening prayers are ordinarily said in common. Experience proves that prayers at these times are most suitable and necessary.

(1) **Morning prayers.** When first awaking, we should make the sign of the cross attentively. Let us say a brief prayer to God, so that every stain of sin may be blotted out, and God may help and bless us in all the labors of the day. Let us try to foresee every task of the day and offer it to God with the purest intention. Let us prepare ourselves, arm ourselves for all eventualities, by carefully considering the places, duties, companions and occasions we shall encounter; what we are to do, what we must avoid, what words we intend to speak, with what modesty we should associate with others. Let us renew our vows and good resolutions, and elicit an act of the particular virtue we need more than any other.

(2) **Evening prayers.** "Prayer ascends more readily, more purely during the profound silence of night, the time when most men are asleep. How untroubled the prayer that rises during the night! God alone observes it — God and His holy angel. The angel receives it and presents it before the heavenly altar! How quiet, how peaceful it is with no disturbing noise or din!"[13] We should thank God for all the natural benefits and the supernatural gifts we have received; for instance, the blessings bestowed on our home, our country and our Order; we should pray for the rest of mankind, for friends and enemies, for the living and the dead. Let us also briefly run through the points of the next morning's meditation, outline the duties of the following day, provide for what is to be done, or may be said, and generally purify our intentions.

Morning and evening devotions will be more fully treated in the chapter on daily exercises.

---

13. St. Bernard, *In Cant.,* Serm. 86, n. 3, in Migne, *P. L.,* t. CLXXXIII, col. 1196.

B. SPIRITUAL RECOLLECTION

187. "Religious should fervently persist in prayer," says the *Mirror of Discipline,* "not only in church, but everywhere, since they themselves are temples of God."[14]

We find an example of this in the life of St. Catherine of Siena. When the parents of the bride of Christ had eliminated every place suitable for prayer and every period assigned to meditation, this was done with God's permission, so that He Himself might build an oratory in her soul. Here she could mentally entertain Him during the performance of her external duties, and be mentally at leisure in her holy solitude.

We should also build a temple in the solitude of our hearts, where we can entertain the Lord Jesus while our body is busy with its tasks. It is written of our Seraphic Father that while "walking, sitting, eating and drinking, he was intent upon prayer."[15] Thomas of Celano also says of him that "while praying in the forests and wildernesses, he filled the meadows and groves with his sighs, he watered them with his tears, he beat his breast with his hand. . . . There he responded to the Judge, there he prayed to the Father, there he spoke with the Spouse. . . . He directed every consideration and affection to that one petition to the Lord; so that he became, not so much a man praying, as one whose whole being had changed into prayer personified."[16] We must follow our Seraphic Father in this spiritual recollection; train ourselves in the practice of the presence of God, eliciting acts of love and other virtues. Would that we could always reply in the words of St. Elzéar of Sabran to his wife, Blessed Delphine, when she anxiously wrote her absent husband about his health: "Seek me in the most holy wound in the side of my sweet Saviour, for there is my dwelling place; there you will find me, and nowhere else."

---

14. Part. I, Chap. XII, n. 1.
15. Thomas of Celano, *Legenda Prima,* cap. XXVII, p. 73.
16. *Legenda Secunda,* cap. LXI, p. 241.

C. EJACULATORY PRAYERS

188. In spiritual recollection we seek God, we aspire to Him. We must therefore approach Him through brief and ardent ejaculatory prayers, for they are like sparks in our hearts, like arrows in the heart of God.

Prayers said in common, particularly the canonical hours, cannot be shortened; but it is not so with individual prayers. We should *frequently* and *continually* pray, throughout the day, but not at great length, not with display, not with many useless words.

(1) **Frequently.** This was always the practice of St. Francis and of all spiritual men, and particularly of the monks of Egypt. Of these monks St. Augustine could write in his letter to Probas: "The brethren in Egypt are known to recite numerous prayers, but these are very short, and are quickly recited as if an arrow were shot from a bow. These do not demand the degree of attention required by longer prayers, which weaken and blunt the keenness of the intention."[17]

(2) **Continually.** Ejaculatory prayers should be used continually: (a) primarily in order *to arouse pious affections.* "Just as when preparing a dinner we stir up the fire to heat the water if it is cold," says St. John Chrysostom, "so too in prayer must we repeat the process and apply our lips, as it were, to the burning coals, that this contact may again enkindle our minds to piety."[18]

(b) *To overcome and repel temptations.* Ejaculatory prayers are called the impregnable wall, the invulnerable armor against temptations.

(c) *As the remedy for all diseases of the soul,* evil inclinations, attraction to vices, especially the carnal ones; against the

---

17. *Epist. 130,* cap. X, in *P. L.,* t. XXXIII, col. 501.
18. *Homil. IV, de Anna,* n. 5, in Migne, *P. G.,* t. LIV, col 666, 668.

itch of the baser emotions, against irritations, dangers, and the occasions of sin.

(d) As a defense against *nocturnal disturbances and diabolical illusions.*

(e) Finally, ejaculatory prayers are efficacious for our retaining a perpetual remembrance of God, for such aspirations easily join continual prayer with our occupations.

Thus constantly, in every place, at night, by day, in prosperity or adversity, in every spiritual undertaking and in every temptation, ejaculatory prayers should at least be formulated and repeated in our minds, if not spoken with the lips. Some of these are: "My God and my all!"; "For love of God"; "Incline, O God, unto my aid,"[19] and so forth.

(3) **Without a multitude of empty words.** "We know that we shall be heard, not because of a multitude of words, but because of the purity of our heart and our tears of compunction," says the *Mirror of Discipline,* "and therefore our prayer should be brief and simple, unless perhaps it is prolonged through devout affections or by the inspiration of divine grace."[20]

Abbot Macarius, when asked by his monks how they must pray, replied: "An abundance of words is not necessary, but stretching forth our hands we should say: 'O God, as You will and what You will, let that be done!' If temptations assail us, we should say: 'God, help us'; for He Himself knows what is expedient for us."[21] Christ Himself says in the Gospel: "But in praying, do not multiply words, as the Gentiles do; for they think that by saying a great deal they will be heard. So do not be like them."[22]

---

19. Cf. Cassian, *Coll. X.,* in Migne, *P. L.,* t. LIX, col. 832, 833.

20. Part I, Chap. XII, n. 3.

21. Commentary on the Rule of St. Benedict, cap. XX, in Migne, *P. L.,* t. LXVI, col. 479, 480.

22. Matt. 6:7-8.

(4) The difference between a many-worded prayer and one of long duration. What does it mean to pray with many words, and in what way does this differ from a lengthy prayer? St. Augustine gives us the answer: "Praying for a longer period of time is not praying with a multitude of words, as some people believe. A multitude of words is one thing, lengthier affections another. It is written of our Lord Himself that He spent the whole night in prayer and that He prayed the longer. He who is the best intercessor in time and who is eternally heard by the Father, meant to set us an example."[23] And in the same letter: "Do not pray in many words, but pray at length, as long as your fervent intention will last. Do not multiply your expressions, for many will be superfluous. As far as God is concerned, to pray much means that we throb with a sustained and pious sentiment. This is done with sighs rather than with words, with tears rather than with speech."

§ III. Precautions against the Soul's Instability — Conditions for Praying in a Becoming Manner

189. There are many changes in the things around us, many alterations in the human mind, besides the manifold workings of Divine Providence. "A troubled night follows the serenity of the day," says Cardinal Bona, "and want succeeds the greatest abundance of all things. Often music is turned into mourning, joy into sorrow; and scarcely is divine sweetness tasted on the tip of the lips when it is changed into the greatest bitterness."[24] For the psalmist who in his abundance had said: "I shall never be disturbed," soon sighed with tears: "When You hid Your face, I was terrified."[25]

According to St. Gregory, a man of prayer passes through the following phases: "In the beginning there are sweet attractions; in the middle, the struggle of testing; toward the end,

---

23. *Epistola 130*, cap. X, in Migne, *P. L.*, t. XXXIII, col. 501.
24. *De discretione spirituum*, cap. XIII, 4.
25. Ps. 29:7, 8.

complete perfection. At first we experience sweetness which is for our encouragement; later bitterness for our trial; and then at length delight and sublime favors for our strength."[26]

These are the usual phases, St. Gregory continues, for: "Sometimes almighty God temporarily abandons those whom He loves from all eternity. Hence it is written: 'For a small moment have I forsaken thee; but with great mercies will I gather thee. In a moment of indignation have I hid My face a little while from thee: but with everlasting kindness have I had mercy on thee' (Isa. 54: 7-8). The Lord helps His saints by coming to them, He tests them by leaving them, He strengthens them with gifts, and tries them with tribulations."[27]

For a better understanding of this, we shall explain: (1) consolations; (2) desolation. Because of the importance of the matter, we shall treat it at length.

I. CONSOLATIONS

190. (A) **Various kinds of consolation.** Before listing the various kinds of consolation, we must understand the meaning of the term itself.

Consolation, in the sense in which it is used here, is a certain sweetness, an internal joy and delight. Since consolations affect the soul in different ways, they are classified under different names.

Consolations are of three kinds. First, those perceived in the mind only; second, in the senses only; and third, those experienced in both the mind and the senses.

"Consolations of the first kind are called spiritual," says Cardinal Bona, "when they are experienced in the mind only, and do not overflow into the sensitive part of man. It may occasionally happen that the lower part is dry and desolate, while the higher enjoys a great peace and delight."[28] "A truly

---

26. *Moralia,* Lib. XXIV, cap. XI, in Migne, *P. L.,* t. LXXVI, col. 302.
27. *Ibid.,* Lib. XX, cap. XXIV, in Migne, *P. L.,* t. LXXVI, col. 168.
28. *Loc. cit.,* cap. XIII, n. 1.

spiritual consolation is experienced," teaches St. Ignatius, "when by means of a certain interior movement the soul breaks forth in a love of its Creator which excludes love of any creature except in God."[29]

Consolations of the second kind, when only the lower part of man is affected, are called sensible consolations. Consolations of the third kind overflow from the spirit into the senses and the body, and take possession of both, as is written: "My heart and my flesh have rejoiced in the living God."[30] As for example, "when tears inciting to divine love flow in abundance, either out of sorrow for sin or from meditating on the Passion of Christ, or from any other cause well ordered to the worship and honoring of God."[31]

These last consolations are the more frequent, since through mutual agreement between the higher and lower faculties one part enters into the feelings of the other, so that the two communicate their joys and sorrows to each other. Yet it can happen that little or nothing flows from one part into the other, as when the lower faculties of Christ were deprived of all consolation during His Passion; as when a sick person who must drink bitter medicine prescribed by the doctor, experiences repugnance in his lower appetite and recoils from the nauseous remedy. Yet, knowing that it concerns the return of his health, the sick person not only desires the bad-tasting drink, but consumes it and is pleased with it. This spiritual delight, by which the will attracts the lower appetites to the good, although these appetites are reluctant to respond, is also called substantial. For the sake of clearness we shall reduce consolations to two kinds: substantial and sensible. The term "substantial" covers only spiritual consolations, but the term "sensible" covers both sensible and mixed consolations.

---

29. *Exercitia Spiritualia* (Roothaan edition, Paris, 1865), Reg. ad spiritus dignosc., 1 hebd., reg. 3.
30. Ps. 83:3, Challoner-Douay version.
31. St. Ignatius, *loc. cit.*

191. (B) Causes of consolations:

(1) **The causes of substantial consolations.** A substantial consolation can come only from God, who alone can enter the human mind.

(2) **The causes of sensible consolations.** (a) A sensible consolation can be derived from a substantial one. This can happen naturally yet through an abundance of divine liberality so that the sensible consolation comforts our weakness by its sweetness, says Cardinal Bona. In this case the consolation evidently proceeds from God. If we are not exalted when such consolations are present, nor afflicted when they are wanting, but use them with humility and gratitude as seasoning by means of which the lower appetites may be induced to eat more solid food, then the consolation is certainly from God.

(b) But when a sensible consolation does not proceed from a substantial one, it is caused sometimes by God, occasionally by the devil, and at other times by the very nature of man. The origin of a consolation can be discerned by its effects.

(a) GOD. "It is proper and customary," says St. Ignatius, "for the Good Spirit to add alacrity and strength to good actions, to console, to arouse tears of devotion, to enlighten the mind and to give peace, so that having overcome all obstacles, through good works men may with greater liberty and expedition always tend to higher things."[32]

But the motive for bestowing these consolations on God's part is not the abundance of grace, but the indigence of the human mind. Cassian declares that this grace of God "inspires the unworthy, awakens the sleeping, enlightens the blind and the ignorant, and mercifully urges and reproves the souls of men. Grace is poured into our hearts to arouse us from the sleep of idleness by the remorse of conscience which it stirs up."[33]

---

32. *Exercitia Spiritualia,* Reg. ad spiritus dignosc., 2 hebd., reg. 2.
33. *Coll. IV,* cap. V, in Migne, *P. L.,* t. XLIX, col. 589.

The effects by which we can determine whether a consolation actually is from God are the following: It illumines the mind, strengthens patience, builds up confidence, inflames the will, excludes mental digression, invigorates the senses, diverts them from earthly things, and finally turns into genuine substantial consolation.

(b) THE DEVIL. "It is the practice of the evil spirit," says St. Ignatius, "to transform himself into an angel of light. For once he knows the pious inclinations of a soul, he first acts in compliance with them, but soon afterwards entices the soul toward his perverse desires. At first he appears to conform to and foster the holy thoughts of a man, so that afterwards he may gradually ensnare him in the dragnet of his guiles."[34]

Father Roothaan maintains that this rule of St. Ignatius is of the greatest importance in penetrating the camouflage worn by the appearance of good in the attempt of the devil to have it confused with the truly good: "The devil observes every virtue which the soul is striving for, and with satanic malice continually tries to annoy, hinder and dissipate the soul, by the empty shadow of the same virtue or through some excess induced by other artifices. Let us consider, for instance, how many are tricked by imprudent zeal, how many are destroyed or hindered by the ruse of inordinate devotion; this happens every day, and is due to the wiles of the devil. But the truly humble and particularly the obedient soul will easily overcome his stratagems. For a powerful external enemy makes very little progress unless self-love within conspires for the same downfall."[35]

St. Ignatius indicates the signs betraying the devil's action: "When the train of thoughts he suggests shifts to something evil, distracting, or less good than that which the soul had

---

34. *Op. cit.*, Reg. pro plenior. discret., spirit., 2 hebd., reg. 4.
35. *Ibid.*, 2 hebd., nota 6 in reg. 4, p. 189 of the Roothaan edition.

originally presented to itself; or when the soul is disturbed and becomes restless, losing the peace, tranquillity and calm it had enjoyed, we have clear signs that these thoughts proceed from the evil spirit, the enemy of our progress and of our eternal salvation."[36] The enemy is identified by his serpent tail. If the consolation really comes from the devil, he pours darkness and obscurity into the mind, making a man proud, stubborn, impatient, unwilling; and finally he dangles before the soul the baited hook of fleshly enticements.

(c) THE NATURE OF MAN. Since nature always seeks its own good in all circumstances, it always has itself as its end and finds its repose in itself.

192. (C) **What to do to prevent consolation from injuring the spirit of prayer and devotion.** We should discover what must be done: (1) at the time of sensible consolation; (2) at the time of substantial consolation.

(1) **At the time of sensible consolation.** Sensible consolations may contain many dangers if they do not come from the substantial, even though God may bestow them on beginners and on the imperfect. Hence the following warnings:

(a) *We should humble ourselves.* When beginners are flooded by interior sweetness, they may have a tendency to judge and despise others, believing themselves to be holy and close to God. They speak of themselves as true contemplatives. All this, of course, is very harmful. Anyone enjoying consolations should, according to St. Ignatius, "humble and censure himself as much as he can, recalling how weak and cowardly he still is in times of desolation unless he is supported by grace and divine consolation."[37]

---

36. *Loc. cit.,* reg. 5.
37. *Op. cit.,* Reg. ad spiritus dignosc., 1 hebd., reg. 11.

(b) *We should foresee the time of desolation.* Imperfect souls regard sanctity as consisting in sweetness and consolation rather than in mortification. As long as they actually enjoy sensible devotion and the grace of tears, they serve God eagerly. But as soon as God takes these away, they become disturbed and abandon prayer and other holy practices. Since they do not feel the interior consolations they like, they are tempted to return to external, earthly things opposed to the spirit. "Anyone who enjoys consolation should look ahead and consider how he will behave when desolation follows. For then during the period of heavenly joys he will be gathering vigor and strength of soul in preparation for the assault of desolation," says St. Ignatius of Loyola.[38]

(c) *We should avoid imprudence.* Thomas a Kempis has an excellent doctrine on imprudence: "Some imprudent souls have ruined themselves by abusing the grace of devotion: As they wanted to do more than they could, and forgot the limits of their own weakness, they followed the inclinations of their heart rather than the judgment of their reason. And as they presumptuously undertook greater things than were pleasing to God, they soon were deprived of grace. They were left in need, and miserably abandoned, who had built themselves a nest in heaven, so that, humbled and impoverished, they might learn not to fly with their own pinions but to trust in My wings."[39] At times of consolation we must be careful not to torment ourselves with external works of penance over and beyond our strength, or rashly to settle upon many other things and to bind ourselves to them by vow. Father David of Augsburg has some solid advice for those who act indiscreetly while they are filled with sensible devotion. He admonishes them occasionally to relinquish vehement consolations of this kind. "For it is more useful," he says, "to enjoy the grace of

---

38. *Loc. cit.,* reg. 10.
39. *Imitation of Christ,* Book III, Chap. VII, n. 2.

devotion moderately for an hour than, having exhausted one's strength and destroyed natural virtue, to lose it entirely and to be irreparably deprived of it. Those who have injured themselves in this way will later begin to have too much pity for themselves and in trying to recover the strength they have lost through their indiscretions will become not only over-indulgent, but even lax. They are like a broken vessel, from which the liquid has been spilled: 'My flesh and my heart waste away' (Ps. 72:26); for when physical strength is entirely lacking, the heart is unable to make the effort required by devotion."[40]

"The best disposition," says Cardinal Bona, "is never to desire sensible consolations, for the life of a Christian consists in doing good and suffering pain. We are often deceived and led to believe that a consolation is from God when it actually is from nature or from the devil. 'How frequently,' exclaims Richard of St. Victor, 'people who are imperfect and ignorant of grace, when they are moved by worldly joy or by natural eagerness, believe they have been affected by spiritual consolation' (*In Cant.*, cap. XXXIII). From whatever source consolation proceeds, man ought not to depart from his own nothingness nor cling to self, but to God alone, who always directs man toward good."[41]

(d) *Sensible consolations.* Sensible consolations are also given to those who are more advanced in virtue, says Father David of Augsburg, "as an overflow of interior sweetness. The soul communicates its passions to the body, as to a companion and partner in life; in the same way it shares its consolations with the body. . . . This is from the overflowing measure of heavenly joy given to the elect. This overflow, which would be lost if it were uncontrolled, is intercepted by the body as a reward for its share in the labor."[42] More advanced souls

---

40. *De exterioris et interioris hominis,* cap. LXIX, Quaracchi edition, pp. 367, 368.
41. *De discretione spirituum,* cap. XIII, 2.
42. *Loc. cit.,* p. 366.

should not seek these consolations purposely, but rather heed the warnings given above.

Those who are truly advancing in charity do not seek self but instead seek God; they do not desire their own consolation but God's good pleasure. They remain unperturbed whether it pleases God to pour a stream of heavenly sweetness into their hearts, or to deprive them of it. In the peace of their soul, they cease not to love and to praise God. And when God enriches them with still greater blessings, they do not become proud, they do not look down upon others, but would gladly suffer for God and be held in contempt by those around them, as our Seraphic Father often explained.

(2) **During substantial consolations.** Spiritual consolation, which is perceived by the mind alone, is more enduring than sensible consolation and is attendant upon mature virtue. Cardinal Bona says that it causes souls to grow in love. When it is absent, saintly souls long for it; when it is present, they jealously guard it; when it is taken from them, they suffer in patience, since they seek only God and not His gifts, and are always ready to do without them. It is a teaching of St. Bernard that there is nothing more efficacious for meriting, retaining and recovering grace than to stand always before God not with the attitude of one who considers himself wise but with an attitude of reverence.[43]

When spiritual consolation is present, we must be on our guard lest we fail to draw full benefit from it. When it recedes, we should be even more anxious since this grace wanes only when we have been negligent in our watchfulness. Therefore, in all consolations, sensible or substantial, "happy the man who is always on his guard."[44]

---

43. Cf. *In Cant.*, Serm. 54, in Migne, *P. L.*, t. CLXXXIII, col. 1042.
44. Prov. 28:14.

II. DESOLATION OR ARIDITY

193. The opposite of consolation is desolation or aridity, a darkness of the mind and a dryness of the affections. We shall: (1) explain the different kinds of aridity; (2) investigate its causes; (3) set forth certain counsels by way of preventing harm to the spirit and to devotion.

(A) **Kinds of aridity.** There are two kinds of aridity: one is called sensible, the other substantial.

(1) **Sensible aridity** is limited to the inferior part of man. It arises from weariness, mental anguish, or a physical disorder during which one does not derive any joy or sensible consolation from prayer, meditation, or spiritual things in general. This is called "the night of the senses" in the writings of the mystics.

(2) **Substantial aridity** envelops the higher part of man with sadness, oppressing him with discouragement, so that he undertakes spiritual exercises painfully and only with incredible difficulty. Such a state is properly referred to as the dark night of the soul or despondency of the will.

There is a great difference between sensible and substantial aridity. Sensible aridity can be experienced together with substantial consolation. Consequently, it can be easily borne by advanced souls, all the more so as they have learned from experience that sensible consolation is taken away for a time only to be restored more generously, and always as a help to salvation. But substantial aridity utterly crushes and dejects the superior part of man. Thus Cardinal Bona describes it when he says: "A dense fog clouds the mind, a languor weakens the will, which finds no consolation in God or in creatures. The fire of love grows cold, and worst of all, the temptations by which the soul is beset are so numerous that it often imagines that it has consented to unfaithfulness, blasphemies, despair. Those who have experienced this horrible torment compare it to the pains of hell."[45]

Sensible aridity afflicts the body only, but substantial aridity affects both body and soul. The same author writes: "Such a man is often despoiled of earthly goods, deserted by his friends, laughed at by everyone, and despised as insane, while his life and morals are everywhere in bad repute. He is attacked by serious illness, troubled by the devil, and wherever he turns, he finds nothing but afflictions, derision, persecution and the terrible prospect of death."[46]

194. **(B) The causes of aridity.** Aridity, like consolation, may come from God, from the devil, or from nature.

Hence we must investigate: (1) why God sends us aridity or permits it to occur in our souls; (2) how it proceeds from our nature; (3) why the devil makes war on souls by means of aridity; (4) the signs by which we may recognize whether aridity comes from God or from the devil.

I. Aridity resulting from the action or permission of God

(a) SENSIBLE ARIDITY. It is possible that precisely when we strive to increase the grace of devotion we may receive less of it, and the more strenuously we persevere, the more arid and hard of heart we may become, particularly when we earnestly try to prepare for Holy Communion or for important feasts. God Himself is often the cause of this dryness. Father David of Augsburg, seeking to explain why God permits this desolation, has this to say: "Since, according to the divine disposition, 'love from hatred man cannot tell' (Eccl. 9:1); since each man's merits are known to God alone; and, further, since we cannot arrive at a correct conclusion as to how each individual should feel and act in occurrences of this kind, we can at

---

45. *Loc. cit.,* cap. VII.
46. *Loc. cit.,* cap. XIII, n. 7.

least make some conjectures as to why God takes away from good and earnest souls the grace of devotion at the precise moment when they aspire to possess it more fully and tirelessly seek it. We can offer five reasons."[47]

These reasons are: (1) humiliation; (2) purgation from sin; (3) training in grace; (4) restraint of impetuosity; (5) the meriting of more grace and glory.

(1) *Humiliation.* The smallest degree of self-satisfaction is always displeasing to God. For, as Father David remarks: "Faithful souls fall into pride in four ways: Either they glory in the fact of having merited the grace of devotion by their studies and labors; or they extol themselves as more beloved by God than others who do not seem to have this grace; or they think that they have received greater graces than is actually the case; or they are proud of the fact that they know how to use this grace to better advantage, to receive it more graciously, to expend it more fruitfully, and to neglect it less than others who have received a similar gift."[48]

Hence it pleases God to destroy this complacency and haughtiness in humiliating us by means of aridity. "Not without cause," says St. Bernard, "have this languor of soul, dullness of mind and strange inertia of spirit assailed me. I was running along in good style: but all of a sudden a stone blocked my path; I tripped over it and fell to the ground. The Lord saw that I was proud, and turned away from His servant. Hence this dryness in my soul; this lack of devotion from which I suffer . . . I have no taste for the Office; I find no pleasure in reading, no delight in praying; I cannot meditate as usual. As a result, I am slack in the performance of manual labor, drowsy at vigils, quickly angered, persistent in my hatred and over-indulgent to my stomach and my tongue. . . . Woe is me! For

---

47. *Loc. cit.*, Lib. III, cap. LXIX, n. 2.
48. *Loc. cit.*, n. 5.

the Lord visits all the mountains that surround me, but stays away from me."[49] And so the punishment of pride is a loss of grace.

When a self-complacent man aspires to obtain the grace of devotion, God afflicts him with dryness, because, as Father David says, "A soul is more humbled then than at any other time."[50]

(2) *Purgation from sin.* "Since a man may be insufficiently purified by other spiritual exercises, or guilty of sins which he does not recall, and as he has to become more worthy of receiving Holy Communion and more perfectly free from sin, he is afflicted with depression; and the more serious this desolation and sorrow, the more efficacious the purgation. And if perhaps at another time he did not earnestly seek the grace of devotion, or if he was negligent in receiving it, not offering himself generously for such favors, he is punished now according to his negligence in the past; and thus he is deprived of this grace when he desires it, because he formerly neglected it when he could have had it; and all this that he may be more careful in the future."[51] In other words, "we are deprived of spiritual consolation because we are tepid and sluggish and negligent and sinful."[52]

(3) *Training in grace.* Another reason why God allows dryness is that man "may be trained in the ways of grace and learn that it comes from God and not from man. For man cannot acquire grace by his own free choice. Only God can bestow it and infuse it when He wills, and withdraw it also according to His good pleasure, as He judges best for the recipient. He bestows it gratuitously, and not according to a

---

49. *In Cant.*, Serm. 54, in Migne, *P. L.*, t. CLXXXIII, col. 1042.

50. *Loc. cit.*, n. 3.

51. David of Augsburg, *loc. cit.*, n. 3.

52. St. Ignatius, *Exercitia Spiritualis*, "Reg. ad spirit. disnosc.," 1 hebd., reg. 9.

man's merit. For if it were always given when requested, and not given unless requested, man would suppose that God bestows grace with regard to the merit of the petitioner and not according to His liberality."[53]

We must conclude, therefore, that this gift of consolation is not a matter of the will or effort but of the mercy of God.

(4) *Restraining of impetuosity.* "Violent action interferes with breathing, and labored breathing is harmful to the heart," says Father David of Augsburg. "Feverish impetuosity likewise affects freedom of mind." When a devout man "is unable to obtain the desired grace according to his wishes, he becomes sad and ever more obdurate. And the more impetuously he tries to force the grace of devotion, the less he succeeds and the drier he becomes, just as the man who by might and main crushes grapes or olives in the press, squeezes out a more unsightly and insipid juice than one who presses them gently."[54] A spirit of liberty and spontaneity should prevail in the quest of devotion — a grace that cannot be forced.

(5) *Greater merit of grace and glory.* "The soul is purified by affliction. The patient endurance of desolation and the humble suffering of sorrow, like a refining instrument renders the soul more bright, more open to the divine splendor, and capable of greater grace and glory."[55] Aridities coming from God are singular gifts of Divine Providence and indications of God's great love for us.

(b) SUBSTANTIAL ARIDITY. This desolation of the soul is ordinarily sent or permitted by God to test our virtue, as it is written, "Because thou wast acceptable to God, it was necessary that temptation should prove thee."[56] "The Lord tests us to see how much we can endure," says St. Ignatius, "and to see

---

53. David of Augsburg, *loc. cit.*, n. 3.
54. *Loc. cit.*, n. 7.
55. David of Augsburg, *loc. cit.*, n. 8.
56. Tob. 12:13.

to what length we will go in His service and honor without the reward of consolations and special graces."[57] The manifold purposes of substantial aridity, according to Cardinal Bona, are: "that the magnitude of consolation may not make us proud, and that we may not claim consolation as a hereditary right; that a man may more truly know himself, fear his own frailty, and so remain always humble; that he may with greater diligence guard the grace he has, and seek it more fervently when lost; that he may learn to have compassion when others are afflicted; that by the practice of patience he may atone for his sins; that he may prevent infirmity of the body, since it cannot for a long time endure the sweetness of the spirit; that man may uproot a too-great attachment to the gifts of God; that he may serve God free of charge, as it were — that is, without payment by way of consolation";[58] and that he may become more like the Son of God.

II. **Aridity resulting from human nature.** Aridity may also be the result of human nature. For nature seeks itself in all things, is saddened when consolation ceases, and shrinks from exercises of piety while it seeks the deceptive joys of creatures. "Since you satisfy yourself with pleasures that are altogether worldly," says St. Francis de Sales, "it is no wonder that you lose spiritual consolation. Those who are filled with mundane pleasures cannot hold anything spiritual."[59] "Duplicity and craftiness with our director in confession and spiritual direction," says the same saint, "result in dryness and sterility."[60] For if we lie to the Holy Spirit, it is no wonder that He denies His consolation. If we have not the will to be as simple and candid as children, we shall not receive the sweets that are reserved for them.

---

57. *Loc. cit.*, 1 hebd., reg. 9.
58. Cf. Cardinal Bona, *De discretione spirituum*, cap. XIII, n. 6.
59. *Introduction to a Devout Life*, Part IV, Chap. XIV.
60. *Ibid.*

III. **Aridity resulting from the action of the devil.** St. Ignatius says: "The evil spirit afflicts men who earnestly strive to purge themselves of vices and sins and to advance more and more each day in the service of God. He injects into such souls worries, scruples, sorrows, false reasonings, and many other annoyances calculated to impede their progress."[61]

We must not be too astonished at this, for our Seraphic Father said that since spiritual joy is of inestimable benefit for the soul's advancement, the devil opposes this joy; he disturbs the soul dedicated to God with every trick in his bag. Father Roothaan expresses the idea very well: "Since he is an enemy, he does not expect to lead a soul into sin without a struggle; but he does try at least to impede progress or to annoy and persecute her. In his hatred he is content in the beginning only to trouble the soul. But he inflicts even this slight evil with the hope of frustrating a greater good, and in the end even of drawing the soul into sin."[62]

IV. **Signs by which we can tell if aridity comes from God or the devil.** (a) SENSIBLE ARIDITY. Cardinal Bona says that when sensible aridity comes from the devil a person becomes impatient, tepid, inconstant, fainthearted and despairing. If someone dares to mention the Cross, patience, or humility, he shows signs of weariness and dread. Shrinking from the practice of virtue, he turns to the unhealthy consolations of the world and the flesh.

When aridity is from God, however, one does not turn to creatures or find in them any consolation. He experiences no confusion or distaste; steadfast in God, he perseveres in his spiritual exercises. And the more severe the sensible desolation, the greater his substantial consolation, and the more he rejoices because now he knows that he is serving God for Himself and not for any sensible sweetness.

---

61. *Exercitia Spiritualis*, Reg. II ad spirit. dignosc., 1 ae hebd.
62. *Ibid.*, Reg. aliae vel 2ae hebd., nota in reg.I.

(b) SUBSTANTIAL ARIDITY. To discover whether substantial aridity comes from God or the devil, we should pray and consult our spiritual director. For, as St. Ignatius aptly notes: "Satan is most desirous that the soul he wishes to encompass and destroy should keep secret the fraudulent suggestions implanted in his heart. Satan is indignant and very grievously tormented if his efforts are disclosed to a confessor or spiritual director, for he knows that they will defeat him. Therefore, if you are unwilling to disclose the facts to a spiritual director, it is a sign that the dryness is from the devil."[63]

195. (C) Some advice in order that aridity may not harm prayer and devotion. We must be faithful and assiduous at prayer even if we are tormented at times with aridity. "Often," says St. Bernard, "we approach the altar with a tepid and dry heart, and yet we apply ourselves diligently to prayer. And those who persist in prayer are suddenly granted grace, their hearts are enlarged and a flood of devotion inundates their souls. Upon those who persevere, the milk of devotion is not slow to flow."[64]

The following is the golden advice of masters in the spiritual life:

Before prayer

(1) In the first place, we must conduct an accurate investigation into the causes of desolation. If it proceeds from a fault or negligence or especially from pride, we must overcome this defect by penance and amendment. To overcome pride "one needs a thorough knowledge of his own unworthiness, tepidity, negligence, ingratitude and vainglory. There is also need for a reverential fear of the account we must render for graces received and neglected, and a fearful apprehension that God will withdraw His grace and Himself from us on account

---

63. *Ibid.*, Reg. ad spirit. dignosc., 1 ae hebd., reg. 13.
64. *In Cant.*, Serm. 9, n. 7, in Migne, *P. L.*, t. CLXXXIII, col. 818.

of our vices, vices that He has for a long time tolerated so that we might change — yet we have never amended. There is need, finally, for considering other souls who, in grace, virtue, and all good works, excel us beyond comparison."[65]

If aridity proceeds from the attacks of the devil, he must be resisted according to the warning of the Apostle: "Resist the devil, and he will flee from you."[66] If aridity is from God, we must manfully endure the chastisement and patiently await consolation. Father Sigismund Neudecker says that a man in this condition should "consider himself totally unworthy of all heavenly and spiritual consolation; and on account of his sins, imperfect life and tepidity, he should say with David, 'I know, O Lord, that Your ordinances are just, and in Your faithfulness You have afflicted me' (Ps. 118:75)."[67] Thomas a Kempis teaches the same thing. In one passage of his works he enjoins that we must pray with a sincere heart and real affection: "Lord, I am not worthy of Thy consolation, nor of any spiritual visitation; and therefore justly dost Thou deal with me, when Thou leavest me poor and desolate. For could I shed a sea of tears, yet I would not be worthy of Thy consolation. Wherefore I deserve nothing but to be scourged and punished, for I have grievously and often offended Thee, and in many things have very much sinned against Thee."[68]

(2) Father Sigismund also warns us that we should by no means omit our works of piety and other customary exercises. Rather, we must believe with all certainty that the prayers, labors and pious exercises which we perform in time of desolation, without any sensible devotion, are just as pleasing to God, if not more pleasing and meritorious than those we perform with the greatest ardor and sensible devotion. For

---

65. David of Augsburg, *loc. cit.*, n. 6.
66. James 4:7.
67. *Schola religiosa*, by P. Sigismund Neudecker, Pars II, cap. XXII, p. 440, n. 51.
68. *Imitation of Christ*, Book III, Chap. LII.

when such labors and devotions are performed without any feeling and consolation, they are performed purely out of love for God.

During prayer

(1) *Peaceful efforts must be made during prayer.* Violent thoughts that strain or fog the mind should be avoided, particularly during recitation of the Divine Office, lest by turmoil, fatigue, and confusion, we close the door of our heart to God.

In a quiet, tranquil, watchful spirit, without disorder, let us persevere in the praise of God. "Wait for the Lord with courage," says the psalmist; "be stouthearted and wait for the Lord."[69] "If it delays," says Scripture in another place, "wait for it; it will surely come, it will not be late."[70] God will come as He plans, at a time more profitable or necessary for each soul.

If we cannot restrain our hearts from distractions, we should not be disturbed, but calmly do as much as we can and commit the rest to the divine will.

(2) *A firm will to pray makes up for involuntary inattention.* As long as we pray reverently and with a constant desire to be attentive, we satisfy God, even though we do not always succeed in lifting our minds to Him. For He will not blame us for this disorder if we do not consent to it through negligence, and if we are disposed for prayer by the custody of our senses. Even if we have not more to offer than a body and soul ready to serve God in holy fear, we can be confident that we shall not lose our reward.

(3) *The soul must by no means be grieved by desolation and temptations.* Holy Scripture says, "Cursed be he who does the Lord's work remissly."[71] Woe to our souls, then, if we

---

69. Ps. 26:14.
70. Hab. 2:3.
71. Jer. 48:10.

are negligent and remiss, and do not care to pray and chant the divine praises. But if we are diligent and do what we can, we shall be on the safe side. We should never complain that we are abandoned by God or say that our submission is not pleasing to Him, for such are the complaints of children lacking confidence. In St. Bernard's writings we read: "The Lord departs from us so that we may desire Him more ardently; and as our desire grows, so does our quest for Him; and when we seek Him for a while, He will more happily be discovered. If consolation never left us, we would be prone to think that we have here a lasting city and be less inclined to seek our future home."[72]

The same argument holds also for temptations. Among the sayings of Blessed Giles there is his response to a question from one of his confreres: "Why is it that a man suffers more temptations at prayer than at any other time?" To this the holy friar answered: "When a man has a case against an adversary in the court of a prince, he will go to the prince to present the case against his enemy. But when the enemy discovers this, he will proceed against this man with all possible energy, lest the decision be given in the man's favor. The devil proceeds against us in the same manner. Therefore, if you engage in conversation with others, you will notice that you are little bothered by temptations; but if you betake yourself to prayer in order to refresh your soul, you will experience the attacks of the enemy. However, you should not give up prayer on this account, but firmly persevere, for this is the way to your heavenly abode. One who gives up prayer at this time is like a soldier who flees from battle."[73]

We must contain ourselves in holy longanimity and wait in patience until it shall please Almighty God to arrange other-

---

72. *Scala claustr.*, cap. VIII (not actually St. Bernard's but found among his writings in Migne, *P. L.*, t. CLXXXIV, col. 480).

73. *Dicta B. Aegidii Assisiensis*, cap. XII.

not restraining his tongue, . . . that man's religion is vain."[78]
Cajetan of Bergamo says, "The Fathers of the desert maintained
that one who does not know how to hold his tongue does not
know how to pray; and one who does not observe silence cannot practice poverty, chastity, obedience and humility. For the
Spirit of God, the Spirit of virtue, loves silence and will not
dwell in a heart where silence is not respected. The spirits
of wine quickly evaporate because of their subtility, unless the
bottle in which the wine is kept is well sealed. When it does
finally evaporate, nothing but scum and dregs remain. The
same can be said of the Spirit of God and of virtue. For in
one hour of idle gossip, a religious man can lose more merit
and virtue than he can acquire in a whole month of prayer
and meditation."[79] But to observe silence well, we must love
to abide in our cell.

II. LOVE OF ONE'S CELL

198. The Fathers of the Church and masters of the spiritual life relate truly wonderful things about love of one's cell.
Guigo the Carthusian says that the cell and heaven are related
dwellings because there seems to be a certain connection between them. "*Cella* — cell, and *coelum* — heaven, are both
derived from the same Latin word *celare*, which means to keep
secret or hidden. What is hidden in heaven is hidden also in
the cell; and what occurs in the cell occurs also in heaven. All
of which simply means that to be occupied with God is to
enjoy God. For one often ascends from the cell to heaven,
but scarcely ever does one descend into hell. Those who die in
the cell seldom if ever go to hell because one who perseveres
unto death in love of his cell is predestined to heaven."[80]

---

78. James 1:26.
79. Cajetan of Bergamo, *Dic. pract.,* II diei V.
80. *De vita solitaria,* Epist. ad Fratres de Monte Dei. This is found in
Migne among the writings of St. Bernard but is actually by Guigo. See Migne,
P. L., t. CLXXXIV, col. 314.

Advantages of a cell. "The benefits derived from one's cell cannot be praised sufficiently," says Thomas a Kempis, "and no harm will be done if we speak extravagantly on this subject. For the safety of the cell is the safety of the tongue, as well as freedom from whispered distractions, rumors, vanity and levity. Whoever loves to dwell in his cell is a good citizen of heaven, a friend of God, a companion of the angels, a discoverer of secrets, a witness to the supernatural, and, a man in possession of peace, . . . a man of constant prayer, one devoted to holy meditation. . . . Imagine that God and you are the only ones on this earth, and you will enjoy great peace of soul. Remember likewise that the angel found Mary praying in her chamber and not outside conversing with others. He who would know the secrets of heaven must separate himself from men. Moses acted in this way when he left the multitude and remained alone on the mountain, there to receive the Law of the Lord. You should at times consider these facts so that you may like to remain in your cell."[81]

Love of one's cell is a necessity in the formation of apostolic men. "Many saints have found tranquillity of soul in solitude and silence, and therein have learned whatever they preached to others."[82] St. Anthony of Padua first remained hidden, and only later appeared as the glorious and eminent preacher of the people. This has usually been the case with holy, saintly Franciscan heralds of the Gospel.

Blessed is the man to whom it is given to remain in his cell and who perseveres in so doing to the end of his life. For he who loves his cell and willingly spends his time there is protected against many sins and temptations. The more he sets his mind to live in his cell, the more it pleases him and the more he appreciates it. But the more negligent he is in this matter and the less frequently he remains in his cell, the

---

81. *Discipl. claustr.*, cap. VII, n. 4.
82. Thomas a Kempis, *Sermo ad fratres*, Serm. 8.

more displeasing and irksome will this obligation become. All is well for the man who loves his cell and dwells therein, for the Holy Spirit will instruct him. The cell is a paradise to the steady man; it seems a prison and a tomb to the rover.

We must love that solitude ardently in which, as St. Jerome says, "God speaks and holds familiar conversation with His own." The same saint is quoted as saying: "Solitude to me is paradise."[83] Unless a religious remains in his solitude and loves it he will have the appearance but not the spirit of a monk.

CONCLUSION. We can never give enough praise to the apostolate of prayer, for no undertaking is more excellent and noble, no work more acceptable to God and more profitable to man. "Happy the monasteries in which the religious continually ascend to heaven through prayer and upon which the graces and mercy of God in turn descend from heaven. Such a monastery is truly a house of God because it is a house of prayer. There all the virtues flourish; there one finds joy and peace and happiness because there the religious live the life of angels rather than of men."[84] The Minister General of the Capuchins wrote: "Since our Seraphic Father insisted on prayer above all else, we have, beloved brethren, chosen the better part not only for ourselves and made provision for our salvation, but also for the salvation of others. Hence it happens that when men of our age spitefully ask: 'What do you do?' we answer: 'Day and night we cry: "Spare, O Lord, Thy people"; we are here to pray for you; we pray that you may do no evil.' But who can begin to enumerate the numberless benefits that religious invite God to bestow on the Church and the Christian state through their prayers and works? What the angel said of Jeremia also applies to prayerful religious: Behold those through whom salvation is wrought!

---

83. Quoted by Clement XIV in the Apostolic Constitution *In vinea Domini.*
84. Cf. Pacificus a Sejano, *Analecta O. M. Cap.,* t. XXVII, p. 145.

'This is a lover of his brethren and of the people of Israel: this is he that prayeth for the people and for all the holy city!' (2 Mach. 15:14). If only this were true of every religious, then all the excitement and confusion among nations, all the misfortunes in the world would cease immediately. These happen because men pray so little. And since fervent and frequent prayers do not ascend to the throne of the Lord from the sanctuary as they should, we must deplore, with the Church, defections among priests and religious."[85]

*Article IV — Franciscan Devotions

199. Certain devotional exercises customary in the Seraphic Order are another means of conforming our will to the divine will. These exercises are derived from the example and customs of our beloved Father St. Francis. Thomas of Celano says, "Although this man was devout in all things, as one enjoying the unction of the Holy Spirit, yet he was moved with a special affection for certain devotions."[1] With a very special devotion St. Francis honored: (1) Christ our Redeemer; (2) Mary immaculate; (3) the saints reigning with Christ.

§ I. The Cult of Christ Our Redeemer

200. Concept of cult. Cult (or worship) is the honor and subjection shown another because of his excellence. The worship offered to God and God alone on account of His infinite and uncreated excellence is called *latria.*

The worship offered to creatures on account of their supernatural excellence in the order of sanctification and union with God is called *dulia.*

Since a more excellent cult is due to the Mother of God, theologians have assigned *hyperdulia* to her.

---

85. *Ibid.,* p. 148.

---

1. *Legenda Secunda,* cap. CXLVIII, p. 316.

The worship of *latria* is applicable to Christ, the Word Incarnate (a term which signifies that He has a divine and a human nature). Such worship must be given to the *human nature* of Christ as well as the divine, on account of the hypostatic union of Christ's human nature with the Divine Word. St. John Damascene writes: "I fear to touch the glowing charcoal because the fire united to the wood makes it burn. I adore both natures of Christ on account of the divinity united to the flesh."[2]

The *general* (common) *material object* of the cult of Christ, therefore, is the *person of the Incarnate Word,* or the whole Christ, and not a certain part only. We do not speak of a man's hand as being honored; it is the whole man who is honored. Even if sometimes it happens that someone's hand or foot is declared honorable, it does not mean that the individual parts are honorable in themselves, but only in so far as the whole is honored in them. For instance, if we strike someone's body unjustly, we do not perpetrate the injury simply upon the part that has been struck but on the whole person.

The *general formal object* or the ultimate objective reason on which all cult of latria depends is the divine excellence of the Word, or the infinite dignity of the Incarnate Word, which together with Christ's whole human nature and all its parts is made one through the hypostatic union.

The object of the manifestation, or the special material object, can and should be summed up as follows:

(1) Christ's human nature itself is the means in and through which the divine excellence, i. e., the Word, is manifested in an admirable and incomprehensible manner. The Word veiled beneath the flesh, discloses Himself to us for adoration and worship.

(2) The mysteries of the life of Christ.

---

2. *De fide orthodox.,* Lib. III, cap. VIII, in Migne, *P. G.,* t. XLIV, col. 1014.

(3) The individual parts of His sacred humanity. These parts of His human nature, since they are the special material object of the worship, call for a special worship of our Lord. Worship of this type is something particular — for example, the worship of the Sacred Heart of Jesus.

201. Devotions of our Seraphic Father. The Seraphic St. Francis was attracted with special devotion to:

1. The human nature of Christ; hence his devotion to the most holy name of Jesus.

2. The various mysteries of the life of Christ, especially (a) the mystery of the Incarnation; and (b) the Passion and the Cross.

3. The most Blessed Sacrament.

4. The most Sacred Heart of Jesus, symbol of the love of Christ.

Here we wish to enlarge on the forenamed devotions. Devotion to the most Blessed Sacrament will be treated in a subsequent article.

Franciscan devotion to Christ is a result of Franciscan Christology, which maintains the absolute primacy of Christ. God created the universe because He willed to have a perfect lover, a perfect adorer. In God's eternal and absolute decree Jesus Christ was willed. From Him God would receive love, adoration and praise in an infinite degree. Through Christ, in whom all creation is summed up, God receives perfect glory. All else is created for Christ, so that through Him, as absolute Primate of creation, the whole universe would finally give glory to God. "All [things] are yours, and you are Christ's, and Christ is God's."[3]

Or, as Father Faber puts it, "The Eternal Word lived in the bosom of the Father. . . . The Babe of Bethlehem was that

---

3. 1 Cor. 3:23.

eternal person, and in some sense He was eternally the Babe
of Bethlehem. . . . This first-born creature, this sacred humanity,
was not only the primal creature; it was also the cause of all
other creatures."[4]

I. THE MOST HOLY NAME OF JESUS

202. (A) **The meaning of the name of the Incarnate
Word.** Since the giving of a name implies dominion over the
one who is named, no one could give a name to the Incarnate
Word except the Father, and those to whom the Father should
wish to reveal it. This imposition of the name of Jesus was
a wonderful thing which the Evangelist described in the following manner: "And when eight days were fulfilled for His
circumcision, His name was called Jesus, the name given Him
by the angel before He was conceived in the womb."[5]

This mellifluent name "Jesus" is a Hebrew word which
means "saviour" or "salvation," and together with the name
Christ has a considerable signification.

"Christ," is a Greek word equivalent to the Hebrew "Mes-
sias" and the Latin "Unctus" (anointed), and is a name of
dignity. " 'Christ' is interpreted as meaning 'Anointed,' " says
St. Thomas, "according to the verse: 'Therefore God, your God,
has anointed you with the oil of gladness' (Ps. 44:8), this
anointing designating the *dignity* of Christ. And since priests
were anointed, as is evident from Exodus (Ch. 27), it reveals
Christ's *sanctity*. Since kings too were anointed, as is evident from the lives of David and Solomon, the anointing
likewise signifies Christ's *power*. It has reference to His
knowledge also, because the prophets were anointed, as is
plain in the case of Eliseus."[6] Whatever is said of the name
"Christ" applies also to the name "Jesus." Hence the angel

---

4. *Bethlehem*, Chap. I.
5. Luke 2:21.
6. St. Thomas, *Comment. in Epist. ad Rom.*, cap. I, Lect. I, in medio.

joined the two when he said to the shepherds: "Behold, I bring you good news of great joy which shall be to all the people: for today, in the town of David, a Saviour has been born to you, who is Christ the Lord."[7] He proposes the name of Saviour first, because it is more characteristic of the Child. As the angel had said to Joseph: "Thou shalt call His name Jesus, for He shall save His people from their sins."[8]

The name "Jesus" is proper to the Divine Word. Although the work of salvation is common to the three Divine Persons, who are the one and only cause of our salvation, yet the name "Jesus" is proper only to the Divine Word made man, from the fact that He alone, having assumed a body of flesh, fulfilled the function of a Saviour by satisfying the Divine Justice and by discharging our debts through His precious blood, which He shed for us.

203. (B) **The name "Jesus" is a powerful name.** The Holy Spirit, says St. Bernard, properly compares the name of the bridegroom to oil when He teaches the bride to cry to her spouse: "Thy name is as oil poured out (Cant. 1:2, Challoner-Douay version). For oil illumines, nourishes and anoints. It enkindles fire, feeds the body, soothes sorrow; in other words, it is light, food and medicine. The same activities apply to the holy name: it gives light when invoked, nourishes when meditated upon, and heals and soothes when implored."[9] Indeed, the honors and prerogatives attached to this great name in Sacred Scripture are almost innumerable. In this name we have a *sure defense:*

"The name of the Lord is a strong tower," says Solomon.[10] Miracles are performed in this name: "In My name they shall

---

7. Luke 2:10-11.
8. Matt. 1:21.
9. *In Cant.*, Serm. 15, n. 5, in Migne, *P. L.,* t. CLXXXIII, col. 846.
10. Prov. 18:10.

cast out devils; they shall speak in new tongues; they shall take up serpents; and if they drink any deadly thing, it shall not hurt them; they shall lay hands upon the sick and they shall get well."[11] In this name we ask whatever we wish from God and we receive it: "Amen, amen, I say to you, if you ask the Father anything in My name, He will give it to you."[12] In this name we have received the remission of sins: "To Him all the prophets bear witness, that through His name all who believe in Him may receive forgiveness of sins," says St. Peter.[13] "Whatever you do in word or in work," writes the Apostle of the Gentiles, "do all in the name of the Lord Jesus."[14] In this name all things should be done so as to be made good and holy.

204. (C) **The name "Jesus" is a sweet name.** Nothing is sweeter and more precious than the name of Jesus. Even if the things pertaining to it were repeated over and over a thousand times, they would not be tiresome to the man who understands, for the holy name will always yield new meanings. Such is the sweetness of this name, such its delight, that the Apostles were most happy to suffer for it. "They departed from the presence of the Sanhedrin, rejoicing that they had been counted worthy to suffer disgrace for the name of Jesus."[15] The Apostle Paul, as well as John the Evangelist, wished to use the holy name as often as possible. For in the Epistles of St. Paul it appears 220 times, and in the Gospel of St. John more often still, since it was so desired, so sweet and so delightful on the lips and in the hearts of the Apostles. "All food for the soul is dry," says St. Bernard, "if that oil is not poured over it; it is unsavory if it is not seasoned by this salt. If you write to me, it will not be pleasant to read unless I

---

11. Mark 16:17-18.
12. John 16:23.
13. Acts 10:43.
14. Col. 3:17.
15. Acts 5:41.

see there the name of Jesus. If you talk with me or discuss something with me, I find no relish in the conversation unless I hear the name of Jesus. Jesus is honey in my mouth, a melody in my ears, joy in my heart."[16]

205. (D) A Franciscan devotion. Thomas of Celano could write of our Seraphic Father: "He was affected beyond human comprehension when he spoke Thy name, O holy Lord, and overflowed with gladness and with the purest joy. At such times he seemed to be a new man, a man of another world. Therefore, whenever he found any writings, whether of divine or human origin, on the road, in a house, or in his pathway, he most reverently gathered them up and placed them in a holy and worthy place, for fear that they might contain the name of the Lord, or something pertaining to it."[17]

This is confirmed in the *Testament* of St. Francis, in which he writes: "And whenever I find our Lord's most holy names and written words in any unseemly place, I like to gather them up, and I beg that they be gathered up, and put in a becoming place." Moreover, devotion to this most holy name was propagated far and wide by St. Bernardine of Siena and St. John Capistran, and it first grew into an ecclesiastical devotion in the Order of Friars Minor.

CONCLUSION. The most holy name of Jesus affords strength and constancy against the devil and against evil men, as well as against many and varied temptations. We must devoutly invoke it in times of temptation and of difficulty, particularly by reciting the litany of the holy name. If we would but fly to Jesus at the proper times, He would disperse our darkness by His grace and light, He would banish our weariness and soften our hardness of heart. Then our sighs would quickly change into tears, accompanied by heavenly joy, so that we

---

16. *Loc. cit.*, n. 6, col. 847.
17. *Legenda Prima*, cap. XXIX, p. 83.

would be able to cry out with the Apostle: "It is now no longer I that live, but Christ lives in me."[18]

II. MYSTERIES FROM THE LIFE OF OUR LORD

1 — The Birth of Our Lord

206. (A) **Devotion to the Infant Jesus is a Franciscan devotion.** "He celebrated the feast of the birth of the Infant Jesus with heartier rejoicing and sweeter devotion than the other great feasts. He called it the feast of feasts, because on that day the Most High Son of God became a poor little child. With insatiable delight he would kiss the images of the Babe; his tender pity for the Little One poured itself from his heart in the form of melting, stammering words like the crooning of an infant. One year Christmas occurred on a Friday. Brother Morico remarked casually that this time no meat could be placed on the table. 'Thou art in error, Brother,' replied Francis; 'on Christmas there is no Friday. I wish that on this day even the walls should eat meat, and since they cannot do so, it should at least be rubbed on them.' He wished that better food should be given to cattle and asses on this day."[19]

Our Seraphic Father was the first to make a crib and to kiss the image of the little child reposing in it.

"The holy man of God," says Thomas of Celano, "stood before the Babe in the manger, shedding tears of love and overflowing with joy. To the people standing around, he announced the birth of the poor King of Heaven, and spoke of the little town of Bethlehem in honey-sweet words. And often, when he was about to pronounce the name of Jesus, the immense fire of love overcame him, and he called Him only the Babe of Bethlehem. And as he spoke the word 'Bethlehem,' his

---

18. Gal. 2:20.
19. Thomas of Celano, *Legenda Secunda*, cap. CLI, pp. 318-319.

voice and his whole being were filled with deep, burning affection. And when he had said the word 'Jesus' or 'Bethlehem,' he let his tongue pass over his lips, as if to taste the sweetness of the word and to rejoice in it."[20]

207. (B) Purpose of this devotion. By means of this devotion, we can learn the dignity of our souls and acquire love for the Franciscan Order.

The birth of Christ makes us realize the dignity of our soul. For in this mystery "the goodness and kindness of God our Saviour appeared . . . ; according to His mercy, He saved us . . . that, justified by His grace, we may be heirs in the hope of life everlasting."[21]

St. Leo exclaims: "Recognize, O Christian, your dignity: You have been made a sharer in the divine nature. Do not return to your former degenerate manner of life. Remember of whose head you are a member. Recall that, torn away from the power of darkness, you have been transferred into the light and the kingdom of God."[22]

It fosters love for the Franciscan Order. After the example of the Seraphic Father, we must often contemplate the Infant Jesus as He lies in the manger and try to realize the great misery with which He was surrounded, out of love for us. This consideration will be an efficient means of increasing our love and devotion for our life of poverty. With the pious affection and holy thoughtfulness of a good Franciscan, we should enter that public shelter for animals, open as it is to stormy winds and to the most inclement weather, freezing with the ice, the cold, and the snows of winter. There we will find nothing superfluous. We shall be amazed at the appalling lack of even the necessities of life. From the example of the Divine Infant we should acquire a greater love of most high poverty.

---

20. Thomas of Celano, *Legenda Prima,* cap. XXX, p. 85 et seq.
21. Epistle for the Second Mass at Christmas, taken from Titus 3:4, 5, 7.
22. Second nocturn for Matins, Office for Christmas Day, taken from *Sermon 21,* I, by St. Leo.

We should recall this mystery every day, and annually observe the fast from the feast of All Saints to Christmas as the Rule prescribes, so that we may celebrate the birthday of the most sweet Infant Jesus with joy and gladness.

2 — The Passion and the Cross

208. Meditation upon the Passion of Christ is a most effective means of enkindling love. Love is best enkindled by consideration of the benefits received; and the greatest benefit of God toward men is the Passion of Christ. As St. John says: "God so loved the world that He gave His only-begotten Son";[23] and St. Paul: "But God commends His charity toward us, because when as yet we were sinners, Christ died for us."[24]

209. (A) Devotion in honor of the Passion and Cross of Christ is a Franciscan devotion. Our Seraphic Father continually meditated on the Passion of our Lord in order to conform his own will most perfectly to the divine will. "The humility of the Incarnation and the charity of the Passion so occupied his memory that he scarcely wished to think of anything else."[25]

(1) *From the beginning of his conversion Francis meditated upon the Passion of Christ.* In the church of San Damiano, "he prostrated himself humbly and devoutly before the crucifix and, favored with unusual visitations, found himself completely changed. A miracle occurred: the image of the Crucified spoke to him. From that hour his soul melted whenever his Beloved spoke to him. The sufferings of Christ were ever before his eyes, and filled them with ever-flowing tears.

---

23. John 3:16.
24. Rom. 5:8, 9.
25. Thomas of Celano, *Legenda Prima,* cap. XXX, p. 85.

Everywhere one heard his weeping; at the thought of Christ's wounds he was inconsolable."[26]

(2) *His habit assumed the form of a cross.* "Did he not clothe himself with the Cross, choosing a garment of penance which had the shape of a cross? Although he chose it because of its poverty, he also desired it to express the mystery of the Cross. He wished his entire body to be clothed with the Cross of Christ, even as his spirit had put on the Crucified; and since God had vanquished the powers of hell in this sign, so also the Franciscan army should do battle for its liege Lord under this standard."[27]

(3) *He used the letter "T" (Tau) to recall the Passion of Christ.* According to St. Jerome, the letter T signifies the mystery of the Cross. Thus he interprets the passage in Ezechiel wherein the prophet says that those who had a T marked on their foreheads would be spared. Our Seraphic Father also "esteemed this sign above all other signs: with this sign he sealed all his writings, with it he marked the walls of the cells. Pacificus, a man of God who enjoyed celestial visions, one day beheld the sign of Tau shining with dazzling splendor on the forehead of blessed Francis."[28]

(4) *Love for the crucified Jesus with which he inwardly burned, at times appeared outwardly.* "Did not Brother Sylvester, one of the first friars and a man of consummate holiness," remarks Celano, "behold a golden cross proceeding from the mouth of the Saint, its beam growing upward into the heavens, and its arms reaching unto the ends of the earth? It is written, and proved by faithful witnesses, that Brother Monaldus, distinguished in manner and deed, saw Francis fixed to the Cross while St. Anthony of Padua was preaching on the mystery of the Redemption."[29]

---

26. Celano, *Legenda Secunda,* cap. VI, p. 176.
27. Celano, *Tractatus de miraculis,* II, p. 343.
28. *Ibid.,* pp. 343, 344.
29. *Ibid.*

(5) *The sacred stigmata were the reward of his love for the Passion of Jesus.* Since every pursuit of the man of God both in public and in private centered on the Cross of our Lord, Celano could write: "How worthy, therefore, of human credence and universal acceptance it is, that one who was so gifted with a marvelous love of the Cross should also be distinguished with the marvelous reward of the Cross! Therefore, nothing can with greater truth be proclaimed of him than the marks of the Cross."[30]

THE FRANCISCANS HAVE ALWAYS PRACTICED THIS DEVOTION. "Was it not always a custom, " asks Celano, "established by a pious practice of his first sons, that wherever they saw a likeness of the Cross they showed all due reverence and honor toward it?"[31] Is it not still the glory of the Franciscans to have the custody of the Holy Land? Was it not by their industry that devotion of the Way of the Cross has been propagated everywhere in the Catholic world?

Since our legislators exhort all friars to practice special devotion to the Passion of our Lord after the example of our Seraphic Father St. Francis, it will be good to consider the necessity and manner of meditating on Christ's Passion, according to the teaching of St. Bonaventure.

210. (B) **The necessity of meditating on the Passion of Christ.** Whoever wishes to keep his soul in a permanent state of devotion must frequently, even continually, set the eyes of his heart on Christ dying on the Cross. For this reason, the Lord says in Leviticus: "The fire on the altar is to be kept burning; it must not go out. Every morning the priest shall put firewood on it."[32] The *Altar of God* is your heart, upon which the fire of fervent devotion must always burn. You must daily nourish it with wood from the Cross of Christ and the memory of His Passion.

---

30. *Ibid.*
31. *Ibid.,* p. 343.
32. Lev. 6:5.

With the movements of your affections draw near to the wounded Jesus, to Jesus crowned with thorns, Jesus fastened upon the gibbet of the Cross; with St. Thomas the Apostle see not only in His hands the marks of the nails; do not stop at putting your fingers into the place of the nails; go farther than putting your hand into His side; enter even into the very heart of Jesus through the door of His side, and there, by a most ardent love of the Crucified, be transformed into Christ.... Seek nothing, desire nothing, find your consolation in nothing but in yielding yourself to die with Christ on the Cross. And exclaim with St. Paul the Apostle: "With Christ I am nailed to the Cross. It is now no longer I that live, but Christ lives in me."[33]

211. (C) **Manner of meditating on Christ's Passion.** The vision of the Passion of Christ should imprint itself so deeply in our memory that we see the Man of Sorrows before our very eyes. For this we must consider the length, the breadth, the height and the depth of His sufferings.

(1) THE LENGTH OF CHRIST'S SUFFERINGS. "From the first day of His life even to the day of His death, He was always surrounded by sufferings, as He testifies through the prophet, saying: 'I am afflicted and in agony from My youth' (Ps. 87: 16); and elsewhere: 'I suffer affliction day after day, and chastisement with each new dawn' (Ps. 72:14)."[34]

(2) THE BREADTH OF CHRIST'S SUFFERINGS. We must try to realize the utter cruelty which surrounded our beloved Saviour at the time of His death. "The more widespread the pain, the greater it is. Christ's sufferings and pains were in every part of His body, so that not one member, even the least, was free from its own particular sting; no portion, no matter how small, was free from bitterness. 'From the sole

---

33. Gal. 2:19-20.
34. St. Bonaventure, *De perf. vitae ad sorores,* cap. VI, n. 8.

of the foot to the top of the head, there is no soundness therein' (Isa. 1:6)."[35]

(3) THE HEIGHT (INTENSITY) OF CHRIST'S SUFFERINGS. Cruelty causes the highest degree of suffering. "The more sensitive a thing is, the more grievously it suffers. But never was a body so sensitive with regard to suffering as the body of the Saviour, for the body of a woman is more tender than that of a man and the body of Christ was wholly virginal; He was conceived of the Holy Spirit and born of the Virgin. The sufferings of Christ were all most cruel, because He was more tender than any virgin."[36]

(4) THE DEPTH OF CHRIST'S SUFFERING. We can judge the depth of Christ's sufferings from the fact that His was suffering in its entirety and at its purest, unmixed by any consolation whatsoever, and from every aspect the most ignominious. "As a thief, He is hanging between thieves, and in the middle as if the prince of thieves. He is lifted up into the air, suspended between heaven and earth as if He were not even worthy to live or die upon earth. The death of the Son of God was most ignominious, first of all because of the kind of death He endured, suspended upon a gibbet; then, on account of His companions in death, since He was placed among the wicked and condemned; because of the place of His death, since He was crucified upon the infamous Mount Calvary."[37]

CONCLUSION. What shall we give to God in return for all He has given us? We shall offer Him our contrite and humbled hearts; we shall offer our hearts — that is, our wills — ready to accomplish anything He may ask. For, says St. Bonaventure, "He has endured these things in order to enkindle in you love for Him; in order that in return you may love Him

---

35. *Ibid.*, n. 6.
36. *Ibid.*, n. 5.
37. *Ibid.*, n. 3.

with your whole heart, your whole soul, and your whole mind. . . . So beware lest you be ungrateful for such a great benefit; set the crucified Jesus 'as a seal on your heart' (Cant. 8:6); and just as a seal is impressed on soft wax so should you imprint Jesus on your heart. . . . Place Him also 'as a seal on your arm' (Cant. 8:6), so that you may never cease doing good, never tire of working for the name of the Lord Jesus; but when you have done everything, begin again to work as if you had done nothing. If at times sadness, oppression, fatigue, bitterness shall befall you, or if doing good has no appeal, run immediately to the crucified Jesus hanging upon the cross; and there contemplate the crown of thorns, the nails of iron, the pierced side; contemplate the wounded feet and hands, the head and side, the wounds of the whole body; remember that He suffered all this for you, and endured so much for you because He loves you so very much. Believe me, such a meditation will immediately turn every sorrow into joy, make every burden light, every annoyance lovable, and bitterness will become sweet and agreeable."[38]

The daily making of the Stations of the Cross is therefore a most excellent practice.[39]

---

38. *Ibid.*, n. 9.

39. The faithful who with a contrite heart make the Way of the Cross may gain:

A plenary indulgence as often as they make the Stations;

Another plenary indulgence if they receive Holy Communion on the same day or even within a month after having made the Stations ten times;

An indulgence of ten years for each Station if, for some reasonable cause, they are unable to complete the entire Way of the Cross. (*Raccolta,* # 194, 1952 edition.)

Conditions: Confession and Holy Communion are not required.

a. One must meditate on the Passion of our Lord; it does not matter how short the meditation may be. A meditation according to one's capacity to meditate suffices. (*S. C. Indulg.,* Monit. VI.)

b. Movement from one Station to the next is required, so that when there is no impediment each Station must be visited individually, except when the group is too large or the place too narrow. (*S. C. Indulg.,* Monit. VII, Decr. auth., n. 287.)

c. The Fourteen Stations must be made without interruption, that is, without notable or moral interruption. (*Ibid.,* n. 385, ad 1; 223, ad 4.)

III. DEVOTION TO THE SACRED HEART

212. Origin and propagation of this devotion. In its *spiritual* object — that is, as a devotion to the divine and human love of Jesus — devotion to the Sacred Heart flourished during the early years of the Church. Even in its *material* object, that is, devotion to the wounds and especially to the wound in the sacred side of Christ, it was not entirely unknown at the beginning of the Church, as we can conclude from the Acts of the martyrs. From the words of St. Bonaventure it is apparent that it flourished in the Seraphic Order from the first. Devotion to the heart of Jesus, says Father Pacificus of Sejano, can be called a "sweetly scented flower which came forth from the heart of the admirable Francis, flourished in the Franciscan garden, and was fostered by the sons of the great Assisian with the most zealous industry and love. Our Redeemer Himself, revealing divine secrets to St. Margaret Mary Alacoque, told her that St. Francis had an extraordinary devotion to His Sacred Heart: Francis had continually endeavored to be totally conquered by and entirely conformed to this most Sacred Heart. Our Seraphic Father bequeathed to his sons a love which they should guard as a sacred fire, and increasingly enkindle in their hearts. He also commanded them to manifest a particular love and adoration for the Sacrament of the Eucharist. In this Sacrament, as in a furnace of charity, the Divine Heart is immolated and burns with a perennial love which sweetly draws us to return love for love."[40] Finally, in the seventeenth century, through the efforts of St. Margaret Mary and St. John Eudes, devotion to the Sacred Heart of Jesus spread over the whole world in a wonderful manner. In 1874 the Order of Friars Minor and the Capuchins were solemnly consecrated to the Sacred Heart. Here our purpose is to explain: (a) the nature of this devotion; (b) the promises of the Sacred Heart to His

---

40. Pacificus a Sejano, *Analecta O. M. Cap.*, t. XXV, p. 25.

faithful ones; (c) the manner in which we should honor the heart of Jesus.

213. (A) **Nature of devotion to the Sacred Heart of Jesus.** Each and every part of the human nature of Christ, as we have seen, must be adored with the worship of *latria,* because all are hypostatically united to the Word in an equal manner, although it is not good to show any individual part a particular worship without a special reason, lest we give unbelievers an occasion for derision. It is most fitting to honor the heart of Christ in a special manner, that is, more than the other parts of His sacred humanity. This is especially evident from the apparitions and revelations of Christ to St. Margaret Mary: "Disclosing His Sacred Heart, He said: 'Behold the heart that has loved men so much.... I request that the Friday which follows the Octave of Corpus Christi be dedicated to the worship of My heart.' "[41]

Material object

(1) The material object, or that toward which the devotion is directed, is the real heart of Christ our Lord, the symbol of His human and divine love.

This material object contains in itself two elements, truly distinct in themselves, yet associated in reality: a sensible or visible element, the very heart of the Saviour; and the spiritual or intelligible element, the love of Christ. The object of the devotion is really one, although consisting of two components, and may be described as the heart of Christ manifesting His love, or as the charity of Christ demonstrated by the symbol of a real heart.

(2) Although the real heart of Christ in itself may be considered a symbol of love for God as well as love for men, in this devotion it is in the proper sense of the word

---

41. Cf. Nilles, *De Rationibus festorum Cordis Jesu et purissimi cordis Mariae.*

regarded as a symbol, and indeed a natural symbol, of God's love for men, as is evident from the institution of the devotion.

(3) Proximately, the created love — that is, the love of the human nature of Christ for men — is the object of this devotion; the Sacred Heart is the natural and proper expression of this cult. Remotely, the uncreated love, which is the love of the divine nature for men, is also represented in an appropriate manner because the person of the Saviour is one, and most assuredly created love in Christ is in a certain sense an imitation and derivation of uncreated love.

FORMAL OBJECT. The formal object or objective reason for worshiping the heart of Jesus is both the dignity of the Word, to whom the heart is hypostatically united, and the divine-human love which He lavishes upon us. In other words, the love or charity of our Saviour is worshiped in a singular manner: (1) because that love is distinguished by the highest perfection; (2) because we owe every good gift to this love; (3) because, in recalling the love of Christ our Lord, we recall all the mysteries of His life in a most fitting and appropriate manner.

214. (B) The promises of Christ to those who honor His most loving heart. We shall do well to meditate frequently on the promises of Christ to those who honor His Sacred Heart, so that we may incite ourselves to a greater love for that heart. The following are the promises; they were made to St. Margaret Mary for souls devoted to the Sacred Heart:

1. I will give them all the graces necessary in their state of life.

2. I will establish peace in their houses.

3. I will comfort them in all their afflictions.

4. I will be their secure refuge during life, and above all in death.

5. I will bestow abundant blessings upon all their undertakings.

6. Sinners shall find in My heart the source of an infinite ocean of mercy.

7. Fervent souls shall quickly mount to high perfection.

8. Tepid souls shall grow fervent.

9. I will bless every place where a picture of My heart shall be set up and honored.

10. I will give to priests the gift of touching the most hardened hearts.

11. Those who shall promote this devotion shall have their names written in My heart, never to be blotted out.

12. I promise thee in the excessive mercy of My heart that My all-powerful love will grant to all those who communicate on the First Friday in nine consecutive months the grace of final repentance; they shall not die in My disgrace nor without receiving their Sacraments; My Divine Heart shall be their safe refuge in this last moment.

215. The manner of honoring the most Sacred Heart of Jesus. While these stupendous promises still ring in our ears, we shall eagerly, joyfully hearken to the voice of God urging devotion to the most amiable heart of Jesus Christ.

(1) In order that this most precious gem left by our Seraphic Father as a legacy to his sons may be safeguarded, all the brethren should remember on the First Friday of every month to renew, both privately and publicly, their consecration to the Sacred Heart of Jesus.

(2) All the brethren should perform, with deepest affections of devotion, the pious exercises prescribed in their Province, "that the most sweet heart of Jesus, which the sons of this ungrateful age most wickedly afflict with injuries and

revilings, may be attended by us with honor and praise in a manner as worthy as possible; lest He complain of our lack of love as He lamented to St. Margaret Mary Alacoque: 'The most bitter grief of all that I suffer,' He said, 'is when My most beloved sons, priests and religious, souls consecrated to God, refuse to respond with love for Me.' Urged on by these complaints, we should promote this most outstanding devotion in our Order, and propagate it abroad; and may our brethren love and worship the heart of Jesus with the seraphic ardor of charity with which Francis loved and worshiped it."[42]

§ II. Devotion to the Blessed Virgin Mary

216. Devotion to the Virgin Mary is a most efficacious means for joining the wills of men to that of Christ. Well does Pius X say, "Because it pleased Divine Providence to give us the God-Man through Mary who, made fruitful by the Holy Spirit, bore Him in her womb, there remains nothing for us but to receive Christ from the hands of Mary. And Scripture also, whenever it foretells the future graces to be given us, clearly points at one and the same time to the Redeemer and to His peerless Mother. A lamb, the Lord of the earth, shall be sent out, but from a rock of the desert; a flower shall spring up, but from the root of Jesse."[43] After reflecting on the nature of devotion to Mary, we shall, if we realize its importance, be entirely devoted to her, as was our Seraphic Father; we shall diligently honor her through the Marian devotions customary in the Franciscan family. With this in mind, we shall briefly consider: (1) the nature of devotion to the Blessed Virgin Mary; (2) Franciscan devotion to the Blessed Virgin Mary; (3) the various exercises of this devotion customary in the Seraphic Order.

---

42. Pacificus a Sejano, *loc. cit.,* t. XXV, p. 26.

43. Encyclical Letter *Ad diem illum laetissimum,* Feb. 2, 1904.

I. NATURE OF DEVOTION TO THE BLESSED VIRGIN MARY

217. The reasons for special devotion to the Blessed Virgin Mary are the following: (a) Mary is the Mother of God; (b) Mary is our Mother; (c) Mary is the secondary Reparatrix of the whole human race; (d) Mary is the Queen of all creation.

(A) **The Virgin Mary is the Mother of God.** A woman is truly the mother of someone from the fact that she gave birth to him. Mary gave birth to Jesus Christ, as is evident from the Sacred Scriptures; and Jesus Christ is truly God. Therefore, Mary is truly the Mother of God.

Furthermore, all the privileges granted to the Blessed Virgin Mary flow from the dignity of the divine maternity. "Just as the humanity of Christ, because it was united to the Word, receives from it the endowments and privileges worthy of such a union and close association, . . . so, in like manner, God endowed the Blessed Virgin with all the charismata and favors condign with her status as the Mother of Christ and Spouse of God. Hence we draw these conclusions: The Blessed Virgin is the Mother of God; she is therefore by far more excellent than all the angels, even the Seraphim and Cherubim. She is the Mother of God; she is therefore most pure and most holy, so much so that under God a greater purity cannot be conceived. She is the Mother of God! Therefore, whatever is granted to any of the saints as a privilege (that is, grace making one pleasing in God's sight — *gratia gratum faciens*) must be granted to her above all."[44]

Furthermore, because of her dignity as Mother of God, the Blessed Virgin has acquired special claims on Christ Jesus. Since the natural law ordains that sons love and revere their parents, the Blessed Virgin has the personal right to be loved and honored by Jesus, her Son. And although she does not have the absolute right to His obedience, since Christ by reason

44. Cornelius a Lapide, *Commentarius in Matt.,* I, 16.

of His hypostatic union was superior to His own Mother and could have withdrawn Himself from her authority, the truth is that He was willingly obedient to her, as it is written: "He ... was subject to them."[45] Nor did this obedience flow from anything but the natural reverence prescribed for a son toward his mother.

218. (B) The Virgin Mary is the Mother of men. Mary is the Mother of Jesus. But Jesus deigned to become our brother according to nature, by assuming flesh; and according to grace, by adopting us as His brothers. "Heirs indeed of God and joint heirs with Christ":[46] thus we are made His members, and become one mystical body with Him — "In one and the same womb of the most chaste Mary, Christ both assumed flesh to Himself, and likewise joined to Himself the mystical body, formed from those who were to believe in Him. So that, bearing the Saviour in her womb, Mary can be said to have borne all those whose life the life of the Saviour contained. Therefore, each and all of us, as many as have been joined with Christ in the same way that the body is joined with the head, have come forth from the womb of Mary. For, as the Apostle says, we are 'members of His body, made from His flesh, and from His bones' (Eph. 5:30). Hence, in a spiritual and mystical manner, we can be called sons of Mary, and she can be called the Mother of all of us."[47] As St. Augustine reminds us: "Mother indeed in the spirit, ... but certainly mother of the members of Christ, which we are."[48]

219. (C) The Virgin Mary is the secondary Reparatrix of the whole human race. Mary, our sweet Mother, has always been associated with her first-born Son in the work of the

---

45. Luke 2:51.
46. Rom. 8:17.
47. Pius X, *Ad diem illum laetissimum.*
48. St. Augustine, *De sancta virginitate,* cap. VI, in Migne, *P. L.,* t. XL, col. 399.

redemption of fallen humanity. For from her own flesh she furnished the material for the human members of the only-begotten Son of God. She provided the victim for the salvation of men. It has been the common belief that the office of Mary was to guard and nourish this victim, and even, when the time came, to present Him at the altar of sacrifice. From henceforth the life and labors of Mother and Son were never dissociated. And when the last moment of the Son approached, "there [was] standing by the Cross of Jesus His Mother,"[49] not only rapt by this tremendous spectacle, but openly rejoicing that "her first-born was offered for the salvation of man; and she felt such great compassion that if it had been possible she would have sustained with great willingness all the torments her Son endured."[50]

As a result of this union between Mary and Christ, she was most worthy to become reparatrix of this profligate world and therefore the dispensatrix of every one of the gifts which God earned for us by His blood and His most cruel death.

Mary therefore is the dispensatrix of all graces. She is mediatrix, not the principal one but the secondary one — mediatrix to the mediator, Jesus; she is the mediatrix, not a necessary one but a most useful one. The font of grace is Christ, and "of His fullness we have all received."[51] But Mary, as St. Bernard notes, "is the aqueduct."[52] She is the neck by which the body is joined with the head and through which the head imparts power and strength to the body. "For she is the neck of our Head, through which all the spiritual gifts are communicated to His mystical body."[53]

---

49. John 19:25.

50. St. Bonaventure, *In I Sent.*, Dist. 48, ad Litt., Dul. 4.

51. John 1:16.

52. *Serm. de Temp. in Nativ. B. M. V. de Aquaeductu*, n. 4, in Migne, P. L., t. CLXXXIII, col. 440.

53. St. Bernardine of Siena, *Quadrag. de Evangelio aeterno*, Serm. 10, a. 3, cap. III.

We must not attribute to the Mother of God the power of producing supernatural grace, for this power belongs to God alone. However, since she surpasses all in sanctity by her union with Christ, and as she was associated with Christ in the work of man's salvation, she merited by a certain propriety ("de congruo") what Christ merited for us in strict justice ("de condigno"). She is the chief dispensatrix of the graces God wills to bestow. He "has taken His seat at the right hand of the Majesty on high."[54] But Mary the queen stands at His right hand, "the most safe refuge of all the imperiled and our most faithful assistant in all our needs. None need fear, none lose heart, with Mary as our leader, our patroness, our promoter, our protectress."[55]

220. (D) Mary is the Queen of all creation. Just as the royal mother of a king is called a queen and exercises at least a jurisdiction of benevolence and charity in the kingdom, so, too, the Mother of Christ the King wields this power in her son's kingdom. With St. Bernardine of Siena we can say: "As many creatures serve the glorious Virgin Mary as serve the Trinity."[56] With Holy Mother Church we salute Mary, "Hail Holy *Queen*, Mother of mercy."

The Seraphic Doctor, speaking of the Assumption of the Blessed Virgin, says, "By all means we should believe and in no way doubt that today in her Assumption the Virgin is met in solemn procession not only by the King, but by the entire heavenly court. The angels fly ahead to see their mistress; the Patriarchs leap down to see their daughter; the Apostles run to see their teacher; the Martyrs come with speed to behold their comforter."[57] And St. Bernard says: "Surely the eyes of all creation are upon you, because through you and of you the

---

54. Heb. 1:3.
55. Pius IX, Bull *Ineffabilis Deus*, of December 8, 1854.
56. *Serm. 61.*
57. *Sermones de Assumptione B. M. V.*, Serm. 3, n. 1.

hand of the Almighty created all that He had made. In truth . . . the entire Trinity hastened to meet you. . . . The Father regarded Blessed Mary as the palace of His majesty, the Son recognized her as the principle of His humanity and of His humility, the Holy Spirit acknowledged her as the sanctuary of His goodness, wherein He stored charismata of graces in plenitude and beyond measure. In this sanctuary, as in a public oratory serving the universe, He gathered the harvest of His gifts, that they might be obtained by the poor in time of necessity. . . . Now of Christ her Son is understood in a proper sense what is written: The king shall rise at the coming of His mother"[58] — that is, at the coming of the Queen of the whole creation. No wonder, then, that our Seraphic Father commended his Order especially to Mary immaculate.

*II. FRANCISCAN DEVOTION TO THE BLESSED VIRGIN MARY

221. Our Seraphic Father loved Jesus most ardently; but he realized that the Child was inseparable from Mary His Mother. "He loved the Mother of Jesus with an unspeakable love," says Thomas of Celano, "because she made the Lord of Majesty our brother. . . . He gave her singular praise, poured forth prayers, offered signs of affections of such number and quality as no human tongue can tell."[59] All true Franciscans have learned from St. Francis this heartfelt veneration of the Virgin Mary, which simply consists in devotion to: (1) the Immaculate Conception of the Blessed Virgin Mary; (2) the Sorrowful Mother; (3) the Mother of the Divine Shepherd.

222. (A) The Immaculate Conception of the Blessed Virgin Mary

(1) This devotion is the glory and honor of the Seraphic Order. No one is ignorant of the fact that devotion to

---

58. *Serm. II in Pent.*, n. 4., in Migne, *P. L.*, t. CLXXXIII, col. 328.
59. *Legenda Secunda*, cap. CL, p. 318.

Mary immaculate is truly Franciscan. "Enumerating the sources from which Pope Pius IX of immortal memory drew this delightful dogma seems almost like narrating the glory and honor of the Franciscan Order. For from its earliest beginnings, your Order," says Raphael Cardinal Merry del Val, "has imbibed like sweet milk deep piety toward the Immaculate Virgin. Later, proceeding according to the teaching of the Venerable Doctor Duns Scotus, [your Order] so enkindled and enriched this doctrine that it became the champion of the dogma declaring Mary to be free of original sin, and became at once worthy to be received into her singular patronage."[60]

(2) Mary Immaculate, the principal Patroness and Protectress of the Order. That the seraphic Francis himself actually constituted Mary the principal patroness of his Order, Celano testifies when he writes: "It gave him much joy to establish her as advocate over the Order, and to place under her protection those whom he would leave as her sons, that she might give them warmth and shelter unto the end."[61] Through a decree of the General Definitorium (October 15, 1712), the Mother of God under the title of the Immaculate Conception was chosen as the principal patroness and protectress of the entire Order. The Sacred Congregation of Rites (March 10, 1714) confirmed this choice and attributed and granted to her all prerogatives due to principal patrons. On June 13, 1912, Pope Pius X deigned to grant under the usual conditions a plenary indulgence applicable to the souls in Purgatory, to those who on the first Saturday of any month in a spirit of reparation perform special exercises of devotion in honor of the Immaculate Virgin. Moreover, in order to invoke the special assistance of the Immaculate Virgin, he ordered all members of the Franciscan family to add "Queen of the

---

60. Cf. Analecta O. M. Cap., t. XX, p. 264.
61. *Legenda Secunda,* cap. CL, p. 318.

Seraphic Order, pray for us," in the Litany of Loreto after the invocation, "Queen of the most holy Rosary."[62]

223. (B) Devotion to the Sorrowful Mother. Another devotion flourishing in the Seraphic Order is that of the Sorrowful Mother. And small wonder! For the Passion of Christ and the co-passion of His Mother are inseparable. Our holy Father St. Francis was accustomed to recall with tears the sorrows of Mary. "While he was sitting at table one day," say Thomas of Celano, "a friar described the poverty of the Blessed Virgin and brought to mind the utter want of Christ her Son. Immediately Francis rose from the table and with increasing sobs of sorrow and profuse tears, ate the rest of his bread on the bare earth."[63]

224. (C) Devotion to the Mother of the Divine Shepherd. (1) *Origin.* Father Isidore of Seville, O. F. M. Cap., was the first to publicly and solemnly call upon, honor, implore and proclaim the most glorious Virgin Mother of God under the most pleasing mystical title Shepherdess of Souls — that is, Mother of the Divine or Good Shepherd. This happened on September 8, 1703. The use of this title was later to develop into a splendid devotion. (2) *Fitness of this devotion.* Certainly Mary, the Mediatrix of all graces, like a shepherdess leads the flock of Christ, gathers the sheep with her own hands, lifts them onto her lap, and carries the little ones. These words of Ezechiel apply directly to Christ: "I myself will pasture My sheep. . . . The lost I will seek out, the strayed I will bring back, the injured I will bind up, the sick I will heal."[64]

Since these things were spoken of Christ they may be applied in their proper degree to Mary. For things proper

---

62. Motu proprio of September 8, 1910; cf. *Acta Apost. Sedis* (1910), p. 720.

63. *Legenda Secunda,* cap. CLI, p. 319.

64. Ezech. 34:15, 16.

to Christ are by participation common to Mary, the Mother of God and Queen of the Church of Christ. Wherefore our Seraphic Father, in greeting the Blessed Virgin, says, "Hail, Mother of God, and all you holy virtues which are poured forth into the hearts of the faithful through the grace and illumination of the Holy Spirit, that you may make the un- faithful faithful to God."[65] It is as if he had said that Mary is the dispenser of all virtues and the shepherdess of Christ's flock. Therefore, with the approval of the Church, the friars have fostered devotion to the Mother of the Divine Shepherd in Spain, in Central America, and also in various dioceses of Europe and in Mesopotamia; and they have chosen Mary patroness of their missions under this most pleasing title.

*III. PRACTICE OF MARIAN DEVOTION IN THE SERAPHIC ORDER

225. Piety and devotion to the Blessed Virgin Mary con- sist in a certain prompt and pious will to embrace all things that pertain to the submission, service and praise of the Blessed Virgin. We accomplish this: (A) by careful avoidance of all sin; (B) by external acts of devotion; (C) by internal acts of devotion.

226. (A) Careful avoidance of all sin. Sin offends the Son of God, and therefore offends His Mother also, so that a client of the Virgin Mary certainly cannot for any length of time remain truly devoted to her if he causes her grief by mortal sin. "Mary desires no greater honor, nothing pleases her more, than that we duly know and love Jesus. Therefore, it is well that crowds of the faithful should flock to the churches, prepare for her feasts with pomp and splendor, re- joicing throughout the city; all of this fosters piety. Yet, unless the will exerts itself in these externals, we shall merely have the empty form, the veneer of devotion."[66]

---

65. *Opusc. S. P. Francisci* (Quaracchi edition, 1904), p. 123.
66. Words of St. Pius X, cited by Bernard of Andermatt in *Analecta O. M. Cap.*, t. XX, p. 78.

227. (B) External acts of devotion

I. Daily recitation of the LITTLE OFFICE of the Blessed Virgin Mary has been the pious custom from the beginning of our Order, for it is a tribute of love from the sons of St. Francis to the Mother of God conceived without original sin, a love introduced and always faithfully cherished even to this day.

II. Daily recitation of the *Franciscan Crown of the Seven Joys*

METHOD OF SAYING THE FRANCISCAN CROWN

We should begin at once with the first decade, saying one Our Father and ten Hail Marys. Then we continue in the same manner with the remaining six decades, reciting each in honor of the joy commemorated, namely: (1) the Annunciation; (2) the Visitation; (3) the Birth of Our Lord; (4) the Adoration of the Magi; (5) the Finding of Jesus in the Temple; (6) the Apparition of Our Lord to His Mother; (7) the Assumption and the Coronation of the Blessed Virgin.

When we have finished the seventh decade, we say two Hail Marys (on the two beads near the link), in honor of the seventy-two years Our Lady is supposed to have lived on the earth. Finally, we say one Our Father and one Hail Mary (on the two beads nearest the cross) for the intention of the Pope, in order to gain the indulgences. There is no Creed nor any other prayer on the Cross.

To gain the indulgence, it is not necessary to *meditate* on the various mysteries but merely to recite the decades in honor of them. Moreover, the Crown may be interrupted at will, as long as the entire rosary of seven decades is recited within the same day.[67]

---

67. Joseph Campelo, *De Indulgentiis Seraphici Ordinis* (2nd edition, Compostela, 1943), no. 356.

HISTORY OF THE FRANCISCAN CROWN

The Franciscan Crown, called also the Rosary of the Seven Joys of the Blessed Virgin, dates back to the year 1422. The famous historian Luke Wadding relates that a very pious young novice who had been admitted to the Franciscan Order in that year, had, prior to his reception, been accustomed to adorn a statue of the Blessed Virgin with a wreath of fresh and beautiful flowers as a mark of his piety and devotion. Not being able to continue this practice in the novitiate, he was very sad and finally decided to leave the cloister and return to the world.

Our Lady then appeared to him and prevented him from carrying out his intention. "Do not be sad and cast down, my son," she said sweetly, "because you are no longer permitted to place wreaths of flowers on my statue."

"I will teach you to change this pious practice into one that will be far more pleasing to me and far more meritorious to your soul. In place of flowers that soon wither and cannot always be found, you can weave for me a crown from the flowers of your prayers that will always remain fresh and can always be had.

"Recite one Our Father and ten Hail Marys in honor of the joy I experienced when the angel announced to me the Incarnation of the Son of God. Repeat these prayers in honor of the joy I felt on visiting my kinswoman Elizabeth. Say them again in honor of the supreme happiness that filled my heart on giving birth to Christ the Saviour without pain and without loss of my virginity. Recite the same prayers a fourth time in honor of the joy I felt when presenting my Divine Son for the adoration of the Magi. Repeat them the fifth time in honor of the joy that thrilled my soul when, after seeking Jesus with deep sorrow for three days, I found Him at last among the doctors in the Temple. For the sixth time recite the Our Father

and ten Hail Marys in honor of the joy I experienced on beholding my Divine Son gloriously risen from the grave on
Easter Sunday. Finally, for the seventh time, repeat these
prayers in honor of my own glorious and joyful assumption
into heaven, when I was crowned Queen of heaven and earth.
If you recite these prayers as I have directed, rest assured, dear
son, you will weave me a most beautiful and acceptable crown
and will merit for yourself innumerable graces."

When Our Lady had disappeared, the overjoyed novice at
once began to recite the prayers in honor of her Seven Joys, as
she had directed. While he was deeply engrossed in this devotion, the novice master happened to pass by and saw an angel
weaving a marvelous crown of roses, and inserting after every
tenth rose a lily. When the wreath was finished, the angel
placed it on the head of the praying novice. The master
then demanded under holy obedience that the youth tell him
the meaning of the vision. Joyfully yet fearfully the novice
complied. The good priest was so impressed with what he had
seen and heard that he immediately made it known to the
brethren. Thus the practice of reciting the Crown of the Seven
Joys of the Blessed Virgin soon spread throughout the Franciscan Order and became one of the favorite devotions of the
friars.

Later it became customary to add two Hail Marys in honor
of the seventy-two years Our Lady is said to have lived on
earth, and one Our Father and Hail Mary for the intention
of the Pope, in order to gain the indulgences attached to recitation of the Crown.

List of Indulgences for Recitation
of the Franciscan Crown

Members of the three Orders of St. Francis, including the
Third Order Secular (Leo XIII, September 11, 1901), gain a

plenary indulgence each time they recite the Franciscan Crown. No beads are necessary. This plenary indulgence can be applied to the souls in Purgatory.

The faithful in general must have rosaries specially blessed for the purpose in order to gain the indulgences listed below. In the *public recitation* of the Crown, however, in churches of the three Orders, all who join in prayers gain the plenary indulgence, whether they have blessed beads or not. Moreover, if two or more say this rosary in common, as, for instance, at family prayers, it suffices if the leader holds a blessed rosary. (S. C. Indulg., September 12, 1906.)

INDULGENCES GRANTED BY PIUS X
FOR RECITATION OF THE FRANCISCAN CROWN

A. *Plenary Indulgences.* The faithful gain:

1. *A plenary indulgence* for taking part in the public recitation of the Crown in any church of the three Orders of St. Francis.

2. *A plenary indulgence* if, after confession and Communion (no other conditions), they recite the Franciscan Crown on the following feasts: Christmas, Epiphany, Easter, Immaculate Conception, Annunciation (March 25), Purification (February 2), Visitation (July 2), Assumption (August 15), Feast of the Seven Joys of the Blessed Virgin (August 27), Nativity of the Blessed Virgin (September 8).

3. *A plenary indulgence* once a month on any day after confession and Communion, if they say the Franciscan Crown every Saturday.

4. *A plenary indulgence* at the hour of death if they have the rosary in their possession and have used it often; and if, having confessed and received Holy Communion — or if this is impossible, being truly sorry for their sins — they say the

name of Jesus, with their lips if possible, or at least mentally, and accept death as the just punishment for their sins.

B. *Partial Indulgences.* The faithful can gain a *partial indulgence* of:

1. *Seventy years and seventy quarantines* every time they say the Crown on any day of the week except Saturday.

2. *One hundred years* every time they say it on any Saturday of the year.

3. *Two hundred years* when they say it on the holydays of obligation.

4. *Three hundred years* when they say it on any feast of the Blessed Virgin not mentioned above for the plenary indulgences.

5. *Ten years* for every good work they perform for the honor of God or for the love of their neighbor, provided they carry the rosary about their person and often recite it.

6. *Ten years* every time they say seven Hail Marys in honor of the Seven Joys of the Blessed Virgin, provided they carry the rosary about their person and often recite it.

All these indulgences, except the one to be gained at the hour of death, can be applied to the poor souls.

External Acts of Devotion (*continued*)

III. *Recitation of the Chaplet of the Immaculate Conception* was begun around the year 1845. Father Bonaventure of Ferraria, O. F. M. Cap., was inspired, as he himself relates, by the Blessed Virgin herself to pray this chaplet in order that through an infallible declaration the Vicar of Jesus Christ might soon proclaim as a dogma of faith the fact that the Blessed Virgin Mary, by a special privilege of God, was preserved free from all stain of original sin from the very first instant of her existence. (This Chaplet generally consists of three parts, each of which is made up of the ejaculation: "Blessed be the holy and immaculate conception of the Blessed Virgin Mary," followed by the Lord's Prayer, four Hail Marys, and finally the doxology, Glory be to the Father, etc.)

IV. The occasional recitation of the *Crown of the Seven Dolors* is also recommended, in order to continue the special devotion which the Seraphic Order always offered to the Most Sorrowful Virgin Mary.

V. The recitation of the *Angelus* three times a day at the signal of the bell.

VI. The performing of some *act of mortification* or devotion on Saturday.

VII. A pious *preparation for Our Lady's feast days,* especially the Immaculate Conception, the Assumption and the feast of the Seven Dolors.

VIII. The zealous promotion of *devotion to Mary* among other persons, in order to lead them by word and example to love and imitate her.

IX. Thinking about Mary in time of temptation, anxiety and doubt and calling upon her name.

X. The strengthening of our love for her, especially by avoiding habitual faults and doing other things the nature of which individual piety will suggest.

228. (C) Internal acts of devotion

1. Like true sons of the Seraphic Father, who was so completely devoted to the most pure Virgin, we should embrace her with a tender love, and prove our affection by our manner of life.

2. With the true affection of sons we should often dedicate ourselves to the Virgin Mary, whom we have chosen as our

Mother from our tender years, and whom we have later accepted as very special patroness and protectress of the Order.

3. We should meditate frequently on the joys and sorrows, and other sacred mysteries of Mary's life.

4. We ought to rejoice wholeheartedly with her more often, celebrate her eminent prerogatives, and thank the most Holy Trinity for the stupendous gifts lavished upon Mary.

5. We ought lovingly to have compassion for the sorrows she suffered at the foot of the Cross.

6. We should ascend to the highest degree of devotion to Mary: imitation of her life and her virtues.

In a word, friends of Mary, let us love her, let us love our Mother, and with Thomas of Celano often say to her out of filial love: "Come, O Advocate of the poor: fulfill in us thy office of protectress even to the time determined by the Father."[68]

§ III. Devotion to the Holy Angels and Saints Reigning with Christ

229. Besides the devotion which our Seraphic Father had for Christ and His most loving Mother, "with great affection he venerated the angels, who are with us in the line of battle and who walk with us in the darkness of the shadow of death"; and "with a divine sense of worship he showed himself most devoted to God, leaving nothing that was of God unhonored through neglect."[69] In other words, he had great reverence for the saints of God. In order to imitate our Seraphic Father in these devotions, we shall here treat first of the angels, and secondly of the saints of God.

---

68. *Legenda Secunda,* cap. CL, p. 318.

69. Thomas of Celano, *Legenda Secunda,* cap. CXLIX, p. 317, and cap. CLII, p. 320.

I. THE HOLY ANGELS

230. (A) Our guardian angels. "Man is placed in this life," says St. Thomas Aquinas, "as if on a road, upon which he should direct his course to his heavenly home. And along this way, many are the dangers that threaten him, both from within and from without, as it is written: 'In the way along which I walk, they have hid a trap for me' (Ps. 141:4). Just as guides are given to men who travel unsafe roads, so a guardian angel is assigned to every human being as long as he is alive."[70] We should always be mindful of this favor: that God wishes the angels to be attentive not only to Himself but also to us.[71] According to the teaching of the Seraphic Doctor, the angels help us in four ways: "The angels come down to perform in our regard a fourfold office: first, to draw us away from sin; secondly, to fortify us in temptation; thirdly, to direct us along our way; and fourthly, to lead us to our heavenly home. We cannot be led to our heavenly home unless we are guided along the way; nor can we be directed on our way unless we conquer the enemy; but we cannot overcome enemies without assistance, and so there is reasonable order in the process."[72]

231. (B) We must honor our guardian angels. "Our Seraphic Father used to say that such companions should be honored with reverence at all times, and such guardians should likewise be frequently invoked. He taught that we should do nothing offensive in their sight, nor presume to do anything before them that we would not do before men. Since in choir he chanted the psalms in the presence of the angels, he wished all who were able, to assemble in the oratory and there to sing wisely."[73] In every place, in every circumstance,

---

70. *Summa theol.*, I, q. 113, a. 4.
71. Cf. Exod. 23:20-21; cf. also, Mal. 3:1.
72. *Sermones*, Serm. 1 de S. Angelis, Collatio, circa medium.
73. Celano, *Legenda Secunda*, cap. CXLIX, p. 317.

we should revere our guardian angel. We should fear and love him and always remember that no matter where we may be we are in the presence of our angel, and indeed not only of our own, but of many angels; for we are in the midst of angels as much as we are in the midst of men. There are angels of Provinces, of places, of churches. We should often salute our angel, especially in the morning and evening, by saying this prayer: "Angel of God, my Guardian dear, to whom His love commits me here: ever this day (night) be at my side, to light and guard, to rule and guide."[74]

232. (C) **Special honor should be shown to St. Michael.** Franciscans should specially honor St. Michael after the example of their Founder. He often said that "St. Michael, because of the office he has of presenting souls to God, should be given a more special devotion. In honor of St. Michael he fasted with great devotion for forty days between the feast of the Assumption and the archangel's feast. Indeed, he used to say that everyone should offer some praise or special gift to God in honor of so great a prince."[75] We should therefore follow the advice of our Father, and often say with confidence: "St. Michael the Archangel, defend us in battle, lest we perish in that fearful judgment."[76]

---

74. For this prayer the indulgences are: 300 days; a plenary indulgence once a month, under the usual conditions, for the daily recitation of this invocation; a plenary indulgence under the usual conditions on the Feast of the Holy Guardian Angels, if this invocation has been said frequently in the morning and evening throughout the preceding year; a plenary indulgence at the hour of death, to be gained by the faithful who have been accustomed to say this invocation frequently during life, provided they go to confession and Communion, or at least make an act of contrition, invoke the holy name of Jesus, orally if possible, or at least mentally, and accept death with resignation from the hand of God as the just punishment for their sins. (*Raccolta,* # 452, 1952 edition.)

75. Celano, *Legenda Secunda,* cap. CXLIX, p. 317.

76. An indulgence of 300 days; a plenary indulgence, under the usual conditions, for the devout recitation of this invocation every day for a month. (*Raccolta,* # 442.)

II. DEVOTION TO THE SAINTS REIGNING WITH GOD

233. With devotion and love we should honor all the saints reigning with Christ. "If you wish to please God and the saints," says Thomas a Kempis, "look into the lives of the saints, read their teachings. In order to be sanctified with the saints, trained by the saints, helped through the saints, heard by the saints, and crowned with the saints, you must be devoted to the saints."[77] "Reasonably enough," adds St. Bernard, "the festive memory of the saints is effective, dispersing clouds of anxiety, tepidity, and error: for our infirmity is aided by their intercession, our negligence spurred by consideration of their blessedness, and our ignorance instructed by their example."[78] All saints are therefore to be honored, but especially those whose name we have received, either in baptism or on becoming a Religious. Next, we should honor the saints of our Seraphic Order, among them St. Anthony of Padua and St. Margaret of Cortona. And, finally, we should reverence all saints to whom we are attracted by reason of a greater confidence and more tender affection. But, above all, St. Joseph, spouse of the Blessed Virgin Mary, and our Seraphic Father St. Francis should be honored with a singular devotion.

1 — Devotion to St. Joseph

234. (A) **Franciscans have always highly honored St. Joseph.** Franciscans have at all times propagated and cultivated devotion to the Blessed Virgin Mary and her most holy Spouse. St. Teresa herself borrowed her devotion to St. Joseph from the Friars Minor. Propagation of devotion to St. Joseph was entrusted to the Capuchins by the Holy See.[79]

---

77. *De discipl. claustr.*, cap. XV.

78. *Serm. 2 in fest. omn. Sanct.*, n. 1, in Migne, *P. L.*, t. CLXXXIII, col. 462.

79. *Analecta O. M. Cap.*, t. IX, p. 161.

235. (B) **This devotion is to be promoted by Francis-cans.** We should always wear the Scapular of St. Joseph as well as the Scapulars of the Blessed Virgin Mary, with the greatest devotion. Let us be diligent in saying the prayers commonly used by the Order, but let us also enkindle in the hearts of others love for the Spouse of Mary.

The conditions for gaining indulgences attached to the Scapular of St. Joseph are given below:

To gain the indulgences which Leo XIII granted, through a rescript of the Sacred Congregation of Indulgences, June 8, 1893, and which are annexed to this scapular, there is required nothing more than the wearing of this small scapular by the faithful, day and night, after receiving it from a duly author-ized priest, and the fulfilling of the conditions on the stated days as indicated.

A plenary indulgence is granted to those mentioned above:

1. On the day in which they received the aforesaid scapular.

2. On the feasts of the Nativity, Circumcision, Epiphany, Resurrection and Ascension of our Lord.

3. On the feasts of the Immaculate Conception, Purification and Assumption of the Blessed Virgin Mary.

4. On the feast of St. Joseph, March 19. (It is also required, in order to gain the indulgence on these days, that the faithful fulfill the conditions of confession and Communion, visit their parish church or another church or public oratory, and there pray for the intention of the Holy Father.)

5. At the moment of death, if they have gone to confession and received Holy Communion; or if, truly contrite, they in-voke the most holy name of Jesus at least in their heart, if they cannot say it orally, and accept death as the just punish-ment for their sins.

Moreover, those faithful who visit the above-mentioned church or oratory, observing those things which are to be observed, on the days of the stations mentioned in the Roman Missal may gain the indulgences called *Stational*.

Finally, an indulgence of 100 days, once a day, is granted to those wearing the scapular, if, rightly disposed, they recite the Our Father, Hail Mary, Glory be to the Father, etc., adding the invocation, "St. Joseph, pray for us."[80]

"Let us go to Joseph, then, with fervor of devotion and most tender trust, not indeed alone but surrounded on all sides by devout faithful whom our zeal has attached to our holy Protector."[81]

2 — Devotion to Our Holy Father St. Francis

236. How can we ever sufficiently recommend devotion to St. Francis, our most sweet Father? Of St. Francis, Blessed Giles says: "One should never pronounce the name of Francis without tasting its sweetness on his lips."[82] God glorifies him, the Christian people honor him, the Church of Christ exalts him. So it is good for us to love our Seraphic Father and to honor him with a worthy devotion. Since blessed Francis took the last place when called to the nuptial feast of Christ, the words of the psalmist are fulfilled in him: "He raises up the lowly from the dust; from the dunghill He lifts up the poor to seat them with princes, with the princes of His own people."[83]

237. (A) God exalts Francis. God exalted His servant Francis even on earth with such immense, ineffable gifts, like precious jewels, as to make him, especially through the impres-

---

80. Joseph Campelo, O. F. M., *De Indulgentiis Seraphici Ordinis Hodie Vigentibus,* n. 959.

81. Cf. Bernard of Andermatt, *Analecta O. M. Cap.,* t. IX, p. 162.

82. *Dicta B. Aegidii* (Quaracchi, 1905), App. I, p. 108.

83. Ps. 112:7-8.

sion of the sacred stigmata, another Christ. In him was seen the form of the Cross and the Passion of the Immaculate Lamb, for his hands and feet were pierced by nails and his right side opened as if by a lance. "O singular gift, O mark of extraordinary love!" exclaims Thomas of Celano. "The soldier is adorned with the royal coat of arms, whose excellent dignity belonged to the King alone! O miracle worthy of eternal remembrance, memorable sacrament deserving admirable, unending reverence, because veiled it represents that mystery in which the blood of the Immaculate Lamb, copiously flowing from the five wounds, washed away the sins of the world!... This man so gloriously decorated by You has loved You with his whole heart!"[84]

And what of his place in the eternal home above? "Blessed Pacificus, who first introduced the Order of Friars [Minor] into France, was a man of great sanctity," writes St. Bonaventure; "and when he was praying with St. Francis in church one day, in a vision he saw the heavens opened, and there in paradise beheld a throne of exquisite beauty. He asked whose throne it was, and there came to him the answer: 'This seat of glory, lost by Lucifer because of his pride, is reserved for blessed Francis because of his humility.' "[85]

238. (B) **The Christian people honor St. Francis.** The faithful have always paid great reverence to our Seraphic Father. For even while he walked on earth, "so great was the faith of men and women, so great their inner devotion to the holy man of God, that they considered themselves happy indeed who were able to touch even his garment. And whenever he entered a city, the priests were gladdened, bells were rung, men were exultant, women rejoiced, children clapped their hands and often, taking the branches of trees, went forth singing to

---

84. *Legenda Prima,* cap. IX, p. 117.
85. *Sermones de Sanctis,* Serm. 2 de S. P. N. Francisco, n. 1.

meet him."[86] Such was the veneration St. Francis received while he still lived among sinners. "But now that he reigns with the angels in heaven . . . , the whole concourse of people honors, extols, and glorifies him."[87] The Christian people have erected to the excellent Francis, our Father, a perennial monument; not one built merely with squared and cut stones or decorated with massive marble, but traced with golden letters. This memorial is solidly fashioned with the historical truth of his deeds; it is adorned with paintings, engravings, even elegantly woven fabrics. "O Seraphic Father, poor and humble, you entered heaven with great riches, you are honored with celestial hymns; and on earth glorious works of art are engraved, sculptured, painted in your honor; golden words are spoken of you. May you receive these grateful offerings as a testimony and token of the song which we, with affectionate and devoted fidelity, pledge to you in our heart of hearts."[88]

239. (C) **The Church exalts our Seraphic Father.** Our most glorious Father Francis deserved to be exalted not only by the faithful but by the Church itself, by the Roman Pontiffs. Gregory IX rejoiced over his son Francis, whom he bore, cherished, nourished with the word and fed with the food of salvation; all the Vicars of Christ, and especially Pope Leo XIII, St. Pius X, and other guardians of the Church and shepherds of the flock in our age, have glorified the Saviour in honoring St. Francis. In his encyclical letter *Rite expiatis* (April 30, 1926), Pius XI recounted and praised the work and influence of St. Francis. And in his address to members of the Third Order of St. Francis on July 1, 1956, Pius XII urged Tertiaries to cultivate the spirit of St. Francis and to imitate his apostolic zeal. For the Saviour in His ineffable wisdom, incomprehensible grace, and inestimable goodness, chose in St.

---

86. Celano, *Legenda Prima*, cap. XXII, pp. 64, 65.
87. Celano, *De Canonizatione S. P. Franc.*, 128.
88. Cf. *Analecta O. M. Cap.*, t. I, p. 51.

Francis what the world regarded as foolish and lowly, in order to draw the wise and mighty to Himself.

240. (D) **It is our duty to honor and love our holy Father.** We, the sons of this most exalted and glorious Father, are bound to love and honor him. We may show our love for and honor toward St. Francis by willingly undertaking the prayers and devotions prescribed in the Order, and the spiritual exercises assigned for the month of October.

(A plenary indulgence may be gained on the feast of St. Francis or one of the days within the octave by fulfilling the usual conditions and having the intention of gaining the indulgence. As often as some pious exercise or novena devotions in honor of St. Francis are performed during the month of October, an indulgence of three years may be gained; a plenary indulgence may be gained at the end of the novena or exercises.[89])

We should also follow the spiritual exercises recommended for the five Sundays immediately preceding the feast of the Stigmata. For this devotion we may gain a plenary indulgence; we may also gain this plenary indulgence once again during the year by performing the recommended exercises on any five consecutive Sundays.[90]

Another and truer sign of devotion to St. Francis consists in observing his precepts with the greatest diligence. "No one should be loathe to imitate the one whose praises he delights to celebrate."[91] May the words which our Seraphic Father wrote in his letters to the General Chapter near the end of his days never fade from our memory: "If any of the friars refuse to observe these things [the established regulations] I will not consider them Catholic nor my brethren; nor do I

---

89. Cf. Campelo, *De Indulgentiis Seraphici Ordinis,* n. 612.

90. *Ibid.,* n. 611.

91. S. Caesarius, *Serm. 225,* found in the Appendix of the works of St. Augustine; in Migne, *P. L.,* t. XXXIX, col. 2161.

wish to see or speak with them until they repent. I say this of all those friars who go wandering about to the disregard of regular discipline, since our Lord Jesus Christ gave His life rather than fail in obedience to His most holy Father." We should, then, honor our Seraphic Father by imitating him. We should not hesitate to approach him with heartfelt confidence, saying: O most sweet Father, "we do not believe you to be so inebriated with the riches of the house of God that you have forgotten your sons; especially since He with whom you are filled is mindful of us. O draw us to you, worthy Father, that we may run in the sweet odor of your ointments! For you must surely observe how tepid, how idle, how languid and sluggish we have become — half-dead through our negligence. . . . Renew our days as in the beginning, O mirror and exemplar of perfection. Do not permit us to be so unlike you in our life, who are like you by the similarity of our profession."[92]

Article V — Devotion to the Holy Eucharist

241. The Sacraments are like channels through which, as Christ decreed, countless benefits of divine grace flow down to us. By this grace the will is moved to the greatest possible good and man is conformed to Christ.

But the Holy Eucharist is pre-eminent among the Sacraments. All the other Sacraments are directed toward it as toward their end. "It is indeed manifest," says St. Thomas Aquinas, "that the Sacrament of Holy Orders gives the power to consecrate the Eucharist; the Sacrament of Baptism admits one to the reception of the Eucharist; and one is given strength through Confirmation, lest he fear, lest he shrink from approaching such a tremendous Sacrament. Through Penance and also through Extreme Unction man is prepared to receive the Body of Christ worthily. And Matrimony, at least in its

---

92. Celano, *Legenda Prima*, cap. CLXVII, p. 337.

signification, is close to this Sacrament in so far as it signifies the marriage of Christ and the Church, a union which is sealed through the Sacrament of the Eucharist."[1]

The Sacrament of the Eucharist is, as it were, a compendium of the mysteries of the life of Christ. Just as the Incarnate Word, under the veil of flesh, appeared among men, was laid in a manger, and led a hidden though divine life in the home of Nazareth, so Christ in this Sacrament under the species of the Eucharist lies hidden; and in the tabernacle (1) He leads a hidden though truly divine life; (2) just as He traversed Palestine doing good and healing all, so in Holy Communion He pours His grace into our souls; (3) and just as He offered Himself in sacrifice by dying on the Cross, so on our altars He is daily offered as a victim.

A threefold aspect must therefore be considered in this single mystery: (1) the ineffable presence of Christ in the Sacrament of the Eucharist; (2) Holy Communion; (3) the Holy Sacrifice of the Mass.

§ I. The Ineffable Presence of Christ in the Sacrament of the Altar and the Obligation of Visiting Him

242. We believe with an unshaken faith that at the priest's utterance of the words of consecration bread and wine are changed and transubstantiated into the body and blood of our Lord Jesus Christ; and this by divine power and not through the merit of the one offering the Sacrifice. We believe that Christ is truly present in the Eucharist, although at the same time His most blessed body also remains at the right hand of His Father in heaven. "Behold," says our Seraphic Father, "He daily humbles Himself as when from His royal throne He came into the womb of the Virgin; daily He Himself comes to us with like humility; daily He descends from the bosom of

---

1. *Summa theol.*, III, q. 65, a. 3.

His Father upon the altar in the hands of the priest. And as He appeared in true flesh to the holy Apostles, so now He shows Himself to us in the sacred Bread; and as they by means of their fleshly eyes saw only His flesh, yet contemplating Him with their spiritual eyes believed Him to be God, so we, seeing bread and wine with bodily eyes, see and firmly believe it to be His most holy body and true and living blood. And in this way our Lord is ever with His faithful, as He Himself says, 'Behold I am with you all days, even unto the consummation of the world!' (Matt. 28:20)."[2]

This most holy mystery can be grasped by faith alone, because it is above nature. As long as we remain on earth our intellect is weak and dull and cannot fully comprehend the works and plans of the Divine Majesty; hence we should not rashly try to understand them, far less be so bold as to find fault with them. Let us respond to such unspeakable love by visiting Jesus in this most august Sacrament. Here we shall: (1) discuss the reasons for visiting Christ; (2) study the requisites on our part for making a visit fruitful; (3) consider the affections that should be aroused during the visit.

I. REASONS FOR VISITING JESUS IN THE MOST BLESSED SACRAMENT

243. Jesus Christ sits on a throne of glory at the right hand of His Father. There He receives the tribute of our prayers through the ministry of His angels. But by instituting the Holy Eucharist He has established a throne of grace among us. For in the tabernacle He is substantially present to us just as He is in heaven. Since He longs for nothing more than to pour out upon us the effects of the generosity of His heart, we may confidently present our pleas and supplications to Him, for He is truly present in the tabernacle.

---

2. Paschal Robinson, O. F. M., translator, *The Writings of Saint Francis of Assisi* (Philadelphia, 1906), p. 7.

Jesus does not remain in our churches so as to lead a solitary life, but rather to open for us poor creatures an easy approach to Himself. We should try often to visit Him who descended from heaven to remain with us.

(1) **A visit is most acceptable to Jesus.** Just as nothing is more pleasing to a loving father than to be greeted often by his sons and to find them frequently near him, ready in filial submission to obey his behests; so it must be pleasing to Jesus, who "found delight in the sons of men,"[3] to accept the visits, adoration, praise, and requests of His beloved sons, who day and night dwell under the same roof with Him.

(2) **Efficacy of Eucharistic visits.** Jesus pours forth superabundant blessings on His sons who adore Him humbly and devoutly, who meditate in His sight on the profound Treasure of such a Saviour, and regard Him with a truly living faith. He looks on us when we contemplate Him, and in that glance He pours out His gifts on us; He takes away our iniquities, and inflames our hearts with divine love.

(a) HE TAKES AWAY OUR INIQUITIES. "A king seated on the throne of judgment dispels all evil with his glance."[4] Jesus sits on a throne of grace and mercy for sinners, in a seat of justice and judgment against sin. He gives life to sinners but dispels and scatters sin as He looks on us with eyes of unbounded kindness.

(b) HE INFLAMES OUR HEART WITH DIVINE LOVE. The Blessed Sacrament, more than any other mystery, exerts the power of drawing us to divine love. In order that the truth of this promise, unshaken as a rock, might stand perpetually, even to the consummation of the world, Christ exclaimed: "And I, if I be lifted up from the earth, will draw all things to Myself."[5] Christ, in a perennial memorial of His exaltation on

---

3. Prov. 8:31.
4. *Ibid.* 20:8.
5. John 12:32.

the Cross, has instituted this venerable Sacrament that He might draw the hearts of all the faithful to Himself and sweetly vanquish them. For Jesus is the true King Solomon, burning with charity and aflame with love for the daughters of Jerusalem — that is, for our souls, that He might set them aflame with the fire of His love.

Christ our Lord in the Eucharist is a most rich Fountain of all graces, the accessible Font of the house of the Lord. Those who approach Him never depart from Him still thirsting. All the saints held it as their greatest delight to pour out their prayers night and day before the Blessed Sacrament, whenever they could. They would hasten in all their difficulties and dangers to the throne of Christ's love. This was the practice of our Seraphic Father, of St. Lawrence of Brindisi, of Blessed Benedict of Urbino, and of so many other true saints of our Order who harvested such great spiritual fruits.

(3) **Gratitude demands Eucharistic visits.** Christ wished to remain with us for our consolation; "For this mystery makes a heaven of earth,"[6] says St. John Chrysostom. In His incomprehensible love He abides with us also to protect us and to heap spiritual gifts upon us. Would it not be unspeakable ingratitude scarcely ever to look upon Christ our God who is truly present there? What thanklessness! While He awaits us, we forget Him entirely!

If we cannot continually dwell in His presence, we should at least visit Him the number of times a day that is suggested in each Province; we ought to go beyond this, however, and visit Him as often as possible. On leaving or reaching a friary, we should, like true sons of the eternal Father, first visit Jesus in the Holy Eucharist. If we are sent on a journey, the *Mirror of Discipline* says, "we should always first visit the church, if we

---

6. *Homil. XXIV in I Corinth.*, n. 5 in Migne, *P. G.*, t. LXI, col. 205.

conveniently can, after the example of our saintly Fathers who are our predecessors in the Order, and more so after the example of our Saviour Himself, who, according to St. Matthew, first entered the temple of the Lord after coming to Jerusalem."[7]

II. WHAT MUST BE DONE ON OUR PART
TO MAKE A FRUITFUL VISIT TO THE MOST BLESSED SACRAMENT

244. When we approach the throne of the Son of the living God, three special acts are to be performed:

(1) **We should set a definite purpose for ourselves.** This purpose will vary according to the circumstances: (a) Sometimes during such a visit we are overcome by sentiments of gratitude for all our benefits in general, or for some particular favor received from God during the day; (b) at other times affection toward God burns within us, and we desire to inflame our heart more and more with a great ardor of love; (c) often when we are depressed by temptations, sorrows or difficulties, we hasten to Christ as to our heavenly physician, that we may receive some consolation or remedy; (d) finally, when suffering doubts or perplexities as did the Apostle St. Thomas, whether they be internal and concern our conscience, or external, affecting others, we seek counsel from the Father of lights.

(2) **We should show due reverence, both interior and exterior, and the greatest devotion our weakness permits.**

(a) EXTERIOR REVERENCE. On entering the church, let us say with the Seraphic Father: "We adore Thee, most Holy Lord Jesus Christ, here and in all the churches throughout the world, and we bless Thee, because by Thy holy Cross

---

7. Part I, Chap. XXIX, n. 1.

Thou hast redeemed the world."[8] Our early Fathers observed this counsel with the greatest diligence, as Thomas of
Celano testifies. "Wherever they saw a church, even if they
were not close to it and were able only to behold it from afar,
they would cast themselves upon the ground in its direction,
and when all of them had done so, they would adore the
omnipotent God, saying: 'We adore Thee . . . ,' as their holy
Father had taught them to do."[9]

(b) INTERIOR REVERENCE. We should approach Jesus in
the spirit and with the eagerness of a pauper drawing near a
wealthy, generous man; let us come to Jesus as a hungry man
goes to a banquet; as one parched with thirst runs to a fountain; as the disciple goes to his master; a son to his father;
the infirm to a physician.

We should approach Him with a devotion made up of
various acts of virtue; faith, humility, trust and especially love.
Let us say to Jesus with the Seraphic Francis, from the depths
of our heart: "I beseech Thee, O Lord, that the fiery and
sweet strength of Thy love may draw my soul away from all
things that are under heaven, that I may die for love of Thy
love, as Thou didst deign to die for love of my love."[10]

(3) We should ask for a definite grace. Since Christ
dwells in the holy tabernacle as on a throne of love and mercy,
let us approach Him in order to receive help in time of need.
We should always determine what we should ask on our own
behalf and for others. With confidence we shall present our
miseries before the Lord. We shall pour forth our heart, our

---

8. From the *Testament of St. Francis.*

This prayer carries with it an indulgence of 7 years, if it is recited on
bended knees when one is entering or leaving a church, a public oratory or
semi-public oratory (in the case of those who are permitted to use the latter).
A plenary indulgence once a month may be gained by saying this prayer if it is
recited at least once a day and the usual conditions are fulfilled. (*Raccolta,*
95.)

9. *Legenda Prima,* cap. XVII, p. 47.

10. *Opusc.,* P. III, Quaracchi edition, p. 125.

prayers, begging Him for help and for counsel in our doubts; and then we shall earnestly desire whatever He wills.

III. DISPOSITIONS THAT SHOULD BE AROUSED DURING THE VISIT

245. Jesus Christ remains with us in this Sacrament, so that by His example he may encourage us in the practice of all the virtues. For here we see the profound humility which clothes our Lord completely with so humble, so plain a vesture: the Eucharistic species. Here, in the sacred host, we behold the unlimited patience with which He bears so many injuries from sinners. Here, in the Eucharist, we find the immeasurable mercy and generosity with which He replenishes the hungry. Here is that prompt obedience by means of which Christ becomes present, without delay, at the word of the consecrating priest. And in all this, Jesus shows a never-wearied perseverance which will last until the end of the world. And powerfully and sweetly, reaching from end to end, binding all these virtues together with the bond of perfection, Jesus burns with a fathomless charity by which He communicates His entire self, the Greatest Good, so much so that substantially He could not possibly give us more. The following dispositions are suggested to help make our visit more efficacious:

(1) Sometimes we may assume the dispositions of the shepherds or of the Magi, who hurried to the newborn Child Jesus and fell down before Him; let us, like them, express our acts of faith, humility, hope, and oblation.

(2) At other times we may approach like the Publican, with a soul contrite and humble. Like him let us sigh, let us pour forth our grief; in the bitterness of our soul let us strike our breast and lament: "I have sinned, O Lord, I have sinned. I am not worthy to lift my eyes to heaven. O God, be merciful to me, the sinner."

(3) At times we could imagine that we are like St. Mary Magdalene, who at the table anointed the feet of Christ, bathed them with her tears, and dried them with her hair; or we might take her place at Jesus' feet, receiving as she did the savory words of the divine teachings, and burn with devout interior affections when we hear them.

(4) We might approach Jesus with full confidence, as did the blind or the lepers or the other infirm; and even if consolation is delayed, we could cry out all the more: "Lord, Son of David, have mercy on me; behold he whom You love is sick."

(5) Like the Canaanite woman crying out after the Apostles, we may approach the Saviour and say: "O Lord, Son of David, have pity on me." We should seek the crumbs that fall from the master's table — that is, the spark of devotion which true sons will feel in the presence of the Blessed Sacrament.

(6) Let us remember with shame how justly we have deserved the wrath of the Eternal Father and His punishment for our many sins. Let us offer Him His beloved Son in propitiation for our offenses and as a token of complete reconciliation with Him.

(7) Every Friday we should offer some acceptable prayer, some act of reparation to the most Sacred Heart. On our knees before the Sacrament of the Altar, in a spirit of readiness to make atonement on our own behalf and on that of all people, let us seek pardon with a contrite heart.

(8) During Lent, in memory of the Passion of our Lord, let us visit Christ in the seven places where He suffered most: at night in the garden, at early morning in the court of the high priest; in the praetorium of Pilate, where He was accused; in the palace of Herod, where He was mocked; in the dungeon where He was scourged and crowned with thorns; on the Way of the Cross; and finally, on Mount Calvary.

After our adoration of the most Blessed Sacrament, let us receive Jesus with great devotion in spiritual communion, and arouse grateful, generous affections. (We shall consider spiritual communion later.) Finally, when we are about to regretfully leave the altar, let us sincerely beg a blessing from Jesus, a blessing better than that which Jacob demanded from the angel.

§ II. Holy Communion

246. It is a great act of mercy that the Word of God assumed our flesh, and an inestimable boon that the Son of God, existing before all time, was born in time as the Son of a Virgin. It is also a great and admirable favor that Christ bestowed on us when, about to ascend to the right hand of His Father, and desiring not to leave us as orphans, He granted us His sacramental presence until the end of time. Here we can behold Him, not indeed in heaven, but among us in the Blessed Sacrament — really, truly, and substantially present. And yet, not even in this way did He satisfy the great love with which He loved us unto the end.

He desired us not only to look upon Him in the Sacrament, but to have and possess Him intimately within our body; He gave us His body and blood as food for our souls. By this real union we remain in Him, and He indeed in us, "O Sacrament of piety," exclaims St. Augustine, "O sign of unity, O bond of love. . . . He who wishes to live has here the Source of Life. Let him approach, let him believe: let him be incorporated that he may be vivified."[11]

St. Thomas states that the Eucharist is, so to speak, a renewal of the Incarnation for each individual, in so far as Christ, God and Man, enters the heart of the recipient to apply the effects and the fruits of His redemption.

---

11. St. Augustine, *Tractatus 26 in Joan.*, cap. VI, n. 13, in Migne, *P. L.*, t. XXXV, col. 1613.

"I would describe to you, to the honor of this most excellent Sacrament," says the Seraphic Doctor, "a way in which you can be gently guided to the contemplation of so great a mystery and be appropriately disposed for its reception. This you should not read hurriedly. Rather, impress its meaning efficaciously on your heart, ponder solicitously, deeply on each single thought in whole or in part as it is mentioned."[12] When about to approach the table of the heavenly banquet, let a man prove himself, as the Apostle says, by considering what this divine Sacrament contains, and then prepare himself and partake.

We shall consider: (1) the nature and the effects of the Eucharistic banquet; (2) frequent and daily reception of the Eucharist; (3) the conditions required for frequent Communion; (4) the manner of approaching the sacred table.

I. THE NATURE AND EFFECTS OF THE EUCHARISTIC BANQUET

247. No time was more bitter, more painful to Christ than that in which He passed to the Father through His ignominious Passion and His most violent death on the Cross. Yet in that very time He bestowed on us the gift of supreme love. For He took bread, and giving thanks, broke, and gave to His disciples saying, "This is My body which shall be given up for you."[13] What could be more precious than this gift? The Good Shepherd gives His own flesh and blood for His sheep, that those whom He has redeemed He might also satiate with His own flesh. "What shepherd," asks St. John Chrysostom, "nourishes his sheep with his very own members? Shall I call Him shepherd? Mothers, after giving birth, often put their child in the hands of a nurse, but He does no such thing: He gives us the nourishment of His own blood and unites us to Himself in all possible ways."[14]

---

12. St. Bonaventure, *Tractatus de praeparat. ad Missam,* Prol.
13. 1 Cor. 11:24.
14. *In Matt.,* Homil. LXXXII ad LXXXIII, in Migne, *P. L.,* t. LVIII, col. 744.

248. (A) **The nature of Holy Communion.** When we approach the holy table, we should firmly believe, and by no means doubt, says St. Bonaventure, that beneath the accidents of bread and wine there actually exists:

"First, the most pure flesh of Christ, that sacred body which, through the action of the Holy Spirit, was formed in the womb of the glorious Virgin Mary, that body which hung on the Cross, was placed in the sepulchre, and is glorified in heaven.

"Secondly, since flesh does not live without blood, there is necessarily present that most precious blood which flowed from the Cross for the salvation of the world.

"Thirdly, as there can be no human being without a rational soul, there is also present the glorious soul of Christ, exceeding in its grace and glory all virtue, beauty, power; that soul in which are 'all the treasures of wisdom and knowledge' (Col. 2:3).

"Fourthly, since Christ is true man and true God, God is consequently present, resplendent in all His majesty."[15] The entire divinity is present; therefore the Father also and the Holy Spirit, who can never be separated from the Son.

Each little host contains Christ, and Christ in His entirety, no matter how small the particle. The whole Christ is present at the same time and in as many places throughout the entire world as there are offerings of the Sacrifice of the Mass and consecrations of the host and the wine. When eaten, Christ is not broken, not consumed, but remains whole and entire for all eternity. What can be more wonderful than this Sacrament in which the merciful and compassionate Lord has left a memorial of His wonderful works, giving Himself as food to those who fear Him, so that when receiving this Sacrament

---

15. St. Bonaventure, *loc. cit.*, cap. I, § 1, n. 1.

we can truly say: "Whom else have I in heaven? And when I am with You, the earth delights me not."[16]

"When you approach, then," continues St. Bonaventure, "beware lest any doubt make you begin to waver; take heed that you be not like a blind man groping with your hands, for a staff which is no more than a reed — that is, for natural arguments and human reasons; do not question the possibility of these things, as the Jews of old argued with one another and as did 'many of [Jesus'] disciples [,who] turned back and no longer went about with Him' (John 6:57). Rather, subject yourself to God, subjugate your mind to the yoke of faith which you see confirmed with such great testimonies."[17] We should remember that Jesus in this divine Sacrament is not only the banquet ("convivium") but also the guest ("conviva"); for He it is who eats and is eaten; He feeds Himself and feeds His disciples; Jesus spiritually takes food with those who worthily partake of Him, and is deeply delighted and refreshed by their progress. For this reason we should every day worthily and devoutly approach this Sacrament, and refresh Him who refreshes us, nourish Him who invites us, and give great joy to Christ, who is so wonderfully pleased by the fruit we receive in this Sacrament.

When Christ is consumed, He does not immediately depart, but abides and remains with us as long as the sacramental species endure. When these are dissolved, He still remains in another manner through grace for, according to St. John: "He who eats My flesh and drinks My blood, abides in Me, and I in him."[18]

249. (B) The effects of Holy Communion. The effects of the Eucharist are innumerable, but two — refreshment of

---

16. Ps. 72:25.
17. *Loc. cit.,* n. 3.
18. John 6:57.

the soul and union with Christ — are essential, while the others are accidental.

(I) Spiritual refreshment of the soul. This essential effect consists in an increase of sanctifying grace with the right to special actual graces. These special graces are granted through the reception of Holy Communion for the conservation, increase, and perfecting of the supernatural life by good works. Since this Sacrament has the nature of spiritual refreshment, it produces the same effects in the soul that material food and drink bring about in the body. "Just as the animal body is given energy and growth, warmth and life by food," says St. Bonaventure, "so the rational soul is fully nourished, filled with energy, inflamed and vivified in affection and understanding by the spirit of Christ, in which it should take its delight. But there is a difference between corporal and spiritual assimilation. Through corporal assimilation the digested food passes into the substance and nourishment of the one who eats, but in spiritual assimilation the partaker is incorporated in Christ, and passes into the unity and love of the spirit of Christ."[19] St. Augustine, voicing the sentiments of Christ, expresses the same idea: "You will not change Me into you, but you will be changed into Me — that is, into the likeness of Me, into goodness, holiness . . . , as fire changes iron into its own likeness."[20]

The Fathers of the Church express this effect of the Eucharist with other striking comparisons: St. Cyril of Alexandria, for instance, declares that just as a little leaven, according to St. Paul, ferments the whole mass into which it is immersed, flavors it and renders it pleasing to our taste and fit for our nourishment, so the little blessing of the Eucharist draws to

---

19. *Loc. cit.,* cap. I, n. 12, 13.
20. *Confessions,* Book VII, Chap. X, n. 16, in Migne, *P. L.,* t. XXXII, col. 742.

itself the whole man and fills him with grace, making him pleasing to God.

Our Lord referred to this when He said that "the Kingdom of heaven is like leaven, which a woman took and buried in three measures of flour, until all of it was leavened."[21] The Eucharist is that leaven which the worthy recipient hides within himself so that his soul, his spirit, and even his body may be leavened, sanctified, and united by the presence of the flesh of Christ.

The same saint uses another example to explain the salutary efficacy of the Eucharist. As the vine gives its own branches the power of growth, of producing leaves and flowers, so Christ is the Vine in relation to us, who are the branches. And just as a branch cannot bear fruit unless it remains on the vine, neither can we be fruitful unless we remain in Him. When Jesus Christ is intimately present to the soul through reception of the Eucharist, He imparts to it a particular vigor by which it flowers with holy desires and brings forth the fruits of good works.

Just as the body receives from the soul its vital energy and its senses, and all its weakened members are revived and resume their strength for work, so the flesh of Christ joined to our soul floods it with genuine, vital forces which we call enlightenment and inspiration. By these the soul is stimulated, by these it is strengthened to do and to dare, to pursue with ever-increasing fervor the things of God. "So he who eats Me," says our Lord, "he also shall live because of Me."[22] By virtue of the heavenly food, the soul with its restored powers passes from earthly things and goes forward to those of heaven, from the temporal to the eternal; walking like Elias in the strength of this food even to Horeb, to the Mount of God, where there is eternal rest. With St. John Chrysostom

---

21. Matt. 13:33.
22. John 6:58.

we can say: "Let us then arise from that table like lions breathing fire, terrible to the devil."[23]

250. (II) **Intimate union:** (a) of the soul; (b) of the body with Christ.

(a) UNION OF THE SOUL. All love naturally tends toward union, and the greater the force and inclination of love, either in both lovers or at least in one of them, the more perfect the union. Although Divine Goodness has gathered its creatures unto itself in an infinite variety of ways, yet none is more efficacious, none richer than this holy banquet in which the soul is intimately joined to Christ through grace and through love. This union, because of its very perfection, constitutes the essential effect of Holy Communion. For by its very institution, Holy Communion has for its purpose that Christ, permeating our being with His own body, should make Himself one with us. In other words, Christ in Holy Communion grafts the members of the Mystical Body more closely to the Head, which is Himself. Through Communion Christ is indeed within us. He is present, not figuratively, but actually; He is present with His body and with His blood, not merely virtually but corporally, existing under the accidents of bread and wine. St. Cyril of Alexandria says that if anyone has mixed one kind of wax with another he will plainly perceive that the one exists in the other; that in the same way whoever receives the flesh of our Saviour and drinks His precious blood will find, as our Lord says, that he is commingled into one whole with Him, as Christ is joined in a certain manner to the communicant through the participation of the Sacrament; so that the communicant truly finds himself in Christ, and in turn finds Christ in him.

Through Holy Communion the just man becomes a temple in which Christ truly dwells. We can say with St. Cyril of

---

23. *Homil. XLVI al. XLV in Joan.*, in Migne, *P. G.*, t. LXXIII, col. 583.

Jerusalem that communicants are true Christophers — that is, bearers of Christ, who works wonderful effects of grace in them and unites them more perfectly with His own soul.

Now in this union: (1) a wealth of spiritual gifts is granted to the soul; (2) the worthy communicant experiences a sweet and heavenly delight.

(1) *Wealth of gifts.* A worthy communicant obtains pardon for his sins, be they few or many. For through this Sacrament small offenses are forgiven, punishment is remitted, and grace increased. O how admirable is the goodness of God! Grace does not cease to flow as long as there is an empty vessel ready to receive it. Whatever the size of the vessel, it will be filled to the brim. The more pure the chalice of the heart, the more emptied of earthly cares, the more it will contain, the more abundant will be its refreshment. Through Holy Communion beginners in the spiritual life receive the purgation of their vices and the mortification of their flesh and of their passions; the more proficient receive an increase of virtue, the perfect, ardent affections of love, and the crowning of union. The Eucharistic banquet demands a worthy preparation by all who partake of it, so that all may enjoy so splendid a gift.

(2) *Sweetness and delight.* This Sacrament contains the Bread which has within it every delight, and the heavenly Wine that gladdens the heart of man and drives away all coldness of spirit. As joy and pleasure abound at an earthly banquet, so this spiritual banquet fills the soul with sweetness and delight. In the first place, it gives man the grace to bear the ordinary toils and trials of this life, not only with an untroubled soul, but even with spiritual joy. Moreover, this Sacrament fills the soul with love for Christ. For some it is manna because of its pleasantness; for others it is bread because of its strength; for still others it is pardon because of their compunction; for many it is oil because it affords comfort and

healing to the soul. The leaven of the elect has a flavor to suit everyone's spiritual taste. Holy Communion infallibly produces this effect unless hindered by the negligence of the communicant or by distractions and temporal cares. In fact, by way of overflow from its interior abundance, this sweetness is at times perceived sensibly also.

(b) HOLY COMMUNION AND THE BODY. (1) In regard to the present life, the Eucharist has some effect on the body and on the sensitive appetite through the restraint it places on concupiscence. (2) In regard to the next life, the Eucharist is the pledge of future glory, for it confers the right to a glorious resurrection of the body.

(1) *Mitigation of concupiscence.* This Sacrament, as the Fathers declare, sanctifies soul and body. This sanctification consists in the fact that Christ, after Communion, considers our flesh as His own, joined to Him by a certain affinity. He loves and protects our bodies and makes them conformable to Himself. By a special providence He destroys the "worms" and "serpents" with in us, that is, our inordinate passions; He subdues the law of the members, strengthens piety, extinguishes the flames of vice. Our Lord effects this lessening of concupiscence in either one of three ways, or possibly by a combination of factors. The first way by which He diminishes concupiscence is by the abundance of devotion imparted to the soul, which overflowers into the sensible part of man, so that both our heart and our flesh may rejoice in the living God. Again, concupiscence is moderated by the intimate union of our flesh with the sacred flesh of the Divine Word in Holy Communion; this curbs the passions, stimulates devout reflections in the imagination, awakens pious emotions in the sense faculties, so that the body is made more eager and willing in its obedience to the spirit, and both body and spirit are prepared to do whatever is right and good. Finally, Jesus, re-

ceived in Holy Communion, modifies the bodily tendencies which stir up the passions, so that the flesh is subjected to reason and the spirit. The mere hem of Christ"s garment healed the sick and cured persons suffering from hemorrhage; Christ's whole body heals and moderates the physical powers of man whenever they hinder the exercise of virtue. Extreme Unction often brings the body back to health. Why should not Christ, anointed as He is with divine oil, bestow health even more bountifully when He touches the body of man with His own flesh to strengthen it, that it may work what is good?

(2) *It is the pledge of a glorious resurrection.* By sanctifying our body, the glorified flesh of Christ makes it share in His incorruptibility. This is why Christ says: "He who eats My flesh and drinks My blood has life everlasting, and I will raise him up on the last day."[24] "It is but just," says St. Cyril of Alexandria, "that death, which has come upon us through the Fall, should subject the human body to corruption; yet, because Christ is in us by means of His own flesh, we shall all rise again. For it is incredible—indeed it is really impossible— that life should not return to those in whom it has dwelt. Just as we set a spark to a heap of chaff so that we may husband a little fire, so by His own flesh our Lord Jesus Christ fosters life in us, and as it were applies to us the spark of immortality which completely burns away whatever corruption may be in us."[25] Therefore our body, because it has been worthily joined to the body of Christ our Lord, deserves to rise on the last day to a life immortal, impassible, and glorious. The Council of Nicaea and the Church Fathers call this divine Sacrament the "Symbol of resurrection," the elixir of immortality, the food that nourishes us to immortal and eternal life, and the pledge of future glory not only for the soul but also for the body.

---

24. John 6:55.
25. *In Joan.,* Lib. IV, in Migne, *P. G.,* t. LXXIII, col. 582.

II. FREQUENT AND DAILY RECEPTION OF THE EUCHARIST

251. Holy Communion is eminently useful, productive of multiple benefits for soul and body. Hence it should be received frequently with great reverence. St. Augustine, in speaking of the reception of the Eucharist, says: "I neither praise nor blame the daily reception of the Eucharist."[26] Blessed Angela of Foligno says: "St. Augustine was both holy and wise; and seeing the good mixed with the bad in the Church of God, he did not condemn daily Communion so as not to hinder the good. But so as not to give any false confidence to evil men, he did not praise the practice. As a matter of fact, no one can estimate how much grace the soul receives in merely one worthy Communion, as long as the defects of the soul place no obstacle in the way."[27]

The reasons in favor of frequent, even daily reception of Holy Communion are given in the following paragraphs.

(1) **It is the desire of the Church.** The Council of Trent, with marvelous insight into the wealth of grace which Christians obtain through reception of the Eucharist, declares: "The holy Council desires that in every Mass the faithful present should communicate not only by spiritual desire, but also by the sacramental reception of the Eucharist."[28] These words explain sufficiently the wish of the Church that all Christians should daily partake of this heavenly food, and draw great fruits of sanctification from it.

(2) **It is the desire of Christ our Lord.** The longing to receive Holy Communion is in full accord with the desire with which Christ our Lord was ardently filled when He instituted this Sacrament. He Himself frequently and clearly explained the necessity of our often eating His flesh and drink-

---

26. *In Epist. 54, ad Januarium,* cap. III, in Migne, *P. L.,* t. XXXIII, col. 201.
27. *Angela de Fulgineo* (Paris, 1598), p. 409. In this book we are shown the way by which we may follow in the footsteps of our Saviour.
28. Sess. XXII, cap. VI.

ing His blood, especially by the words: "This is the bread that has come down from heaven; not as your fathers ate the manna, and died. He who eats this bread shall live forever."[29] From this comparison of the angelic food with bread and manna, the disciples could easily understand that just as the body is nourished daily by bread, and as the Hebrews were fed daily on manna in the desert, so the Christian should be fed and nourished daily by heavenly Bread. Furthermore, the Fathers of the Church almost unanimously teach that when we are told in the Lord's prayer to ask for "our daily bread," we should not interpret it so much as the material bread or food for the body, but as the Eucharistic Bread which we should receive daily.

(3) **From the nature of this Sacrament.** Jesus Christ and the Church truly desire that Christians should partake of the sacred banquet every day. And the main reason for this desire is that Holy Communion unites the faithful to God, and from this union they derive strength to overcome concupiscence, to wash away small, daily faults, and to ward off the grievous sins to which human frailty is exposed. Here also the saying is true that "the Sacraments are for man, not man for the Sacraments." For even in the case of the Blessed Sacrament, the primary purpose is not the honoring and glorifying of God, nor a reward of virtue, but the immense benefits man obtains. Hence the Council of Trent calls the Eucharist the antidote whereby we may be liberated from our daily faults, and preserved from mortal sin.

(4) **The practice of past centuries.** Correctly interpreting the divine intentions, the early Christians daily approached this table of life-giving strength: "And they continued steadfastly in the teaching of the Apostles, and in the communion of the breaking of bread."[30] The Fathers and ecclesiastical

---

29. John 6:59.
30. Acts 2:42.

writers testify that this was also the practice in following centuries, to the great increase of perfection and holiness.

III. CONDITIONS REQUIRED FOR FREQUENT AND DAILY COMMUNION

252. According to the decree of the Sacred Congregation of the Council cited above, frequent and daily Communion is permitted: (1) to all who are in the state of sanctifying grace; (2) whose intention is upright and pious; (3) who are detached from any affection for venial sins; (4) who follow the advice of their confessor.

253. (A) **State of grace.** Everyone should determine before going to Holy Communion whether he is a friend or an enemy of Jesus; whether he is clothed with the wedding garment or does not have it; whether or not he is free of mortal sin. "Seriously consider," St. Bonaventure warns, "that although mortal sin may not have been present after your last confession and penance, yet some grievous sin or the intention of sinning may still be in you, whereby your miserable soul may be dead and hence cut off from Christ the root and from His Church. For this life-giving Bread and divine Food has no vivifying influx, provides no nourishment to branches that are severed and dead. Such receive the Sacrament, but not the benefits of the Sacrament — that is, the grace of Christ and His divine charity. It is eaten with the mouth, but does not nourish the spirit; it enters the stomach, but not the soul. Some men partake of the Eucharist like brute animals, though the Body of Christ is in no way injured. Such reception does not revive the soul, nor does it unite and incorporate the soul; but rather, Christ Himself, impelled by nausea, vomits the bad communicant from His mouth as if he were a putrid corpse, so much carrion to be devoured by beasts and vultures. Christ delivers the wretched soul to be tormented by Satan, as it is written of

Judas: 'And after the morsel, Satan entered into him' (John 13:27). Therefore, if you have been ensnared by such evils beware lest for some cause or other you presume to receive without due contrition, purpose of amendment and confession, for 'it is a fearful thing to fall into the hands of the living God' (Heb. 10:31)."[31]

254. (B) An upright and pious intention. The Sacred Congregation of the Council explains this condition when it says: "An upright intention exists in the person who approaches the sacred table not out of routine or vanity or for human respect, but to fulfill the will of God, to be united to Him more closely in love, and to partake of this divine remedy for his weakness and defects."

If we are so soul-sick that we have no hunger for this Bread of heaven, if we have no taste — or worse, if we have distaste — for this Food, we may be certain the languor is not that of love — it is torpor. If we do not desire the presence of Christ and do not mourn His absence, we suffer from the wound dealt not by charity but by tepidity. Yet we must not, because of these weaknesses, abandon Holy Communion. For who will wound us with this wound of love, and who will make us languish with the languor of love? Christ, as our Physician and Medicine, while He heals us, while He perfects us in charity, must inflict pain on our souls. He thus wounds souls who receive Him with an upright intention. For the effect of the Eucharist is to wound the soul with love, so that the soul may desire it more ardently, as it is written: "He who eats of Me will hunger still, he who drinks of Me will thirst for more."[32]

255. (C) The cleansing of souls from venial sins. Everyone should carefully cleanse his soul not only from

---

31. *Loc. cit.,* cap. I, § 2.
32. Sirach 24:20.

mortal sins but also from venial sins, so that there is at least
no deliberate affection for them. Jesus Christ expressed this
at the Last Supper. Pouring water into a basin, He washed the
feet of His disciples to show them that they must be entirely
cleansed, not only from more grievous sins, but also from the
dust of lesser sins, before receiving this most pure Sacrament.
"It suffices that those who receive Communion daily should
be free from mortal sins and have the intention of never committing such sins in the future; and thus it cannot but come to
pass that they will gradually rid themselves also of venial sins
and their affection for them."[33] Although sometimes daily
communicants are subject to certain venial sins, they should
keep in mind the words of Blosius: "The Lord our God is
faithful, even when, as He often does, He leaves a man of
good will with some noticeable defect over an entire lifetime.
For He permits this fault to remain, so that, humiliated not
only inwardly but also in the eyes of those with whom he
lives, he is led to the knowledge of his own nothingness.

"No one should therefore abstain from receiving the
blessed Eucharist because of his minor defects. Whoever has
good will, even though he is weak and imperfect, should approach with joy and love. He should beg to be entirely
cleansed by the precious blood of Christ which perpetually
inundates those who desire it, and he should yearn to be
clothed with the virtues and merits of the Lord Jesus."[34]

But since, according to the directive of the Apostle, we
ought to prove ourselves before Holy Communion,[35] sacramental confession will be fitting and sometimes necessary.

256. (D) Sacramental confession. In general, the advice of a confessor concerning frequent Communion should be
sought. Our legislation and canon law prescribe that all the

---

33. Cf. Decree cited.
34. *Sacellum animae fidelis,* Pars III, cap. XVI, n. 5.
35. Cf. 1 Cor. 11:28.

friars should confess at least once a week. As to this confession, let us keep in mind the words of St. Bonaventure: "When you go to your spiritual physician and father, tell your sins not by way of a general confession as some hardhearted persons do. These wrap their grievous sins in the folds of commonplace words in general confessions, and thus tell them without true sorrow, so that they could even confess publicly in the street in this manner without shame. This is not a confession but a deception and mockery. If you truly wish to be healed, expose your wounds. Confess, clearly, delve to the bottom of your heart, reveal whatever you have committed since your last confession. Confess not only actions but also sinful thoughts, for taking pleasure in such thoughts defiles the mind. Reveal not only mortal sins but also the more serious venial sins which trouble and disturb your conscience. Mention the rest briefly, lucidly, but in a general way."[36] If you follow these admonitions of the Seraphic Doctor, you will always approach the heavenly banquet clothed in a clean nuptial garment fragrant with virtues, that is, with a radiant, joyful soul.

IV. THE RECEPTION OF HOLY COMMUNION

257. We may receive the Holy Eucharist in two ways, namely: (A) sacramentally; (B) spiritually.

(A) **Sacramental reception.** Whoever receives this Divine Food sacramentally must: (1) prepare himself worthily; (2) approach devoutly; (3) give thanks fervently.

(1) **Preparation for Holy Communion.** A twofold preparation or disposition is necessary for receiving Communion, the one remote, the other proximate.

REMOTE PREPARATION. This prepares the soul at a distance, as it were, and is nothing other than a holy and spiritual life, a life free of vice and licentiousness, the avoidance of

---

36. *Loc. cit.*, cap. II.

all that could defile a devout man. St. Lawrence Justinian speaks of this disposition: "Be assured that the best way to receive Holy Communion is in humility of spirit. For the more humble of heart you are, the more pure of soul, fervent in love, and eager for virtue, the more worthy you will be to receive the Holy Eucharist and the more holy your life will become."[37]

We highly recommend the pious practice handed down to us by holy religious of our Order. The entire interval between one Communion and the next was filled by them with preparation and thanksgiving, by means of fervent aspirations and ejaculatory prayers. Before Communion they were accustomed to say: "O blessed day, the day of love in which I shall fully enjoy Thee, O my Jesus, O God, my God, 'to Thee do I watch at break of day; for Thee my soul hath thirsted' (Ps. 62:2, Challoner-Douay version); my flesh longs for Thee. In Thy arms, O my Jesus, I shall take refuge, in them I shall hide and repose. O there let me remain! Come, good Jesus, and do not delay! Come into my heart, take possession of it and conform it to Thy own!"

After Communion: "I give Thee thanks, O Jesus, for the singular grace whereby You have fed me, a most vile sinner, with the Food of angels. O most generous God, who hast offered Thyself for me on the Cross, and hast given Thyself to me in the Eucharist: I also offer myself entirely to Thee. Let my heart, in which Thou, O my God, art dwelling, admit nothing worldly. Thee alone do I love, who alone art all. . . . "

Our efforts toward holiness are better founded and our soul more ardently inflamed by these fervent and constant aspirations than by lengthy prayers and spiritual exercises.

PROXIMATE PREPARATION. The proximate preparation consists not only in the state of sanctifying grace but also in

---

37. *De triumphali Christi agone,* cap. IV ad med.

various acts of virtue which stimulate and invigorate the soul, particularly acts of living faith, profound humility, filial confidence, and divine love.

The morning meditation before Holy Communion should often center on the Sacrament of the Holy Eucharist. Three things should be especially considered: an ardent love of our Lord, who is about to visit us; the extreme insufficiency of man, who is visited; and the fullness of love with which Christ visits His poor servants.

When about to approach the heavenly banquet in which Christ is received, devoutly recall:

(a) *The benefits of God,* particularly the Lord's Passion, in which the unspeakable love of Christ for us is especially resplendent. For He Himself spoke of this banquet, saying: "Do this in commemoration of Me." Therefore, according to our allotted time, we should reflect and meditate on all the Lord Jesus has done and suffered for us; and at the same time beg Him to prepare for Himself a rich and pleasant abode in our heart.

(b) *The insufficiency of man.* We should also consider the manner in which Christ in His loving kindness comes to rescue us who are so often wretched and miserable sinners. Salvation might have been obtained merely by gazing upon the Sacrament of His love, as the Israelites were cured of the bites of poisonous snakes by gazing upon the brazen serpent. But His bounty is so great that He prefers the intimate and penetrating communion in which His bodily form is joined to that of man. He deigns to unite Himself with us who are but nothingness, and who so little deserve such a tremendous favor. He will help us to turn our gaze upon ourselves, to consider the disproportion between our merits and the gift, and thus to have ever better reasons for praising His infinite goodness.

(c) *The purpose of Christ's coming.* This purpose can be understood by considering the functions which Christ fulfilled in the world. He came, as we have seen above (*a*) as a Saviour, to take away our sins; (*b*) as a physician to heal us, to cure us absolutely of all our spiritual ills; (*c*) He came as a teacher, to show us the light of His inspirations; (*d*) He came as a high priest, to communicate the fruit of the bloody sacrifice which He offered on the Cross; (*e*) He came as a shepherd, to nourish and sustain our souls.

With such thoughts in mind, we are easily led to acts of faith, of humility, of confidence and of love.

We should yearn for this divine food with insatiable desire, with vehement hunger and thirst. For if Christ our Lord "desired with desire"[38] — that is, yearned with the greatest love — to institute this pasch for us, how much more ardently should we long to eat it, that we may become partakers of His divine nature.

The better the preparation we make for Holy Communion, the richer the fruits we shall carry away from the holy table, and the more our soul will be elevated to lofty heights of perfection. St. Paul, speaking of the Jews in the desert, says: "And all ate the same spiritual food, and all drank the same spiritual drink. . . . Yet with most of them God was not well pleased";[39] they did not use this spiritual food in a spiritual way — that is, with sincere faith and humble obedience. Many find no taste for this heavenly manna because they take more delight in earthly foods and pleasures. They cannot stand its sweetness, for they have spoiled their taste with the flavor of material nourishment.

258. (2) **Devout reception of the Eucharist.** At the time of Communion, we should approach as if we had been invited to a banquet. Let us go to the holy table with humility,

---

38. Cf. Luke 22:15, Challoner-Douay version.
39. 1 Cor. 10:3-5.

but with eagerness even greater than that of people of the world hastening to a sumptuous feast. Our heart should be inflamed with the greatest desire, our attitude reverent, our hands joined and our eyes cast down.

We should consider our Lord as a living Being, as though with our own eyes we could see Him coming to us surrounded by saints and angels. Sometimes we should consider Him as a boundlessly loving Father; at others as a most dear brother, as a physician, as a shepherd, and so forth. Yearning for Him with a most fervent desire, let us tell Him, not so much with our lips as with our heart: "My Lord, who art Thou to come to me? Who am I to receive Thee? Of myself I am but the most miserable of sinners, for even though I have received the fullness of Thy revelation and of Thy grace, I have so often failed to love Thee and to obey Thy word. But in Thy infinite mercy, Thou hast looked upon me, a sinner; Thou hast called me with words of penance and of peace; Thou hast taken all darkness out of my soul. O come into the dwelling made by Thy own hands, come into the light of Thy own love, come into the abode Thou hast desired to find in me!"[40]

At the "Domine, non sum dignus," let us recite the prayer and strike our breast with sincere humility like another publican who, acknowledging his guilt, does not dare to lift his eyes to heaven. They with strong faith, hope and love, let us receive Him in whom, by whom and for whom we believe, we hope and we love.

259. (3) Worthy thanksgiving. After receiving Holy Communion we should return to our place with a glad and joyful heart, with the same attitude as before. Let us kneel at our place, with our eyes closed, and think only of Jesus, our God. Let us try to give every honor to our King, and then

---

40. St. Bonaventure, *loc. cit.*, cap. II, oratio.

treat with Him about whatever concerns our soul; considering
Him within ourselves, where He abides for our benefit. Finally,
to the best of our ability, let us listen to Him and deal with Him
in an intimate and friendly way.

These are golden minutes with Jesus in our heart. No other
time is better for dealing with our Lord on the subject of our
salvation than when we have Him actually within us. Let us
voice our sentiments of humility, of reverence, and of self-
distrust, exclaiming: "How is it my Lord and my God should
come to me?" Then let us proceed at once to expressions of
praise and of gratitude. Finally, let us offer some gift to the
Lord out of thankfulness for the benefits received, and wel-
come Him who welcomes us. Above all, we should give Him
our soul with all its powers and our body with all its senses.

Let us renew our holy profession, and offer Jesus something
special, such as some internal or external mortification, then
finish our thanksgiving by conversing confidently with our
most loving Guest, as a friend would talk to a friend.

Our gratitude should appear in our behavior. Let there be
an increase of modesty in our ways, greater fervor in religious
exercises, better observance of silence, and more moderation
in food and drink. Such should be the sacrifices which we place
before the supreme Lord of heaven and earth who in the morning dwelt in our heart.

When we have no time for immediate thanksgiving, or
when we must read, sing, or be occupied with other things
according to the custom or rules of the Order, let us be sure
to make a proper thanksgiving after these obligations have been
fulfilled.

260. **(B) Spiritual communion.** Christ can be received
not only sacramentally, but also spiritually, and with great
profit to the soul if He is received in the right way.

(1) NATURE OF SPIRITUAL COMMUNION. Spiritual communion is the holy desire to receive Christ and to be united

to Him with stronger ties through the imitation of His virtues. He who seeks Christ with great faith, with earnest meditation, with fervent love, and with the desire to partake of Him, receives Him spiritually and reaps much fruit from this spiritual communion.

Spiritual communion involves three acts: (1) an act of lively faith in the real presence of Christ; (2) the devout recollection of the spiritual graces which the Lord merited by His Passion and death and which He dispenses to the well-disposed communicant; (3) love for Christ and the desire to receive Him in Holy Communion if possible, so that we may be made partakers of His virtues and become like Him.

(2) THE BENEFITS AND ADVANTAGES OF SPIRITUAL COMMUNION. The benefits of this holy practice are sufficiently apparent from the fact that it has always been appreciated by God's saints and recommended to the faithful by the Council of Trent. And rightly so, for if God rewards even a pious desire for any virtue, how much more will He reward the desire of man to possess Him.

"He has filled the hungry with good things, and the rich He has sent away empty."[41] As often as we wish to communicate we shall always find the Son of God, our Lord, ready to nourish us spiritually.

We can practice this holy exercise at any time, in any place. It is most appropriate during Holy Mass, particularly at the time of the Communion of the priest. For while the Blessed Sacrament is exposed to view and vividly present, our heart is more ardently moved by divine love.

(3) MANNER OF MAKING A SPIRITUAL COMMUNION. When we attend Holy Mass but cannot actually receive Holy Communion, we should proceed in this way: After the Lord's

---

41. Luke 1:53.

Prayer, let us direct our attention to Jesus, then to our weakness and our defects, meditation on the majesty of God who is here present. Repeating the Agnus Dei three times with the priest, we should be truly sorry for our sins and beg for peace with God, with our neighbor, and with ourselves. While saying with the most intense love, at the same time as the celebrant, "Domine, non sum dignus," let us consider ourselves entirely unworthy of the sublime condescension of our most loving Saviour, who is prepared to come to us; unworthy, indeed, because of our many sins, the enormity of our ingratitude for so many benefits, the corruption of our body and soul, and the abysmal depths of our nothingness. Then, relying on the infinite goodness of Jesus, let us invite Him with an ardent longing to cleanse and adorn our heart and to possess it forever. Soon we shall be making acts of faith, love, and all the other virtues, and shall express our gratitude for our spiritual refreshment as though we had communicated sacramentally.

If we desire to communicate spiritually outside the time and place of the Holy Sacrifice, we should recall our last sacramental Communion and unite ourselves in intention with all the priests who are offering the Holy Sacrifice; with fervent desire let us make acts of faith, love, and so forth as described above.

Through Holy Communion our Lord Jesus Christ gives to us, as to beloved sons, His own substance, His flesh and blood, His soul and His divinity, and all the riches of His grace. He, as it were, makes very little of His infinite being, hiding it under the lowly covering of the accidents of bread and wine so as to offer it to us as food and drink. To obtain this love of Christ, let us lavish upon Him our earthly possessions, despising them as nothing.

§ III. The Sacrifice of the Mass

261. We have considered the Holy Eucharist as a Sacrament instituted for man, but now we must examine it in relation to God as a sacrifice. We should consider, then: (1) the excellence of the Mass; (2) the effect of this divine sacrifice; (3) the fruits which accrue to us by its celebration; (4) the method of devout and fruitful assistance at Mass.

I. THE EXCELLENCE OF THE SACRIFICE OF THE MASS

262. Since sacrifice is the primary duty of religion, it was evidently proper, says Cardinal Bona, that the Christian religion, which has no peer, should have the most noble sacrifice. The excellence of this sacrifice can be gathered from many sources:

A. **Because of the Victim offered.** That which is offered is Christ the Lord, true God and true Man. Therefore, the Sacrifice of the Mass, by reason of that which is offered, does not differ from the bloody sacrifice which Christ offered on the Cross, for in each of them the same body and blood are offered. The only difference between the sacrifice of the Cross and that of the altar is the manner of offering; for we acknowledge that the former is bloody and the latter unbloody. On the Cross the Son of God was subject to suffering and death; but on the altar, although His sacred humanity is in all truth offered in sacrifice, He still enjoys an immortal and impassible existence, since His blood is not shed physically: "Christ ... dies now no more; death shall no longer have dominion over Him."[42]

B. **Because of the value of the sacrifice.** The Sacrifice of the Mass is infinite in value, as are the merits and the Passion of Christ. The Mass is therefore as pleasing to God

---

42. Rom. 6:9.

as Christ's death on the Cross, although the effects of the Mass may be limited. For God has determined all things in the supernatural order according to certain laws just as He has in the natural order; the Mass produces only a finite effect, and, through the will of Christ, a certain determined effect. But in itself the value of the Mass is, and must be considered, infinite. The Mass is not a mere memorial and representation of the sacrifice of the Cross. For Christ Himself is truly present as the Principal Agent and Chief Offerer of the Mass — He who offered Himself both at the Last Supper and on Calvary. The Sacrifice of the Mass is therefore of the same value as that of the Cross; for He who then sacrificed Himself for our salvation is the same as the one who now offers Himself continually in the Mass through the ministry of the priest. As proof of this, let it be remembered that the priest at the consecration does not say: "This is the body of Christ"; but, knowing well that Christ is the Principal Offerer, Sacrificer and Consecrator, he speaks the words of consecration in His name: "This is My body."

C. **Because of the purpose of the Mass.** Christ our Lord instituted this mystery of the altar for two reasons: first, that it might be, as a Sacrament, the nourishment of the soul, by means of which He might preserve, restore and renew the spiritual life; secondly, that the Church might have a perpetual sacrifice for God, to be offered with a fourfold end:

(1) *Adoration* — that through sacrifice we may render the cult of supreme worship ("latria") to God our Creator, and humbly demonstrate our servitude and subjection to Him.

(2) *Thanksgiving* — to render Him unfailing and worthy of thanks for all His benefits.

(3) *Impetration* — to implore the help of divine grace and God's protection, inspiration and direction.

(4) *Propitiation* — to make satisfaction to God, who is offended by sin that, being appeased, He may grant us mercy and grace and the remission of our sins, and thus relieve both the living and the dead in this respect.

The Sacrifice of the Mass contains in itself elements of all the sacrifices of the Old Law. No greater or more efficacious action can be performed by human beings in this life than the offering of this sacrifice.

II. THE EFFECTS OF THE SACRIFICE OF THE MASS

263. The fourfold end of the Sacrifice of the Mass from its very institution corresponds to the fourfold effect which it produces in regard to God and in regard to man.

In regard to God, it renders the most perfect worship ("latria") to the most Holy Trinity and fulfills the debt of gratitude for benefits received.

In regard to man, it implores all supernatural and natural benefits in so far as they lead to salvation and are pleasing to God, and it obtains the remission of the guilt of sin. The Mass, then, produces the effects of praise, thanksgiving, impetration and propitiation.

A. **Praise.** Every rational creature is bound to acknowledge the supreme dominion of God, that is, to give to God the worship that is due Him. This must be done by offering sensible objects as a sign of due subjection and honor, in the form of a sacrifice. From the very beginning of the world we find that Cain and Abel offered sacrifice to God in compliance with a law of their very nature. And in the Mosaic Law God Himself appointed priests and instituted sacrifices and various oblations.

These sacrifices were but a figure and a foreshadowing of the supreme sacrifice which the Son of God offered in His own Person on the altar of the Cross. St. Paul shows us Christ addressing His Eternal Father thus: "In coming into the world, He says: 'Sacrifice and oblation Thou wouldst not, but a body Thou hast fitted to Me' ";[43] as though He would say: "O Eternal Father, in so far as I perceive that Thou dost abhor and despise the offerings and victims of former times, I offer Thee as a true sacrifice this body Thou didst give Me when I entered this world by means of the Incarnation, this body which will not only be equal to the victims of former ages, but will exceed them in an infinite number of ways." To render to God the supreme worship we owe Him, nothing more pleasing, more useful, or more efficacious can be offered to God than this unbloody sacrifice.

B. **Thanksgiving.** In a prophetic vision the psalmist foresaw the unbloody sacrifice of the Church as an offering of thanks and as the occasion of innumerable benefits from the hand of God, for further thanks have to be given. He said: "How shall I make a return to the Lord for all the good He has done for me? The cup of salvation I will take up, and I will call upon the name of the Lord."[44] Incarnate Wisdom devised this sacrifice for His most holy humanity, that by means of His continual oblation He might unceasingly recall to our minds the goodness of God and might give continual thanks to the Eternal Father in our name. It was perhaps for this reason that the Saviour, before He proceeded to the consecration at the Last Supper, gave thanks to the Father, as the Gospel says: "And taking a cup and giving thanks, He gave it to them."[45]

We have no more excellent means of thanking God for His benefits than the Holy Sacrifice of the Mass. St. John Chrysostom says: "The best safeguard of a favor is the remembrance of this favor and continual thanksgiving for it. We

---

43. Heb. 10:5.
44. Ps. 115:12-13.
45. Mark 14:23.

should celebrate these wonderful and salutary mysteries of the Eucharist in each assembly, because these mysteries are the commemoration of many favors; they represent the fountainhead of Divine Providence, and they lead us to thanksgiving for all things."[46]

C. **Impetration.** Christ, moved with a continual desire to obtain favors for us from the Father, uses this sacrifice as a most efficacious means of presenting His sacred humanity to the Father, and this the Almighty can never reject. He who is offered on the altar sits at the right hand of the Father as our Advocate. "Christ Jesus . . . also intercedes for us,"[47] and as the Second Person of the Blessed Trinity He, together with the Father and the Holy Spirit, accepts, as He is, clothed in this mortal body, this worthy and meritorious oblation. Woe to us if Divine Providence and love had not given us this sacrifice; we are in need of many graces in this valley of tears, and yet we continually offend the Divine Goodness and make ourselves utterly unworthy of the very graces we need and which we could never obtain by our own power. Still we know from experience that although we are sinners and rebels we participate in God's benefits. Most certainly the only cause to which these benefits can be attributed is the fact that in the Sacrifice of the Mass Jesus Christ is offered somewhere on earth at every hour, indeed every minute. He "intercedes for us," He continually intervenes for us, and asks whatever is necessary for our salvation.

D. **Propitiation.** The Apostle clearly declares that the Sacrifice of the Mass has the power of propitiation: "For if the blood of goats and bulls, and the sprinkled ashes of a heifer sanctify the unclean unto the cleansing of the flesh, how much more will the blood of Christ, who through the Holy Spirit offered Himself unblemished unto God, cleanse your

---

46. *Homil. XXV in Matt.*, in Migne, *P. G.*, t. LVII, col. 331.
47. Rom. 8:34.

conscience from dead works?"[48] But this same precious blood is offered daily to the Eternal Father in the Sacrifice of the Mass. And Christ Himself declares: I have poured out the eucharistic chalice "unto the forgiveness of sins."[49]

It is important to know that "the Sacrifice of the Mass cannot have greater efficacy than the sacrifice of the Cross, since the Sacrifice of the Mass derives its power from the sacrifice of the Cross; however, the sacrifice of the Cross did not immediately and efficiently justify, but only by way of impetration and merit. Otherwise all men would be automatically made just and holy — since the Lord offered Himself to God as a sacrifice for all men. Therefore, the Sacrifice of the Mass does not justify men immediately; it petitions justification so that, from the merit of the sacrifice of the Cross, grace and the gift of penitence may be given to men."[50]

When treating of this divine Sacrament and pondering on the words which Christ spoke to His Apostles at the Last Supper: "As often as you shall do these things, you shall do them in memory of Me," Abbot Rupert could write: "Take away the daily commemoration of the death of the Saviour and see how justly the Saviour Himself would lament: 'Of what use is My blood?' If the memory of this sacrifice, now ardent, were to grow cold, all love would freeze, faith totter, hope waver, and at the same time the loud cry of the second Abel would be silenced, whereas now it resounds perpetually from so many altars, daily opens and refreshes the mouth of the thirsty, clamoring earth which is the Church. . . . Since this memorial is so frequently renewed, the charity of Christ glows, the edifice of faith stands firmly on its foundation, hope is restored by the daily remission of sins."[51]

---

48. Heb. 9:13-14.
49. Matt. 26:28.
50. St. Robert Bellarmine, *De Missa*, Lib. II, cap. IV.
51. *De divinis officiis*, Lib. II, cap. X, in Migne, *P. L.*, t. CLXX, col. 42.

We can say with the Seraphic Doctor: "Take away this Sacrament from the Church and what will you have in the world but error and infidelity? The Christian people would be like a scattered herd of swine, and would soon be given over to idolatry, as infidels are. But through this Sacrament the Church abides, faith is strengthened, the Christian religion and divine worship flourish, and Christ can say: 'Behold, I am with you all days, even unto the consummation of the world' (Matt. 28:20)."[52]

III. THE FRUITS OF THE SACRIFICE OF THE MASS

264. We have already discussed the impetratory, propitiatory and satisfactory fruits which can be gained by the very fact that the Mass is celebrated or attended ("ex opere operato"). But there are fruits of the Mass which can be increased by the activity or devotion of the priest and those assisting at the Mass — that is, by their greater fervor and closer union with Christ ("ex opere operantis").

This fourfold fruit of the Mass is (1) general; (2) special; (3) personal; (4) ministerial.

(1) THE GENERAL FRUIT is that in which the whole Church participates. All are aided by this general fruit, both the living and the dead, provided there is no impediment on their part. The Mass is substantially the same as the sacrifice of the Cross, which was offered for all. By divine right the priest was constituted by God to offer sacrifices for the sins of the people.

(2) THE SPECIAL FRUIT is gained by those who concur in the sacrifice in a special manner, as do those who offer it together with the priest, those who offer it with him by an internal disposition, those who serve at Mass, or those who gave an alms so as to have it celebrated. All these participate

---

52. St. Bonaventure, *Tractatus de praeparat. ad Missam*, cap. I, § 1, n. 3.

in the special fruit by the design of Christ and the will of the Church. "Those who assist at several Masses at the same time, partake of the fruits of all — because the only conditions required for participation in these fruits of the Mass are corporal presence and devout attention. If while in church one can devoutly attend several Masses at the same time, there is no reason to deny that the fruits of each sacrifice are obtained."[53]

(3) THE VERY SPECIAL or PERSONAL FRUIT is gained only by the priest who celebrates the Mass; just as he is the personal offerer, so he in a singular way offers the sacrifice for himself. At the Offertory he must say, "For my sins and offenses."

(4) THE MINISTERIAL FRUIT is gained by those for whom the Sacrifice of the Mass is offered in particular; for the sacrifice was so constituted that of its very nature it is offered for men, and so it benefits those for whom it is offered.

We should be happy to minister to the priest as his server, says David of Augsburg, for this is the office of angels. "Not only is the priest whom you serve bound to pray for you, but so are all who are in attendance, whose place you take, and even the whole Church, everywhere on earth; for you take the place of all the faithful. In truth the faithful wherever they live would be bound with most cordial thanksgiving to serve their God descending from heaven, if they could be present at Mass. You take their place when you serve."[54]

"It is a great misfortune and a sorry fault," says our Seraphic Father, "to have Him thus so near you, and to be thinking of anything else in the world. Let all mankind tremble, let the whole earth quake and heaven rejoice, when Christ, the Son of the living God, is on the altar in the hands of the priest. What admirable power and stupendous dignity! O sublime humility! O humble sublimity! The Lord of the uni-

---

53. Noldin, *Summa theologiae moralis* (Innsbruck, 1906), De Sacramentis, p. 192.

54. *De exterioris et interioris hominis compositione*, Lib. I, Pars I, cap. X.

verse, God Himself and the Son of God, humbles Himself so far as to hide Himself for our salvation under the feeble appearances of bread. See, brothers, the humility of God and 'pour out your hearts before Him' (Ps. 61:9), and humble yourselves in your turn, 'that He may exalt you' (1 Pet. 5:6). Keep nothing of yourself for yourself, so that He who has given Himself wholly to you may possess you entirely."[55]

From the excellence, the fruits and the effects of the Sacrifice of the Mass, we can gather that it is the *center of our entire religion,* the heart of the divine worship. For the Divine Office and other devotions merely supplement the sacrifice of the altar. With what great uprightness, devotion and admiration, and with what seraphic longing and jubilation, we should assist at Mass, especially the conventual Mass! To this end, we should follow the Mass either according to the missal or according to the method of St. Bonaventure, which we shall explain.

IV. MANNER OF HEARING MASS

265. With sinless hands, with pure and tranquil hearts, the faithful should stand with the priest before the altar of God to assist at the most holy Sacrifice of the Mass. There, lamenting and sympathizing with Mary, John, and the devout women, and meditating on the crucified Christ, let them stir up ardent affections in order to gain all the fruits of the Holy Sacrifice.

From the Beginning of Mass to the Offertory

266. We should consider the dignity of this sacrifice and determine to assist at it reverently, humbly requesting this grace from God. Then let us imagine Christ prostrate in the garden, preparing for the sacrifice of the Cross; after briefly

---

55. *Opuscula,* Epistola 2, Quarrachi edition, p. 103.

reviewing our sins, let us renew our resolutions to amend our lives, and then recite the Confiteor; for when the Confiteor is said with contrite heart, venial sins are remitted.

From the Offertory to the Consecration

267. During the Offertory we should watch Jesus on Mount Calvary, waiting there until the Cross is brought forth and He is immolated; then, united with Him, let us willingly offer ourselves and all our good desires and generous resolutions to God, especially the things we shall do during the day.

From the Consecration to the Agnus Dei

268. During the Consecration we should meditate on the raising of the Cross and the immolation of Jesus. Let us look up to Christ hanging on the gibbet. For if the Jews of old, looking upon the brazen serpent, immediately perceived its power to heal (a power it had because it was a symbol of Christ crucified), how much more should we experience the fruits of this divine sacrifice when we stand in the presence of the reality and not the figure. For Christ Himself is hidden in this Sacrament which renews His death. With all possible devotion and humility let us, together with the whole Church, triumphant and militant, adore Jesus, and offer Him who suffered so much for us, to God the Father, for ourselves and for those for whom we are bound or intend to pray, pouring forth our heart in the sight of the Lord.

From the Agnus Dei until the End of Mass

269. Here we should recall the death and the burial of the Lord Jesus. Let us prepare ourselves for spiritual or sacramental Communion by devoutly asking Christ to come into our soul, which has been cleansed of its defects and adorned with virtues. Then let us receive Communion with the priest, with ardent desire, asking the sweet Saviour Himself to live in us, to rule us and to govern all our thoughts and actions.

After Communion, we should make our thanksgiving, renew our vows and resolutions, particularly those concerned with an increase in the depth and intensity of our love; then let us offer God the practice of some virtue. If we do this after hearing Mass, we can say for the rest of the day: " 'I live, now not I, but Christ lives in me'; I have offered everything to God the Father through Jesus, and He will direct my external senses so that nothing but what Christ desires will pass through them. He will observe through my eyes, hear through my ears, detect through my sense of smell; He will speak with my tongue, and perceive through my senses of taste and touch, because I do not intend to do anything except under His direction; He will move my internal senses and appetites with noble thoughts and devout affections."

Let us then devoutly receive the blessing which our Lord imparts through the priest.

CONCLUSION. It is fitting to add a few words on the devotion of our Seraphic Father to the most Holy Eucharist and his reverence for priests, the ministers of this holy mystery.

270. (A) Devotion of St. Francis to the Holy Eucharist.

In his life of St. Francis, St. Bonaventure, to renew our ardor, describes the admirable piety and love of this man of God for the Holy Eucharist: "Every fiber of the heart of Francis was aglow with love for the Sacrament of the Altar, and with exceedingly great admiration he marveled at the loving condescension and the condescending love of the Lord. He received Communion often and so devoutly that he enkindled devotion in others, and at the sweet taste of the Immaculate Lamb he was transported into an ecstasy of mind, just as if he were spiritually inebriated."[56] Thomas of Celano says, "He considered it an unpardonable negligence not to attend

---

56. *Legenda S. Franc.*, cap. IX.

at least one Mass each day whenever possible."[57] In his last days he wrote a letter to the General Chapter and to all the brethren, in which, among other serious and useful considerations, he wrote: "Kissing your feet, I implore you all, my brothers — and with the utmost affection of my heart I beseech you — to show the greatest possible reverence and honor to the most holy body and blood of our Lord Jesus Christ."[58] And he says in his *Testament:* "These most holy mysteries I desire to venerate and honor above all things and to reserve them in precious tabernacles." And although he loved his holy mistress Poverty, still he desired that "chalices, corporals, altar decorations and everything pertaining to the sacrifice, be of precious material."[59] "Therefore he wished at times to send the brethren into the world with precious vessels, so that wherever they noticed any consecrated host in an unbecoming place they would put it in the best place they could find for it."[60] He showed special love toward all those who venerated this most holy Sacrament. "Therefore he loved France as a friend of the body of the Lord, and he wished to die there because of her reverence for the sacred species." He called to sanctity his brethren, the priests and clerics, who were to be future ministers of the altar. "I also implore in the Lord," he said, "all my friars who are, shall be, or who desire to be priests of the Most High, that when they intend to celebrate Mass, being pure, they offer with great reverence the true sacrifice of the most holy body and blood of our Lord Jesus Christ. . . . Listen, my brethren: If the most blessed Virgin Mary is honored as she deserves for having borne the Lord in her most holy womb; if the blessed Baptist trembled and did not dare to touch the holy head of God; if the sepulchre in which our Lord was laid for a time, is venerated; how much more,

---

57. *Legenda Secunda,* cap. CLII, p. 319.
58. *Opusc.,* Epistola 2, Quaracchi edition, p. 100.
59. *Ibid.,* Epistola 5, p. 113.
60. Celano, *Legenda Secunda,* cap. CLII, p. 320.

then, should he be holy, just, and worthy who touches Christ with his hands, who takes Him into his mouth and heart, who gives Him to others — no longer a mortal Christ, but a glorious Victor forever, 'on whom the angels desire to look!' " (1 Pet. 1:12, Challoner-Douay version).

"Consider your dignity, friar priests, and keep yourselves holy because He is holy (cf. Lev. 11:44). And as the Lord God honored you above all through this mystery, so also should you love, revere and honor Him above all other things."[61]

271. **(B) Devotion of St. Francis to priests.** Our Seraphic Father not only honored the sacrament of the Altar, but out of love for this divine mystery, he, with great faith, also reverenced priests. In his *Testament* he says: "And these priests I am resolved to hold in respect, love, and honor as my masters; and I will not consider any sin in them, because I behold in them the Son of God and they are my masters. I act thus because in this world I see nothing corporally of the most high Son of God except His most holy body and blood, which they consecrate, receive, and which they alone administer to others." And Thomas of Celano testifies; "He desired that great reverence be shown to priestly hands, upon which divine power is conferred for the purpose of consecrating. Frequently he said: 'If a saint from heaven and a poor priest came to meet me at the same time, I would first go to honor the priest and kiss his hands affectionately. For I would say: "Wait, St. Lawrence, because these hands touch the Word of Life, and they possess something beyond the human." ' "[62]

We must imitate our Seraphic Father, for there is nothing more precious on earth than Jesus hidden in His Sacrament, united to our soul and body in Holy Communion, and offered to the eternal Father for us in the Sacrifice of the Mass.

---

61. *Opusc.,* Epistola 2, Quaracchi edition, pp. 101, 102.
62. *Legenda Secunda, loc. cit.*

Article VI — Means Used Occasionally

272. So far we have covered the daily means by which we conform our will to the will of God. There are others which are only used occasionally, such as: (1) the chapter of faults; and (2) spiritual recollection.

§ I. The Chapter of Faults

273. This ancient practice of monks, the chapter of faults, has been followed by Franciscans since the beginning of the Order. Bernard of Andermatt says that through this pious exercise of humility the charity of superiors toward their subjects is sincerely demonstrated, and their firmness turns everything into a blessing for the community. For a better understanding of this subject, we shall consider (1) the purpose for which the chapter of faults was instituted; (2) the faults which should be revealed; (3) the manner in which subjects should conduct themselves in the chapter.

I. THE PURPOSE OF THE CHAPTER OF FAULTS

This exercise of humility was instituted in religious Orders for a twofold purpose: (A) for the common good, that is, to safeguard the practice of religious discipline; (B) for the individual good, that is, to stir up the desire for virtue in the souls of religious.

A. **The common good.** According to our legislation, the common good is the principal purpose of the chapter of faults, for the Constitutions show that the chapter of faults should be used to preserve discipline among religious, to prevent violations of the Rule and Constitutions, and to correct and amend transgressors and negligent friars. From love of justice every religious superior should strive to promote religious perfection and spiritual progress, and do away with whatever hinders them. The superior should take care that: (1) the precepts of God and of the Church and the religious vows be observed; (2) all scandals be avoided; (3) a spirit of prayer, the strength of every true religious, be fostered; (4) external discipline flourish, for this, as St. Bonaventure observed, "is prescribed, not as the only way of life but because it is so much more conducive to the observance of discipline and uniformity for the brethren, lest one live and do as he please and disturb the others."[1] The chapter of faults was introduced in the Order so that the superior might be given the opportunity to perform his duty in this respect. The Seraphic Doctor explains: "The praiseworthy Orders and those already in decay are distinguished not by the fact that no sinners can be found in the former, but that none is allowed to remain unpunished, that occasions for further sins are carefully removed, that all incorrigibles and all vicious elements are prudently eliminated, and the good are favored and encouraged so that they may persevere and always progress toward higher aims. Since even in the assembly of angels, before their final choice, and in the assembly of the disciples, at the time of the teaching of Christ, some fault was to be found, which Order of virtuous men on earth would presume to claim the prerogative of being without sin?"[2]

B. **Individual good.** The religious derive a threefold benefit from the chapter of faults:

1. Humility;

2. Amendment of life;

3. Spiritual advancement.

(1) *Humility.* As fire melts ice, this excellent practice of humility dispels self-exaltation and self-love.

(2) *Amendment.* As the purgatory of the cloister, the chapter of faults destroys the evils contracted by negligence.

---

1. *De sex al. Seraph.,* cap. II, n. 11.
2. *Ibid.,* n. 13.

For the religious, publicly acknowledging his transgression, makes reparation for his fault through the penance he humbly accepts and performs. Paul V, in his Constitution *Romanus Pontifex*, of May 23, 1606, granted an indulgence of forty days for fulfilling this religious exercise with a contrite heart, making a spiritual communion, and making an act of one of the virtues.

(3) *Spiritual advancement,* especially for the younger religious. Dorotheus writes that the novice and newly professed are most fervent as regards fasts, vigils, solitude, obedience, and other good practices. But after a while, when the first fervor wears off, if there is no director or sponsor to stir up the dying embers, the recruit withers and fails; and then, completely destitute, is taken captive by his enemies.

II. MANIFESTATION OF FAULTS IN CHAPTER

The chapter of faults is not sacramental confession. Its primary purpose is to preserve public order and to remove obstacles to the common good. Hence the disclosing of external and public violations of the vows, the Rule and Constitutions and religious discipline is within the scope of the chapter. We must accuse ourselves of these, make reparation for violated order, and atone for faults by public penance. But internal and secretly committed sins should always be excluded from the chapter. The Church does not pass judgment on internal matters of conscience in the external forum; much less does the superior in the chapter of faults. The more grievous sins and certain heinous crimes are reserved to an ecclesiastical judge. In these matters the superiors act according to a judicial process. A commentator writes: "It cannot be tolerated for the brethren to mention any faults besides those which they consider negligences; hence whatever regards conscience or confession should be formally excluded from the chapter of faults, without, however, breaking the law requiring reparation for public scandal according to the norms of moral theology."

III. MANNER OF CONFESSING FAULTS

The subject should confess his faults in a place and on the appointed days and in the manner customary in his Province. According to the *Mirror of Discipline,* a religious should tell his faults with:

(1) Respect;

(2) Caution;

(3) Humility.

(1) *With respect.* The recitation of faults should be performed with head uncovered, without grinning or looking around, or making any motions with the hands.

(2) *With caution.* The words should be few, and nothing should be said which might involve another.

(3) *With humility.* In attitude and in words: in attitude, for according to custom the brethren humbly bow toward the floor; in words, for they should express subjection and repentance. From the beginning of the Order, the novices were taught that whenever in the chapter or outside it they were accused too harshly or unjustly, they should not become vexed, but should rejoice in the Lord and be glad. For the first brethren knew that St. Francis had said that those who patiently endured reprehension were blessed with a triple blessing. For he used to say: "Blessed is the servant who endures correction or accusations as patiently from another as from himself. Blessed is the servant who does not fret over blame, who submits modestly, humbly confesses, and willingly makes satisfaction. Blessed is the servant who is not too quick in excusing himself, and who humbly accepts the shame and the blame for

an offense he has not committed."[3] To better enforce these admonitions of St. Francis, our legislation imposes a penalty on those who dare to answer back in chapter, unless they first have sought and obtained permission. Let us consider these excellent warnings of St. Francis, and write them deeply in our heart. From the perfection with which we practice this doctrine, we can know to what degree we are Friars Minor and sons of the Seraphic Father.

Subjects should assist in the chapter of faults in a humble manner and should be careful not to reveal anything that was said or done in it; each one should take care of his own particular spiritual progress. "If all religious but knew," exclaims Trithemius, "how much merit for eternal life the willing acceptance of capitular reprimands earns for them, they would joyfully endure all accusations and injuries for love of God."[4]

§ II. Spiritual Recollection

274. Spiritual recollection or solitude is another instrument occasionally used.

Men seek solitude for various reasons:

(1) "There are some," says St. Ambrose, "who for the sake of rest take their mind away from business cares and withdraw from the crowd. They either seek a place of retirement in the country or the peace of open lands, or keep an unoccupied mind in the city, in order to enjoy peace and tranquillity."[5]

(2) Others, like all the real philosophers and wise men of the true religion, regard a place of retirement as a condition for the refreshment of mental and corporal powers, a field for reaping the fruit of human liberty, an aid for the composition and study of letters, a place which provides the right atmos-

---

3. *Opuscula,* Quaracchi edition, p. 16.
4. *De tripl. Reg. claustr.*
5. *De officiis Ministrorum,* Lib. III, cap. I, n. 6, in Migne, *P. L.,* t. XVI, col. 155.

phere in which to prepare themselves for further activity, the haven where they can calm their soul and reform their behavior.

(3) Saintly men, enlightened by God, both in the Old and in the New Testament, secluded themselves so as to become better and more holy, to confer with God, to walk with Him.

It is of this type of retirement and recollection that we shall treat, as regards:

I. Its excellence and necessity;

II. The time for recollection;

III. The prescribed manner for members of the Franciscan Order, that they may fruitfully perform this pious exercise.

I. THE EXCELLENCE AND NECESSITY OF SPIRITUAL RECOLLECTION

275. By means of spiritual recollection and solitude, a religious retires from the company of his fellow men and puts aside all distracting cares. He can devote himself entirely to the things of God through frequent meditation, spiritual reading, examination of conscience, the chapter of faults, corporal penances, and other spiritual exercises. God Himself declared that spiritual recollection and solitude are very effective for conquering vice and acquiring virtue. When speaking of the just soul, He said through the prophet: "So I will allure her; I will lead her into the desert and speak to her heart."[6] That is, speak to the soul with words of life and of eternal salvation.

A. **Excellence.** The Fathers of the Church understood the excellence of both solitude and spiritual retreat. St. Jerome exclaims: "O desert, nourishing the flowers of Christ! O solitude which produces the firm rocks mentioned in the Apocalypse with which the city of the great King is constructed. O barren

---

6. Osee 2:16.

waste, rejoicing in familiarity with God!"[7] St. Basil says: "A solitary life is the school in which heavenly doctrine is learned and a preparation for the practice of divine arts is given. It is a paradise of delights which emits the perfumes of virtue. There the roses of charity are enveloped in crimson flame and no sudden squalls are able to destroy the violets of humility. There the myrrh of perfect mortification diffuses itself, and the incense of constant prayer hangs heavy on the air. . . . O workshop of spiritual exercise, in which the human soul rebuilds in itself the image of its Creator, and returns to its original purity."[8]

B. **Necessity.** By His own example, Christ teaches us the necessity of spiritual retreat. St. Luke tells us that "He . . . was in retirement in the desert, and in prayer."[9] Not only for a few days but for forty days He separated Himself from all human companionship in order to contemplate the divine mysteries. In St. Mark's Gospel we read that Jesus advised His disciples to seek a little rest from the turbulent crowd, and to turn their gaze inward, so that they might understand what the Holy Spirit had taught them. When, therefore, "the Fountainhead of absolute sanctity withdrew for the purpose of possessing purity, He was not outwardly lacking in the good effects produced by such retirement and solitude, for the fullness of purity in Him who cleanses and sanctifies the polluted world could neither be tainted by the dust of the worldly crowd nor contaminated by human companionship. He desired to instruct us by the example of His retirement."[10] St. Bonaventure says: "He undertook such a hard and solitary life for Himself in order that He might raise the minds of the faithful to the

---

7. *Epist. ad. Heliodorum monachum,* Ep. 14, in Migne, *P. L.,* t. XXII, col. 353.

8. *De laude vitae solitariae,* cap. XIX, Opusc. 11, found among the works of St. Damian; in Migne, *P. L.,* t. CXLV, col. 246 et seq.

9. Luke 5:16.

10. Cassian, *Coll. X,* cap. VI, in Migne, *P. L.,* t. XLIX, col. 827.

pursuit of perfection and strengthen them for greater endurance."[11] "After the example of Christ," says St. Gregory, "holy men, forced by the necessity of duty to devote themselves to distracting occupations, seek refuge in the secret recesses of their hearts, where they ascend to the height of intimate thought, and see the law as if it were on a mountain. Disregarding the allurements of transient affairs, they investigate on high the tenor of the heavenly will."[12] Thus our Seraphic Father Francis spent forty days in solitude, praying and performing spiritual works. Following the example of Christ, many entered such spiritual retreats that they might liberate their souls from bodily desires and attune themselves to the Divine Wisdom. "In the silence which replaces the usual clamor of worldly activities, they delighted in holy meditation on the eternal truths."[13]

Holy men, such as our Seraphic Father, St. Bonaventure, St. Bernardine of Siena, and others outstanding in their regular observance held this solitude to be so necessary to preserve and renew a fervent spirit that they sought refuge in the solitude of their hearts and for a time occupied themselves only with the problems of their salvation. How much more should we esteem this holy practice, we who have not as yet attained such perfection, and are so easily distracted by occupations, and who so easily abandon our first fervor and good resolutions! St. Leo asks, "Is there anyone so arrogantly proud, so flawless, so presumably guiltless that he has no need of renovation? Such an opinion is absolutely false and whoever advances in years with such foolish vanity inanely presumes himself immune from all the harm proceeding from the temptations of this life."[14]

---

11. *Lign. vitae fruct.*, III, n. 10.

12. *Moralia,* Lib. XXXI, cap. XXV, n. 49, in Migne, *P. L.,* t. LXXVI, col. 600.

13. Pope St. Leo the Great, *Serm. 8, De jejunio;* in Migne, *P. L.,* Serm. 93, t. LIV, col. 457.

14. *Serm. 5 de Quadrag.;* in Migne, *P. L.,* Serm. XLIII, t. LIV, col. 282.

Even though the mechanism of a watch runs smoothly, we must occasionally remove whatever dust may have found its way inside. The religious cannot live entirely apart from the spirit of the times; and although through pious meditations he winds the mainspring of his spiritual life every day, he gradually gathers dust which, according to St. Gregory, can soil even the most pious hearts. But he is cleansed of this dust by a period of solitude in which eternal salvation is seriously considered. When we examine ourselves on how we are advancing in the practice of our religious duties, we find that although every day we do the things required of us, an exaggerated number of other occupations prevent us from doing them as we should and become a cause of distraction to the soul and of a slackening of its holy work.

*II. TIMES OF SPIRITUAL RECOLLECTION FOR THE FRANCISCAN RELIGIOUS

276. Definite periods of recollection are prescribed for certain persons in the Franciscan Order.

(a) For postulants: before receiving the habit;

(b) For novices: before pronouncing their vows;

(c) For the professed clerics: before receiving Holy Orders;

(d) For all religious there are two periods of recollection: one every year for a number of consecutive days; the other each month for one day only.

A. The Recollection or Retreat Made before Receiving the Habit

277. Before a candidate is admitted into the Order, he must make a spiritual retreat of eight full days and pray with piety under the direction of the novice master. At the discre-

tion of his confessor, he may make a general confession of the sins of his past life, and on the day of investiture receive Holy Communion. The candidate must be approved in regard to those things which the friars observe, in order that he may show his good will and obtain greater light before entering upon so great an undertaking. The purpose of the retreat is not to choose a state of life but (1) to make certain of the choice already made; and (2) to put away "the old man" and put on "the new man."

Making certain of the choice. An affair of such importance as admission into the Franciscan Order should be given much serious thought, so that the beginner will with great fervor commence his service of the Lord. He should listen to the voice of the Lord inviting him to follow. But if he is not free of all temporal cares and worldly concerns, he may not perceive the gracious invitation. St. Bernard advises: "O beloved, if you are preparing the ear of the spirit for this voice of your God, a voice sweeter than honey and honeycomb, then flee external cares; so that when your inner sense is disentangled and free, you may say with Samuel, 'Speak, Lord, for Thy servant heareth' (1 Kings 3:10). This voice does not speak amid the din and bustle of the world, nor is it heard in any public gathering. Secret counsel seeks to be heard also in secret. Joy and happiness will certainly be given you if you listen with a chastened ear. Abraham was commanded to leave his own country, so that he might deserve to behold and possess the land of the living. . . . You also must in a sense flee your brethren if you wish to secure your salvation."[15]

If at this time the candidate is disturbed by the devil about his vocation, he should remember what St. Gregory wrote to a certain nobleman, who hoped that the Emperor would appoint him to serve in public affairs: "Why, O my illustrious son, do

---

15. *Epist. 107 ad Thomam,* in Migne, *P. L.,* t. CLXXXII, col. 248.

you not consider that there is an end to this world? Every day we approach closer to the time when we must render an account to the eternal and almighty Judge. Then why should we be mindful of anything but this all-important moment? Our life can be compared to sailing in a boat. Whether he stands, sits, or lies down, the sailor continually moves, for the ship is driven onward by the wind. While awake or asleep, speaking or silent, at every moment of each day we come closer to our end, whether we want it or not. When our final day arrives, of what advantage will be those things which we sought with so much care and gathered with such solicitude? If we seek what is good, then we love what is of endless value. If we hate evil, we fear that which causes the damned to suffer eternally. How ardently we wish for temporal favors! As soon as we have them, how much we fear to lose them, even in the service of a good prince. Consider, therefore, what a punishment it is to be strained by the desire for success, or tortured by the fear of adversity.

"I further recommend," St. Gregory told the nobleman, "that for a short time Your Grace should set aside a period for studying how to live as a recipient of the only things of any value in this short journey of life: a suitable time for giving yourself to a quiet and peaceful life, to reading holy books, meditating on inspiring words, enkindling within yourself a love of eternity, performing good works according to your ability, and as a reward for them hoping for an everlasting kingdom. Living in this way is the beginning of eternal life, already obtained on earth.

"I tell you all these things, my beloved son, because I highly esteem you, and because now you are drifting toward rough waters and dangerous storms, and I hope to rescue you with the life line of my words. If you grasp this life line, once you are safe on the shore you yourself will realize how great were the dangers from which you escaped, and how happy and peaceful is your present joy."[16]

The candidate should diligently examine and meditate on these words of St. Gregory in so far as he needs to overcome the obstacles to his vocation. By doing this he will learn to despise riches and honors and to abhor the vanity of the world and its enticing pleasures. He will stabilize his resolution to serve God by a life of perfection, he will cheerfully and wholeheartedly embrace Franciscan poverty and humility.

Putting off "the old man." Before assuming the Franciscan habit, the postulant must try to improve his interior life so as to serve God diligently under the standard of our Seraphic Father and to fulfill the expectations of the Order. He should heed the advice of the Apostle: "Be renewed in the spirit of your mind, and put on the new man, which has been created according to God in justice and holiness of truth."[17] "May you walk worthily of God and please Him in all things."[18]

In this holy retreat the postulant should apply himself to the spiritual exercises under the direction of his master so that in silence and in the presence of God he may realize through frequent reflection the purpose of man's creation. He should meditate on the greatness of God's love in creating him and in calling him to the true faith. God must appear to him as a Father. The remembrance of past sins will then grieve him because he has offended such a loving parent. Even his meditations on the last things — death, judgment, heaven and hell — must be colored by this more endearing view of God.

The better one understands these last things the more he will despise the things of earth and the more grateful to God he will be for the grace of a vocation to the Seraphic Order. He will realize that anyone who wishes to reach the Promised

---

16. St. Gregory, *Epist.*, Lib. VII, cap. XXIX, in Migne, *P. L.*, t. LXXVII, col. 884.

17. Eph. 4:23-24.

18. Col. 1:10.

Land, to obtain the glory of his heavenly home, must leave
Egypt and enter the desert, crossing the Red Sea by the power
of the Cross. He must abandon the life of pleasure and the
shadow of sin, and take up a life of labor; he must be ready
to die with Christ on the Cross of penance, in order to have the
right, at the hour of death, to hear the words addressed to the
repentant thief: "This day thou shalt be with Me in paradise."[19]

B. The Retreat before Profession

278. The novitiate itself could pass as a sort of daily retreat, since every day two periods are devoted to mental prayer,
rigorous silence and various penances and devotional exercises.
However, a retreat before profession is really necessary: (1)
in order to regain baptismal innocence; (2) for a better understanding of the obligations and the excellence of the life promised by profession.

(a) **Regaining baptismal innocence.** According to the
opinion of the Doctors of the Church, novices who pronounce
their vows with the requisite dispositions regain the freedom
from guilt received at baptism. "You wish to hear me explain,"
remarks St. Bernard, "how among other expiations, monastic
observance merits this prerogative which we call a second
baptism. I believe that on account of the complete renunciation of the world and the singular excellence of the spiritual
life, which surpasses all other ways of life, God makes those
who take vows and love Him, like unto angels and unlike other
men. In these He refashions the divine image, forming Christ
in them as at baptism."[20]

To help the religious obtain this priceless fruit, the laws
of the Franciscan Order prescribe special exercises for the
novices in this retreat. By following them, the novices will be

19. Luke 23:43.
20. *De praecepto et disp.*, cap. XVII, in Migne, *P. L.*, t. CLXXXII, col. 889.

well prepared, after Communion, confession and fervent prayers, for the all-important act of profession.

(b) **Necessity of meditation on the obligations and excellence of the religious state.** Before a novice consecrates himself to God in a life of perfection, he should again consider in what the life of a perfect Christian and a true Friar Minor consists, and should weigh the obligations he will assume in the religious state. He should give much thought to the gift of a religious vocation, to its excellence, and to the conditions for a faithful response to it after profession.

He should consider the means the Order prescribes to help him control and conquer his passions, acquire virtue and strive for perfection. He is to reflect on the spirit of humility, poverty, and angelic purity, the spirit of self-denial and mortification which should animate a son of St. Francis. With a full realization and deliberation he will choose to remain forever in the house of the Lord, to carry the Cross willingly with Christ, and in the end to enjoy eternal happiness with the blessed in heaven. A novice can find the answer to these questions only in a spiritual retreat.

C. The Retreat before Reception of Holy Orders

279. Before the friars are elevated to Holy Orders, it is important that they should realize and meditate seriously on the great dignity to which they are being promoted, so that they may be inspired by this thought to lead a life worthy of an ecclesiastic. Each aspirant should know what Holy Mother Church expects of him.

(a) **Tonsure.** The Church, in selecting the chosen ones for the sacred militia, demands that they profess: "O Lord, my allotted portion and my cup, You it is who hold fast my lot."[21] St. Jerome adds, "They have been called to the clerical state,

---

21. Ps. 15:5.

either because they are the Lord's by choice, or because the Lord Himself is their choice; that is, He is the portion — the allotted share — of the clergy. But he who is either the portion of the Lord or who has the Lord as his portion, should conduct himself as such, so as to possess the Lord and to be possessed by Him."[22]

(b) **Subdiaconate.** The Church seriously addresses those who are to be elevated to the subdiaconate with the words: "Again and again you must carefully consider the burden which you today, of your own free will, wish to take upon yourselves. . . . Therefore if until now you have been remiss in your duties toward the Church, from now on you must be fervent; if until now you have been heedless, from now on you must be watchful; if until now you have been open to censure, henceforth you must be without reproach. . . . Behold what a ministry is entrusted to you."[23]

(c) **Diaconate.** For those who are to be elevated to the diaconate, the Church, through the bishop, prays to God: "May virtue abound in them in all its beauty, in unassuming authority, in unchanging modesty, in spotless purity, and in the observance of spiritual discipline. Let Thy precepts shine forth in their lives, so that by the example of their holiness the faithful may be drawn to holy emulation."[24]

(d) **Priesthood.** Even more earnest is the admonition addressed to candidates for the priesthood: "It must be with great fear that you ascend to so high a station; and care must be taken that heavenly wisdom, blameless conduct, and long-continued righteousness shall commend the candidates for it. . . . Let the odor of your lives be a delight to the Church of Christ. May you thus build up, by word and example, the

---

22. *Epist. 52 ad Nepotianum,* n. 5, in Migne, *P. L.,* t. XXII, col. 531.
23. *Roman Pontifical,* Admonition given at the ordination of a subdeacon.
24. *Ibid.,* Prayer recited over the deacons.

House that is the family of God."[25] A most serious exhortation is then given: "Be you imitators of Him whom you handle." Literally: "Imitate what you handle — Imitamini quod tractatis." The candidates must be the fulfillment of Paul's precept: "that we may present every man perfect in Christ Jesus" (Col. 1:28).

Everyone who is about to receive Holy Orders should prepare himself by means of the spiritual exercises of a retreat — if not by force of law or a decree in the Rule or Constitutions of the Order, certainly by reason of the very nature of the priesthood.

D. The Retreat Made by the Community

280. All the friars, particularly those who preach and those who must have many associations in the world and are thus more exposed to spiritual stains, are obliged to purify their minds in solitude. St. Bonaventure, speaking of our Seraphic Father, says that in order to wipe off any dust that might have clung to him from his association with men,[26] he would recollect himself for a time in solitude. St. Francis himself chose the places of recollection for the brethren, and it is in one such solitary place that he rewrote the Rule. To ensure the holy silence of the friars and to allow them more freedom in prayer, he obtained permission from Pope Innocent III to have Mass celebrated in these places of retreat.

Clerical students have a greater need for recollection than others, for their studies are often a source of lukewarmness. According to St. Thomas Aquinas, "Science and anything else conducive to greatness is to man an occasion of self-confidence, so that he does not wholly surrender himself to God. The result is that sometimes such things occasion a hindrance to

---

25. *Ibid.,* Exhortation given at the ordination of a priest.
26. Cf. *Legenda S. Franc.* cap. XIII, n. 1.

devotion."[27] An unknown writer, whose works are published with those of St. Peter Damian, relates of himself: "Formerly Tullius seemed sweet to me, the poets' songs pleased me, philosophy sparkled with golden words, and enticing sirens utterly enchanted my intellect. The Law, the prophets, the Gospel and the Epistles, and all the glorious thoughts of God and of His servants seemed insignificant or of no importance."[28] For in the course of our studies we are often tempted to take credit for our knowledge instead of using it for the glory of God. Our Seraphic Father carefully avoided learned, proud friars, for he feared they might destroy and tear down the Order which God had established through him. He was right in this, for the ruin or dissolution of some religious Orders has been caused by learned but self-satisfied men.

III. MANNER OF MAKING A SPIRITUAL RETREAT

A. Annual Retreat

281. To be able to gather fully the fruits of our annual retreat, we must understand: (1) its purpose; (2) how to prepare for it; (3) what to do during the exercises; (4) how to obtain results; (5) what to do when it is over.

282. (A) **The purpose of the annual retreat.** *The ultimate purpose* of spiritual recollection, as of all human actions, is God Himself; for love of Him and in His honor we should undertake these spiritual exercises. However, the *immediate or intrinsic end* to which this recollection tends by its very nature is and must be the renovation of ourselves and of our whole spiritual life.

Our personal renovation consists in two things: (1) the rooting out of improper affections and inclinations, whether habitual or actual, innate or acquired; (2) pursuing the per-

---

27. *Summa theol.*, IIa IIae, q. 82, a. 3 ad 3.
28. *In Nat. Salvatoris*, Serm. 61, in Migne, *P. L.*, t. CLXIV, col. 852.

fection of our state, and thus becoming men after the heart of God, conformed in all things and through all things to His divine will.

The renewal of our spiritual life consists in the perfect performance of all the spiritual exercises which are imposed upon us daily by reason of our profession, our position or office, such as the morning intention, the particular or general examen, recitation of the Divine Office, Holy Communion, Mass, meditation, or any other means of acquiring perfection prescribed by the Rule or by custom.

It is most important that *we see where we have failed.*

Father Joseph Anthony points out that, "either before these exercises or immediately upon beginning them, you should devote one or two meditations to finding out your predominant passion and those vices toward which you are particularly inclined by the weakness of your nature. Then, select the virtue opposed to this same vice or passion. As an example, if you feel inclined to anger, you should choose meekness, if you cater to pride, take humility; if you experience excessive dryness in prayer and other spiritual exercises, try zeal and love of God; and during these exercises make every effort to overcome your predominant passion and to acquire the opposite virtue. If no occasions are offered for practicing the virtue selected, at least make frequent internal acts of that virtue."[29]

THE PARTICULAR PURPOSE. Besides making this intrinsic principal resolution, we should strive for still other particular purposes, such as comfort in sorrow, preparation for death, and so forth.

Comfort in sorrow. Since the words of the Apostle, "And all who want to live piously in Christ Jesus will suffer persecution,"[30] are also verified in the religious life, it is no wonder

29. Fr. Joseph Anthony Caesaremontanus, O. M. Cap., *Spiritualis decem dierum solitudo.*

30. 2 Tim. 3:12.

that religious suffer many afflictions. "If you do not suffer persecution," says St. Augustine, "you do not wish to live piously in Christ. And if you wish to test the truth of this statement, begin to live piously in Christ."[31] The burdens of these tribulations are lightened only by prayer and by solitude. Anyone who is driven and tossed by tribulations from whatever cause, or who endures with intense bitterness the misfortunes of the times, will do well to seek solitude, as St. Augustine teaches. "Often a burning desire for solitude arises in the heart of the servant of God from no other cause than the storm of tribulations and scandals, and he cries out, 'Had I but wings like a dove, I would fly away and be at rest' (Ps. 54:7)."[32] That St. Augustine's doctrine was applied in early Franciscan practices Luke Wadding shows: "There frequently arose among the early friars a desire for solitude, this desire originating from nothing else than the many fiery tribulations which oppressed them."[33]

Preparation for death. Every Christian and, more so, every religious should always live as if death were close at hand — as if any day might be his last. When sickness besets him, he should in good time do with fervor and virtue whatever is necessary in danger of death, so that at his final hour he may be found well disposed and well prepared. No one knows the hour of death nor how suddenly it will strike; so special preparation should be made in the annual retreat and during the monthly recollection. St. Bonaventure describes how St. Francis, after many labors, was led by Divine Providence to a high place called Mount Alverno, so that he might prepare himself for death.

---

31. *In Ps. LIV*, no. 8, in Migne, *P. L.*, t. XXXVI, col. 634.
32. *Ibid.*, col. 633.
33. *Opusc.*, t. III, col. 3, fol. 291.

283. (B) **Preparation before the retreat.** As the time for the retreat approaches, it will help to pay special attention to the following instructions.

(1) *Be joyful.* St. Bonaventure writes of St. Francis: "When he had come into the solitude of Alverno to keep a fast in honor of the Archangel Michael, many different birds fluttered around his cell, and seemed, by their joyous flight, to rejoice at his coming, and to invite and entice the holy Father to tarry there. Seeing this, he said to his companion, 'I perceive, Brother, that it is in accord with the divine will that we should abide here a while, such great comfort do our sisters the little birds seem to take in our presence.' "[34] Perhaps the birds do not rejoice when we enter into solitude, but the angels and saints of God certainly do, and most of all our Seraphic Father. Let us ardently anticipate the time of recollection, realizing that it is one of the best means of perfection. Let us come to it with the firm intention of gathering much fruit. Let us enter into it with holy eagerness, not in a spirit of sadness nor because it has to be done, but with joy: "God loves a cheerful giver."[35]

(2) *Pray.* From the heavenly Father who gives "the Good Spirit to those who ask Him,"[36] we should ask for the grace of the Holy Spirit through the only-begotten Son.

(3) *Selection of patrons.* It is advisable to choose certain patrons, either those whose feast is celebrated at the time of the retreat or other saints toward whom we have a special devotion. But first we should seek the aid of the "one Mediator between God and men, Himself man, Christ Jesus,"[37] and also the intercession of Mary, His most holy Mother, and devoutly commit all our good works and offerings to God through her.

---

34. *Legenda S. Franc.,* cap. VIII, n. 10.
35. 2 Cor. 9:7.
36. Luke 11:13.
37. 1 Tim. 2:5.

(4) *Right intention.* We should form the good intention of accomplishing all the spiritual exercises for the honor of God alone. We should wish to acquire the merit of holy obedience for a more effective and secure pursuit of our own salvation, and in order to gain the plenary indulgence granted by the Sovereign Pontiffs to those who make a retreat. We should firmly intend to do everything under divine inspiration for God's honor and for our own good and for the good of our neighbor.

(5) *Resignation to God's good pleasure.* Before undertaking the retreat, we should prepare our souls to overcome temptations and give ourselves completely to the divine good pleasure, accepting in advance anything God may wish to send us. We should deem ourselves unworthy of consolations or special favors, and firmly determine to persevere constantly and assiduously in the exercises, even though no sweetness relieves the strain of dryness and of spiritual aridity.

From the very beginning we should make up our minds to control ourselves, until by this endurance, this lowliness and resignation it is given us to taste the manna of divine consolation and to enjoy the sweetness hidden in the solitary life.

(6) *Laying aside ordinary occupations.* We must, above all, lay aside our ordinary occupations, projects, and such things, so that during the time of the retreat we may be disengaged from all other tasks but the one thing necessary: our own salvation. Francis Maggio maintains that "during these days of the spiritual exercises all other duties, cares and occupations must be laid aside and not permitted under any pretense, not even under the plea of piety or inconvenience to others. All this, however, according to the dictates of prudence."[38]

---

38. Maggio, *Secessus ad exercitia spirit.,* cap. III, § 6. The author is here quoting *Ex circa perfect.,* by Joannis Suffrani.

If more than three hundred and fifty days a year are spent in helping and serving others, does it seem too much to devote eight or ten to God and to our own soul?

"I give you this advice," says St. Ephrem: "live in peace and silence, keep the fear of the Lord before your eyes, collect your thoughts and preside over them as a judge. Examine the reason why you have entered on a solitary life in the past; understand what this state should have meant to you; see what guilt is in your heart and from what cause this guilt arose."[39] In other words, observe silence and examine your conscience.

Whenever we happen to get sick, we forget all other occupations and cares, and attend only to our state of health, and no one blames us if during all the time of our illness we visit no one, or talk to no one. Why, then, do we not do the same during the time set aside for curing the infirmities of our soul and recovering spiritual health? Does not our soul have more value than our body? Are the diseases of the soul not more dangerous than those of the body? We must be careful to remove all impediments, and to devote ourselves entirely, with perfect liberty of mind, to the care of our salvation.

284. (C) During the retreat. In general we should conscientiously observe the timetable of the spiritual exercises as determined in our Province.

(1) *Before meditation* and the other exercises, we should say some devout prayers that God may bestow on us abundant graces to help us know Him and to fulfill His divine will, repeating with Samuel the prophet, "Speak, Lord, for Thy serv-

---

39. T. II, p. 323, of the Antwerp edition (1619) of St. Ephrem's works.

ant heareth."[40] We should also kneel before our Eucharistic Saviour and speak to Him or to the saints.

(2) *Throughout the day* we should frequently examine our conscience to discover any defects in our performance of the spiritual exercises, and determine the means needed to correct them. This should be done particularly before each canonical Hour. For as Paul says, "If we judged ourselves, we should not ... be judged."[41] For this reason we should go to the choir early enough to make privately a short preliminary recollection — an expression of regret for our defects — and to say some prayers to our Eucharistic Lord.

(3) *Concerning imperfections during the spiritual exercises.* We should atone for them by imposing upon ourselves some penance, such as the recitation of the *Miserere* or the *De Profundis,* or the performance of some kind of mortification. Even if we often fail through human weakness, we should not lose heart, but, realizing our frailty, should humble ourselves before God and earnestly implore His help, for He knows the weakness of our nature.

(4) We receive *special lights* during the time of retreat in order to help us form resolutions for the future. We shall also learn what to avoid and, in case we fall again, how to amend.

(5) If we resolve to make a *general confession* for peace of conscience and greater perfection, we should first consult our spiritual director. We have already submitted a form for an examination of conscience according to the ten commandments and the precepts of the Church. To these we must now add points of examination that apply to the Rule and Constitutions.

---

40. 1 Kings 3:10.
41. 1 Cor. 11:31.

PRECEPTS OF THE RULE AND ORDINANCES
OF THE CONSTITUTIONS

285. (1) As to the Order itself. Have I been well-disposed toward my vocation? How do I regard it?

Do I value it highly? Do I thank God for such a priceless gift?

Do I really wish to strive for perfection and to reach that proposed goal?

Do I place this purpose before me as the rule of all my actions?

Do I without mature deliberation lightly, indifferently employ any means at all, as chance may present them?

Am I negligent in using the means I once selected, procrastinating or executing them with a certain amount of sluggishness or unwillingness?

Do I persevere in my undertakings or cease through cowardice?

Do I bear ills and adversities with equanimity?

Have I become lax in my way of living, and have I by my example weakened religious discipline?

Do I impede the progress of reforms? Do I become irritated when I am censured or forced to perform a penance because of violated rules?

Do I wholeheartedly seek to promote the good of the Order?

Have I presumed to divulge secrets concerning our life to outsiders?

(2) The vows. *Poverty:* Am I strict in my observance of most high poverty?

Am I going to the limit in seeking and desiring every comfort and convenience? Do I hanker after sumptuous feasts, greater quantities of food, and delicately prepared foods?

Am I easily disgruntled about the lack of things, even in small matters? Have I procured and accepted foodstuffs, or kept any food in my cell without permission from the superior?

Have I through feigned necessity received and stored up without permission various things given me by outsiders?

Have I retained anything superfluous?

Chastity: Have I tolerated anything against chastity?

Am I negligent in repelling evil thoughts?

Do I ever surrender to morose delectations?

Have I given occasion for improper thoughts by not controlling my eyes, even though I fully realize that mortification of the senses is of great importance for me?

Have I violated the precept of the Rule concerning suspicious dealings with women?

Have I spoken too freely with any person of the other sex?

Have I brought about occasions for temptations against chastity through curiosity, bad literature, or particular friendship?

Have I used scurrilous language or told jokes not in accord with religious decorum?

Do I conduct myself modestly at home and abroad?

Vow and virtue of obedience: Have I always considered the superior as taking the place of God?

Have I conceived an evil opinion of him or magnified his imperfections?

Have I held him in contempt? inasmuch as he is the superior? or on account of some imperfection?

Have I shown him the respect due to him, or have I spoken too freely to him?

Have I ridiculed him by any external action or derisive laughter, especially in the presence of others?

Have I shown perfect internal obedience — that is, in the will, in judgment and in the intellect? Or have I obeyed with repugnance and murmurs, and have I outwardly manifested this repugnance?

Have I shown absolute external submission in every way by a prompt, cheerful and humble obedience? Or have I disobeyed any of the superior's commands? out of contempt or mere negligence? Have I executed all the orders of the superior, but performed them slowly and lazily, according to my own opinion and intentions rather than the judgment and purpose of the superior?

Have I shown a frank and sincere disposition toward my superior? Am I hostile to him?

Do I wish him every good of mind and body, every advantage that may aid him in fulfilling his office successfully? Have I helped him as much as I could?

Have I earnestly prayed for him?

Have I always spoken honorably of him? Defended him in the presence of others, taken his part?

(3) THE CONSTITUTIONS AND THE ORDINANCES OF SUPERIORS: Although the Constitutions do not bind under pain of sin, nevertheless transgressions are rarely without sin if perpetrated without justification, or from laziness or negligence. Formal contempt for the Constitutions is always a mortal sin, for it is opposed to the strict obligation by which we are bound to strive for perfection. I must examine myself and see whether or not there is any ordinance of the Constitutions which I am accustomed to violate rather frequently, and whether or not my conscience admonishes me and prods me on to observe this ordinance.

Have I ridiculed those who observe the Constitutions exactly, by calling them simpletons, scrupulous or foolish people?

Have I complained against superiors who insist on the strict observance of the Constitutions, and who punish and correct transgressors?

Do I brand such superiors as indiscreet and too rigorous? even in the presence of seculars?

Have I boldly contradicted any paternal correction of the superior, justly deserved by my lax observance of the Constitutions? Or have I been guilty of greater audacity when, surprised and angered at a correction, I retorted in some such fashion as: "Why so many regulations in the Constitutions? Why so many ordinances? Isn't it enough to observe the essential vows?"

Have I at any time induced others to break the Constitutions? Have I caused others to pay little attention to many fine points of the Rule, to disregard them as matters of no importance?

Have I defended a more lenient view in regard to regular observance, and continued to hold my opinion with biting words before other friars and even against the superior?

Have I accepted the general and provincial ordinances with due respect?

Do I diligently observe the approved customs of the Order and of the Province?

Do I faithfully observe and punctually perform the customary penances, austerities, fasts and disciplines?

(4) MORTIFICATION: Do I observe proper internal and external temperance in regard to food, drink, sleep and treatment of the body?

Have I kept the prescribed fasts, abstinence, and acts of discipline in the friary and also outside it?

Do I look upon the control of my senses as a duty?

(5) SPIRITUAL EXERCISES: Have I the deplorable custom of reciting the Divine Office distractedly, irreverently, and with little devotion?

Am I usually lukewarm, without diligence in giving myself to prayer?

Do I allow my mind to dwell on vain and useless thoughts for a considerable time?

Have I contracted the bad habit of spending a good deal of time in idleness and in useless talking? Do I neglect spiritual reading, examination of conscience and, in general, whatever leads to spiritual perfection?

(6) FRATERNAL CHARITY: Do I frequently sin against charity?

Have I, for any length of time, built up a feeling of aversion toward certain confreres? Do I avoid their company and conversation? Do I speak ill of them? Is my conduct so wrong in this respect that I have given bad example to many others?

Have I wished evil on any friar?

Have I inflicted injury on him or other people by my reproaches, detraction or contumely, destroying his peace of mind and bringing on defection? Le Gaudier says, "There are five ways in which one can offend in this matter: (1) whenever there is a certainty or a positive doubt that a neighbor's good name has been notably injured among others; (2) whenever the good opinion others have had of a person is diminished so that he becomes less capable of maintaining his social position, working for the glory of God, or performing any good work; (3) when not only hatred is stirred up among others, but also when their friendship is diminished, or when the close relationship among religious is strained so that these will not even speak to each other; (4) when a less grievous sin of reproach or detraction affects anyone with a grave mental disturbance, or causes him sadness, especially when we know that he is already suffering mental anguish and therefore is easily disturbed; (5) when the victim of the uncharitableness cannot administer the affairs of his office properly and justly on account of the reproach or detraction."[42]

---

42. *De perfectione vitae spirit.*, Vol. II, p. 229.

Have I displayed my anger toward another by censure or insulting remarks?

Have I been envious? That is, have I been sad because of another's progress, grieved by someone's temporal or spiritual success?

Have I shown proper politeness and friendliness in conversation? or have I been contentious in word and rude in action?

Have I always tried to give good example to others?

Have I been too affectionate, overfamiliar with certain individuals?

As a final question: Remembering that this may be my last confession, do I find anything else still weighing on my conscience?

286. (D) The fruits of an annual retreat. A retreat made devoutly and in the spirit of faith produces a twofold fruit: a renovation of our spiritual life, and a good disposition for meeting death at any hour. Comforted by a good confession and Holy Communion, we may properly close our retreat with the renewal of our religious profession and a humble acceptance of death.

(1) *A renewal of vows,* or of religious profession, performed with sincere affection and the right intention of keeping the promises we have made, obtains the same grace concerning remission of sin as the original promise by which we consecrated ourselves completely to God. Denis the Carthusian says that St. Bernardine and many other spiritual writers teach that as often as a religious renews his profession with such eagerness that, for love of God, he would at once bind himself by means of his vows if he had not already done so, he obtains the remission of all temporal punishment due to his sins. Anyone who takes such pleasure in a past sin that he would be willing, if possible, to commit it again, incurs as much guilt as in the

original act since, before God, it is the evil intention that is the sinful element. In the same way, anyone who is glad that he performed a past good deed and who, for love of Jesus Christ, would be willing to perform it again, obtains the same measure of merit and remission as occasioned by the original deed. If we obtain full remission of our sins by our first profession, we shall obtain the same benefit by renewing it, since God, because of His divine clemency, is more prone to dispense mercy and forgiveness than to punish.

Before this renewal of profession, we should consider the great blessing of our vocation, and thank God for it.

Every religious should consider his entrance into religion as a great privilege. With these and similar sentiments let us reconsecrate ourselves entirely to the service of God.

FORMULA FOR THE RENEWAL OF VOWS

I give Thee thanks, most benign Jesus, for that singular grace by which Thou hast led me, a most vile sinner, out of an evil world. I am sorry from the bottom of my heart that until now I have responded so poorly to this great grace and that I have been so ungrateful for this special benefit. I detest all the transgressions and negligences committed in this state of life, and I sincerely regret that I have aspired so feebly to its perfection. Forgive me, O God, gracious pardoner and lover of human salvation, and grant that, having completed the spiritual exercises, entirely reconciled to Thee through (a general) confession, I may begin this hour to put on "the new man," created in justice and holiness. At this moment, renew within me that burning will and devotion I had at the moment of my holy religious profession. I desire again to offer the sacrifice I made to Thee when I pronounced my vows. I desire to arouse myself once again to a most exact and faithful observance of these vows. I call upon heaven and earth and all the angels and saints as witnesses to the sincerity of my sentiments. Come, all ye blessed, into the presence of Jesus Christ, of the most holy Virgin Mother, and of my holy Father St. Francis, and be witnesses to my renewal of vows, which I promise to the most august Trinity, the Father, Son and Holy Spirit, to observe.

I, N..., am inflamed with the most ardent desire of con-secrating my whole soul to Thee alone, O my Lord! Therefore "I vow and promise to almighty God and to the Blessed Virgin Mary, to our blessed Father Francis and to all the saints, to observe all the days of my life the Rule of the Friars Minor, confirmed by our lord Pope Honorius, living in obedience, without property and in chastity."

Behold, O Lord, the sacrifice whereby I offer Thee my en-tire self. True, I have offered this same sacrifice on other occasions, but I make it now as never before, with the fullest consent of my will. Would that I had greater fervor, that my offering might be more acceptable. But I beseech Thee, Holy Father, Eternal God, do not receive me in my present condition, but receive me hidden in the heart of Jesus Christ, Thy Son, who sacrificed Himself to Thee on the Cross. In this heart of Jesus I strip myself of all that is of self, and to this most holy heart of Jesus I direct all my affections, that in it I may glorify Thee always, in time and in eternity. Amen.

In an abbreviated form we should make this renewal daily, for as St. Francis Xavier says, "I propose that at meditation you daily renew the vows of poverty, chastity and obedience; because for a man consecrated to God there is hardly a more efficacious remedy against the snares and treacheries of the devil."[43]

(2) *Acceptance of death.* In the same spirit of fervor we should devoutly recite, in the presence of the Holy Eucharist, an

---

43. *Epist. ad Joan. Bravium.*

act of acceptance of death. All who express the intention of accepting calmly and gladly from the hand of God whatever death He may send them, with all its pain, anguish, and suffering, may gain a plenary indulgence at the hour of death if they have made such an act at least once during their lifetime after having fulfilled the usual conditions for gaining a plenary indulgence.[44]

It is not necessary to use any set formula of words to gain this indulgence, but the following brief act will serve the purpose:

"My Lord and my God, I, being truly sorry for my sins and loving Thee above all things, now profess my willingness cheerfully to accept from Thy hand whatever kind of death it may please Thee to send me, with all its pains, penalties and sorrows."

Below the translator offers a longer, contemporary formula by José de Vinck which might be used during retreats by those who wish to follow a more lengthy form.

An Act of Acceptance of Death

In the name of the most holy Trinity, I, N..., with complete sincerity of heart and with faith, hope, and love in my soul, declare in thy presence, O Angel of God, my holy guardian, that with thy assistance I will accept without revolt any form of death which the providence of God may have in store for me, at this very moment, or after many more years of toil in His vineyard, in this very place or in any distant corner of the earth. I resign myself to dying in peace or violence, surrounded by friends or enemies, or even abandoned and alone, for I know that death will always come to me as God's final gift on earth: for death is the gate, and the dawn, the end of the pilgrimage, and the accomplishment of the promise.

---

44. Sacred Cong. Ind., March 9, 1904; Holy Office, Nov. 16, 1916; S. P. Ap., March 18, 1932.

I do not pray that my death may be painless, for I wish to bear my share of the sufferings of Christ, and at the final hour, when all is about to be accomplished, I wish to offer again the only thing I can truly give because it is truly mine: my pain. Let this hour be the crowning of my life, the richest moment of my time on earth: let it summarize my every effort toward Thee, O Lord, by being part of Thy own death on the Cross.

Yet I am weak, and life is good, and I may fail when the time of trial comes; and so I pray to thee, my patron saint, to thee, O holy Joseph, the patron of a happy death, and most of all, to thee, O most holy Virgin Mother of God, to come to my rescue in time of need, so that, through the merits of Christ I may, when death is close, make good the promise I have made today; that I may live in expectation of this hour, and never fall away from grace through mortal sin; that I may always rise to greater faith, and greater hope, and greater love of God and my neighbor, until such time as I am called upon to give an account of all my thoughts and words and deeds; and that, when all is done I may, with the repentant thief, hear these words of pardon and of love: "Amen I say to thee, this day thou shalt be with Me in paradise."[45]

287. (E) Father Joseph Anthony recommends that when the retreat is finished we: (A) thank God, (B) beware of relapses; (C) faithfully fulfill our good resolutions.

(1) THANKSGIVING. "How shall I make a return to the Lord for all the good He has done for me?"[46] We should recall the many special benefits God has granted during these spiritual exercises, consider the lights, the pious inclinations to good, our peace of conscience, etc. Truly, how shall we repay the Lord for all these aids to eternal salvation and for such

---

45. Luke 23:43.
46. Ps. 115:12.

singular graces? "The cup of salvation I will take up," says the psalmist, "and I will call upon the name of the Lord. My vows to God I will pay in the presence of all His people."[47] This will also be our fitting thanksgiving to God: that we take up the chalice of salutary mortification — by enduring, for love of Christ, every adversity on the path of perfection, every temptation, tribulation; and by calling upon the name of the Lord through prayer and meditation. "Praised be the Lord, I exclaim, and I am safe from my enemies,"[48] says the psalmist. We shall pay our vows to the Lord in the presence of all His people by fulfilling our good resolutions so that all may clearly see in us a change for the better, a renewal in Christ. St. John Chrysostom explains Psalm 149, an invitation to glorify the Lord, by saying: "Verbal gratitude is not sufficient; it has to be accompanied by the complement of deeds."[49] If we let the light of our life, the fulfillment of our retreat resolutions shine before men, that they may see our good works and glorify our Father in heaven, we shall live, says the same saint, a life that will glorify God. This is the best and most acceptable gratitude to God, the complete renovation of our spiritual life in justice and holiness of truth. We maintain this grateful attitude over our whole lifetime by faithfully pursuing whatever resolutions we have offered to God during these spiritual exercises.

(2) A HOLY FEAR. A state of grave disorder exists when we know the will of God and fail to obey it. "But that servant," says our Lord, "who knew his master's will, and did not make ready for Him and did not act according to His will, will be beaten with many stripes."[50] "For this is the will of God, your sanctification,"[51] declares St. Paul. The knowledge,

---

47. *Ibid.* 115:13-14.
48. *Ibid.* 17:4.
49. See Migne, *P. G.*, t. LV, col. 493.
50. Luke 12:47.
51. 1 Thess. 4:3.

the means and the motives to fulfill the divine will were all proposed to us during the retreat. But what does it profit us to have the means if through culpable negligence we fail to use them? We are in danger of becoming one of those cold and tepid religious who are concerned about everything except their spiritual perfection. They shoulder their crosses complainingly, obey unwillingly, seldom remain in their cell, and continually break silence. They avoid work but love idleness; they shorten their prayers but extend their useless talk; they incline toward externals but are averse to the internal; are indolent in regard to good thoughts but quick to harbor evil thoughts; eager to eat and drink, but plainly dejected when they must fast; they desire honors but shy away from any form of humiliation; are vehemently opposed to strict discipline, but always disposed to laxity. The man of God is faithful to the resolutions he has made under the inspiration of divine grace.

(3) FIDELITY. St. Paul advises: "Therefore, my beloved brethren, be steadfast and immovable, always abounding in the work of the Lord, knowing that your labor is not in vain in the Lord."[52]

True love is not satisfied with the first degree of perfection but always aims higher, continually desires what is more perfect. We must daily offer to God the spiritual sacrifices flowing from various virtues and always aspire to greater perfection. We must gird ourselves to run the way of perfection by means of the unceasing practice of a chosen virtue or an unrelenting battle against a determined vice. This labor will not be in vain in the Lord. We must frequently address our beloved Saviour: "Confirm, O God, this work which Thou hast wrought in me through the retreat. Strengthen my frailty, for I intend to pursue my enemies, to war against my flesh and its concupiscences, and I shall not desist until they are overcome.

---

52. 1 Cor. 15:58.

I would rather die than ever fail in the resolutions with which
Thy love has inspired me. So help me, Lord, with Thy grace!"

B. The Monthly Day of Recollection

288. Nearly everything that has been said of the yearly
retreat also applies to the monthly recollection. However,
James Alvarus suggests a few thoughts specifically applying
to the latter: "To grow in virtue it will be very useful to
select one day each month during which you remain free from
external occupations and devote yourself to an examination
of your ways and actions." He goes on to explain: "During
this day, pray long and devoutly, and recite the psalms with
attention and devotion. Set aside a longer period for spiritual
reading; act the part of a discriminating umpire, a strict judge
when you review your actions. Regarding the supernatural,
try to determine if you worship God simply and fervently,
whether you venerate the saints and aspire to the things of
heaven. Regarding your internal life, see whether you subjugate your body, check your senses and restrain your feelings.
Regarding your surroundings, examine yourself as to whether
you remove all superfluities, accept necessities with restraint,
and set a good example for your brethren. Regarding things
that are beneath you — material goods — find out if your
thoughts are becoming more detached, if you are growing in
virtue and living a tranquil life. These are the things that
should be done on the day of recollection: to correct our faults,
to strengthen our good points, and to spur ourselves on to
more heroic acts of virtue."[53]

---

53. *De vit. relig. inst.*, Lib. IV, cap. III.

CHAPTER III

THE MEANS OF SUBJECTING THE SENSES AND THE PASSIONS

289. The Supreme Author of all things created man as a composite of two elements: the spiritual and the animal. The spiritual principle is opened to God and conformed to Christ when the intellect, instructed in the divine law, and the will, aided by the grace of God, abandon themselves to the divine will and goodness. We obtain this desirable end by availing ourselves of the various means outlined in Chapters I and II.

The animal or lower part of man must also be opened to God's influence and conformed to Christ by subjecting the passions and senses to right reason and to faith. St. Augustine says, "Man received his body for the sake of service. God is the Master, the body the servant. Above man is the Creator; below him that which is created inferior to him. The rational soul is stationed in the middle position. The law of the soul is to adhere to what is superior, and to rule what is inferior to it."[1] If the superior part of man tends toward divine and spiritual things, the lower part, on the contrary, misled by concupiscence, searches for gratification, pleasure and worldly advantages; it grovels in vain and earthly things, thus holding back the superior part from a greater good. As a result, there is a continual battle between the two, as the Apostle teaches: "For the flesh lusts against the spirit, and the spirit against the flesh."[2]

ABNEGATION is the act of the will controlling the appetites and desires of man's lower nature by refusing to yield to their inordinate demands.

---

1. *Enarr. in Ps.,* CXLV.
2. Gal. 5:17.

RENUNCIATION goes further than abnegation in so far as it is the premeditated intention of depriving oneself of natural satisfactions. In a purgative sense, it means the elimination of all inordinate satisfactions. In the perfective sense it means the voluntary surrender of even legitimate pleasures. Perfective renunciation can be limited to a particular field, or can be total in an act of absolute sacrifice. Total renunciation does not mean that no pleasure or satisfaction will be had, but that none will be sought. It leaves to the will of God the distribution of His riches, unhindered by any human desire or effort directed toward an immediate reward of man's choosing. It opposes God's generosity to human greed.

MORTIFICATION applies to the senses or to the faculties rather than to their object. We renounce the world, but we mortify our flesh. The result of mortification is not the death of our senses, but their purification. Through the practice of abnegation and renunciation, our senses are *dead to the world,* cleared from the distortions of sin, burned and made luminous to the point of being increasingly sensitive to the signs of God's presence in His creatures.

Mortification consists in fighting concupiscence by performing directly opposite acts. The fires of the ensuing pains and sufferings will reduce and burn out the desires of the flesh.

CRUCIFIXION exceeds mortification. Here the will accepts, and often spontaneously increases, its share of suffering, not out of a desire for self-perfection, but out of that very highest of charities: the love of Christ, and Him crucified. Many saints have prayed for increased sufferings so that Christ would not be alone on the Cross. In crucifixion, man not only suffers: there is a form of mystical identification with Christ, the most perfect union of victims with the Victim on the Cross.

Crucifixion is not limited to mere unqualified acceptance of the cross. It is also the result of a vow on the part of the victim by which every pain is accepted in advance and related to the pain of Christ. It is a sublime participation of man in the sacrifice of the Son, eminently acceptable to the Father and blessed by the Spirit.

These four acts of virtue should be used together, for they assist each other. They are commonly designated by the term "mortification," used in a general sense.

Mortification in this sense is not a particular virtue, but rather an act of all the virtues combined; it is love by which we pursue what is truly good, our salvation and the glory of God. This love inclines us to live right and to work for our salvation and for the greater honor and glory of God; at the same time it helps us to deny, renounce, mortify and crucify whatever is an impediment to our final end.

Love is accompanied by the moral virtues. In a similar way mortification, which cannot develop perfectly without acts of moral virtue, avails itself of penance, humility, poverty, chastity, obedience, temperance, patience and modesty, so that love may be free to reach its full development.

Mortification is of two types either *active* or *passive*.

It is *active* when it is self-imposed; *passive* when adversity is calmly accepted as being sent or permitted by God.

Either of these types of mortification can be *internal* or *external*.

Mortification is *internal* when the internal powers, the intellect, the judgment, evil internal passions and inordinate affections, are subjected to right reason and to the divine will.

Properly speaking, *mortification* is external when the body is afflicted or chastised for a supernatural purpose. We say "properly speaking," for although mortifications of the senses are referred to as external, they are not all truly external. When we mortify any external sense, we do not, for the most part, mortify that particular sense so much as the internal passion: For instance, we mortify not so much the eye or the ear as our inordinate inclination to see and to hear. True external mortification is found only when the body itself is afflicted or chastised, as with hair shirts, flagellations, etc.

Now that we have clarified our concept of mortification, it remains for us to examine the different tools we shall use to achieve this work in the most perfect way. These tools are the moral virtues, particularly penance, temperance, fortitude and patience.

Among the many forms of penance practiced in the Seraphic Order, the following are the most important: the wearing of the religious habit, the use of the discipline, and nocturnal vigils.

Fasting is the most important act of temperance. With the aid of God's grace man is able to use these penances and acts of abstinence to subordinate his lower nature to the higher and to attain to conformity with Christ. God goes so far as to help man in this battle, either directly or through others, especially through superiors. By means of a hidden yet most admirable providence, and being mindful of the pliability of our souls, God — like an experienced farmer who prunes his trees to make them bear more fruit in their season — sends or allows various trials and adversities over and above what a man ordinarily expects. He breaks the shell of pride with hard but salutary blows, or sweetly tempers the sway of inordinate passions. To endure these, man stands in need of fortitude and patience, and through their exercise subjects his lower nature to the higher. Bodily infirmities are the most prominent of these adversities.

Since mortification is of such importance, let us consider its necessity before elaborating on the various means of mortification. We shall consider: (1) the importance of mortification in general; (2) the religious habit in particular; (3) the use of the discipline; (4) nocturnal vigils; (5) fasting; (6) the bearing of bodily infirmities.

Article I — Importance of Mortification

290. According to the teaching of Christ, the whole life of a Christian, and particularly of a religious, is a cross and a martyrdom. (1) Our Lord Himself imbued His disciples with the true notion of mortification. (2) He insisted on the necessity of practicing it. (3) He gave the reasons for its necessity.

§I. Meaning of Mortification for a Disciple of Christ

291. Speaking of the importance of subjecting our lower nature to the higher, our Lord not only declared it useful but necessary. He gave His followers reasons for abnegation, renunciation, mortification and crucifixion.

(1) **Concerning abnegation,** Jesus said: "If anyone wishes to come after Me, let him deny himself, and take up his cross daily, and follow Me."[3] We deny ourselves when, by a sincere conversion, we turn away from our former vices — for instance, by becoming temperate and restraining ourselves from whatever is licentious. "We abandon ourselves," says St. Gregory, "when we avoid what we were of old and try to attain that to which we are called by our new birth."[4] To deny ourselves, according to the doctrine of Christ, is to have no will of our own, to despise ourselves, to condemn our lives when necessary for the sake of Christ, to renounce our attachments and desires. It means avoiding what self-love suggests to us, but pursuing the prescriptions of the divine will. It implies that we are not to seek ourselves but God, that we have to avoid and banish whatever is opposed to the law of God, and put aside worldly and carnal desires and affections. In a word, abnegation signifies rejection and repudiation of anything, even if it is pleasant and agreeable, that is not in perfect agreement with the will of God.

---

3. Luke 9:23.
4. *Homil. XXXIII in Evang.,* 2, in Migne, *P. L.,* t. LXXV, col. 1233.

(2) **Renunciation.** Our Lord requires renunciation of His followers when He says: "Every one of you who does not renounce all that he possesses, cannot be My disciple."[5] With these words Jesus warns everyone who wishes to be associated with Him, that it takes great courage to give up all the things that might keep us from following Him. It could mean bearing with an untroubled mind the loss of all earthly goods, incurring the wrath of our neighbor, or even losing our very life.

(3) **Mortification.** In clear words, Jesus taught His disciples that mortification is a necessity: "He who loves his life loses it; and he who hates his life in this world, keeps it unto life everlasting."[6] A disciple of Christ should oppose his rebellious appetites and mortify them with appropriate measures. "I live, yet not I," is the cry of a man who mortifies himself. It is the cry of a man who would lose his own life to gain Christ, living in Him as it were through justice, wisdom, grace and peace.

Jesus confirmed the necessity of mortification when He said: "He who would save his life" — that is, preserve his life when it should be given up for Christ, or indulge in and satisfy his appetites and evil desires — "will lose it."[7] Again, "He who loses his life for My sake" — that is, he who, for the sake of Christ, either accepts death or bravely overcomes and stifles the evil desires of the flesh — "will save it."[8] He will acquire the life of the soul, the life of grace in time, and the life of glory in the future. St. Gregory illustrates the meaning of the text with an example: "We could say to the farmer: 'If you save your grain, you will lose it; but if you sow it, it will multiply.' For everyone knows that the seed disappears from sight and decays in the ground. However, after it de-

---

5. Luke 14:33.
6. John 12:25.
7. Luke 9:24.
8. *Ibid.* 9:24.

cays in the earth, new fruit springs forth. The soul goes through a period of persecution, but after it has cast off earthly desires a time of peace follows."[9]

(4) **Crucifixion.** Our Lord Himself indicated that crucifixion is the supreme degree of discipleship. "He who does not take up his cross and follow Me, is not worthy of Me."[10] The cross is the most severe and ignominious of trials. By the word "cross," our Lord means any torment, ignominy or death. And since many smaller acts of suffering are included in this highest offering of crucifixion, Jesus, having endured them Himself, demanded that His disciples bear the tribulations and afflictions which may arise from zeal for virtue, from the struggle against evil inclinations, from the ill-will of others, or from sickness, adversities and other difficulties.

Christ presented the true idea of mortification when He taught His followers that they cannot be His disciples without abnegation, renunciation, mortification and crucifixion. For these acts of virtue contain not only passive and internal mortifications but also active and external mortifications.

Our life as religious is a life of mortification. This mortification is not regulated by certain periods or extraordinary circumstances, but is a daily necessity. Jesus urges His disciple: "Let him deny himself, and take up his cross daily, and follow Me."[11] "By 'daily,'" Luke of Bruges explains, "Christ means that as day succeeds day, so cross follows cross. There is no end to adversity until we depart from this world. Otherwise a man might consider himself exempt from bearing the cross after having borne the first one with resignation. When a man has sustained many adversities, he is better prepared to endure each new one."[12] We must observe that our Lord adds:

---

9. *Homil. XXXII in Evang.,* 4, in Migne, *P. L.,* t. LXXVI, col. 1235.
10. Matt. 10:38.
11. Luke 9:23.
12. *In Lucam:* in Migne, *Scripturae sacrae cursus,* t. XII.

"And follow Me." We must follow Him so that He may
supply us with grace and teach us how to carry our cross. And
while it is consoling for us to know that in carrying the cross
we are made associates with Christ, it also mitigates the bitterness. To gain any merit from our cross, we must bear it in
the spirit of Christ: with resignation and patience, willingly,
for justice' sake, and finally, for the purpose of giving glory
to God."[13]

§ II. Purpose of Mortification

292. Our Lord, after establishing His doctrine on mortification and prescribing it as a requisite for discipleship, explained its necessity by adding: "For what does it profit a man
if he gain the whole world, but ruin or lose himself?"[14] that
is, if he falls prey to eternal damnation.

Now if the whole world — that is, control over the whole
world — all its wealth, pleasures, delights, and any other good
it may contain — can procure no true advantage, how worthless can a mere portion of it be?

The reason why man rejects Christ and thus loses himself
is indicated in Jesus' declaration: "Whoever is ashamed of
Me and My words, of him will the Son of Man be ashamed."[15]
In other words, Jesus will not recognize him as one of His
disciples, but will indignantly cast aside him who is ashamed to
carry his cross, to practice self-abnegation, to mortify his flesh
and to follow in the way of the Cross.

This teaching of our Lord on the observance of mortification has been handed down to the faithful, from the very
beginning of the Church even to the present day. The Apostle
writes: "If you have risen with Christ, seek the things that are
above, . . . not the things that are on earth. For you have died

---

13. Luke of Bruges, *loc. cit.*
14. Luke 9:25.
15. *Ibid.* 9:26.

and your life is hidden with Christ in God. . . . Therefore mortify your members which are on earth."[16] "Strip off the old man with his deeds."[17] He also writes: "And they who belong to Christ have crucified their flesh with its passions and desires."[18]

Convinced of this doctrine, all the saints have followed Christ crucified. When our Seraphic Father understood this doctrine, filled with the spirit of God he cried out, as Celano tells us: "This is what I want, this is what I seek, this I will do with all my heart." And, as Celano adds: "Overflowing with happiness, the servant of God began to put into practice the salutary counsel he had heard, neither permitting delay nor allowing anything to interfere. He removed the shoes from his feet, laid aside his staff and, content with a single tunic, he exchanged his belt for a cord. Clad in this tunic which he formed in the shape of a cross, he prepared himself most austerely so that he would be able to crucify his flesh with its vices and sins."[19]

To be a disciple of Christ consists in pursuing the way of abnegation, renunciation, mortification and crucifixion. "Just as the body preserves life by a twofold action: (1) by aspiration, the taking in of pure air to expand the lungs and thus purify the blood; and (2) by expiration, or the expelling of impure and harmful air which is detrimental to health; similarly there is a twofold process," says Father Le Gaudier, "by which the vicissitudes of the spiritual life are overcome: prayer and mortification. Through prayer the spirit is drawn to the things of God, and the life of the soul, the life of the inner man, is strengthened. Mortification expels the unhealthy air of our lower nature which corrupts the will; the poisonous exhalation which induces spiritual death."[20]

16. Col. 3:1, 2, 3, 5.
17. *Ibid.* 3:9.
18. Gal. 5:24.
19. Celano, *Legenda Prima*, cap. IX, p. 25.
20. *De perfectione vitae spiritualis*, Pars V, sect. XIII, cap. II.

We must learn to master ourselves, to get used to subjection, to rejoice in humiliations and to glory in the correction given us. These are matters we wish to develop more fully.

*Article II — The Franciscan Garb

293. Our particular habit is prescribed for many reasons. The change from secular clothes to the habit indicates a change of ways. In a sense the habit makes it necessary for the members of an Order to lead a devout life. For their holy attire marks them as religious by profession, signifies their separation from the world, and so removes them from the danger of useless wanderings. Moreover, the religious garb is an outward expression of the vow of poverty. And, by poverty in dress the religious professes his contempt for the world.

The habits of the various Orders in the Church differ from one another, so that the particular work for the glory of God performed by the wearer may be determined at sight.

When a Franciscan thinks about his habit, he should consider it with regard to its (1) nature; (2) quality; (3) signification; so that seeing himself in the same Franciscan habit which so many saints of the Seraphic Order have worn, consecrated as it were by their merits and life, he may be ashamed of himself for being so different from them and thus arouse a sincere desire to imitate the holy confreres who wore the habit worthily.

§ I. The Nature of the Franciscan Habit

The habit consists of one tunic with a capuche and another, an inner tunic, if desired; the cord, and the Rosary.

The friars should be content with as few and as simple handkerchiefs and drawers as necessity demands.

What St. John Chrysostom said of the religious garb of his time is also applicable to the Franciscan habit: "The cloth becomes these men, for they are not dressed like unmanly and effeminate people who make a show of their apparel, but rather as messengers of God, as an Elias and an Eliseus, as John and the Apostles might be dressed."[21]

§ II. The Quality of the Franciscan Habit

Our holy Father St. Francis, who made most exalted poverty the foundation of his Order, prescribed that the brethren should be clothed in coarse garments. Poverty and austerity must be reflected in the Franciscan habit; not, however, to such an extent that anyone seeing it would be horrified or led to ridicule.

(1) In regard to the rough and coarse garments, the brethren should wear the commoner and coarser material that can be conveniently procured in the places in which they live.

(2) The cord should have simple knots and should have no singularity.

(3) The sandals should be simple and plain and should conform to poverty, having no ornamentation. "It is becoming for religious to wear coarse attire," says St. Thomas, "since the religious state is a state of penance and of contempt for worldly glory."[22]

§ III. The Signification of the Franciscan Garb

(1) The habit with the capuche has the form of a cross, reminding us that we are crucified to the world and the world to us.

(2) The capuche or cowl, the particular mark of the Franciscan habit, reminds the religious that he should not fasten his gaze upon the world, but must be mortified and guard against the deceits of the devil.

---

21. *Serm. 68 in Matt.*, n. 3, in *P. G.*, t. LVIII, col. 644.
22. *Summa theol.*, IIa IIae, q. 187, a. 6, in corp.

(3) The cord with which we gird our loins signifies the mortification with which the Franciscan must surround the bodily members that contain the seeds of licentiousness. "Our cincture is a rope," says St. Bonaventure, "and ropes are generally used to bind up sackcloth. However, I believe the reason that St. Francis chose a rope for himself was that he read in the Gospel: 'They bound Him and led Him away, and delivered Him to Pontius Pilate' (Matt. 27:2). And in his usual manner of following the holy Gospel to the letter, Francis made the coarseness of the rope harmonize with the coarseness of the habit, thereby effecting greater mortification of the flesh."[23]

(4) Sandals. No footgear other than sandals is allowed. According to St. Jerome, "Plato said that the two extremities of the body should not be covered, lest the head and the feet become too tender. For when these have become hardened, the rest of the body is more robust."[24] The Seraphic Doctor St. Bonaventure maintains that St. Francis wished to imitate Christ, who told His Apostles to wear sandals.

St. Gregory Nazianzen declared that the early monks observed this precept: "I desire to behold that holy choir singing psalms. They set an example of a better life for everyone else. They silently preach the laws of God and of the Gospel. Their dress itself is a sign of virtue for, like the Apostles, their hair is untrimmed and their feet are bare."[25]

§ IV. The Obligation of Living
According to the Signification of the Garb

If the Franciscan habit is a symbol, "let everyone take diligent care that he does not bear the sign without the signifi-

---

23. *Exp. Reg.*, cap. II, n. 11.
24. Quoted by St. Bonaventure in *Exp. Reg.*, cap. II, n. 17.
25. *De recol. monachi*, oratio 6 (alias 12), quoted by St. Bonaventure in *Exp. Reg., loc. cit.*

cation, that he does not wear the garment without the virtue, lest he become like a sepulcher whitened on the outside but full of filth within. Whoever is clothed in these sacred garments but not vested in upright conduct will be the more despicable before God, the more venerable he appears before men."[26]

To practice mortification we must:

(1) *Flee vanity and superfluity.* "A vain heart impresses the mark of vanity upon the body," says St. Bernard, "and exterior superfluity is an indication of interior vanity."[27] St. Basil teaches that "we should not seek fine clothing, but choose the coarser, so that even in this matter we may show humility, lest we appear to be elegant, lovers of self and lacking in fraternal charity. For whoever desires splendid attire loses charity and humility."[28]

(2) *Cherish the annoyances inherent in our garment* as means well suited to mortifying the flesh and subjecting ourselves to God. St. Bonaventure writes, "Those who rely on their own inclinations rather than on the dispositions of Christ, say that it is better to be shod rather than unshod, when teaching divine truths, so as not to impede the word of God. But let these people remember that no manner of spreading the Gospel is more fitting than that in which the Gospel was first preached — with bare feet. I admit that it is an arduous penance to go about with bare feet. . . . Yet the friars like the Apostle Paul went rejoicing 'in cold and nakedness' (2 Cor. 11: 27). Disregarding winter rigors and summer heat, they traveled unshod to the most remote parts of the world. Tartars, barbarians, Saracens, Catholics or schismatics, in every part of the world that knew the friars, were witnesses to this fact. In their case unshod feet were not an impediment to

---

26. Innocent III, *De myst. altar.*, Lib. I, cap. LXIV, in Migne, *P. L.,* t. CCXVII, col. 799.

27. *Apol. ad Guilelm. abb.*, cap. X, n. 24, in Migne, *P. L.,* t. CLXXXII, col. 913.

28. *Const. monast.*, cap. XXX, in Migne, *P. G.,* t. XXXI, col. 1419.

spreading the word of God."[29] And what St. Bonaventure asserts of bare feet can be confirmed by the example of countless friars.

"A man must take care," says St. Augustine, "to renounce completely the devil and his pomps, lest after profession he fall victim to the demon through fine clothes, and he whom Christ wished to liberate by His grace become chained by trappings of sin."[30]

"Lay people judge us by our habit," says Father Neumayer. "We even become venerable in their opinion when our life corresponds to our habit; if it does not, they consider us hypocrites. All will rise to seek the humble Franciscan, but they will scoff at a proud one, and say: 'Change either your habit or your life.' Although certain actions may be harmless and innocent in themselves, they often appear indecorous when they do not conform to the way of life which the habit signifies. The habit is a sort of mouthpiece, bespeaking who you are and what kind of person you profess to be."[31]

Article III—Use of the Discipline, or Chastisement of the Body

294. Various corporal chastisements are recommended to keep the body from rebelling against the spirit, and to make certain that the body will always be subject to the spirit in all things. The friars, clad in poor garments, sleeping on coarse beds, should strive to conform to their Seraphic Father, whose bed was often the bare ground, and with our Lord, who used a similar resting place in the wilderness. Mindful of the need for mortification of the flesh, they should imitate their sweet Saviour Jesus and try to experience in themselves, by

---

29. *Exp. Reg.,* cap. II, n. 18.

30. *Serm. de Symb.,* in the appendix to t. VIII of the works of St. Augustine; in Migne, *P. L.,* t. XLII, col. 1119.

31. Neumayer, *Via compendii ad perfectionem* (Munich, 1757), Part II, p. 179.

the salutary use of the discipline, a small portion of His sufferings while He was bound to the pillar. This and similar penitential exercises should be carefully observed, for corporal chastisement: (1) is a law of Christian life; (2) produces many good results; (3) must be performed with due moderation.

§ 1. The Necessity of Corporal Chastisement

Since our nature is such that the flesh wars against the spirit, every Christian, and particularly every religious, must assume the obligation of controlling his mind and chastising his flesh in order to bring it into subjection. St. Basil teaches: "The body must be chastised and restrained; not led about and driven by its animal impulses. These disorders by means of which the body disturbs the soul, must be subjected to reason with a lash; the mind must never give free rein to voluptuousness or it will be led like a rider on an unbridled horse and violently thrown."[32] St. Paul, writing to the Corinthians, says: "I chastise my body and bring it into subjection, lest perhaps after preaching to others I myself should be rejected."[33] This means: I beat this body of flesh with vehement strokes. I persevere despite difficulties and dangers, in plagues, in prisons, in labors, in sleepless nights, in fastings, and so forth. And I use these stripes, molestations, torments and sufferings so as to chastise my body and make it entirely subject to the spirit, that, like a conquered slave, it may faithfully serve its master. St. Paul wrote these words not only to the Corinthians but to us also, so that following his example we may learn how to act in the arena of this life. This struggle of which St. Paul speaks extends over the whole lifetime of a Christian without any truce.

---

32. *Homil. de legend. gent. libr.,* n. 7, in Migne, *P. G.,* t. XXXI, col. 583.
33. 1 Cor. 9:27.

§ II. The Good Results of Bodily Chastisement

Inspired by the Holy Spirit, nearly all the saints imposed scourgings on themselves and, by subjecting the body to the spirit, obtained many salutary benefits, among which were: (1) the remission of sins; (2) a holy fervor in the service of God.

(1) **The remission of sins.** One day when St. Mechtilde was carried in spirit to heaven before the throne of God, she heard a most pleasing sound re-echo in the firmament of heaven from the sound of the discipline, which some Sisters were taking in common. At this the angels joyfully manifested their delight, demons fled from tormented souls, other poor souls were relieved of punishments, and the chains of the guilty broken.[34] What is more excellent and magnificent than willingly to offer satisfaction to Divine Justice for sins while we are still on earth. "There will be no punishment in the next life for those who in this life scourge themselves with a penitential discipline," says St. Isidore; "for if we strike ourselves now on account of our sins, we shall at that time be found without sins."[35]

(2) **Holy fervor.** By means of corporal punishments and chastisements, a religious demonstrates his contempt for carnal pleasures, aspires to the things of heaven, acquires perseverance in prayer and diligent obedience to authority. He burns with a zeal like that of the martyrs and desires to be associated with them, which is in effect martyrdom by desire. "Is it absurd," asks St. Peter Damian, "for the Church to use in time of peace what she formerly used in time of strife? Even if the hand of the executioner is checked from delivering the fatal blow to the martyrs, what difference does it make as long as the same holy devotion, deserving fellowship with the holy

---

34. Cf. *Lib. Spec. grat.*, II, cap. XXVI.
35. *De Veteri et Novo Testamento quaestiones,* Quaestiones in Deut., cap. XXII, n. 2, in Migne, *P. L.,* t. LXXXV, col. 370.

martyrs, is evident? If I willingly chastise myself in the sight
of God, I would manifest the same flame of true devotion to
God if I met an executioner. If this punishment is so sweet
to me that I inflict it upon myself when it is lacking, how
willingly I would accept it also from the hand of the persecu-
tor! For Christ I wish to endure martyrdom, but because of
my lack of zeal I have not the opportunity. At least, then,
I can show the readiness of my will by dealing myself some
blows."[36]

St. Thomas teaches that this corporal chastisement must be
inflicted with discretion or it is not pleasing to God. When
its purpose is to restrain concupiscence without being too
detrimental to our nature, it is pleasing to God.

§ III. Discretion in the Use of Corporal Chastisement

Everyone must adapt corporal chastisements to his capacity
for endurance. Blosius advises novices not to try extraordinary
penances even though they know that many saints led extremely
rigorous lives. The saints knew that they lived in a way pleasing to God, for they were enlightened by the Holy Spirit.
Many are led by the fervor they experience in the beginning
of their conversion to overburden nature in this matter of
corporal penances, and as a result become unfit for the service
of God. "We must act discreetly in this matter," warns St.
Bernard, "lest the desire for flagellations cost us our eternal
salvation, and in our endeavor to subdue an enemy we bring
death to a citizen. Take your physical constitution and its
capabilities into account. Consider your build and impose
corporal penances on yourself accordingly. Preserve your body
as an unimpaired offering to your Creator. We have seen
many so abuse their poor flesh at the beginning of their spiritual life and so exceed the limits of discretion that they were

---

36. *Epistola 27,* in Migne, *P.L.,* t. CXLIV, col. 416.

rendered unfit for divine services, and required better and warmer clothing for a long time."[37] Hair shirts, a hard bed, flagellations, and similar acts of penance performed solely for the honor of God will certainly be pleasing to the Lord. For taming the flesh of robust youths they have no equal. But in the final analysis, true love of God will unite men much more intimately with God.

Article IV — Nocturnal Vigils

295. Among the more austere penitential practices for subjecting the body to the spirit, nocturnal vigils should by no means be omitted. We will, however, more eagerly perform these if we realize: (1) their background and antiquity; (2) their utility.

§ I. Background and Antiquity of Vigils

Both the Old and New Testaments recommend the practice of night vigils.

(1) *In the Old Testament.* Isaia cried to the Lord, "My soul yearns for You in the night, yes, my spirit within me keeps vigil for You."[38]

David the Prophet admonishes: "Come, bless the Lord, all you servants of the Lord who stand in the house of the Lord during the hours of night."[39] And lest we imagine that only the early evening hours are meant, he says in another place:[40] "At midnight I rise to give You thanks because of Your just ordinances."

We find these and many similar passages in the Scriptures written by holy men like so many alarms to arouse us from our

---

37. *Serm. 40 de divers.,* n. 7, in Migne, *P. L.,* t. CLXXXIII, col. 652.
38. Isa. 26:9.
39. Ps. 133:1.
40. *Ibid.* 118:62.

sleep of torpor so that, heeding their admonitions and examples we too may undertake these salutary night vigils.

(2) Nocturnal vigils are also mentioned in the New Testament. St. Luke, speaking of our Redeemer, says that Jesus "continued all night in prayer to God."[41] He spent the night praying, certainly not for Himself but that we might know that we all have to watch and pray. He reproached Peter at the time of His Passion, saying: "Could you not, then, watch one hour with Me?" And He admonished the other Apostles: "Watch and pray, that you may not enter into temptation."[42]

Instructed by these exhortations and strengthened by these teachings, the Apostles kept vigils and commended their observance to others. On the night Peter was freed from prison by an angel, he went to a house where he found many of the faithful gathered together, not for a good night's rest or in order to celebrate the event, but for the purpose of watching and praying.

In his Epistle St. Peter admonished us: "Be sober, be watchful!"[43] St. Paul exhorts the Corinthians to keep vigils: "Watch, stand fast in the faith, act like men, be strong."[44]

Keeping vigils is an old devotional practice, one with which nearly all the saints were familiar. The members of some religious Orders recite Matins and Lauds at midnight, according to the example of the royal psalmist and of the saints, that their houses may echo, day and night, with the praises of the Lord.

The Nocturnal Adoration Society of the United States keeps the practice of vigils alive among the laity also. This Society was founded in 1882 to provide for public adoration of the Blessed Sacrament during the hours of the night. The Society has 70,000 members in three hundred and forty branches in thirty-three states, the District of Columbia and Panama.

---

41. Luke 6:12.
42. Matt. 26:40-41.
43. 1 Peter 5:8.
44. 1 Cor. 16:13.

§ II. The Utility of Vigils

Devout and fervent religious understand what St. Nicetas means when he asserts: "It is easier to feel the usefulness of this exercise than to explain it."[45] For we "taste and see how good the Lord is."[46] If we taste, we shall see how many annoyances these vigils remove, how much mental apathy they dispel, what great lights they pour upon the vigilant and prayerful soul, what graces they readily bring, to fill his whole being with joy. The flesh is chastised, vices are subdued, chastity is strengthened by vigils. Long meditations and fervent prayers are good, but nocturnal meditation is far more acceptable and efficacious. During the day our many needs prove a disturbance, our many occupations dissipate the mind, our many cares divide our attention. The time of night, by contrast, is solitary, quiet, and made for prayer and vigils. Since the hours of the night are free from worldly occupations, we can more easily collect our senses, more readily direct our whole attention to the service of God. Most certainly vigils are pleasing to God and bring choice blessings.

In order to gain these results, it is important not only to keep watch with the eyes but also with the heart. While our lips are praying, our mind must also be elevated. For a vigil to bear fruit, our heart must be closed to the devil and opened wide to Christ, and the words of our lips should flow from our heart. Such are the vigils which God will accept. Such are the nights of prayer which, carried on under the eyes of God with diligence and true devotion, will be eminently salutary.

Like the saints, we should appreciate these nocturnal vigils as much as we can, lest it be said of us, "They have slept their sleep; and ... have found nothing in their hands."[47] It

45. Cf. *Opusc. I,* in Migne, *P. L.,* t. LXVIII, p. 370 et seq.
46. Ps. 33:9.
47. Ps. 75:6, Challoner-Douay version.

is better to be able to say: "By night my hands are stretched out without flagging."[48] And again, "It is good to give thanks to the Lord, and to sing praise to Your name, Most High, to proclaim Your kindness at dawn and Your faithfulness throughout the night."[49]

*Article V — Fasting in the Franciscan Order

296. Concupiscence of the flesh is increased according as the flesh is pampered through luxuries and fancy foods and drinks. The Christian, and particularly the religious, should, as a contemporary of St. Bernard says, "eat to live, not live to eat."[50] We shall now discuss the necessity and usefulness of fasting and indicate the fasts prescribed and recommended in the Seraphic Order.

§ I. The Necessity and Value of Fasting

The necessity of fasting can be proved from the fact that it was imposed upon man by God, sanctioned by the example of Christ, handed down to us by the Apostles and prescribed by the Church. We can judge the value of fasting by the effects it produces.

Imposed upon man by God. When God installed our first parents in Paradise, He commanded them not to eat of the fruit of the forbidden tree and strengthened His order with the penalty of death. The transgression of this command broke open the floodgates of continuous calamities. The same Almighty God announced through His prophets that fasting was a penitential work acceptable to Him.

Sanctioned by the example of Christ. Before He began His public life, our Saviour fasted forty days even though

---

48. Ps. 76:3.
49. *Ibid.* 91:2-3.
50. *Lib. de Pass. Dom.,* or *Vitis Myst.,* cap. XLIV, n. 139; found among St. Bernard's works in Migne, *P. L.,* t. CLXXXIV, col. 719.

He had no need for the helps of penance. In like manner He charged the Apostles with the obligation of fasting after He, the bridegroom of the parable, would leave them.

Apostolic tradition. The practice of fasting became common in the Catholic Church so that the faithful might sanctify certain days through its use, prepare themselves for celebrating the feasts, and at the same time more easily dispose themselves for prayer by curbing concupiscence. Sacred Scripture is our proof that the Apostles set the example by fasting together with the other Christians. The Fathers of the Church devoted entire books to the subject of fasting.

Legislation of the Church. The Church has accepted fasting as an Apostolic tradition, sanctioned it in her canonical legislation and prescribed it for all the faithful.

The effects of fasting. The bestowal of extraordinary gifts unmistakably proves how eminently pleasing fasting is to God. Through the prayers of persons who fasted, God delivered besieged cities. He has received into His favor cities once destined for annihilation. Humble souls have obtained remission of sins through their fasting. Hence the Church sings in her Lenten Preface: "On those who chastise their bodies by fasting, [God] bestows the restraining of evil passions, uplifting of heart, virtues and heavenly favors." St. Bonaventure remarks that fasting is the life of the angels, the death of sin, the destruction of vices and the remedy leading to salvation. By its observance, we follow the perfect way of holiness, we reach a clear knowledge of truth and we acquire constancy in virtue.

It is no wonder, then, that our Seraphic Father has prescribed the rigorous fasts described in the following paragraphs.

§ II. Fasts in the Seraphic Order

297. FROM THE RULE. The Rule of the Friars Minor speaks of three fasts: Two imposed by precepts, the fast from the feast of All Saints to Christmas, and the Lenten fast of the Church; and the third, a voluntary fast on the forty days following the Epiphany, for those who wish to keep such a fast.

At other times the friars are not bound by rule to fast, except on Fridays, kept as a day of fast because our Lord chose to be crucified on that day.

CONCLUSION. These are some of the means of mortification used in the Seraphic Order to bring the body into conformity with Christ. Quoting the words of St. John Capistran, we can say, "Who can doubt that at the time of the first friars not only St. Francis, but even his companions and brothers zealously observed greater penances than we do today? Where are the breastplates of iron that the friars of those days wore on their bare bodies? Where are the garments made of hair cloth? Where the frequent fasts on bread and water? Where the many vigils? What has happened to the disciplines which subdue the flesh, the flagellations which recall the sufferings of Christ? . . . Is there anyone in our day who sincerely looks down upon gratifications and earnestly desires to be despised by everyone? Who among us now persists in prayer from late at night until dawn as did the early friars, drawn as they were by excessive spiritual sweetness? . . . When I think of these things, my tongue is unable to describe the fervor of the first fathers, my hand is at a loss as to what to write, my heart and mind are unable to express themselves. Oh, if we could only return to that austere life of old! If we cannot perform all these penances because of our human frailty, would that we might walk in their holy footsteps as best we can! For it is written: 'Those who will not imitate the holy martyrs to the best of their ability will likewise not be able to reach the blessed state of the martyrs.' (The latter is an excerpt found among the works of St. Augustine; see Migne, *P. L.,* t. XXXIX, col. 1261.)"[51]

Article VI — The Bearing of Bodily Infirmities

298. Our Seraphic Father manifested a sincere concern for the sick and strove to impress a similar attitude on his spiritual sons. The Rule states: "And when any friar falls sick, the other friars shall serve him as they would wish to be served themselves."[52]

The Rule itself seems to set aside all its regulations when it treats of the sick. Yet the sick friar should see to it that the infirmities serve his spiritual advancement. We shall therefore discuss how the sick friars should be treated: (1) They should avail themselves of a physician and medicines;(2) they should not be too solicitous regarding their recovery; (3) the other friars should not form a judgment concerning the seriousness of the sickness; (4) the superior's solicitude should be paternal; (5) superiors should be of service to the sick; (6) the sick friars should implore divine aid; (7) they should patiently bear their infirmity.

§ I. The Services of a Physician, and Medicine

299. Holy Scripture teaches us not to neglect the aid of a physician in sickness. "Hold the physician in honor," says Ecclesiasticus, "for he is essential to you, and God it was who established his profession. From God the doctor has his wisdom. . . . God makes the earth yield healing herbs which the prudent man should not neglect."[53]

---

51. Letter of St. John Capistran, dated January 2, 1455; found in Van Loo's *Stimulus Seraphicae conversationis,* p. 176 et seq.

52. Chapter VI.

53. Sirach 38:1-2, 4.

St. Basil outlines various reasons why we should avail ourselves of the services of a physician in case of serious sickness:

(1) Sacred Scripture enumerates medicine among the gifts of God, and orders physicians to be honored by reason of their necessity.

(2) We use other sciences without harm to ward off physical inconveniences, such as agriculture to dispel famine, weaving to cover our nakedness, architecture for protection against the elements; so also the science of medicine to prevent sickness.

(3) God placed healing powers in herbs and in many other things He created on the earth and in the sea, so that human industry might use them to cure sickness.

(4) The medical arts commend temperance, since they object to luxuries, condemn drunkenness, frown on sumptuous banquets, delicately prepared sauces, and so forth.

The religious should use medicines as needed to overcome sickness; St. Basil himself prescribed medicines for his monks. St. Augustine, in his Epistle to the Virgins writes: "If sickness requires the body to be bathed, this should not be postponed too long. Upon the advice of a physician it should be done without complaint. Even if the patient is unwilling, the order should be carried out for the sake of health. . . .

"And if a servant of God definitely tells of suffering from a hidden pain, she must be believed without a doubt. But when it is a case of requiring pleasant remedies and the sickness is doubtful, a physician should be consulted."[54]

Summing it up, then, St. Augustine warns of two things: (1) that the sick should not manifest too great an anxiety about their recovery; (2) that the healthy brethren should not murmur against the sick or against their superiors.

---

54. *Epistola 211*, n. 13, in Migne, *P. L.*, t. XXXIII, col. 963.

§ II. Excessive Care of Health

300. People who take too much care for their health, says St. Bernard, are on the watch for good food, but neglect good morals. "They display their character by remarks such as, 'This is bad for the eyes, this for the head, this for the chest, or stomach. Beans form gas, cheese weighs on the stomach. Milk harms the head, drinking too much water weakens the chest. Cabbage fosters melancholy and leeks cause cholera. Fish does not agree with my constitution.' What fastidiousness! All the streams, fields, gardens or cellars together could scarcely furnish the food you wish to eat! Remind yourself that you are a monk, not a medic; you are not to base your judgments solely on your physical constitution but primarily on your religious profession."[55] St. Bernard nevertheless mentions that if anyone complains of a hidden pain, he should be believed without doubting.

§ III. We Should Not Misjudge the Sick

301. Healthy friars who regard the sicknesses of their brethren as imaginary often torture the sick. Such friars, who by their taunts and annoyances add to the misery of the sick, take the risk of being punished by God with the same infirmity. St. Bonaventure warns that "all kindness must be shown to the sick and crippled, because they have been struck by the Lord. If others afflict them with additional pains, their very misery cries aloud to the merciful Father against those who abuse them. . . . A sick person who cannot accept his suffering is still more troubled when he is not consoled by the persons who could help him . . . and have compassion for him. The strong and healthy cannot know the tortures of the sick; therefore, they do not know how to show compassion. But when they themselves suffer, they will then understand. If they object

---

55. *In Cant.,* Serm. 30, n. 10, 11, in Migne, *P. L.,* t. CLXXXIII, col. 938.

because some always exaggerate their sickness, should all be judged hypocrites on that account?"[56]

§ IV. Paternal Solicitude of the Superiors for the Sick

302. According to the teaching of the Seraphic Doctor, a good superior realizes that he is the father of his brethren and that all, particularly the sick, the feeble, and the weary, have a special claim to his paternal affection. St. Bonaventure divides the sick into three classes. "To the first class belong the bed-ridden, suffering from serious illnesses. The second class is composed of those who are able to move about the house or around the grounds, but frequently suffer severe pains, such as gallstones and the like. The third class is made up of those who do not suffer from definite sickness, but whose body is crippled and without strength. Old people, those exhausted by work, and those afflicted with natural infirmities which temporarily incapacitate them, belong to this class."[57]

Superiors are bound, the Seraphic Doctor continues, to assist the sick according to the example of our Seraphic Father. Superiors should supply medical care; they should relax the rigor of our life in regard to food, clothing, vigils where health demands; and should exempt as much as needed, in such cases, from duties of office and other things of this kind. Thomas of Celano writes that Francis manifested compassion for the infirm and a deep solicitude for their needs. "He was earnestly concerned about the condition of each sick friar, offering words of compassion when other aid was impossible. He even used to eat on fast days so that the sick might not fear to do the same, and he was not ashamed to beg meat publicly for the infirm. Once when he learned that one of the sick friars had a particular liking for grapes, he immediately

---

56. *De sex al. Seraph.*, cap. III, n. 3, 4.
57. *Ibid.*, n. 2.

led him into a vineyard and, seating himself under the vine, he began to eat first to encourage the other."[58]

Friars who complain about the paternal solicitude of the superior when it is in regard to the weak and infirm, sin against charity. For, as St. Bonaventure explains, "They [the sick] should be refreshed lest they become downcast. To act otherwise would be against the virtues of mercy, charity and prudence, because the sick by their counsel, zeal and pious example sustain the Order in its vigor and prevent it from losing its pristine purity. Although their bodily strength is gone, their value lies in their weakness itself. At least no one should be allowed to fail to have mercy for them, for by such an action carnality is fostered in the Order. Any healthy youth brought up according to prudence of the flesh, seeing such actions would say to himself, 'If such men, who deliver up their bodies to many labors for the building up of the Order, are permitted to perish without mercy once they are incapacitated, I will take care to spare my body and carefully cherish it lest the same happen to me.' And so no one will be willing to give himself completely to the service of God."[59]

We should guard against criticizing our superior even if he has recourse to money for the relief of the infirm. This is not only permitted, but at times the superior is bound by grave obligation to use money, as our holy Father Francis has written in the Rule, since charity is more precious than poverty.

The Seraphic Doctor affirms that it is well for "a superior sometimes to have experienced the sicknesses others must endure so that he may learn compassion."[60] The healthy friars should not form evil judgments concerning the care which superiors lavish on the infirm, but should rather offer every service of charity to their sick confreres.

58. *Legenda Secunda*, c. XXXIII, p. 300.
59. St. Bonaventure, *Determinationes quaest.*, Pars I, q. IX.
60. St. Bonaventure, *De sex al. Seraph.*, cap. III, n. 6.

§ V. Relieving the Burdens of the Sick

303. All the expositors of the Rule agree that if superiors and infirmarians do not manifest a sincere care for the sick, the other friars are obliged to supply for this defect. Even if there is no neglect, the friars are bound in charity to visit their sick brethren. "Neglect not to visit the sick," says Sirach; "for these things you will be loved."[61] We should be of assistance, not only to those who are sick in the convent, but to all men, either by spending some time with them or by some other service of piety or charity. The friars should take care that they do not become a nuisance, bothering the infirm with tedious conversations, babbling worldly news and supplying other useless and annoying distractions. D. Maurus Wolter writes, "Your brother is a chosen member of Christ, a beautiful image of Him. He is a companion of Christ in His Passion, he plays a role in the drama of Calvary. Whenever proper, you should approach the sick with holy reverence and piety, adoring Jesus present in him and serving him in gratitude, zeal and charity. . . . You should take the place of . . . an angel and be a most obliging friend. In case of a serious illness, when it is clear that the time of the death struggle is fast approaching, you should prove a loyal companion in the fight, comforting the other's afflicted spirit, elevating his mind, consoling and fortifying him with prayers and other aids."[62]

But if the superior, the infirmarian, and every friar is bound to show charity, meekness, and benevolence to the sick, the sick also are bound to implore divine aid and patiently to bear their infirmities.

---

61. Sirach 7:35.

62. *Praecipua ordinis monastici elementa,* VI, Opera pietatis (Bruges, 1880), pp. 617 et seq.

§ VI. Seeking Divine Aid

304. As we have already seen, it is not wrong to seek medical aid when we are sick; but we must place our greatest confidence in divine assistance. Sirach advises, "My son, when you are ill, delay not, but pray to God, who will heal you."[63] St. Ambrose warns, "Let us beware, lest we seem to place more confidence in the skill of the physician and in the healing power of herbs than in the power of the Lord. We must first fly to Him who is able to cure the infirmities of our souls. Certain persons acting in the opposite way seek first the aid of man and then, as a last resort, the aid of God."[64] St. Jerome says, "The skill of a physician is valueless without the mercy of God."[65] St. Basil confirms this statement of St. Jerome and gives the following reasons:

(1) We must primarily trust in the mercy of God. He wishes us to be cured also through natural means, so that we may more clearly recognize His beneficence. God is the Creator of all medicines.

(2) There are some diseases sent by God as scourges for our sins. Not all sicknesses have their origin in natural causes or in unhealthy living conditions. Those which spring from natural causes readily yield to medical care, but the others are often inflicted by God as punishment for sin. Hence the Apostle could say: "This is why many among you" — namely, unworthy communicants — "are infirm and weak, and many sleep."[66] We should imitate him who in the prophecy of Michea says, "The wrath of the Lord I will endure because I have sinned against Him,"[67] and I will bring forth fruits of penance.

---

63. Sirach 38:9
64. *De Cain et Abel,* cap. X, n. 40, in Migne, *P. L.,* t. XIV, col. 355.
65. *In Isaiam,* Lib. VIII, cap. XXVI, versus 14, in Migne, *P. L.,* t. XXIV, col. 310.
66. 1 Cor. 11:30.
67. Michea 7:9.

(3) God afflicts some people with sickness in order to test their virtue, as in the case of Job; He afflicts others like Lazarus, so that He may reward them more abundantly in the next life.

Those afflicted by the Lord should implore divine aid, and if the sickness is serious they should have recourse to their superiors and to their confessors so as to receive the Last Sacraments. "Is any one among you sick? Let him bring in the presbyters of the Church, and let them pray over him, anointing him with oil in the name of the Lord. And the prayer of faith will save the sick man, and the Lord will raise him up."[68]

§ VII. Patience in Sickness

305. Supported by divine help, a sick person should be able to bear with patience the diseases of the flesh, and many other excruciating torments, and should not too readily consider himself despised and neglected. Our Seraphic Father advises the sick: "Patiently bear your illness and do not fall into temptation if everything does not go your way." Thomas of Celano says that Francis once wrote: "I beg all my sick friars not to become irritated by their infirmities nor infuriated against God or their brethren."[69]

The sick friar should observe, to the extent that he can, the Rule, statutes, laws and customs. It is not required that the aged friars and those suffering from illness be strictly observant of the fasts, vigils and other externals, but they should zealously observe silence as best they can at the prescribed times and places, for no one can truly understand or sufficiently realize how fruitful and useful are such practices.

"Resign yourself to God," says Blessed John Ruysbroeck, "and do not grumble about the infidelity of men or the lack of comforts or the painfulness of your sickness. Even if no

---

68. James 5:14-15.
69. *Loc. cit.,* p. 300.

one at all should visit you, do not complain or judge anyone, but receive whatever happens as coming from the hand of God, no matter what He wishes to give you. Eat and drink the things you are served, . . . even if the food is too salty, or is burned or tasteless. Remember how our Lord, plagued by a parching thirst and tormented in the worst way, tasted gall and vinegar and was silent. . . . Perhaps something desirable and necessary may be lacking. Then you may speak of it to those around you. If you obtain it, thank God; but if not, be patient and gladly go without it for love of God, and God will be your reward."[70]

Sickness can be a remarkably effective way to subject man's lower nature to his higher nature, to make the latter conform with Christ. "I believe it is good for you to continue to suffer," says St. Gregory Nazianzen, "and to be cleansed in spirit. Consider the disease merely as a useful discipline, a discipline extending to the body and everything that pertains to it, despising and considering as nothing whatever is transitory, disturbing, and perishable. Give yourself up entirely to heavenly things. Live not for the present but for the ages to come, the world without end. Regard this miserable life as a meditation on death, as Plato did."[71]

St. Bonaventure tells of some marvelous occurrences in the life of St. Francis. "Now, to increase his merits, . . . which had been perfected in patient endurance . . . , the man of God began to suffer so grievously from various ailments that scarcely one of his limbs was free from pain and acute suffering. . . . While afflicted with such severe bodily suffering, he would not call his pangs punishments, but 'sisters.' And once when he was harassed more than usual by sharp pains, a simple friar said to him, 'Brother, pray the Lord that He deal more gently with thee, for it seems that His hand is laid more heavily upon

---

70. *De septem custodiis,* cap. VI, p. 371.
71. *Ad Philogr.,* Epist. 31, in Migne, *P. G.,* t. XXXVII, col. 67.

thee than is right.' Hearing this, the holy man groaned and cried out, saying: 'Did I not know the simple purity that is in thee, I would henceforth have shunned thy company, for thou hast dared to deem blameworthy the divine counsels concerning me.' And kissing the ground, he cried, 'I give Thee thanks, O Lord God, for all these pains, and I beseech Thee, my Lord, that if it please Thee, Thou wilt add unto them a hundred-fold, ... since the fulfilling of Thy holy will is unto me an overflowing solace.' Thus he seemed to the brethren like another Job, whose powers of mind increased, even as did his bodily weakness."[72]

CONCLUSION. Bodily sickness is often a remedy to the soul, and sickness itself proceeds from the God of lights and the God of all consolation. It is God "who comforts us in all our afflictions,"[73] God the Father Almighty, who sends His children nothing but what is good for them. Therefore we should accept illness not only without complaint but with heartfelt gratitude. We should be encouraged by the example of our Saviour: "Shall I not drink the cup that the Father has given Me?"[74] A sick religious, says Humbertus, should recognize the purpose of sickness and not be less intelligent than a beast of burden which seems to know why he is whipped. He has gone off the road but returns to it; or he is proceeding too slowly, and he must quicken his step. . . . One whom the Lord has struck down should examine his conscience. If he finds himself wandering from the road to paradise, he should acknowledge this and confess his fault. If he finds that he is still on the road to paradise, he should find out whether he has been slothful in doing good, and should plan to do good more

---

72. *Legenda,* cap. XIV, n. 2, in *Opera omnia* t. VIII (Quaracchi, 1898), p. 545 et seq.

73. 2 Cor. 1:4.

74. John 18:11.

fervently in the future, as directed in the Psalm: "Their infirmities were multiplied: afterwards they made haste."[75]

We should keep in mind the advantages of sickness and remember its foremost grace — that of strengthening the interior man, and at the same time weakening that familiar enemy, the flesh.

---

75. Ps. 15:4, Challoner-Douay version.

CHAPTER IV

MEANS FOR THE PROPER ORDERING OF OUR ACTIONS

306. Besides the means for instructing the intellect, confirming the will in good, and subjecting the body to the spirit, there are others for the proper ordering of our actions and the conforming of them to Christ. This constitutes as it were the fourth key for "opening" man's life, so that Christ may enter in. "Performing your ordinary, everyday occupations is an exceedingly powerful means to perfection," says Cardinal Bona, "for spiritual life is nothing else than a series or chain of good exercises from morning to evening, and from evening to morning. Scripture's comment is to the point: 'For this command which I enjoin on you today is not too mysterious and remote for you. It is not up in the sky, that you should say, "Who will go up in the sky to get it for us and tell us of it that we may carry it out?" ... It is something very near to you, already in your mouths, and in your hearts; you have only to carry it out' (Deut. 30:11-12, 14). Perfection, then, does not consist in doing a great number of sublime and extraordinary deeds; it resides in everyday acts, faithfully, virtuously performed. 'Justice and justice alone shall be your aim' (Deut. 16:20)."[1]

This doctrine, "the little way," was practiced in a wonderful way by St. Thérèse of Lisieux during her whole lifetime, and is clearly explained in her *Autobiography.*

For our actions to appear good and perfect before God, they must be directed to our last end by a right intention.

We must, then, properly use such an important means of perfection. It is also fitting for us to examine various actions

---

1. *Horol. ascet.,* cap. II, 1.

in detail so that we shall know how to perform them for the glory of God. We shall therefore explain: (1) a right intention; (2) certain actions which occur frequently.

Article I — A Right Intention

307. When aided by habitual grace, man as such and in a general way directs his whole life toward God; and his actions, provided they are not disorderly, tend to God by their very nature. Yet spiritual progress is much easier when we frequently and explicitly offer all our thoughts, our affections, our words, and our deeds to God out of love for Him. This is the more noble, the more secure, and the shorter way to perfection. "If a man earnestly and perseveringly makes use of this simple means, he will easily and pleasantly reach the apex of Christian perfection in his state of life; and immediately after this life he will attain a sublime and extraordinary degree of glory. On the other hand, if he neglects this, no matter what other pious practices he observes, he will scarcely be able to make notable progress in his spiritual life."[2]

To determine the best way to use this means of perfection, we must examine three things: (1) the nature of intention; (2) the importance of a good intention; (3) its practice.

§ I. The Nature of Intention

308. Intention is an act of the will by which that faculty pursues any previously planned end, and directs itself and all its energies toward that end.

Diverse intentions. The heart of man in paradise before the fall was steadfast and fixed upon eternity through love for God, and retained its unity by means of this singleminded love. As soon as it began to be afflicted by earthly passions, it was

---

2. Cardinal de Aguirre, *S. Anselmi Theologia,* t. III, Tract. VII, disp. 130, n. 149 et seq.

torn in as many directions as there are desires. Hence there will be as many intentions, of concupiscence or of love, as there are desires.

These intentions are generally classified as: (1) bad intentions; (2) pure or right intentions.

(1) **A bad intention.** THE BAD INTENTION IS THREE-FOLD. Vain, sensual and mercenary intentions are really bad, even though they may appear to be good.

In the first, a man seeks his own honor and glory. He desires delight and pleasure in the second, and in the third he seeks reward.

All worldly-minded men strive after these three, as St. John testifies, "For all that is in the world is the lust of the flesh, and the lust of the eyes, and the pride of life."[3] Any action motivated by one of these intentions, although it may have the outward appearance of being good, has only an image and a shadow of virtue, for it is not a true and essential act of virtue. Men seem to imagine that virtue is a slave, serving their delight, their convenience and their pride. True virtue is not a slave of temporal things, but their superior and their ruler, ordering all things and subjecting them to herself, but in such a way that they serve God more faithfully through her influence.

To get a better grasp of this imperfect disposition, we must study two elements of the intention. These are the matter and the motive; or the intended thing and the reason why. "From these two," says St. Bernard, "anyone can judge the beauty or deformity of a soul. If we intend to seek the truth and only out of love for the truth, does it not seem that both the matter and the motive are good? If we cast aside the desire for truth and are motivated by vainglory or some other temporal satisfaction, no one will hesitate to form an unfavorable judgment

---

3. 1 John 2:16.

of us. For instance, any time we notice a man without any worthy pursuits entangled in the allurements of the flesh, as are those 'whose god is their belly, and whose glory is in their shame' (Phil. 3:19, Challoner-Douay version), will we not agree that both the matter and the motive in this case are most destestable?"[4]

(2) The right intention. DEFINITION. In regard to virtue, the right intention is that which seeks and practices virtues for themselves, and not for temporal gain, earthly pleasures or unworthy motives. For true virtue is conformable to right reason, the law of God, and the divine will. Virtue unites us to God, greatly pleases Him, and increases His external glory. To tend toward the virtues in this manner is to tend toward God Himself and to direct ourselves toward Him.

Why the right intention can be called the simple intention or the simple eye. The intention is spoken of as a right intention when it aims at God without turning aside. So the intention can be called simple when it strives after Him without any admixture of what is contrary or adverse to God. For simplicity, as St. Thomas teaches, is a virtue by which the soul does not incline toward various objects, but toward the same thing interiorly and exteriorly. Whatever it performs exteriorly agrees with the intention it has in its heart.

(3) Simple and multiple intention. An intention which, when it operates, seeks only the glory of God is a simple intention, even when the good works are diversified. For in such a case all the good works are performed out of love for God. As St. Paul says: "Whether you eat or drink, or do anything else, do all for the glory of God."[5] A truly Christian life is a simple life, a striving for only one thing: the glory of God.

---

4. *In Cant.,* Serm. 40, in Migne, *P. L.,* t. CLXXXIII, col. 982.
5. 1 Cor. 10:31.

But this simple intention is at the same time manifold and varied, for it is a combination of many right intentions. We can have as many pure intentions as there are virtues. For instance, we may do something in order to acquire chastity and its goodness, or we may perform a task with justice, mercy, or any other virtue or end in mind. We shall have done good under the sway of each virtue. The intentions of the wicked are manifold and in many ways contradictory. They cannot be reduced to one intention unless it be an inordinate love of self. On the other hand, the intentions of the just, although they have many particular purposes, all converge on one ultimate end — God, and an increase in His external glory.

(4) **Different degrees of the simple intention.** We can distinguish three degrees of the simple intention. The FIRST DEGREE excludes every culpable adherence to anything *seriously displeasing* to God — in other words, every grievous sin. This is the intention common to all the just.

The SECOND DEGREE seeks to avoid all *smaller offenses;* yet it contains traces of self-love, which, however, may be a well-regulated self-love. For a man who earnestly seeks God may also seriously strive to avoid the pains of hell, set his mind on the possession of heaven, and endeavor to obtain a share of the wonderful gifts granted to God's friends. Even David once exclaimed: "I have inclined my heart to do Thy justifications forever, for the reward."[6] Hence working for an eternal reward is lawful, just as it is also allowed to work for benefits already received. Nevertheless, the intention whereby a man directs his labors to God merely and solely to gain a reward, even an eternal one, smacks of the mercenary. We are sons, not servants. There is another degree of intention more becoming, more proper to sons, an intention by which we act out of love of God.

------

6. Ps. 118:112, Challoner-Douay version.

The THIRD DEGREE. The most simple as well as the most excellent of all right intentions is the one based on *Love of God*. Love is friendship with God. Friendship draws us to the friend because of the friend himself, not because of the useful and delightful things he has. Therefore, the most simple and best intention is love of God, by which we love God because of Himself and His infinite perfections.

We must never exclude the desire for eternal happiness from this intention. For the desire for heaven only supports the intention of love of God, not by subordinating love of God to the desire for heaven but by eliciting a desire for our true happiness, which is God.

This very simple intention can gain such complete control over our heart that we seem to desire nothing, to seek nothing from God but God Himself; so that if it were expedient for His glory we would be prepared to suffer eternal or temporary loss of the vision of God. St. Paul expressed the same thought in his Epistle to the Romans, "For I could wish to be anathema myself from Christ, for the sake of my brethren."[7] These and similar expressions do not exclude the desire for happiness with God, but merely express the ardor of love.

We do not recommend these extraordinary acts to those who are still somewhat imperfect and tepid. They might fall and fail, unprepared for such splendid acts, and might even quit the religious life. But when they have arrived at greater perfection such exalted acts of love may be very profitable.

Meanwhile, let us study the importance of a good intention.

§ II. Importance of a Good Intention

309. We can estimate the importance of the good intention by realizing: (1) that it is the basis of good works; (2) that Christ particularly recommended it; (3) that the devil

---

7. Rom. 9:3.

plots against it. Hence it follows that (4) we should never deviate from our good intention and that (5) beginners should be on guard lest the devil deceive them under the appearance of good.

(1) **The good intention as the foundation of good works.** An intention is the basis of good works, the foundation of the spiritual edifice. As a column depends upon its base, so our life depends upon our virtues. But our virtues are in turn dependent upon our internal intention. If the base has been set upon sand or soft ground and not upon firm rock, the building will soon collapse. If the intention rests upon temporal or apparent good, virtue will not be strong enough to endure. Neither will it be true virtue, for by its very nature virtue demands firmness and stability. The intention should be founded upon stable and eternal good, upon Christ Himself, upon God. Then our virtue will abide eternally. St. Augustine says: "We must not so much consider what we do but the spirit in which we do it."[8] Even the noblest deeds are worthless if the intention is not heavenly. "If a man afflicts his body with fasts, flagellations, and other penances, not for the sake of God but to receive praise from men, it profits him nothing. If with the same intention he travels to far-off India and there with much labor converts all unbelievers to God, he is like 'sounding brass or a tinkling cymbal.' For, as the Fathers of the Church teach, the motive and not the sufferings make the martyr."[9]

(2) **The right intention highly recommended by Christ.** In the sermon in which our Lord promulgated the evangelical law, He ascribed the greatest value to the right intention in prayer, fasting, almsgiving, and in every holy and virtuous deed. He enjoined a certain secrecy or privacy in the per-

---

8. *De Serm. Dom. in Monte,* Lib. III, cap. XIII, n. 4-6, in Migne, *P. L.,* t. XXXIV, col. 1289.

9. Cardinal Bona, *Horol. ascet.,* cap. II, § 7, n. 1.

formance of good works. Not that He objected to our engaging in good deeds before men. What He desired is that while we pursue good works we at all times retain the secret, interior intention by which we seek to please God alone, as truly as if God alone and no one else beheld our good deed. Jesus gave an extreme example when He said: "Do not let thy left hand know what thy right hand is doing."[10] In other words, our intention should not deviate to the left or any other angle but only to the right — that is, to God. Jesus immediately put off those who sought Him from some unworthy motive, saying: "You seek Me, . . . because you have eaten of the loaves and have been filled. Do not labor for the food that perishes, but for that which endures unto life everlasting."[11] His meaning was: "Seek Me for a supernatural motive, not for the hope of receiving perishable goods." And yet, while temporal benefits should not be the motive, those who seek first the kingdom of God and His justice will also receive the goods of earth.

(3) **Diabolical plots against the right intention.** Since the right intention is so pleasing to God, the devil will leave no stone unturned in his attempt to spoil the intention of a good deed. For if he can only lead the heart away from a good intention, he can easily vitiate and lay waste the accomplishment and end of the action that follows. In the same way he does not wish the full benefit of the deed to be given to God. For when he sees the whole tree about to bear fruit for God, he sinks his poisonous fangs into the roots. We must be as prudent as a serpent, which is concerned chiefly about its head. In the same way we must be concerned about the good intention, from which proceed our actions and the life of our whole body. We should not be content merely with forming the intention at the beginning of our work, for we

10. Matt. 6:3.
11. John 6:26, 27.

may be deceived by the demon during the work itself. "Be careful," says Cardinal Bona, "that no improper intention asserts itself during the course of your work and that no sadness or impatience with the labor, nor delight or self-satisfaction in the work, becomes mixed up with your intention. Otherwise you will complete for your own gratification what you really began for God. Therefore frequently raise your mind to God by means of aspirations or ejaculatory prayers."[12]

(4) **We should avoid deviations from the right intention.** Since it is so important to direct our actions properly to God, we must take the greatest care to avoid any swerving or deviation of the intention, lest the whole work become corrupted. It is in this sense that the Fathers of the Church interpret the following words of Christ: "The lamp of the body is the eye. If thy eye be sound, thy whole body will be full of light. But if thy eye be evil, thy whole body will be full of darkness."[13] For what does "eye" mean here, asks St. Gregory, except the intention of the heart, anticipating its work? Before the mind engages in action, it contemplates what it seeks. And what is meant by "body" except every action? Our actions follow the intention as if it were an intuitive eye which, if it is simple and pure, illumines and directs the whole body; but which, if it is evil, makes the whole body detestable and full of darkness.

(5) **Salutary admonition for beginners.** The enemy is accustomed subtly to deceive beginners. They may seek and desire virtue, or practice it, not for the sake of the virtue itself but because of a certain good attached to it, such as spiritual delights, distinction and honors, or the great opportunities associated with virtue. They might hear or perhaps feel what Solomon said of divine wisdom: "So I determined to draw her

---

12. *Horol. ascet.,* cap. II, § 1, n. 3.
13. Matt. 6:22, 23.

into fellowship, knowing that she would be my counselor while
all was well, and my comfort in care and grief. For her sake
I should have glory among the masses, and esteem from the
elders, though I be but a youth. I should become keen in
judgment, and should be a marvel before rulers."[14] Since these
good qualities are associated with wisdom and virtue, some
people strive for virtue because of the benefits associated with
it. They abuse the things God has attached to virtue to make
its pursuit more pleasant. Partaking of food is pleasurable.
But we do not eat for inordinate pleasure, for that is the vice
of gluttony. We eat because food is necessary to sustain life
and we take it with good manners yet without fastidiousness.
Now in the same way we must not strive for virtue on account
of the delight associated with it, even if it is spiritual, but
because of virtue itself. Otherwise the needle of the pure intention will waver, it will turn toward mixed motives, and we
shall be guilty of spiritual gluttony, which is the source of
many imperfections. "God often takes away sensible consolations," says St. Bernard, "so as to make us pursue virtue not
for any sensible delight, but simply for the sake of the virtues
themselves and in order to please God alone. Those who pursue
virtues because of the delight associated with them soon become sad, murmur and loudly complain against God; and
shortly either omit the deeds of these virtues or perform them
negligently."[15]

§ III. The Practice of a Pure Intention

310. A pure intention for love of God is the most excellent of all intentions. "How happy we would be," says Blosius,
"if whatever we did or omitted were done or omitted out of
sincere love for God — that is, having God in view more than
ourselves. It is certainly well to do good out of fear of punish-

---

14. Wisd. 8:9-11.
15. *Serm. 5 de quadrag.*, in Migne, *P. L.*, t. CLXXXIII, col. 180.

ment, or out of the desire for virtue or heavenly glory, but it is not perfect. Since love of God is infinitely more excellent than love of ourselves, we do far better when we are motivated by love of God than by self-love."[16]

We must now (1) determine whether or not a right intention directs our actions; (2) learn how to direct our actions to the glory of God; (3) renew our intention at certain times during the day.

(1) **Various signs of a right intention.** We can discern whether or not the right intention directs our actions by the following signs: (1) If we start to work on our duties in a tranquil spirit, without anxiety or confusion. (2) If it is all the same to us whether our tasks are undignified or honorable, hard or easy. If we are not upset whenever our work seems less effective and if we apply ourselves to our work whether or not we are bound to it by our vows. (3) If we are not given to vainglory over our accomplishments, and not elated by the praises of others, nor depressed by censures and contempt. (4) If we perform our duties with equal diligence, whether in public or in private, before our superiors or in their absence, in the presence of many spectators or only a few. (5) If we accept everything with equanimity, wishing only to please God and dreading nothing but to displease Him. (6) If, when we hear others being commended, praised or highly esteemed, we do not become saddened or disturbed, but remain calm and at peace.

We should examine all our deeds, words, thoughts and omissions to find out whether or not they are entirely dedicated to the praise and glory of God. Before any action, work, thought, or omission we should examine our motive for the action or omission and discover whether it is love of God or self-love. If we find that the motive is self-love, we must

---

16. *Sacell. animae fidelis,* § 4, n. 3.

desist without delay or change our intention, deny ourselves, and direct the entire intention to God alone.

In this way we shall be interiorly disposed to consider God first in all things, and we shall learn to recognize and to love God in every creature, and every creature in God. We will look upon creatures in an eminently noble way, that is, as springing from one common source: God. We propose the following method of forming this good intention:

311. (2) **Method of forming the good intention.** The best method of forming a right and pure intention is: (A) to use various means which, although (B) they seem rather difficult in the beginning, become easier by use and (C) produce much fruit and many consolations.

A. THE VARIOUS MEANS. Some of these principal means are: (a) To make our intention *correspond with God's intention* working in and through us. "For God," says Cardinal Bona, "concurs with you in all your actions as the First Cause and the Primary Principle of nature and of grace, and without His operation in you, you can do nothing. Therefore, the most perfect intention consists in assuming in every single action the very same intentions the all-wise God has when operating through you. Direct your mind to God by saying: 'O Lord, my God, I intend to undertake and accomplish this task for the very same reasons which You have; and I direct my intention to the same object You have — to Your love and glory, so that Your will may be entirely accomplished in heaven and on earth. Would that I might always attain this same end with the uprightness which I desire and which You deserve.' "[17]

(b) To unite your intentions *with the intentions of Christ.* It may be difficult, even with the greatest effort, to make our intentions correspond with the intentions of God. We therefore propose another way to obtain God's help, a way which

---

17. *Horol. ascet.,* cap. II, § 7, n. 4.

is very pleasing to the Divine Majesty. This is simply to unite every one of our deeds, words and thoughts to the deeds, words and thoughts of our Lord Jesus Christ. We should offer ourselves and all our labors to God in union with the offering which Christ our Lord made of Himself to the Father while living with us on earth. Let us join our prayers with His, our fasts with His, our afflictions with His Passion, and all our undertakings with His, considering all these things as being offered now by Christ Himself to God the Father together with His own actions.

We thus include our offering with His, making the two, as it were, one; for Christ is the way by which we go to the Father.

(c) To form *many intentions at the same time.* Learned theologians assert that by multiplying intentions we can multiply the merits of individual acts to the extent that, by one deed, provided with, let us say, three or more intentions, we can merit as much as if we repeated that same deed three or more times. But since we cannot form multiple intentions before all our occupations, we shall do well to pause slightly before our principal undertakings, and select in each instance only those intentions which the nature and the circumstances of the occupation suggest.

(d) To *avoid* every *wrongdoing* in our actions. We must discover what we love in each of our actions and transform every intention of self-love into the pure intention of love of God. For instance, when we wish or desire anything because of a natural craving for our own convenience, we shall do well to change to a better intention, so that we may proceed not because this thing is especially useful to us but because it is what God wills and approves. If we long for heaven, then let us aim to enter it because God, out of the overflowing abundance of His goodness and charity, intensely desires us to reach it, and because in that ever blessed kingdom we can love and praise God. Even while sleeping we can honor God, if before sleep we intend to seek not our own comfort but the divine will. Before our repose we can say to God: "I desire, O my God, that while I sleep, my every breath may praise and glorify Thee, as if with the affection of all the angels and saints I were forever saying, 'Praise be to Thee, O Lord, King of eternal glory.'" Likewise during meals we can offer God every morsel we eat, every drop we swallow, as if we were saying over and over: "Blessed be God." When reading or writing we can offer every letter for the same intention, as if each were crying out with a loud voice, "Holy, Holy, Holy, Lord God of Hosts." Many of our other activities can be transformed in the same way.

B. DIFFICULTIES WITH THE RIGHT INTENTION. This exercise of the right intention may appear difficult to beginners. To them it seems troublesome to perform all their labors for God. They should remember that the beginnings of any art are difficult, for only by continual practice can it be learned. In the beginning we must expect a certain apathy among those who have previously been accustomed to labor for their own pleasure according to a natural inclination, but who now desire to labor for love of God alone, exchanging their inertness and selfishness for the pleasure of another: the glory of God. Since to work for God's glory is supernatural and man is unaccustomed to it, we need not be surprised that at the beginning he has little taste for it. If one suffers severe aridity, it does not mean that his labors are less meritorious. When he becomes accustomed to the practice of the right intention, consolation will return.

C. RESULTS AND CONSOLATIONS DERIVED FROM A RIGHT INTENTION. The practice of a pure intention ennobles our most insignificant acts, even those we perform for the rightful comfort and licit pleasure of our body. Those of our labors which appear to us sublime and of great importance might be displeasing to God if performed with an improper intention; other occupations, which seem indifferent in themselves and of no importance, are very pleasing to God when performed with the right intention. We shall receive an abundant reward for such small devotions as a bow before an image of Jesus crucified, or an offering of flowers for the altar of the Mother of God, or the proper use of our feet, hands and tongue for love of God, and even for the most insignificant charitable thought or desire. Our Lord told St. Gertrude that she demonstrated an extraordinary love for Him when in His honor she thought, saw, heard, said or did anything useful. Even little actions such as picking up a piece of straw from the ground or taking one step are pleasing to God and worthy of a reward when done for the honor and love of God. Whenever we take food with the holiest intention and at the proper time, we obtain more merit than through fasts or fierce chastisements performed for another intention, even if it is a good one, but not one proceeding entirely from love of God. If we have purity of intention in all the services we must provide for our body in caring for its health, our spiritual merit will increase.

A certain holy virgin, says Blosius, rejoiced while taking reasonable care of her body because she did it as if she were serving Christ, who said: "As long as you did it for one of these, the least of My brethren, you did it for Me."[18] For she considered herself one of His least. We should revive and refresh our body with discretion, for the eternal glory of God, in union with that love by which our Saviour became man for our sake, deigned to eat, drink, rest and sleep while on earth; and offer Him, in union with that same love, the bodily comforts we allow ourselves. In this way all our actions are made pleasing to God and abundantly fruitful for ourselves.

18. Matt. 25:40.

Oh, with what peace and joy we shall abound if we seriously and perseveringly endeavor to perform this heavenly and angelic art, if we are of one spirit and of one will with God! We shall be exceedingly joyful, and shall exult in the immense majesty, glory, charity, and other amiable perfections of God. This will be our lot, perhaps even in the present life, and most certainly in the one to come.

312. (3) **Proper time for making or renewing the right intention.** To form the right intention at the proper time, we shall do well to observe the following counsels:

(a) IN THE MORNING. In accordance with the ancient and pious Christian custom, we should form a general pure intention in the morning, referring all our actions, works, words, thoughts, sacrifices, sorrows, and so forth, to the love and glory of God alone, excluding every reference to our own glory or comfort. This general intention has such force that it virtually influences all the other actions of the day.

(b) DURING THE DAY. The best time to renew this pure intention is: (1) before spiritual exercises, so that they may become more meritorious and be performed with more devotion; (2) before a difficult task, or one of greater importance or longer duration, so that such tasks may be committed to the worthy and sweet heart of Jesus; (3) before employing the lowly activity of the senses in actions such as eating, etc. (when we notice that we desire anything connected with the sense operations according to our own will or natural cravings; when we are aware of seeking merely our own comfort or satisfaction, we must quickly make ourselves desire this from a better motive — for instance, because God wills it); (4) before troublesome, vile and abject occupations (when things go contrary to our wishes, we must remember that they come from the hand of God, and try to bear them as patiently and humbly as possible); (5) before honorable occupations, lest they be infested with the worm of vanity. Then we must recall the examples of humility which our Lord Jesus Christ gave us, and hope with all our heart and soul that the most gracious will of God may be always accomplished in us.

CONCLUSION. Just as the sinner always turns his face, that is, his mind and heart, away from God and toward creatures or himself, so we must turn ours away from earthly and worldly affairs. We shall behold God, and God will consider us so that there will be no aversion between us. Instead, we shall see things as He does and dwell in His grace and friendship. With this in mind we shall examine various occupations in detail.

Article II — Various Actions Which Occur Frequently

313. If we fulfill the duties of the religious life, and do so with a good intention and in the prescribed order, they will be marvelously fitting means for arriving at perfection and the happiness of our heavenly home. We have already considered many of these duties in detail when treating of conforming the intellect, the will and the body with Christ. Hence only the following remain for our consideration: (1) rising from sleep; (2) eating; (3) working; (4) taking recreation; (5) external conduct; (6) retiring, and sleeping at night.

§ I. Rising from Sleep

314. Our first task of the day is to rise from our bed and to apply our mind to vigilance and work. Often we rise not only before the sun, but even at midnight, and in the morning long before the dawn, so that during these quiet hours we may be occupied with God for longer periods without any disturbance. This first exercise deserves special attention, for divine visitations and devotion, zeal and promptness during the day usually depend upon it. To accomplish this task perfectly,

three conditions in particular are required: (1) perseverance; (2) eagerness; (3) devotion.

(1) PERSEVERANCE. Each day, at the appointed time we must punctually rise from bed. Continual perseverance in little victories is most praiseworthy, for it is in this way that habits are formed and the will gains control over the flesh. But if we accept any excuse to extend our sleep — cold weather, or a restless night, or a headache — our body becomes an unwilling servant and we are deceiving ourselves with lies. Let us listen to Sirach: "At the time of rising," undoubtedly from bed, "be not slack: but be the first to run home to thy house."[19] That is, to the house of prayer; and precede all your brethren so as to receive the first blessing from God and to perform certain little duties for them, such as putting on the lights or opening the windows, etc.

In the early hours of the morning only a few beloved sons of God are imploring between the vestibule and the altar, saying, "Spare, O Lord, Your people."[20]

(2) EAGERNESS. When the signal for rising is given, we should rise immediately, without delay or hesitation, with great fervor and eagerness. Immediately let us say, "for the love of God," and then let us "get up quickly,"[21] as the angel told Peter to do. And if we rise without delay, the chains of tepidity and slothfulness will fall from our hands. Sleep is the brother of death. Does anyone raised from the dead deliberate whether he should come forth from the tomb or not? When the trumpet sounds, "Rise, O ye dead!" the reprobate will indeed move slowly, but the elect will swiftly come forth from their tombs. We should observe which of these we imitate when we are slothful in rising. We shall do well to

---

19. Ecclus. 32:15, Challoner-Douay version.
20. Joel 2:17.
21. Acts 12:7.

recall here what has already been said concerning the preparation for Divine Office.

(3) DEVOTION. Immediately after awaking, during the night or in the morning, we should offer God our first thoughts. Just as the eyes of the body are opened to sensible light in the morning, so too the eyes of the soul should be opened to spiritual and divine light.

(a) We should immediately make the sign of the Cross. By virtue of its power we shall be protected against the dangers of night and day, against corporal as well as spiritual perils. St. Cyril of Jerusalem earnestly urges all Christians: "Never be ashamed to make the sign of the Cross. It should be made as an introduction to everything we do — before eating and drinking, upon entering and leaving a room, before sleeping and upon rising, while traveling and resting. It is a great protection, ... a sign of the faithful and a terror to the demons. ... When they see the Cross, they think of the Crucified. They fear Him who crushed the heads of the dragon (cf. Ps. 73:14)."[22]

(b) Let our first words be those which one day will be our last: "Jesus, Mary, Joseph, Francis!" Then, let us prostrate ourselves and kiss the floor as an acknowledgement before God that we are dust and ashes and that we shall shortly return to the earth; meanwhile we may say with our heart rather than with our lips: "My God and my All! Behold, I am ready to do Thy will!"

(c) While washing ourselves in the morning, we should reverently adore the Holy Trinity and invoke the Blessed Virgin, our guardian angel, and our patron saints. Let us also ask for fervor in prayer, purity in the reception of the Holy Eucharist and diligence in the performance of our duties.

---

22. St. Cyril of Jerusalem, *Cateches.*, XIII, in Migne, P. G., t. XXXIII, col. 815.

(d) Then we should proceed to the choir, genuflect in the presence of our Lord, and recite our morning prayers with as great fervor as possible. We shall have begun the day as *fervently* as if it were our first, and as *carefully* as if it were our last.

§ II. Eating

315. Eating, to say the least, requires great caution; for it is surrounded by many grave dangers. Many men, even religious, are at times drawn to the table more by the enjoyment of food than by a good intention.

Burdening the stomach with unnecessary food dulls the mind. "Who is there, O Lord," exclaims St. Augustine, "who does not sometimes exceed the limits of necessity? Whoever he is, he is great. He glorifies Thy name. I, however, am not great, because I am a sinful man."[23] We must (1) avoid gluttony while eating; (2) learn to take our food and drink with religious propriety.

(1) AVOIDANCE OF GLUTTONY. To safeguard the spirit of mortification, only what is sufficient and befitting our poverty should be served at the table. The friars must remember that whereas little is needed to satisfy necessity, nothing can content sensuality. We shall do well to recall what was written above concerning the custody of the sense of taste. There are two more points to be stressed:

(a) We must deem ourselves unworthy of God's benefits, and remember that many people better than ourselves are satisfied with poorer and less food than we have. What we discard, they may consider suitable for their nourishment.

(b) An act of mortification, no matter how small, at each meal is a highly commendable habit. For example, to deny our senses and to offer up to Christ any small measure of the

---

23. *Confessions,* Book X, Chap. XXXI, in Migne, *P. L.,* t. XXXII, col. 799.

things placed before us and for which we have an immoderate appetite. Another mortification consists in leaving the table with the appetite not quite completely satisfied, so that after dining we can read or pray without serious inconvenience or difficulty. To do otherwise "is not the life of a man who professes poverty,"[24] says our Seraphic Father. And speaking of himself, he said, "It does not behoove you to become accustomed to such" — that is, delicate foods — for "little by little you will return to contemptible things, and again give yourself up to delicacies. Rise then with diligence and beg from door to door for your mixture of leftovers."

Love soothes all things, says Thomas of Celano, and makes sweet all that is bitter.

(2) MANNER OF TAKING FOOD AND DRINK. Although it is necessary to insist on mortification at meals, far greater stress must be placed on a good intention. Listen to what her guardian angel told St. Bridget: "Christ the Lord does not pay much attention to what kind of food is eaten, as long as it is not forbidden, and everything is taken with a pure intention, from a motive of love, with moderation and without any inordinate desire." Therefore, besides the rules that must be observed in the refectory, which we have covered under the "reformation of the body," it is necessary to observe the following:

(a) We should eat and drink with a right intention. St. Gertrude was given to understand by divine inspiration that it was most pleasing to God and useful for man to form on his lips or at least in his heart, the following or a similar prayer before eating and drinking: "O Lord, grant that I may partake of this food for the glory of Thy name alone, in union with that love with which Thou didst partake of such necessities

---

24. Celano, *Legenda Secunda,* cap. IX, p. 179.

while on earth, for the praise of God the Father, and for the salvation of the whole human race."[25]

(b) We should have Christ present at the table. "May your superior be in the midst of the brethren as a true vicar of Christ," says Thomas a Kempis, "while the other brethren eat with him as holy apostles."[26]

(c) We should observe decorum. If we are occupied with higher considerations while at table, it will be easy for us to observe the proper decorum. We must pay more attention to the sacred reading than to the food. And, like good religious, we should partake of food as if it were medicine, not a luxury. We must provide for the needs of the body out of necessity and in order to fulfill the divine will.

§ III. Work

316. Whenever God establishes a religious family, He goes out like the householder to hire laborers, to call men to conform their lives to Christ through a definite kind of work. We who are called to the Seraphic Order must discover what work the divine will has imposed upon us by reason of our vocation.

Various things must be considered: (1) the necessity of work; (2) the kinds of work prescribed in the Franciscan Order; (3) the special obligation to study; (4) the manner in which we must work and study.

I. THE NECESSITY OF WORK

317. When God created man, He did not want him to be inactive and unoccupied, says St. Basil, for God commanded Adam to work in paradise and to guard it. This duty of working, at first pleasant and honorable, was turned into a punish-

---

25. Found in the work of Blosius, *Conclav. anim. fid.*, Pars. II, cap. VIII, n. 3.

26. *Exercit. spirit.*, cap. VI.

ment by sin in such a way "that in the sweat of his brow" man was subsequently to eat his bread.

By grace we are indeed the sons of God. But by nature we remain slaves and servants of our Creator. If Adam while in the state of innocence was originally put in a place of enjoyment and given work, says St. Bernard, who would intelligently suppose that Adam's sons were put in a place of affliction to be at leisure? No one, for man is born to labor as the bird to fly. Therefore, the words of St. Paul certainly apply to one who disapproves of work. "If any man will not work, neither let him eat."[27]

Besides his good example, our Seraphic Father offers two reasons in particular which should encourage us to work: (1) the good of the *soul*. This is effected when we flee from idleness, for he says in his Rule: "The friars shall work in such a way that, avoiding idleness, the enemy of the soul, they yet do not extinguish the spirit of holy prayer and devotion."[28] His second reason is: (2) *bodily* support. For in the same place he says: "In payment for their work, let them receive whatever is necessary for their bodily support and that of their brethren."[29]

A. **Avoidance of idleness.** By word and example St. Francis condemned idleness on account of the disorders it causes in the mind as well as in the body.

(1) *Words and example of our holy Father:* "I worked with my hands," St. Francis says, "and I still desire to work, and I earnestly desire that all the other friars occupy themselves in fitting work." And to a friar leading an indolent life in the Order, he said: "Go thy way, Brother; fly";[30] in other words: return to the world. And lest this saying seem too

---

27. 2 Thess. 3:10.
28. Chap. V.
29. *Ibid.*
30. St. Bonaventure, *Legenda S. Franc.*, cap. V, n. 6.

hard, he adds the reason: "lest through idleness your heart and tongue indulge in what is illicit."[31]

(2) *The effects of idleness.* Gerson stated: "There is no thought . . . too foul, too abominable or evil to have its source in detestable idleness. For the heart given to idleness is like a mill which, because it does not have good grain to grind, grinds and consumes itself since it is in constant motion. It grinds away even to its own destruction and doom unless it is stopped by some occupation. And it grinds filthy flies just as readily as choice grains."[32]

(a) *Idleness disables the body.* An idle and inactive body is more susceptible to disease. A man who moves and works and is occupied with labors is in better condition and is healthier. St. John Chrysostom explains: "Unless the eye, the mouth and the stomach, and every other organ performs its particular function, it becomes seriously ill. Which is the useful horse: the pampered one or the one which is exercised by work? Which is the useful ship: the one which navigates or the one lying idle? And which is the useful plough: the one which moves or the one which stands unused? Is it not the one which shines like silver? The unused one is consumed by rust and disintegrates."[33]

(b) *Idleness corrupts the mind.* The rust of idleness not only corrodes the body but also the soul and consumes its splendor and its virtue. St. Augustine says: "Drive away all idleness and always do something good. Whoever becomes tired of praying or reciting the psalms, should not hesitate to work with his hands, recalling that as long as David was engaged in battle he did not pursue immorality; but as soon as he remained idle in his home, he fell into adultery and com-

---

31. Celano, *Legenda Secunda,* cap. CXX, p. 290.

32. *Tractatus de exercit. discret,* Pars. III.

33. *Homil. XXXV et XLIV* in *Act. Apost.,* in Migne, *P. L.,* t. LX, col. 256 et 378.

mitted murder. As long as Samson fought the Philistines, the enemy could not seize him. But as soon as he slept in the embrace of a woman and remained idly with her, he was captured and imprisoned by the enemy. As long as Solomon was occupied with the building of the temple, he had no inclination to sensuality. But soon after he ceased laboring he fell into the clutches of sensual excesses. . . . Be on your guard, therefore, my brethren, and do not weaken; for I know that you are neither holier than David, braver than Samson nor wiser than Solomon."[34]

We shall do well to keep working so that the devil will find us occupied. If he should tempt us to sin, we shall easily overcome him. The Fathers of the Church have left us this holy thought: "The monk who works is tempted by one evil spirit, but the idle monk is ravaged by innumerable spirits."[35]

B. **Bodily support.** If the Order binds itself by an agreement at the time of profession to provide us with the necessary food and clothing, we have, by the same agreement, assumed the obligation of serving the Order by our work. This agreement is all the more binding on members of the Seraphic Order because we live on alms.

Working for the Order. Every religious should be mindful of the words of Thomas a Kempis: "You have come to serve, not to rule; know that you have been called to suffer and to work, not to be idle and chat."[36] Our Seraphic Father had a special loathing for all idlers. "No one," says Celano, "could appear idle before him without receiving a severe censure. He gave such serious reproofs because he desired us to be less burdensome to other men."[37]

---

34. *Serm. 17 ad fratres in eremo,* in App.; in Migne, *P. L.,* t. XL, col. 1264.

35. Cassian, *De coenob. Inst.,* Lib. X, cap. XXIII, in Migne, *P. L.,* t. XLIX, col. 394.

36. *Imitation of Christ,* Book I, Chap. XVII.

37. Celano, *Legenda Secunda,* cap. CXX, p. 290.

Begging is allowed only in case of necessity. We must remember that we are permitted to have recourse to the table of the Lord only when the wages for our labor are not given us or when the payment is not at all sufficient for our needs. We must work in such a way that each one of us daily acquires his right to eat. We should earn whatever is necessary for an honest livelihood. To this St. Francis bears witness in his *Testament,* saying: "Should the wages of our work be not given us, then shall we have recourse to the table of the Lord, asking alms from door to door."

In his First Rule Francis called the friar blessed who worked assiduously, using the words of the psalmist: "For you shall eat the fruit of your handiwork: happy shall you be, and favored."[38]

We must work by reason of the alms we receive. We must consider this truth carefully. "If there are any religious," says St. Thomas Aquinas, "who without necessity and advantage wish to live idly on the alms given to the poor, they must realize that this is dishonest. For privileges (such as begging alms) are given to religious to allow them more freely to attend to their religious duties. Those who give of their temporal goods wish to have a share in the merit gained by the religious for performing these duties. Hence, if the religious neglect their obligations, the things given as alms should be denied them; for as far as they are concerned, they frustrate the intention of the donors."[39]

II. DIFFERENT TYPES OF WORK

318. St. Francis in his *Testament* exhorts the friars to work, and admonishes them to undertake nothing but honest work. This honest work in our Order may be either manual or spiritual.

---

38. Ps. 127:2.
39. *Summa theol.,* IIa, IIae, q. 187, a. 4, 5.

By manual labor we understand the servile work done in or even outside the friary, such as begging, etc.

Spiritual labors comprise the pursuits and charges by which religious strive to promote the salvation of souls.

Manual labor is prescribed for all. Although the greater part of the servile work is imposed upon the lay Brothers, nevertheless, according to St. Basil, manual labor is necessary for the perfect imitation of Christ, and this imitation we Franciscans openly profess. "I shall now proceed to the life of our Saviour," he says, "that life which He lived in the flesh in order to be an example and model of virtue to all who desire to lead a good life. Everyone should endeavor to follow His example in his own life. In early youth Jesus was subject to His parents. Together with them He bore every physical hardship in a kind and obedient spirit."[40] It is our duty as Franciscans to manifest a willingness for every kind of work, even the most humble manual labor which may be assigned to us on account of some natural ability or because of some need of the convent.

It is our personal duty at least to keep our cell and clothing clean, unless we are excused through sickness. And as good Franciscans, we must be willing to serve meals to all the brethren, particularly to the sick.

The clerics and priests must be occupied principally with spiritual labors. St. Thomas holds that those who are publicly occupied with spiritual labors are by reason of these spiritual labors excused from manual labor. But to avoid idleness, the mother of vice and the enemy of virtue, those who are not fitted for studies should employ themselves in some honest manual labor becoming to the priestly and religious state. In dependence upon our superior we can all be employed according to our state: the priests in their sacred ministry, the clerics

---

40. *Const. monast.,* cap. IV, n. 486, in Migne, *P. G.,* t. XXXI, col. 135.

in their studies, the lay Brothers in their temporal duties and labors, in caring for the sick, or in seeking alms.

III. STUDIES

319. Since spiritual labors are by far the most important in our Order, we must consider in detail: (a) the necessity of studies in general; (b) studies in the Seraphic Order in particular.

(A) **The necessity of studies in general.** Everyone knows how necessary studies are in all religious Orders dedicated to the salvation of souls. The most eminent and saintly Doctors, such as St. Bonaventure and St. Thomas Aquinas, agree that studies well arranged help religious discipline, close the door to abuses, and guard against evils arising from ignorance.

(1) *Studies help religious discipline.* "How can anyone," asks Mabillon, "remain in his cell for a long time, lead a solitary life and preserve silence without aid of studies? To be occupied constantly with prayer and contemplation is a very special gift of God, hence not given to everyone. Even prayer itself or contemplation needs to be nourished on pious thoughts and devout affections from time to time. These are supplied and sustained by reading. When this prop is removed, prayer necessarily becomes dry, languid, dissatisfying; silence and solitude become almost unbearable. At this point the monk often seeks external solaces coming from useless occupations or from material objects, with consequent loss of the interior spiritual refreshment which God bestows only upon those who direct all their labors to Him alone."[41]

(2) *Studies prevent abuses.* Where studies are taken seriously, useless excursions from the friary are avoided, worldly

---

41. *De studiis monasticis,* Pars I, cap. VIII; cf. B. Van Loo, *Stimulus Seraphicae conversationis,* XXXII.

conversations are despised, love of earthly things is excluded, and idleness, the plague of religious houses, is banished. Many who have observed the causes of ruin in religious Orders write in this strain, as did Trithemius: "There are two things which maintain regular observance in an Order: love of God and study of the Scriptures; and when these things were lacking, monks have left their religious institutes. For some ignorant and inexperienced religious, lacking a knowledge of Scripture, without anything interior to hold their interest, have turned to a love of the world and unhappily have destroyed the discipline of the Order."[42]

(3) *Evils arising from ignorance are avoided.* Nothing is more unfortunate than an uneducated religious or cleric. Ignorant of the Rule of his institute and of the obligations of his state, he neglects and transgresses them. Trithemius says that to commend the neglect of studies under the pretense of piety and to call ignorance humility is a deception of the devil. If we take the light of doctrine away from religious Orders, what can we hope for but Cimmerian or Egyptian darkness? If we take away from the soldiers of Christ their arms, the sword of the word of God, how can they stand steadfast in faith against the phalanxes of various sects? It is surprising to note the degree of blindness in an illiterate cleric; for he often mistakes vice for virtue. These words of St. Bonaventure fit him perfectly: "The unlettered in religious Orders, who do not appreciate the interior life, place all the importance of the spiritual life on external signs of goodness (which have the appearance of good before men but internally lessen the purity of the religious life before God). They defend this external goodness with great zeal and are unconcerned about true virtue and spirituality."[43] Father Pacificus of Sejano says that neglect of studies consigns religious to obscurity, like the dead

---

42. *De viris illust.,* Lib. I, cap. VIII.
43. *De sex al. Seraph.,* cap. V.

of past ages. "Woe to religious who indulge in idleness. They are like children who poison their own mother — that is, they inflict death upon the Order. On their account the name of God is blasphemed, the holy Founders of religious Orders are submitted to disgrace, and their Orders are rendered useless to God and the world, and the Church is made hateful to society."[44] A more accurate consideration of the necessity of studies in the Seraphic Order is imperative in order to refute the objectors who maintain: Studies must be abandoned and condemned according to the wish of St. Francis.

*320. (B) Necessity of studies in the Seraphic Order. Confounding the enemies of learning, the Seraphic Doctor clearly proves that studies are not contrary to the mind of St. Francis. On the contrary, studies are even recommended by the Rule and are necessary for fulfilling the very purpose of the Seraphic Order. And all this applies not only to theology but to all the other sciences in some way associated with theology.

(1) St. Francis recommended studies. That the Friars Minor might be ministers of the New Testament and faithful dispensers of the mysteries of God, our Seraphic Father wished and commanded that they add knowledge of the Scriptures to sanctity of life. He compelled the clerics to provide themselves with such knowledge, by a statement in the Rule: "No friar shall by any means dare preach to the people, unless he has been examined and approved by the Minister General of this Fraternity and the office of preacher has been conferred upon him. Moreover, I admonish and exhort the same friars that when they preach, their language be well considered and simple, for the benefit and edification of the people, discoursing to them of vice and virtue, punishment and glory, with brevity of speech, for our Lord when on earth used few words."[45]

---

44. *Analecta O. M. Cap., loc. cit.,* pp. 159, 160.
45. *Rule,* Chap. IX.

"It is evident from this chapter," says St. Bonaventure, "that the friars must study according to the intention of St. Francis, for without study they cannot consider their words in a proper way."[46] "In order that you may know," he says in another place, "how much study of Sacred Scripture pleased him — and I heard this from a friar who is still living — when a New Testament fell into his hands he divided it according to pages and shared it with each of them, since so many friars could not have the entire book at the same time. He also held the clerics whom he received into the Order in the highest esteem; and when dying he ordered his friars to regard the Doctors of Sacred Scripture with the greatest reverence as persons from whom they receive the words of life."[47] For in his *Testament* he says: "Theologians and those who minister to us the most holy word of God, we must honor and revere as those who minister to us spirit and life." What are we to think, when according to Celano, "he desired ministers of the word of God to be such as to give themselves to spiritual studies, and to be hindered from studies by no other duties . . . "? And when he once wrote to blessed Anthony, he began the letter: "To my brother Anthony, my bishop."[48] While it is true that almost all the first Franciscans were simple and unlearned, from the very beginning of the Order men of letters most willingly joined St. Francis, and public chairs of theology were established from the first. If our Seraphic Father at times reproved the abuses connected with studies, yet he could always say with St. Bernard: "Perhaps I may seem excessive in my condemnation of learning and perhaps I may appear to censure the learned and forbid the study of letters. Far from it. . . . I am not ignorant of how much they have benefited the Church and how much her learned men have accomplished by refuting

---

46. *Exp. Reg.,* cap. IX.
47. St. Bonaventure, *Epist. de tribus quaest.*
48. Celano, *Legenda Secunda,* cap. CXXII, pp. 291, 292.

the enemy and teaching the simple. Finally I have read in Osee: 'Since you have rejected knowledge, I will reject you from My priesthood' (Osee 4:6)."[49]

(2) *Studies are necessary to fulfill the purpose of the Seraphic Order.* St. Francis established his Order especially for the support and increase of the entire Church. Public preaching is necessary to attain this goal. But since the Order is made up of two categories — lay Brothers and clerics — our holy Founder forbade studies for the lay Brothers, but recommended them to the clerics. The Seraphic Doctor clarifies this point in his letter to an anonymous instructor. He explains the passage in the Rule which says: "And those who are illiterate shall not be anxious to learn; but let them endeavor to have what is to be above all things desired, the spirit of the Lord and His holy operation."[50] St. Bonaventure says: "The Rule does not forbid studies to the literate, but to the illiterate who are lay Brothers. It directs that no lay Brother should ascend to the clerical state; neither . . . is it desired that clerics become lay Brothers by refusing to study."[51] Elsewhere Francis wrote that "since the duties of preaching and hearing confessions as a regular practice have been given to the Order, it is evident that we must study Sacred Scripture and have recourse to instructors. For these duties require a knowledge of Sacred Scripture, and the subtle passages of Scripture require an explanation, lest out of ignorance we teach error instead of truth. And this knowledge is advantageous not only for the education of others but also for our own instruction. With this knowledge a servant of God will know how to govern himself well, he will be able to distinguish virtue from vice, he will acquire a better knowledge of God and the future reward, and in all things will proceed more cautiously

---

49. *In Cant.*, Serm. 36, n. 2, in Migne, *P. L.*, t. CLXXXIII, col. 967.
50. *Rule*, Chap. X.
51. St. Bonaventure, *Epist. de tribus quaest.*

and produce better fruits."[52] St. Bonaventure further said: "I condemn the pretentious Friar Minor and declare him utterly unfit for the office of teaching. But I commend the studious friar and believe that no one is more competent to teach the Gospel with authority than he."

(3) *Necessity of acquiring other sciences.* St. Bonaventure demands not only the necessary theological studies for the Friars Minor but also all the other sciences which minister to that sacred doctrine, and serve for its understanding or its defense. Hence his reply to the anonymous professor who objected to the study of philosophy in the Order: "I see that empty curiosity displeases you. It also displeases me and all good friars, and even God and His angels. I do not defend those who babble on and on in puerile treatises: I detest them as much as you do. Here is a bit of pertinent advice both for myself and for you: that we be zealous for knowledge. Let us not be too critical in this respect; let us not be too hasty in rejecting, lest we root out the good grain with the chaff. But wherever these philosophical discourses make for a better understanding of the truth and the refutation of error, a man who studies them does not wander from the purity of the Franciscan ideal; for there are many questions of faith which are unintelligible without these discourses. Therefore, if we want to be too strict, we might even consider the saints guilty of curiosity — surely an impious thought! For no one describes the nature of time and matter better than St. Augustine in his *Confessions.* No one tells the development of forms or the origin of things better than Augustine himself in his work on Genesis. No one answers questions about the soul and God better than he in his book on the Trinity. No one explains the nature of the creation of the world better than the same Augustine in his book *The City of God.* Read Augustine on

---

52. *Determinationes quaestionum,* q. 3.

Christian doctrine, in the passages wherein he proves that Sacred Scripture cannot be understood without a knowledge of other sciences. He proves also that just as the children of Israel took with them the vessels of Egypt, so the doctors of theology make use of the doctrines of philosophy. Therefore, we learn many things from the saints which we do not learn from philosophers and the maxims of philosophy."[53] What St. Bonaventure said of philosophy can be applied to all the other useful sciences.

(4) *Other studies must be associated with theology.* To avoid having the friars absorbed by the natural sciences alone, the Seraphic Doctor composed a short treatise on the reduction of all arts to theology. In this little work he clearly shows how to associate the natural sciences with theology, and how by means of them we may find a clue to the understanding of the sacred mysteries. He says in the conclusion: " 'The manifold wisdom of God' (Eph. 3:10), which is clearly treated of in Holy Scripture, is hidden in all knowledge and in all nature. It is also evident that all knowledge is the handmaid of theology; and therefore theology uses examples and terms pertaining to every type of knowledge. It is also evident how broad the illuminative way is; how God Himself is hidden deep within everything which is thought or known."[54]

CONCLUSION. The enemies of learning, the opponents of liberal studies, are therefore either ignorant, deceived, or illwilled.

The ignorant are opposed to studies either because they do not understand the advantages and necessity of studies or because they wish to cover up their own ignorance. "The ignorant," says St. Gregory Nazianzen, "wish everybody to be like themselves. If the learned were deprived of their knowledge,

53. *Epist. de tribus quaest.*, n. 12.
54. *De reductione artium ad theologiam*, in *Opera omnia*, t. V (Quaracchi, 1891), p. 325.

they would be reduced to the lowly, common standard of the unlearned, and no one would be able to discover or disclose the lack of knowledge in the ignorant."[55]

The spiritually deceived are foolishly opposed to learning because they consider it contrary to virtue. They imagine that the religious life cannot preserve its humility and purity together with learning. Their error is evident from what has been said above.

Finally, the *ill-willed* are opposed to learning, not because they deem it useless or dangerous, but in order to excuse their own negligence.

All these opponents of science and learning have been vigorously condemned by the Sovereign Pontiffs, who have never ceased to commend and promote studies with all their authority. But if we must work and study, then there must be a way in which to conform our manual labor and especially our studies to the example of Christ.

IV. MANNER OF WORKING

321. (A) **In general.** St. Francis himself prescribed the manner of working for his sons when he said; "Let them work faithfully and devotedly."[56] He meant, says St. Bonaventure, "faithfully in respect to themselves and their neighbor and devotedly in regard to God."[57]

(1) In order to work *faithfully*, we should first of all devote ourselves to the tasks to which we are bound by our vocation or by the command of our superiors. A special occupation is assigned to each one of us lest we fall into idleness. A cleric who, instead of studying, devotes many hours of the day to manual labors suited to his own taste, does not

---

55. *In funere S. Basilii*, Oratio 43, n. 11, in Migne, *P. G.*, t. XXXVI, col. 510.

56. *Rule*, Chap. V.

57. *Exp. super Reg.*, cap. V, n. 1.

labor faithfully, but abuses the graces given to him. A lay Brother does wrong who studies while he should be engaged in manual labor. "In the same way in which all the bees of a hive ingeniously fall to work with consummate skill and admirable order at the job established for them," says Father Pacificus, "so must all friars of our convents work in an orderly, assiduous, and skillful manner, for our convents are not the dwelling place of idlers but of devoted servants of God. These will produce honey, that is, provide good things for themselves and others in time and in eternity. Hence the wise mandate of the ancients: 'Work and pray.' "[58]

(2) In order to work *devotedly* we should "direct the work to the greater glory of God."[59] The friars must be careful not to make work their sole object, nor to set their heart too strongly upon it, nor to become so engrossed in it as to extinguish or weaken "the spirit to which all things should be subservient." Ever fixing their mind on God, they should take the higher and the more direct road, so that labor, imposed on man by God, accepted and commended by the saints as a means of preserving interior recollection, may not become an occasion of distraction and wordliness.

322. (B) **Manner of studying correctly.** To study in an orderly and effective manner, three conditions are to be fulfilled: (1) The studies themselves must be useful; (2) they must be pursued for a fitting purpose; (3) they must be accompanied by the practice of the other virtues.

(1) USEFUL STUDIES. True usefulness is necessary for the perfection of studies. It is wrong to spend time reading and learning useless things. Concerning this evil, St. Thomas, citing these words of St. Jerome, says, "We see priests who, neglecting the Gospels and the prophets, read comedies and

58. Pacificus a Sejano, *Analecta O. M. Cap.*
59. St. Bonaventure, *Exp. super Reg.,* cap. V, n. 1.

sing bucolic love songs."[60] "In our day," says Bernardine van Loo, "there are only a few priests to whom the words of Jerome apply. However, there are some who skip the more arduous studies, occupy themselves entirely with politics, and waste their time in reading newspapers and magazines. Besides neglecting studies, such religious inflict great harm upon their own souls; for they easily take in the affections and passions of the authors they read. Let those who study with this or any other inordinate desire carefully weigh the words of St. Thomas: 'It is in accordance with their state for religious to engage primarily in studying doctrine that is according to godliness, as St. Paul told Titus' (*Summa theol.*, IIa IIae, q. 188, a. 5 ad 3). Religious whose entire life is dedicated to divine service should study worldly matters only when they pertain to sacred doctrine."[61]

(2) THE PURPOSE OF STUDY. The true purpose of study is growth in charity. "Learning, when used to increase charity, is marvelously helpful," says St. Augustine; "but of itself, without such a purpose, it is not only superfluous but pernicious."[62] "For," says Richard of St. Victor, "what is knowledge of holiness without the good intention but a statue without life? Knowledge that does not produce sanctity and goodness is but a vain idol that cannot move."[63] Knowledge, says the Apostle, puffs us up. "Should you therefore flee from knowledge," asks St. Augustine, "and choose to know nothing rather than be puffed up? You should esteem knowledge, but value charity even more. Where charity does not build, there knowledge puffs up; but where charity builds, the foundation is solid. There is no puffing up where there is a rock."[64] We must

---

60. *Summa theol.*, IIa IIae, q. 167, a. 1, in corp.
61. *Stimulus Seraphicae conversationis*, XXXII.
62. *Epist.* 55, cap. II, n. 39, in Migne, *P. L.*, t. XXXIII, col. 223.
63. *De erud. hom. int.*, cap. XXXVIII, in Migne, *P. L.*, t. CXCVI, col. 1292.
64. *Serm. 354*, cap. VI, in Migne, *P. L.*, t. XXXIX, col. 1566.

always make a good intention before studying; and while studying elicit some pious aspirations to God.

(a) *The intention.* "Some wish to learn only for the purpose of knowing: this is vain curiosity. Some wish to learn in
order to make themselves known: this is shameful vanity. Still
others wish to learn in order to sell their knowledge for money
and honors: this is simply base gain. But there are some who
wish to learn so as to be able to serve their neighbors: this is
charity. Likewise some wish to learn for self-improvement:
this is prudence."[65]

(b) *Prayer.* We read of St. Thomas Aquinas that he never
read or wrote without first praying. Whenever he was faced
with difficult passages of Sacred Scripture, he added fasting to
prayer. And he used to say to his confrere Reginald, that
whatever he knew he had acquired not so much from his own
study and labor as from divine revelation. In the same way
St. Bonaventure admits that he obtained the best of his doctrines through prayer. "A man," says Blessed Roger "who raises
his mind to God before every action and directs all things to
God discovers God in everything. Therefore, when you wish
to read sacred books, you should raise your heart to God
saying: 'O Lord, I, Thy most vile servant, unworthy of any
good, wish to enter in to see Thy treasures. Though I am unworthy, may it please Thee to conduct me within; and by these
most holy words grant that I may love Thee as much as I
come to know Thee, for I do not wish to know Thee unless
it be to love Thee, my Lord God!' A mind disposed in this
way will find God as soon as the book is opened."[66]

Without prayer it is almost impossible to grasp and penetrate the secrets of sacred theology, for, as St. Augustine says:

---

65. St. Bernard, *In Cant.*, Serm. XXXVI, n. 3, in Migne, *P. L.*, t.
CLXXXIII, col. 968.
66. *Analecta Franc.*, t. III, p. 387.

"God is the source and origin of all knowledge. The more a man drinks at this source, the more he will thirst."[67]

(3) *Study must be combined with virtue.* Another condition is necessary for the proper ordering of studies. They must be united to the exercise of other virtues. St. Gregory expresses it well when he says: "Proud and learned men, although they do not live good lives, are prompted to preach correct doctrines. They often become heralds of their own damnation; for their actions contradict what they say, so that they condemn themselves with their own voices."[68] St. Francis, as Celano writes, "said that even a great cleric should stop his studies for a while after he has entered the Order, so that, unhindered by such duties, he may offer himself entirely dispossessed into the arms of the Crucified."[69] And St. Gregory justifies St. Francis when he says: "Perfect knowledge means knowing all things and yet in a certain sense being unaware of one's knowledge."[70] If a Franciscan cleric out of humility despoils himself in this way, can you imagine, asks St. Francis, what the future holds for one who begins by doing it? He will be like an unchained lion, attacking all obstacles with vigor, and the pleasant draught which he has enjoyed in the beginning will make him continue to progress with rapid strides. Whoever has entered the school of perfection in this way will quickly attain perfection.

CONCLUSION. We should set a high value on our time, and be careful not to waste it in idle words. St. Bernard says[71] that a word speeds away never to be recalled. Time spent never returns. And the foolish man does not realize what he has

---

67. *De tripl. habit.,* cap. V, in App., in Migne, P. L., t. XL, col. 996.

68. *Moralia,* Lib. XXVII, cap. XXXVII, n. 62, in Migne, *P. L.,* t. LXXVI, col. 442.

69. *Legenda Secunda,* cap. CXLVI, p. 315.

70. *Moralia,* Lib. XXVII, cap. XXXVII, n. 62, in Migne, *P. L.,* t. LXXVI, col. 436.

71. *Serm. 17, De divers,* n. 3, in Migne, *P. L.,* t. CLXXXIII, col. 584.

lost. He gossips until a whole hour is lost, wasted. A whole hour is lost which the mercy of the Creator granted for the purpose of doing penance and obtaining pardon, of gaining grace and meriting glory. "Go to your work and labor in the vineyard of God for the denarius of eternal life, lest the Master upbraid you, saying, 'Why do you stand here all day idle?' (Matt. 20:6)."[72] Love your work. For St. Augustine says, "The labors of those who love work are in no way burdensome but are even delightful.... For what is loved either is no burden or the burden is loved."[73]

§ IV. Recreation

323. When on a certain day the Apostles mentioned that they had labored much, Jesus our Saviour took them into a desert place, saying: "Come ... and rest."[74] And it was well that He did so, for it is necessary to all to have relaxation now and then. Recreation — peaceful, legitimate recreation — lightens the burden of arduous labor. Let us, therefore, consider: (1) the advantages of recreation; (2) the conditions necessary for relaxing in a pious and religious manner.

I. ADVANTAGES OF RECREATION

324. The advantages of recreation can be established: (1) from the life of the Fathers in the desert; (2) on the authority of the Doctors of the Church; (3) from the practice of nearly all the religious Orders.

A. FROM THE LIFE OF THE FATHERS IN THE DESERT. Although joviality and diversion may seem offensive to some religious, and may appear as something to be avoided, says Cassian, yet they must be deemed advantageous to both body and soul.

---

72. Thomas a Kempis, *De discipl. claust.*, cap. VI.
73. *De bono vid.*, cap. XXI, in Migne, *P. L.*, t. XL., col. 448.
74. Mark 6:31.

They must not be considered something to be patiently tolerated but something to be accepted with a joyful heart. A legendary account about St. John the Evangelist illustrates the point. When a hunter asked him why he, who seemed so faultlessly dignified and holy, would condescend to pet a partridge, he replied: "And why do you not always carry your bow taut?" The hunter answered, "If the bow were forever bent and taut, it would not keep its springiness, it would not be of service in an emergency." "Then," the Apostle responded, "do not be surprised that I relax and recreate my mind, for I do it so as to give myself to contemplation with greater ease later on." Cassian maintains that "unless a little recreation occasionally unbends and relieves the rigor of one's efforts, the spirit will slacken under the constant strain, and will not be able to practice virtue when necessity demands it."[75]

B. ON THE AUTHORITY OF THE DOCTORS OF THE CHURCH. (1) "Man needs rest to refresh his body," says St. Thomas.[76] He cannot work continuously. For his strength is limited and capable of only a certain amount of labor. The strength of the mind is also limited, and the mind capable of only a certain amount of work. Bodily rest relieves bodily fatigue; in the same way mental rest or recreation relieves mental fatigue. A delightful object is restful for the mind; so, too, the remedy for mental weariness consists in seeking something delightful, such as a period of rest and recreation after work. To confirm his point, St. Thomas quotes the example of St. John given above.

(2) St. Gregory also uses this example to prove the necessity of relaxation. He says, "Much energy is lost because work is overdone. But when work is discreetly discontinued for a time, much energy is saved. It is not surprising to discover the

---

75. Cassian, *Coll. XXIV*, cap. XX et XXI, in Migne, *P. L.*, t. XLIX, col. 1314.

76. *Summa theol.*, IIa IIae, q. 168.

same principle in incorporeal energy as in the corporeal. For the bow is loosened that it may be taut at the proper time. A man who does not take time to relax loses his ability to overcome tension; so, taking proper recreation is a virtue. Although the practice of taking recreation can with discretion be omitted, it should in general be preserved; for a man will all the more powerfully battle against vices if he has prudently taken time off to relax."

C. FROM THE PRACTICE OF RELIGIOUS ORDERS. It is almost a universal custom with all religious Orders for the superior and the other religious to gather at a common place for recreation after meals. In this way they prevent the disadvantages arising from the desire of some members of the community to relax their minds and hearts apart from the others.

In the Seraphic Order. Our legislation states that proper and moderate recreation is granted to all on certain days and at certain hours. At times extra recreation is permitted provided it is not worldly. Ordinary recreation should not be denied to novices and clerics when it is granted to others. It is always preferable to make concessions to the younger members of the Order rather than to the rest. The same can be said in the matter of extra recreations, for the superiors and masters are as fathers to the younger members. They should prudently see to it that, strengthened by joy and cheerfulness at the proper times, the beginners willingly bear the yoke of the Lord. Superiors should also see to it that the younger members become genuinely devoted both to the Order and to the superiors, in whom they behold paternal love associated with religious fellowship.

All things proceed with due order in well-established communities. Those who labor must have proper quiet and diversion to preserve strength of body and soul. Where common recreation is neglected, private recreation and useless and extemporaneous confabulations spread like a contagious disease. The idle and negligent care little for ordinary recreation because they are forever seeking distractions, and are occupied with a thousand trifles. Recreation should be taken at a fixed time, and should be regulated and well ordered. No one should be excluded. Usually all the friars should be obligated to attend common recreation.

II. NECESSARY CONDITIONS

325. Many fail to spend their recreation time in the right way. Some do not know how to leave off studies nor how to begin studying again. Some apply themselves to work too strenuously: they are at it day and night. Others leave off studies and are scarcely able to resume. The necessity of mental diversion we can readily grant, but there is no need for dissipation. For wholesome recreation St. Thomas in the *Summa theologica* (IIa IIae, q. 168) gives three conditions which we must never omit. Even the best things become evil when they exceed the bounds of reason.

A. THE FIRST CONDITION is "that we do not seek to enjoy ourselves in unbecoming or harmful conversation or occupations."

(1) We must avoid all words which are not in full accord with the religious state nor fit to be uttered in the presence of God. We should speak ill of no person or thing, vex no one, and not argue with others. By no means should we spread news or rumors that contain not a single grain of edification. Let us not laugh in indecorous guffaws, nor speak in a loud voice. In short, let us repress all the evils of the tongue. "But if at times there is need for cheerful words to banish sorrow at least for a while," says St. Basil, "let your speech be imbued with spiritual charm and seasoned with evangelical salt."[77]

---

77. *Const. monast.*, cap. XII, in Migne, *P. G.*, t. XXXI, col. 1375.

(2) It is bad and even dangerous if two or three religious go to someone's cell or to an unfrequented place of the house or into the garden to take their recreation apart from the others. "For this is not charity," says St. Basil, "but discord and division, and a proof of the dishonesty of those who assemble in this way. For if they cared for the common good and religious discipline, they would without doubt have a common and equal love for all. But if by isolating and separating themselves they form another community within the community, such an isolated friendship is wrong. Such companionships must not be tolerated in convents. Nor may anyone, for the purpose of preserving friendship, be the companion of a friar who wishes to do wrong and violate the laws of common discipline. As long as all remain good, everyone ought willingly to associate with and be united to all the others."[78]

(3) It is equally unlawful to transgress the norms established by the laws and ordinances of one's Order as to the manner of taking recreation — that is, priests with priests, clerics with clerics, and novices with novices. "Otherwise charity, obedience, peace and hierarchical reverence will suffer."[79]

B. THE SECOND CONDITION is that a certain dignity must be preserved. We may play and jest and it is indeed lawful. But we must be reasonable about it just as in regard to sleep and rest. If more than a reasonable amount of time is spent, it is no longer recreation but occupation; body and mind become confused and oppressed rather than relieved and refreshed. "I do not say," writes St. Francis de Sales, "that while speaking and playing you should not take delight in the speech or sport. Otherwise recreation would be boring. But I do say that the mind must not be so engrossed in them that

---

78. *Ibid.*, cap. XXIX, in Migne, *P. G., t.* XXXI, col. 1418, 1419.
79. *Analecta O. M. Cap.*, t. IV, p. 302, n. 2.

we wish to stay at this forever."[80] And St. Thomas says: "There is also virtue in playing games. The philosopher calls it *eutrapelia*. And a man is said to practice this virtue when he has a happy turn of mind, whereby he gives his words and deeds a cheerful twist. And inasmuch as this virtue restrains a man from immoderate fun, it is included under modesty."

C. THE THIRD CONDITION. "Like all other human actions, recreation must be suited to the person, the time and the place, and be duly arranged according to other circumstances."[81]

We shall do well to recall what was said about the reformation of the members of the body. Here we shall only add some words about the matter and manner of conversation during recreation.

We should converse on subjects which will be least detrimental to our spirit and yet procure some recreation for our natural constitution. Let us omit anything too serious or too deep. Should a serious topic present itself, we can discuss it amiably and cheerfully. We should never start a "heavy" discourse or debate, but talk with a light heart, gaily, genially. The main thing is the motive of charity. If we cannot think of anything else, let us speak harmless nonsense. During recreations, clerics should be particularly careful not to philosophize, but rather exercise themselves physically so as to be able to return with more vigor to spiritual and intellectual pursuits. Young friars who do nothing but sit and read during recreation make a mistake. Whenever possible, it is better to walk around the garden or to engage in some other moderate physical exercise according to the approved customs of the place. But all immoderate and fatiguing exercises which would impede intellectual activities should be avoided.

Finally, as soon as the signal is given, let us stop at once. Let us even interrupt the conversation we may have just begun,

---

80. *Introduction to a Devout Life,* Part III, chap. XXXI.
81. *Summa theol.,* IIa IIae, q. 168, a. 2.

impose silence on ourselves, and quietly proceed to church with the others. If we have said anything wrong during recreation, we should be sorry for it and humbly beg pardon, asking for the grace to live in holiness and to work strenuously for the remaining hours of the day.

§ V. External Associations

326. We should always cherish the spirit of solitude and foster a love for it, flee from the distractions of the world, and appreciate a life hidden in God. Peace, quiet, solitude and retirement from the world are the surest proof of an interior life and of religious spirit. We must be careful not to wander about in the world nor to let the world enter the cloister or the cells. But since the Franciscan life is a mixed life, it is sometimes necessary to associate with the world. We shall, therefore consider: (1) the danger of associating with the world; (2) legitimate reasons for going out into the world; (3) the safeguards to be used.

I. THE DANGER OF GOING OUT INTO THE WORLD

327. The Fathers of the Church and current experience demonstrate how much superfluous departures from the monastery and visits to the cities (a) corrupt the good morals of religious; (b) extinguish fervor in religious Orders.

A. Useless wanderings destroy good morals. "The world is a sea," says St. Augustine, "dangerous not only because of storms and rocks but also because of the many beasts of concupiscence which lie in ambush."[82] "If you love the world, it will absorb you; for the world knows not how to support, but only how to devour its admirers."[83] A contem-

---

82. *De cataclysmo,* cap. I, in Migne, *P. L.,* t. XL, col. 693.
83. *Serm.* 76, cap. VI, n. 9, in Migne, *P. L.,* t. XXXVIII, col. 482.

porary of St. Bernard, writing to a Sister, has this to say:[84] "In a monastery, life is contemplative — in the world, laborious; in a monastery, holy — in the world, reproachful; in a monastery, spiritual — in the world, carnal; in a monastery, heavenly — in the world, earthly; in a monastery, quiet —in the world, turbulent; in a monastery, peaceful — in the world, quarrelsome; in a monastery, chaste — in the world, voluptuous....In a monastery life is filled with virtues — in the world, with vices."[85]

Further on, he adds: "Behold good and evil before your gaze; behold before your eyes the damnation and salvation of your soul; behold before you life and death. Behold fire and water. Stretch forth your hand and choose the one you wish." Thomas a Kempis writes: "He is truly a religious who willingly renounces the world and does not return to it in spirit."[86] In another place: "Seldom will he remain good for a long time who freely mixes with people of the world"; and especially "injurious is it for youths, the recruits, to visit secular friends and to return to the home they have left."[87] Elsewhere he exclaims: "Behold how many have perished by wandering outside the monastery! How many slaves there are to worldly curiosity who bring back from their useless journeying not a single degree of holiness."[88] "The longings of sensuality prompt you to roam abroad; but when the hour has passed away, what do you bring back with you but a weight on your conscience, and a dissipated heart? Often

---

84. *De modo bene vivendi ad sororem*, cap. XX, in Migne, *P. L.*, t. CLXXXIV, col. 1237.

85. The saintly authors quoted here seem to be going to extremes. They seem to give the impression that the monastery has the monopoly on virtue. Actually they are merely endeavoring to stress a point. For there are saintly and virtuous people in the world — the world taken in the physical sense. But to the saints quoted here "the world" meant only one thing — the spirit of the world which, according to St. John, is the concupiscence of the eye, the concupiscence of the flesh and the pride of life.

86. *Serm. 14 ad Novit.*, n. 10.

87. *Dial. Nov.*, cap. IV, n. 4.

88. *Serm. 11 ad Novit.*, n. 4.

a joyous going abroad begets a sorrowful return home: and a merry evening makes a sorrowful morning."[89] Our own experience has probably proved to us that when we return from the world, more often than not we return with our soul filled with vain, dangerous images and with a distaste for more serious work. The devil often tempts religious in this way. He does not dare to propose sin immediately, but causes the religious to become negligent and off guard and slowly lures him into his snares. For the religious may abhor grave sin, but may perhaps not loathe worldly conversations, in which there seems to be a certain virtue and uprightness. The saints give this wise advice: just as fish die when they tarry on dry land, so monks who leave their cells to linger with seculars are turned away from their proposed life of solitude and fervor.

(B) **Going out destroys regular observance and fervor.** The letdown since the beginning of the Order, the present-day diminution of fervor, demonstrate the amount of harm done to religious discipline by unnecessary departures from the convent.

(1) *Cause of relaxation.* In his letter to the Provincials, in which he speaks of the causes of relaxation since the beginning of the Order, St. Bonaventure shows that pointlessly wandering about was the chief cause. "The bodily comforts required by many who wander about become an annoyance to the people where these religious sojourn. Such friars leave behind them not the example of a good life, but rather scandals which injure souls."[90] He seriously warns superiors against this abuse, saying, "Keep wanderers in check!"[91]

(2) *Present-day decrease in fervor.* In our own day, leaving the monastery without necessity is still a most dangerous

---

89. *Imitation of Christ,* Book I, Chap. XX, n. 7.
90. *Epistolae officiales,* Epist. I, n. 2.
91. *Loc. cit.,* n. 4.

practice, leading to the cooling of fervor. "Today, to our sorrow, we are too frequently in the world, and the world all too often in our cloisters; and therefore we often think, speak and act like worldlings in our life, in our duties, and the like; we more or less follow in the footsteps of the worldly. The Scriptural saying: 'You are not of the world' (John 15:19), is not entirely true in our regard, and hence regular observance suffers. But whoever is filled with the spirit of devotion and prayer and is animated by it, lives far from the world. He lives in God and for God."[92] "They are certainly mistaken," says Albert of Bulsano, "who think they please seculars by their useless visits and empty conversations, and who think they thus win their love and esteem; for experience teaches that the very opposite usually happens, according to the old adage: 'Appear rarely if you wish to be appreciated.' "[93] We may, however, sometimes be compelled by necessity to go out into the world.

II. REASONS FOR GOING OUT INTO THE WORLD

328. The dangers arising from association with the world are less when we go out only through necessity or to fulfill the will of God. God protects us with the shield of good will and extends His right hand to us even as to Peter, when only at His command we walk upon deep and turbulent waters.

We must always ask ourselves: Is it God Himself who is calling me out? In other words, from what motives and for what purpose am I going out into the world? Three kinds of motives are discernible: (A) evil motives; (B) apparently indifferent motives; (C) holy motives.

A. **Evil motives.** We can omit treating of evil motives, for they are entirely out of place for religious.

---

92. Bernard of Andermatt, *Analecta O. M. Cap.,* t. XVII, pp. 277 seq.
93. *Exp. super Reg.,* cap. III, § 47, n. 1.

B. **Apparently indifferent motives** can be: (1) going out for a walk, for a pleasure trip after work; (2) visiting seculars who seem to have some difficulties.

(1) There is nothing reprehensible in ordinary walks which are undertaken moderately according to the custom of the Order. For it is evident that a man cannot be constantly occupied with serious affairs. And all will admit that walking relieves both the body and the mind.

Concerning pleasure trips after work and extraordinary traveling, superiors will do well to be prudently strict. For these cannot easily be undertaken without expense, interference with the spiritual life, disedification of seculars and disturbance of regular observance. All the friars have the obligation of considering seriously whether or not there are sufficient reasons for asking such things from their superiors.

(2) Visits to seculars for festivities or recreation are to be discouraged. Worldly feasts and association with seculars easily defile a religious. When we need recreation, is it ever necessary to seek it among people in the world? Is it impossible to find men who are reasonable, learned, of good disposition and of tried virtue among our confreres and ecclesiastics, with whom we can share the joy of pious conversation and innocent recreation?

C. **Holy motives.** These are motives which can make our appearance in the world truly safe. Jesus Himself entered the house of a publican to make him a son of Abraham; He went up to Jerusalem on a feast day to restore His Father's glory, which had been violated by the sinful irreverence of those who bought and sold in the temple. On the advice of our Lord, the Apostles entered secular houses to communicate His peace. Our Rule demands that we lead not only a contemplative life but also an active life. And to carry on the active life according to the example of Christ and our Seraphic Father, we at times must leave the monastery. These and other motives dictated by charity and obedience are just and holy.

III. SAFEGUARDS WHICH MUST BE USED

329. St. Francis admonished his friars[94] that when they go out in the world, according to the example of Christ and His disciples they should neither quarrel, nor dispute, by obstinately asserting their opinion, nor judge others, by interpreting doubts in their more evil aspect; but remain interiorly and exteriorly free from guilt. He wanted them to be meek, by suffering blame; peaceful, by preserving the rules of their humble Order; and modest, by guarding their senses, actions, and words; gentle, by avoiding impetuosity in their ways; and humble by seeking no honor, fleeing every vestige of glory. And as a special check to the tongue he adds: " . . . speaking courteously to everyone as is becoming, that is, sincerely reverencing every man according to his rank. And into whatever house they enter for the purpose of saving souls, . . . they shall first say, 'Peace be to this house' (Matt. 10:12, Challoner-Douay version) and according to the holy Gospel they may partake of whatever food is set before them."[95]

According to the *Mirror of Discipline* all these things can be explained under three headings: our behavior (A) with our companion; (B) in regard to our own person; (C) in regard to the houses which we enter.

A. **Our companion.** Although conditions have changed somewhat in our times, and more liberties are taken for granted now than formerly, nevertheless, as a rule, religious should not go out alone for recreational purposes, unless it is a question of visiting their own relatives. But, following the example of the disciples of our most holy Saviour, they should take a companion with them. They should not part company on the

---

94. Cf. *Rule*, Chapter III.
95. According to St. Bonaventure, *Exp. super Reg.*, n. 11, 12.

way or quarrel, but, as brothers in Christ and following the example of our Saviour, should endeavor with all humility and charity to obey and serve each other spiritually. When necessary, they can correct each other in a brotherly spirit; and if there is no improvement one should make the other's faults known to the superior.

All the friars should heed the words of our holy Father: "In the name of the Lord go two by two on your journeys, humbly and modestly. . . . Let no idle and useless words be spoken among you, but even as you walk let your conversation be as humble and edifying as if you were in your monastery or your cell. . . . For Brother Body is our cell, and the soul is the hermit who dwells therein to praise God and meditate on Him; and if the soul does not remain in the quiet of this cell, other cells built by man will be of little profit to it. Conduct yourself among people in such a way that whoever hears or sees you may devoutly praise the Most High God, our heavenly Father."[96]

B. **Our own personal conduct.** Let us see how we should behave (1) in respect to our actions; (2) to our words.

(1) IN ACTION. We must always observe: (a) modesty; (b) devotion; (c) discretion.

(a) *Modesty* requires, says the *Mirror of Discipline*, that we avoid all unrestrained movements of hands and arms and other bodily members, such as may occur while running here or there. People who even inadvertently see such conduct are deeply disgusted. The arms must not be noticeably bared and the habit not gathered up or in any other way held irreligiously.

(b) *Devotion* demands that when we pass a church, a crucifix or the image of a saint, we demonstrate our reverence by bowing to them. Nor should we ever pass a cemetery without saying a prayer for the dead.

---

96. *Opusc.* (Wadding edition, Cologne, 1849), Collat. 22.

(c) *Discretion* demands that in all we have to do while on a journey we let ourselves be guided by the advice of the senior friar. Before all else, the obligation of saying the Divine Office must always be devoutly fulfilled, lest the friars appear to be worldlings rather than religious. Otherwise they could be accused of putting secondary things before what is of first importance — their religious profession.

(2) As to the use of WORDS, we must be concerned about: (a) the subject matter; (b) the tone of voice.

(a) SUBJECT MATTER. Upon meeting people we should first humbly greet them. And since in his *Testament* our Seraphic Father Francis says that it was revealed to him by the Lord that after the example of Christ we should greet others with: "May the Lord give you His peace," the friars should use this evangelical salutation or any other pious greeting. Then, says the *Mirror of Discipline,* "it is the duty of the older friars to propose some edifying and comforting topics of conversation for their companions and others with whom they may at times chance to speak. . . . If there are no seculars present, the words of the Friars should be about God; for He becomes the traveling companion of disciples who speak of Him. It is disgraceful to occupy the time with mere chaff, trivialities, and invented stories."[97] St. Bonaventure mentions three topics which should be omitted in conversation:

(1) *Personal endowments.* We must avoid babbling about our own gifts or those of our brethren. Such boasting is detestable to God and man, and usually begets contempt instead of honor, according to the adage: "Self-praise is contemptible."

(2) *Sins and faults.* We must be even more careful not to speak to others about serious disorders which may perhaps reflect on the Order. For those who reveal such things commit

---

97. Part I, Chap. XXVIII, n. 3.

the worst kind of detraction and give the greatest scandal. Besides the penalties established by the Order's legislation and the General Chapters, they incur the divine wrath; they are like the impious Cham.

(3) *Private matters.* We must be silent not only about the more serious disorders, but also solicitously avoid revealing the less serious faults of one or the other religious, for such revelations might expose them to contempt and laughter. Finally, it is often very imprudent to tell seculars about the things pertaining to regular discipline. For seculars who have no idea about monastic affairs, may easily draw the wrong conclusions.

(b) TONE OF VOICE. The voice should usually be low. The *Mirror of Discipline* continues: "Let them entirely avoid loud speech, which is never becoming to religious, especially when they walk among groves or orchards. For according to the common proverb, the forest is said to have ears and the field or the plain, eyes. I cannot proclaim as devout and possessed of religious zeal persons who when among men fail to avoid boisterousness, clamorous disputes, quarrels, or other things which can give offense to strangers."

C. **In the houses of seculars,** circumspection and caution must always be used, in regard to: (1) persons; (2) undertakings; (3) food.

(1) PERSONS IN GENERAL. We must always behave as servants of God. Let us be serious, religious, and modest in appearance, in posture, and in every action. As the status and nature of the people differ, so too our manner of dealing with them. Let us be prudent, acting differently with different people, but cautiously with all. Let us be simple but not stupid; humble but not downcast; gentle but not spineless; cheerful but not wanton; affable but not boastful or scurrilous. It is a sign of wisdom to be able to relax the rigor of discipline occasionally, when circumstances demand it, in such a way that the

boundaries of modesty are not overstepped. Such relaxation is blameworthy, however, when it is neither becoming nor advantageous.

We do well to keep in mind the admonition of St. Paul when he instructs Timothy how to treat various kinds of people: "Do not rebuke an elderly man, but exhort him as you would a father, and young men as brothers, elderly women as mothers, younger women as sisters in all chastity."[98]

In accord with further instructions of St. Paul, the religious will keep himself from becoming involved in worldly affairs that do not pertain to his state: "Conduct thyself in work as a good soldier of Christ Jesus. No one serving as God's soldier entangles himself in worldly affairs, that he may please Him whose approval he has secured."[99] In particular, the friars will be careful when visiting the homes of women. Our Seraphic Father, who knew how necessary chastity was for all and especially for religious, whose life should be an instruction and a powerful sermon to others, established in his Rule the precept of avoiding suspicious dealings or conversations with women. And rightly so. For we bear within ourselves the same seeds of corruption as other men. Custody of the senses and vigilance offer the only remedy. As soon as we neglect these, we are undone, we perish. We must never imagine that we are safe. For this false security is a snare of the devil. If St. Paul, though raised to the third heaven, prayed three times that the sting of the flesh be taken from him; if the holy anchorites living in the desert amid the most rigid penances, and our Seraphic Father himself, fought so much against dangerous imaginations, can we, who observe none of their austerities, feel secure in the midst of a corrupt world? "I flee, lest I be conquered," says St. Jerome. "There is no security in sleeping

---

98. 1 Tim. 5:1-2.
99. 2 Tim. 2:3-4.

near the serpent. It may be that he will not injure me; but it may happen that sometime he will."[100]

(2) BUSINESS AFFAIRS WITH SECULARS. We should always proceed carefully in business affairs. It is unbecoming for a religious to act rashly in these matters. "If affairs of the soul are concerned, those who have the duty and ability to counsel must give advice. Otherwise it is not being a soldier of God to entangle ourselves with the secular business of relatives and friends. For one dying to the world gives up these things."[101]

(3) CONCERNING FOOD AND DRINK. Although according to the Rule we may partake of whatever food is set before us, it must be noted, says St. Bonaventure, that these words are not without limitations. In saying: ... "according to the holy Gospel," St. Francis restrains licentiousness, and maintains that our partaking of food must be done according to the law of evangelical virtue. We must partake of food and drink with temperance and due modesty.

(a) *Concerning food.* We must be careful not to be guilty of gluttony by reason of the quantity or quality of our food. The Seraphic Doctor maintains that "where there is a superfluity of courses, there is not a superfluity of evangelical holiness but more truly an abuse. After what is necessary has been eaten, evangelical holiness demands that we prudently leave untouched what cannot be taken without bad example."[102] Let us recall also the words of Bernard of Besse, "Is it not indeed unseemly for poor men to seek more elegant food, to be discontented with what is placed before them, to give orders concerning the way in which the food is to be prepared, ... to praise some particular food so that more of the same will be served?"[103]

---

100. *Adv. Vigil.,* n. 16, in Migne, *P. L.,* t. XXIII, col. 368.
101. *Mirror of Discipline,* Part I, Chap. XXX, n. 6.
102. *Exp. super Reg.,* cap. III, n. 15.
103. *Mirror of Discipline,* Part I, Chap. XXXII, n. 4.

(b) *Concerning drink.* Let us be particularly careful about the observance of temperance. For it is shameful to be marked as an excessive drinker. The friars "ought to be careful," says the *Mirror of Discipline,* "not to drink wine too frequently after meals, even if it is frequently served. Sitting by the fire causes thirst and compels drinking, which wearies the body and exhausts the soul. . . . How often is it necessary to correct in the morning what has been unwisely babbled out the evening before. The wise preach in the morning. The unwise harangue in the evening."[104]

CONCLUSION. Since associations with others are open to many dangers, we should follow the advice of St. Basil: "If an urgent reason should compel you to leave your cell, then fortify yourself with love of God as a defense; place your hand into the loving hand of Christ, and with perfect restraint overcome every attack of voluptuousness. Return home immediately after fulfilling your duties. Never loiter, but return on swift wings, like an innocent dove returning to the ark from which you have been released. Be entirely convinced that your ark is the monastery, that you can find salutary rest in no other place."[105]

§ VI. Sleep and Nocturnal Rest

330. After the examination of conscience and preparation for the morning meditation, we can prepare ourselves for the night's rest. But in order to be able to say with the psalmist, "As soon as I lie down, I fall peacefully asleep, for You alone, O Lord, bring security to my dwelling,"[106] it is necessary: (A) to take our rest at the appointed time; (B) in a manner proper to religious; (C) and to resist the temptations of the devil, if perchance they occur during sleeplessness.

---

104. *Ibid.,* n. 2 and 3.
105. *Serm. de renunt. saec.,* n. 5, in Migne, *P. G.,* t. XXXI, col. 638.
106. Ps. 4:9.

A. **The time for sleeping.** We should try to strike a prudent mean between sleep and vigils, says St. Vincent Ferrer. And yet it is quite difficult to set up a universal norm. There are two things by means of which danger to the body and consequently to the soul, becomes particularly imminent — when we exceed the bounds of discretion, by abstaining from sleep too frequently, and by excessive vigils. In the evening we should observe the foregoing rule, that we may not lengthen our vigils too much; for a late vigil impedes our attention and devotion at the morning Office. A person who keeps excessive vigils is usually sleepy, tired, indevout. In fact he must at times absent himself from the morning and evening Office altogether.

We should take the sleep we need, but at the appointed time and not before.

B. **In a manner proper to religious.** We must go to sleep with the right and pure intention — that is, to regain our strength in order to serve God better. The following advice should be of assistance:

(1) BEFORE LYING DOWN. Even if we have recited night prayers with the community, we should kneel in the direction facing the Most Blessed Sacrament and say three Hail Marys in honor of the Immaculate Conception of the Blessed Virgin Mary, Patroness of the Seraphic Order; then thank God for the benefits received that day; make an act of contrition from the depths of our heart for the sins we have committed; and finally, bowing humbly, ask the blessing of the most sweet Jesus.

Then, rising from our knees, we should sprinkle our bed with holy water, saying: "May the Lord grant me a peaceful night; may He keep my enemies far from me; and may His angels guard me in peace. I intend to praise and glorify God with every breath." After this, having devoutly made the sign of the cross, let us get into bed with the proper decorum.

(2) WHEN IN BED our body and our soul should be well disposed.

Disposition of body. We should conduct ourselves most becomingly in bed, and remain decently covered, even in the greatest heat.

Disposition of soul. Our bed should be like a tomb in which we rest a little while, and from which we shall rise in a short time to keep vigil and sing the praises of God. The better prepared we are when we fall asleep, the more quickly shall we be able to rise. While lying in bed before falling asleep, let us recite psalms, or meditate on something advantageous or, better still, think of Jesus in His Passion. Our Lord said to St. Mechtilde: "When anyone wishes to go to sleep, let him meditate on something concerning Me or speak with Me. For, although the body sleeps, the mind will watch with Me; and if he should experience anything less becoming in sleep, and on awaking find that it is displeasing and troublesome, it is a sign that he is not separated from Me in the least. When going to sleep he should desire that I accept every breath that he breathes that night as ardent praise of Me. And I who cannot fail to hear the holy prayers of a pious and loving soul, will truly fulfill his desires."[107]

C. **Sleeplessness and deceits of the devil.** (1) *Sleeplessness.* When we cannot sleep at all, and are extremely weakened and deprived of energy, we should offer this trial for the salvation of souls. When St. Gertrude spent a virtually sleepless night, Jesus said to her: "When one weary from sleeplessness and devoid of energy asks Me to give him sleep so as to regain his energy in order to praise Me, and I have not answered his prayer and he has borne this lack of sleep humbly and patiently, he pleases Me very much. And when a sick person, whose strength has been sapped by sleeplessness, humbly bears and

---

107. Blosius, *Conclav. animae fidel.,* Pars II, cap. IX, n. 3.

offers this lack of sleep to Me, he is by far more acceptable to Me than any healthy person who is well able to keep vigil and who spends the entire night in prayer."[108]

(2) *The deceits of the devil.* During sleeplessness we often experience the temptations and deceits of the devil. Whenever we wake we should immediately raise our mind to God by means of pious aspirations. If the flesh tempts us or a foul image presents itself or any other passion is aroused, we may not remain indifferent. We should make the sign of the cross on our forehead, mouth and heart, so that God may preserve our heart from all evil and curb our unruly flesh. Meditating on the eternal fire of hell and the sufferings of the holy martyrs will help. And thus, with the assistance of God, and by reflecting on such thoughts, we shall conquer fire with fire; we shall confound the devil. But before all things, as we have already said, let us remember the Passion of our Lord. The Seraphic Doctor writes: "If you will diligently meditate on the Passion, the devil will never or hardly ever be able to molest you, because devout meditation on the Passion of Jesus Christ will rout every attack."[109]

All this requires discretion. Otherwise sleep, so necessary to nature, will only be the more disturbed by excessive conflict.

---

108. *Ibid.,* n. 4.
109. St. Bonaventure, *Reg. Nov.,* cap. VII, n. 1.

INDICES

Index to Scriptural References

Index of Authors Quoted

Topical Index